*ALEXIS LICHINE'S GUIDE
TO THE WINES
AND VINEYARDS OF FRANCE*

by

ALEXIS LICHINE

in collaboration with
Samuel Perkins

Alexis Lichine's
GUIDE
TO THE WINES
AND
VINEYARDS
OF FRANCE

THIRD EDITION, REVISED

Alfred A. Knopf   New York   1986

THIS IS A BORZOI BOOK
PUBLISHED BY ALFRED A. KNOPF, INC.

Library of Congress Cataloging in Publication Data
Lichine, Alexis.
Alexis Lichine's guide to the wines and vineyards of France.
Bibliography: p.
Includes index.
1. Wine and wine-making—France—Guidebooks.
2. France—Description and travel—1975-   —Guidebooks.
I. Perkins, Samuel.   II. Title.
III. Title: Guide to the wines and vineyards of France.
TP553.L48   1986   641.2′22′0944   85-45943
ISBN 0-394-55335-7
ISBN 0-394-74440-3 (pbk.)

Manufactured in the United States of America
Published April 18, 1979
Second Printing, July 1979
Revised Edition, May 1982
Second Printing, further revised
and updated, April 1984
Third Edition, May 1986

TO SACHA AND SANDRA
raised in the vineyards of France
and now grown to be my companions
in the enjoyment of wine

Contents

CONTENTS

CONTENTS

Maps

xi

MAPS

Author's Note

This book was originally conceived as a revision of my earlier work *Wines of France*, first published in 1951. But as the writing progressed, I became increasingly aware of the vast changes that have taken place in the world of wine over the past quarter-century. In fact, it was my privilege to be the instigator of some of these changes and the willing advocate of others. It was clear that the time was ripe for a completely new book about French wines and wine-making.

A project of this scope could not have been realized without the help of a number of people:

First, Émile Peynaud, one of the greatest of oenologists, who was generous in lending his experience and expertise, and who shares with me an abiding belief in, and love for, the greatness of Bordeaux wines;

Henri Meurgey, like his father before him, is an oenologist and a broker in Beaune, and former estate manager in Chambertin-Clos de Bèze. M. Meurgey allowed me to draw on his detailed knowledge of the growers and soils in the Côte d'Or—the region he knows so well;

Few people in France know their districts and their *métiers* as intimately as Jean-Pierre Moueix and his son, Christian. Had they lived a century ago, Saint-Émilion and Pomerol could have been classified in 1855, as the Médoc was in the great classification of the wines of the Gironde. Many thanks go to Georges Dubœuf, and to his assistant, Michel Brun. In our thirty years of friendship, M. Dubœuf has helped immeasurably to deepen my understanding of his beloved Beaujolais and Mâconnais;

Maurice Ninot was one of the artisans who assisted me when I first began estate-bottling on a large scale in Burgundy. His close friendship with the growers of the region has been a help in unraveling the intricate patterns of ownership among the Burgundy vineyards;

Patrick Léon is one of the few people in France with a knowledge of the wines of the whole country. Thanks also to Rosemary Barry for her contribution in time and interest; and to my editor, Charles Elliott, for his ready guidance;

The professional eye of Sam Perkins collaborated with me at all stages of the project. His enthusiastic and imaginative research was invaluable; his interest in every facet of wine was untiring. This book would not have come to fruition without him. My appreciation also to Katie Philson, for her faithful help at various stages of the book; to Victoria Foote, who gave me very valuable assistance with the new itinerary chapter in this book; and similarly to Elizabeth Schumann for further revisions. Above all, my sincere gratitude goes to Pierre Bréjoux, retired vice-president of the French National Institute of Place Names (I.N.A.O.), whose dedicated attention in the final stages of this project proved an immense help.

I am no less grateful to the many others who helped me and whose names are listed in the Acknowledgments at the back of the volume.

A.L.

Preface

As an inveterate insomniac, I've often counted corks instead of sheep, and if it hasn't made me any wiser (it certainly didn't put me to sleep), it has at least given me many opportunities to mull over my own years with wine and to think about all the changes I have seen—and lived through. What are these changes?

I hardly know where to begin. Few people are aware of the upheavals that have occurred in the last thirty years of wine. Indeed, only now, in the course of writing this book, have I fully realized the chasm that yawns between the wine-innocent world that existed before World War II and the sophistication of today's consumers.

I have often been asked to write my autobiography, but I have always preferred the story of wine to that of my own exploits. On the other hand, much of the time I find that the two stories are one. I was born in Russia on the eve of the Revolution and, having toured the globe, came with my family to France, where I spent my childhood in Paris. After completing the courses at a *lycée,* I traveled in my late teens to the United States, where I enrolled at the University of Pennsylvania. On returning to Paris I found part-time work with the Paris edition of the *Herald Tribune.* The biggest news of 1933 was the repeal of Prohibition in the United States, and I took on an assignment that changed my life. Sensing that Americans would discover wine, the editor of the *Tribune* wanted to attract potential wine and spirit advertisers with editorial profiles of France's major vineyard regions. Off I went in 1934, up and down the vineyard roads, from Champagne to Bordeaux. Although I had been an enthusiastic *amateur* of wines all my young life, my research and travels revealed to me the richness, the culture, and the subtlety of wine, to say nothing of the complexity of the wine business. I had found my calling.

In 1935, I returned to New York and took a job selling wine—at a store where bottles were hidden behind wooden paneling. The owners thought them too rare and refined for display! I soon began a Wine-of-the-Month Club, sending subscribers a bottle of wine every month, with background information and instructions for serving each selection.

Two years later, when working for a New York wine importer, I met Frank Schoonmaker, who at that time had a very fine retail wine shop in New York and circulated beautiful catalogues of wine to a mailing list of real *aficionados*—the hard-core oenophiles of the day. Schoonmaker's wines were bought for him in France by Raymond Baudouin, founder of the *Revue des Vins de France* and compiler of wine lists for, among others, Fernand Point's famous restaurant La Pyramide and Alexandre Dumaine's Hôtel de la Côte d'Or in Saulieu.

Baudouin was very knowledgeable about (and therefore unpopular with) the French wine shippers (*négociants*), not least because he was an early promoter of château- and estate-bottling. Traditionally, shippers bought wine in bulk, often disfiguring it by blending it with Algerian wines, and did the bottling themselves, collecting large profits. In 1939, I traveled throughout France with Baudouin. During the journey we stopped at a restaurant in the south, where the menu listed Romanée-Conti '29 for a dollar a bottle. After a bit of talk and a bottle of the superb vintage with our meal, we learned that the proprietor had eleven more bottles of this extraordinary—and virtually unobtainable—wine, and had never sold any. We bought his entire stock for $11! Back at Frank Schoonmaker's in New York, we sold each bottle for more than all eleven had cost.

I recall on the same trip holding a newspaper and trying, in the glaring sun of the Beaujolais, to read the headlines announcing the declaration of war between France and Germany. Even that news took second place to my career in wine! Nor, in a way, was I alone: even after war was declared, Frank Schoonmaker continued to receive requests from Eleanor Roosevelt from the White House for good German wines. Like art, wine knows no ideology.

By 1941 our business was exclusively wholesale. Since, for obvious reasons, our stocks of European wines were beginning to run low, Schoonmaker and I set out for California. We approached the then leading wine-makers: John Daniel of Inglenook, Louis M. Martini, Carl and Herman Wente, Fountaingrove, Tony Korbel, and F. Salmena. Subsequently, we were the first to market American wines under American names east of the Rockies. At the time, most American wines were sold (as many of them still are to this day) as so-called European equivalents, under such names as "Burgundy," "Sauterne" (without its final "s"), and "Chablis"—which they are not. As part of our efforts to root out this misleading practice, Schoonmaker and I introduced the word "varietal," indicating the grape variety along with the name of the county where it was grown.

After Pearl Harbor, when the United States entered the war, Schoonmaker went into the O.S.S. and I into the U.S. Army military intelligence. We sold our stocks of American wines to Charlie Berns, of Jack and Charlie's "21" Club and 21 Brands. Our French wines were sold off by the carload to several restaurants, among them Antoine's in New Orleans.

My recollections of the day-to-day aspects of military intelligence are much less vivid to me now than my memories of my other main wartime duty—taking charge of wines and other "V.I.P. requisitions" for the likes of Churchill, Patton, and Ei-senhower, acting as aide-de-camp for the latter after VE-day. Then as now, as much diplomacy took place around the dinner tables as in the conference rooms.

Later in the war I "liberated" some extraordinary clarets—a 1906 Haut-Brion among them—for the table of Eisenhower and his guests, including Churchill and Averell Harriman. Eisenhower's taste ran to sweet wines, his favorite being Château Coutet, which I later supplied to him at the White House.

As a major and wartime aide-de-camp, I often shared in the enjoyment of my finds, which sometimes led to other remarkable experiences. It was, for example, over some claret at the Hôtel de Paris in Monte Carlo, after the liberation of France, that Winston Churchill, to whom I had been attached on several occasions, gave me a rambling discourse on the complexities of wine. I listened silently until I could stand it no more and then chimed in with my own remarks. Churchill sat bolt up-right and said, "Boy, from now on you do the talking and I'll do the listening!"

Upon my return from Europe in 1946, I went to work as import-export man-ager for United Distillers of America, a group of distilleries owned by Armand Hammer, later of Occidental Petroleum fame. I put together some comprehensive lists of wines and spirits, but left Hammer in 1948 and started selecting wines for shipment to important customers in the United States. In this endeavor I had the help of H. Seymour Weller, a cousin of Douglas Dillon, Ambassador to France under President Kennedy, later Secretary of the Treasury, and who with his late fa-ther Clarence Dillon, was owner of Château Haut-Brion.

Arriving in the Médoc soon after the war, I discovered the châteaux in disrepair and the owners with little hope of finding buyers for their wines. There was no rec-ognition on the part of the shippers or the growers of any markets beyond their old, familiar ones, now wrecked by the war. Visits to vineyards were discouraged and foreign wine merchants rarely were able to push beyond the warehouses of the shippers in Bordeaux. Philippe de Rothschild, of Château Mouton-Rothschild, was unusual among growers of the time for inviting visitors to his property.

In 1955, in order to coordinate my selections from all over France and to expand my clientele throughout the world, I started a shipping company in Margaux. I dealt exclusively in château-bottled Bordeaux and estate-bottlings from Burgundy, Beaujolais, and other regions of France. At that time château- and estate-bottling, with the wines then centralized under one roof for combined shipments, was not a general practice. But it soon caught on. Alexis Lichine and Company became a success and I moved its offices to the famed Quai des Chartrons in Bordeaux.

In Burgundy, only a handful of producers were bottling their wines at the *domaine* and it was an uphill fight to persuade the rest to follow suit. Today, not only are they doing their own bottling—a job the *négociants* used to do after blending—but they are further cutting out the shippers by selling wine directly to the consumer.

Estate-bottling of Burgundies won acceptance in England much later than in the rest of the world. Until 1967, as the largest shipper of estate-bottled Burgundies in France, I had not sold so much as a single case to an English buyer. No doubt this was due to the system of the English wine merchants, who "interpreted" wines for their clients, providing certain "styles" of Pommard, Clos de Vougeot, and so on. Although legal at the time (only because Britain did not belong to the Common Market and was not subject to the Appellation Laws of France), this practice usually made for wines that were heavy, thick in the mouth, with little nuance and often no more than a faint hint of the complex and delicate Pinot Noir grape of Burgundy. It's a blessing that this situation has changed since Britain has become part of the Common Market.

As a neophyte buyer in Burgundy, I accepted numerous invitations to eat with the growers at their midday meal. But after a couple of experiences of drawing up a chair at one o'clock for lunch only to rise at six, then to have to sit down again at eight with another grower for dinner, I soon learned that there was a better way to do business. I'd leave the lunch hours open for the haggling that always goes with buying wines, especially at the estates in Burgundy. At least I always knew I could find the growers at home, returned from the vineyards at the sacred hour of noon.

Resentful of attempts by outsiders to penetrate their stronghold, the shippers offered resistance at every level. Outsiders faced the difficulty of traveling not only from the United States to France by ship but also within France from one vineyard area to another. There was no regularly scheduled commercial trans-Atlantic air service, and not until 1961 was it possible to fly from Paris to Bordeaux. The French wine establishment was a closed society, with family and business ties interwoven through many generations. Only with great difficulty could it be breached.

Moreover, at that time the export wine market consisted largely of people who drank only Bordeaux First and Second Growths (then cheap), without any desire to broaden their experience.*

Around 1950, I conceived the idea of a book to explain estate-bottled Burgundies, which had become a specialty of mine. Most wine books then available were patterned closely on works like George Saintsbury's *Notes on a Cellar-Book*. They tended to be esoteric cellar records of great bottles—lavishly praised—rather than practical accounts of the story of wine from vine to bottle for the consumer. Indeed, many of the authors hardly acknowledged the part that grapes played in winemaking. Still, there were great ones among them, particularly the late André Simon, one of wine's finest writers, who contributed greatly to the reputation of wine as the highest expression of nature. The scope of my book quickly grew to include the wines of Bordeaux, and from there it was only a short jump to the *Wines of France,* whose publication brought me over a quarter-century of friendship with publisher and wine buff Alfred A. Knopf. (I should note in passing some help I received in preparing the index in 1951 from another good friend, a lady whose name then was Grace Kelly.)

In 1951, with the book safely off my hands, I began to look about the Médoc for a property of my own. A large number of châteaux were on the market, including some of the most illustrious names of Bordeaux, but it was Château Cantenac-Prieuré which fired my imagination. Hoping for endorsement of my idea from men with experience in such matters, I sought the advice of the Duc de Montesquiou-Fézensac, owner of the beautiful Château de Marsan, in Armagnac, and of Georges Delmas, *régisseur* (vineyard manager) of Château Haut-Brion. Pierre de Montesquiou took one look at the ruinous state of the house and warned me that it would take decades and a fortune to restore. Delmas was equally emphatic after an informed inspection of the state of the vineyard. Luckily I disregarded their well-intentioned warnings, and took a plunge I have never for a minute regretted. Although the technical aspects of running a château may appear complicated, available local expertise, ripened over centuries, makes the task comparatively easy.

It is a long-standing tradition in the Médoc for the owner of a vineyard to join his name to the established title of the property. By law, the names laid down in the Classification of 1855 belong to the Committee of Classified Growths. I applied to the Marquis de Lur-Saluces, then president of the commitee, who, in 1953, officially

* See the chapter "Shall the Old Order Change?" for an explanation of "First and Second Growths," and of wine classifications in general.

authorized the change of name to Château Prieuré-Lichine. This will remain the château's official name long after I'm gone, although I still see columns by English wine writers who refuse to acknowledge the change that took place more than thirty years ago!

Soon after the Prieuré had become mine, Château Lascombes came on the market. With a group of enthusiastic and supportive shareholders, including David Rockefeller, George F. Baker Jr., Paul Mannheim, Warren Pershing, and Gilbert Kahn, I plunged for a second time, with equal pleasure and success. We finally sold Lascombes in 1971, and the sale enabled me to increase my holdings at Château Prieuré-Lichine. That property, which began as 11 hectares, now covers 62 hectares (155 acres) of vineyards.

By 1953, I owned small parts of Latricières-Chambertin and Bonnes-Mares in Burgundy, as well as the two châteaux in Bordeaux. The export company which bore my name soon grew to be one of the largest dealing in fine wines in France, and in the United States my activities as an importer, distributor, and all-round crusader on behalf of wines expanded at the same rate as the burgeoning interest in (and consumption of) wine. I was spending much time in helping to convert the United States to wine. For many years I faced six-week trips three or four times a year by propeller plane, train, and bus from coast to coast, deep into the grass roots of the U.S., which started to bear fruit. It was at about this time that I began the protracted labors that finally resulted in the publication of my *Encyclopedia of Wines & Spirits* in 1967 (revised and expanded in 1974 and every year thereafter, with a third edition published in 1981 and revised in 1982 and again in 1984, and a fourth updated and revised edition in 1985).

It became increasingly obvious to me in the mid-fifties that the 1855 Classification of the wines of the Bordeaux region had, after a hundred years, outlived its usefulness. It seemed high time to make the relative standings of the châteaux more accurate and comprehensible to buyers, especially in view of the boundary changes that have occurred with almost every sale of a property. Therefore, after consulting over seventy of the most knowledgeable palates in the Bordeaux wine trade, I devised my own classification system, published for the first time in 1962 and updated periodically since then. It is fully explained in the chapter "Shall the Old Order Change?" in this book.

Quite apart from the difficulties of *buying* wines in postwar France, the American market for wine after the Second World War was hard to crack. As an importer, I found my influence severely curtailed by the complicated legal system that controls the distribution of wines and spirits in the United States to this day. The wine and spirit laws, being different in each state, barred in many states an outside importer from having any contact with the client, whether as wholesaler or as retailer.

Many of the wholesale liquor distributors in the late 1940s were onetime boot-leggers, reluctant to take on a product for which they foresaw no market. Retailers, for the most part, apparently felt the same way. My only recourse was to take the crusade for wine directly to the consumer.

My campaign followed a pattern that was adapted to circumstances as I found them. In Detroit, for instance, I went to the city's best restaurant, where I met Lester Gruber, the proprietor, on the eve of his departure for Europe. I tore up his proposed itinerary and gave him a revised version, based on a trip I had made two years earlier with Alfred A. Knopf. My high-handed methods produced a lasting friendship and eventually helped to establish wine as an indispensable feature of the Detroit restaurant scene. It was not long before bottles began to appear on the tables of private homes as well. This scenario, recast and rescripted as necessary, repeated itself from city to city across the country.

In 1959, I spent two days in an attempt—ultimately successful—to sell 42 assorted cases of wine to the largest retail spirits company in Milwaukee. The shipment (the first French wines the company had ever stocked) sold out in a week, and the next order, unsolicited this time, was for 350 cases. Shortly thereafter, the then Governor of Wisconsin, Warren Knowles, responded enthusiastically to my suggestion that he lay down a wine cellar—a task in which I was delighted to serve as consultant—and in no time it seemed that all of Wisconsin wanted wine. The hundreds of thousands of bottles now sold annually in the state can be traced in a direct line to that first sale of 42 cases. The Wisconsin example was typical of what happened not only in the Middle West, in the East, and in California, but also throughout the United States.

The problem of customer resistance was nothing in comparison to the legal bottlenecks that impeded the wholesaler, the retailer, and the restaurateur. Interstate and intrastate licensing systems were so complicated that businessmen felt they could hardly spare the time to unravel the red tape that accompanied a shipment. In time, I am glad to say, I showed them that the complexities of selling and stocking wine were no greater than those of selling spirits. Fear of wine—the great unknown—had been at the root of the problem.

The 1959 vintage was probably the turning point for wine sales in the United States. In that year some of the press, fearless of the pressures of the dry lobby, finally discovered wine as something newsworthy, and since then there has been a gradual but inexorable improvement in attitudes and taste. It is unfortunate that this change has not been matched by similar and equally necessary changes in the United States legal code. The laws, which still reflect a narrow-minded intolerance reminiscent of post-Prohibition days, treat wines as a suspect commodity, controlling them even more rigidly than firearms. Among the most backward are the sections restricting licenses issued to importers, wholesalers, and retailers for the sale and distribution of wines and spirits.

In the 1930s, after repeal, many wine drinkers—although not the true oenophiles—in the United States tended to prefer sweet white wines, especially Sauternes. Taste gradually swung to dryness, until it eventually became an almost obsessive expression of *chic*. People equated "dryness" with sophistication (what better example than the dry Martini?), and it became fashionable to be known to like dry wines—although to this day wines embodying a certain touch of sweetness evoke the most positive market response.

My personal view is that the current fad in the United States for white wine will lead, in time, to increased consumption of red, by far the more popular accompaniment to food in the major wine-producing countries. In France, for instance, red wine accounts for close to 90 percent of all wine consumed. A similar majority applies in Italy, Spain, Argentina, and Chile. The only exceptions are South Africa and Australia, where, in any case, more white wine is produced than red.

The appetite for white wine seems to be related to the American predilection for all things chilled. When I began my crusade on behalf of the grape, the "wines" of the United States were coffee, tea, milk, or cola. Alcoholic beverages—liquor or beer—were drunk either before or after meals, never with. The beer drinker who took that light alcoholic beverage with his food was already on his way to discovering wine. The cocktail drinkers have been a good deal harder to win.

Interesting changes have taken place in French wine consumption simultaneously with the development of wine appreciation in the United States. The average French consumer of *vin ordinaire*—usually a simple red wine from the Midi—was at first hardly aware of the "hierarchy" of French wines, and even to this day most of the top wines of France are exported to the United States, England, and the Benelux. However, the switch to direct consumer sales is symptomatic of the growing French interest in their own wines. In this connection it is interesting to note that while, overall, the per capita consumption of wines in France has fallen over the past few years, the consumption of better wines has shown a marked increase.

With the jet age and the concomitant influx of tourists into Europe, there has been an unprecedented upsurge of interest in wines of every kind all over the Western world. In the United States there is hardly a city of any size that does not have its wine—or wine and food—society, whose members meet regularly to taste wine, to talk about it, to hear invited lecturers, and to exchange ideas. No bookstore is without its wine-and-food section, and adult education programs offer courses in tasting and appreciating fine wines. Weekly wine columns are now commonplace in newspapers, whereas twenty years ago they were virtually unheard of. In England, always a mainstay of the Bordeaux wine trade, there has been a proliferation of books and writers on wine. I have attended and spoken at wine tastings throughout the world, and, in this connection, have been interviewed on radio and television in the United States, Great Britain, Scandinavia, the Far East, and France. In 1968, I even made a dramatized recording, *The Joys of Wine,* which was released by MGM and sold widely. I made a new recording in 1982.

In 1966, I sold my shipping firm—Alexis Lichine and Company—to Charrington United Breweries, now Bass-Charrington, an English brewery group. Two years later, I was completely out of the wine export business and concentrating my energies on wine-making at Château Prieuré-Lichine and Château Lascombes in Margaux. Thus, during the 1973-74 Bordeaux wine crash, I was in the enviable position of being a grower and not a shipper. By the mid-seventies I was thirsting to get back into the trade, but repurchase of the Alexis Lichine name was beyond my resources at the time. It happened, however, that Norton Simon, Inc., in New York, decided in 1975 to develop a prestige wine division in their wholly owned spirit subsidiary, Somerset Importers. I was asked to join Somerset as a consultant and director; the firm contracted for the exclusive agency of the company which bears my name in Bordeaux, and I was able to control its Lichine selections from 1975 to the end of 1980.

This made me busier than ever, incessantly commuting between Europe and the United States, buying the wines for the new selections that had my name, as well as supervising the vineyard and wine at Prieuré-Lichine. Having sold Lascombes in 1971, I have found time here and there to enjoy congenial talk among friends. Over the years love of wine has attracted writers, musicians, painters, statesmen, politicians, and some of France's great chefs to the Prieuré, where I manage at last to leave the overworked world of wine behind. After all, it is only by appreciating civilization in its many expressions of art, lively company, and good food that we develop our senses and understand the role that fine wine can play in life. For close to thirty years I have organized exhibits of paintings on "La Vigne et le Vin" in the midst of the vineyards of Margaux; the latest, in 1985, were large enamels scattered through the grounds and courtyard of the Prieuré.

My own experience in wine-making, though it has spanned scarcely more than a generation, covers a period of almost incredible change. For example, scarcely more than thirty years ago in the Médoc, in Margaux as in the rest of Bordeaux, horses were still used for plowing and general transport. In Saint-Julien, it was considered *de rigueur* to have mules, and in Saint-Estèphe, where heartier wine was always made, oxen were used. I myself was first to bring a vineyard tractor to the Médoc from Burgundy (where, although the growers may often look poorer, they are usually richer). The Loiseau vineyard model, which I introduced in the Médoc through a garage in Pauillac, has now sold throughout Bordeaux for over thirty years.

Since the 1940s I have witnessed tremendous advances in the technology of wine-making. Haphazard methods of vinification, storage, and shipment have almost entirely disappeared, to be replaced by scientific techniques that, without altering the essential quality of the wine and though powerless to augment the extraordinary peaks of the truly great vintages, can do a great deal to eliminate the valleys of the poorer years.

Today the young person entering the trade—it might more properly be termed an art—learns scientific methods of vinification at modern schools with up-to-date equipment for assessing chemical characteristics, including acid and alcohol content. Twenty or thirty years ago, the only place for a student to learn was at his father's elbow, and his chemistry was in his mouth.

Greater care—even in terms of much needed simple hygiene—is now exercised in the cellars and *chais* throughout the entire duration of a wine's development. Science has brought about a fuller understanding of the fact that wine lives. It is born, it breathes, it grows from adolescence to maturity. The greater the wine, the longer its life-span. But eventually, all wine dies, returning, like man, to the separate elements that formed its initial substance.

Improvements in vinification have been applied at least as much to the lesser wines of France as to the great, where, in any case, there was not such a compelling need. Before the war, one used frequently to hear of simple *vins de pays* that could be enjoyed only in their place of origin. Excellent examples were Beaujolais, some Côtes du Rhône, and such wines of the Loire Valley as Muscadet and Vouvray. A similar caution applied to Pouilly-Fumé. With some notable exceptions, these wines were all too poorly vinified and too badly cared for to be worth shipping or to catch the interest of foreign buyers. They usually expired rapidly, oxidizing or often having an excess of acidity and incomplete secondary fermentation. But today these same wines are more than respectable, bringing high prices (and frequently high praise) from consumers not only in France but also abroad. And through improvements in quality control, many "new" wines in a lower price range have made noteworthy inroads into the market.

The costly sacrifice of carefully selecting barrels or vats in many of the top vineyards of Bordeaux has eliminated lesser wines in deficient vintages, hence adding to the reliability of a great label or château from year to year. The increased awareness of high-quality wines and subsequent greater demand for them have created scarcity among the top growths, with an over-indulgent aura for their labels. Total yearly production of the Bordeaux First Growths is under 150,000 cases and since a sizable proportion of this is required to stock the wine cellars of good restaurants all over the world, the consumer must compete as best he can. None of these top growths could actually be called "rare," but sustained high costs have made them much less accessible to the average wine lover. At the same time, though, the rise in quality of the lesser wines means that more good wine is increasingly available to all. To those of us in the business of wine, who have discovered its joys and wish above all to share them, this is good news indeed.

ALEXIS LICHINE'S GUIDE
TO THE WINES
AND VINEYARDS OF FRANCE

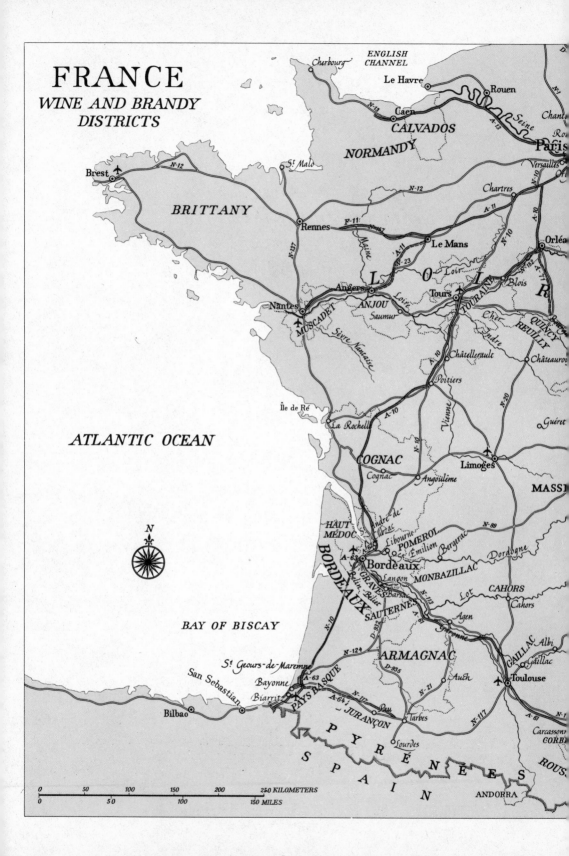

FRANCE
WINE AND BRANDY DISTRICTS

ATLANTIC OCEAN

ENGLISH CHANNEL

Cherbourg

Le Havre

Rouen

Caen   N-13   Seine

CALVADOS

NORMANDY

Paris

St Malo   N-12   Versailles

Chartres

BRITTANY

Brest   N-12

Rennes   F-11   N-157   Le Mans   Orléa

Maine   A-11   N-10   Blois

L   O   I   R

N-23

Angers   Loire   Tours   TOURAINE   QUINCY   REUILLY

ANJOU   Saumur   Cher   Indre

Nantes   MUSCADET   Châtellerault   Châteauro

Sèvre Nantaise   A-10

Poitiers   Vienne

Île de Ré

La Rochelle   Guéret

Limoges

COGNAC   **MASSI**

Cognac   Angoulême

N-89

HAUT-   St André-de-

MÉDOC   Cubzac   Libourne   Dordogne

POMEROL

A-63   Émilion   Bergerac

BORDEAUX   Bordeaux

GRAVES   Langon   MONBAZILLAC   Lot   **CAHORS**

Julien-Beau   Barsac   N-113   Cahors

SAUTERNES   Agen

N-10   Garonne   GAILLAC   Albi

BAY OF BISCAY   D-932   Gaillac

N-124   **ARMAGNAC**   Toulouse

St Geours-de-Maremne   D-935

San Sebastian   A-63   Auch   N-21

Bayonne   PAYS BASQUE   N-117   A-61

Biarrit   A-64   Pau   N-117   Carcassonn

Bilbao   JURANÇON   Tarbes   CORB

N-   Lourdes   ROUS

P Y R É N É E S

S P A I N   ANDORRA

N

0   50   100   150   200   250 KILOMETERS

0   50   100   150 MILES

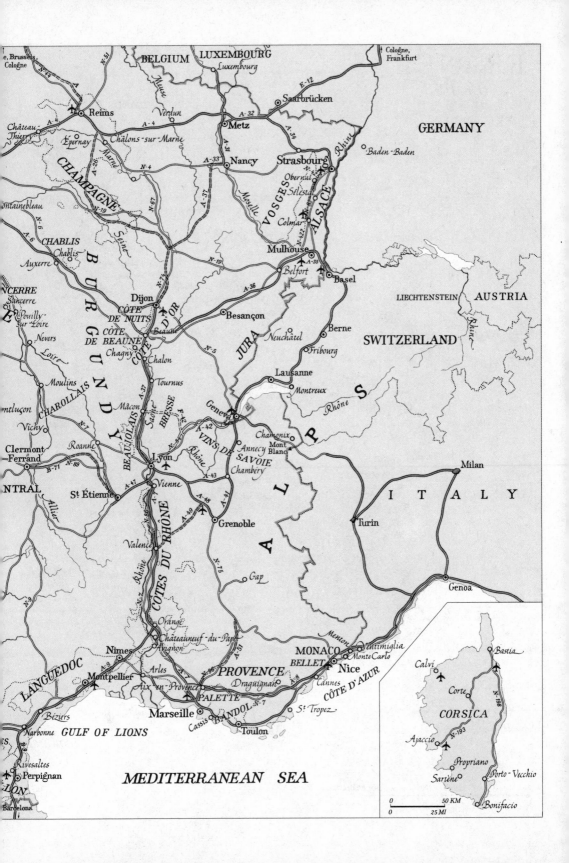

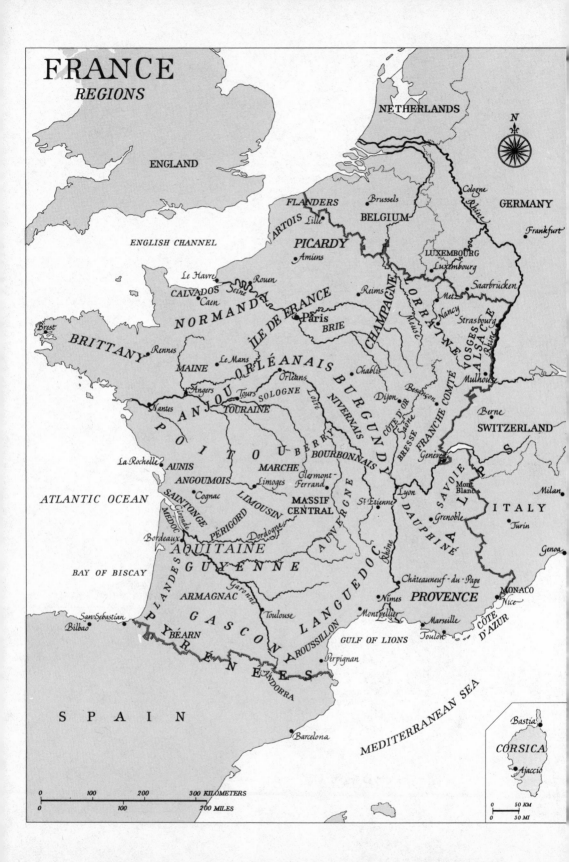

FRANCE
REGIONS

NETHERLANDS

ENGLAND

GERMANY

Cologne

Frankfurt

ENGLISH CHANNEL

FLANDERS

Brussels

BELGIUM

Lille

ARTOIS

PICARDY

Amiens

LUXEMBOURG

Luxembourg

Saarbrücken

Le Havre

Rouen

Seine

CALVADOS

Caen

NORMANDY

ÎLE DE FRANCE

Paris

BRIE

CHAMPAGNE

Reims

LORRAINE

Metz

Nancy

Meuse

Strasbourg

VOSGES

ALSACE

Brest

BRITTANY

Rennes

MAINE

Le Mans

ANJOU

ORLÉANAIS

Orléans

Chablis

BURGUNDY

Dijon

CÔTE D'OR

Besançon

FRANCHE COMTÉ

Mulhouse

Berne

SWITZERLAND

Angers

Tours

TOURAINE

SOLOGNE

Loire

NIVERNAIS

Saône

BRESSE

Genève

Nantes

POITOU

BERRY

BOURBONNAIS

La Rochelle

AUNIS

MARCHE

Limoges

Clermont-Ferrand

MASSIF CENTRAL

AUVERGNE

St Etienne

Lyon

SAVOIE

Mont Blanc

Milan

ATLANTIC OCEAN

ANGOUMOIS

SAINTONGE

Cognac

LIMOUSIN

Grenoble

Turin

ITALY

MÉDOC

Gironde

PÉRIGORD

Dordogne

Bordeaux

AQUITAINE

GUYENNE

DAUPHINÉ

ALPS

Genoa

BAY OF BISCAY

LANDES

ARMAGNAC

Garonne

Toulouse

LANGUEDOC

Rhône

Nîmes

Châteauneuf-du-Pape

PROVENCE

MONACO

Nice

CÔTE D'AZUR

San Sebastián

Bilbao

GASCONY

BÉARN

PYRÉNÉES

ANDORRA

ROUSSILLON

Montpellier

Marseille

Toulon

GULF OF LIONS

Perpignan

SPAIN

Barcelona

MEDITERRANEAN SEA

Bastia

CORSICA

Ajaccio

| 0 | 100 | 200 | 300 KILOMETERS |

| 0 | 100 | 200 MILES |

| 0 | 50 KM |

| 0 | 30 MI |

THE WINES
OF FRANCE

From time immemorial, the world's greatest wines have come from France. Though not large in size, for the diversity and quantity of wines it produces France could be a continent. From some 1.1 million hectares (under 3 million acres)* of vines, more than half a million French growers extract 75 million hectoliters (2 billion gallons) of wine each year—25 percent of all the wine produced in the world. Wine is made in at least 80 of the nation's 95 continental *départements*. A great deal of it is coarse, rough stuff, which is nonetheless downed in huge quantities throughout France; the annual French wine consumption amounts to fewer than 100 bottles for every man, woman, and child in the country. Of this vast vinous outpouring of 75 million hectoliters—10 billion bottles—less than one-fifth is worth the serious attention of wine lovers. The better wines, controlled by Appellation Contrôlée laws, amount in an average year to the equivalent of some 13 million hectoliters of fine table wines—150 million cases of twelve bottles each. These are as richly varied as the landscape. There is hardly a corner of the country that does not offer its own distinctive wines and cuisine, history and scenery, in almost equal measure.

The first of those four attractions was, until recent decades, the least reliable of

* One hectare equals about 2.5 acres.

5

all. Until the 1930s, a great deal of wine outside of the château-bottled wines of Bordeaux was fraudulently labeled. Now virtually every variable that goes into the making of wine is strictly regulated by the rigorous and enlightened laws known as the Appellation d'Origine Contrôlée, or A.O.C., meaning "controlled name of origin." The laws are in fact decrees formulated by the growers, who are supervised by the I.N.A.O., the Institut National des Appellations d'Origine (National Institute of Place-names). The conclusions determined by the growers and the I.N.A.O. are made official by the Ministry of Agriculture, and influence the wine laws of the member nations of the Common Market.

These laws control every factor that contributes to the wine, every process that may affect it; in fact, under these laws every detail literally from the ground up is regulated until the bottle of wine is sold to the consumer or leaves the boundaries of France. The fraud inspectors ensure that the law is enforced. While each control law will be adapted to its specific area, all are governed by broad general principles, which are the result of two thousand years of trial and error, of matching hundreds of grape varieties with the multitude of soils and microclimates in France.

With this experience in mind, the first task is to delimit the area of production for each place-name. The geological composition of the land is studied and marked out by experts in the region, and only vineyards within the delimited area are permitted to use the place-name. The boundaries are reflected on the property land map, or *cadastre,* kept in the town hall of every village with Appellation Contrôlée vineyards.

Grape varieties are specified by law, because in different soils and under different skies the same vine will produce grapes with different characteristics. The selection of grape varieties follows the traditional practices of each area.

Methods of pruning and other practices of vine culture are outlined where necessary. Minimum alcoholic content of the wine is specified because alcohol helps to give wine its staying power—its ability to live long enough to develop into greatness. If not properly pruned, the vines will overproduce and the grapes may develop so little sugar that the wine will end up unbalanced, with too little alcohol to match its other characteristics. Stipulation of minimum natural alcohol content before enrichment of the wine is thus an assurance of quality.

This principle is further pursued by limiting the maximum harvest per hectare. Since quality is inversely proportional to quantity, the amount of permissible harvest is specified. This is expressed in hectoliters per hectare (which may be converted into maximums of tons or gallons per acre). This maximum yield decreases (thus promoting quality) as the place-names get geographically more specific and smaller.

Other vinicultural practices are specified, including a total prohibition of irrigation. The ban on irrigation remained steadfast even through the great drought of

1976, when not a drop of rain fell on France from June until the end of August, and a government-levied drought tax to subsidize stricken growers evoked a furious outcry from the public. Still, 1976 was a very good vintage.

The A.O.C. laws apply to about 33 percent of France's wines. Less stringent laws govern the lesser wines, about 5 percent of total production, that are classed as Vins Délimités de Qualité Supérieure, or V.D.Q.S., identifiable as such by the V.D.Q.S. emblem on the label. Some of these wines, such as Corbières and Vins de la Moselle, can be a good value. The remaining 62 percent of French wine production is officially lumped together as *vins ordinaires* or *vins de consommation,* meaning generally cheap, common wines with little claim to distinction.

The A.O.C. laws have required growers to match soils and microclimates with the most promising vines until the nearest thing to a perfect marriage is achieved. This has given France in the past an incomparable advantage over the other fifty or so wine-growing countries of the world, none of which had a body of wine law as long established or as toughly enforced as the Gallic A.O.C. Moreover, these laws have clearly benefited the grower of French wine as well as the consumer. While the amount of land used to produce *vins ordinaires* not subject to A.O.C. regulation has steadily decreased in recent years, the area devoted to wines that are made under A.O.C. laws has expanded. While it is a certainty that the production of A.O.C. wines is rising, it is equally certain that world demand for some of the finest will continue to outstrip supply.

Two conclusions are evident. One is that buyers of French wine (including the French) are demanding higher quality: since the late 1970s, French consumption of A.O.C. wines has grown from 7 to 20 percent of their total wine diet, the rest being in V.D.Q.S., *vins de table,* or mediocre brand-name wines. The other is that growers and shippers are responding with greater self-discipline and striving to make better wines. This is not to deny that a lot of French wine is still sold under misleading labels or that, on occasion, it can be overpriced. However, as a gauge of consumer awareness, when prices of Bordeaux wines soared through the roof in 1973 as the result of a speculative boom, American buyers in particular, and the French, English, and Belgians as well, virtually boycotted them until they returned to reasonable levels.

In other, more constant ways every bottle represents a battle against poor weather, disease, and insects that perennially threaten the harvest. In this respect, the art and science of making wine has progressed enormously in the past two decades. Although the vines are still plagued in some years by mildew (as in 1977), frost, hailstorms, drought, and overabundant rains, growers today know infinitely more about viticulture than did their parents. In the old days, Burgundians had a saying: "One-third of the grapes for plant sickness, one-third for insects, one-third for the wine." Now they have nearly three-thirds for the wine and the grapes are healthier and better. And when it comes to harvesting the crop, modern growers rely less on the feel and taste of the grape; patrolling the vineyards before the harvest with mustimeters, they can tell accurately when the grapes are approaching ripeness. Most important of all, there is a constant dialogue between the grower and the oenologist. By harvesting too soon, the grower risks making a thin wine, low in alcohol and too high in acidity. On the other hand, by waiting too long, there is the risk of rain, which can swell the grapes to bursting point, diluting their character, and bring on rot. Today, the chances of making the correct choice are far better than they were before.

In the cellars or aboveground *chais* where the wine is left to ferment, the great old oaken *cuves* (vats) are rapidly being replaced by stainless steel, glass, and concrete vats. These are less romantic, certainly, but they permit fermentation under finely tuned, controlled temperatures and clean conditions.

Throughout France, the most dramatic changes in this arcane business have been brought about by oenology, the application of science to the making of wine. Only quite recently in the six-thousand-year known history of wine has advanced technology come to the aid of the man in the cellar or *chai*. Émile Peynaud, the distinguished oenologist, professor emeritus of the Station Oenologique de Bordeaux, notes that the chemical compounds identifiable in wine have risen in a few years from four to some seven hundred; not until after World War II did scientists begin to explore the biochemistry and microbiology of wine. Laboratories, once dismissed by tradition-bound growers as expensive frippery, have become at least as essential to wine-making as human intuition. Every step in the production of fine wine is monitored by scientific methods. The men in the white smocks are not alchemists; they will never be able to transmute pallid wines into heroic vintages. They can, however, help to minimize the faults of an average wine and heighten the virtues of a great one. Unfortunately, oenologists were not around to help with the disastrous trio of vintages: 1930, 1931, and 1932—years when the wine made was hardly drinkable. Better viticultural and vinicultural techniques might have produced light, thin, fast-maturing, but correct wines which would have found a market. The chemical analysis of wine is like breaking down the pigments in an Impressionist painting: it tells you what colors the artist used, not what makes the painting great. As Professor Peynaud observes, "Technology and taste must work together." Today, even brokers like Henri Meurgey of Beaune rely on the lab to test the wines they handle; his father, who was a broker before him, probably never in his life resorted to the test tube.

Science and the wine laws can only go so far, however. It is the combination of four main factors that determines the quality of wine: the soil, the microclimate, the grape variety, and the man behind the bottle. In one happy respect, that ancient formula may be changing. In recent years, women have been entering the world of French wine, which, from ancient times, has been a jealously guarded bastion of masculine skills and prerogatives. More than once at dinner with one of the venerable shipping families of Bordeaux, I have heard the patriarch exclaim over a newly decanted bottle, "Excellent! Excellent! *None for the ladies!*" Today, armed with diplomas in oenology, women are engaged in every area of wine production and shipping. Not only in France but throughout the world, women are also doing more of the buying of wine for the home. Statistics show that in the United States, for example, around 80 percent of all table wine is bought by women. This reflects the sales of gallons and half-gallons of domestic wines for daily use, which forms the bulk of all wine consumption in the United States, and the accessibility of wine in supermarkets, which has made shopping for the daily wine, along with other daily supplies, the responsibility of women. As a result, until recently these figures did not hold true for French wines, which continued to be bought predominantly by men.

Another socioeconomic factor influencing wine-making is that wine buyers today tend to be younger—between 25 and 49 years old; few of them have the money, patience, or space to store precious bottles for years before they can be consumed. As Paul Bocuse, the renowned author-chef, points out: "In the old days, you bought wine at the birth of your child and drank it at his or her wedding. Now there's less ceremony, people have less time. Tastes have changed, as fashions have changed, toward the light and informal, and spontaneous." Additionally, with financing charges that can run to 15 percent annually, or more, few producers and shippers have the resources to keep slow-maturing wines for years in inventory. Hence the trend toward lighter, softer, suppler wines that can be drunk fairly young, yet continue to develop in the bottle.

To appreciate the benign impact of technological change on this ancient trade, one only has to recall that many of the French wines we consumed in the 1930s and '40s—the Maconnais, Beaujolais, Muscadets, Côtes du Rhône, Anjous, Vouvrays, and other Loires—were little more than country wines, or *vins de pays*. Most vineyards were like convents, sealed to tourists. Nowadays, however, there is hardly a wine-village in France that is not festooned with signs inviting the passer-by to come in, inspect, sip, and buy a few bottles of the local vintage. The growers have reaped enormous benefits from this casual trade, not only in public relations but also in the sheer volume of wine sold, without benefit of middleman, to drop-in tourists from all over Europe. Burgundy, in particular, is rapidly becoming a vast retail wine market, with signs proclaiming "Vente Directe" or "Dégustation et Vente" everywhere you look. Occasionally, a sign will deliver the same invitation to taste and buy in English or German. This lively trade, and indeed the general elevation of quality, has been made possible to a large extent by the widespread adoption of the system of estate- (*domaine-*) bottling, initiated by Bordeaux vintners with their château-bottlings. In Burgundy, especially, few producers in the immediate postwar years were bottling their own wines, leaving that task to the shipper, who bought his wines in barrel from the producer and, too often, turned out blends and permutations that bore little relation to the original wine. As a mark of honesty, and usually of quality, any estate-bottled French wine is labeled as such.

However, a word of caution is necessary. The present huge demand for French wine throughout the world is a threat to this tradition of quality. The present cry is for more of everything turned out at a faster rate. Wine can be made inexpensively, but it will not then be fine wine. The best wines have always been made from relatively unproductive vines, deliberately pruned to reduce output and channel the plant's energy into the production of superior fruit. The general boom period for French wines has also resulted in large planting of vines in new or previously abandoned areas. Some of these new plots are not suitable for good grape varieties. Another trend with serious consequences for French vineyards is the recent tendency to overfertilize. Some growers have been dumping enough phosphates and rich loam into their vineyards to create a truck garden. In addition, the growers, especially in the Midi and outside the Appellation Contrôlée areas in the Languedoc-Roussillon vineyards on the Mediterranean coast, prefer to plant the more productive vine varieties, sacrificing quality for quantity. And many growers have also been playing it safe by advancing the dates of the harvest, and thereby producing lesser wines. Only by gambling—waiting to get the most out of the weather and risking the rainfall that may overswell and damage the grapes by rotting—can one hope to achieve the best results.

As the market for French wines has expanded, so has the demand for a more standardized product. The far-flung clientele of French wines has at times been slow to appreciate the variations in wines as they occur from vintage to vintage. Wines will be different in different years, and rarely is there a vintage without some virtues. The catechism of the plastic vintage card cannot be taken as an infallible *diktat,* as it too often is. Vintages are not the most important quality factor.

A major obstacle to the full understanding and acceptance of French wine lies in the 1855 Classification of the wines of Bordeaux, based on long-outdated boundaries, defunct ownership, commercial rivalries, and what appear today to have been, in many cases, arbitrary and inconsistent standards. The system—however sensible it may have seemed at the time—totally excludes such districts as Pomerol, with its great Château Pétrus, and Saint-Émilion, with its Cheval-Blanc and Ausone, and classes certain superior vineyards as only Fourth or Fifth Growths, in some cases because they may not have had the standing at the time or the social "pull" of their neighbors. (This subject is discussed at greater length in the chapter "Shall the Old Order Change?") The only discernible advantage of this system to the consumer is that many wines that are rightly or wrongly given lower rankings by the 1855 Classification are fun to seek out and frequently may be good buys.

Though the names of the famous French wines conjure up visions of vast and lordly estates, they are grown for the most part on minuscule plots. For example, the great Chambertin vineyards, Le Chambertin and Chambertin Clos-de-Bèze, are large by Burgundy standards, yet cover only 28 hectares (70 acres) and are owned by over two dozen different families. Le Montrachet, the greatest of white Burgundies, is even smaller at 7 hectares (17.5 acres). Even in Bordeaux, taking in the entire region, where properties tend to be larger, most owners are wine peasants and their wine-making continues as artisanry. It is by drinking the small wines, rather than beginning with the great ones, that the consumer can best get to know the great array of French wines. I have always argued that specific and rigid classifications mean little: only by tasting and comparing and classifying wines by your own standards can you appreciate their merits. Learning about wine is one of the pleasantest educational pursuits known to man.

The pursuit has been made infinitely easier in recent years by France's extensive new network of expressways, or autoroutes. These superhighways make most of the wine regions quickly accessible from Paris:

• The vast, chalky plain of Champagne, with its large corporate or family-run firms and huge cellars, is less than a ninety-minute drive to the east of Paris.

• Three hours east of Champagne lies Alsace, which makes the Alsatian Rhine wines of France and is one of the country's most attractive regions.

• Driving south from Paris on Autoroute A-6, which after it splits leads to the Côte d'Azur or into Spain, it takes only about ninety minutes to reach Chablis, the northernmost of all winegrowing slopes in Burgundy and one of the world's most famous wine names.

• Another hour or so will bring you to the ancient city of Beaune, which rightfully calls itself the capital of Burgundian wines and is well worth a visit.

• Detouring to the north, on N-74, you can visit the great red-wine vineyards of the Côte de Nuits. To the south lie the slopes of the Côte de Beaune and its varied reds and whites.

• Getting back onto the autoroute at Chalon, it takes only forty minutes to reach Mâcon, whose most famous wine is the dry white Pouilly-Fuissé. Bordering Pouilly-Fuissé on the south, and well worth a detour, lies the charming Beaujolais country, whose red wines are now among the world's best-known.

• Traveling south on the autoroute, you come to Lyon, capital of France's richest gastronomic region, and beyond it the Côtes du Rhône, whose distinctive wines are finding favor increasingly in France and abroad. Farther south you can either branch off to the east to explore the sunny vineyards of fabled Provence and the beach resorts of the Côte d'Azur, or veer west on the road to Spain to visit the Languedoc-Roussillon, a beautiful and sometimes wild region.

• Or, starting again from Paris and heading southwest, it takes less than two hours to reach Tours, the heart of the magnificent, château-lined Loire Valley, whose vineyards and seigneurial domains stretch for hundreds of kilometers from Pouilly-Fumé to the Muscadet district on the Atlantic Ocean.

• Less than two hours southwest from Tours, on A-10, brings you to Cognac and Jarnac, home of the great Cognac firms that distill and age the world's most elegant brandy.

• Continuing south on A-10 at Saintes, one hour's drive takes you into the Bordeaux district, one of the world's greatest—if not *the* greatest—winegrowing regions, and the most diversified. It takes under two hours to drive through the Bordeaux region, from the tip of the Médoc to Sauternes—much longer if you detour northeast to Saint-Émilion, the oldest and one of the most picturesque wine towns in France. I have also said a few condensed words about many of the towns, their sights, and their specialties.

In all the vineyard regions and along all the roads, you will find good restaurants that pride themselves on the local gastronomic specialties. Some in the vineyard regions are among the best in France; and many out-of-the-way places serve good food with care and courtesy. Hotels, from the modest to the grand, especially recently, are generally clean and hospitable. In the wine country, after all, they have been feeding and bedding strangers for many centuries. To travel through these regions as leisurely as possible is as much a part of a wine education as sipping the vintages.

Finally, it must be understood that the list of restaurants and hotels that follows each chapter does not attempt to cover all that is available in the entire region. I have restricted my choices to the hotels and restaurants in the wine districts themselves and their main cities. Wherever possible, I have favored the establishments in the vineyard villages rather than the cities, simply as a matter of convenience to the traveler—even though, in some cases, this involved an unavoidable compromising of gastronomic standards. Some areas are more blessed than others when it comes to a choice of establishments; some of the restaurants listed in the Médoc, for example, are not meant to be taken as comparable in overall quality with those listed in Lyon, one of France's greatest centers of *grande cuisine*. But I have tried to supply the wine tourist with a useful selection, even in regions where the choice is necessarily limited.

The hotel and restaurant lists at the end of most chapters should be used in conjunction with the maps of the vineyard districts; together they will make any vineyard tour easier than has been the case in the past. For further clarity, each town or city heading is accompanied by the departmental number and name. Distances of each vineyard town and village from important cities of the region are listed in parentheses as reference points. *The distances are given in kilometers.*

The hotels and restaurants which have been chosen are of three types. Hotels with no restaurant, or just a snack-bar, are indicated by **H**, with the occasional comment "restaurant available" to indicate that one *can* eat at the hotel, although the food is not of special interest. Restaurants, indicated by **R**, range from the simplest to the most grand; some are indicated as having rooms, but not of a sufficient number or quality for the traveler to search them out when a better alternative is available. Hotel-restaurants, indicated by **HR**, are so designated because they offer both a sufficient number of comfortably furnished rooms and a restaurant of at least passing interest. *A point to keep in mind:* In season a number of hotel-restaurants *require* you to take your meals in their restaurant; if you don't, you are charged just the same. If in doubt, call ahead.

Street addresses are given for most establishments; for some of the tiny vineyard villages, however, the actual street name (if there is one) has little relevance. Once you reach the village, there are often signs pointing the way, otherwise ask directions; it's bound to be well known among the locals. In November 1985 all the area codes of France were integrated into the phone numbers. The telephone system in France is explained more fully in a separate chapter toward the end of the book, on pages 417–18.

Finally, a point of terminology: In French the term *menu* not only refers, as in English, to the comprehensive listing of a restaurant's offerings but also designates, more narrowly, a meal of three to five courses (depending on the establishment) at a given overall price. The menu (in the more usual sense) may list a variety of such "menus." Since there is no precise English equivalent for this second meaning of the word, I have followed the French in using *menu* in both senses.

Naturally I hope that the sense of adventure and anticipation that accompanies a new dining experience will be fulfilled. If the descriptions I have offered do not correspond to your experiences, or if you have suggestions or discoveries of your own, I would appreciate hearing from you at:

Château Prieuré-Lichine
33460 Margaux
France

Or, instead of writing, why not visit Château Prieuré-Lichine and contribute your applause or criticisms orally? This is another way I can add your evaluations to mine for future editions. Furthermore, the Château (25 kilometers outside of Bordeaux) is open every day, including Sundays and holidays. English-speaking guides take you through the cellars, explaining the background and wine-making processes, and I have been told that this is alone well worth a special trip.

BORDEAUX

In the southwest corner of France, on a curve of the Garonne River, lies the world capital of wine, the oenophile's Athens and Rome. Physically, Bordeaux is a city of some grandeur, and it boasts some noble buildings; but its real greatness lies rather in its history and its wines. For nearly two thousand years the Bordelais have been involved in the tending of vines and the making, selling, sipping, and shipping of wine. As the city's well-filled restaurants and well-fed citizens attest, wine is still big business in Bordeaux, and long may it prosper.

For more than a thousand years, Bordeaux has also been a major port. Indeed, its function determined its name: *au bord de l'eau,* at the water's edge. Its Roman name was Burdigala, which means the same thing, and in the days of the Caesars the town was a strategic and convivial headquarters for the Roman troops assigned to Gaul. Indeed, one can well imagine Bordeaux as a rest-and-recreation center for legionnaires on leave from the Frankish fronts. But, first and last, Bordeaux is a port, and therein, as much as in the great vineyards that encompass it, has lain its destiny.

Like the Port of London, Bordeaux is not on the ocean: it lies 100 kilometers (60 miles) upstream from the Atlantic, sheltered from storms. Although it is on the banks of the Garonne, its access to the world is through the Gironde, a wide, lazy, and muddy river formed by the confluence of the Garonne and the Dordogne, flowing in from the east. The Gironde, so peaceful-seeming, has been a vital artery of transportation and supply in most recorded European wars. It has also been the great funnel of wine to the world.

The port area of Bordeaux, the long *quais* that curl around the river's bend, was originally on the outskirts of the city; over the years it forced the city to the river, bending it into the shape of a crescent moon. Originally, the medieval walls placed the port beyond town limits, leaving the waterfront to the Carthusian monastery; after the good monks abandoned the site, the waterfront took on their name, becoming the Quai des Chartrons. Still off limits, it became the ghetto of the foreign Protestant traders, forerunners of today's wine merchants who set up shop there in the seventeenth, eighteenth, and nineteenth centuries. But the advantages of the city as an exporting center had been recognized centuries before foreign shipping firms settled along the banks of the river. To the loading docks of Bordeaux came wine from all over the Garonne and Dordogne basin. From Agen, Gaillac, Moissac, and Cahors far inland, came the hearty, full red wines that in the twelfth, thirteenth, and fourteenth centuries often rivaled the section known as Entre-Deux-Mers just outside Bordeaux. Whatever their origins, the wines passed through the dockers' hands at Bordeaux, and so were known as "Bordeaux" wherever they went (although in England they have always been dubbed "claret," a corruption of *clairet*—an old French word meaning wines made from red and white grapes combined).

Then, as now, the market for the Bordeaux wine trade was "foreign," whether the wine was shipped to the northern ports of France or to Belgium, Holland, or England. It was only natural that the other port cities of western Europe should be the first converts to this finest consummation of the grape. Of all the countries exposed to wine, the English took to it with the greatest alacrity and went to rather extreme measures to get more of it. In 1152, Eleanor of Aquitaine, whose first marriage to King Louis VII of France had been annulled (he suspected her of infidelity), was married to Henry Plantagenet, Count of Anjou and heir (as Henry II) to the English throne. Eleanor's dowry included territories in Poitou and the Limousin, to the north and northeast of Bordeaux, and, most importantly, in the Guyenne, the area that covered nearly all the Aquitaine wine-producing country in the southwest of France. Two years later, in 1154, when King Stephen died and Henry and Eleanor became King and Queen of England, they held between them a fabulous fiefdom all the way from Normandy and Brittany to Spain. This was not unusual at a time when the vassals who held a few hundred square miles could find themselves changing nationality overnight after a battle, a bedding, or a coup.

It was not exactly the intention of Henry and Eleanor to make vassals of their French subjects. The English court began by appointing a governor and various other officials, both for the city of Bordeaux and the province of Aquitaine. Soon

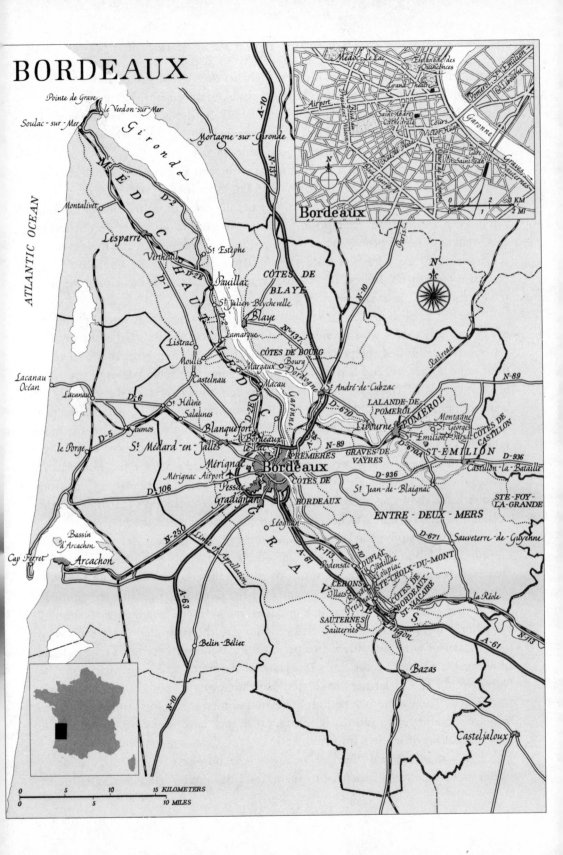

BORDEAUX

Pointe de Grave
le Verdon-sur-Mer
Soulac-sur-Mer
Mortagne-sur-Gironde

Gironde

ATLANTIC OCEAN

Montalivet

MÉDOC

Lesparre

Verthuil
St Estèphe
Pauillac
St Julien-Beychevelle
Blaye
Lamarque
Listrac
Moulis
Margaux
Bourg
Castelnau
Macau
Lacanau-Océan
Lacanau
St Hélène
Salaunes
Blanquefort
Saumos
St Médard-en-Jalles
le Porge
Mérignac
Mérignac Airport
Pessac
Gradignan
le Lac

CÔTES DE BLAYE
CÔTES DE BOURG
Dordogne
St André-de-Cubzac
LALANDE-DE-POMEROL
Libourne
POMEROL
St Georges
Montagne
St Émilion-Parsat
CÔTES DE CASTILLON
ST-ÉMILION
Castillon-la-Bataille
GRAVES-DE-VAYRES
PREMIÈRES
BORDEAUX
St Jean-de-Blaignac
STE-FOY-LA-GRANDE

CÔTES DE BORDEAUX

BORDEAUX

ENTRE-DEUX-MERS
Sauveterre-de-Guyenne

Léognan

Bassin d'Arcachon
Cap Ferret
Arcachon

Podensac
CERONS
Villats
Dupiac
Cadillac
Loupiac
STE-CROIX-DU-MONT
CÔTES DE BORDEAUX-ST-MACAIRE
la Réole

SAUTERNES
Sauternes
Langon

Belin-Béliet

Bazas

Casteljaloux

Bordeaux

Médoc, Le Lac
Esplanade des Quinconces
Grand-Théâtre
Airport
Saint-André Cathedral
Garonne
Saint-Jean
Graves, Sauternes
Bordeaux

0 1 2 KM
0 1 2 MI

0 5 10 15 KILOMETERS
0 5 10 MILES

the resident bourgeoisie was granted the right to elect a lord mayor and select a regional governing body, the Jurade, from the local establishment. There was no communication barrier between London and far-off Bordeaux; the language of the
English court at that time was French, and remained French up to the time of John
of Gaunt, who was named Prince of Aquitaine in 1390.

Thus, the Bordelais felt a closer kinship with their English rulers than they did
with the equally remote French crown. The English allowed them to manage their
own affairs, and where they intervened they usually came in on the side of the local
burghers, granting them exemption from various sales taxes and trade restrictions
that were required of other merchants from outside Bordeaux. By the middle of the
fourteenth century, wine was Bordeaux's greatest export and the English were its
best customers by far. Indeed, the English were quick to see that by helping the wine
trade they would, in every sense, be helping themselves.

The first English monarch to espouse the cause of wine was King John, the son
of Henry and Eleanor, who ascended the throne in 1199. For political and economic
reasons, he established the practice of favoring the Bordeaux merchants over those
from outside the city, and laid down rigid rules about the selling-dates of the wine.
Since methods of conservation were but vaguely understood at the time—wine
being bought and sold only in the barrel—the wine that had been most recently
casked, bought, and sold was considered the most palatable and, therefore, the most
valuable. Growers and merchants from outside the city were not allowed to sell their
wines until November or December, to allow adequate time for the Bordelais to
unload their stocks of newly made wine. Over the years, the decrees sent out from
London made the business so favorable for the Bordeaux shippers that traders from
outside the area clamored to be admitted to the inner elite of the bourgeoisie.

To be sure, ships sailed from Soulac, on the Atlantic near the mouth of the
Gironde, and Libourne, on the Dordogne, in the fourteenth and fifteenth centuries.
However, because of the strict control of river traffic up and down the Gironde,
Dordogne, and Garonne, Bordeaux remained the dominant port of the region. In
early winter, when the wine was just in barrel, the Garonne swarmed with ships all
vying for position at the leading harbor. In 1350, the equivalent of 1 million of
today's cases of wine was shipped in barrels from Bordeaux, going to England and
all along the Channel coast from Le Havre to Amsterdam; from Amsterdam, the
Dutch would take it farther yet to the Hanseatic ports in northern Germany and
Scandinavia. There were two periods for wine shipments: one in autumn, called the
"vintage" shipping, and another in spring, called the "rack" shipping, after the wine
had been drawn off its lees into fresh casks.

When the Hundred Years War began, the burghers, quite happy under a
régime so commercially beneficial to them, took the English side, fearing naturally

that an end to English rule would mean an end to their privileges. The war raged on and off from 1337 to 1453, punctuated by the Plague. It ran from the hills of Pauillac in the Médoc, where the fortress of Latour was razed, upriver as far as Castillon on the Dordogne, where England's General John Talbot was finally defeated in 1453. This victory made Aquitaine French once again. The Bordeaux wine trade passed through a period of uncertainty; its privileges were suspended and the trade with England came to an end. But with the coronation of Louis XI in 1461, the commercial and financial advantages traditionally accorded to the Bordeaux merchants were reinstated and, in some cases, increased. The next two centuries were marked by a great expansion of the wine trade, particularly with the Dutch, who had replaced the English as the foremost maritime power. Every October the ships from Holland would arrive by the thousands in the Gironde, for claret and for the cheaper white wines of the Charente around Cognac, for consumption that winter, and also for trade and resale the following spring. The Dutch were aided in their rise to pre-eminence in the trade by the continuing hostile relations between the French and the English, whether in the form of outright war or punitive excise taxes.

The eighteenth century under Louis XIV and Louis XV was the *belle époque* for both the wine trade and the city of Bordeaux. Better methods of conservation—the blown-glass bottle and the cork stopper—opened new overseas markets, including the British Colonies in North America, the West Indies, and French Canada. The first glassworks in Bordeaux was founded in 1723, and by 1790 the total output had grown to 2 million hand-blown bottles per year. The oldest bottle remaining of château-bottled wine in the Médoc is a 1797 in the cellar of Lafite. Although the great Mme de Sévigné had predicted that Bordeaux would go out of style like "coffee and Racine," by the late eighteenth century wine snobs in England and France were savoring and treasuring their Bordeaux, quoting not Sévigné, but perhaps Samuel Johnson's dictum: "He who aspires to be a serious wine drinker *must* drink *Claret.*"

In this time of economic expansion, other commercial goods began to gain on wine in importance. Bordeaux prospered from a version of the "triangular" trade: slaves from Africa to the West Indies, which in turn shipped mahogany, tobacco, rum, sugar, coffee, cotton, and indigo to Bordeaux, which then sent arms, as well as other manufactured goods and luxury items, including wines, back to Africa. As trade flourished, it financed for the Bordelais some of France's finest eighteenth-century architecture, much of it commissioned by the king's appointees in charge of governing the city, who were called the king's intendants. From Louis XV to the Revolution, the intendants set about changing the body and face of Bordeaux. The greatest of them all was the Duc de Richelieu (1692-1788), who was banished from the court of Versailles to govern Guyenne by Louis XV. To his credit, Richelieu swallowed, so to speak, his pique. A fervent lover of Burgundy, he became a convert to the wines of Bordeaux. And he commissioned Victor-Louis to design and construct the Grand Theatre in Bordeaux. Not only were great public buildings conceived and executed at this time, but throughout the city the boulevards were lined with private mansions, *"hôtels particuliers,"* which stand to this day as monuments to the wealth, taste, and confidence of their age. Many of the wealthier shippers and château owners have kept them as townhouses.

The economic boom brought more than great architecture to Bordeaux; it also attracted the foreign tradesman-shipper. The daring, energetic Protestants from England, Holland, Denmark, and Ireland all saw the opportunity for profit in the fine wines of Bordeaux. Their firms sprouted up along the Quai des Chartrons, which became the shippers' exclusive, isolated quarter of Bordeaux, gray-and-white stone houses with flat façades hiding beneath and behind them a warren of tunneled warehouse and *chai* space. Far back in the dark recesses of the *chais,* the shippers would age, store, and care for their wine in vats or barrels. When ready for shipment, the wine would be put into cheaper shipping barrels and rolled across the wharf, then loaded directly aboard ship. Not content to let the markets come to them, the shippers, intrepid salesmen at heart, traveled throughout Europe on horseback and carriage, often risking their lives to find new customers and make new converts to Bordeaux wines.

The French Revolution and the Napoleonic Wars brought particularly hard times for the Bordeaux wine trade, closing the traditional market of England and impeding trade with America and the West Indian colonies, as well as cutting off all overland traffic. To this injury was added a further insult: Napoleon preferred Chambertin and Clos de Vougeot to claret. The growers could only wait and hope, while the shippers began handling more mundane commodities for a livelihood. When Napoleon was finally exiled to St. Helena, the wine trade picked up again. The big boost to the trade came, as before, from England. In 1860, the English Chancellor of the Exchequer, William Gladstone, drastically lowered the duty on imported wines. The boom in "Gladstone's Claret," as it came to be called, continued for the rest of the century. Englishmen laid down bottles of claret as never before, and some of England's great collections of fine Bordeaux vintages date from this time. Although her soil has never been regarded as particularly favorable to the production of wine, England has been shown again and again to be one of the happiest homes of fine French wines. Indeed, a substantial part of the Bordeaux wine trade was sustained by the eager and knowledgeable English market of the mid-nineteenth century. As Edmund Penning-Rowsell reports in his book *The Wines of Bordeaux,* British imports of French wine more than tripled in the two years after Gladstone lowered the duty. On the French side of the Channel, well-stocked cellars can be found in the north of

France, particularly in the cities of Lille, Roubaix, and Tourcoing, and especially in Belgium. Other markets for Bordeaux wine opened up in the last half of the nineteenth century in Scandinavia, Russia, and Argentina—these last two now eclipsed.

This boom era for the trade soon suffered its greatest setback with the arrival of phylloxera. Although there had been vine maladies as long as vines existed, they were minor compared to the destruction of a century ago. *Phylloxera vastatrix,* a root-eating parasite of American origin, appeared in France in the 1860s and spread through the vineyards of Europe with breathtaking speed. Among various conjectures one writer recently offered an intriguing fantasy explanation of why phylloxera did not arrive sooner. Vines had been sent from America to Europe since 1629, but because the sea voyage before the age of steamships was too slow, the louse died en route.

By 1878, the Médoc was overtaken, and the devastation continued until about 1890. The tiny louse came from the eastern part of the United States, where the root-stocks of the native *Vitis labrusca* vines were immune to its ravages. The more delicate European vine species, *Vitis vinifera,* succumbed easily; the destruction was one of the greatest agricultural holocausts since the biblical seven lean years. Dozens of experiments were made to save the vines, to no avail. One writer estimates phylloxera probably cost France more than did Bismarck's armies in the Franco-Prussian War (1870–1871). The eventual solution was to graft the *Vitis vinifera* plants onto the roots of American *Vitis labrusca,* but it was not until the First World War that the vineyards had fully recovered from phylloxera. Some growers, like the Domaine de la Romanée-Conti in Burgundy, succeeded through heroic efforts in maintaining their dwindling vineyard of ungrafted vines up to the Second World War. But now virtually all French grape varieties are grafted onto American root-stocks, reproduced in nurseries throughout the world.

The history of the Bordeaux wine community since the Second World War is essentially that of the Bordeaux shipping families. Most of the important firms can still be found along the quais of the Garonne, with offices in their wine-filled warehouses. They carry on business today much as they did in the past—in the low-keyed, dignified manner that has come to be a hallmark of the Bordelais spirit. But this is not to say that business for the shippers has not changed: it has, and greatly so—as we will see later on.

Despite these recent changes, however, the basic pattern of the shippers' trade has not altered significantly since it was first set up nearly three centuries ago. The shipper or *négociant* buys wines from the vineyard (and, to a small extent recently, from the regional cooperatives) through a broker immediately following the harvest, when the price should be at its lowest. After the wine has been bottled, the shipper sells it to customers in France and abroad. For a period around the late fifties and early sixties, some châteaux, with the brokers' help, offered their wines *before* the harvest, a practice called *sur souche* (literally, "on the vine"). Shippers who bought before the harvest gambled on the quality of the vintage by buying low. The châteaux, selling at the low prices, were assuring themselves a quick and sure return. Sales *sur souche* do not exist anymore, because growers are not so pressed financially as they once were and they naturally prefer to hold their wines to appreciate in value.

Nowadays, the classified Bordeaux châteaux do not put their wine on the market until some months after the vintage. The opening date for sale to begin is never officially set, but arrived at by unspoken mutual consent. "It can be March, April, or May after the vintage," says one broker. "The wine will be in barrels, lying peacefully in the *chais,* and you won't hear a word from the châteaux. Then, out of the blue, one of us brokers gets a call from, say, La Lagune, though it could be anybody. They offer one or a number of brokers an opening lot of 60 or 100 *tonneaux* [each *tonneau* is four barrels, or the equivalent of one hundred cases] to sell to the shippers. They may consult with us on the opening price, as well as terms of payment, both of which depend on the quality of the vintage and the market conditions at the time. We then contact several shippers by telephone to sell them the wine. If the vintage was a good one and their inventories are low, they jump to buy quickly, before the price goes up. The news spreads around that the selling is beginning and a few days later we hear from, say, Calon-Ségur, who also wants to sell. Within a week or so, we can tell by the reaction of the shippers and the size of their purchases whether a realistic market has been set. This is often based on the reaction they receive from the hundreds of telexes they send to their customers throughout the world. Word travels fast throughout the Bordeaux region, and in a few weeks' time we find ourselves offering one wine after another."

Depending on the château and its reputation, the brokers may sell out the first offering, the first *tranche,* or "slice," in a few days' time; sometimes the sale may drag on for three or four weeks. Of the sixty-three classified Médoc growths, some are sold exclusively to one shipper. Château Giscours is sold exclusively to Gilbey's, Château Lascombes to Alexis Lichine and Company (I sold this company in the late '60s), Mouton-Baronne-Philippe through La Bergerie, Rausan-Ségla by Eschenauer, Palmer by Sichel and Company and Mahler-Besse, Kirwan by Schroeder and Schyler, Cantenac-Brown by Hiram Walker and Curlier. Châteaux Gruaud-Larose, Talbot, and Cantemerle are only sold by Cordier. J. P. Moueix is the only firm to sell the wines of its properties, Châteaux Pétrus, Trotanoy, La Fleur Pétrus, and Latour à Pomerol, and Magdelaine and Fonroque at Saint-Émilion.

The better *négociants* maintain large stocks of back vintages in their labyrinthine *chais* for customers in search of rare bottles. Some shippers, such as Duclot, Des-caves, and Dubos specialize in older vintages, three to five years old. Others may be strong in regional wines, which they keep in vats or barrels and blend and bottle themselves. Up until the 1950s, "foreign" buyers—anyone from beyond the Bordeaux area—would buy the wines from the shipper without ever going to the property or seeing a vineyard. All tasting took place at the shippers' offices in Bordeaux.

To maintain significant stocks of wine, even for a short period, is always expensive. Shippers build up their stocks by borrowing money from the banks, hoping that the future sale of the wine will more than cover the high interest rate on their loans. Most of the time, the shippers have bought sufficiently cheap and sold sufficiently dear for the trade to be a profitable one, and many of the great firms which began in the eighteenth century have descendants along the Quai des Chartrons.

But few tradesmen as traveled and established as the shippers of Bordeaux have been so far removed from the realities of their market. After the Second World War, the shippers, along with the rest of France, were in complete disarray. Reliable prewar markets had shrunk, and some, like Argentina and Germany, had disappeared completely. Blinded by their respect for past practices, the established shipping families neglected their responsibilities to increase the existing markets and explore the new ones, such as the United States and even France itself, which, until this last decade, has been as ignorant of its great wines as any country.

This shortsightedness and obstinacy is the result of generations of inbred values and inbred blood. Intermarriage has long been the rule in the snobbish, closed world of the Bordeaux shipping firms. Matchmaking between the de Luzes, Cruses, Johnstons, and Calvets, to mention a few, was the standard operating procedure. These families, as well as a few others, were the important ones; while around them, like so many pilot fish, were the smaller firms, often older, most of which made a great point of the date of their founding, which was prominently displayed on their letterhead. Irrespective of blood alliances, rivalry has always been bitter. This was especially true after the war, when the many family firms competed for the business of the relatively few domestic and foreign buyers active at the time. Family snobbery was passed from generation to generation, and each new wave vied for the furniture and estates that deceased aunts and uncles left behind.

These shippers, along with the established brokers who followed in the wake of the big firms, kept a stranglehold on the winegrowers of Bordeaux, from the largest château to the smallest peasant. Smaller satellite shipping firms and brokerage houses were cold-shouldered by the inner circle. This pattern of local family control endured until the late fifties and early sixties, when I and some foreign companies, many of them British, recognized that wine was more than just refined esoterica and that new markets, particularly the United States, had great potential for growth. By settling the shippers' bank debts, foreign investors could convert the interest paid on loans into increased profits. Even with only modest growth, once freed from debt, shipping companies could, in fact, be profitable. Many offers were too good to refuse: Barton and Guestier became a property of Seagrams, of the U.S.A. and Canada; Delor was bought by Allied Brewers of the United Kingdom, and eventually liquidated; the warehouse was taken over by the Dutch-controlled Dourthe-Kressman group; Cruse by Société des Vins de France; Eschenauer was taken over by Holt, a British shipping consortium who in turn were taken over by Lonrho of London; de Luze was acquired by Bowater, the British paper company. It was resold to Rémy-Martin Cognac in 1980. Calvet was sold in 1982 to the British brewers Whitbread. Cordier was taken over by the group La Hénin; La Loudenne, owned by Gilbey's, was acquired by I.D.V. (International Distillers and Vintners); and Beyermann by Atkinson and Baldwin of London. As I noted in my preface, I sold Alexis Lichine and Company, which I had formed after the war, to Bass-Charrington, the British brewers. From 1975 to 1980 I made the selections for the United States market on behalf of Somerset of New York, the importers of the Bordeaux company that bears my name.

These changes were carried to a dangerous extreme in the early 1970s. Folly was in the air: in auction rooms in London and New York, gavels were coming down on record prices for First and Classified Growth Médocs. One Texas retailer paid $36,000 for a magnum of Mouton-Rothschild 1929 at a Chicago auction. For whatever reasons, great vintage Bordeaux were recognized as investments, not for uncorking and drinking but strictly for buying and selling. In short, too many people—some of whom had only the vaguest understanding of wine—began buying wines on speculation, certain that the market, which was healthy enough then, would continue to grow. Well, it grew only because everyone from French banks to English brewing companies, from Swiss chocolate firms to American multinationals, continued to buy the wine without thinking of where, or when, they might sell it. The prices rose to extraordinarily high levels.

This speculation, plus a worldwide economic slowdown aggravated by the so-called oil crisis, came hot on the heels of a local scandal in Bordeaux, involving a shipping firm with dubious blending practices. It all hit the customer at once. Resentful to begin with at the grossly exaggerated prices for the fair-to-medium 1972 vintage, wholesalers, retailers, and consumers refused to go along. Cases of wine piled up in the warehouses of Bordeaux and abroad, and no one was pulling the corks from French bottles. The bottom fell out practically overnight. Many foreign speculators were wiped out—never, fortunately, to appear on the wine scene again.

The shippers lost less in the debacle than the foreign speculators, but, still, the episode dealt a devastating blow to many firms that were, so to speak, already on the brink of foreclosure. It is safe to say that no traditional shipping company today wields the same power it used to. The Cruses, as a result of their trial in 1973, were forced to sell their cherished Château Pontet-Canet and to divest themselves of their old wine stocks, as well as their Burgundy firm. The Ginestet company was saved by the sale in 1977 of the Château Margaux, which had been in the family since the 1930s, to Laura and André Mentzelopoulos for $17 million. Many of the smaller firms merged to keep from going under.

For a few of the smaller shippers, the dark cloud of the Bordeaux wine crash had a silver lining. A number of these smaller firms were relatively unscathed: Janoueix and A. Moueix in Libourne; Coste in Langon; Dourthe and Kressmann in Bordeaux; and Bertrand de Rivoyre in Ambarès. Because their markets were traditionally stable (the Benelux countries particularly), they had sufficient wines in stock to meet their needs before the prices rose. They were therefore not obliged to resupply themselves by borrowing money from the banks—they simply sold off their stocks at higher prices. Meanwhile their better-heeled (and more greedy) competitors, who had the money but too little wine, tried to catch up with what they thought was increased demand by buying wines at high prices, often borrowing money at usurious interest rates to lay in bigger stocks of wine for simple speculation. The smaller firms, whose assets were in wine and not in cash, could only afford to buy what they knew they could sell, so when the crash came in 1974 whatever losses they took were relatively small. Those who speculated were forced to dump their wines at a fraction of the cost.

After the dust cleared, a number of the smaller firms found their share of the market considerably increased. Of those mentioned above, Coste and de Rivoyre emerged stronger than before; Gilbey's at Château Loudenne (whose losses for a time were large) and Dubos and Société des Vins Fins of Hernandez in Bordeaux also found their relative positions in the marketplace greatly improved over what they had been in 1971. A few rare firms with large vineyard holdings, such as J. P. Moueix, in Libourne, and Philippe Rothschild's La Bergerie, in Pauillac, with its branded wine, withstood the crisis, took their losses, and continued in the trade stronger than ever.

Whatever their size and however they fared as a result of the crash and the scandal, shippers, as a profession, suffered a great loss of reputation and of public confidence in their reliability. One consequence of this, not only in Bordeaux but through all the French wine regions, has been the growth of direct sales. Not only are continental tourists and French vacationers flocking more than ever to the wine properties to replenish the home cellar, but wholesalers and even retailers from abroad are making the journey to the thousands of properties that surround Bordeaux to place their orders. Although the wine still passes through the shippers' hands on its way from the château to the foreign buyer, the individual shipper's profit is often reduced considerably from what it would be if he had the desired wines in his stock. However, unless foreign wholesalers and retailers purchase thousands of cases at a time, the amount of money they save by this kind of direct sale is minimal.

One way to gauge the health of the shippers and the Bordeaux wine trade in general is to count the number of brokers, or *courtiers*. Although they do deal with wines from the great Bordeaux châteaux, the brokers' main service is to find generic and regional wines from small properties to make up the shippers' blends. From growers all over Bordeaux—referred to in the trade as *la propriété*—the brokers bring samples to the shippers, who taste and select among them to make up their blends of "Bordeaux," "Graves," "Margaux," "Saint-Émilion," and so on. For this service of seeking out the vats and barrels from the vast array of growers and cooperatives, the brokers charge 2 percent commission on the sale. The broker also acts as the intermediary between the larger châteaux and the shipper, still getting his 2 percent on the sale.

The sale itself between shipping company and producer is attested by a sales certificate, called a *bordereau,* which the broker makes up and mails to buyer and seller. If, when the sale is being negotiated, the price of the wine is disputed, it is the broker's job to reach a compromise between the parties, who do not know one another's identity.

Essential to the Bordeaux market is the heavy trading and bidding on wines in the two years between the vintage and the time the wine is bottled. As prices rise, certain shippers in search of easy and early profits resell their wines (still in barrel at the château) through a broker to another shipper at the new, increased market price. If another shipper buys this wine, the broker makes out a new *bordereau,* again adding his 2 percent fee, and sends it to the château. At bottling time, eighteen to thirty months after the vintage, the wine may have passed through several hands, usually increasing in price with each transaction.

The grower or château owner naturally resents this kind of price spiral—of which he gets no part—within the Bordeaux market. The château owner's aim, after all, is to have his wine distributed to restaurants and hotels within France and to importers, wholesalers, and retailers in foreign markets. In short, he wants the customers to pull the corks, instead of seeing his wine used as a commodity for simple speculation. Yet, after all, the foreign markets are immensely important to him: nearly 65 percent of all the wine produced in the Haut-Médoc district is consumed outside France.

Hence the sales procedure described earlier, using the example of La Lagune and its first *tranche* of wines. A few months after the grower sells his first *tranche* and has seen how the market is behaving, he releases his second *tranche* of, say, forty or fifty *tonneaux* at a higher price to the broker . . . who, again, contacts the shippers. In this way the grower can participate in the increased prices of his wines, possibly holding back a certain quantity in bottles to be sold several years later at a still higher price. In recent vintages, the opening sales included all the wine—in one of-fering—with the exception of the First Growths.

Although the brokers were not directly hurt financially when the Bordeaux bubble burst—for they never actually buy the wines—over the longer term they suf-fered from the region's loss of face and trade. In 1965, there were 1,200 brokers in France dealing in wines; by 1978 only 500 remained, perhaps 15 percent of them in and around Bordeaux. And they work hard at their trade.

The period of euphoria, as I call it—from the end of 1971 to the end of 1973—did have two positive effects. Château owners, with some cash in their pockets at last, could make long-needed improvements in their vineyard and vat-room equip-ment. They bought new tractors, planted new vines, replaced wooden vats with new ones of stainless steel or concrete. Some installed refrigeration and a host of other devices that modern oenology had revealed as useful but that had been beyond the means of most of them until then. The second result of all this quick cash was the spreading practice among the Second, Third, Fourth, and Fifth Growths of selecting their vats of wine more carefully, known as *assemblage,* and rejecting those judged to be below the standards of the château, thereby improving the château-labeled wines. (The lighter, inferior vats are then sold under a lesser label.) Although conscien-tious growers have always selected their vats, they could now afford to be more dis-criminating, and some who previously had not selected at all now began to do so.

The wines of Bordeaux, for all their renown, are not exactly at the city's doorstep. Aside from Haut-Brion and a couple of other Graves vineyards on the Arcachon road, all the vineyard areas require at least a half-hour's drive from the center of the city.

The heart of the Médoc, starting with Margaux, lies 25 kilometers (15 miles) northwest of the city; Saint-Émilion and Pomerol require forty-five minutes of driv-ing to the northeast; Barsac and Sauternes are a forty-five-minute drive to the south on the autoroute. Thus to call the wines of Saint-Émilion and Pomerol "Bordeaux wines" took a pretty broad outlook in the horse-and-carriage days. From Bordeaux to Libourne and Saint-Émilion there are the Garonne and the Dordogne rivers to cross; and the Dordogne, until the early nineteenth century, had only frail ferries to take the traveler from shore to shore.

Although it put the city on the map and is its most illustrious product, wine is no longer Bordeaux's top money-spinner. Three-quarters of the business of the port of Bordeaux, France's sixth largest in cargo tonnage handled, is now in petroleum products. A great deal of wood is still exported. Clustered around the city in metropolitan Bordeaux are industrial zones where factories make Ford gear boxes, IBM computers, and jet planes. The Dassault aerospace company, whose Mirage jets flash across the sky and break the sound barrier with great booms (a source of complaint among winegrowers of the area), is, in fact, Bordeaux's most lucrative industry. To accommodate all of this, plus small shipbuilding and chemical-manufacturing plants, a new, large hotel and conference center has been constructed just 3 kilometers (2 miles) outside of town, at Bordeaux-Le Lac. With its many hotels, numerous conference halls, and a huge exhibition pavilion, Bordeaux-Le Lac is ready to receive thousands of visitors and businessmen from all over the globe. In the center of Bordeaux itself, the new Mériadeck development boasts new office buildings, apartments, and hotels—all signs of a business community whose dynamism belies its stuffy exterior.

Jets and autos and computers may come and go, but the wines of Bordeaux will probably be with us as long as there are eyes and noses and palates to appreciate them. The wine business, in all its ramifications, still employs at least a fifth of the region's population.

Yet, amazingly, when you consider the obvious connection of Bordeaux with wine, the city fathers show little awareness of their past, present, and future fame as the world's great wine capital. From the chamber of commerce to city hall to the all-encompassing wine association of Bordeaux, the C.I.V.B. (Comité Interprofessionel des Vins de Bordeaux), the Establishment appears to lack enthusiasm and pride for its wines and their renown—the wines on which the city is literally built. It is almost as if there were no mention of William Shakespeare in the thriving tourist town of Stratford-on-Avon, or no mention of Champagne cellars in the city of Reims.

In the entire city of Bordeaux, there is little to tell the traveler that just beyond the suburbs lies the glory of wine. Unlike Beaune, the self-appointed capital of Burgundy, Bordeaux hardly teems with wine shops and information bureaus. It is not that easy to find a map of a vineyard tour, although they are available at the Maison du Vin, on the Allées de Tourny, and at the nearby Syndicat d'Initiative. Even the route to the great Médoc vineyards is not all that obvious. From the center of Bordeaux, follow signs for Soulac; if you lose your way, ask for the Barrière du Médoc. After 3 or 4 kilometers, less than one kilometer past the turnoffs for the Paris Autoroute, the road branches to the right, in the direction of Pauillac. This is your Route des Grands Crus, D-2. It may not be easy to locate at the start, but the vineyard tour it leads to is definitely worth a journey and will be a memorable experience in anyone's lifetime.

BORDEAUX VINTAGES

1952   A good year for red wines. The top wines, slightly on the hard side, were slower to mature than the '53s. In Saint-Émilion and Pomerol, the '52s were much greater than the '53s, not so in the Médoc. Many of the '52s have lasted longer than the '53s.

1953   This was a very great year for red wines. The '53s had great softness, roundness, and perfect balance. Not as long-lasting as the '52s, but certainly sheer perfection until recently.

1954   Short-lived, the red wines were good value.

1955   A great year for red wines. Magnificently balanced.

In white wines this was a perfect year for those who find Sauternes over-sweet.

1956   Red wines were poor to fair. Curios now of little interest.

1957   Good vintage for red wines. A tendency to hardness made the wines relatively slow-maturing, harsh, and lacking in roundness. In 1984 I enjoyed an excellent Leoville-Barton. If you can find a bottle, they have matured beautifully.

1958   Very light, fast-maturing. Expect faded bottles today.

1959   The '59s made banner headlines throughout the civilized world. This was a very good vintage. The red wines were and are full, harmonious, and slow-maturing.

For those who like Barsacs and Sauternes, 1959 is the year. Perfectly balanced, the '59s helped to re-establish a dying custom, the serving of Sauternes with desserts.

1960   A large quantity of good red wine, now fading.

1961   The flowering during the cold and rainy month of May resulted in a diminution in production of 50 to 60 percent in comparison with the previous year. Then a hot summer, followed by a superb September, gave us (in quality if not in quantity) the greatest red wine vintage since 1945.

This was a good vintage for the sweet wines of Sauternes and Barsac. Sauternes produced great bottles which will last another ten, twenty, or thirty years.

1962   Beautiful, soft, well-rounded, fast-maturing red wines. These pleasing wines were ready long before those of 1961.

The great sweet white wines were rather on the light side, but fruity and pleasant.

1963   A vintage to forget.

1964   A very plentiful year for red wines. A magnificent summer was followed by an excellent September, and the grapes achieved maturity in good conditions. Certain châteaux in the Médoc waited to harvest late, but unfortunately it rained incessantly from October 8 onward, and these late-harvested wines were disappointing. Those harvested earlier, however, made 1964 an excellent vintage overall.

Fair for sweet white wines, but for the Sauternes growers who waited until the end of October, it was a disaster because the *pourriture noble* turned to ordinary gray rot.

1965   The summer was rainy. A few vineyards harvested late under fair conditions. When well selected, there were some fair-quality wines which did not last long.

1966   Uniformly a great vintage. A very dark deep color with perfect balance made these full wines outstanding. Hard, slow-maturing, they are just now starting to be ready and will last for a long time.

Barsacs and Sauternes—one-third very good. The remainder disappointing.

1967 Softer than the '66s, hence faster-maturing. A good vintage requiring selectivity—Will not last much over twenty-five years. Sauternes and Barsacs were excellent. Yquem produced a superb and memorable wine.

1968 Light, due to a rainy summer.

1969 Fair in the Médoc; disappointing in Saint-Émilion and Pomerol. July and August had abundant sun followed by freakish rains in September. The quality was saved by an unusual burst of a hot spell just before and during the late harvest in October. As a whole, wines were not pleasing because of a lack of balance.

The sweet Barsacs and Sauternes are only fair.

1970 A great vintage. Unquestionably the best since 1966, with an abundance not seen since the beginning of the century. Many of the wines will mature at different ages, and a selection should be made accordingly; some wines are just now coming into their own.

1971 A very good vintage, lighter and faster-maturing than the '70s. The reds are light but round. Some growers preferred the '71s to the '70s because of the elegance, breed, and perfect balance of the former. 1971 matured and afforded pleasure before the 1970s.

The white wines are generally good, with some very exceptional highs in Sauternes, which will be delightful until the '90s.

1972 After a disastrously rainy summer, the vintage was somewhat saved by the hot sunny weather from late September through the October harvest. The reds showed too much acidity when young, and even when mature they will not be very good. These wines were originally sold in Bordeaux at ridiculously high prices, the highest on record.

Barsac and Sauternes did not approach the quality of the '71s.

1973 An extremely large harvest, even more plentiful than the record produced in 1970. The reds are round, lacking in the tannic acid sufficient to give them longevity. They will be light and pleasant drinking up to the late 1980s. The better red wines resemble those from 1967.

The dry white wines were fair to good, the sweet ones barely average. Hail destroyed the Sauternes vineyards several times throughout the summer.

1974 For red wines, a fair to very good vintage, with deep color, good character and finish.

The dry whites were good—fruity and well balanced. Unfortunately the harvest in Sauternes was a disaster.

1975 A very great vintage for red wines; rich, harmonious, very slow-maturing. The quality is the best since 1961, and it may eventually overshadow the '66s and '70s. The great wines should not be uncorked until the late 1980s or, preferably, the 1990s. *Crus Bourgeois* and minor châteaux are now good drinking wines. Only a small quantity was produced (50 percent less than in 1974).

Superb sweet Barsacs and Sauternes were produced due to the good weather which continued through late October and early November.

1976 The dry, hot summer, which caused the most serious drought in the last hundred years, brought high hopes for a memorable vintage. The vineyards which started to pick the faster-maturing Merlots at the end of the first week of September, and which were able to hold off harvesting the rest of the crop during the intermittent rains of the second half of September, produced very fine wines in abundant quantities. The better of the '76s will be enjoyable before the slow-maturing '75s from the great vineyards. Hence, the '76s compare to the '75s as the '71s did to the somewhat harder '70s. Very drinkable. Some '76s are weakening.

Sauternes and Barsacs were spotty owing to the October rains. Rot set in before the *Botrytis cinerea* could exercise its "noble rot" process. Many excellent, sweet '76s were produced.

1977 The tragedy of the 1977 vintage was the spring freeze which killed the buds and resulted in the smallest crop in twenty years. Of the Médoc, Pomerol, and Saint-Émilion, the Médoc was spared the greatest damage and suffered only 50 percent loss, whereas the other two regions took losses of 80 percent. Concerning the quality: after a rainy summer, the 1977 growing cycle performed something of a miracle. At the end of a cool August a warm, dry, sunny period began, lasting until the completion of the late harvest, which took place under very good conditions through October. This late hot spell produced wines dark in color, fruity, and slightly on the hard side, which have, however, matured fairly rapidly. Although it requires selectivity, 1977 can be rated quite well, definitely superior to the '72s. Here is an example of the rating of vintage charts having destroyed the possibility of enjoyment of many good wines.

Of the sweet wines of Barsac and Sauternes, only a minute quantity was produced, a few of them quite acceptable.

1978 Euphoric is the best way to describe the Bordeaux mood as the greatness of the 1978 vintage became a reality. The elation was due to the surprising late hot summer weather which saved the vintage from being merely average and turned it into top quality. After a long cool spring and summer, the sun and heat arrived in mid-August and continued through September and October lasting through the harvest, which was the latest since 1926. The reds, with their deep color and high sugar content, are rated as comparable to, and in some cases superior to, the excellent '70s. Some have a tannic hardness that may make them resemble some 1975s, though they are less hard than some 1975s.

Barsacs and Sauternes made luscious sweet wines.

1979 An exceptionally abundant harvest, especially for red wines. The wines are of generally very good quality, although varying from region to region. They are round and soft, and will mature faster than the '78s. They are characterized by the softer Merlot grape, which ripened more completely than the harder Cabernet Sauvignon. For this reason, the wines of Pomerol and Saint-Émilion are of very good quality. Many producers compare the '79s to superior '62s. And some now claim that the 1979 vintage is better than the '78s. This is true at Château Margaux, Château Lafite, and Château Prieuré-Lichine.

For sweet Sauternes and Barsac, noble rot developed well, and the wines are characteristic and fine without achieving the concentration of the '71s or the '67s.

1980 Vested interests of *négociants* and importers, abetted by an irresponsible press, inspired an attempt to run down the reputation of the vintage as early as July 1980, before the wine was even born.

Good, sunny September weather preceding one of the most delayed harvests on record, beginning around the 9th of October in the Médoc, and as late as October 23rd at Château Pétrus in Pomerol. Sunny, hence favorable, weather conditions produced pleasant, fast-maturing wines which will be very good values, especially those from the properties where château owners carefully selected the vats for their name wines. The fruit and aroma, as well as the softness and roundness of body in these wines, are good.

October and November were especially favorable to the sweet white wines of Sauternes and

Barsac, which are very good. At Château d'Yquem, for example, where they are very selective, 80 percent of the harvest was sold under its label, compared to only 40 percent in 1979.

1981 A very good vintage, slightly superior to 1979. It is fuller and firmer than the 1979; as compared to the 1978, it is softer, less even, with a little more fruit, and surprising quality. Both the sweet whites of Barsac and Sauternes and the dry whites have produced an outstanding vintage.

1982 This great vintage will be remembered for its superb red wines—round, perfumed, and long on the palate, particularly among the better estates, where a strict selection was applied to the choice of the vats. Experts predict great affinity to the wines of 1947, 1955, and 1959, best since 1961, but whichever it may be, a very great vintage is assured.

Excellent dry whites; while the Barsac and Sauternes were partly ruined by the mid-October rains, some good sweet whites were produced.

1983 The miraculous, record-beating hot weather—starting in mid-September and continuing to the very end of the harvest, without a drop of rain—unexpectedly produced a vintage that some growers think may prove even better than 1982. The intense, dark color and high density signal the birth of a great, pleasant, and classic vintage, one that will be superior to 1978.

In Sauternes and Barsac, Châteaux d'Yquem, Guiraud, Coutet, and other vineyards, by pruning sufficiently to curb abundance and patiently waiting to pick late, made another very great vintage, which is now affirmed to be excellent.

1984 Maligned and prematurely condemned by the press because the Merlot grape variety experienced poor flowering; hence its production was cut by 80 percent in Pomerol and by as much as 40 percent in the Médoc; therefore a confusion of quantity and quality occurred, further prejudiced because of some torrential rains in the second half of September, before the harvest. Those who picked under very sunny conditions after October 8 in the Médoc and Graves made wines which are pleasant, fruity, and which are better than the 1980s, although not quite as good as the 1981s. Fruity, the Médocs will be pleasant drinking before the '83s and '82s. Disappointing wines were made in Saint-Émilion and Pomerol.

1985 A great vintage. After a long, hot drought a small harvest of fairly hard wines was predicted. Because of the considerable amount of grapes and contrary to expectations, a large harvest of this great vintage was produced. The quantity helped to dilute the hardness and the agreeable, subtle tannins may, at this early stage, liken this vintage to a cross between 1982 and 1983.

Although the success was very marked in the Merlots in the Médoc, this was less evident in Saint-Émilion and Pomerol. In Sauternes there was perfect maturity. In November the needed mist slowly helped the development of *botrytis*. The sugar was high. The picking went on into December and Sauternes has enjoyed a great vintage which may be similar to the excellent 1983s.

BORDEAUX

(33000—Gironde)

(Margaux 25—Saint-Émilion 39—Langon 46—Angoulême 108—Saintes 118—
Cognac 120—Agen 139—Biarritz 184—La Rochelle 189—Auch 190—Cahors 200—
Toulouse 250—Lyon 550—Paris 568)

Hotels and Restaurants

H = *Hotel;* R = *Restaurant*

Numerous air connections from major cities in France to Mérignac Airport, a half-hour from
Bordeaux. Approximately one hour's flight from Paris, Lyon, Marseilles, Nantes, Nice, Geneva,
and Madrid; eighty minutes from London. Flights also available from Lisbon, Tunis, Algiers,
Milan, and Las Palmas.

Excellent rail connections from Paris, taking less than five hours.

To drive: 568 kilometers from Paris by *autoroute* through Tours and Poitiers, to Bordeaux;

up from Spain on A-63 to Bayonne and from Bayonne to Bordeaux on the N-10, a major highway. The trip from the Spanish border will take a little over 2 hours.

From the Côte d'Azur, there is an autoroute to Aix-en-Provence, Nîmes, Narbonne, and Carcassonne which continues via Toulouse and Agen through to Bordeaux.

Good, functional rooms available. Bordeaux lacks luxurious rooms. The pleasantest, with a limited number, are available in Margaux.

Bordeaux is not only the most splendid eighteenth-century city in France, but has become one of its hubs of gastronomy. No matter how short your visit, you must not miss a glance at the Palais de la Bourse and the Grand Théâtre in the center of town. Stroll past the quaint shops and winding walkways of Old Bordeaux where no cars are allowed, or for the latest in twentieth-century French fashions head for the Cours Clemenceau and the Cours de l'Intendance. For a mouth-watering finale, pay a visit to the Marché des Grands Hommes where stands vaunt choice cheeses, fish, pâtés, and other edible goodies. Just be sure to go before noon, and never in August.

BORDEAUX/TOWN CENTER

HR GRAND HÔTEL DE BORDEAUX: 2, Place de la Comédie. Tel.: 56.90.93.44. Tlx.: 541658. 98 rooms.
Centrally located across from the Opera House, with parking in nearby underground garage. The rooms, with the exception of 4 suites of an acceptable size, are small, but modern. No restaurant. Brasserie. Café.

HR FRANTEL: 5, rue Robert-Lateulade. Tel.: 56.90.92.37. Tlx.: 540565. 196 rooms.
In Bordeaux, but not in midtown. Sizable, modern, air-conditioned rooms, though the hotel service has been criticized. Le Meriadeck restaurant is good, if lacking in charm. English spoken.

H LE NORMANDIE: 7, cours du 30-Juillet. Tel.: 56.52.16.80. Tlx.: 570481. 100 rooms.
Excellent central location. No restaurant. Breakfast available. Warm welcome. English spoken.

H MAJESTIC: 2, rue Condé. Tel.: 56.52.60.44. 50 smallish rooms. No restaurant. Breakfast available. A smile would be welcome.

H ROYAL MÉDOC: 3, rue de Sèze. Tel.: 56.81.72.42. Tlx.: 571042. 45 rooms. 37 toilets. Very central. Small but comfortable, entirely remodeled. Breakfast available. English spoken.

R JEAN RAMET: 7, Place Jean-Jaurès. Tel.: 56.44.12.51.
Jean and Raymonde Ramet stand at the top of Bordeaux gastronomy. They opened their small, excellent restaurant in 1982. Among the various good dishes, start with the *feuilleté d'huîtres*. Reservations required. One star in Michelin.

R CHRISTIAN CLÉMENT/DUBERN: 42, allées de Tourny. Tel.: 56.48.03.44.
This elegant restaurant is one of the best in Bordeaux. M. Christian Clément, who took over in 1986, has helped to reestablish the city as a gastronomic center. Excellent service, appreciated by the leading wine merchants of Bordeaux. English spoken. *Relais et Châteaux.* One star in Michelin. "Le petit Dubern" has a simplified, reasonably priced menu, wine included.

R BRASSERIE LE NOAILLES: 12, allées de Tourny. Tel.: 56.81.94.45.
Very centrally located. Informal restaurant serving up to midnight from sandwiches to more-than-adequate dishes. Not one of the gastronomic highlights of Bordeaux.

R LE ROUZIC: 34 bis, Cours du Chapeau-Rouge. Tel.: 56.44.39.11.
Located to a side of the Grand-Théâtre, Le Rouzic is the newest among Bordeaux's better restaurants. Under the talented direction of its chef/owner, Michel Gautier, Le Rouzic is fast becoming one of the pillars of Bordeaux's gastronomic renaissance. For quality and price, the menu-surprise is not the least of Le Rouzic's attractions. Warm welcome from Josette Gautier. One star in Michelin.

At the beginning of 1985 they opened a bistro above Le Rouzic that offers Russian specialties: Le Bolshoi.

BORDEAUX/NEAR SAINT-JEAN TRAIN STATION

HR L'ARCADE: 60, rue Eugène-Le-Roy. Tel.: 56.90.92.40.   Tlx.: 550952.   140 rooms.
Directly across from train station, modern, clean, inexpensive, and functional. Simple restaurant. Snacks available. If you expect little, you won't be disappointed.

HR MAPOTEL TERMINUS SAINT-JEAN: At train station. Tel.: 56.92.71.58.   Tlx.: 540264.   80 rooms. Large and comfortable rooms. Good, simple restaurant.

R CLAVEL: 44, rue Charles-Domercq. Tel.: 56.92.91.52.
Facing the railway station. Underground parking. Excellent restaurant, superb cuisine. Francis Garcia's talents rank him among the most brilliant chefs of the Bordeaux area. Try the gratin of oysters with foie gras, the pot-au-feu of duck, a perfect filet of bass with tomato butter and the dessert plate with an assortment of goodies. In the summer, try the lobster gazpacho. Tastefully redecorated. Very good service. One star in Michelin. Deserves two.

R BISTRO DE CLAVEL: 44, rue Charles-Domercq. Tel.: 56.92.91.52.
In a modest setting, the good, reasonably priced food is prepared by the adjoining kitchens of Clavel.

R PÉRIGORD SAINT-JEAN: 202, cours de la Marne. Tel.: 56.91.42.80.
Small restaurant run by M. Biard, who has among his specialties seafood and an assortment of Landes dishes such as *foie de canard*. Reservations recommended. Air-conditioned. Reasonable, good value.

R RELAIS DE MAÎTRE KANTER: 27, rue Charles-Domercq. Tel.: 56.92.29.83.
Facing station. An inexpensive brasserie with fair Alsatian dishes. Open until 2:00 a.m.

R CELLIER BORDELAIS: 30-31, quai de la Monnaie. Tel.: 56.31.30.30.
On the waterfront, between the Pont de Pierre and the railway station. The few, very simply served dishes are popular among Bordeaux wine merchants for the large selection of very fairly priced château-bottled Bordeaux which accompany them and which M. René Laffargue also sells at retail.

BORDEAUX/VIEUX BORDEAUX

Old Bordeaux has been delightfully refurbished. Pedestrian streets make it a must to visit, especially the gorgeous sixteenth-century buildings of Place du Parlement.

R LE BISTROT DE BORDEAUX: 10, rue des Piliers-de-Tutelle. Tel.: 56.42.92.32.
Good food and reasonable prices. The wine bar offers a selection of good wines sold by the glass. Some wine merchants lunch daily, being served at the bar.

R LA CHAMADE: 20, rue des Piliers-de-Tutelle. Tel.: 56.48.13.74.
The chef here is a fine cook and the atmosphere of this restaurant, located near the Place du Grand-Théâtre, is pleasing. The wine list could do with a better selection of Classified Growths. One star in Michelin.

R CHEZ JOËL D, LE BISTROT DE L'HUÎTRE: 13, rue des Piliers-de-Tutelle. Tel.: 56.52.68.31.
Joël Dupuch specializes in the best oysters available in the Southwest of France, which would make, taken by themselves, an excellent light dinner any time of the year, not waiting for a month with an "r." In the last guide I recommended another oyster bar, belonging to Joël's mother. I have revised my oyster palate. Joël likes being on the move. He has left his wife to manage the oyster bar, preferring the warmer climes of Martinique.

R CHEZ PHILIPPE: 1, Place du Parlement. Tel.: 56.81.83.15.
A well-decorated, intimate bistro, specializing in seafood dishes sold at fairly high prices. Closed July, August, and September.

R LA TUPINA: 6, rue Porte de la Monnaie. Tel.: 56.91.56.37.
A small, charming restaurant close to the waterfront. (Travel along the quai toward the Gare Saint-Jean; after the Elf gas station on left, rue Porte de la Monnaie will be on the right through the archway.) Good regional specialties are grilled over an open wood fire. Jean-Pierre Xiradakis has put together a wine list with a good selection of Armagnacs. Fairly expensive; open late.

R LE VIEUX BORDEAUX: 27, rue Buhan. Near the big bell, between the Cours d'Alsace and the Cours Victor Hugo. Tel.: 56.52.94.36.
The menu shows to advantage the talents of the owner/chef, Michel Bordage. The service is supervised with charm and a smile by his wife, Nicole. The quality/price ratio is good.

R LA TENARÈZE: 18, place du Parlement. Tel.: 56.44.43.29.
If you like foie gras, duck, goose, and all of the dishes which may lay claim to the gastronomy of Gascony, then you may like the specialties of Madame Dubois, who trained under the expert eye of André Daguin, the master of this realm at the Hôtel de France at Auch. La Tenarèze is simple and reasonably priced.

R LE CAILHAU: 3, place du Palais, near the Porte Cailhau gate, a remnant of the old wall which surrounded what is now old Bordeaux. Tel.: 56.81.79.91.
A good, small restaurant, taken over by Alain Juillard, who learned his trade behind the ovens of L'Archestrate in Paris. He excels in many dishes and charges what some consider a rather hefty price.

BORDEAUX/NEAR MÉRIGNAC AIRPORT

HR NOVOTEL MÉRIGNAC (1 km east of airport, 12 km from center of Bordeaux): Tel.: 56.34.10.25. Tlx.: 540320. 100 rooms. Simple, modern, well-appointed, well-soundproofed.

HR LA RÉSERVE (at l'Alouette-Pessac, 4 km southeast of airport, 0.5 km from the No. 13 exit on the *rocade,* or expressway, skirting Bordeaux on the west). 74, Av. de Bourgailh. Tel.: 56.07.13.28. Tlx.: 560585. 20 rooms.
Pleasant small hotel in the Bordeaux area, with good service. Isolated, but close to Haut-Brion and other Graves vineyards. Good restaurant, owned by M. and Mme Flourens. Good wine list. English spoken. *Relais et Châteaux.* One star in Michelin.

BORDEAUX/LE LAC–PARC DES EXPOSITIONS

෬ This convention and exhibition center and hotel enclave can be reached by following the signs to Le Lac, 5 km northwest of Bordeaux. Not close to airport, but the autoroute or *rocade* makes these hotels speedily accessible.

HR AQUITANIA: Tel.: 56.50.83.80.   Tlx.: 570557.   210 rooms, including 8 suites.
Remodeled modern, air-conditioned hotel, heated pool. Provides easy access to Bordeaux, the Médoc, Saint-Émilion. Decent seafood restaurant, Le Flor, and coffee shop. English spoken.

HR IBIS: Tel.: 56.50.96.50.   Tlx.: 550346.   119 rooms.
Modern, moderately priced. Very simple restaurant.

HR NOVOTEL BORDEAUX-LE-LAC: Tel.: 56.50.99.70.   Tlx.: 570274.   173 rooms.
Modern, air-conditioned hotel with pool. So-so restaurant for simple, quick meals. As it is far out of town, you will need your own transportation; bus service at intermittent hours.

HR MERCURE: Tel.: 56.50.90.30.   Tlx.: 540077.   108 rooms.
Modern, air-conditioned, with pool, discothèque, and vinothèque of wines from the region. Restaurant and snacks.

HR SOFITEL: Tel.: 56.50.90.14.   Tlx.: 540097.   100 rooms.
Modern, air-conditioned hotel with pool. The restaurant, La Pinasse, produces good seafood fare, but the service is slow. There is also a snack bar. The Sofitel and the Aquitania, although devoid of charm, seem to me to be the best in the area.

IN THE BORDEAUX ENVIRONS

R SAINT-JAMES (at Bouliac, 5 km southeast on D-10 from center of Bordeaux on the right bank of the Garonne, D-113 in the direction of Langon): Place Camille-Hostein, near the church. Tel.: 56.20.52.19.

The renowned chef, Jean-Marie Amat, has an out-of-town restaurant, 25 minutes away from the center of Bordeaux. Prettily located on a hill overlooking the Garonne river, this is one of the best restaurants of Bordeaux and is a gastronomic showcase for the talents of M. Amat, whose dishes are, unfortunately, slowly served. *Relais & Châteaux.* Two stars in Michelin.

R AUBERGE DU MARAIS: 22, Route de Latresne, at Bouliac. Tel.: 56.20.52.17.
Turn immediately right after crossing the bridge, drive 4 km until second Bouliac sign, turn left, drive until you reach traffic lights, turn right into Route de Latresne. If you don't get lost, you will find good food and wine value.

MÉDOC

The châteaux of the Médoc, in all their diversity of architecture and in the great variety of wine they produce, are among the great sights that France offers. Any time you can spend in this country will be well repaid in knowledge of the district and the wine. A day or even an afternoon devoted to the châteaux along the vineyard road through the villages of Margaux, Saint-Julien, Pauillac, and Saint-Estèphe will be an unforgettable introduction to the family of Médoc wines, to the role that geography plays in their excellence, and to the great difficulties that must be overcome to produce the finest of them.

At many châteaux there will be someone to greet you, give you a short tour of the *chais,* and perhaps invite you to taste the most recent vintage from the barrel. An appointment is rarely necessary these days. Bottles of recent vintages are sometimes for sale, though generally not available for tasting on the spot. The *maîtres de chai,* whether voluble or taciturn (the latter more likely), will be united in their love of their wine. Most of them speak only French, so come prepared. Like most French institutions, especially in the countryside, the châteaux are generally closed between noon and two o'clock. If in doubt you may want to call ahead: in the telephone book most will be listed under "Château X," or in some cases, under "Société Civile du Château X," or some other illogical prefix.

Until quite recently in wine time—that is, until the beginning of this century—vines grew right up to the city limits of Bordeaux on the north, south, and west. But as the city has pushed out, particularly since the end of World War II, suburban development has devoured the old encircling farmland, swallowing up melon field and vineyard alike. In Blanquefort, on the northeast of town, vines used to flourish where there is now an industrial zone centered on a Ford transmission-assembly plant. It is just after Blanquefort that the Haut-Médoc vineyards begin following the west bank of the Gironde, some 3 kilometers back, along the narrow strip of gravelly soil, rarely more than 12 kilometers (7.5 miles) wide. The best wines of the district are grown in the place-names of Margaux, Saint-Julien, Pauillac, and Saint-Estèphe. These lands were taken from forests centuries ago. Converted to vineyards, in summer they look at first glance like billiard tables: row on orderly row of well-pruned greenery. At second glance, you see that the soil beneath is like a gravel bed.

As noted earlier, four essentials go into a great wine: the proper soil, the suitable microclimate, the grape varieties that will flourish in both of these, and, finally, the man behind the bottle who tends the vineyard and makes the wine. Of these four, if one excludes year-to-year weather variations, the most variable element is the human factor. Owners and vintners change, but soil, microclimate, and grape varieties remain much the same, and nowhere in the world will you find an area in which these three factors unite in such harmony as in the Haut-Médoc. Vines, like poets, produce their best when they must struggle for survival. In the Haut-Médoc, a marginal climatic area, soil and climate push the vine to its limit. In the anemic soil that is typical of the best growths, the roots must delve deep for nourishment, while the vine above grows slowly. This way, the vines live to a great age, up to eighty years, with roots going down 3 to 4 meters (10 to 12 feet).

All things being equal, the age of the vines will be the distinguishing feature of *all* great vineyards. There is no way that even the best soils, best microclimates, and the best wine-maker can overcome the handicap of young vines. To produce their best wines, they must be at least ten years old, and the older the better. To maintain these old vines entails great sacrifice on the part of the vineyard owner because, as the vine ages and produces better and better quality, with a higher sugar content, the quantity falls off steadily to an uneconomic trickle. The vine varieties Cabernet Sauvignon, Merlot, Cabernet Franc, and Petit Verdot are the four that remain in use after centuries of efforts to match grape varieties with the character of the soil and the rigors of the local climate.

The microclimate works in conjunction with the thin soil, providing borderline weather conditions from year to year, with grudging rations of sun, cool nights, and rain. However, sun is far from being the only climatic factor necessary for quality. In

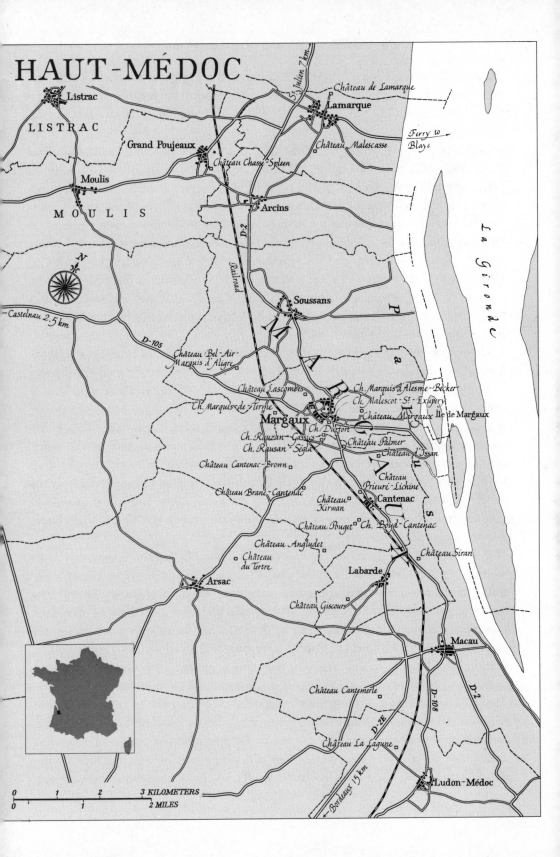

HAUT-MÉDOC

Listrac

LISTRAC

Grand Poujeaux

Moulis

MOULIS

Château de Lamarque

Lamarque

St. Julien 7 km

Château Malescasse

Ferry to Blaye

Château Chasse-Spleen

Arcins

D-2

Railroad

Castelnau 2.5 km

D-105

Soussans

La Gironde

Château Bel-Air-Marquis d'Aligre

Château Lascombes

Ch. Marquis de Terme

Ch. Marquis d'Alesme-Becker

Ch. Malescot-St-Exupéry

Margaux

Château Margaux

Ile de Margaux

Ch./Durfort

Ch. Rauzan-Gassies

Ch. Rausan-Ségla

Château Palmer

Château d'Issan

Château Cantenac-Brown

Château Brane-Cantenac

Château
Prieuré-Lichine

Château
Kirwan

Cantenac

Château Pouget

Ch. Boyd-Cantenac

Château Angludet

Château
du Tertre

Château Siran

Arsac

Labarde

Château Giscours

Macau

D-2

D-108

Château Cantemerle

D-28

Château La Lagune

Bordeaux 15 km

Ludon-Médoc

0   1   2   3 KILOMETERS
0   1   2 MILES

the sun-drenched vineyards of Andalusia, the French Midi, or southern California, the grapes bake in the hot sun, acquiring large amounts of sugar, which fermentation turns to alcohol in a proportion that makes the wine out of balance and lacking in finesse.

The good Haut-Médoc vineyards start on D-2, 19 kilometers (11 miles) from Bordeaux, at Château La Lagune, a Third Growth. The château itself is behind a pretty wrought-iron gate, off to the right of the vineyard road, alongside its functional *chai* and well-kept vineyard. It is now owned by the heirs of the Ayala Champagne firm and is very ably run by Jeanne Boyrie, one of the few female *régisseurs,* or vineyard managers, in all of France. Mme Boyrie oversees the production of about 20,000 cases of wine a year and has maintained a high quality. With the Graves region only 20 kilometers (12 miles) to the south, the southern Haut-Médoc combines some of the Médoc elegance with Graves's earthy richness, and some brokers claim that, as a result, La Lagune is not completely typical of the Haut-Médoc wine from a bit farther north.

I first saw La Lagune in the 1950s, when staying at Château Haut-Brion which, through the kindness of its president, H. Seymour Weller, I made my headquarters in Bordeaux. Hearing that La Lagune was for sale, Mr. Weller and I went to look it over. We were discouraged to find a broken-down château and a tiny, badly neglected vineyard. Not long after that, the vineyard and château were bought by Georges Brunet, who repaired the château, planted new vines, and set the winemaking aright. With La Lagune's reputation re-established, Brunet then sold it to the Chayoux family, owners of the Ayala Champagne firm, and headed southeast for the Riviera sun, where he became a successful real-estate agent. Ever the impassioned vintner, Brunet later built up yet another vineyard property, Château Vignelaure, outside Aix-en-Provence.

A couple of kilometers up the vineyard road from La Lagune is the other noteworthy classified Haut-Médoc vineyard, Château Cantemerle. The large stone, manor-like château is buried in the trees off to the left of the road, at the end of a beautiful park. Since 1981, Château Cantemerle has been owned by an insurance group and the vineyard is managed by M. Jean Cordier. In 1980, it was bought by a grocery chain, and the vineyard plantings were more than tripled. In a revised classification, they would certainly rise well above their present Fifth Growth status.

The wine-proud village of Margaux not only is the home of one of the most famous wines in the world, Château Margaux, but it also lends its name to an entire area, including parts of four other villages—Arsac, Labarde, Cantenac, and Soussans—and some 1,000 hectares (2,500 acres) of vineyard, 70 percent of which is held by the village's twenty-one Classified Growths. In 1983, seventy-six individual growers pro-

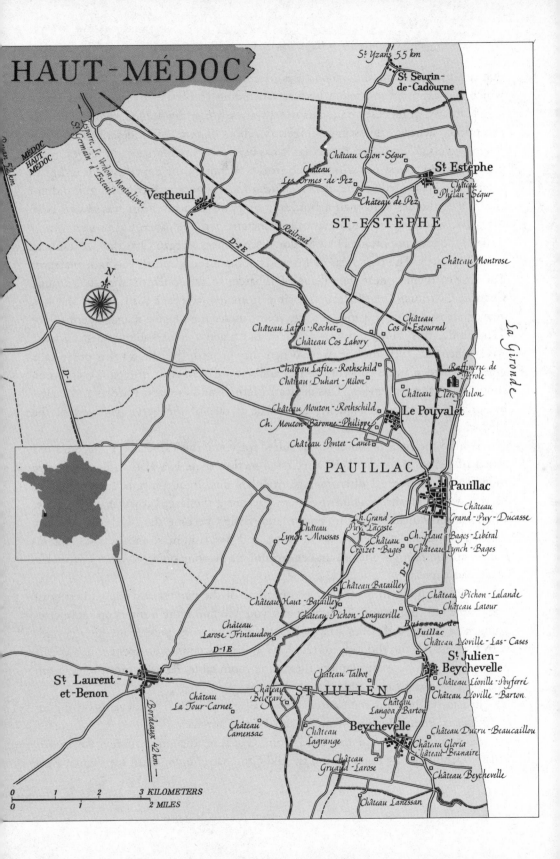

HAUT-MÉDOC

St. Yzans 5.5 km

St. Seurin-de-Cadourne

MÉDOC
HAUT-MÉDOC

Lesparre, Le Verdon, Montalivet, 52 km.

St. Germain-d'Esteuil

Château Calon-Ségur

St Estèphe

Vertheuil

Château Les Ormes-de-Pez

Château de Pez

Château Phélan-Ségur

Railroad

D-2 E

ST-ESTÈPHE

Château Montrose

N

D-1

Château Lafon-Rochet

Château Cos d'Estournel

Château Cos Labory

Château Lafite-Rothschild

Château Duhart-Milon

Raffinerie de Pétrole

Château Clerc-Milon

Château Mouton-Rothschild

Le Pouyalet

Ch. Mouton-Baronne-Philippe

Château Pontet-Canet

PAUILLAC

Pauillac

Château Grand-Puy-Ducasse

Ch. Grand-Puy-Lacoste

Château Lynch-Moussas

Château Croizet-Bages

Ch. Haut-Bages-Libéral

Château Lynch-Bages

D-2

Château Batailley

Château Pichon-Lalande

Château Haut-Batailley

Château Latour

Château Pichon-Longueville

Ruisseau de Juillac

Château Larose-Trintaudon

Château Léoville-Las-Cases

D-1E

St Julien-Beychevelle

Château Léoville-Poyferré

Château Talbot

ST-JULIEN

Château Léoville-Barton

St Laurent-et-Benon

Château Belgrave

Château La Tour-Carnet

Château Langoa-Barton

Bordeaux 42 km —

Château Camensac

Château Lagrange

Beychevelle

Château Ducru-Beaucaillou

Château Gloria

Château Branaire

Château Gruaud-Larose

Château Beychevelle

Château Lanessan

La Gironde

0   1   2   3 KILOMETERS
0   1   2 MILES

duced a total of around 450,000 cases of *appellation* Margaux wine, 65 percent of which was exported to foreign markets, including 30 percent to the United States.

Margaux, at its best, represents the quintessence of the Médoc, characterized by exceptional delicacy, finesse, and lingering echoes of taste, often described as evocative of violets. No wonder, then, that it has been said that Margaux, in its best years, produces the greatest red wine in the world. Although my experience in trying to acquire the Haut-Médoc vineyard of Château La Lagune was discouraging, it did not cure me of the desire to own a Bordeaux vineyard, and my heart was always with Margaux, whose wines I automatically associated with elegance and finesse.

Of the four important Haut-Médoc place-names, Margaux has the deepest beds of pebbly earth. The best areas of Margaux soil are found on three slight plateaux. The first of them is near the village of Labarde, to the south of Margaux, around Château Giscours. The château is visible from the vineyard road, off to the left, viewed across a broad expanse of vines. Now under the capable management of the Tari family, this Third Growth vineyard has made a remarkable comeback since 1954, when the Taris took it over. When they arrived, they found this potentially great vineyard planted in hybrid vines and the vat rooms in disrepair, a common condition in the early fifties. This dedicated father-and-son team, Nicolas and Pierre, has greatly improved the quality and made it one of the better growths of the Médoc.

Behind the château, on land not suited for vines, the Taris have 25 hectares (62 acres) of beautiful parkland. In a secluded section there is a virtual forest of huge rhododendrons, where I often take afternoon walks. In autumn, at the end of the harvest, we go mushroom-hunting there, gathering the large brownish *cèpes,* which, when sautéed quickly in garlic, butter, and parsley, become the Bordeaux specialty *cèpes à la bordelaise. Cèpes* flourish in warm and wet summers, and in 1968, for instance, all the rain gave us a bumper crop of them—our only consolation for that year's bad harvest.

Also beginning in September, at the time of the harvest and the gathering of *cèpes,* is the hunting season. Once it opens, you will find more hunters on mobilettes going *à la chasse,* with rifles strapped to their backs, than pickers in the vineyards with baskets. All the shooting terrified my collie, Bacchus, who spent much of the month of September hiding under the dining-room table. He was unfortunately run over by a speeding car outside my gate.

Just to the north is the Cantenac knoll of gravel with the vineyards belonging to Châteaux Prieuré-Lichine, Palmer, and Brane-Cantenac.

As you come around the bend from Giscours, the first château you see is Prieuré-Lichine, located just behind the old Cantenac church. Until the French Revolution, Prieuré-Lichine was an old Benedictine priory, attached to the church (hence its name), and it was a vineyard long before that. After much searching, I bought the Prieuré, then called Château Cantenac-Prieuré, in 1951, and eventually, through some sixty purchases and exchanges of vineyard, brought the estate up from a mere 11 hectares to 62 (155 acres). The archway and the interior court of Prieuré-Lichine are decorated with dozens of ornate cast-iron firebacks, which I have collected from all over Europe. The vat room, built by the monks, still features the original beams set in place in the sixteenth century and is one of the oldest in the Médoc, while the vats themselves and the other wine-making equipment, installed since 1977, are among the most modern of the Médoc.

Like most Médoc châteaux, the Prieuré has two wings to its *chai*—one for the wine of the most recent vintage and the other for the barrels of wine from the previous one, waiting another year before being bottled. The newly fermented wine is put into oak barrels, which, in Bordeaux, hold 225 liters (59 U.S. gallons), or the equivalent of 300 bottles of 75 centiliters each. The barrels, made of Limousin, or Nevers Allier, oak, preferably new, to impart the oak tannin to the newly vintaged wines, are kept seven months with the bunghole, or the opening, loosely closed with a glass stopper. A certain amount of oxidation is encouraged, allowing the residual carbon dioxide to escape. Due to the evaporation, referred to as ullage, the barrels must be refilled twice a week to keep the wine at the brim. This is called "topping-up." In the early summer, following the vintage, the bunghole is tightly sealed with a burlap-wrapped wooden bung, and the barrel is rotated so the hole is on the side, restricting as far as possible the passage of air. Oxidation continues to take place through the pores of the wood at a barely perceptible rate.

To taste the wine during this second year, the *maître de chai*, M. Armand Labarrère, first drills a small hole in one end of the barrel; because of the vacuum in the tightly sealed barrel, the wine will not spurt out. He then jams a metal claw resembling the back of a hammer under the crossboard at the end of the barrel, and lifts it until the pressure is sufficient to force a stream of wine through the hole into your glass. When finished, M. Labarrère fits a small wooden peg into the hole. Thus, the wine is tasted, the vacuum is preserved, and future tastings will be easily accomplished by removing the peg. The bottling will take place in the second summer following the vintage.

Since I've had the Prieuré, it has been a tradition to welcome visitors at all hours, any day of the week, all year round. They receive a guided tour of the *chai* and a briefing on the wines of the Médoc.

Across the road from Prieuré-Lichine, at the end of a long alley of plane trees, is a property belonging to the Cruse shipping family of Bordeaux—the moated sixteenth-century Château d'Issan with its pretty and recently renovated *chai*. The château's wine is fuller-bodied than that of its neighbors. Like most of the vineyards of Margaux, they excelled in the 1983 vintage.

Before leaving Cantenac, on the right side of the road is Château Palmer, whose vineyards are also on the Cantenac plateau. One look at Palmer will go a long way to explaining its popularity over the years. A small mansion with graceful lines, it flies three flags from its peaked roof, one for each of its owners: the British flag for Peter Sichel, an Englishman who lives in nearby Château Angludet, a good Bourgeois Growth (*Cru Bourgeois*); the French flag for the Miailhe family; and the Dutch for the Mähler-Besse shipping firm. At the base of the courtyard walls, along the Médoc road, roses are planted in a garlanded extension of the Bordeaux tradition of planting roses at the end of each vine row that borders the road. Although a Third Growth, Palmer has sold at the price of a better Second Growth. It is a big, full wine for a Margaux, developing more slowly than many of its neighbors.

Immediately to the left from the road one sees Château Rausan-Ségla and its adjoining Rauzan-Gassies, two second growths which had fallen in quality and whose 1855 classification has been questioned. Very recently the former is making a slow comeback and its vineyard, largely replanted, should in the late 1990s start producing wines which made this vineyard famous. Still further back on the other side of the railway tracks one sees the large Tudor structure of Cantenac-Brown, which belongs to Monique du Vivier and her son Aymar. The third and last area of fine, gravelly vineyards includes those of Château Margaux, some of the village of Margaux itself, and the good vineyards of Château Lascombes, to the north of town, which I sold in 1971. As the Labarde and Cantenac gravel knolls did, the "plateau" around the village of Margaux rises slightly above the surrounding countryside, perhaps no more than 5 or 10 meters, and lies a good distance from the river, away from the marshy soil that continues to border the Gironde. In this low riverside region, the vineyards of heavy, rich earth are called *palus*. These consist of alluvial loam, quite clear of stones, which produces huge quantities of heavy, common wines not entitled to the Haut-Médoc place-name but only to the *appellation* Bordeaux. The old Médoc saying went that if you could see the river or across it and had pebbles under your feet, you could surely make good wine. The pebbles are of critical importance; thus the significance of these tiny little swells in the land, where the soil becomes firm and stony. They are as important—as more than one Frenchman has noted—as the curves in a woman's body.

On the same Route des Grands Crus, before reaching the village of Margaux, a sign to the right directs you to the great Empire-style Château Margaux. Magnificently situated at the end of a long lane of fine plane trees, the enormous pillared château with its majestic front entrance is the perfect symbol of a Médoc Great First

Growth. The vineyards, the Empire-style château, and the beautiful surrounding parklands were bought from the Ginestet family in 1977 by Laura and André Mentzelopoulos, financiers and former owners of Felix Potin, one of France's largest grocery chains, and now part owners of Perrier, the soda water. Although new to wine, they showed great dedication in restoring Château Margaux as a great wine. The greatness of the 1979, 1982, and 1983 and the excellence of the 1980 are proof that Château Margaux is again a candidate to produce one of the greatest of all Bordeaux wines.

Mme Mentzelopoulos, before and after the loss of her husband in December 1980, has had the wisdom to surround herself with talented advisers, and in 1978 courageously began the lengthy, painstaking restoration of the château, literally stone by stone. I regret the departure of Margaux's former owner, Pierre Ginestet, one of Bordeaux's great gentlemen. In 1955 M. Ginestet generously offered me free use of his warehouses at Château Durfort, which served as my first base in establishing Alexis Lichine & Co., which I sold in 1966; for this, I shall be forever grateful.

Of surpassing delicacy and finesse, Château Margaux has produced wines of legendary excellence. One of the greatest wines I have ever tasted was the 1900 vintage of Château Margaux. Near the château is the great *chai,* among the biggest in the Médoc, lined with long rows of tall pillars.

In Burgundy, every grower takes you down into his cool, low-ceilinged cellar, carved out of the limestone bedrock; in Bordeaux, the cellar master takes you into a long, low-slung structure with a sloped roof of red tiles, the *chai.* Since the Médoc is bordered by the Gironde, in certain places, especially Margaux, the water table is too high for the châteaux to dig the traditional deep wine cellars. Yet in the winter of 1981, Laura Mentzelopoulos, with the help of her daughter Corinne, undertook the construction of a huge underground cellar, despite the difficulties, to achieve better storage conditions.

So, with a few notable exceptions, the Bordelais have sheds, not cellars. In the airy, dimly lit confines of what looks like a warehouse, with a long, central colonnade and whitewashed walls, the barrels are stacked two and three high and arranged in long, neat rows. In the most impressive *chais,* such as those of châteaux Margaux, Lascombes, and Mouton-Rothschild, the barrels are not stacked; one enters from slightly above the floor level, with the long rows stretching out below, the glass bungs all perfectly lined up. There is a cathedral-like hush in these environs, and even the most garrulous visitors will pause for a moment of silence. In 1980, a separate facility was built to handle the white wine. The Pavillon Blanc du Château Margaux is vinified, just as is the red, under the skillful supervision of Émile Peynaud.

Just at the edge of Château Margaux's vineyards lies the namesake village where, at the entrance of town, a billboard proudly claims "MARGAUX—Les Vins Rouges les plus Célèbres du Monde" ("The World's Most Famous Red Wines"). At the other end of the village is the last expanse of gravelly vineyard, shared by châteaux Margaux and Lascombes, which stands right on the knoll overlooking its great sweep of vineyards. Bought in 1952 by a group of wine-loving Americans, including the author, Château Lascombes was sold in 1971 to Bass-Charrington, the British brewing and liquor conglomerate. The quality of Lascombes had improved in the last thirty years. Northeast of Soussans, the final village of the Margaux place-name, is a good, non-classified vineyard, La Tour-de-Mons, efficiently run by M. Bertrand Clauzel, who until 1979 was also responsible for the wines of Château Cantemerle.

North of Soussans, the land begins a slow descent, and within a couple of kilometers (a mile or so), the quality vineyards have ended. From Margaux to Saint-Julien, the land is low-lying and partly marshy, with an occasional gravel rise, where some of the better Haut-Médoc Bourgeois Growths may be found, among them Lamarque, with its landmark feudal castle, Malescasse, acquired in 1979 by the Tesseron family, owners of Pontet-Canet and Lafon-Rochet, and Lanessan, owned by the owners of Pichon-Longueville-Baron. There is also the fine vineyard in Moulis with the strange name of Chasse-Spleen (literally, "banish despair"), which has produced wines of a quality that has often surpassed many Classified Growths. Maucaillou is another fine vineyard, which belongs to the Dourthe family.

In Listrac Baron Edmond de Rothschild has built a vineyard from the ground up: Château Clarke, which lies off the main vineyard road, has 120 hectares (300 acres) planted and boasts a modern, well-equipped *chai*. His first vintage was '77, but as the vines grow older, and with the Rothschild name, the vineyard cannot help but make a reputation for itself despite the soil. In summer there is a small restaurant on the premises.

The approach to Saint-Julien on the vineyard road affords the most graphic example of the importance of elevation in the Médoc. On the low-lying field below Château Beychevelle, the first Saint-Julien vineyard, the rich soil makes fine pasture land where herds of fat cows munch. Up the rise, by contrast, the Great Growth vineyards again take hold, flourishing in paltry, gravelly soil. Just as the outstanding vineyards of Margaux were clustered together on the hills of gravel, so the vineyards of Saint-Julien lie nearly on top of one another, all grouped on the highest ground. The late Aymar Achille-Fould, erstwhile politician and part-owner of Beychevelle, described the individuality of Saint-Julien this way: "As you climb the hill toward Saint-Julien and continue through it, the wines become fleshed-out and full, and perhaps less elegant, but richer and rounder than those of Margaux. Saint-Julien is, in fact, a transition between the elegance of Margaux and the bigness of Pauillac."

Château Beychevelle stands on the site of a medieval fortress that was rebuilt in great style in 1757. From the river side, the château, with its classic symmetrical garden, presents a memorable sight. From the back terrace one can see to the river, where centuries ago the mariners who sailed up the Gironde, loaded with wood to trade for wine, would shout in Gascon (*"Baisse voile"*: "Lower the sail") to salute the Duc d'Épernon, Grand Admiral of France, when he was lord of the domain in feudal times. Hence the name of the château and the design of the Beychevelle label, which shows a boat lowering its sail. The classic architecture and this charming story about the etymology of the name have made Beychevelle one of the best-known Médoc châteaux. In 1983 the Achille-Fould family decided to keep one-third of the shares and management, and sold two-thirds to an insurance group.

Across the road from Beychevelle, but somewhat overshadowed by its celebrated neighbor, is Château Branaire-Ducru. Also, like Beychevelle, classified a Fourth Growth, Branaire-Ducru makes a sturdy, big wine. The château is owned by the Tari family, owners of Château Giscours, and Mme Tari's brother, M. Jean-Michel Tapie.

Leading directly out of the Beychevelle vineyards are those of Ducru-Beaucaillou. The name Beaucaillou means "beautiful pebbles," and outside of the Margaux vineyards, none has as many. Jean-Eugène Borie, the owner of Ducru-Beaucaillou, has improved the vineyard remarkably since he took over in 1953. The wines are supple, full-bodied, and typically Saint-Julien, more than deserving of their Second Growth classification. More than Beychevelle, Ducru-Beaucaillou strikes the perfect balance between the suave elegance of Margaux and the full-bodied classicism of Pauillac wines. This is not to say that Saint-Julien wines are simply the sum of these characteristics. Far from it. Still, as a broad outline of the Saint-Julien type, this is a generally accurate picture. M. Borie, whose family has long held Château Haut-Batailley in Pauillac, should have even greater opportunity to assess the differences between the wines of Pauillac and Saint-Julien now that he's bought (in 1978) the Pauillac vineyard Grand-Puy-Lacoste. Because the château is situated on the knoll of Saint-Julien, the *chais* of Ducru-Beaucaillou are built slightly underground, giving them an added measure of dampness that is particularly advantageous in the keeping of old wines. An excessively dry environment will cause the corks of old bottles to dry out and shrink, exposing the wine to air; humidity helps to keep the corks healthy and swollen.

Off the main road toward Saint-Laurent are the two fine Cordier properties, Château Talbot and Château Gruaud-Larose. In 1983, the banking group La Hénin, owners of the Midi beach-grown wine branded "Listel," acquired control over those vineyards.

One of the few promotional projects of the entire Médoc is found just up the road from Beychevelle and Branaire, in the form of a huge bottle of Saint-Julien wine that stands on the edge of the road and the vineyards. Five meters high, perched on a small pedestal, this Bacchic symbol serves as a kind of icon to the wines of the commune. In the staid Médoc, it is blatantly out of character.

Just across from the monstrous magnum are the headquarters of a non-classified vineyard, Château Gloria, the most renowned Bourgeois Growth in the Médoc. The owner, Henri Martin, has put together a collection of vineyard parcels from the surrounding châteaux and created an excellent wine. In 1982, he bought Château Saint-Pierre. In 1983, the Japanese wine and spirits firm Suntory acquired Château Lagrange, another Classified Growth in Saint-Julien. Despite its being run down, Suntory's ambitious plans hopefully will revive a potentially good property.

The three Léoville vineyards in Saint-Julien, all classified as Second Growths, were once the property of Blaise Alexandre de Gasq, lord of Léoville and a president of the Bordeaux Parlement in the eighteenth century. He acquired the vineyard through marriage, and the land took his name. When the property was split up after the French Revolution, part of it remained with Jean de Las-Cases, a member of the Léoville family, and the rest was divided between Hugh Barton—an Irish wine merchant who bought parts in 1821 and 1826—and the Poyferré family. Barton's descendants continue to run the excellent Barton vineyard today. Léoville-Las-Cases, Léoville-Poyferré, and Léoville-Barton now are all separately owned and run.

In the twenties, Poyferré used to be rated the best of the three, and its '29 was legendary in Bordeaux. Since then, it is generally agreed that Poyferré's wines have been surpassed by the others. After the war and into the early fifties, when new vines were planted, the quality of Las-Cases suffered. In 1959, however, new vinification methods were introduced by the eminent Professor Émile Peynaud, Bordeaux's top oenologist, new cooperage was purchased, the vatting of the newly fermented wines was increased from ten days to three weeks (thus making the wines characteristically harder and achieving a quintessence of harmony), and the wines quickly reached a level of excellence. The 1966 Las-Cases, followed by many vintages in the 1970–85 period, were outstanding. The vineyard is entered through a tall, grim stone arch, a sketch of which appears on the Las-Cases label. Going back some ten to fifteen years, Las-Cases has a reputation and a standing watched and somewhat rivaled by Ducru-Beaucaillou and Pichon-Lalande competing for an intermediate place above the Classified Growths and just below the First Growths.

Under the laws of the Appellation, growers are not allowed to make wine from a vine less than four years old. Even at that age the plant is really too young to produce top-quality wine. At around eight to twelve years, the vine roots will have penetrated deeply enough into the soil to extract nourishment evenly and the vine itself will have grown out sufficiently to concentrate its energies on producing grapes, rather than new branches. From twenty years on, if the vine is properly pruned (this process is also controlled by the Appellation laws), it will produce less and less wine but of increasingly fine quality. To maintain even quality from year to year, growers stagger the planting of new vines, gradually replacing the plots of old ones. Rotated planting thus maintains an equilibrium, avoiding the problem that Las-Cases and many other vineyards had in the early fifties, when the vineyards were catching up after a couple of decades of neglect. Léoville-Las-Cases is now one of the most respected Classified Growths of the Médoc.

The "intermarriage" of vineyards continues to this day with the two Barton properties in Saint-Julien: Léoville-Barton and Langoa-Barton. The estates adjoin and have been in the Barton family since the 1820s. The harvest is now vinified under a single roof at Langoa, where the late owner, Ronald Barton, lived. Léoville-Barton produces the superior wine. Langoa is a much smaller property, perhaps a third the size of its neighbor, producing wine similar in many respects to the Léoville-Barton, but generally less refined. Since 1969, when mandatory château-bottling for all classified vineyards became the rule, the wine has been château-bottled. Ronald Barton's nephew, Anthony, with the help of his daughter, Lilian, is continuing in the good Barton tradition, doing an admirable job in running the two estates. Anthony and his Danish wife, Eva—now comfortably ensconced at Château Langoa, as Château Léoville-Barton is often called—have been close friends of mine ever since I settled in the Médoc.

Within jumping distance of Léoville-Las-Cases, the last Saint-Julien vineyard, is the great estate of Latour, the southernmost of the Pauillacs. The vineyards of Las-Cases slope down to a tiny gully. The hill climbs a few meters, the vines begin again, and we are now in Pauillac, in the vineyard of Latour.

Both pirates and the Hundred Years War had a hand in shaping the features of Château Latour—the first were responsible for its being built, and the second very nearly saw to its destruction. La Tour, the tower of the name, now stands alone at the center of the vineyard, where it was once part of a fortification built against marauding brigands. During the Hundred Years War (1337–1453), the English, French, and Gascons took turns at occupying the fort, until it was reduced to little more than a heap of stones. The *chais* of Latour stand in its place today.

Only the grower of an aristocratic and expensive wine like Latour can afford to vinify the wine to be so hard and long-lived. The must, or fermenting juice, is left in the stainless-steel vats for from twenty-five to thirty days. In addition to the long vatting period, the high percentage of Cabernet Sauvignon grapes (around 80 percent) makes for a wine of great quality, but one that must be waited for. Unfortunately, the great majority of Latour's average production of 20,000 cases is drunk before the hard, young wine has had a chance to assume the full grace and breeding that can only come with age.

The new chairman of Latour is Mr Alan Hare, while the day-to-day operations of the château, as of 1986, are the responsibility of Christian Le Sommer; until 1983 they were expertly managed by Jean-Paul Gardère, a former broker. The Pearson Group—the London investment group then headed by Lord Cowdray, now by Lord Blakenham—acquired the majority share of the vineyard in the early 1960s for the bargain price of $2.7 million. The minority share is divided between Harveys, the Bristol wine merchants, and the de Beaumont family, the previous owners.

When discussing his favorite wines, M. Gardère is never at a loss for words. "Describing the wines of Pauillac can be as difficult as you want to make it: it depends on where you look. Do you want to describe Latour or Lafite? Lafite is a svelte and elegant Madame Récamier, while Latour is more like a Rubens heroine. Then there's Mouton, situated between the two, also a hard wine with great elegance that is long in maturing." Certainly much of Latour's greatness comes from the demanding selection of vats: on the average only 60 percent of most vintages is bottled as Latour; the rest is sold under the label Les Forts de Latour or simply as *appellation* Pauillac. This selection takes place in the spring and is called *assemblage*. Not enough can be said about *assemblage*. It is this sacrifice that indicates which proprietors are really dedicated to making wines of quality.

A sense of individuality carries through the rest of the Pauillac growths: the greater they are, the more individual they will be. One characteristic they do share is great full-bodiedness. They are also bigger, harder wines than the delicate, elegant Margaux and Saint-Juliens, and they are less hearty and more nuanced than Saint-Estèphes. Each of Pauillac's three First Growths—Latour, Mouton-Rothschild, and Lafite—expresses its "Pauillac-ness" in a unique way, as three artists would have three different visions of the same countryside.

My son, Sacha, now in his mid-twenties, has become a very good wine salesman. He has started a small company on his own, and represents wine-producers of quality. He sells their wines throughout the U.S. and the Caribbean. He has visited, tasted, and worked in the vineyards of California, France, and Germany.

The one message I have constantly tried to impart to him is that to make good wines you have to sacrifice. The main sacrifice which has not been sufficiently recognized by wine buyers and well-initiated wine lovers, is for the grower to be very rigorous and disciplined in the selection of the ultimate blend.

A château has dozens of fermentation vats. For instance, at Château Prieuré-Lichine we have thirty vats. Not all of the wines fermented in these vats are the same, nor equal in quality. They do all come from the same vineyards belonging to Château Prieuré-Lichine, but each grape variety is picked separately, starting with the Merlot, the fastest-maturing of Bordeaux's four grape varieties, followed by the Cabernet Sauvignon, and usually finishing with the small quantity of Cabernet Franc and Petit Verdot. Even within each variety, maturity is not always the same. The grapes come from diverse areas, scattered in Cantenac, Labarde, Margaux and Soussans, all within the *appellation* of Margaux. This means a variation of soils, and vines of different ages, as well as minute differences in microclimate, and the grapes are picked at different intervals over sometimes as long as a three-week period.

In Bordeaux, which is a marginal climatic region, the sun is not a constant: there may be cooler or hotter, dry or rainy days, and the weather which prevails during the harvest is crucial, very often determining the "highs" in the quality of the vintage. Therefore these vats are not going to be of equal quality. It is this rigorous selection which I perform with my oenologist friend Émile Peynaud, sometimes as often as four times, as was the case with the 1984.

In 1984 as in most years, the first tasting was made after the first fermentation at the end of October, the second after the second or malolactic fermentation in November. Both were purely to get an insight into the wines, and not a selection.

And then finally comes the main tasting, known as the *assemblage,* in late March or early April, when by this time the vats will be set aside to be sold as our second wine, at half the price and below our cost of production, as Château de Clairefont.

This sacrifice of rigorous selection is what really permits the large properties in Bordeaux to be very discriminating, thus enabling them to make top wines. Château Margaux, our neighbor, set aside their lesser wine and call it Pavillon Rouge du Château Margaux. Château Latour has Les Forts de Latour. Château Lafite has Moulin les Carruades. Haut Brion sells their second wine as Bahans. Léoville Las Cases has Clos du Marquis. Pichon-Lalande has Réserve de la Comtesse, and at Château Prieuré-Lichine, my second wine is Château de Clairefont.

Selling part of your production at half price is a discipline demanding a sacrifice that not many châteaux are willing, or can afford, to make. But this discipline is what sets certain châteaux apart from others.

The vineyards of Pichon-Lalande abut on Latour's and spill over into Saint-Julien; and just across the road are those of Pichon-Longueville-Baron. These two vineyards were once joined under a single ownership. They came into the Pichon family through marriage in the seventeenth century: Pierre des Mésures de Rausan, of Rausan-Ségla and Rauzan-Gassies in Margaux, owned the entire property and made it part of his daughter's dowry in her marriage to Jacques de Pichon, Baron de

Longueville, and one of the presidents of the Bordeaux Parlement. It remained in-tact until the middle of the nineteenth century, when it was split between a son and daughter of the family—Sophie, Comtesse de Lalande, receiving two-thirds and her brother, the Baron de Pichon, the rest. Until recently the names were as difficult to keep straight as the history, but now the comtesse's share is labeled Pichon-Lalande, while the baron's portion is labeled Baron de Pichon-Longueville (usually referred to as Pichon-Baron), with a busy coat of arms adorned with rampant griffins instead of a picture of the nineteenth-century "Renaissance" château, which would be a per-fectly distinctive label. The ownership and management of the two vineyards are now totally separate. Both are classified as Second Growths, and both are good wines, though during the past generation Pichon-Lalande has gained in quality and hence in popularity over Pichon-Baron. The 1970, 1975, 1979, 1981, 1982, and 1983 Lalande were of surpassing excellence, and will certainly help its continuing rise in reputation. Lalande's situation close to the river, and with some of its vineyards on the Saint-Julien side, means that the soil has a greater proportion of the fine gravel of the Latour type, and that is probably why Lalande is lighter and more supple than Pichon-Longueville-Baron, which is less harmonious and more full-bodied. It is from the terrace that one sees one of the most beautiful views, overlooking endless rows of vines, with the Gironde in the distance. Mme Eliane de Lencquesaing is the present owner of Pichon-Lalande, after a drawn-out court case won from her brother, Alain Miailhe.

Between the two Pichons and the town of Pauillac are two of Pauillac's Fifth Growths which would certainly be moved up in a new classification: Lynch-Bages and Grand-Puy-Lacoste. They both have vineyards set back from the river, on the west side of the vineyard road. Because they reach a sufficient elevation, their soil composition is still largely gravel, though there are also significant sections of heav-ier, sandier soil. This combination gives the wines long life and a full-bodied vigor which, in their early years, may make them seem rough or hard. Lynch-Bages is the property of Jean-Michel Cazes and of André Cazes, Pauillac's energetic mayor—and owner, as well, of the fine Saint-Estèphe Bourgeois Growth (a Cru Bourgeois) Les Ormes-de-Pez. "Bages" is the name of the particular gravel knoll near Pauillac, and the "Lynch" comes from the family of Thomas Lynch, who emigrated from Ireland to settle in the Médoc in the early eighteenth century. For a century the Lynches were a prominent family; their last descendant was president of the Bordeaux Parle-ment in the early nineteenth century. (One wonders, finally, if the number of presi-dents of the Bordeaux Parlement who became large vineyard owners did so because they were already rich—nearly all were at least comfortably off—or because they enriched themselves by being Parlement presidents.)

M. Cazes emphasizes the changes in the way in which the region's wines are now vinified. "There is no doubt," he observes, "that we are making wines that are finer, more supple, and faster-maturing than we did in the past. The increase in knowledge of all wine-making principles has allowed us to lower the acidity and bring out the fruit and delicacy of the grapes. So the wines are now easier to drink at the end of five years, without necessarily being shorter-lived over the long haul."

Until he sold Grand-Puy-Lacoste in 1978 to Jean-Eugène Borie, also owner of Ducru-Beaucaillou in Saint-Julien and Haut-Batailley, a nearby Pauillac château, the vineyards and château were in the hands of the late Raymond Dupin, who died in 1980. Even in his eighties M. Dupin was ever the *grand gourmet* of the Médoc. During the German occupation, his château served as a barracks and a stable for German soldiers. When he returned to it after the war, he found that the wooden paneling and wainscoting had been torn out and used for firewood to fight off the damp Médoc winters. Although a wealthy man, with extensive forest holdings in the Landes, M. Dupin spent little on repairing the house, preferring, instead, to give exquisite dinners, with some of the Médoc's oldest and finest wines. For a characteristic image of the Médoc, picture a beautifully set table with fine china, delicate linens, magnificent crystal and silver, and sublime food and wines in the middle of a nearly empty room, lit by a naked bulb.

From Margaux to the end of the Médoc peninsula, all of the little villages along the vineyard road dedicate themselves to wine. In small workshops, squirreled away off the village squares, artisans put together wine cases, and the countryside and towns are filled with small vineyard owners or the workmen who tend the vines. The big exception to the rule is the town of Pauillac, which, though it gives its name to the most regal of the four Médoc place-names, is the least dependent on wine for its livelihood.

After a long sleep, the town of Pauillac recently awoke under the vigorous leadership of André Cazes, its present mayor. Popular M. Cazes is a busy man. He is dedicated to the Médoc, both as owner of the fine Château Lynch-Bages, which he runs with his son, Jean-Michel, who is a motivating spirit of the Commanderie du Bontemps de Médoc. In addition to everything else, father and son are the Médoc's largest insurance brokers. As mayor, André Cazes was instrumental in having the Shell refinery come to Pauillac. The refinery and all the jobs were certainly welcomed in the sixties, when fewer people were attracted by agriculture and there was some fear that the châteaux of the region would have difficulty finding trained vineyard help. That is no longer an issue. More worrisome now are the three towering smokestacks of the refinery, clearly visible from Lafite, Mouton, and Cos d'Estournel. Shell commissioned oenologists to investigate the potential effect of the refinery's fumes on the wine, and later reported that the grapes are in no way harmed. Let us hope Shell is right. Luckily, the prevailing breezes carry most emissions far out over the river, though the refinery itself certainly offends the eye. Shell decided to close the refinery in 1986. The eyesore remains, but the fumes have ceased being a subject of controversy.

At least Pauillac was spared open warfare with the oilmen. In wilder times, river pirates frequently raided the port and many battles of the Hundred Years War were fought along the banks and through the fields above the town. Moreover, the Pauillaçais proudly point out that the Marquis de Lafayette embarked from their port for America in 1777. In Lafayette's day, there were some eighty shipbuilding firms in and around Pauillac. None remain today. The port still has a certain charm, with a long, tree-lined promenade along the Gironde. At this point, halfway between Bordeaux and the Atlantic, the Gironde is more of an estuary than a river; nearly 2 kilometers (1 mile) across, sluggish and muddy, wider than the Rhine and as majestic as the Mississippi.

Up to May 1984, to get a better feel of the Médoc after traveling the vineyards, one could pay a visit to the Maison du Vin of Pauillac, located at the beginning of the Pauillac waterfront in a big modern building. Unfortunately, a fire destroyed this headquarters of the Commanderie du Bontemps de Médoc, Bordeaux's main promotional society and counterpart to Burgundy's Chevaliers du Tastevin. Inside, you could find a large room with a map, covering three walls, that showed the road and the châteaux along it leading from Bordeaux to Pauillac and beyond. It has been reconstructed, and was reopened in the summer of 1986. It is worth a visit.

Just above Pauillac, on the left of the vineyard road, is Château Pontet-Canet, one of the largest vineyards of the Médoc. It was the pride of the Cruse family until 1975, when it was purchased by Nicole Cruse's husband, Guy Tesseron, owner of the Saint-Estèphe vineyard Lafon-Rochet and of a Cognac firm possessing one of the greatest collections of rare old Cognacs.

Stretching north from Pontet-Canet is the cluster of Rothschild vineyards and dependencies. First, the Philippe de Rothschild properties: the recently renamed Fifth Growth Mouton-Baronne-Philippe, his cherished First Growth Mouton, and the Fifth Growth Clerc-Milon. Bordering them are the vineyards of the banking branch of the Rothschild family: the First Growth Château Lafite-Rothschild and the Fourth Growth Duhart-Milon.

Until 1730, Mouton was all part of the property belonging to Prince Nicolas de Ségur, another president of the Bordeaux Parlement and owner, as well, of Latour, Calon-Ségur and Phélan-Ségur, and many other lands in the Médoc. It was bought as Château Mouton by the Baron Nathaniel Rothschild in 1853. His great-grandson, the present Baron Philippe, took over the management in 1926 and ownership shortly afterwards. Since the early eighties, he has enjoyed the able assistance of his daughter Philippine. By putting himself on the map, he helped to put the entire Médoc district there as well. Just about everyone from Blanquefort to Pauillac has profited from the tens of thousands of people who journey up the peninsula each year to visit his incomparable Mouton Wine Museum. In addition, he holds two other Pauillac vineyards: Mouton d'Armailhacq, whose name he changed to Mouton-Baron-Philippe in 1956 and then, in 1977, to Mouton-Baronne-Philippe, in memory of Pauline, his recently deceased wife; and Clerc-Milon-Rothschild, which he acquired in the sixties.

The great *chai* at Mouton is the most impressive in all of Bordeaux. Twin glass doors swing open onto a small platform from which one sees ten rows of barrels stretching out nearly a hundred meters. On the far wall, perfectly centered and lit from behind, is the seal of Mouton.

Baron Philippe and his late wife, Pauline, spent many years assembling the Mouton Wine Museum. Opened in 1962, it features a priceless array of ancient drinking vessels, goblets, tapestries and paintings, and hundreds of works of art connected with wine and its lore. Its galaxy of superb art objects is inspiring testimony to the civilizing symbol that wine has been throughout the ages. The pieces are beautifully lit and displayed, and may be seen now by appointment with the curator. Beneath the museum and *chai,* in moss-blackened cellars (some of the few true cellars in the Médoc) lies one of the most extensive collections of old vintage bottles from fine châteaux all over Bordeaux. Mouton-Rothschild of nearly every vintage is kept here, going as far back as 1859 and totaling in all some 100,000 bottles.

My friendship with Philippe has been a long one, and I regard him as undoubtedly the Médoc's greatest asset, a man of enormous culture, taste, and charm. Philippine, his daughter, is actively promoting the vineyards and the wines of the shipping company called the Bergerie, anticipating the help of her son, Philippe Sereys de Rothschild.

The next adjoining vineyard is that of the rival Château Lafite. The name is said to derive from the old Médoc word *"la hite,"* meaning "the height." The Château does, in fact, sit on the highest knoll of Pauillac. The owners are descended not from Nathaniel Rothschild but from his brother, James, who bought Lafite in 1868. It has remained in the family since that time. In relative terms, however, the Rothschilds are newcomers to Lafite, for, as a wine-making château, it has eight centuries of history behind it. Lafite was reputedly served by Madame de Pompadour, and required by Madame du Barry, at her dinners. The Château's royal connections ended with the Revolution, however, and in 1794 it became public property and passed into the hands of a Dutch syndicate. The oldest bottles in its cellar date from this period, the earliest being a 1797.

Besides possessing the oldest bottle of its own wine of any château in the Médoc, Lafite also has the famous Bismarck desk, brought from Château Ferrière, the Rothschild residence outside Paris. It was at Ferrière that the Iron Chancellor learned of the Rothschild agreement to advance the funds for payment of the huge indemnities he had demanded as a condition to end the Prussian occupation of France in 1870. Apparently, the chancellor had fully expected his demands to be impossibly high, but the combined financial muscle of the Rothschild banks provided the money. On hearing the news, the enraged Bismarck slammed his fist on the desk with such force that the inkwell jumped from its stand, spilling ink all over the top. The desk, complete with ink stain, is now in one of the private rooms of Lafite.

Lafite's other notable German connection came during World War II, when the status-seeking Göring, awed by its reputation, declared his intention of taking Lafite as his own after Germany won the war.

Deep in Lafite's vast cellars lies one of the world's outstanding wine libraries. In the best years, such as the legendary ageless and expensive '61s and '70s, Lafite can be supreme. It has great finesse and a particular softness imparted by the relatively high percentage of Merlot grapes.

A word should be said about the celebrated Rothschild rivalry between Lafite and Mouton. This reached a peak of a sort in the 1960s, when the cousins began holding an informal contest each year to see whose château could sell its wine for the higher price. The idea was to gain prestige. The winner's luster was considerably dimmed by the time the wine reached the consumer, however, since bottles of the same vintage vary widely from country to country and store to store as a consequence of duties, the idiosyncrasies of distribution, judicious buying, and price-cutting. In any event, the yearly bidding war between the châteaux was a good publicity device. Eventually other châteaux in Bordeaux got into the act, holding out for the higher prices in order to reap even greater fame. The greatly inflated prices that resulted played a part in the "bubble" of 1973, and the comedy ceased to amuse. When the bottom fell out in 1974, prices returned to more sensible levels. This informal pricing competition is now being played in the mid-eighties by three second Classified Growths. Let us hope that this is not the foreboding of another 1974 Bordeaux wine crash.

In 1977, after a few dubious vintages, Château Lafite came under the management of Eric de Rothschild, who engaged a new *régisseur,* Jean Creté, formerly of Léoville-Las-Cases. M. Creté oversees the day-to-day production of Lafite, as well as of Lafite's second wine, Moulin des Carruades. The vineyards of Lafite include small parcels in Saint-Estèphe, just as Pichon-Lalande overlaps with Saint-Julien. The other vineyard of the Lafite branch of the Rothschilds is Duhart-Milon, which is separately cultivated and vinified, although it is managed by the same personnel.

* * *

The good, gravelly soil that distinguishes Pauillac disappears abruptly after the vine-yards of Lafite, resurfacing only in a narrow *croupe,* or hill, for Cos d'Estournel and again, farther north, just above the village of Saint-Estèphe, where the vineyards of Calon-Ségur are found. The soil also becomes slightly heavier, with greater amounts of clay, which retains moisture longer. As a result, if the wines of Saint-Estèphe have any fault, it will be a barely perceptible lack of finesse. With every step north, the Pauillac characteristics fall away and the heavier Saint-Estèphe nature emerges.

Although Saint-Estèphe has the smallest amount of gravel, it is the most pro-ductive of the four Haut-Médoc place-names, covering some 1,000 hectares (2,500 acres) and making the equivalent of 670,000 cases, of which less than a fifth is in Classified Growths. Of the five Saint-Estèphe vineyards classified in 1855—Château Cos d'Estournel, Château Montrose, Château Calon-Ségur, Château Lafon-Rochet, and Château Cos Labory—the first three have been the most respected and most widely distributed.

With the possible exceptions of Cos d'Estournel, Montrose, and Calon-Ségur, one doesn't look for any great mystery and subtlety in Saint-Estèphe wines, which usually lack the breeding or finesse that are hallmarks of Pauillac, Saint-Julien, and Margaux, and sometimes incline to be rustic. However, they can be beautifully gen-erous, full wines, appealing to the consumer who is fond of a big mouthful that lin-gers on the palate long after the wine is swallowed.

The hands-down winner of The Weirdest Château of the Médoc Award is Cos d'Estournel, a pagoda-turreted, nineteenth-century fantasy fort, complete with wooden carved doors from the palace of the Sultan of Zanzibar. Until the sixties Cos was part of the Ginestet family holdings, but in 1970 some of the property was split up among the relatives, and the owner is now the dedicated Bruno Prats, who also functions as head of the Committee of Classified Growths. Under his direction, Cos has greatly improved and now makes a first-rate wine that faithfully reflects its inter-mediate position between Saint-Estèphe and Pauillac, being somewhat lighter and more supple than the other important Saint-Estèphes but still full and rich, with a marked characteristic fatness—what the French call *gras*—which comes, in part, from the natural glycerines in the wine. A few kilometers north of Cos is Château Montrose, its vineyards all of a piece overlooking the Gironde River.

The wines of Montrose are less inviting in their youth, but are renowned for the great class and vinosity they take on with years of bottle-aging. In 1970 I came across a magnum of 1865 Montrose that was as firm and alive as a 1970 would be today. Since that time, Château Montrose has lightened up considerably, although its distinctive character is still one of long life and deep fullness. The 70 hectares (175 acres) of vineyards are now owned by Jean-Louis Charmolüe. In the mid-fifties,

Mme Charmolüe (his mother) became the first woman to be inducted into the formerly all-male Commanderie du Bontemps de Médoc.

All alone above the village of Saint-Estèphe is Calon-Ségur, the northernmost of the Médoc's Classified Growths. The "Calon" is taken from the word for a small riverboat that was used in the Middle Ages to ferry timber across the Gironde. (In fact, on account of the extensive tracts of cultivated forest in the area of the château, the entire Saint-Estèphe district was known until the eighteenth century as Calones.) The "Ségur" part comes from Nicolas de Ségur, the ubiquitous eighteenth-century president of the Bordeaux Parlement, who was then the owner of the château, as well as of Lafite and Latour. The heart on the label signifies his preference for Calon over his other wines, as expressed in this motto on the château's archway:

I make wine at Lafite and Latour
But my heart is at Calon

The wine so close to his heart is characterized by robustness and full body, with traces of suppleness. Along with Château Montrose, Calon-Ségur produces the longest-lived wines of Saint-Estèphe. To counteract the increasing heaviness of the soil, Calon uses a higher percentage of Merlot grapes. Recently, Calon-Ségur has had a tendency of keeping their wines in barrels for twenty-four to twenty-five months before bottling. This is four to five months longer than some of their neighbors, which may be why some of their vintages were prematurely oxidized.

The fame of Calon-Ségur wine was made largely by the late Édouard Gasqueton, who was one of my closest friends in my early days in the Médoc. His generosity and hospitality were without equal. His nephew, Philippe, has succeeded him and now runs the adjoining Bourgeois Growth Château Capbern, while managing Château du Tertre in Margaux and Château d'Agassac, a medieval fort partly in ruin, in Ludon. Calon-Ségur recently added an underground cellar which helps the control of temperatures.

More than the other three Médoc place-names, Saint-Estèphe is rich with fine Bourgeois Growths, some of which would certainly be included in any new classification. Phélan-Ségur, Château de Pez, Les Ormes-de-Pez, Marbuzet, and Haut-Marbuzet are among those worthy of more attention than they currently receive. They are rather elegant wines whose depth and fullness make them attractive choices for those searching for moderately priced, good-quality Saint-Estèphes or Haut-Médocs.

In addition to the four Haut-Médoc place-names just described, there are two other Haut-Médoc appellations which deserve mention as producing wines often approaching the minor châteaux of Margaux, Saint-Julien, Pauillac, and Saint-Estèphe. Moulis and Listrac lie together to the west of Saint-Julien and the northern part of

Margaux along the Médoc's other highway, D-1. Far as they are from the Gironde, the vineyards of Moulis and Listrac have little of the gravel found elsewhere in the Haut-Médoc. The better area, and the smaller of the two, is Moulis, whose clay and limestone soil marries well with the favored Merlot grape to produce wines of fair delicacy. Listrac has sandier soil more apt for the Cabernet grape, and its wines, however pleasing, will lack the finesse of its neighbor. Some of the better châteaux include: in Moulis, the above-mentioned Chasse-Spleen, Maucaillou, and Poujeaux-Theil; in Listrac, Clarke, with its 120 hectares (300 acres) of vines; Edmond de Rothschild courageously started the vineyard from scratch and is selling his wines today at high prices, as if they were of proven quality, with a great following; and the Châteaux Fourcas-Dupré and Fourcas-Hosten, the latter ably managed by Bertrand de Rivoyre, one of Bordeaux's more successful shippers.

Geographically speaking, the Médoc usually means the entire peninsula. For the purpose of classifying the wines in 1855, however, two regions were distinguished: the Haut-Médoc, where the six place-names Margaux, Saint-Julien, Pauillac, Saint-Estèphe, Moulis, and Listrac are found; and the Bas-Médoc, the region north of Saint-Estèphe continuing nearly to the tip of the peninsula. The Bas-Médoc (Lower Médoc), though it lies to the north, was so named because it is downstream on the Gironde. The unpleasant, and occasionally justified, connotations of *"bas"* were no help when it came to selling wines, so the growers from the area agitated for a change in name, and the distinction is now made between the Haut-Médoc (from Blanquefort to a few kilometers north of Saint-Estèphe, containing the six place-names) and the Médoc (everything north to the tip of the peninsula).

In the Médoc, the wines are mostly undistinguished, though some are of quite good quality considering the soil, which, this far downstream, becomes more alluvial and heavier. All of the gravel that might have been carried here millions of years ago is deposited instead along the intervening narrow strip of vineyard running from south of Margaux to Saint-Estèphe. Individual so-called *"petits châteaux"* continue to make wines in this region, as do many commune cooperatives, some of which bottle their wines under a château name. Active communes in the region include Blaignan with Château La Cardonne, Bégadan, home of Château La Tour-de-By and Château Greysac; Saint-Germain d'Esteuil with Château Castéra, and Saint-Yzans with Château Loudenne. The apogee of wine-drinking pleasure may not be found in this region of the Médoc, but honest, well-made wines are not rare—and most often are not expensive.

For the tourist, this northern stretch of the Médoc is somewhat more appealing to the eye than the more famous Haut-Médoc. The region is hillier and covered with vines, forestlands, and fields of corn and potatoes. It has a backwoods feeling. As the land narrows to the point where the Gironde meets the sea, at Le Verdon one feels and smells the salt breeze and coastal vegetation: scrubby pines and *maquis* fill the air with their faintly exotic aroma. Fine for a summer vacation, but less than perfect for the production of the greatest of wines. Now at le Verdon-sur-Mer, at the tip of the peninsula, a huge container and petroleum port has been developed that is diverting much of the shipment of wines from the port of Bordeaux. Shipped by rail from Bordeaux in large metal and wooden containers, much of the region's wine leaves from this port which is located directly on the sea, rather than way upstream from Bordeaux.

MÉDOC
Hotels and Restaurants
H = *Hotel;* R = *Restaurant*

From Bordeaux the road to the Médoc is not well marked. Follow signs to Soulac and Pauillac from the center of town; if you lose your way, ask for the Barrière du Médoc, which will lead you out of Bordeaux. About 1 km after passing the entrance to the Paris Autoroute (on your right), there is a small turn-off to Blanquefort and Pauillac on the right. This is D-2, the beginning of the great vineyard road of the Médoc.

The Médoc, with one exception, has little to offer in the way of grand cuisine. Most of the restaurants and inns indicated below may be compromises, offered to save the vineyard-visiting traveler a trip back to Bordeaux to eat.

BLANQUEFORT (33290—Gironde)
8 km north of Bordeaux off D-2.

HR AUBERGE DES CRIQUETS: On D-108, just north of Blanquefort, 4 km from the exhibition/hotel complex, 12 km from Margaux. Tel.: 56.35.09.24. 8 rooms with baths. Assorted menus with regional specialties. Warm welcome. English spoken.

MARGAUX (33460—Gironde)
25 km northwest of Bordeaux on the vineyard road,
in the heart of the great Haut-Médoc vineyards.

This small village, with its 1,400 inhabitants, belies the greatness of the Margaux wines. On weekdays, with the exception of August, you can visit Château Margaux by special appointment. At Cantenac (2 km before you reach Margaux) Château Prieuré-Lichine is open from 9:30 a.m. to 6:30 p.m. every day of the year. Bilingual guides explain how wine is made in the sixteenth-century Benedictine priory. Margaux boasts the best combination of eating and sleeping in the Bordeaux region at the newly built Relais de Margaux.

HR LE RELAIS DE MARGAUX: Tel.: 56.88.38.30. Tlx.: 572530. 18 luxurious, well-decorated rooms, plus 3 suites.
This beautiful auberge-restaurant opened in the summer of 1985. Overlooking the Gironde river in the midst of a 50-hectare park behind Château Margaux, it is perhaps the most comfortable hotel in the Bordeaux region. The good, elegant restaurant is under the personal daily supervision of Jean-Paul Mâle, an excellent chef who moved from his restaurant at Saint-Jean-de-Blaignac, near Saint-Émilion, to Margaux in June of 1985. One Michelin star.

R LE SAVOIE: Place Trémoille. Tel.: 56.88.31.76.
In 1980, M. and Mme Fougeras took over this restaurant, perfectly situated in the heart of the Médoc vineyards. The good cuisine, at what were fair prices, promises to make this the best quality/price restaurant in the Médoc. Understaffed, Mme Fougeras could improve the warmth of her welcome.

SOUSSANS-MARGAUX (33460—Gironde)
2 km from Margaux, 27 km northwest of Bordeaux on D-2,
the Route of the Grands Crus.

R LA RIGAUDIÈRE: Tel.: 56.88.74.02.
In 1980, chef Dominic Pradet leased this wine château and transformed it into a garden-restaurant situated in a pretty park. Specialties include fair fish and regional dishes. Fairly expensive for what it is. Slow service.

LAMARQUE (33460—Gironde)
(Bordeaux 33—Margaux 8)

If driving north to Cognac, you may choose to cross the Gironde by ferry, which runs infrequently in winter but several times a day in summer. The half-hour crossing will take you to Blaye, which boasts a fort built by Vauban, Louis XIV's war minister. A lunch in the arresting citadel will add flavor to your trip.

R RELAIS DU MÉDOC: Tel.: 56.58.92.27. Between Margaux and Saint-Julien, just off D-2. Very good, simple, inexpensive restaurant.

SALAUNES (33160—Gironde)
(Bordeaux 21—Margaux 30)
From Bordeaux, take D-6. From Margaux, take D-105 direct via Castelnau.

HR DOMAINE DES ARDILLIÈRES: Tel.: 56.05.20.70. 24 rooms.
Quiet, comfortable inn between the vineyard region and the pines and sands of the Landes. The food, unfortunately, is very uneven.

LISTRAC (33480—Gironde)
(Bordeaux 34—Margaux 12)
From Bordeaux, take D-1. From Margaux, take D-105 to Castelnau.
Listrac 6 km north of Castelnau.

Château Clarke is open for visitors on weekends during the summer months.

HR HOTEL DE FRANCE: Tel.: 56.58.03.68. 7 small, quiet, reasonably priced rooms not worth a detour.
The owner serves good-quality lunches and dinners at fairly reasonable prices, with a warm smile. There has been a change of management, though, in 1986.

SAINT-LAURENT-ET-BENON (33112—Gironde)
(Bordeaux 45—Margaux 21)
6 km west of Saint-Julien-Beychevelle

R LA RENAISSANCE: Tel.: 56.59.40.29. 8 rooms: 2 medium-good and 6 barely fair.
Simple, good, and reasonable. M. Dutrey, the owner, was my caterer for the pickers during the harvest.

LESPARRE (33340—Gironde)
(Bordeaux 63—Margaux 40)

This is the most important shopping town in the Médoc, and that's not saying much. Picnickers will find a good pastry shop and a good charcuterie in the center of town. The wine fair held in July is worth a small detour. At the northern tip, Le Verdon, you can take a ferry to Royan, a bombed-out and reconstructed summer resort town that will give you access to the oyster beds of Marennes. From there you can head north to La Rochelle.

R LA MARE AUX GRENOUILLES: Tel.: 56.41.03.46.
Pierre de Wilde offers a good wine list and justifies a short trip after visiting Mouton, Lafite, Latour, and many of the other great châteaux of Pauillac and Saint-Estèphe.

PAUILLAC (33450—Gironde)
(Bordeaux 50—Margaux 19—Lesparre 20—Le Verdon 55—Mouton-Rothschild 3)

❧ If you want to have a decent meal, do not be tempted by the cafés and so-called restaurants on the waterfront of the Gironde. It's from this waterfront that Lafayette's ship set sail for the American colonies.

. . .

SHALL THE OLD ORDER CHANGE?

The Case for Reclassification

The 1855 Classement des Grands Crus de la Gironde, as it was called, was an ambitious work from the outset. Napoleon III was adamant in his desire for a classification of the wines of Bordeaux, the greatest of French wines, for the Exposition Universelle de Paris—the world's fair of the day—where the best France had to offer would be put on display. Charged with the task of drawing up the rankings, the Bordeaux Chamber of Commerce delegated the work to the Bordeaux Brokers' Association, an official body attached to the Bordeaux Stock Exchange. What was required in effect was a listing of the wines of the Bordeaux region in order of excellence as demonstrated by the prices they had fetched over the years.

This type of list according to price existed long before 1855. From the time that wines began to emerge under their own names in the eighteenth century, price hierarchies had been established, based on the demand for the wine in the market. By the end of the eighteenth century, the four wines that were later designated First Growths in 1855 were already recognized as the very best that Bordeaux had to offer and the prices paid for them were correspondingly high. Brokers often made informal classifications of their own to serve as buyer's guides of a sort. In 1824 and 1827 individual brokers drew up classifications with four major categories of growths (the

1855 list has five). The lists differed in significant ways from each other and from the 1855 Classification—each reflecting the limitations of its compiler.

Still, no group was better qualified to rank the wines of the region than the brokers. Since their job was (and is) to act as the intermediary between the *propriété* and the shipper, they were familiar with all the wines of any commercial importance on the Bordeaux exchange. But this familiarity led to one inevitable and distorting limitation—wines which had little or no exposure in the Bordeaux marketplace received no attention, no matter what their quality. Therefore the great districts of today—Graves (except for Haut-Brion, which was classed along with the First Growths of the Médoc), Saint-Émilion, and Pomerol—were out of the running, because in 1855 they had no commercial or public recognition. The fact is that they were minor wines at the time. The brokers had no way of knowing that a century later Pétrus, Cheval-Blanc, and Ausone would all command prices equal to and often surpassing those of the First Growth Médocs. Whether these wines were in fact so little worthy of attention remains debatable, however—after all, the world of the Bordeaux wine trade was closed and snobbish and Saint-Émilion and Pomerol were on the wrong side of the river, so to speak. Between Bordeaux and Libourne (the wine center for Saint-Émilion and Pomerol) there are the Dordogne and Garonne rivers to cross, and until the early nineteenth century there was no bridge across the Dordogne. More than one château owner in Saint-Émilion and Pomerol has insisted to me that the only reason his region and wine were excluded in 1855 was that the Bordeaux trade in those days considered Libourne a social backwater. But that is another story.

The fact remains that there were only two notable wine regions at the time: the Médoc for the red wines and Sauternes-Barsac for the sweet whites. Château Haut-Brion in Graves was an exception to the all-Médoc line-up because it was too well known and too well sold to be ignored by the brokers.

In establishing the criteria for the new classification, although price was the most important factor, the prestige of both the wine and the owner was taken into account. The quality of the soil and the exposure of the vineyard were also considered, because they remain more or less constant from generation to generation regardless of who the owner is. In 1867, only twelve years after the official classification, Charles Cocks, author of his own respected rating of the wines of Bordeaux, underscored the need for ongoing reassessment:

> Like all human institutions, this one is subject to the laws of time and must, at certain times, be rejuvenated and kept abreast of progress. The vineyards themselves, in changing ownership, may often be modified. A certain vine-site, neglected by a careless owner, or by one who has run

into debt, may fall into the hands of a rich, active, and intelligent man, and because of this, give a better product. The opposite can also happen. . . .

It is apparent that Cocks was and is right, and the time for a new classification is very much at hand.

Although the quality of the vineyard soil will remain the same, the owner may be forced to sell it or rent it out, or he may trade it for better vineyard parcels elsewhere. For these two reasons alone—the changes in ownership and the changes in vineyard holdings—updating is constantly necessary. The vineyard area of a Médoc château is not fixed in the same way as the boundaries of a Great Growth (*Grand Cru*) vineyard of Burgundy, such as Latricières-Chambertin. Any of the First Growths of Pauillac, for instance, could buy hectares of the poor land within the Appellation Pauillac Contrôlée (all communes have select as well as less desirable areas of soil) and include the wine made from that land in the château-bottling. Given the character of the owners, this is not likely to happen, but the point is that no plot of vines within Pauillac (or Saint-Estèphe or Saint-Julien or Margaux, for that matter) is reserved for or classified under a specific château name. Instead, each vineyard parcel takes on the prestige of the château that owns it. Hence it is not uncommon for a given vineyard parcel to change classification from a First to a Fourth to a Second to a Fifth Growth as it is bought and sold by different châteaux. The character and quality of the château's wine are directly affected as a result.

The greatest variable in the greatness of a wine, however, is ultimately the owner himself and the effectiveness of his management as reflected in the know-how and dedication of his workers in the vineyards and the cellars. Hundreds of small but crucial steps have a bearing on the quality of the wine. Does the owner see to it that the vines are properly pruned to limit the harvest, and properly safeguarded against disease? Is his vinification equipment clean and in good repair? Is he willing (and able) to buy new vats and barrels as they are needed? Is he prepared, in his search for the best quality, to sacrifice the lesser vats of his wine and reserve only the best to go out under the château label? The *assemblage,* or the selection of vats, is a proprietor's responsibility. His diligence in discarding lesser vats will directly reflect on the quality of the wine. Will he take the trouble to make soil analyses in order to ascertain the right types of fertilizers and vine clones to use? Will he buy only the best parcels of land within the *appellation* to plant with vines? The answers to all of these questions and more will indicate the depth of the grower's dedication, and determine the excellence of his product. Although the most conscientious grower in the world cannot overcome poor soils and unfavorable climate, he can have an influence—for the better—on all other aspects of the wine-making process.

With the changeability of these two factors—geography and management—in mind, it is especially remarkable that the form of the 1855 Classification was in strict order of merit, even within the five categories of growths. Within the Second Growths, for instance, the châteaux Ducru-Beaucaillou, Cos d'Estournel, and Montrose were listed in that order of excellence. But the owners themselves—even, probably, in 1855—would have hesitated to maintain that this order was the correct one year in and year out.

In recent years, after much agitation on all sides, the Syndicat des crus classés petitioned the INAO for an update of the 1855 classification. There were two choices: either the 1855 classification should be amended to reflect changes in production and market value, or else it should be left untouched and a completely new classification drawn up. In 1960 the INAO declared that the rankings in the 1855 classification had been prizes for quality at a given time and that they had no authority to, in effect, take the prizes back. So the INAO established guidelines for a new ranking; but even these were hotly disputed, and the Institut lost heart in the project.

In the meantime, four prominent and extremely able wine brokers were delegated the task of a new classification. The result was three categories of excellence, instead of the five used in 1855. Eighteen of the châteaux classified in 1855 were omitted and thirteen new ones were added. The judges concluded that it would be necessary to update the classification every five years.

The reaction was explosive outrage. Château owners demoted or entirely deleted gave vent to their intense distress and condemned the ranking as malicious, incompetent, and unjust. The fact is that at present Bordeaux simply lacks the men of courage and leadership required to push through the necessary modifications. Moreover, the economic wine crisis of 1973-74 left Bordeaux badly shaken and—ironically—more apprehensive than ever of change, however urgently needed.

I was a member of the original committee on amending the rating, and when I saw that progress was not being made I decided to move ahead on my own. My classification, in its first version, was completed in 1959. In the course of preparing it, I interviewed more than seventy experts privately and off the record. We found that there were no real differences on the key issues. Investigations of the land records in the various communes revealed that some of the châteaux no longer occupy the same terrain they held in 1855, and in some cases no longer made any wine. Some classified as Fourth or Fifth Growths deserved to be sold as Seconds or Thirds, while certain Bourgeois Growths (the general group of vineyards which were not included in the 1855 classification) had earned elevation to Fourth or Fifth Growth status. Here the grower and consumer (who is misled by the wine's rating) lack a realistic basis for evaluation. It should be emphasized that even in 1855 a wine ranked as a Second, Third, Fourth, or Fifth Growth was *not a second-, third-, fourth-, or fifth-rate wine.* This terminology has always been confusing. Actually, since only sixty-one among approximately three thousand vineyards in the Bordeaux area were considered worthy of being named Great Growths—whether First or Fifth—as a group they comprise a majority of the world's finest red wines. To be second only after Lafite, Latour, Margaux, and Haut-Brion is vastly different from being second-rate. Moreover, it is only on average that the First are the best; in certain years others equal or even surpass them.

I thus found general agreement on avoiding the invidiousness of a ranking by number—First, Second, Third, and so on. It goes without saying that in today's age of publicity and competitive salesmanship a Second, Third, Fourth, or Fifth Growth would be unfairly handicapped. When the vineyards of Saint-Émilion were classified in the fifties, the officials at that time used the simpler categories of "First Great Growths," "Great Growths," and "Other Principal Growths." I adapted this format to my needs. It was also decided that within each category the listing should be alphabetical rather than strictly hierarchical. This, too, is patterned on the classification of Saint-Émilion.

In my life with wine over the decades, I have often felt that an updating and simplification of the 1855 classification would improve consumers' understanding of the ratings of the better Bordeaux wines, would enhance the ratings' credibility, and would encourage many growers in uplifting the quality of their wines. But when one considers the outcry, disputes, and lawsuits brought about by a new classification proposed for Saint-Émilion in 1985 (see Appendix IV), one must reluctantly conclude that no such new classification—however much needed—is likely to win adoption; the messy controversy that will inevitably ensue seems to be more than the government, the wine traders, and the growers themselves are prepared to face.

To measure the effect of changes in ownership of vineyard châteaux demanded great delicacy, to say the least. It often happens that vineyards are passed on to less energetic sons or to inexperienced owners, and the change is reflected in the wine, as Cocks correctly foresaw. If there is no reassessment, the wine will coast along on its former reputation and ranking. For some châteaux, the problem remains chronic; in others the difficulty passes quickly, in the time it takes to find a new *maître de chai* or to employ a top oenologist and listen to him. Happily, vineyards that have fallen on hard times will frequently pull themselves together and surpass the wines of their rank. It was to encourage and reward those who work hard for the best quality that I undertook the new classification.

My ranking was published for the first time in 1962, and has been brought up to date many times since then—most recently in March 1981, with some further changes in 1985—and always in collaboration with the local experts of each region.

We should note, of course, the official reclassification of 1973 that gave Mouton-Rothschild the long-deserved accolade of First Growth status. Unfortunately, the Ministry of Agriculture stopped there. Others who deserve upgrading or even initial ranking are still waiting.

The following is the only classification that dares to combine the best red wines of all four important Bordeaux regions. In assimilating wines with varying characteristics it becomes increasingly difficult to identify peers as one moves toward the lesser growths. It is easy, for example, to compare the very best wines of Saint-Émilion and those of the Médoc, as one might contrast the masters of different schools of painting; but the more common and undifferentiated the wine, the narrower the base for comparison.

Because wine is a product both of nature and of man's skill, any such classification is bound to be ephemeral and somewhat arbitrary, and several wines in the following list could be raised or lowered for any particular vintage.

With the exception of the Outstanding Growths, the wines in each category have been listed in alphabetical order.

PERSONAL CLASSIFICATION OF BORDEAUX

OUTSTANDING GROWTHS
(*Crus Hors Classe*)

HAUT-MÉDOC
Château Lafite-Rothschild (*Pauillac*)
Château Latour (*Pauillac*)
Château Margaux (*Margaux*)
Château Mouton-Rothschild (*Pauillac*)

GRAVES
Château Haut-Brion (*Pessac, Graves*)

SAINT-ÉMILION
Château Ausone
Château Cheval-Blanc

POMEROL
Château Pétrus

EXCEPTIONAL GROWTHS
(*Crus Exceptionnels*)

HAUT-MÉDOC
Château Brane-Cantenac
(*Cantenac-Margaux*)

Château Calon-Ségur (*Saint-Estèphe*)
*Château Cos d'Estournel (*Saint-Estèphe*)
Château Ducru-Beaucaillou (*Saint-Julien*)
Château Gruaud-Larose (*Saint-Julien*)
Château Lascombes (*Margaux*)
Château Léoville-Barton (*Saint-Julien*)
*Château Léoville-Las-Cases (*Saint-Julien*)
Château Léoville-Poyferré (*Saint-Julien*)
Château Montrose (*Saint-Estèphe*)
Château Palmer (*Cantenac-Margaux*)
*Château Pichon-Lalande (*Pauillac*)
Château Pichon-Longueville (Baron)
(*Pauillac*)

GRAVES
*Domaine de Chevalier (*Léognan*)
*Château La Mission-Haut-Brion (*Talence*)
Château Pape-Clément (*Pessac*)

SAINT-ÉMILION
*Château Figeac
Château Magdelaine

* *These wines are considered better than their peers in this classification.*

POMEROL

Château La Conseillante
Château l'Évangile
Château Lafleur
Château La Fleur-Pétrus
Château Trotanoy

GREAT GROWTHS (*Grands Crus*)

HAUT-MÉDOC

Château Beychevelle (*Saint-Julien*)
Château Branaire-Ducru (*Saint-Julien*)
Château Cantemerle (*Haut-Médoc*)
Château Duhart-Milon-Rothschild (*Pauillac*)
*Château Giscours (*Labarde-Margaux*)
Château Grand-Puy-Lacoste (*Pauillac*)
Château d'Issan (*Cantenac-Margaux*)
*Château La Lagune (*Haut-Médoc*)
*Château Lynch-Bages (*Pauillac*)
Château Malescot-Saint-Exupéry (*Margaux*)
Château Mouton-Baronne-Philippe (*Pauillac*)
*Château Prieuré-Lichine
                       (*Cantenac-Margaux*)
Château Rausan-Ségla (*Margaux*)
Château Rauzan-Gassies (*Margaux*)
Château Talbot (*Saint-Julien*)

GRAVES

*Château Haut-Bailly (*Léognan*)

SAINT-ÉMILION

*Château Belair
*Château Canon
Clos Fourtet
Château la Gaffelière
Château Pavie
Château Trottevieille

POMEROL

Château Gazin
Château Latour à Pomerol
*Château Petit-Village
*Vieux Château Certan
Château Nénin

SUPERIOR GROWTHS (*Crus Supérieurs*)

HAUT-MÉDOC

Château Batailley (*Pauillac*)
*Château Boyd-Cantenac
                       (*Cantenac-Margaux*)
Château Cantenac-Brown
                       (*Cantenac-Margaux*)
Château Chasse-Spleen (*Moulis*)
Château Clerc-Milon-Rothschild (*Pauillac*)
Château Durfort-Vivens
Château Gloria (*Saint-Julien*)
*Château Haut-Batailley (*Pauillac*)
*Château Kirwan (*Cantenac-Margaux*)
Château Lagrange (*Saint-Julien*)
Château Langoa (*Saint-Julien*)
Château Marquis d'Alesme-Becker
                       (*Margaux*)
Château Marquis de Terme (*Margaux*)
Château Pontet-Canet (*Pauillac*)
Château La Tour-Carnet (*Haut-Médoc*)

GRAVES

Château Carbonnieux (*Léognan*)
Château de Fieuzal (*Léognan*)
Château La Louvière (*Léognan*)
*Château Malartic-Lagravière (*Léognan*)
Château Smith-Haut-Lafitte (*Martillac*)

SAINT-ÉMILION

Château l'Angélus
*Château Balestard-la-Tonnelle
Château Beau-Séjour Bécot
Château Beauséjour-Duffau-Lagarrosse
Château Berliquet
Château Cadet-Piola
Château Canon-la-Gaffelière
Château La Clotte
Château Croque-Michotte
Château Curé-Bon-la-Madeleine
Château La Dominique
*Château Larcis-Ducasse
Château Larmande
Château Soutard
Château Troplong-Mondot
Château Villemaurine

* These wines are considered better than their peers in this classification.

POMEROL

Château Beauregard
Château Certan-Giraud
*Château Certan-de-May
Clos l'Église
Château l'Église-Clinet
Château Le Gay
Château Lagrange
Château La Grave
Château La Pointe

GOOD GROWTHS (Bons Crus)

HAUT-MÉDOC

Château d'Agassac (Haut-Médoc)
*Château Angludet (Cantenac-Margaux)
Château Beau-Site (Saint-Estèphe)
Château Beau-Site Haut-Vignoble
    (Saint-Estèphe)
Château Bel-Air-Marquis d'Aligre
    (Soussans-Margaux)
Château Belgrave (Saint-Laurent)
*Château de Camensac (Haut-Médoc)
Château Citran (Haut-Médoc)
Château Clarke (Listrac)
Château Cos Labory (Saint-Estèphe)
*Château Croizet-Bages (Pauillac)
Château Dauzac (Labarde-Margaux)
Château Ferrière (Margaux)
Château Fourcas-Dupré (Listrac)
Château Fourcas-Hosten (Listrac)
Château Grand-Puy-Ducasse (Pauillac)
Château Gressier-Grand-Poujeaux (Moulis)
Château Hanteillan (Haut-Médoc)
Château Haut-Bages-Libéral (Pauillac)
Château Haut-Marbuzet (Saint-Estèphe)
Château Labégorce (Margaux)
Château Labégorce-Zedé (Margaux)
Château Lafon-Rochet (Saint-Estèphe)
Château Lamarque (Haut-Médoc)
Château Lanessan (Haut-Médoc)
Château Lynch-Moussas (Pauillac)

Château Marbuzet (Saint-Estèphe)
Château Maucaillou (Moulis)
*Château Les-Ormes-de-Pez (Saint-Estèphe)
Château Pédesclaux (Pauillac)
*Château de Pez (Saint-Estèphe)
Château Phélan-Ségur (Saint-Estèphe)
Château Pouget (Cantenac-Margaux)
Château Poujeaux (Moulis)
*Château Saint-Pierre (Saint-Julien)
Château Siran (Labarde-Margaux)
Château du Tertre (Arsac-Margaux)
Château La Tour-de-Mons
    (Soussans-Margaux)
Château Villegeorge (Haut-Médoc)

GRAVES

Château Bouscaut (Cadaujac)
Château Larrivet-Haut-Brion (Léognan)
Château La Tour-Haut-Brion (Talence)
Château La Tour-Martillac (Martillac)

SAINT-ÉMILION

Château l'Arrosée
Château Bellevue
*Château Cap-de-Mourlin
Domaine du Châtelet
Clos des Jacobins
Château Corbin (Giraud)
Château Corbin (Manuel)
Château Corbin-Michotte
Château Coutet
Château Dassault
Couvent-des-Jacobins
Château La Fleur-Pourret
Château Franc-Mayne
Château Grâce-Dieu
Château Grand-Barrail-Lamarzelle-Figeac
Château Grand-Corbin
Château Grand-Corbin-Despagne
Château Grand-Mayne
Château Grand Pontet
Château Guadet-Saint-Julien
Château Laroque
Château Moulin-du-Cadet

These wines are considered better than their peers in this classification.

Château Pavie-Decesse
Château Pavie-Macquin
Château Saint-Georges-Côte-Pavie
Château Tertre-Daugay
Château La Tour-Figeac
Château La Tour-du-Pin-Figeac
Château Trimoulet
Château Yon-Figeac

POMEROL

Château Bourgneuf-Vayron
Château La Cabanne
Château le Caillou
*Château Clinet

Clos du Clocher
Château La Croix
Château La Croix-de-Gay
Clos de l'Église
Château l'Enclos
Château Gombaude-Guillot
Château La Grave-Trignant-de-Boisset
Château Guillot
Château Moulinet
Château Rouget
*Clos René
Château de Sales
Château du Tailhas
Château Taillefer
Château Vraye-Croix-de-Gay

These wines are considered better than their peers in this classification.

SAINT-ÉMILION

The Wine and Its Charming Town

Perched above the Dordogne, Saint-Émilion is one of the lovelier wine towns of the world. Its hill-hugging houses are built from the soft rock of the plateau, and the cellars are carved deep into the limestone below. A walk through narrow, winding, cobbled, precipitous streets takes you past shops of artisans and craftsmen, cafés, and antique stores.

The town is named for Saint Émilion, a pious eighth-century Breton wanderer who can hardly have been a winebibber but liked the countryside well enough to settle there. In the lower part of town is the cavern where he lived, beneath the ruins of a small chapel. Beside the carved niche is a block of stone. The townspeople say that if you sit on it, lean far back, and make a wish, the wish will come true.

In the Middle Ages, the village of Saint-Émilion was a stopover for the valiant pilgrims from Brittany—along with hundreds of thousands of others from all over Europe—who went every year to receive the benediction at the shrine of Spain's patron saint, Santiago de Compostela, in northwest Spain. The French popes, wishing to establish Avignon as the capital of western Christendom, promoted this particular pilgrimage over others in order to divert masses of voyagers from Rome. Their propaganda—whatever its methods—was extremely successful, and for a time as many as 500,000 people a year made the journey—the more affluent on horse or carriage, the majority on foot, plodding from village to village, threading their way south and west like columns of ants, in spite of highwaymen and bandits, lice, starvation, and disease.

Today, those busy times have faded almost entirely from Saint-Émilion's memory, but there still exist many evidences of the past. In addition to the houses, whose old stone fronts and weathered tile roofs give the town much of its charm, there are the walls of a Gothic church, abandoned in the fifteenth century during the Hundred Years War and still standing forlornly at the entrance of town. Much better preserved is the Église Monolithe, the largest church of its kind in France. Its devout builders began, a thousand years ago, by carving the chapel, pillars and all, out of existing grottoes and the quarries that had been dug into the limestone plateau beneath the town. Work continued on and off for over three centuries. Above the church is a terrace overlooking the town of Saint-Émilion. The vineyards stretch out below like a patchwork quilt in shades of green—beyond the picturesque jumble of tile roofs and cobbled streets—and the sight is almost too pretty to be true, like a Hollywood replica of the typical medieval French village.

The beauty of the town and the variety of the wines continue to attract thousands of visitors to Saint-Émilion each summer, many of them leaving weighed down with wine or the local semi-sweet macaroons that are nearly as famous. Not that there aren't enough châteaux to visit. Saint-Émilion claims (without exaggeration) to be the region of the thousand châteaux. And the total is beyond this number easily if one includes the lesser so-called satellites of Saint-Émilion: Saint-Georges, Puisseguin, Lussac, and Montagne—all regions (named, in fact, for villages) that border Saint-Émilion proper and that are allowed to add "Saint-Émilion" after their name, as in "Montagne-Saint-Émilion."

To simplify things for the wine buyer and traveler, the châteaux were classified in 1955, exactly one hundred years after the classification of the wines of the Gironde—twelve as First Great Growths and seventy-two as Great Growths or Grand Crus. Two among the top twelve, Cheval-Blanc and Ausone, were distinguished as superior to the rest, and the other châteaux were listed alphabetically following them. Whereas the 1855 Classification of the Gironde encompassed too few vineyards, omitting all of Pomerol, Saint-Émilion, and Graves (though Haut-Brion was included), this new one mentions too many. Nonetheless, it is to be applauded for being the first classification in the region that is subject to periodic review and amendment. It was reexamined in 1958, 1969, and 1985. So far, few châteaux have been dropped in rank, but Château Berliquet is one that has been elevated to Great Growth, or Grand Cru, status. Even if this system has not yet penalized many growers who have lapsed, it performs the invaluable service of rewarding quality and effort. Such recognition is essential if a wine region is to remain vital. In this, and

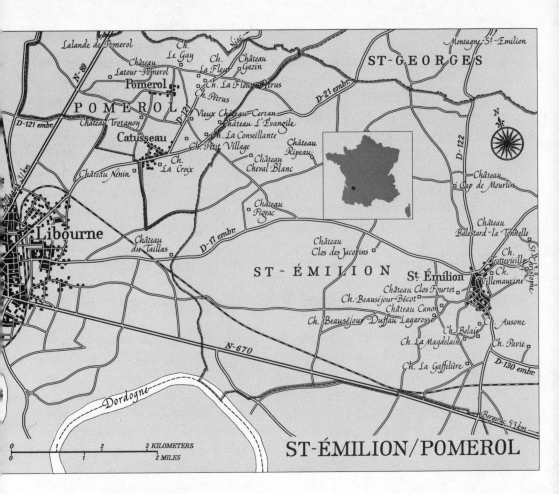

many other ways, the Médoc had a lot to learn from this wine district on the Dordogne. Moreover, in striking contrast to the Médoc and to the city of Bordeaux, Saint-Émilion and its people are exuberant promoters of their wine and their region.

The area covered by Saint-Émilion's twelve First Growth vineyards is split into two main regions totaling 200 hectares (500 acres). The first in importance is the plateau around the town of Saint-Émilion, where the vineyards cling to the few centimeters of topsoil above the limestone bedrock. The excellence of any of the plateau vineyards will depend on the balance between vines of the steep slope and those of the plain. From each sector the grapes take a certain character: finesse and subtlety from the slope, body and depth from the plain below.

The other area for the best growths of Saint-Émilion is far smaller—only 70 hectares (175 acres). Bordering on Pomerol, this low-lying land is divided between châteaux Cheval-Blanc and Figeac. The character and composition of the soil here are very different from those of the plateau, as these vineyards contain more gravel and clay in the way that the better Pomerol vineyards do. Thus the wines of Cheval-Blanc and Figeac have much in common with the Pomerols.

Another difference between the gravelly sector and the plateau of Saint-Émilion was shown with tragic force in the winter of 1956, when frost devastated the vineyards of Pomerol (some almost totally) and those of the low-lying area of Saint-Émilion, killing large sections of vines. Cheval-Blanc and Figeac lost their 1956 crops, and most of their 1957s, and continued to feel the effects of the frost for years to come, as many of the vines slowly withered and died. The plateau vineyards, on the other hand, survived without much damage, depending on their position on the slope. Château Ausone, for example, escaped unhurt.

Driving up to the plateau and village of Saint-Émilion from the Libourne–Bergerac road, you first pass La Gaffelière, on the right, and Château Pavie. As the defile narrows and you climb higher, Belair and Ausone will be on your left, with the town up off to the right. Farther around the slope of Belair is Château Magdelaine.

Ausone and Belair are both owned and managed by the Dubois-Challon family, and both have been ranked among the finest of the wines of the plateau. Despite Ausone's special status, together with Cheval-Blanc, as a sort of super-First Growth, in my opinion its pre-eminent claim to quality has been challenged by other good vineyards, particularly Figeac and Magdelaine. Ausone's decline from its pre-World War II greatness has been partly due to lack of care, particularly the practice of aging the wine in old barrels, which contain little of the tannin or oak flavor necessary to develop the balance and depth of any fine wine. As a result, in the decades following the war, although it remained a wine of distinction, Ausone was uncharacteristically light for a Saint-Émilion. Now, however, after a long period of indifferent management, there seems to be proof that this great vineyard will be able to re-establish its reputation. I consider that a turning point came with the 1976 vintage, when Ausone was perhaps the best of all the 1976 Saint-Émilions that I have tasted. But it may take until the late eighties to prove that I am right.

Belair's 13 hectares (33 acres), though adjacent to Ausone, differ from their neighbor in exposure to the sun and produce a slightly lighter wine. Until recently, the two were both vinified and aged in the dark, moldy cellars of Ausone, dug out of the plateau's soft rock centuries ago. Belair is generally thought to be the older of the two vineyards—in fact, it may be the oldest in the region, its terraces having been created in primitive fashion by gouging out terraces in the rock and filling them with earth to plant vines. People of a romantic turn of mind contend that Ausone was planted even earlier by Ausonius, the fourth-century poet and Roman governor, a native son of the area. But whenever or wherever the first vine was planted in the area, both Ausone and Belair are magnificently placed on the edge of the plateau, overlooking the terraced and sloped vines.

Just below the Belair slopes, facing more directly to the south, are 20 hectares (50 acres) of vineyard of Château La Gaffelière. Although the château is potentially one of the greatest Saint-Émilion growths, its owner, Comte Léo de Malet-Roquefort (who in 1978 acquired the Château Tertre-Daugay), has been criticized for wine-making methods that do not do credit to the excellence of the soil and exposure of his land.

Across the road and reaching the top of the terraced plateau are the vineyards of Château Pavie, the largest of the better Saint-Émilion growths, also blessed with southern exposure. Surrounding Pavie, lower on the plain, are two spin-off (and lesser) vineyards which use the name Pavie as part of their own: Pavie-Decesse and Pavie-Macquin, both classified as Great Growths. I have found the Pavie-Decesse in certain vintages not only to be up to Pavie in quality but to exceed it.

Around the twist of the ridge that extends from Ausone and Belair is Château Magdelaine, the excellent property of Jean-Pierre Moueix, part-owner of the great Pomerol vineyard Pétrus. Magdelaine is a beautifully made, consistently dependable wine. M. Moueix, in addition to being one of Bordeaux's largest shippers of wine, is a tasteful and shrewd collector of great modern paintings. Until his retirement in 1978, he was, more than any other *négociant-propriétaire,* an economically vitalizing force for the wines of the Saint-Émilion and Pomerol region. Today the Moueix tradition is being ably carried on by his two sons, Christian and Jean-François. Christian not only oversees the Moueix properties but is also involved in a vineyard in Napa.

In order to reach the next vineyard area, which includes the two Châteaux Beauséjour, Château Canon, and Château Clos Fourtet, you have to take a small, winding road from the Saint-Émilion village, barely wide enough for two tractors to pass; as you continue along the ridge, there will be signs to Château Canon. Canon is owned by the Fournier family. In her time, the late Mme André Fournier was the great lady of Saint-Émilion and leading figure in its Jurade, a promotional organization mainly concerned with giving banquets and holding induction ceremonies at which only Saint-Émilion wines are served. Canon is a supple wine, perhaps lapsing into over-softness, justifying recent criticism that its vintages, with the exception of the '75s, '82s, and '83s lack the character of bygone days.

By contrast, Château Beau-Séjour Bécot—not to be confused with Beauséjour-Duffau-Lagarrosse—has achieved distinction through the efforts of its owner, Michel Bécot. In the late sixties Bécot took the vineyard over from the late, eccentric Docteur Jean Fagouët. Some of M. Bécot's improvements to his former First Growth vineyard included a modern *chai,* in which he housed his stainless-steel fermentation vats, and a large adjoining reception hall where banquets of the Jurade are held.

Not far from Beau-Séjour Bécot is Château l'Angélus, one of the Great Growths of Saint-Émilion that has been very popular. It is a reliable, well-made wine, though lacking the breeding of a top-rank vineyard.

Among the seventy-two Greats are two good growths that may one day deserve higher rating: Château Villemaurine and Château Balestard-la-Tonnelle. Besides producing fine wine, Château Villemaurine boasts huge and most impressive cellars, scooped out of the Saint-Émilion bedrock. The château, vineyards, and cellars were bought in 1970 by Robert Giraud, owner of Château Timberlay and Château Cadillac.

During the harvest of 1977, while walking through Villemaurine's dramatic grotto-like cellar, I came upon a hidden niche of old vintages set aside by the former owners. With M. Giraud looking over my shoulder, I gently lifted a cobweb- and mold-covered bottle of Villemaurine 1899 and offered to buy him lunch if we could open the bottle. So, we went around the corner to Chez Germaine for some *jambon de Bayonne* and cheeses. Having extracted the crumbling cork, Giraud and I were elated: the bottle was superb. A month later, now privy to this cache, we took another bottle of 1899 to the nearby Hostellerie de Plaisance. Our lunch of *lamproie à la bordelaise* (lamprey—an eel-like fish—cooked in a red-wine sauce) was more elaborate. This second bottle of 1899 was good, even excellent, but not as memorable as the first we'd tried, and we realized how two wines of the same vintage can with age become absolutely separate and distinct from one another. This is a point one should always keep in mind when purchasing very old wines.

At Balestard-la-Tonnelle, Roger Capdemourlin is putting much effort and dedication into the property and the *chais,* and we may soon see this vineyard upgraded. Not far from Villemaurine and Balestard is the last of the important First Growths on the plateau, Château Trottevieille. It is owned by the Borie-Manoux family, who have recently been improving the wine, already well made, so that it may well become a challenger to the top four or five. Another good value in Saint-Émilion wines is Château Laroque. From the terrace of its Louis-XIV-style château, one has a splendid view of the Dordogne valley.

Honors for the best Saint-Émilion wine are hotly contested by the two great vineyards from the gravelly region of Saint-Émilion, near Pomerol: the super-First Growth Cheval-Blanc and its neighbor and close contender, Château Figeac. Cheval-Blanc, which produces some of the 15,000 cases of the most expensive wines in Saint-Émilion, was, like the rest of the vineyards of Saint-Émilion and Pomerol, overlooked in the 1855 Classification of the Gironde. Though this may have been a fair assessment at the time, it is one more instance where the 1855 Classification is at odds with present-day standings.

The cellar master at Cheval-Blanc still tells the story of the spring of 1961, when alternating warm and cold spells caused the vines to blossom in two or three successive periods. When this occurs, the vines always produce fewer grapes. The critical time for any vintage, whether in Saint-Émilion, the Médoc, or elsewhere, is the two-week period in June when the tiny green pinheads form that will eventually develop into grapes. During this interval of pollination and incubation, the weather must be warm and dry and not excessively windy. If the temperature swings wildly from day to day, the tiny grapes-to-be can be literally nipped in the bud. This is called *coulure,* aborted pollination, and leads to a drastic drop in quantity, as in the Merlots of 1984. It does not, however, affect the quality, as can be plainly seen in the supreme but minuscule vintage of 1961. In contrast to '61, the pollination periods of '75 and '76 went off without a hitch and were followed by hot weather straight through the harvest, producing a great vintage for Cheval-Blanc and the rest of Bordeaux. The 1975 Cheval-Blanc is a very big wine with considerable tannin; the 1976 is already enjoyable.

Poor flowering is only the second problem a grower faces in terms of the quantity of the harvest. The first hurdle in determining quantity is the period from late March to early May, when the vines bud, and when the temperature can suddenly drop below freezing. Unlike a winter freeze, which could kill the vine itself, the spring freeze kills only the buds—as happened most recently on March 30, 1977, and April, 16, 1978.

Figeac borders on Cheval-Blanc, sharing the precious gravel of Saint-Émilion; it is one of the largest and most respected of the Classified Growths of the region. Figeac's owner, Thierry Manoncourt, makes a point of reserving a barrel of each grape variety from certain vintages, and bottling them separately for his own tasting. "This way," he explains, "we can see how each grape variety—Cabernet Sauvignon, Cabernet Franc, Petit Verdot, and Merlot—develops as it ages. This helps me in my choice of grape when it comes to replanting rows of vines. Each grape gives a different characteristic to the wine, both at the moment we make our total blend and, later on, as the wine ages in the bottle." Since assuming responsibility for the wine after World War II, M. Manoncourt has improved the vineyard by planting as much Cabernet Sauvignon as Cabernet Franc (about 35 percent each), contrary to local tradition; the balance is made up in Merlot. Figeac is now running a very close second to its illustrious neighbor, Cheval-Blanc, and M. Manoncourt's claim that they are equals might someday prove to be true. As is common in both Saint-Émilion and Pomerol many lesser vineyards surround the great ones and take on their name as part of their own. Thus there are five variations on the Figeac name in the vicinity of M. Manoncourt's property.

Nearly one-third of all the wine produced in the region of Saint-Émilion—which takes in all the different Saint-Émilion *appellations*—comes from the "satellites" scattered around the central plateau of Saint-Émilion itself: Puisseguin-Saint-Émilion, Lussac-Saint-Émilion, Montagne-Saint-Émilion, and Saint-Georges-Saint-Émilion. Hundreds of small châteaux dot the countryside for miles around, each consisting of modest vineyards which the owners work themselves—plowing, spraying, planting, pruning, and even harvesting with only a single tractor and the help of family and friends. Depending on the grower, these wines can be well made, though never approaching the excellence of the better châteaux of Saint-Émilion itself. It is generally held that the best satellite châteaux are those of the Saint-Georges- and Montagne-Saint-Émilion. One Lussac-Saint-Émilion château that has managed to separate itself from the crowd and boast quality resembling that of Saint-Émilion proper is Château du Lyonnat, owned by Jean Milhade. Since the suffix "Saint-Émilion" is not always understood to indicate a lesser wine, it has often irritated me to see the first-class passengers of airlines (especially Air France) being purposely deceived by the misleading use of that name.

Bordering the Saint-Émilion satellites on the east are two little-known but surprisingly good red wine *appellations*: Côtes de Castillon centered on the river town

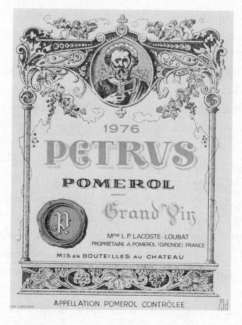

Castillon-la-Bataille and Côtes de Francs centered on the town of Francs. Castillon's red wines are among the best from Bordeaux's minor regions; it produces only about 800,000 cases of wine a year, but the standard is fairly high. The Côtes de Francs makes both red and white, though little white is sold as Côtes de Francs. The cooperative cellar in Francs handles about 90 percent of the *appellation*. In general, the best wines are made from the areas of clay soil where the Merlot grape does particularly well.

In February 1985 the I.N.A.O. proposed a new classification for the wines of Saint-Émilion, with the old classification, as is customary, being canceled beforehand. The new ranking, however, has been legally contested by some of the châteaux that were demoted; moreover, the two cabinet ministers who must by law formally approve the new classification have not yet done so. Therefore, a full year after the I.N.A.O. submitted it, it still has no official standing, and, according to the press, the wines of Saint-Émilion are no longer classified at all.

POMEROL

The Round Wines

Literally in the backyard of the river port of Libourne, the vineyards of Pomerol fan out 2 kilometers or so up to Lalande. Pomerol is a relative newcomer to the Bordeaux wine scene, and its vineyards, unlike those of the Médoc, Graves, Sauternes, and Saint-Émilion, have never been classified. In the middle of the nineteenth century, when the Médoc vineyards were ranked, Pomerol was not even distinguished from its larger neighbor Saint-Émilion, and none of the châteaux had even a local reputation for excellence. Pomerol may have suffered then for the smallness of its production, but today the rarity of its wines and the very fact that they are not classified gives them a certain *cachet* which Saint-Émilion rarely attains. Pomerol's devotees can debate the relative excellence of their favorite châteaux, each believing his choice the best. On the whole, the châteaux of Pomerol maintain a high standard of quality. Indeed, of the five principal vineyard regions of Bordeaux, Pomerol may have the highest average of superior châteaux.

Land in Pomerol is more scarce than in other parts of Bordeaux. The houses, though honorifically called châteaux, are modest by comparison with the large estates in the Médoc and Graves, and parkland surrounding the houses is practically nonexistent. A large vineyard in Pomerol will be 10 hectares (25 acres), and in the top rank of Pomerol châteaux, only Gazin, La Pointe, and Nénin have 20 hectares or more. This situation may change in time, when larger and more successful châteaux buy up land from their neighbors, as Château Pétrus did in 1969, buying up a small sliver of vineyard from Château Gazin across the road. Christian Moueix, who now manages Pétrus, estimates that of the two hundred property owners currently active in Pomerol, only a little more than a hundred will be left within fifteen or twenty years; already more than half of the owners hold a hectare (2.5 acres) or less.

Given such a small area of vineyard, it is easier here than in the other four principal regions of Bordeaux to account for the characteristics of the wines, which are softer and earlier-maturing than the reds of the Médoc, Graves, or Saint-Émilion. In the first place, two-thirds of all the grapes grown in Pomerol are Merlot; the rest of the plantings are almost entirely Cabernet Franc, with practically no Cabernet Sauvignon. Although under perfect conditions the Merlot is a slightly more productive vine than the Cabernet Sauvignon, it is the most vulnerable of any of the three major varieties grown in Bordeaux to the hazards which face a vintner. Since it is the first vine to bud and eventually to mature, it is the most likely to be frozen in early spring and to suffer from poor pollination, as in 1984. Autumn rains can make it susceptible to early rotting. Still, it is especially prized for its appealing, round softness, fine color, and quick maturation.

The other feature of Pomerol that contributes greatly to the character of its wines is the presence of heavy clay in the soil, which otherwise is gravelly and sandy. After rain in Pomerol, this mixture of sand and clay is nearly cement-like in consistency and can be very difficult to plow. Indeed, the name Château Trotanoy is derived from the fact: *trop* (too) *ennuyeux* (troublesome). However, the heaviness of the soil marries well with the elegant roundness of the Merlot grape to create wines of finesse and distinction that, at their best, start giving excellent quality when ten years old and may be at their peak when over twenty, with perhaps a few lasting as long as fifty or sixty years.

The best area for vineyards in Pomerol is on the slight rise above the plain that extends to Libourne itself. As in the Médoc, the lower the vineyard, the higher the proportion of sand and, therefore, the more common the wine. Nearly all of Pomerol's better vineyards are located on the plateau. Along the road from Libourne, the first vineyard of fine quality is Château Nénin, one of the biggest of the region at 20 hectares (50 acres). Its relatively large production—around 10,000 cases—and effective promotion by its owners, the Despujol family, have made Nénin one of the more renowned Pomerols.

Along the edge of the rise on the Saint-Émilion-Pomerol border are the châteaux Petit-Village, La Conseillante, and L'Évangile. Petit-Village is a well-tended vineyard owned by Bruno Prats, also owner of Château Cos d'Estournel in Saint-Estèphe, in the Médoc.

La Conseillante is an example of what can be done with dedication in the vineyard and *chai;* in the past it was not properly managed and the quality of the wine suffered. In the early seventies, however, its owners—the Nicolas family for well over a century—placed the wine-making in the hands of a new team, and since then the wines have regained their stature. The planting mix is an interesting one: 50 percent Merlot, 45 percent Cabernet Sauvignon, and 5 percent Malbec.

L'Évangile borders two Moueix properties, La Fleur-Pétrus and Pétrus, and, like these two, has a greater than average proportion of gravel in its soil and nearly equal amounts of Merlot and Cabernet Franc vines.

Gazin, La Fleur-Pétrus, Pétrus, Lafleur, and Vieux Château Certan are in the heart of the gravelly part of the region where the pebbles and the clay make their happiest match. Château Gazin is one of the better-known properties of Pomerol, mainly because of its comparatively large area—25 hectares (62 acres). However, the quality of Gazin is variable. Château Lafleur is owned by two elderly sisters, Thérèse and Marie Robin (they are also owners of Château Le Gay), both of whom still work the vineyards themselves. Lafleur is only 4 hectares (10 acres), but, in the opinion of the local *cognoscenti,* it is the only vineyard that can stand up to Pétrus itself. Château Lafleur should not be confused with Château La Fleur-Pétrus, one of the Moueix châteaux in Pomerol. La Fleur-Pétrus borders Pétrus on the east and is one of the rare examples of a château that lives up to the connotations of its name. Just a narrow road separates the two vineyards under the same ownership, and yet the Pétrus sells for three times the price of La Fleur-Pétrus—this is where fame, nature, and scarcity combine in a prestigious label.

The recognition gained by Pomerol wines in the past two decades has been greatly helped by Château Pétrus and its owners. Mme Edmond Loubat, who owned the Château Pétrus until her death, a towering character if there ever was one, and promoter of Pomerol, dominated the Pomerol scene through the 1950s with her vivacious personality, and became a legend in her time. After Mme Loubat's death in 1961, Jean-Pierre Moueix took over the management of the château and sale of the wine. From its 12 hectares (30 acres) comes the most expensive of all Bordeaux wines. The château itself is unprepossessing, offering no hint at all of the excellence of the wines it produces. The management of the vineyard is now in the hands of the young and engaging Christian Moueix, the owner's son. In his estimation, it is the average age of Pétrus's vines that raises it above the rest of Pomerol; he judges them to be about forty years old. The soil is the ideal mix of gravel and clay, and it reacts perfectly with the old vines. "In order to maintain that balance," says

M. Moueix, "I never replant a vine if the vines around it are more than ten years old. This way I can keep track of the age of each plot of vines and make a proper selection of the vats after the vintage. Some of the vines date from the turn of the century. They don't produce much, but what they do produce is the secret of our greatness."

Little known until 1960, Pétrus was boosted from obscurity as the "vinous" find of the late, great Henri Soulé, owner of New York's Le Pavillon, then one of the world's most glamorous restaurants. The Duke and Duchess of Windsor, the Niarchoses, the Onassises, the Kennedys, world leaders, and the international society set—Soulé told them all where to sit (if he gave them a seat) and what to drink, and most often he recommended this excellent new discovery of his, Château Pétrus.

The grape variety planted at Pétrus is exclusively Merlot, and the combined effect of old vines and the relatively delicate constitution of the Merlot makes Pétrus particularly susceptible to frost. In 1956, the whole of France was ravaged by a winter freeze, but nowhere was the damage as severe as in Pomerol and the adjoining Saint-Émilion vineyard of Cheval-Blanc. If the cold can reach deep below ground to the sap in the roots, the inner tissues of the plant burst and the vine dies. This is what happened then, and the damage was felt for the next four or five years, as many vines withered, died, and had to be replanted. At Pétrus in 1956 they produced less than a tenth of their normal quantity, and they did not regain full capacity until the mid-sixties. Then in 1977, Pétrus, like all of Pomerol, was again hit badly by spring frost, which this time cut production for that year to fewer than a thousand cases.

The vineyards of Château Latour-Pomerol, just off the N-89 road from Libourne, are tenant-farmed by the Moueix family, which means that they are charged with the making of the wine as well as its sale. The owner is Mme Lili-Pau Lacoste, niece of the late Mme Loubat, former owner of Château Pétrus.

Château Trotanoy, with its clay- and gravel-rich soil, is still another of the Moueix family holdings. Traditionally one of the top Pomerol vineyards, Trotanoy escaped the freeze of 1956 thanks to its excellent southwestern exposure. Its vines are among the oldest in Bordeaux, averaging around fifty years.

Vieux Château Certan borders Pétrus and makes excellent wines; unusually for Pomerol, it also has an exquisite eighteenth-century château. But the most impressive château of Pomerol is Château de Sales, located in the sandy part of the region. Ever since de Sales was built in the seventeenth century, it has remained in the same family, except for a brief interruption during the Revolution. With 46 hectares (113 acres) in vines, Château de Sales is the largest of the Pomerol estates. Its wine is rarely found in the United States, and only occasionally in England. The level of wines from this sandy soil is good at best, but never rises above a certain commonness.

Just to the north of Pomerol is the related *appellation* Lalande-de-Pomerol, which produces red wines of the Pomerol–Saint-Émilion type. The soil of this region tends to be sandy and devoid of gravel. It is important to remember the difference in names, because in 1976, for instance, more wine was sold as Lalande-de-Pomerol than as Pomerol proper. The best-known of all the Lalandes is Château Bel-Air—not to be confused with the Belair of Saint-Émilion (or with the other thirteen Châteaux Belair and Bel-Air in the Gironde!). These wines will be generally similar in kind to their more illustrious neighbors, without achieving their distinction. The quality of the wines from château to château can vary enormously. Yet, as often happens in these adjacent wine regions, the shrewd buyer can turn up some interesting finds.

Just downstream from Libourne on the Dordogne opposite Pomerol are the red wine regions of Fronsac and Canon-Fronsac. Though the quality can be uneven, as is true in all of the less-frequented vineyard regions, the best of Fronsac can be very good indeed. In many cases they surpass Saint-Émilion's wines, displaying unusual fullness and ability to age well, and on the whole are considered out of the ordinary for wines of the region. Château de la Rivière is a good example. High up on a wooded hill, this vineyard and its beautiful medieval château stand out from its neighbors in that the wine is often as good as the beautiful architecture of the château. It stands up with age, and from year to year it is a reliable wine, which is not the case of the sister appellation Canon-Fronsac, nor of many of the other Fronsac wines, although many deserve to be better recognized as full-bodied, long-lived wines. Fronsac deserves to be better known. In the early '80s Christian Moueix affirmed his belief in the wines of Fronsac by purchasing tiny Château Canon (not to be confused with Château Canon of Saint-Émilion), Château de la Dauphine, and Château Canon de Brem. These three attractive properties combined have less than 22 hectares (55 acres) of vines.

In the sincere belief that both consumers and people in the trade may need some guidance with this unranked region of Bordeaux, I have proposed a classification of the Pomerol châteaux, which may be found in Appendix VI. This classification was made with the help of qualified friends in the trade, it being kept well in mind that periodic revisions will be necessary to reflect each château's success in meeting the challenge of the growing season, the age of the vines, the amount of replanting, and, most important, any change in management. Every effort has been and will be made to keep abreast of these changes.

&

SAINT-ÉMILION AND POMEROL
Hotels and Restaurants

H = *Hotel;* R = *Restaurant*

From Bordeaux, follow signs for Paris and the Pont d'Aquitaine to A-10. Once across the Garonne, get off the Autoroute at the Quatre Pavillons exit and, by turning right for Libourne, get on N-89 toward Libourne and Périgueux. The Pomerol vineyards begin just on the other side of Libourne, off D-21. There is an alternate route from Bordeaux via the Pont-de-Pierre (stone bridge) to N-89, and to get to Saint-Émilion, continue past Libourne on the Bergerac road, N-670. Signs will indicate Saint-Émilion, off to the left.

SAINT-ÉMILION (33330—Gironde)
(Paris 556—Bordeaux 38—Libourne 6.5—Langon 49—Bergerac 56)

☙ If you have time after taking in the town's historic sites, you should visit the newly scooped-out cellars of nearby Château Villemaurine.

Less than one hour's drive from Bordeaux and ten minutes' drive from Libourne, you will find the old town of Saint-Émilion in the midst of the vineyards. For its charm Saint-Émilion has been used as a Hollywood set. An hour's walk through this quaint town is a must if you enjoy medieval stone or curio shops with high-priced antiques. The Maison du Vin de Saint-Émilion (located just across the Place du Clocher from the Hostellerie de Plaisance) and the many small wine shops offer minor château bottlings of local wines at prices that are fair to medium—provided you do not have to carry them on a plane. If you have time, you should visit the scooped-out ninth-century monolithic church.

HR HOSTELLERIE DE PLAISANCE: Place du Clocher. Tel.: 57.24.72.32.   12 rooms.
Hotel-restaurant built above ninth-century Église Monolithe. Louis Quilain, the owner, has contributed one of the logical places for lunch when visiting the vineyards of Saint-Émilion. Service can be slow, especially on Sundays.

HR AUBERGE DE LA COMMANDERIE: Rue des Cordeliers. Tel.: 57.24.70.19.   14 small, inexpensive rooms. (10 toilets).
Reasonably priced restaurant. The owner's daughter has remodeled a 15-room functional hotel, Le Logis des Remparts, nearby.

R CHEZ GERMAINE: Place du Clocher. Tel.: 57.24.70.88.
The central location in town compensates for average food.

R LOGIS DE LA CADÈNE: Place du Marché-au-Bois. Tel.: 57.24.71.40.
Reasonably priced, a good value. Close to the Église Monolithe. Good selection of Saint-Émilion wines, and try a Bordeaux specialty, lamprey in red-wine sauce. Lunch only.

R DOMINIQUE: Rue de la Petite Fontaine, centrally located in lower Saint-Émilion off the place du Marché, opposite the entrance to the Église Monolithe. Tel.: 57.24.71.00.
Inexpensive, good, small restaurant run by Dominique and Sabine Lees, who spent five or six years in Washington, D.C.

LIBOURNE (33500—Gironde)
(Paris 550—Bordeaux 31—Bergerac 61—Saint-Émilion 8)

❧ A small and busy town on the Dordogne river. A few wine merchants make Libourne their head-quarters, specializing in the local wines of Pomerol and Saint-Émilion.

HR LOUBAT: 32, rue de Chanzy (near railway station). Tel.: 57.51.17.58.   42 rooms.
A new chef has given a fresh impulse to this traditional hotel and restaurant. Fair quality for a fair price. A good wine list of Bordeaux wines.

GRAVES

The vineyards of Graves lie on the southern fringes of the city of Bordeaux. As the metropolis and its suburbs grow, the vineyards are being constantly thrust back. Since the Middle Ages, the Graves vineyards have followed the western bank of the Garonne, but the area is now reduced to a rough rectangle, at most 8 kilometers (5 miles) wide and 55 kilometers (35 miles) long, stretching south to the town of Langon and encircling the sweet-white-wine enclave of Cérons and Barsac-Sauternes.

Although there is a widespread belief that the wines of Graves are mostly white, in fact the few classified châteaux produce some of Bordeaux's outstanding reds. The balance in production between red and white wine is more even than one might suppose; in 1976, white wine exceeded red by the equivalent of only 40,000 cases out of a combined total of 1,200,000. However, *château-bottled* white wine is a relative rarity. The classified white-wine-producing châteaux of Graves turn out only about 3 percent of the total production of white wine, whereas classified red wines make up around 12 percent of the total production of red.

Aside from its most celebrated vineyard, Château Haut-Brion, which was classified along with the top Médoc châteaux in 1855, none of the Graves châteaux was so recognized until 1953. In that year, twelve other châteaux among those producing the red wine and eight in the white category were classified. (These lists may be found in Appendix V.)

The best Classified Growths are along N-650, the road to Arcachon, a seaside resort 62 kilometers (38 miles) from Bordeaux that is the wine shipper's traditional summer home. In quick succession come the three classified Haut-Brion-suffixed vineyards, La Mission-Haut-Brion, La Tour-Haut-Brion, and the white Laville-Haut-Brion, followed by Haut-Brion itself. A little farther on is Château Pape-Clément. After that, for about 12 kilometers (7 miles) to the south, there are no vineyards of interest before the beginning of the next important group around the commune of Léognan. Surrounding the village on all sides are Domaine de Chevalier, Château Haut-Bailly, Château de Fieuzal, and Château Malartic-Lagravière. Part of the same group, though a bit to the east, are Châteaux Carbonnieux, Bouscaut, and Smith-Haut-Lafitte. South of this area, the great Graves wines stop and the more ordinary—but very pleasant—white wines take over.

"Graves" means "gravel" in French, and, like the best vineyards of the Médoc, those of Graves would look like gravel pits if they were dug out. The pebbly soil occurs elsewhere in the Bordeaux region, most notably in the Médoc and to a much lesser extent in Pomerol and Saint-Émilion. Indeed, the best of the Graves and the best of the Médocs will have recognizably similar features, but they are by no means twins. If the Médocs, especially the Margaux, are more feminine and delicate, the Graves have more body, a distinct character, and a pleasing earthiness. There are probably as many different classifications of gravelly soils as there are special clones for vines, and each type of gravel will produce a different wine. As is true in the Médoc, the changes in soil composition from one hectare of Graves vineyard to another can be startling. Gravel is best thought of as a kind of leavening in the soil, taking whatever character the base soil has and elevating it to great heights. It also provides good drainage, which is important for even nourishment of the vines.

From the Middle Ages, when much of the Médoc was still forest, until the late seventeenth century, most Bordeaux wines were called "Graves." As the vineyard area closest to Bordeaux, it was the best known to the city, and therefore to the wine trade. It was also the safest. In the troubled thirteenth and fourteenth centuries, when country roads left one easy prey to highwaymen, the bourgeois growers of Bordeaux used to hurry back each nightfall to the sheltering walls of the city.

The first vineyard to emerge from obscurity was the great estate of Haut-Brion. The history of Haut-Brion is, to a large extent, the history of Bordeaux, and of France as well. Governors, princes, and presidents of the Bordeaux Parlement all successively owned Haut-Brion, and its fate often hung on the economic and political fortunes of its proprietors. Although there are records of Haut-Brion as a place-name going back to the fourteenth century, the man who, in a sense, founded Haut-Brion and was the most important of its early owners was Jean de Pontac, born in 1488, son of a wealthy Bordeaux merchant. Jean de Pontac expanded his father's profitable shipping business and soon became one of Bordeaux's wealthiest tradesmen and largest landowners, with property scattered from Graves all the way to Saint-Estèphe, in the Médoc. Jean de Pontac bought the major part of what was to become the Haut-Brion property in 1533 and continued to add to it until 1550.

Like much of the red wine from the area, Haut-Brion at that time was sold as "Pontac," because of the great reputation the Pontac's "Haut-Brion" had already achieved locally and also because of the extensive vineyard holdings the Pontac family had around Bordeaux. Meanwhile, the Médoc wines, which later achieved great fame, were still known simply as "Bordeaux," without any more specific indication of origin.

Jean de Pontac died in 1589 at the age of 101, having served as notary and secretary of the province under six kings. At his death, by virtue of his political position and successful business, he was the most famous and most powerful man in the city.

Barely a generation passed without a Pontac holding the position of president of one of the parliamentary chambers of Bordeaux. It was in the last half of the seventeenth century, under the ownership of Jean de Pontac's great-grandnephew, Arnaud de Pontac, that this tradition of power and influence bore fruit among the claret-loving English. In 1663, in early spring, a cantankerous gossip in the person of Samuel Pepys for the first time on record bought, tasted, and appreciated a Bordeaux wine under its own name. Pepys stopped off at the Royall-Oake Taverne before lunch "and here drank a sort of French wine called Ho Bryen that hath a good and most peculiar taste that I never met with." He was soon joined by a chorus of admirers of the Haut-Brion wine.

Arnaud de Pontac's son, François, then conceived the brilliant marketing scheme of acting not only as his own shipper of Haut-Brion to London but also as his own on-the-spot vendor. François de Pontac had neither the temperament nor the aptitude for the legislative life, and he sold his presidency of the Bordeaux Parlement and sailed for London, where his wines were already being sold to the likes of Samuel Pepys. In so doing, he anticipated the valiant shippers of Bordeaux, who, a century later, were to fan out throughout Europe, risking their lives to peddle their wines. His stroke of truly creative enterprise came in the 1680s: he started up a fashionable tavern in London, called the Sign of Pontac's Head, where he served Haut-Brion and other Pontac wines. As England's other great diarist of the seventeenth century, John Evelyn, observed, "The vignoble of Pontaque and Obrien [was the source of] our choicest Bordeaux wine." Defoe, Dryden, and Swift all mention the Sign of Pontac's Head with a certain fondness. François was so successful in boost-

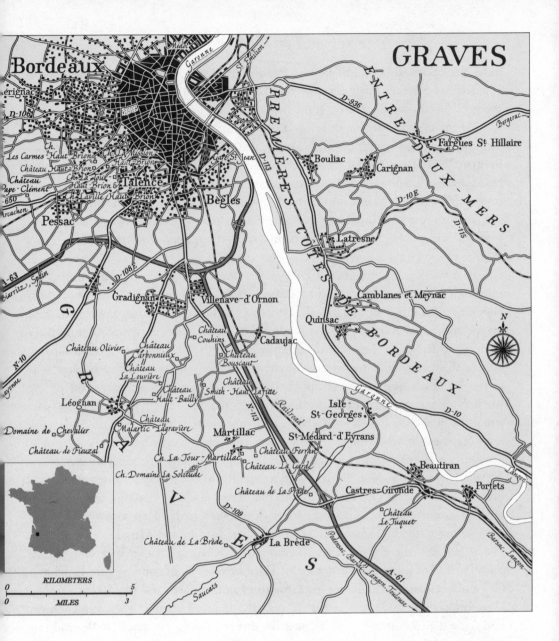

ing Haut-Brion's reputation that the château soon became a necessary stopping place for every wine pilgrim. In 1687, John Locke became the first Englishman on record to pay Haut-Brion a visit. Even then, it is clear that Haut-Brion was recognized as superior to the other wines of the region.

The eighteenth century was the first great boom era for both Bordeaux wines and Bordeaux trade, and from the end of the War of the Spanish Succession in 1713

95

until the upheavals brought by the Revolution (1789–1792), the vineyards prospered as never before. Although during this period the wines of the Médoc overtook those of Graves in popularity, Haut-Brion was never overshadowed.

By the middle of the eighteenth century, Haut-Brion and the rest of the Pontac property had passed twice through the female line, falling into the second great family dynasty after the Pontacs, the Fumels, who held it until 1801. A major turning point under the Fumels was the introduction of the bottle for shipment and the discovery that aging wine in a bottle improved it. (Thomas Jefferson, a lifelong admirer of Haut-Brion, ordered his wine in bottles rather than in casks, as was then the custom, knowing as he did that any wine in barrels that passed through the hands of a shipper risked being adulterated.)

In 1773, the Comte Joseph de Fumel returned to Bordeaux from a military campaign to tend his vineyard and the affairs of the Bordeaux Parlement. Despite his popularity with the Bordelais—after the Revolution he became Bordeaux's first mayor by popular acclaim—he was slandered by informants (his own butler, in fact) during the Reign of Terror and guillotined in 1794. (He was in good company: during this period all four owners of the future First Growth châteaux were sent to the Bordeaux guillotine, set up where the Place Gambetta is today.) Following Joseph's execution, part of Haut-Brion was confiscated by the government, part remained in the family—who later bought back the state's share and, in 1801, sold it to Napoleon's wily counselor Talleyrand, who kept it only until 1804.

After weathering three decades of lackluster ownership, the vineyard was taken in hand by Joseph-Eugène Larrieu, who restored it to prominence. When the Classification of the Great Growths of the Gironde was made in 1855, no other leading wine of Graves was included, but Haut-Brion was rated a First Growth (*Premier Cru*), along with the three great Médocs: Lafite, Latour, and Margaux.

When the rest of the Graves vineyards were at last given a separate Graves classification in 1953, the great red wine of Haut-Brion was, of course, again listed as a First Growth, and it is now a First Growth of both Graves and the Médoc. Today, Haut-Brion's red wines are vatted in specially designed stainless-steel fermentation tanks, installed in the early 1950s under the direction of H. Seymour Weller and former *régisseur* Georges Delmas, father of Jean Delmas, the present manager. Haut-Brion was the first of all the great vineyards of Bordeaux to recognize the superiority of stainless steel over the traditional picturesque wooden vats. The latter have been found to contribute to volatile acidity, the wine-maker's enemy.

Acquired in 1935 by the American financier Clarence Dillon and now owned by his son, Douglas Dillon, former Secretary of the U.S. Treasury, the château and its grounds present a noble, well-tended picture. The outer walls have been burnished to show the beauty of the original stone, the majestic entrance has been restored, and a large, beautiful underground cellar has been built. In 1975, Douglas Dillon's daughter, Princess Joan of Luxembourg—now Duchess of Mouchy—was named president of Haut-Brion, and, with her husband, she is now carrying on the family tradition of excellence and attention to detail that has been the distinguishing feature of the Dillon management.

Just across the Arcachon road, N-650, from Haut-Brion are three excellent and important Haut-Brion-named vineyards, all formerly owned by the Dewavrin-Woltner family, until acquired in September 1983 by Haut-Brion. La Mission-Haut-Brion makes superb red wine, and in a new Classification it would be rated immediately after the First Growths, practically in a class by itself. La Tour-Haut-Brion is a small property, 16 hectares (40 acres), whose wines are perhaps fuller and in a lower class than those of La Mission. Laville-Haut-Brion makes a tiny amount of very good white Graves.

A short distance down the Arcachon road, hidden off to the right behind the trees, are the vineyards and Château Pape-Clément, which claims to be one of Bordeaux's oldest vineyards. In the late thirteenth century, the estate was set aside as part of the episcopal property of Bordeaux by Bertrand de Goth, Archbishop of Bordeaux. When he became Pope Clement V, in 1305, and subsequently moved the Papacy from Rome to Avignon, the property took on his name. Pape-Clément produces only red wine, of a consistently good quality from year to year.

Farther south and slightly east, in the very heart of Graves, there is a bevy of vineyards around the town of Léognan, best reached from Pessac on D-109. Tucked back in the woods is the Domaine de Chevalier. The simplicity of the buildings belies very fine wines—both red and white. In 1983, Paul Ricard sold this property to the Bernard Co., a manufacturer of industrial alcohol. The limited annual production—about 3,800 cases of red and less than 1,000 cases of white—and the superb quality of the wines have made them a connoisseur's favorite.

On the opposite side of Léognan is Château Carbonnieux. True to the custom of Graves, Carbonnieux makes both a red and a fine dry white wine. The white has surpassed the red recently in popularity, and, indeed, its dry, clean, crisp taste is ample reason. Carbonnieux white, as it is vinified by Antony Perrin, is setting a trend for the making of dry white Graves that the rest of the region will no doubt follow. Whereas, in the past, the generic white Graves was often slightly sweet and somewhat flabby, without freshness or charm, the newly vinified white wines, with Carbonnieux as the forerunner, have taken on new life. M. Perrin maintains that by bottling early, usually in the spring five to seven months after the harvest, he can capture the true fruit and vigor of the wine.

Dating from the thirteenth century, Carbonnieux is one of the oldest of Graves's wine-producing châteaux. The château itself is late-fifteenth-century. The property was long in the hands of Benedictine monks, who provided food and lodging to pilgrims on their way to Santiago de Compostela, in Spain. The shell on the label remains today as a symbol of the pilgrimage.

Close by Carbonnieux is Château Haut-Bailly, generally rated better than Carbonnieux and one of the best red wines of the middle Graves district. Still in Léognan, but farther south, is the red- and white-wine-producing vineyard once owned by La Rochefoucauld, Château de Fieuzal. It is well run today by M. Gribelin; the late M. Negrevergne, a Bordeaux pharmaceuticals manufacturer, had owned it since 1974. Another Léognan vineyard is Château Olivier, more important now for its thirteenth-century château—a turreted, buttressed, and moated affair—than for its wine, which only recently became château-bottled. Controlled for many years by the Eschenauer shipping firm, Olivier sells well, but it is far from being one of the best wines the district can offer.

Fifteen minutes' drive east from Léognan, just south of Martillac, is the property of the Kressmann shipping family, Château La Tour-Martillac, making about 5,000 cases of wine a year, nearly all of it white. Just to the north, at Cadaujac, is Château Bouscaut, which was owned from 1968 to 1981 by a group of Americans who put a great deal of money and energy into rebuilding it. In 1981 Bouscaut was purchased by Lucien Lurton of Brane-Cantenac.

Graves differs from the Médoc, Saint-Émilion, and Pomerol in that it has a comparatively small number of châteaux in relation to the amount of land planted in vines. In the entire Médoc, nearly 30 percent of the vineyards are held by top classified châteaux, all of which bottle the wine themselves and sell it under the individual, well-recognized château label. This is in striking contrast to Graves, where classified châteaux hold just over 10 percent of the 2,400 hectares (6,000 acres) of vineyards. The rest of the vast vineyard area is given over to small properties, most of which produce white wine, sold either under a lesser château name or to Bordeaux shippers, who, in turn, market it as generic "Graves." Still, there are a fair number of good properties, including Château Les Carmes-Haut-Brion in Pessac and the especially good Château La Louvière in Léognan, which deserves to be classified. In Martillac are Château Ferran, Château La Garde, and Domaine La Solitude, while farther south there are Château Le Tuquet in Beautiran, Château Magence in Saint-Pierre-de-Mons, and Château de Portets in Portets. In 1984 a decree of the I.N.A.O. set aside the best vineyard lands of northern Graves, those closest to the city of Bordeaux. It decreed that those close to the city could optionally add "Graves de Pessac" on their label and those in northern Graves around the town of Léognan could call themselves "Graves de Léognan" to differentiate themselves from the lesser Graves to the south.

A contribution to tourism, if not wine, is the majestic, moated, fifteenth-century Château de Labrède, in Labrède, birthplace and home of Charles-Louis de Secondat, known to the world as Montesquieu. The château's impressive grounds and library make it a showplace.

SAUTERNES, BARSAC,

and Other Sweet Wines

Set like a jewel in the midst of Graves, south of Bordeaux, is the most acclaimed sweet-wine region in the world: Barsac-Sauternes. With its north end bordering the Garonne and stretching south to the sandy soil of the Landes, the district forms a rough triangle. A small, clear stream called the Ciron bisects it and empties into the Garonne, leaving the Barsac portion to the north and Sauternes on the south.

All the wines from this region are eligible for the *appellation* Sauternes, including those from Barsac. The Barsac growths have the choice between Barsac and Sauternes as *appellations;* the regulations for each, regarding minimum alcohol, sugar content, and so forth, are the same. However, the two regions do differ rather remarkably in the respective personalities of the wines they produce. What is typical of the best Barsacs is a distinctive backbone and an acid nerviness behind the sweetness. Overall, the Barsacs are perhaps a bit spicier and more flowery than the Sauternes, which may be generally characterized as fuller, richer in texture, and seemingly sweeter than the Barsacs. As is the custom, we will use the general name "Sauternes" to refer to both regions, except when discussing the specific character of each.

The state of affairs in Sauternes, so far as sales is concerned, is the sorriest of any Bordeaux wine region. Until 1982–1983 most Sauternes were being sold at ridiculously low prices. Indeed, some experts predicted that apart from its top two or three vineyards, much of Sauternes would not survive this century as a major wine-producing area. As one grower ruefully put it: "You could say that the heyday for Sauternes ended with the Russian Revolution. After the fall of the Czar, gone were the orders at a hundred cases a throw for the grand dukes of Moscow and Saint Petersburg; no more cut-glass decanters with silk ribbons." Whether it is the Russian Revolution, the First World War, the Depression, changed eating habits, or, more likely, the contemporary preference for dry white wines that is to blame, the once big and avid market for Sauternes has all but disappeared. This is a great shame.

In 1855, with the exception of Haut-Brion in Graves, the only two regions of Bordeaux that were classified were the Médoc for its red wines and Sauternes for its sweet whites. Only four wines of the Médoc were considered worthy of the title First Growth; for the Sauternes, by contrast, not only were there eleven in the First Growth category but one was considered so excellent that it was placed in a special category: *Premier Cru Supérieur,* "Superior First Growth." Eleven others were classed as Second Growths. But how many people can name the First Growth Sauternes? A few may be easy to recall. Of course, Château d'Yquem. No one would dispute its *Supérieur* status today. Then perhaps one can recall the two great Barsacs, Coutet and Climens, and then . . . and then . . . ?

In the nineteenth century, not only were there a dozen First Growth Sauternes to four of the Médocs, but they generally kept longer and fetched higher prices. With Sauternes one could be more sure than with many of the reds of having excellent wines in five or ten years' time. In 1787, when Thomas Jefferson was shopping for wines, he bought some from the first Comte de Lur-Saluces, and found that his Yquem lasted "to eight years of age," far beyond the reasonable expectation of a First Growth at that time.

However, one thing the Classification also showed was that *"Sauternes ne supporte pas la médiocrité":* a mediocre Sauternes is of little interest. In an average year a well-made Sauternes will please; in a great year it will astonish. But nothing can correct or compensate for poor vinification, poor weather, or poor soil, and if any one of these is part of the making of a Sauternes, the wine will be ordinary, cloying, flat, lacking in acidity and freshness, totally devoid of grace or charm.

It does not take many experiences with mediocre Sauternes to understand why there are only two classes of the wine. Many of the small Sauternes châteaux and other producers of generic Sauternes have detracted from the glory of the greatest. These lesser properties cannot afford to pick more than once, so not all (frequently much less than half) of the grapes are either properly matured or affected by the "noble rot" that is essential to concentrate the bouquet and sugar. The lack of natural sugar content will be offset by excessive chaptalization—the addition of sugar to the must—producing a thin, sweet, common wine with little bouquet. The great name of Sauternes has also been dragged down by sweet, common, self-styled Sauternes from California and Australia—for their imitation the Californians drop the final "s." This type of fraud (there is no other word for it) has probably hurt the region most of all—even more than the so-called "champagnes" have tarnished the name of Champagne.

Where does that leave us now? With a product that is without equal in the world, that is appreciated by fewer and fewer people each year, and with a glorious region that is doomed unless its wines can be aggressively marketed. Unfortunately, little regional cooperative effort is being mounted. There is a glimmer of hope, however. In the mid-eighties there seems a definite tendency for a Sauternes discovery on the part of some, and a rediscovery on the part of others. Sauternes seems to be making a definite comeback.

Who, after all, is in a position to decree that dry is chic and sweet is out? Let the palate decide. As an aperitif, but most particularly as a dessert wine—indeed, a dessert in itself—a fine Sauternes is as beautiful a glass as you can ever hope to raise.

Driving on the Autoroute which starts in Bordeaux along the Garonne River, you can make the Barsac-Sauternes vineyards—even with traffic—in less than half an hour. Leaving Bordeaux, follow signs for Langon-Toulouse to A-61; exit at the Podensac-Illats-Cerons turnoff and follow signs to Cadillac. Five kilometers from the Autoroute, turn right onto N-113, the old Bordeaux-Barsac road. For a beautiful drive, follow the signs reading *"Circuit du Sauternais,"* which takes you through a network of narrow, weaving country lanes past châteaux of the region, both obscure and august. At most of them you will be well received and have a chance to taste the wines and chat with the owner or the *maître de chai*. One afternoon will go a long way toward unlocking the mysteries of the wine and country.

Though interesting to taste from the barrel, Sauternes are at their best in the bottle. The '67s, '71s, '75s, '78s, '79s, '80s, '81s, '82s, '83s, and, soon, the '85s can nearly always be purchased at the vineyard where they were made.

Just to the north of the tiny village of Sauternes is the great Château d'Yquem, whose wine has been the standard-bearer of the entire region for nearly two centuries. It was here, in 1787, that Thomas Jefferson stopped to buy the great sweet wine of the region from the Comte de Lur-Saluces, who had just bought the property; that noble entrepreneur's great-great-great-grandnephew, the Comte Alexandre de Lur-Saluces, owns and manages the property today.

The château is built like a fortress, in the apparent expectation that barbarian

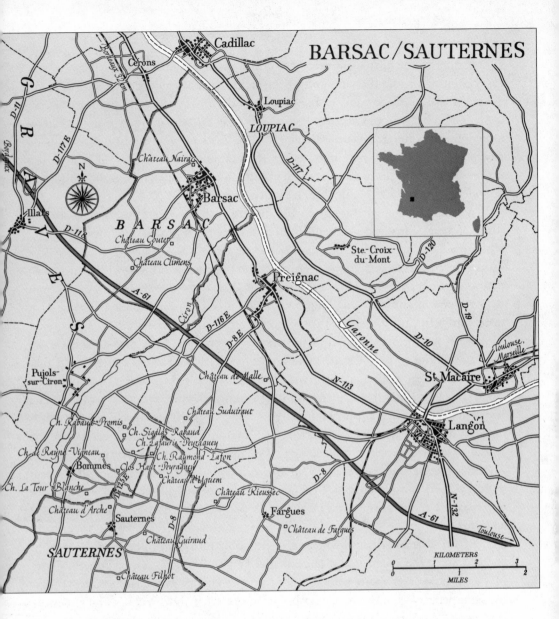

hordes would someday storm its heights for the priceless liquids in its depths. (They fortunately never did.) From its crenellated walls you can look eastward down the gentle slope to the river, a wooded view that embraces the main communes of the *appellation* Sauternes: Bommes, to the west by a kilometer or so, home of the First Growths Rayne-Vigneau and Sigalas-Rabaud; Preignac and its Château Suduiraut, just to the north; and Fargues, to the east, where the vineyards of Château Rieussec are located, bordering on those of Yquem, and Château Guiraud to the south.

Farther to the north, on the old N-113, is the small, unassuming village of Barsac, behind which lie the vineyards of the area's best châteaux: Coutet and Climens. Barsac is also home to some of the best Second Growths, notably Château Nairac.

Yquem has 80 to 90 hectares (200 to 225 acres) in actual production. By careful selection, the vineyard makes only about 7,500 cases of wine a year—if there is no freeze in the spring and no rain or hail in the summer or fall. Château d'Yquem also makes an excellent dry white wine, having much of the superlative Sauternes flavor, yet with no sweetness, being absolutely dry. It is called "Y."

At many dinners in Bordeaux, culminating with the great Sauternes, I have enjoyed Yquems forty years old and more. Philippe de Rothschild at Mouton-Rothschild has an extraordinary collection of old Sauternes from which he is apt to serve a freezingly cold Yquem from the turn of the century—oxidized, with a brownish patina of age, and much of its sweetness lost, but with superb *sève* (a French term whose literal meaning is "sap," but which in this connection implies a fine depth of taste with a lingering trace of fruit)—an unforgettable experience.

What was much less sure, in the days of Jefferson and the first Yquem, was a château's ability to produce the same kind of sweet wine with consistency. In that age, the chemical workings of *Botrytis cinerea,* the "noble rot," were not fully understood. It is likely that the first lessons in the making of white sweet wine came in the late seventeenth century from Hungary, the home of the illustrious Tokay, which is made in a climate quite similar to that of Sauternes. From Hungary the technique spread through Europe and achieved its greatest results in Germany and France. Today France is the only country in the world that produces high-quality sweet white wine in substantial quantity. Great Trockenbeerenauslesen can be had from the northerly vineyards of the Rhine and the Mosel, but only in insignificant amounts.

No one knows precisely when or where noble rot began to be used as a way of concentrating the sugars and aromas of the grapes. The *régisseur* at Yquem, Pierre Meslier, who worked many years for me at Prieuré-Lichine in the late fifties, says that the wine Jefferson bought was probably *liquoreux* (rich and sweet) in the same way it is today. "They probably knew that noble rot helped the grapes and was necessary to make the best wine possible, but they did not know that the mists of autumn were also necessary. In any case their understanding of the process was much inferior to ours today."

The ideal environment for the greatest of all Sauternes would be a succession of blue-sky days—not too dry and not scorchingly hot—through the summer, followed, from the last week in September until November, by morning mist, which clothes the grapes in the moisture needed for the mold to form. The microclimate of the entire area where the Ciron meets the Garonne is perfect for the growth of the all-important *Botrytis cinerea* mold. In simplest terms, the noble rot loosens the skin of the grape, allowing the water to evaporate, concentrating the sugars and pectins inside, and compressing the bouquet- and aroma-enhancing elements in the grape. It is for this reason that a great Sauternes will have a luscious and memorable bouquet.

In 1981, a Canadian, Hamilton Narby, had the laudable courage to buy the run-down Château Guiraud, a couple of kilometers south of Yquem, and still within the Sauternes village limits. He has painstakingly invested some of his share from his Montreal family's assets so that Guiraud can achieve its potential for making a great Sauternes. The Sauternes region needs more such examples of dedication and confidence. Much of the lore of Sauternes can be discovered by visiting Château Guiraud, which is open every day and has English-speaking guides. Château Guiraud also makes a dry white wine called "G."

To the north of Yquem in the tiny village of Preignac, tucked away at the end of a long approach road, is the large historic domain of Château Suduiraut, one of the top First Growths but now also suffering from the world's neglect of these great wines. The château is a marvelous seventeenth-century structure. It has an abandoned air and is seldom occupied by its absentee owners, the daughters of the late M. Fonquernie, Mme Frovin and Mme Olivier. The fine park, designed by Le Nôtre (who also laid out the gardens at Versailles), is better maintained than the residence. When a M. de Suduiraut was still around as mayor of Bordeaux in the seventeenth century, Louis XIV stayed at the château whenever he came to the region, pausing also at his apparent favorite, Château Nairac in Barsac. Suduiraut is about the same size as Yquem, with about 80 hectares (200 acres) of vines under cultivation. The wine traditionally has breed and richness with desirable *sève*.

East and slightly south of Suduiraut on D-25e, also in Preignac, is Château de Malle, which, from 20 hectares (50 acres), makes a fine, clean wine. The château is impeccably maintained by the owner, the Comte Pierre Lespinasse de Bournazel.

Slightly south on D-8 are the vineyards of Château Rieussec, until recently owned by M. Albert Vuilliers, who sold the vineyard to the Rothschild group of Château Lafite in August 1984. The estate is large for the region, covering about 60 hectares (150 acres). An astute agriculturist, M. Vuilliers knew that he was taking a big gamble. "Sauternes," he said, "is coming to a crossroads now. It may get out of its marketing doldrums by selling more of its wine and converting more people to it. Or else, in the not too distant future, there will be far fewer châteaux." A dry white wine is made called "R."

Ranged along the hills of Bommes, on D-125, is another clutch of fine if little-known First Growth vineyards. Two of the best are Sigalas-Rabaud and Rayne-Vigneau, which have maintained consistently high quality and, at their price, are good values, especially the former. Sigalas-Rabaud is one of the smallest of the First

Growth vineyards, comprising only 8 hectares (20 acres). Founded as one vineyard with its neighbor, Château Rabaud-Promis, in the seventeenth century, Sigalas-Rabaud is by far the superior, one of the best of Sauternes: it is a pity that there is so little of it. Rayne-Vigneau also continues to make good wine, though it has been known to falter recently. In 1971, the vineyard was sold without the château by the owner, Vicomte François de Roton, to the Bordeaux shipping firm of Mestrezat-Preller.

Between Rayne-Vigneau and Yquem on D-125e are the two small First Growth vineyards, Clos Haut-Peyraguey, owned by M. Jacques Pauly, and Château Lafaurie-Peyraguey, which belonged wholly to the shipping firm of Cordier, until 1983, when the group La Hénin bought a share in it. Both vineyards produce fine wines.

Among the better Second Growths, more than in the larger and more re-nowned First Growth vineyards, one can sense the strain of struggling to preserve quality in the face of rising costs. At the fine Second Growth vineyard of Château d'Arche, the former *régisseur,* M. Perrisser, lamented the snob-appeal of labels. "It is only with connoisseurs that we have a real chance," he says. "We deal largely with private customers who recognize the excellence of our product and have enough confidence in their own taste." Pierre Perromat, former president of the I.N.A.O., and a property owner in Entre-Deux-Mers, now has taken a lease on Château d'Arche.

Barsac, to the north of the Ciron River, was blessed with only two First Growth châteaux in the 1855 Classification, but it is the home of seven of the twelve Second Growths. The two First Growth Barsacs are Coutet and Climens. These wines are a shade lighter in body and sweetness than Sauternes, retaining more of a backbone of acidity and spice. They are not as overwhelmingly rich in consistency, making up for it with elegance and nuance of taste. Coutet and Climens are the only two growths in the Sauternais that offer a real alternative to great Sauternes such as Yquem, for they are nearly a different type of sweet wine.

Recently the better of the two has been Coutet, a great château that has man-aged to maintain a following by the sheer excellence of its wine. This should not come as a surprise. The uniqueness of Coutet is reflected in its very name, which de-rives from *"couteau"* (knife), signifying the wine's *nerveux,* or piercing, quality. This gives the wine the feeling of freshness in the mouth with a lingering floweriness even from the oldest of bottles. The quality of Coutet is very strictly controlled. Any vintage that is judged to be below the château standard is sold as generic Barsac or Sauternes, as was partly done in 1974. The château and vineyards were bought in 1977 by Marcel Baly of Strasbourg.

Château Climens has produced legendary bottles; the '29 and the '37 were the best of the entire region. Just as Barsac as a whole distinguishes itself from Sauternes, so Climens' more clay-rich soil sets it apart from Coutet, being richer and fuller, with great depth. Climens was cruelly hit in the freeze of 1956, which reduced the vineyard to an expanse of blackened stubs. In 1971, the vineyard was bought by Lucien Lurton, owner of the Médoc vineyard Brane-Cantenac.

Not many of the Second Growth Sauternes are found outside of France, since they are mostly sold directly to consumers and to the local restaurants. One worthy of note, however, is the small Barsac growth of Château Nairac, mentioned earlier in connection with Château Suduiraut and Louis XIV. The owner and manager, Tom Heeter, and his wife, Nicole Tari, of Château Giscours have made an impressive show of resurrecting this fine growth and embody a welcome sign of faith in Sauternes' future.

It bears repeating that Sauternes, as an area and as a wine, is faced with slow death in the next fifteen to twenty-five years. Unfortunately, at present the wines cost much more to produce than the public is willing to pay. The method of picking the grapes is not only expensive—requiring anywhere from three to ten pickings through the vineyard—but is totally unadaptable to any kind of mechanization. Unfavorable weather in the last weeks of summer and the early part of fall can easily wipe out most of a crop—as happened in 1973, 1974, and again in 1977. Furthermore, it should stay in barrel up to three years before bottling. Meanwhile, the interest on the owner's investment is being compounded constantly. Then there is the question of quantity. Whereas the very abundant Bordeaux vineyards can get half a bottle of wine or more per vine, Sauternes, if properly made, is lucky if it gets a healthy glassful. The legal limit allows 25 hectoliters per hectare, or the production of 200 to 250 cases per hectare. Some vintages produce only half that—around 140 cases of wine per hectare, or 50 cases per acre.

The higher the quality, of course, the greater the expense. New barrels should be used as often as possible to give the wine the tannic acid that will save it from being soft and flabby and merely sweet. The care taken in the picking will automatically reduce quantity and raise costs in labor. Some vineyards can no longer afford to pick grape by grape. They wait for a sufficient quantity to ripen and pick all the grapes at once; then they over-chaptalize the wine in the vat, to make up for the lack of natural sugar. One *régisseur* estimated that 90 percent of the area's generic wine is now chaptalized beyond the legal limit. This is not the case with First Growth Sauternes, the majority of which avoid chaptalization whenever possible.

Finally, there is the question of what the public is willing to pay. In Germany, for example, where a bottle of the great rare sweet wine Trockenbeerenauslesen is as expensive to make as a bottle of Sauternes, one finds a public ready and willing to pay fabulous prices for it—the equivalent of fifty to ninety dollars a bottle and up. Unfortunately, the same is not true of Sauternes: demand is small, and the prices at which it sells are depressed accordingly. The combined difficulties of cultivation and financing have proved so overwhelming for at least one owner, M. de Pontac of Château de Myrat, that he was led in sheer frustration to rip out his vines and plow the land under for grazing.

To those who enjoy a sweet aperitif, a bottle of Sauternes can be marvelous. Many growers, and I for one, have often consumed Sauternes with *foie gras*—a superb combination. Regrettably, good *foie gras* is not easily available outside of France, but everyone does have dessert—whether just a ripe pear or a great soufflé—when a fine bottle of Sauternes can provide a grand finale to the meal. One bottle of Sauternes will suffice for six to eight people. If you are only four or six for dinner, a half-bottle of Coutet, Rieussec, or Guiraud will probably do, whereas at least a full bottle of Champagne (at three times the price) would probably be drunk in its place, without providing the same gustatory harmony as a good Sauternes. There are some signs that people are starting to discover these wines and there is still hope that the world will learn the proper use and true value of Sauternes.

Indeed, Sauternes suffers from its virtues. It is rich, sweet, and full—all characteristics that go against the current fad for lightness and dryness. Perhaps another problem is that as far as dessert is concerned, or at least a wine at the end of the meal, Sauternes may be a bit too serious, profound, nuanced for some people. As the Sauternais concede, "It is a particular wine, made for specialists."

But how true is this really? The fact is that there are light Sauternes, the Barsacs particularly, from good years, spiced and fresh, somewhat lower in alcohol and not as overpowering as a great vintage in its second or third decade. These younger Sauternes are not the deep *vins liquoreux* with great echoes of taste, but they can be perfect companions to some hors d'oeuvres and offer no impediment to enjoyment by anyone who likes wines.

The Comte de Lur-Saluces, Château d'Yquem's owner, recommends his wine with any kind of food at any stage in the meal, and in fact all during the meal. Whether or not he finds many to agree entirely with him, the point is that Sauternes has nearly infinite variety and far more adaptability than people give it credit for. It is a wine to be drunk for itself at any time of the day. It is pleasing to the eye—ranging from light, straw-like gold to near amber—and a revelation to the palate.

Interestingly, great Sauternes like d'Yquem require, like the great Médocs, years of aging to exhibit their true greatness.

Also on the left bank of the Garonne just downstream from Barsac is the sweet white wine region of Cérons. As in the Sauternes, part of the Cérons's sweetness and character is due to the noble-rot process. The wines are rather alcoholic and full and at their best approach the quality of generic Sauternes, although they sell for considerably less. From one property to another they have little individuality.

On the opposite bank of the river facing Sauternes, Barsac, and Cérons are two lesser districts of sweet white wine, Loupiac and Sainte-Croix-du-Mont. The region is hillier and the wines are less alcoholic and slightly more acidic than those of Cérons—some can be quite good. The main sales outlets for the cheaper ones are the town fairs in France. All three regions produce 100,000 to 200,000 cases of wine a year, the least expensive and the most common of them being Loupiac. Sainte-Croix-du-Mont also makes a certain amount of dry white wine, sold simply as Bordeaux and Bordeaux Supérieur. M. de Sèze, who sells his dry white wine under the name of Le Fleuron Blanc of Château Loubens, has one of the district's most interesting properties. His cellars are built into the rock hillside and the walls are covered with fossils of oysters and other shellfish.

⚬❧⚬

BARSAC AND SAUTERNES
Hotels and Restaurants

H = *Hotel;* R = *Restaurant*

From Bordeaux, follow signs to the Toulouse autoroute, A-61. After 35 km on A-61, exit for Podensac, and follow signs to Cadillac. Five km from the autoroute exit, turn right onto N-113 to Barsac. The autoroute makes it a quick trip.

BARSAC (33720—Gironde)
(Paris 608—Bordeaux 38—Langon 8—Libourne 45)

❧ Start here for your visit to the sweet-wine country. In Barsac look for and follow the sign for the *Circuit du Sauternais,* which will wind you along country roads and the Barsac-Sauternes vineyards. From Barsac you can also visit the Moulin de la Molle in Labrède (Tel.: 56.20.20.79), a goose farm where you can taste and make a picnic of their special home-made *foie gras* with a glass of Sauternes. The farm is practically opposite the Château de Labrède—worth a visit, but call ahead.

HR HOSTELLERIE DU CHÂTEAU DE ROLLAND: Tel.: 56.27.15.75.   7 rooms.
An old Carthusian monastery with some large, comfortable rooms; well decorated. Good setting for visiting Barsac–Sauternes vineyards. Restaurant's food and service, previously criticized, have improved. English spoken.

SAUTERNES (33210—Gironde)
(Paris 613—Marmande 45—Barsac 12—Bordeaux 50—Langon 8)

❧ This small village with its monumental name has a very out-of-the-way and forgotten feeling about it. Much of the lore of Sauternes can be discovered by visiting Château Guiraud, which is open every day.

HR LE SAUTERNAIS: In the heart of the village, next to the Post Office. Tel.: 56.63.67.13.
Opened in the autumn of 1985 by the owner of Château Guiraud. This small restaurant, dedicated to the local sweet wines of Sauternes and to the foods such as *foie gras* and magret of duck which complement them, is worth visiting. Unusual, but interesting, is a complete array of old vintage Sauternes served by the glass.

R AUBERGE DES VIGNES: Place de l'Église. Tel.: 56.63.60.06.
Rustic, simple, reasonably priced restaurant with a good wine list. Very pleasant. Open at lunch on Sundays, making the discovery of Sauternes a good pursuit on God's day of rest.

LANGON (33210—Gironde)
(Paris 615—Bordeaux 47—Libourne 54—Agen 96—Marmande 37)

❧ The bridge at Langon will lead you in less than one hour to Saint-Émilion, via Entre-Deux-Mers, a vast vineyard country of inexpensive red and white wines. The other attraction is its restaurant.

HR CLAUDE DARROZE: 95, cours Général Leclerc. Tel.: 56.63.00.48.   14 small rooms.
This good, pleasant hotel-restaurant, run by the son of a great chef, the late Jean Darroze, from Villeneuve de Marsan, is very close to the village of Sauternes. After tasting the great sweet wines of France, you will find his regional specialties delightful. The nearby Armagnac brandy district naturally makes the fine selection picked by his brother, Frances Darroze of Villeneuve de Marsan, a pride and a specialty. From Bordeaux, Darroze is easily reached. Thirty minutes by A-61. One star in Michelin.

BAZAS (33430—Gironde)
(Paris 620—Bordeaux 59—Marmande 42—Sauternes 32—Langon 15—Mont-de-Marsan 68)
From Sauternes, take D-8 to Villandraut and then D-11 direct.
From Langon, take D-932.

If you're not especially interested in the intermittent calf fairs (held the first Wednesday of each month), nor in a show of overgrown bulls held each March, do not despair. Find a parking space, preferably on the rue Ausone, and stroll past the old houses along the rue Fondespan. This will lead you to the cathedral, with its Gothic façade and medieval statues—a vision at hand every day of the year.

HR RELAIS DE FOMPEYRE: On the Mont-de-Marsan road. Tel.: 56.25.04.60.   34 rooms. Tlx: 550684.
Pretty setting in a park. Swimming pool. Small, comfortable rooms. Better than fair restaurant.

LESSER WINES
OF BORDEAUX

The entire Appellation Contrôlée area of the Bordeaux region covers 77,000 hectares (192,500 acres) and makes the equivalent of about 40 million cases of wine per year. The sweet and dry white wine accounts for about one-third of the total, the red wines, with a small amount of rosé, making up the balance.

Of those 40 million cases of wine, less than one-third come from the five major place-names discussed in the preceding chapters—the wines to which Bordeaux owes its fame. This leaves 70 percent of all Bordeaux's wine originating from the regional *appellations* such as "Bordeaux," "Bordeaux Supérieur," and "Premières Côtes de Bordeaux," as well as from the smaller regions such as Côtes de Blaye, and Côtes de Bourg, Entre-Deux-Mers, and Côtes de Castillon. Many of the wines—in fact, most—are bought by the shippers to make their house blends and simply sold under the name of the regional *appellation*. A significant share, however, is produced by individual growers and bottled at the property. When well made, these wines can show a certain individuality reflecting the specific microclimate and character of the soil. Invariably they will be cheaper and less fine than the Classified Growths from the top place-names, so they may offer good values to the interested wine drinker.

When sold through a reliable shipper and well selected, these wines are worth discovering.

BLAYE AND BOURG

In the fifteenth century, when the Médoc was still in its infancy, the wines from the opposite side of the Gironde between the towns of Bourg and Blaye were among the most sought-after and coveted of the entire Bordeaux district. Growers who had property on both sides of the river would only agree to sell their Bourg wine if the merchant would take some of the "lesser" Médoc wine along with it. After the vinous fortunes of Bourg and Blaye declined in the seventeenth century, the strategic importance of their position on the river remained. This was especially true of Blaye, whose rock promontory was used as an observation post to monitor river traffic in and out of Bordeaux. In the seventeenth century, the great military architect Sebastien Vauban was commissioned by Louis XIV to build a citadel—a walled fortress town—to stop marauders coming down the estuary and smugglers trying to get out. Overlooking the river from its rocky escarpment, the citadel still stands as a reminder of the days when free-trade was more of a free-for-all than anything else. On the opposite side of the Gironde in the Médoc, Vauban also built the Fort du Médoc. On the riverbank at Blaye there is an elegant retirement home for former river and sea captains, who assemble on the balcony, spyglasses in hand, to salute their former colleagues and capture a bit of the romance of the past.

Until the 1960s Bourg and Blaye were still plowing their vineyards and hauling their grapes by ox and cart, but the arrival of many *pieds noirs* (Algerian French) changed all that. Accustomed to large spreads of vineyard, the *pieds noirs* had long used tractors for many vineyard tasks and lost no time introducing a bit of mechanization to the right bank of the Gironde. "Everyone thought they were crazy," recalls wine broker Maurice Touton, "but before long, everyone had tractors."

The Côtes de Bourg and the Côtes de Blaye, which are separate *appellations,* make 2 to 3 million cases of wine a year, the reds in general being much better than the whites. On average, the reds of Bourg tend to be heavier and more evenly dependable than those of Blaye, though the reds of Blaye reach higher peaks of finesse. They both gain with bottle age, eight to ten years being the general limit. Growers from the region believe that the difference in the wines is due to the difference in the soils: Blaye, lying further downstream and closer to the sea, has more light, sandy soil, while Bourg's is heavier and more alluvial. The criticism that may be cast on the wines of the Côtes de Blaye is their lack of balance and character, a criticism that cannot generally be cast upon the Côtes de Bourg.

In recent years the market value of these wines has risen a little, but hardly enough to make worthwhile the extra effort necessary to produce the best wines. There used to be little difference between Bourg and Blaye and the simple appellation Bordeaux reds, and many growers declassified their wines. During the fifties and sixties many properties were abandoned and the vines pulled up to make way for more profitable crops such as grain. Some of the better properties that do remain in Blaye are the Château Les Chaumes, Château Les Moines, and Château des Petits-Arnauds, while in Bourg there are the Château de Barbe in Villeneuve, Château Beaulieu and Château Rousset in Samonac, Château du Bousquet, Château Caruel, and Château Le Clos du Notaire in Bourg-sur-Gironde, Château Brulesécail and Château Guerry in Tauriac, Château Eyquem and Château Falfas in Bayon, Château Laurensanne, Château Les Rocques, and Château Tayac in Saint-Seurin de Bourg, Château Le Nègre in Bourg, Château Les Heaumes in Saint-Ciers de Canesse, Château Mendoce in Mendoce, Château Mercier in Saint-Trojan, and Château de Thau in Gauriac.

PREMIÈRES CÔTES DE BORDEAUX

Along the northern bank of the Garonne, south of Bordeaux, are the red- and white-wine vineyards known as the Premières Côtes de Bordeaux. Approximately 350 owners produce over 50,000 hectoliters of red wine from approximately 1,300 hectares of vineyards. The majority of these small growers bottle their own wines and offer them directly to the consumer.

Some thirty good properties have brought the level of the red Premières Côtes de Bordeaux to that of Saint-Émilion and to certain wines from Graves at better prices, and they have established the quality of the reds to be generally superior to that of the whites. The Merlot, Cabernet Franc, and Cabernet Sauvignon, in that order, predominate.

The southern half of the Premières Côtes from Langoiran to Saint-Germain-de-Graves is planted predominantly in white grapes. Many producers erroneously still tend to try to make wines on the sweet side, appealing to those who wish a sweetish white at a low price; fortunately, there are some quite decent producers of dry white wines.

ENTRE-DEUX-MERS

The huge area of Entre-Deux-Mers lies just to the north, literally "between two seas"—the Dordogne and the Garonne. Formerly an area of small growers scattered throughout the wooded and rolling countryside, it has become, since the 1960s, increasingly dominated by nearly forty local cooperatives. This, the largest wine-producing area of Bordeaux, with approximately equal quantities of red and white, produces nearly one-half of all the wines of Bordeaux. Of the 30 percent of growers who produce good white wines, there are some who have succeeded in capturing the fruit and making good, likable, fruity white wines when bottled early in the year following the vintage. The Sémillon grape predominates, and the Sauvignon, planted in small quantities, contributes its pleasant, typically strong aroma. Although these wines are not of the quality of Graves they are a very good value.

The reds are predominantly planted with Cabernet Sauvignon, usually to the extent of some 60 percent, with 25 percent Merlot and 15 percent Cabernet Franc. Only the whites of the area have the right to the *appellation* Entre-Deux-Mers, though about half the wine produced is red, sold under the name of Bordeaux and Bordeaux Supérieur. Entre-Deux-Mers white is certainly one of the best inexpensive white wines of France. Some, through greatly improved vinification, are really pleasant good wines which should be drunk when less than five years old. A recently created *appellation* for these wines and other Bordeaux white wines is "Bordeaux Blanc Sauvignon." Co-operatives are responsible for a substantial part of the Entre-Deux-Mers production.

BURGUNDY

Burgundy, with its fertile slopes and fought-over towns, resembles a time capsule: so much history and so many resonant names and noble vineyards compressed into an insignificant amount of space. From Chablis to the Beaujolais, the entire Appellation Contrôlée vineyard area of Burgundy would cover less than half the area of New York City, while the Côte d'Or vineyards that have given Burgundy its great fame would cover less than half of Paris. As you wind your way down the vineyard roads between Chablis and just north of Villefranche-sur-Saône, you can hardly reel off the name of one great vineyard or wine commune before you're halfway through the next.

The ancient Duchy of Burgundy is neither the largest nor, financially, the most important wine region in the world, but it is one of the very greatest. Nowhere else is wine so much a part of daily life, and nowhere is there such voluble expression of honest love of wine and so much discussion of its varieties and perfection.

Burgundy begins with the white wines of Chablis. One hundred forty kilometers (84 miles) to the southeast is the bustling city of Dijon, once only a provincial town whose name could conjure up the scent of mustard, now the commercial capital of Burgundy. It is a full-fledged city, complete with suburbs, heavy traffic, and surrounding industrial complexes. Factories producing shoes, biscuits, and automobile parts line the major roads leading into and out of the city center. Swift and frequent modern trains put Dijon at the door of Paris, Switzerland, and the south of France. Between Dijon and Chagny, 60 kilometers (36 miles) to the south, lie some of the most famous vineyards of the world, the heart of Burgundy itself, the Côte d'Or. If Dijon is Burgundy's commercial capital, Beaune is its wine capital. It is the center for the important shippers who buy, blend, and bottle wines from the region to send all over the globe. But Burgundy does not stop at the Côte d'Or; farther south a transition area, the Chalonnais, leads one to the bountiful Beaujolais, the land of light, fruity wines that are guzzled with enjoyment all over the world.

For centuries Burgundians have been making and drinking wines and shipping them to the earth's four corners. The tradition has been passed from father to son, from priest to nobleman to peasant. Over the centuries, the finest vineyard sites have been carefully tended, and the best vines for the soil—Pinot Noir and Pinot Chardonnay—planted. However, the criticism of this great wine region today is that between pruning for greater quantity and vinifying for quick consumption, Burgundy in the late sixties and seventies has lost considerably in quality, especially in its red wines.

It is unfortunate, but true, that one man's Burgundy is likely to be another man's *ordinaire,* for no other name is so persistently misapplied. In the 260-kilometer (156-mile) stretch from Chablis to the end of Beaujolais at Villefranche-sur-Saône, Burgundy expresses itself through its wine in hundreds of ways. All too frequently, "Burgundy" turns out to mean dark red wine that is sometimes too rough, sometimes too alcoholic. Such wines are not true Burgundies. The red wines from the Burgundian district of Beaujolais, for example, are at their best light, fresh, and fruity, and even Burgundies from the Côte d'Or are more often light, elegant, and subtle wines, particularly those from Chambolle, Vosnes, Volnay, and Beaune.

With some truly great exceptions such as 1969, 1976, and 1985, Burgundy often lacks sufficient sunshine to bring full ripeness and tannic depth to the grapes. The Burgundian grower's classic fault is to chaptalize the wine excessively, adding sugar in the hope of making it taste like the mythical Burgundy the public expects. Whatever the merits of chaptalization, sugar will never replace the rays of the sun in a wine of quality. By over-chaptalizing the fermenting must, and thus raising the alcoholic content of the wine, vintners gain the impression of greater richness and suppleness while robbing the wine of its character. Chaptalization, when judiciously done, is very useful in "focusing" a wine that might have been unresolved because of a lack of body or alcoholic content. Too often, though, there is a heavy, abusive hand on the sugar bag (referred to wryly as "sun in sacks"). The misconception that red Burgundy should be heavy, when in fact it tends to be naturally light in comparison to Bordeaux, continues to be encouraged by buyers all over the world. In

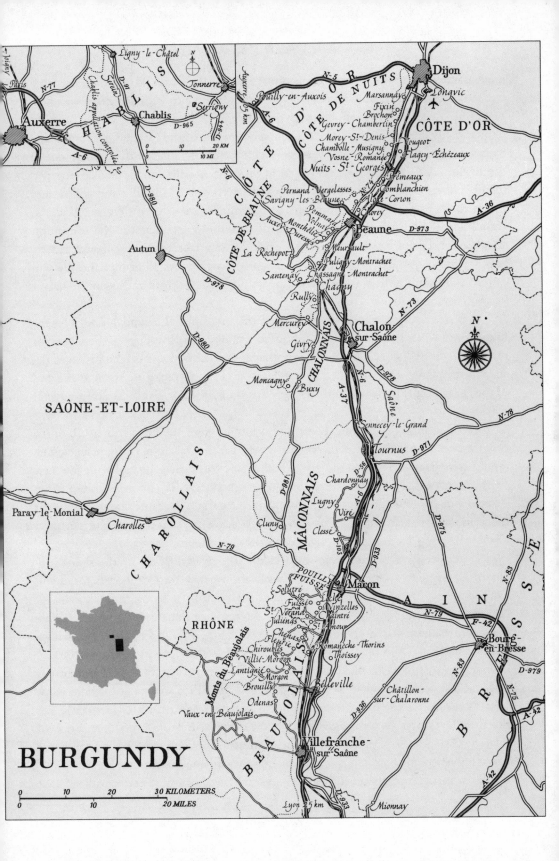

many countries there is no hesitation about putting the name Burgundy on any red wine, no matter where it originates. In fact, the only wines with any historical, geographical, moral, or (in France at least) legal right to the name are those from certain clearly defined sections of the French departments of the Côte d'Or, Yonne, and Saône-et-Loire and the *arrondissement* of Villefranche-sur-Saône in the department of the Rhône. As is the case with all French wines of Appellation Contrôlée, the permissible vines are legally controlled, the yield per hectare is legally controlled, and the methods of pruning, growing, and fertilizing, as well as of vinifying and aging, are all legally controlled—and if the resultant wine does not meet the minimum standards it is not Burgundy. Thus, while bottles labeled California burgundy, South African burgundy, or Chilean burgundy may all have their merits, they will never be Burgundy. In all, the vineyards of Burgundy—the true Burgundy—cover 30,000 hectares (75,000 acres).

It is not known who first introduced the vine into Burgundy. The Romans found vines when they made their conquest, and under their influence the vineyards certainly increased and prospered. It is probable that the barbarians who followed destroyed the plantations, and their descendants began to reconstitute them at the end of the fourth century. In the fifth century A.D. Pliny told of Gauls drinking wine at Auxerre.

In the year 581, Gontran, King of Burgundy, gave the vineyards of Dijon to the Abbey of Saint Bénigne, a move that was to have far-reaching consequences. The monks were happy to receive the gift, which assured a steady source of wine for their religious services. In the centuries that followed, Burgundy changed from a kingdom to a duchy and various nobles, following Gontran's example, gave to different religious orders such vineyards as those of Aloxe, Fixey, Fixin, Santenay, Auxey, Comblanchien, Chassagne, Savigny, Pommard, and Meursault.

To the medieval world, wine was wealth, and, overwhelmed by the sudden influx of liquid riches, some of the clergy began to forget the strict monastic rules and lived too well. By the twelfth century, the great reformer and ascetic Bernard of Clairvaux was denouncing the luxurious and often licentious living of his Benedictine brothers, particularly those at the Abbey of Cluny (the largest religious edifice in Christendom at the time, only surpassed later by St. Peter's in Rome), about 25 kilometers (15 miles) from Mâcon. He came in 1112 to the Benedictine abbey at Cîteaux, just across the plain from Vougeot, and his fervor and spirit for hard work were soon recognized. The Cistercian motto became *Cruce et Aratro* (By the Cross and the Plow), and even though Bernard left Cîteaux in 1115 to establish his own abbey at Clairvaux in Champagne, his dedication to the hard labor of the soil had a direct influence on the establishment of the vineyards of Burgundy.

Even in the twelfth century the monks at the Abbey of Cîteaux realized that their land was not fit for vines, so of all the lands bestowed on them they chose the hillsides 12 kilometers away around Vougeot. They cleared the slope of brambles and planted it with vines. They continued to use the abbey at Cîteaux to store their barrels of wine. For eight hundred years this soil has been producing one of Burgundy's finer red wines. The Cistercians carried their dedication to abbeys all over the world, including Kloster Eberbach along the Rhine, the largest Cistercian monastery dedicated to wine-making, and still in use today. Their greatest accomplishment was the founding of the Clos de Vougeot, built up slowly from grants given by landowners who were impressed by the sanctity and industry of the monks.

Vines flourished throughout the Middle Ages, some of them of dubious quality. In 1395, Philip the Bold, Duke of Burgundy, banned from Burgundian vineyards the grape he referred to as the "disloyal Gaamez," which gives wine in abundance but wine full of "very great and horrible harshness." The introduction into fine wine regions of inferior grapes that produce quantity rather than quality is a recurrent evil. The Gamay vine mentioned by the duke is not unknown in Burgundy today; one of its varieties is responsible for the good wines of Beaujolais, but on the Côte d'Or it gives a wine similar to that described by Duke Philip more than five centuries ago. Another ducal edict of the Middle Ages attempted to ban the storage of wines coming from any other district.

The wines of Burgundy, of Beaune especially, appealed to the kings of France. During the Coronation of Philip VI at Reims, Burgundy flowed from the nostrils of a bronze stag set up outside the cathedral. Louis XI was extremely fond of Volnay, and he achieved the vinous reward in his reign of bringing the rebellious duchy of Burgundy to the French crown.

At that time, in the seventeenth century, it was not yet the wine we know: it was much lighter, and sometimes white grapes were mixed with the red to produce the pinkish, "partridge-eye" color then preferred. Foreign customers, particularly Germans and Dutch, are said to have wanted a heavier drink, and for them, before the practice of chaptalization became generally widespread, sugar was sometimes introduced when the vintage was not heavy enough.

When the French Revolution erupted, a great part of the Burgundy vineyards was in the hands of the Church. So the established ownership of Burgundian viticulture was completely disrupted by the wave of anticlericalism that swept France in the revolutionary 1790s and through the Napoleonic First Empire. The vineyards were seized by the state, and parceled out to the local peasants, who in turn split them up among their children. This set up a pattern of small ownership that prevails throughout the Côte d'Or to this day. The result was and is that the great vineyards continue to exist as entities, but each one is divided among a number of owners. Thus, two bottles of wine coming from the same vineyard, in the same year, may be quite different from each other, their characteristics depending to a large extent upon the age of the vines and the grower's talent and care. The Bordeaux system of large estates unified under one ownership is today practically unknown in Burgundy; with a very few exceptions, there are no Burgundian châteaux in the Bordeaux sense of the word, and a domain may include bits and pieces of a number of widely scattered vineyards, the wines of which are sold under different place-names but made and stored all in one cellar. In Burgundy, there are more than a hundred separate place-names; at first glance the system appears complicated and confusing. The confusion is justified in that the distinctions are real in the taste and the character of the wines.

Of all of France's wine regions, Burgundy was the first to have close attention paid to its subtle differences from vineyard to vineyard. The Clos de Vougeot fathers, for instance, soon recognized at least three grades of wine from their 50-hectare plot.

All this appreciation of distinctions of soil is reflected in the classification of the wines from the region. In 1936 the I.N.A.O. (National Institute of Place-names), under the aegis of the Ministry of Agriculture, set up stringent laws concerning the production of all wines. The system has become a model to the world for distinguishing unique characteristics and establishing standards of quality. The local commissions of the I.N.A.O. for each wine commune set the standards for the various wines produced, first by defining the boundary of the region where the wine would be eligible for the general regional place-name—for example, "Bourgogne"; the district, "Côte de Nuits"; the village area, "Gevrey-Chambertin"; and sometimes the vineyard, such as "Chambertin-Clos de Bèze." Requirements for the vineyard are set out, such as grape variety, the pruning method, and maximum production per hectare, as well as the quality of the wines, including minimum alcoholic content before chaptalization. The Ministry of Agriculture formulates these various decisions into the laws or decrees called Appellations d'Origine Contrôlée.

An important element in the control of wine quality is the limitation of the yield of wine produced per hectare. In each wine-producing village, every November, following the harvest, all growers must file a declaration of the amount of wine they have just produced (*déclaration de récolte*) at the local town hall, or *mairie*. These records are checked by the local tax authorities to see that a vintner does not sell more wine than he produces. This is one safeguard to prevent the grower from blending the wines produced from his own vineyard with those from land that he does not own. Since the grower's vineyard holdings are registered at the *mairie*— down to the last square meter—it is easy to check the amount of wine he is entitled to declare. The Appellation Contrôlée of the region may stipulate, for instance, that 40 hectoliters of wine be produced per hectare. If a grower has 3 hectares, he cannot declare more than 120 hectoliters, the excess being declassified into common table wine without the benefit of any place-name. Each time wines are sold and leave his premises, he is required to go to the local village tax office, the *Bureau de Régie,* to pay a small internal revenue tax (*congé*) and apply for a transport certificate (*acquit*), which must specify the amount of wine sold, even the license number of the transport vehicle and its destination.

The *acquit,* with all this information, must accompany every purchase and transportation of wine. Any wine that is transported without such a certificate is fraudulent and subject to heavy penalties. This control extends to the shipper as well, since, in order to sell his wine to a shipper, the grower must furnish him with the proper *acquit,* which is necessary for any future sale and/or export of the wine.

Wines destined for export are not liable to any internal revenue tax and such shipments are made *"en acquit,"* that is, exempted from tax and checked by customs at the French exit border.

The paperwork and hassle involved in this system have been streamlined, however, for those who wish to buy wines directly from the property in bottle. The grower can purchase lead capsules (the sort used to sheathe the cork) from the *Régie* with a *congé* imprint, showing that the wine tax has been paid.

The laws governing labeling were set up by the Ministry of Agriculture and entrusted to the I.N.A.O. and the Service des Répressions des Fraudes (the Fraud Squad) for supervision and enforcement. All wines produced under the control of the I.N.A.O. must bear the statement "Appellation [place-name] Contrôlée" on the label, as in the village designation Appellation Gevrey-Chambertin Contrôlée, or its vineyard subdivision, Appellation Chambertin Contrôlée.

A further guarantee of authenticity and excellence in Burgundy's great vintages is the system of estate-bottling, by which the wine is produced and bottled by the grower, with the label bearing his name or the words "Estate Bottled."

The Bordeaux label is relatively simple, for a château-bottled wine invariably carries the words *"Mis en Bouteilles au Château,"* a guarantee that this wine was bottled by the vineyard owner at the château. The Burgundy equivalents—I include a list of them near the end of the chapter—carry the wording *"Mis en Bouteilles par le Propriétaire," "Mise au Domaine," "Mise du Domaine,"* or something similar.

French law specifies that an estate-bottled wine, or *"Vin de la Propriété,"* is one of which the bottler is the proprietor, or lessee, of the vineyard. He holds a license to bottle only his own wines and no others.

Little did I realize that the principle of estate-bottling, which had become my main business policy in the late forties and early fifties, would boomerang in the late seventies. Until just after the Second World War, the growers were totally beholden to the *négociants* for the sale and distribution of their wines. They had little incentive to produce better wine because, no matter how good their product, it would end up in the shippers' blending vats. Then, appealing to their egos by featuring the grower's name on the label and to their pocketbooks by paying a premium for their best wines—which became Alexis Lichine Selections—I, along with a few like-minded buyers, liberated the producers from the anonymity of the blending vat and encouraged them to stand on their own. Induced by Alexis Lichine & Cie to bottle their wines themselves for the sake of authenticity and profit, today's Burgundians may give me a small discount from their high retail prices—and that just for old times' sake. Whereas in the late forties and early fifties only a few hundred cases from the whole Côte d'Or were sold by the growers directly to the consumer, today fully 40 percent of the yield is sold that way.

Our erstwhile artisans have become little retailers, transforming Burgundy into an enormous wine bazaar. Signs reading "Vente Directe" have popped up everywhere. Beginning at Easter and continuing in an ever-increasing stream through the summer, the small courtyards of the growers in Chassagne, Meursault, Pommard, Vosne, and Gevrey are filled with wine-thirsty customers eager to meet the *"propriétaire"* personally. All day long the growers who choose to sell direct can be found in their cellars, some no bigger than a hotel bedroom, pipette in hand, filling a multitude of glasses (never forgetting their own *tastevin*) for potential customers—most of whom don't know one wine from another and probably won't buy more than one case at a time, if that. This small-fry operation does not daunt the grower; on the contrary, he loves the recognition, and with every four-bottle sale he squirms with delighted satisfaction that he is cutting out the shipper—the old shipper from whom I freed him—and pocketing a bigger profit. Even during the crucial weeks of the harvest—a time when the human element so important to the quality of wine plays its vital role, a time when every conscientious grower knows he should be out in the vineyard directing his family as to which rows to pick, or in his garage-like vatroom checking the bins full of grapes as they arrive from the vineyard—even then, M. Vente-Directe can be tempted to lead his customer down the stone staircase to the caves to demonstrate, in his Burgundian accent with its rolling R's, the virtues and beauties of his wine.

We take estate-bottling for granted now, but to get it off the ground took a lot of legwork, and in this I was helped by an energetic and resourceful man named Maurice Ninot. When I met him he was a truck driver for a Beaune trucking company, Beaune-Transport. We found a bottling truck and drove it around to the growers' cellars and piped the wine right from the vat into a machine on the back of the truck which filled the bottles and corked them. Maurice would make up a full truckload and drive it down to Bordeaux, where I had my warehouse.

Soon he was making the eight-hour trip across the Massif Central two to three times a week. The trip became so boring, he said, he once counted the number of times he changed gears between Beaune and Bordeaux—around Angoulême he lost count at two thousand! Since then, Ninot has gone on to become a successful *embouteilleur de vin* for shippers and growers up and down the Côte d'Or.

I worked the same system I had used in Burgundy shortly afterward in the Beaujolais; only there my right-hand man was Georges Duboeuf, now a shipper of fine Beaujolais at Romanèche-Thorins.

In spite of the boom in direct sales, the shipper's job goes on as it always has. The *négociant* may buy from many growers, bring the wines into his cellars, blend them as he wishes, and bottle them under his label. There are many honest and good shippers, and the quality of the wine will depend entirely on their integrity. A *négociant* must give his status on the label. Many are shippers who own a vineyard or even several vineyards. Recent French law insists that a shipper may claim to be a proprietor, or *"propriétaire,"* in addition to being a *négociant,* only if the wine shipped is from the township where he owns a vineyard. The label may then state *"Propriétaire"* or *"Négociant et Propriétaire."* If a shipper owns a pocket-hand-kerchief-size vineyard in Nuits-Saint-Georges, he is allowed to buy wines, good or bad, from any part of this township and still state *"Propriétaire et Négociant à Nuits-Saint-Georges"* on the labels. New laws state that if the shipper's address is in a town or region whose name also happens to be an *appellation contrôlée* name such as Beaune or Gevrey-Chambertin, the shipper may only indicate his address by name if the wine in the bottle comes from the same *appellation*. If the shipper has his offices in Gevrey-Chambertin and he bottles wines from outside of the *appellation* area, he may only indicate that he is located in Gevrey-Chambertin by postal code. This regulation outlaws the misleading practice of a number of Burgundy shippers who sold non-*appellation* wines, many of them poor-quality wines from the Midi, with a trademarked name on the label and below it their company address in Gevrey-Chambertin, Beaune, or some other prestigious Burgundy place-name. The consumer, understandably, was misled into thinking that since the shipper's address was in Gevrey-Chambertin, then the wine in the bottle came from there, too.

The Appellation d'Origine laws by no means eliminate frauds, but they do help to reduce them. Many small wines go to market with meaningless phrases that closely mimic the significant ones. A list of phrases appearing on labels, both meaningful and meaningless, appears below. The wise wine buyer knows that the wording of a wine label is not a pretension but a precaution, one that often makes the difference between enjoyment and disappointment.

BURGUNDY LABELS
GOOD HONEST LABELS OF ESTATE-BOTTLING

Mis en Bouteilles par le Propriétaire—Bottled by the vineyard owner or grower.

Mise à la Propriété—Bottled at the estate either by the grower or a bottler.

Mise en Bouteilles au Domaine—Bottled at the *domaine,* or estate.

Mise au Domaine—The same as above.

Grower's name (XYZ) followed by the word *Propriétaire*—Owner or grower.

Grower's name (XYZ) followed by the words *Propriétaire-Récoltant*—Owner or grower.

Grower's name (XYZ) followed by the words *Viticulteur* or *Récoltant*—Wine-maker or vintner.

Grower's name (XYZ) followed by the word *Vigneron*—Vintner.

Vigneron often applies where an absentee owner has a crop-sharing agreement with a wine-maker, the latter getting one-half or two-thirds of the production in payment for his work in tending the vines and making the wines. French law provides that the wines sold by the *vigneron* under his name are just as much "estate-bottled" as those sold under the name of the vineyard owner. Thus the same wine may sometimes be sold legally under two different names.

MISLEADING STATEMENTS

Mis or *Mise en Bouteilles dans Nos Caves* (Bottled in Our Cellars)—If the bottler is not the owner of the vineyard, this statement is meaningless, as all the wines in Burgundy are bottled in cellars. And if the bottler is not the vineyard owner, chances are that by making such a statement he is trying to parade as such. The important thing is that wine labeled this way has not been domaine-bottled.

Mis en Bouteilles au Château [*XYZ*]—This again is meaningless in Burgundy if the so-called château bears no proprietary relationship to the vineyard producing the wine. This phrase is sometimes used by shippers who maintain offices in a château and bottle, in its cellars, wine purchased on the outside. The wine may be good, but this statement carries no guarantee of authenticity except that of the shipper's reputation.

Although the whole of France follows the same general pattern when it comes to vintages, each district has its own deviations and characteristics. Because grapes are a harvested crop, local weather conditions affect them and the resulting wine. When a great vintage comes along, the wines are quickly bought up when too young for drinking. Some great wines may not be fit for drinking for five or ten years, or longer. Each vintage must be considered in relation to specific wines; those that are good in some vineyards may be poor in others. Such considerations should obviously concern those who buy their wines from the vintner. In Bordeaux, when you buy a château-bottled wine, you can be sure you are getting the vintage marked on the bottle. In Burgundy, wines may bear false labels of old vintages. It is best to buy estate-bottlings of a reputable grower or wines of a reliable shipper. Good wines are never cheap. Good old wines cannot be.

What follows is the author's personal listing of major vineyards in order of excellence, with their locations and principal owners.

RED WINES

VINEYARD	COMMUNE	PRINCIPAL OWNERS
La Romanée-Conti	*Vosne-Romanée*	Domaine de la Romanée-Conti; De Villaine et Leroy
La Tâche	*Vosne-Romanée*	(Same as above)
Chambertin-Clos de Bèze and Chambertin	*Gevrey-Chambertin*	(Also see list page 158.)
Richebourg	*Vosne-Romanée*	Domaine de la Romanée-Conti; Gros Frère et Soeur; Jean Gros; Charles Noëllat Domaine Méo; Liger-Belair
Musigny	*Chambolle-Musigny*	Domaine Mugnier; Comte de Vogüé; Domaine J. Prieur; Conrad; M. Drouhin; Roumier; Moine-Hudelot
La Romanée	*Vosne-Romanée*	L'Abbé Liger-Belair
Romanée-Saint-Vivant	*Vosne-Romanée*	Charles Noëllat; Pierre Poisot; Domaine de la Romanée-Conti; L. Latour; R. Arnoux; Cathiard
Bonnes Mares	*Chambolle-Musigny*	Clair-Daü; Mugnier; Drouhin-Laroze; Comte de Vogüé; P. Ponnelle; Groffier; Hudelot; Roumier; R. Newman; M. Roblot; Moine-Hudelot; P. Bertheau; Jean Bart; Peirazeau; Domaine des Varoilles; G. Lignier; Domaine Dujac
Grands-Échézeaux	*Flagey-Échézeaux*	R. Engel; Domaine de la Romanée-Conti; Mlle

VINEYARD	COMMUNE	PRINCIPAL OWNERS
		C. Gros; Vve Mongeard-Mugneret; L. Gouroux; Georges Noëllat Bissey; Sirugue; Collet; H. Lamarche; E. Lenternier; Brosson
Clos de Vougeot	*Vougeot*	(Also see list pages 166–68.)
Latricières-Chambertin	*Gevrey-Chambertin*	Drouhin-Laroze; J. H. Remy; L. Trapet; L. Camus; Consortium Viticole et Vinicole (Faiveley); R. Launay
La Grande Rue	*Vosne-Romanée*	Lamarche
Clos de la Roche	*Morey-St-Denis*	H. Ponsot; A. Rousseau; Ph. Remy; Domaine Dujac; Groffier; Marchand; Mlle Ory; Vve Tortochot; G. Lignier; M. Jouan; Coquard; H. Lignier; Pierre Amiot; Paul Amiot; Rameau-Vadey Mauffré; Peirazeau
Corton-Clos du Roi	*Aloxe-Corton*	Prince de Mérode
Les Bressandes	*Beaune*	L. Latour; P. Gauthrot; D. Senard
Clos de Tart	*Morey-St-Denis*	J. Mommessin
Mazis-Chambertin	*Gevrey-Chambertin*	Camus; A. Rousseau; P. Gelin; Tortochot; Rebourseau; Thomas; Marchand-Simeon; Noblet-Girod; Jacqueson; Seguin; Chouiller; Hospices de Beaune cuvée Madeleine-Collignon; Geoffroy; Consortium Viticole et Vinicole de Bourgogne (Faiveley); Vacher; Newman; Dr. Bizot; Maume; Dupond-Tisserandot; Magnien; Roty; Drouhin-Laroze
Chapelle-Chambertin	*Gevrey-Chambertin*	Domaine Damoy; J. Camus;
Charmes-Chambertin		Drouhin-Laroze; J. H. Remy;
Griotte-Chambertin		L. Trapet; Domaine Tortochot; J. Coquard;

VINEYARD	COMMUNE	PRINCIPAL OWNERS
		Livera; Gaité; Clair-Daü; S. Thomas Dugat; R. Peirazeau; R. Groffier; Rebourseau; Jeantet; Rousseau; Masson; Charlopin; Humbert; Maume; Lucotte; Trapet-Javelier; Bourgeot; Domaine des Varoilles; Raphet; Roty; Dupond-Tisserandot; Richard; Noblet; Sérafin; Seguin; Jousset-Drouhin; F. Pernot; E. Marchand
Clos des Porrets-Saint-Georges	*Nuits-St-Georges*	Domaine H. Gouges
Clos Saint-Jacques	*Gevrey-Chambertin*	Esmonin; Clair-Daü; A. Rousseau; F. Pernot
Les Varoilles	*Gevrey-Chambertin*	Monopole Sté Civile Domaine des Varoilles
Les Amoureuses	*Chambolle-Musigny*	Domaine Mugnier; L'Héritier-Guyot; M. Drouhin; R. Groffier; Peirazeau; Servelle; Bertheau; B. Serveau; Moine-Hudelot; Roblot; Roumier; de Vogüe
Clos des Lambrays	*Morey-St-Denis*	Domaine du Clos des Lambrays
Les Suchots	*Vosne-Romanée*	Lamarche; Mme Blée; Maitrot; Domaine de la Romanée-Conti; J. Confuron; H. Noëllat; Ch. Noëllat; L. Jayer; R. Roblot; R. Arnoux; Manière-Noirot; R. Mugneret; M. Noëllat; H. Lamarche; Cacheux; J. Gros
Clos Saint-Denis	*Morey-St-Denis*	Bertrand; J. Coquard; A. Jacquot; G. Lignier; A. Rameau; E. Seguin; Domaine Dujac;
Rugiens	*Pommard*	J. Guillemard; Pothier; Comte Armand; Clerget;

VINEYARD	COMMUNE	PRINCIPAL OWNERS
		Jaboulet-Vercherre;
		B. Gonnet; J. Voillot;
		Gaunoux; de Montille
Épenots	*Pommard*	Domaine Lejeune; Chandron
		de Courcel; M. Parent;
		Delagrange; J. Monnier;
		Loubet; H. Boillot;
		Domaine Gaunoux;
		L. Ricard; Bouchard Père &
		Fils; L. Chenot; L. Latour;
		Hospices de Beaune
Saint-Georges	*Nuits-St-Georges*	Domaine H. Gouges;
		Morizot-Pelletier; Misserey;
		Hospices de Nuits;
		E. Michelot; Liger-Belair;
		Union des Vins de
		Bourgogne; M. Guilleminot;
		V. Delatraute; Consortium
		Vinicole de Bourgogne;
		L. Bruck; Bocquillon Liger-
		Belair; L. Audidier;
		L. André; de Grammont;
		G. Chevillon; M. Chevillon;
		Marcel Chauvenet
Clos des Corvées	*Nuits-Prémeaux*	Gouachon; Hospices de
		Nuits-St-Georges Noireau;
		C. Renow; J. Cognieux; Ch.
		Viénot
Échézeaux	*Flagey-Échézeaux*	R. Engel; Domaine de la
		Romanée-Conti; L. Gros;
		Groffier; Mongeard-Mugneret;
		L. Gouroux; J. Bossu;
		R. Bossu; Confuron; Jayer;
		Mugneret-Gibourg; Gerbet;
		Noblet; Mugneret-Gouachon;
		Bissey; Cavin; Maire;
		R. Coquard; Bizot; Cacheux;
		Lamadon; M. Noëllat;
		Haegelen; M. Roblot;
		R. Roblot; Zibetti; Galland;
		Magnien; Vve Clerget Bichot
Clos Frantin, Vaucrains	*Nuits-St-Georges*	Domaine H. Gouges;
		Michelot; J. Confuron;

VINEYARD	COMMUNE	PRINCIPAL OWNERS
		Misserey; Chauvenet; Domaine de la Poulette; Mme P. Léger; L. Audidier; A. Chicotot; Union Commerciale des Grands Vins; V. F. Dupasquier
Malconsorts	*Vosne-Romanée*	Massart; A. Bichot; H. Lamarche; Ch. Noëllat
Clos de Thorey,		Moillard
Les Porrets	*Nuits-St-Georges*	J. Jarot; E. Michelot; Hospices de Nuits; Consortium Viticole de Bourgogne; Union Commerciale des Grands Vins; R. Dubois; Sté Civile du Clos de Thorey; Domaine H. Gouges
Renardes	*Aloxe-Corton*	P. Petitjean; Delarche; J. Collin; Gaunoux; Maldant; Gilles; Maillard; D. Senard
Cuvée Dr. Peste	*Aloxe-Corton*	Hospices de Beaune
Les Pruliers, Les Cailles	*Nuits-St-Georges*	Domaine H. Gouges; Marcel Gesseaume; Misserey-Rollet; J. Jarot; Chicotot; M. & R. Chevillon; Pidault Père & Fils; G. Jeanniard; E. Grivot; Union Commerciale des Grands Vins; C. Besancenot; Zibetti Frères
Clos de la Maréchale	*Nuits-Prémeaux*	Domaine Mugnier
Beaux-Monts (or Beaumonts)	*Vosne-Romanée*	Charles Noëllat; Michel Noëllat; G. Noëllat; Lamarche; Grivot; Bissey; Chevallier; Cacheux
Didier, Saint-Georges	*Nuits-Prémeaux*	Hospices de Nuits
Fremiets, Champans	*Volnay*	Marquis d'Angerville; F. Buffet; C. Rapet; P. Emonin; M. Voillot; J. Prieur; R. Caillot; Bouchard Père & Fils; de Montille; Montagny
Les Caillerets	*Volnay*	H. Boillot; H. Bitouzet; Bouchard Père & Fils;

131

VINEYARD	COMMUNE	PRINCIPAL OWNERS
		Bouley-Duchemin; Marquis d'Angerville; Clerget; Delagrange; Vve Fabregoule; Mme Boillerault de Chauvigné; Sté de la Pousse d'Or
Clos des Réas	*Vosne-Romanée*	Jean Gros
Fèves, Grèves, Clos des Mouches	*Beaune*	J. Drouhin; L. Voiret; Bouchard Père & Fils; Champy Père & Fils; Chanson Père & Fils; L. Latour; J. Guillemard; H. Darviot; F. Clerget; Martin-Bourgeot; Goud de Beaupuis; Dard; M. Marion; Hospices de Beaune
Clos de la Boudriotte	*Chassagne-Montrachet*	Domaine Ropiteau-Mignon; André Bachelet et Bachelet-Ramonet; L. Jouard; E. Guillon
Clos Saint-Jean, Morgeot	*Chassagne-Montrachet*	André Ramonet et Bachelet-Ramonet; L. Jouard; E. Guillon; André Colin; J. N. Gagnard; M. Moreau
Clos de la Perrière	*Fixin*	Jehan-Joliet; Bellote
Clos du Chapître	*Fixin*	P. Gelin
Santenots	*Meursault*	Domaine Ropiteau-Mignon; Domaine des Comtes Lafon; Raymand Ballot; Marquis d'Angerville; E. Bouley; Clerget Thévenot; Sté Civ. de la Pousse d'Or; Mme Philippon; Lag; Glantenay; G. Mure
Clos Blanc, Pézerolles	*Pommard*	Jaboulet-Vercherre; Poirier; F. Clerget Cavin; L. Michelot; Lochardet; Grivot H. Bardet; de Montille; Voillot; Virely
Les Angles	*Volnay*	H. Rossignol; Mme Boillerault de Chavigné; Mlle Douhairet; H. Boillot

WHITE WINES

VINEYARD	COMMUNE	PRINCIPAL OWNERS
Montrachet	*Chassagne et Puligny-Montrachet*	(See list page 199.)
Chevalier-Montrachet	*Puligny-Montrachet*	(See list page 199.)
Bâtard-Montrachet	*Chassagne et Puligny-Montrachet*	(See list page 200.)
Corton-Charlemagne	*Aloxe-Corton*	L. Latour; A. Duc; L. Jadot; Jaffelin-Rollin; Louis Cornu; Rapet; Dubreuil-Fontaine; Laleure-Piot; Chabot; Bonneau de Martray; Klein; Hospices de Beaune; Delarche; M. Moine; Mme Duchet; Perronet-Maratray; Nudant; Pavelot; Chevallier; Lessaque; Rollin Marey; Desbrosses; Gordo; Maldant-Pauvelot; M. Voarick; Chapuis; Capitain; Domaine Guyon
Clos des Perrières	*Meursault*	Mme Bardet-Grivault
Musigny-Blanc	*Chambolle-Musigny*	Comte de Vogüe; Domaine Mugnier
Perrières	*Meursault*	Ampeau; Joseph Matrot; Domaine Lafon Lochardet; Domaine Ropiteau-Mignon; Chouet; J. F. Coche; J. Boulard; P. Gauffroy; A. Michelot; J. Belicard; H. Prieur; P. Latour; Boyer; F. Gaunoux; G. Roulot; Pothinet; B. Morey; Château de Meursault
Charmes	*Meursault*	P. Boillot; A. Bouzereau; P. Latour; A. Michelot; Bernard Michelot; E. Jobard; Jean Monnier; Domaine René Monnier; E. Morey; Château de Meursault; Veuve Vitu-Pouchard; Ropiteau; Hospices de Beaune; Domaine J.

133

VINEYARD	COMMUNE	PRINCIPAL OWNERS
		Matrot; Comtes Lafon; Ch. Chouet; C. Martenot; Prieur-Perronet; R. Ampeau; Ch. Patriarche; C. Girard; A. Brunet; G. Roulot; M. Morey; P. Gauffroy; Tessier; M. Germain; M. Rougeot; Pothinet; Bouzereau; P. Millot; R. Ballot; B. Thévenot
Ruchottes	*Chassagne-Montrachet*	Claude Ramonet; Ramonet-Prudhon; M. Moreau
Combettes	*Puligny-Montrachet*	Étienne Sauzet; Domaine Leflaive; Domaine H. Clerc & Fils; R. Ampeau; P. Matrot; Domaine Prieur; Veuve Moroni Carillon
Champ-Canet, les Referts, Folatières	*Puligny-Montrachet*	Fernand Bouzereau; Bernard Belicard; Domaine H. Clerc & Fils; Albert Chavy; Gérard Chavy; Domaine Leflaive; Maroslavac-Tremeaux; Domaine Sauzet; Carillon
Goutte d'Or	*Meursault*	Pierre Bouzereau; Ch. Jobard; R. & B. Millot
Blagny	*Meursault*	C. Blondeau; J. Bondet; Domaine Matrot; Comtesse de Montlivault; Domaine Leflaive; B. de Cherisy; R. Ampeau; Pernot; F. Jobard

BURGUNDY VINTAGES

1959   The red wines had depth and enough sustaining backbone to make them into *vins de grande garde*.

The white wines did not have enough fixed acidity for lasting freshness.

1960   Light and disappointing in both the Côte d'Or and the Beaujolais.

1961   A very great year for red Burgundies. Rich, tannic, and well-balanced wines.

A high degree of alcohol, counterbalanced by acidity, gave the white Burgundies a well-deserved reputation for excellence. This is now a matter of the past.

1962 Very fine, light, and well-balanced red Burgundies.

White Burgundies were excellent, but are now faded.

1963 Red Burgundies were disastrous; white Burgundies barely drinkable, but no more.

1964 The red Burgundies were better than the red Bordeaux. These well-rounded wines could be drunk fairly early, as was the case with the '62s, and had plenty of bouquet.

The white Burgundies were well balanced; they matured quickly.

1965 The floods, which spoiled many vineyards, and the lack of maturity made the red wines a disaster.

1966 Burgundies were similar to '64, being full, round, and somewhat fast-maturing.

The white wines were also exceptional, with that perfect balance that was found in the '62s.

1967 Good vintage, but lacking the body of the '66s.

1968 Light, disappointing wines.

1969 Great vintage in the Côte d'Or with a deep color—round, full, with lasting character. In this particular vintage the Côte d'Or produced the highest quality of all the wine regions of France. The white wines lacked the required acidity and many have now faded.

1970 A good vintage, but not in the same league as the '69s, many of which have faded. (The contrary was true in Bordeaux, where 1970 was a great vintage.)

1971 The harvest was small owing to bad weather during the flowering, followed by storms and hail. The red wines were full-bodied with good color, and not equal to the '69s. The white wines were full-bodied; a fine vintage, now faded.

1972 In spite of the good weather during the late harvest in October, the Pinot Noir and other red-wine grapes lacked maturity. Some reds had good color and balance, but on the whole are only average. The white wines were generally disappointing.

1973 A very large harvest on the Côte d'Or, and therefore the quality was less than it could have been. Not worthy of much consideration today. Whites better than reds.

1974 A rather good vintage, the reds better than the '70s, at the same level as the '71s. Fruity wines with a strong Pinot Noir character. Overproduction as a result of excessive September rains diluted the quality. Good white wines, to be consumed rather rapidly.

1975 Very disappointing vintage. The red wines were too light, had too little color, because of abundant rains at the beginning of September and during the harvest. In the Côte de Beaune there were a few exceptions. In the Côte de Nuits the wines were more successful, and a few of them were good.

The white wines were, surprisingly, of good quality, and in many instances better than the '74s. But most are now dead.

1976 A great vintage. For Burgundy, which suffers from a lack of good vintages, '76 was an exception. The wines were full, round, deep in color and character. These were the best from the region since 1969.

The whites were full-bodied, though lacking in the acidity needed to give them freshness and the ability to last beyond 1987.

Beaujolais enjoyed its best vintage since 1961.

1977 Small in quality and large in quantity, these wines were too light, thin, and short. A few exceptional wines may be found acceptable. The whites were good.

Beaujolais were disappointingly light, especially for export.

1978   The reds are good soft wines, not overly tannic and therefore not slow in developing, the way the '76s have been. For their limited quantities of wine, the Burgundians were engaged in a "price folly."

The whites, too, turned out superbly well, with neither the softness of the '76s nor the tendency toward greenness of the '77s.

Beaujolais produced a very good vintage—fruity, flowery, well balanced. The various growths, or *crus,* were especially good, notably Fleurie, Morgon, Brouilly, and Moulin-à-Vent. There was a huge quantity of lower-end Beaujolais, as there was a marked tendency to overproduce drastically and to make up the alcohol by over-chaptalizing.

The Mâcon white, Saint-Véran, and Pouilly-Fuissé, when well selected, were excellent, with perfect balance and the proper acidity and character. Chablis excelled.

1979   Quality was good but not as good as 1978. The wines are fruity and well-colored, but they sometimes lack depth and body.

Abundant quantities of Beaujolais were produced. Here, quality was very uneven, with 20 percent good, 20 percent acceptable, and 60 percent poor. The situation was the same for the *crus.*

Abundant crop of white Burgundy. Although light-bodied, the wines were well-balanced and fruity. Although not wines for laying down, they were better than the red.

1980   Fair year for the red wines that aged fairly rapidly. As for the whites: Meursault, Puligny, and Chassagne yielded well-balanced and fruity wines.

Fairly passable good light wine in the Beaujolais region.

1981   The deep color of the wines is pleasing, but there is a certain lack of depth of character in the taste of the reds. Some sparse rains during the harvest have reduced the potentially very good quality.

The whites are better than the reds, very fruity and elegant. They have stood up well.

1982   A good year for the red wines. The quality was uniform, with good, deep color and tannic content. An exceptionally large harvest for Beaujolais but, in contrast, having great imbalance in fair quality, requiring skillful selection.

The white Burgundies were supple, elegant, low in acidity, and markedly superior to those of 1981.

1983   The hot, sunny weather in late September and during the harvest produced a very good, rather tannic, hard vintage in red wines, which Burgundy had needed since 1976, despite the hail which destroyed some of the flag-bearers in Vosne-Romanée, the heart of the Côte de Nuits, where top reds can be found.

Because of their richness the 1983 white wines had a tendency to oxydize prematurely, which made the 1982s more appealing for those seeking fruit and freshness.

1983 in the Beaujolais was a prized vintage for those who were willing to sacrifice lightness and fruit for the staying power needed for wines exported to distant shores.

1984   Despite having a good color, the red wines are on the light side and of average quality. In the Beaujolais the quality was good. Some growers compared it to 1973 and 1982. The white Burgundies are good. They have, however, been criticized for a lack of fullness and depth.

1985   A good vintage, good fruit and color. They are better than the '82's and '84's. Some liken them to the '78s and '79s. They could have more subtlety, which would give them more character. A very large quantity of wines was produced, if somewhat diluted as regards the whites in Puligny and Chassagne. A few exceptional highs can be found.

BURGUNDY
Hotels and Restaurants

H = *Hotel;* R = *Restaurant*

For a selection of hotels and restaurants along the route from Paris to the Côte d'Or, see the end of the Chablis chapter, pages 145–49, and Itinerary D, pages 421–22. Chablis is Burgundy's northernmost vineyard district.

Traveling distances in Burgundy are not great; the whole Côte d'Or, from north to south, extends scarcely more than 50 kilometers (30 miles). The traveler will find that, wherever in the Côte d'Or he stays, he has easy access to any of the Burgundy vineyard districts.

With the T.G.V., rail service to Dijon is among the best in France. Regular trains depart from Paris as often as every 40 minutes, with connections to Switzerland and the South of France. If you travel by the new Autoroute A-6, you can be in the Burgundy vineyards within three hours of leaving Paris.

DIJON (21000—Côte d'Or)
(Paris 312—Beaune 38—Auxerre 148—Lyon 192—
Geneva 199—Reims 285—Nevers 190)

Dijon was once the capital of the illustrious dukes of Burgundy. Today it is better known worldwide for its mustard. But Crème de Cassis is also made here, which led Dijon's late mayor, Chanoine Kir—who was at once priest, politician, and promoter—to invent the popular aperitif bearing his name. United in one glass, white Burgundy and Crème de Cassis are a liquid appeal to one's further use for Burgundy wine.

HR HOTEL DE LA CLOCHE: 14, Place Darcy. Tel.: 80.30.12.32. Tlx.: 350498.   80 comfortable rooms, recently remodeled, air-conditioned, and soundproofed. In the center of the city.

137

A good restaurant, Les Caves de la Cloche, has, strange as it may seem, a very fine selection of Bordeaux wines, as they purchased the stock of the Grand Hôtel de Bordeaux, in Bordeaux, which closed its restaurant in 1984. Alain Jacquier, the owner, also operates the Frantel and the Central Ibis, of a lesser standard.

HR HÔTEL CENTRAL-IBIS: 3, Place Grangier. Tel.: 80.30.44.00. Tlx.: 350606. 90 rooms, air conditioned.
Restaurant with grill. Center of town; slightly noisy. Small but decent modern rooms. Restaurant varies from good to adequate.

HR LE MAPOTEL CHAPEAU ROUGE: 5, rue Michelet, near cathedral. Tel.: 80.30.28.10. Tlx.: 350535. 33 rooms, sound-proofed.
Comfortable, sizable hotel rooms with modern bathrooms. Attractive dining room; smiling service. Good restaurant. M. Mornant is a fine host, and he and his chef are dedicated to further improvement of their imaginative dishes. If you are staying in Dijon, Le Chapeau Rouge is the best the city has to offer. One star in Michelin.

HR FRANTEL: 22, Bd. Marne. Tel.: 80.72.31.13. Tlx.: 350293. 124 rooms.
The hotel has air-conditioned rooms, a garden, and a swimming pool. Ten minutes from city center, the restaurant, Château Bourgogne, is respected by local Burgundians.

R LA CHOUETTE BREUIL: 1, rue de La Chouette, pedestrian street behind Notre Dame. Tel.: 80.30.18.10.
In this beautiful ancient house located in old Dijon, M. Breuil's cuisine has won him one star in Michelin.

PRODUCE OF FRANCE

Bourgogne

APPELLATION CONTROLÉE
White Burgundy Wine

Contents 750 ml

Alcohol by volume 12,5%

Jean Claude Boisset

NÉGOCIANT-ÉLEVEUR A NUITS-SAINT-GEORGES (COTE-D'OR)

R LE RALLYE: 39, rue Chabot-Charny. Tel.: 80.67.11.55.
Roger and Yvette Roncin offer a warm welcome, simplicity, and good cuisine which have won them many followers. One star in Michelin.

R THIBERT: 10, Place Wilson. Tel.: 80.67.74.64.
Good and small restaurant run by a capable, smiling couple, with a good wine list.

R LE VINARIUM: 23, Place Bossuet (center of town). Tel.: 80.30.36.23.
A former waiter and his English-speaking wife run this colorful restaurant in an authentic thirteenth-century cellar. Early Gothic arches and wine objects make up the décor. Reasonably priced Burgundian specialties. The Burgundy wines are varied. A wine shop adjoins the restaurant.

R LE CHABROT: 36, rue Monge. Tel.: 80.30.69.61. Near the Place Émile Zola.
Restaurant, wine-bar.

R PRÉ AUX CLERCS ET TROIS FAISANS: 13, place de la Libération (facing the beautiful Place Royale). Tel.: 80.67.11.33.
A traditional restaurant both in decoration and in cuisine, it is here that the priest Kir started his vinous mixture.

CHABLIS

Chablis, the world's best-known white wine, comes from a small core of vineyards 175 kilometers (105 miles) southeast of Paris. This northernmost of the Burgundy vineyards is nestled in the limestone-rich hills of the valley of the Serein—a river and countryside as serene as its name.

After you exit from Autoroute A-6 at Auxerre, continue down D-965 toward the village of Chablis. The plane-tree-lined road winds along sparsely covered slopes of birch and pine past fields of grain and grazing cattle. Small roads branch off to farms and settlements, marked by narrow rows of tall poplars with dark green balls of mistletoe in their higher branches. It is only as you approach the town itself that Chablis's nearly 2,000 hectares (5,000 acres) of vines really come into view.

The village of Chablis (population 2,400) has grown a bit since I first visited it in the thirties, but remains hardly more than a small huddle of stone houses. The slate steeple of the church rises above the sandy walls of split limestone and the black, mossy roofs of the growers' houses. The town faces east to the curving slope, shaped like an oyster shell with the seven Great Growth Chablis vineyards spread along it. From the center of Chablis, the vineyard road takes you across to the right bank of the Serein (here a shallow stream overhung with willows) to the base of the slope, straight to the largest—and some say the best—of the Great Growths: Les

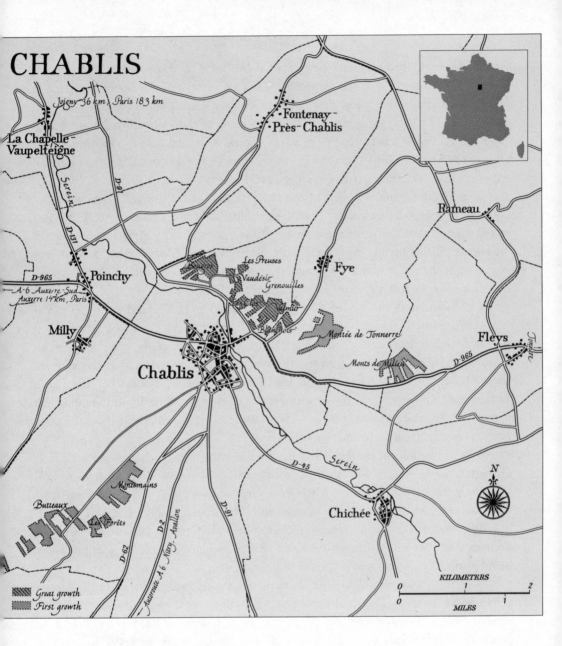

CHABLIS

Jogny 36 km) Paris 183 km
Fontenay-
Près-Chablis
La Chapelle-
Vaupelteigne
Rameau
D-91
Serein
D-131
Les Preuses
D-965
Poinchy
Bougros
Vaudésir
Fye
A-6 Auxerre-Sud
Grenouilles
Auxerre 14 km, Paris
Le Clos
Valmur
Milly
Blanchots
Montée de Tonnerre
Fleys
Chablis
Monts de Milieu
D-965
Tonnerre
Serein
D-45
Montsmains
N
Butteaux
Les Forêts
D-2
D-91
Chichée
D-62
Auxerre A-6 Nitry, Avallon
KILOMETERS
0   1   2
0   1
Great growth
First growth
MILES

Clos. To the right is Blanchots and off to the left are Valmur, Grenouilles, Vaudésir, Les Preuses, and Bougros. In all, the Great Growths cover scarcely more than 100 hectares (250 acres), part of which may be lying fallow at any one time.

The next classification of Chablis wines is the First Growths, a step down in quality from the Greats. Although there are over thirty First Growth vineyards, the growers and shippers have regrouped many of them to keep the names under a dozen. As might be expected, the best of them, such as Vaulorent and Montée de Tonnerre, surround the Great Growths on the right bank of the Serein. On the left bank of the river other good First Growth vineyards are Vaillons, Montmain, and Les Forêts. The total surface area for the vineyards of the First Growths of Chablis has now reached 550 hectares (1,375 acres). To go from vineyard to vineyard tasting among the Great or First Growths is to sense vividly the decisive effect that soil and exposure have in creating the great highs and lows in wine.

The Great Growths have the most distinction and character, with what has commonly been called a *goût de pierre à fusil,* literally a flinty taste. Since I've never tasted flint, I take the description to be a metaphorical approximation of the full "mordant" flavor of the wine; well-made Great Growth Chablis from a good year has an uncanny combination of austere strength and hardness with an elegant fruitiness from the Chardonnay and its chalky soil.

Pat distinctions among Les Clos, Les Preuses, Grenouilles, and the other Great Growths are not as easy to make as, for instance, among the Greats of Montrachet. As for all white Burgundies, the Pinot Chardonnay is the grape, but the wines of Chablis produced by its 250 growers are totally different in style and character from those of the Côte d'Or. Les Clos and Les Preuses vie for top honors here for being the longest-lasting and having the greatest depth of taste. More important than the particular plot will be the exposure—even among the best vineyards there are poor patches—and the care and talent of the grower.

Among the best of the Firsts there is even less to choose; when well made, First Growth Chablis will be fine and memorable wine, always with that characteristic Chablis hardness and elegance. The Great Growths—which, in a good year, now make about 50,000 cases—go to market with the label "Chablis Grand Cru," followed by one of the seven vineyard names. The First Growth label states "Chablis Premier Cru," with or without the name of a particular vineyard, as a shipper may blend a number of First Growth vats together.

"Chablis," without any qualification, means a wine made from any of the lesser slopes in the district. The total surface area for the general *appellation* of Chablis is 1,250 hectares (3,125 acres). An additional 3,000 hectares (7,413 acres) could be planted with vineyards. Since much of this wine goes through shippers' hands, it is best to choose from a reputable one.

Chablis, as the first of the Burgundy vineyards you reach when driving south from Paris, will provide your introduction to the standard Burgundian wine-tasting prop, the *tastevin* (pronounced in French without the "s"). The *"tasse,"* as the growers call it, is a shallow, dimpled silver saucer about the size of a small ashtray. If you haven't got one, the grower will take out some clear, short-stemmed glasses.

In Burgundy, most growers, shippers, and other serious wine tasters use a *tasse,* whether to see the color better or simply out of habit. The *tastevin* is silver—to prevent any foreign taste being imparted to the wine—and dimpled along the sides, so that the taster can see the color of the wine at different depths. Some *tastevins* have ridges along one side to reflect the shimmer of light through the wine. Good Chablis will have characteristic green highlights around the edges, a sign in white wines of freshness and youth.

After unlocking the door to the *cave,* the grower picks up a sort of crowbar from the top of a barrel and takes the glass pipette down from a hook. The pipette is a tapered glass tube with a metal ring at either side of the wide end so that it can be held by the index and second fingers. A Burgundy pipette is usually shorter than the Bordeaux variety—less than a fifth of a meter long. On top of the barrel is the bung, a wooden stopper wrapped in burlap. After working the bung loose with a few smart raps with the crowbar, the grower lowers the pipette into the barrel, tapping on the rounded hole of the pipette with his thumb to create suction. If the pipette does not fill fast enough, the grower sucks air out of it through the thumb-hole, then covers the hole with his thumb. Lifting the pipette out, he allows it to drain into your glass or *tastevin.*

If you taste with a *tastevin,* it should be held in front of you, about waist-high, so that you can see the wine's color under the bare light bulb. The silver of the *tasse* sparkles under the wine, and a good wine picks up and adds to the sparkle. Chablis in barrel are young, green wines, but they should be clear and free of floating particles. The color should be pale yellow, with a faint green tinge. The smell of the wine should be clean, fresh, and fruity, with no unpleasant odor of wood or sulfur.

After looking at the wine and smelling it, you take a small sip and, holding it in your mouth, purse your lips as if to whistle, suck in air, and make a gurgling sound that tumbles the wine about on the tip of your tongue. Young, green wines taste sharp and often acid, but you can recognize the traditional Chablis depth of taste behind the youthful bite: that flinty, clean taste born of the incomparable marriage of the Pinot Chardonnay and the Kimmeridgian clay soil. (This soil, a mixture of clay and limestone, emerges in Pouilly-sur-Loire, Sancerre, and also in Champagne.) Then you spit the wine out on the earthen floor. Both gurgling and spitting are somewhat scandalizing to a novice, but after a couple of *caves,* the rankest of amateurs is spitting like a master. Some of the growers swallow the wine—because it is precious, even when green and undrinkable—but a shipper going from grower to grower to make his selections cannot. Besides the fact that green wine is not very digestible (to put it mildly), for a professional to sample fifty barrels a day and never spit a drop would deaden his sensibilities and probably kill his kidneys in a week.

Wines change in the barrel, one tasting fine the first week and off the next, while the barrel beside it will be just the reverse. These differences are easy to distinguish and vary noticeably not only from barrel to barrel but from vineyard to vineyard and vintage to vintage.

Most Chablis growers, like those in the rest of Burgundy, make wines from several different vineyards, so a visit to a cellar may be a tour of the different Chablis growths. If a grower makes and bottles his own wine, he is an estate-bottler and his name, along with that of the vineyard, will appear on the bottle label.

For the hardworking Chablis growers who, along with their fathers and grandfathers, built Chablis into the name it is today, the exploitation and abuse of the name abroad is an outrage. For millions of people every day, Chablis is accepted as the "idea" of dry white wine, just as the word "Sauterne" (without final "s") stands for slightly sweet white wine. Like a huge brood of ungrateful offspring, the young, burgeoning white-wine regions of California and Australia took on Chablis as a generic name and prostituted it—the so-called imitation of the Chablis style is a sign not of flattery but of contempt. For decades now, insipid whites, and, lately, even rosés, have been given credibility by the Chablis label. The irony now is that just when some people have learned to distinguish the genuine article from the fake, Chablis may yet have a hand herself in compromising her reputation.

For a decade and a half following the Second World War, there seemed to be little future for Chablis. The former clientele that had made the Yonne one of France's most plentiful wine districts had disappeared. The thin, stony vineyard soils, which are hard to work and require long fallow periods, finally became too difficult to cultivate for the money they returned. Of the 4,700 hectares (11,700 acres) designated by the I.N.A.O. as eligible to produce Chablis, less than a fifth was planted; one year in three, spring frosts hit the vines with devastating effect, sometimes cutting production by more than half. The growers were demoralized and few among the younger generation could resist the attraction of surer employment in Paris, just an hour and a half by train to the north.

The sixties were kinder to the growers and their Pinot Chardonnay vines. The first steps were taken to install propane and oil heaters in the vineyards to combat the sudden freezes that can occur until the middle of May. The world that had forgotten Chablis rediscovered it, and by the end of the decade, business was booming. Growers replanted abandoned parcels at a prodigious rate; between 1967 and 1978, the vineyard area jumped by 50 percent, and it now stands at just short of 1,700 hectares (4,250 acres). In that period, production of Great Growth Chablis tripled, and it may grow even more. At the same time, First Growth production increased by half, while simple *appellation* Chablis tripled in volume. Yet all this is still not enough to meet the demand for the Chablis name.

In the rush to rebuy land in the better sections of the Great Growth and First Growth vineyards, the price of simple *appellation* Chablis skyrocketed and forced speculators to look into the lesser region of Petit Chablis, a pale cousin of true Chablis, taking in nearly any terrain not classified as Chablis of some kind. The growers in Petit Chablis hope to capitalize on the happy change in Chablis's fortunes by applying to the I.N.A.O. for admission into the ranks of *appellation* Chablis.

IMPORTED BY : VINEYARDS INTERNATIONAL, PORT CHESTER, N.Y.

PRODUCE   OF FRANCE

Chablis

Appellation Chablis Contrôlée

WHITE BURGUNDY WINE

750 ML   ALC. 12% BY VOL.

MIS EN BOUTEILLE AU DOMAINE

Domaine Jean-Marc BROCARD

Propriétaire-Vigneron à PREHY - 89800 CHABLIS FRANCE

CHABLIS
On the way to Burgundy

Hotels and Restaurants

H = *Hotel;* R = *Restaurant*

The visitor to Chablis should also consult the "Hotels and Restaurants" section for Burgundy on pp. 137-39, plus Itinerary D, pp. 421-22.

SENS (89100—Yonne)
(Paris 119—Auxerre 57—Fontainebleau 53—Dijon 217)

On the old post road between Paris and Burgundy. From Paris on the Autoroute, exit to N-60 north, or straight from Paris or Fontainebleau on N-5.

❧ The Cathedral of Saint-Étienne is the oldest Gothic cathedral in France, having been built between 1130 and 1164. If you are in Sens for more than a meal, it is worth a visit.

HR PARIS ET POSTE: 97, rue de la République. Tel.: 86.65.17.43. Tlx.: 801831.   31 rooms (27 with toilet).
Good restaurant in a pretty town (cathedral and its treasure).

LES BEZARDS (45290—Nogent-sur-Vernisson)
(Paris 137—Auxerre 76—Orléans 70—Gien 16—Montargis 23—Orly airport 132)
See end of section on the Loire, page 292.

JOIGNY (89300—Yonne)
6(Paris 140—Auxerre 27—Chablis 45—Sens 30—Tonnerre 45)
From Paris, take N-6 direct; from the Autoroute A-6, take exit at Joigny to D-943.

HR CÔTE SAINT-JACQUES: 14, Faubourg de Paris. Tel.: 86.62.09.70. Tlx.: 801458.   19 rooms and 15 new rooms, in an annex, overlooking the Yonne River, plus 4 suites. Covered, heated pool. Excellent restaurant, where you will be warmly welcomed by the hospitable Lorain family, consisting of the father, Michel, his wife, their son, Jean-Michel, and their daughter-in-law, Jacqueline. Good stopover when driving between Burgundy and Paris. Small, comfortable rooms, charmingly decorated. Good wine list. *Relais et Châteaux.* In the previous edition of this book, I said that of the two-star restaurants then aspiring to a third star in Michelin, this was one of the most promising; and I am delighted to report that in 1986 Michelin vindicated my judgment, awarding the Lorain family their well-deserved three stars.

HR MODERN'HOTEL: 17, avenue Robert Petit (near railway station). Tel.: 86.62.16.28. Tlx.: 801693.   19 small, air-conditioned, clean, comfortable rooms. Small swimming pool. Tennis. A good restaurant called Les Frères Goddard has, despite its slightly pretentious cuisine, achieved a star in Michelin.

AUXERRE (89000—Yonne)
(Paris 167—Chablis 17—Sens 57—Chalon-sur Saône 175—Auxerre 148—Nevers—112)
From Paris, take the Autoroute A-6 south. Exit at Auxerre Nord.

❧ The bustling new streets of Auxerre contrast markedly with the historic quarter abutting the flamboyant Cathedral of Saint.-Étienne. The Caveaux des Vins de l'Yonne (1, quai de la République), where you can taste and buy wines, may be more interesting for some than the Musée Leblanc-Duvernoy with its fine collection of porcelain, furniture, and Beauvais tapestries. Specialties: Goussard Chocolates, 3, Place Charles-Surugue. Andouillettes, a Burgundian specialty, are especially good at Michel Soulié, rue Auxerroise. If picnicking, try the charcuterie, René Porte, on the same street.

HR MAXIME: 2, quai de la Marine. Tel.: 86.52.04.41.   25 rooms.
Simple restaurant, beautifully sited below the cathedral, on the quai alongside the broad, placid waters of the Yonne River.

R LE JARDIN GOURMAND: 56, boulevard Vauban. Tel.: 86.51.53.52.
Best restaurant in town. If gastronomically inclined, drive 5 km to La Petite Auberge. One star in Michelin.

R LA PETITE AUBERGE: at Vaux, 5 km south on D-163. 2, Place du Passeur. Tel.: 86.53.80.08. Elegant, small inn, overlooking the Yonne River. Considered the best restaurant of the area. Jean-Luc Barnabet oversees good service and a warm welcome. One star in Michelin.

R LA CHAMAILLE: at Chavannes, 7 km southwest. Take N-151 and D-163 at La Borbotière. 4, route de Boiloup, 8 km southwest at Chavannes, taking N-151 and D-1. Tel.: 86.41.24.80. Restored country farm. Pierre Siri has one star in Michelin, and a good recommendation in Gault et Millau.

CHABLIS (89800—Yonne)
(Paris 183—Auxerre 19—Avallon 39—Saint-Florentin 25—
Tonnerre 16—Venizy 30—Joigny 41)

This serene wine town, situated on the aptly named Serein stream, lies in the heart of the most imitated white wine vineyards in the world. Unlike Bordeaux, where the great wines are produced by châteaux with large vineyard holdings, the producers of Chablis own what are virtually small patches of vines. Nevertheless, they will welcome you to have a taste of their wines in their small cellars if you just ring the bell, walk in, and say, *"Je voudrais goûter votre vin, s'il vous plaît."* There is a small wine festival held there on the fourth Sunday in November.

HR L'ÉTOILE: 4, rue des Moulins. Tel.: 86.42.10.50.   15 rooms (3 with toilet).
The fairly competent restaurant is a compromise if you don't want to travel as far as Joigny or Avallon. The rooms are very inexpensive and of rudimentary comfort.

R AU VRAI CHABLIS: Place du Marché. Tel.: 86.42.11.43.
A small, inexpensive restaurant. Specialties are ham and andouillettes.

HR AUBERGE DU BIEF: 2, avenue de Chablis, near the church. Tel.: 86.47.43.42.   11 km north on D-91 at Ligny-le-Châtel.
A country inn where, if you are lucky, you can eat either in the garden or on the terrace. Light food with many local specialties.

HR HOSTELLERIE DES CLOS MICHEL VIGNAUD: rue Jules Rathier. Tel: 86.42.10.63.   26 rooms.
Finally Chablis has impoved its hotel and restaurant accommodations. A restaurant has been installed in a former hospital and 26 small air-conditioned rooms have been built in an old chapel. Since 1986, one star in Michelin.

SAINT-FLORENTIN (89600—Yonne)
(Paris 174—Auxerre 32—Joigny 26—Tonnerre 27—Chablis 25)

This is agreeable countryside for walks, and the stained glass windows of the fifteenth-century church are worth a glance. The abbey at Pontigny, halfway between Auxerre and Saint-Florentin, is a fine example of Cistercian architecture. Situated on the edge of the Serein, the long, austere abbey, without spire or tower, is testament to Saint Bernard's severe creed of reformation.

HR MOULIN DES POMMERATS: 5 km north of Saint Florentin in Venizy, at Brienon-sur-Armençon, on the D-129 and D-30. Tel.: 86.35.08.04.
A small, comfortable inn with a fine garden above a millstream where you can fish trout. Whether you fish it or not, it may be one of the items on the dinner table.

TONNERRE (89700—Yonne)
(Dijon 126—Avallon 52—Auxerre 35—Sens 73—Chablis 16)
Exit Auxerre Sud on A-6 when going south. Exit Nitry when going north.

◆§ In 1292 Margaret of Burgundy, the widow of Charles of Anjou, King of Naples and Sicily, built a hospital. That was 150 years before the famed Hospice de Beaune. The châteaux of Tanlay and Ancy-le-France lie ten kilometers east of Tonnerre and are perhaps two of the finest but unknown buildings of Burgundy. Tanlay is largely hidden from the road by big walls and a thick screen of trees. Inside the château is a mural which depicts, with true *ancien régime* mentality, French nobles disguised as ancient gods. Nearby and clearly visible from the road is the massive Ancy-le-France, one of the finest Renaissance buildings in France.

HR HOSTELLERIE DE L'ABBAYE SAINT-MICHEL: Montée de Saint-Michel. Tel.: 86.55.05.99. Tlx.: 801356.
Seven comfortable rooms and 3 apartments in an old Benedictine abbey in the midst of a large park. This is the most luxurious stopover close to Chablis. Rather expensive. *Relais et Châteaux.* One star in Michelin.

AVALLON (89200—Yonne)
(Paris 224—Auxerre 60—Beaune 107—Chablis 39)
10 km west of Avallon exit on Paris–Riviera Autoroute. Coming south on the
Autoroute, exit at Carbonnières for N-6A and change to N-6 direct.

◆§ If time permits, look at the ramparts of this old town. If heading in the direction of Vézelay, take the valley road along the Cousin River. For this beautiful drive, exit the town on the N-6 and 4 km later turn left on D-957.

HR HOSTELLERIE DE LA POSTE: Place Vauban. Tel.: 86.34.06.12. 24 luxurious rooms.
Converted stagecoach inn with luxurious rooms facing an old cobblestone courtyard full of flowers. In the good (if expensive) restaurant, try the turbot with cucumber, or stuffed pigeon and pigs' feet with turnips. *Relais et Châteaux.* M. René Hure in the past deserved his two stars in Michelin, but now the one star awarded him most likely arises from a cuisine that is overly pretentious. His daughter, Catherine, with a new chef, is now relaunching this hostelry, which dates back to 1707. She has inherited a fine Burgundy wine list.

HR HOSTELLERIE DU MOULIN DES RUATS: Beautiful drive in Vallée du Cousin (6 km southwest of Avallon on D-427). Tel.: 86.34.07.14. 20 rooms. (13 toilets)
An old country mill on the banks of the Cousin River. The rooms are comfortable and charming. Good restaurant, good selection of Burgundy wines.

HR LE RELAIS FLEURI: At Pont de Cercé at La Cercé, on N-6, 4.5 km east of Avallon (exit from Autoroute A-6 at Avallon). Tel.: 86.34.02.85. Tlx.: 800084. 48 motel rooms.
Modern, comfortable rooms and adequate restaurant.

R LE MORVAN: 7, Route de Paris. Tel.: 86.34.18.20.
In this attractive country-inn setting, M. Breton should be proud of his specialties. One star in Michelin.

SAULIEU (21210—Côte d'Or)
(Paris 258—Beaune 76—Dijon 73—Auxerre 98—Vézelay 12)
On road between Paris and Burgundy. Take N-6 direct, or from the Autoroute,
exit at Bierre-les-Semur and take the D-980 south.

HR LA CÔTE D'OR: 2, rue d'Argentine. Tel.: 80.64.07.66. Tlx.: 350778.   17 small rooms have been transformed, and 7 luxurious rooms added, in 1985.

Bernard Loiseau's task in succeeding the great Alexandre Dumaine was not an easy one. With a smile and a warm welcome, M. Loiseau, who has great talent, is a proponent of light and fresh cuisine. Some guidebooks have gone head over heels in praising his cuisine; the more traditional Michelin has given him two stars. Prices are not high compared to other restaurants of the same quality. Also, breakfast here is delicious. Good Burgundy wine list. *Relais et Châteaux.*

CÔTE DE NUITS

These fabled vineyards of the Côte de Nuits, its priceless heart and soil, begin 12 kilometers (7 miles) south of Dijon at Fixin and run for another 20 kilometers or so (about 12 miles), down to just south of Nuits-Saint-Georges, the town which gives the slope its name. From this narrow strip of voluptuous little hills come some of the world's most magnificent red wines.

Of the two slopes that make up the Côte d'Or, the Côte de Nuits produces the wines that share the greater family resemblance; however, the wines of no other district in the world contain such a variety of notes of bouquet and taste. The hills of the Côte de Nuits range side by side with great regularity, all with a similar south-eastern exposure. It is on the middle of the slope (not too close to the hilltop or too far out on the plain) that the best soils combine with the best microclimate to produce the greatest wines with the fullest range of qualities. The vineyards have reddish clay soil full of chalky fragments and mineral-rich subsoil, giving the Pinot Noir grape the best conditions to express itself. In certain vintages these factors combine to produce wines of incomparable depth, balance, and harmony.

The affable, outgoing Burgundians must, year by year, survive a growing season fraught with all the perils of a classic melodrama. From the buds of April to the bunches of September or October, the vine is a fragile creature, infinitely susceptible to attack. As the lovingly nurtured grapes swell and ripen through the three crucial months before the autumn harvesting, their development is sometimes more a matter of poetry, faith, and superstition than of agriculture. Heavy rains in late August and in September can literally water the wine. And then may come, as it sometimes does, a final dazzling week, in which the grapes suck in the sun and make ready to release the final expression of sun-assertive delicacy to the vintner, whose personal skill will put a stamp of individual perfection on the final wine.

All of this skill and care is lavished on a precious small amount of vineyard space. The Côte de Nuits vineyards cover a strip from 200 to 800 meters wide that extends for roughly 20 kilometers. Not all of that is vineyard; the total—around 1,400 hectares (3,500 acres)—produces a yearly average of 650,000 cases of wine.

About one-third of this is sold directly from the grower to individual buyers—mainly French, Belgian, and Swiss tourists—while another 5 percent is kept by the grower, leaving roughly 400,000 cases of Côte de Nuits (of all *appellations*) available annually for the world at large. In the case of Chambertin and Chambertin-Clos de Bèze, for instance, this translates into a total production of 7,000 cases or so, 3,000 of which are already accounted for by local sales. When the hazards of frosts, hail, mildew, and pestilence and the problems of poor flowering and bad management are added to this, it is almost a miracle that some of the smaller *appellations* are ever seen outside of France.

"Weather translates into vintages," so the saying goes.

In early September of 1976, for instance, a supreme vintage was slowly being eaten away by the continuing onslaught of heat, sun, and drought. The quality would be high, but the grapes had so little juice that the vintage threatened to be disastrously small. But at last, at the end of August, the drought broke. Late-summer showers swelled the thick-skinned grapes just enough to give a perfectly balanced vintage. The result: the finest Burgundy vintage since 1969.

Another of the great dangers faced by a Burgundy grower is summer and autumn hail. By a lucky turn in the history of Burgundy, much of the threat of being bankrupted by hail has been eased by the division and re-division of great vineyards. Few properties are now held exclusively by one owner, in what are called *"monopoles."* Before the French Revolution, most properties were held that way, with the owners being mainly nobles and the Catholic Church. After the Revolution, when much state and Church property passed into the hands of the local bourgeoisie, inheritance problems were settled by splitting up the vineyards into smaller and smaller pieces. Depending on their interest in wine, the children would keep, trade, or sell their legacy. Each generation split the vineyards further. Nowadays, though each grower may have plots of vines all over the slope in different *appellations,* the

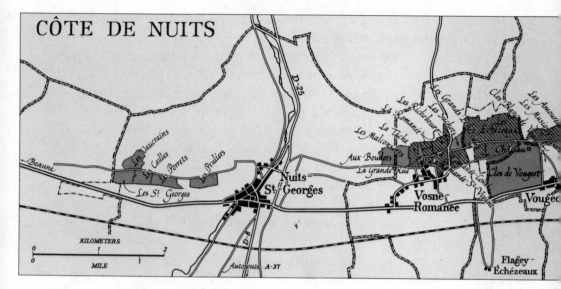

scattering provides some insurance against being totally wiped out by a hailstorm that can destroy a vineyard along with the year's work and investment.

Quirks of weather and disease, though they occur in all vineyards and afflict many other crops besides grapes, are particularly important on the Côte de Nuits. Here grapes are grown that cannot be planted successfully in a more extreme climate. Unfortunately, in 1983 a hailstorm destroyed all the vineyards of the village of Vosne-Romanée, which produces some of the most expensive Burgundies, causing exaggerated talk of the effects this hailstorm would have on France's balance of payments. If the Pinot Noir and Chardonnay were planted farther north, the character of the wine would change, becoming thinner and higher in acid, as in Champagne, where a different wine is made from the same grape varieties. When the Pinot Noir and its varieties are planted farther south, the wine produced is softer and less robust, as can be seen even in the best of the delicate Côte de Beaune wines (with the exception of the better Pommards, the Volnays, and the Cortons). This is why the great vineyards are so small and why the wine from one spot may be good while the bottles from another spot no more than a hundred meters away may be shameful representatives of the Burgundy place-name.

It is for this reason that the vineyards are called *climats,* literally "climates," because each one represents a slightly different exposure to sun, wind, and rain and a different soil composition. The best *climats* are on the middle of the Côte, 200 meters

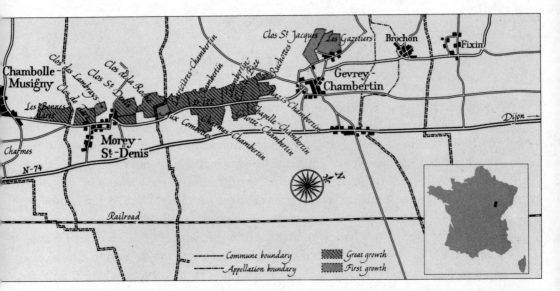

or so upslope from the plain and its richer soil, facing southeast. With such fine differentiations in such a limited space—where a slight slant of the sun's rays or a chemical variation in the subsoil can change the personality of the wine—it is no wonder that vintners speak of their vineyards and wines as artists might speak of their materials and their finished works. The best of the wine-makers are indeed artists, and of a rare kind, giving the world consummate—and consumable—beauty.

To return to the *climat*: nobody knows for sure why the vineyard of Chambertin-Clos de Bèze should be better than that of Charmes-Chambertin, across the road from it. One can only taste the difference in the wine. It may be the tilt of the slope, the way the rain falls on it or runs off it, the composition of the soil itself; but at least part of the difference is the man who makes the wine. A careful and conscientious vintner will plainly produce a better bottle than a careless, sloppy fellow, but the distinction is more subtle. Burgundians like to point to the fact that a racehorse will run better for one trainer or jockey than another, that a great orchestra will sound different in the hands of various conductors. Just as children take on the mannerisms of their parents, a well-reared wine acquires some of the traits of the man who makes it.

When all the minor differences in winegrowing and wine-making reach a conclusion in a particular bottle, the wine will have a character all its own: proud, individual, and distinct.

FIXIN

The northernmost of the eight communes of the Côte de Nuits is Fixin, just above Gevrey-Chambertin. Before the Second World War, the hills between Dijon and Fixin made up what was called the Côte Dijonnaise, but the urban expansion since then has eaten up these lesser vineyards, leaving a trail of commercial warehouses, garages, small manufacturing installations, and furniture showrooms in its wake. Fixin's wines have some of the character of its famous neighbor, Gevrey, although they hardly command the same price. But out on the highway, at the turnoff that leads back to the town, a large sign boasts not of the wines but of a statue of Napoleon, executed in bronze by François Rude, whose most famous work is the adornment of the Arc de Triomphe in Paris. When I first came to Burgundy in the 1930s there were still old-timers who remembered their grandparents' accounts of the unveiling of the statue of Napoleon in 1847. All of Dijon, it seems, came down to Fixin for the day and the streets were jammed with every volunteer artillery company and fire department for miles around. Today the statue stands in a park especially designed for it called the Villa Napoléon.

The wines from the vineyards near Fixin have a deep red color and a strong bouquet. Because of their high alcoholic content, they develop with age. When well made, Clos de la Perrière and Clos du Chapitre can equal some of the lesser *Premiers Crus* of Gevrey-Chambertin.

Fixin is also one of the five communes allowed to make wine with the Côte de Nuits-Villages *appellation*. The other four are Brochon, Corgoloin, Comblanchien, and Prissey.

Within the confines of Fixin there are some 202 hectares (500 acres) growing wines that are allowed to go to market only as Côtes de Nuits-Villages. About 43 hectares (105 acres) produce better wines sold as "Fixin," including the following *Premiers Crus:*

FIRST GROWTHS (*Premiers Crus*)

VINEYARD	HECTARES	ACRES
Clos de la Perrière	6.53	16.3
Clos du Chapitre	4.79	11.9
Les Hervelets	3.83	9.5
Les Meix-Bas	1.88	4.7
Aux Cheusots (Clos Napoléon)	1.75	4.55
Les Arvelets	3.36	7.8

GEVREY-CHAMBERTIN

Not 2 kilometers (1.2 miles) south of Fixin is the first of the Golden Slope's great wine villages. Gevrey-Chambertin and its three thousand inhabitants live from and for their wine, and for the wine-loving traveler it is the Burgundian wine village *par excellence*. Most of the houses belong to winegrowers, each having his cellar underneath—low-ceilinged and cool, with a bare-earth or limestone-gravel floor. With all Gevrey's attributes, it has always seemed most sensible to me, when showing my friends through the Côte d'Or, to begin the vineyard tour there on the Route des Grands Crus, D-122. For 15 kilometers or so (about 10 miles) it zigzags above, below, and through some of the world's greatest red-wine vineyards. Anyone with a sincere interest in wine should make this short trip, if only to see how insignificantly small and closely spaced these noble vineyard plots are. Only paved since the Second World War, D-122 remains a marvelous road out of another century, with an occasional cowpath leading off to a tool shed and iron crosses at the turns to bring good luck and good weather.

At Gevrey there is the fine restaurant La Rôtisserie du Chambertin, run by Pierre Menneveaux and Serge Lanoix. It is a dramatically colorful establishment in a converted wine cellar, reached by passing the doorways of underground rooms with papier-mâché figures dressed in authentic medieval vineyard dress and all engaged in some form of wine-making. Old Burgundian drinking songs playing in the background, along with the models of coopers and vine pruners, add a touch of historical color, welcome in a wine region trying to recapture a sense of its rich past.

Down the vineyard road to the south is the great parcel that gives Gevrey its second name, the Grand Cru of Chambertin.

Around A.D. 630, Algamaire, the Duke of Southern Burgundy, endowed the Abbey of Bèze with some land in Gevrey. The monks turned the land into a vineyard and found that they could produce an extraordinary wine. Some six centuries later, the field next to the abbey was bought by a peasant named Bertin and was called the Champs de Bertin, or "Bertin's field." Inspired by the success of the abbey vineyards, Bertin also planted vines on his field, and the name was soon shortened to Chambertin. But it was not Bertin, nor even the monks of the Abbey of Bèze, who · expanded the fame of the vineyard; that was left to a man named Claude Jobert, who in 1702 acquired not only Chambertin but the Clos de Bèze as well. On account of the quality of his wines and the wealth which made him able to build this *monopole* of excellence, Jobert could not be ignored by the wine merchants of Beaune, Dijon, and Nuits-Saint-Georges. Jobert actually changed his own name to Jobert-Chambertin. The vineyards are no longer united, as they were under Jobert, but are divided up into plots belonging to more than two dozen growers.

Chambertin has a great history and a great reputation, and there can be no wonder that the other vineyards of the town have wished to capitalize on it. Under the present law, the only ones that are allowed to use the name Chambertin attached to their own are several immediately adjoining it. Since the Clos de Bèze is considered on a par with Chambertin—and indeed can sell its wines as Chambertin if it so desires—it is allowed to place the magic name before its own, while the others may only add it after. They are Charmes, Chapelle, Griotte, Mazis (or Mazys), Ruchottes, and Latricières; the Great Growth vineyard of Mazoyères is now sold as Charmes-Chambertin. The plots range in size from 5.4 hectares (13 acres), in Chapelle, to 3 hectares (7 acres), in Ruchottes, and their fame rests on little more than a total of 25,000 cases of wine per year.

Each *climat* has subtle differences, and the Gevrey growers, no matter which ones they own, can be eloquent about them all.

One of the best growers on the slope is Jean Trapet, who has made wine all his life, as his father, grandfather, and great-grandfather did before him. "I guess it shows a certain lack of imagination on our part," he says, "but I wouldn't trade places with anyone." To see his cellar is enough to see why. Barrels of Chambertin, Latricières, and Charmes, some of the world's most sought-after wines, line the walls waiting out the two years or so before bottling. M. Trapet explains some of the differences among the Chambertin wines this way: "Around the central hub of Chambertin and Clos de Bèze all the vineyards are related, differing mostly by their position on the slope—the wines of those higher up being more elegant and of those lower down being more full. Chapelle is very similar to Clos de Bèze, especially with its perfumed nose, but it lacks the depth, body, and final grandeur of Clos de Bèze. Griotte, which is right next to it, gets its name from the whiff of the cherry [*griotte*] it can have. Charmes has a character similar to that of Chapelle and Griotte. Ruchottes and Mazis are related in the same way, with a shade more finesse found in the Ruchottes, which is a bit higher on the slope. The Latricières vineyard is on the same level on the slope as Chambertin and distinguishes itself from its illustrious neighbors by giving a wine of greater finesse and bouquet but a shade less power."

For some fifteen years, starting in the late forties, I was part-owner of a one-hectare parcel at the top of the Latricières slope of vineyard. The easiest access to my vines was through the adjoining Latricières property belonging to a M. Camus. But Burgundian wine-makers are exceedingly strong-minded men: I had once criticized M. Camus' wines; he refused me the right-of-way. My poor *vigneron* was forced to use a roundabout route through the vines of the Trapet family, who then and today make the best Latricières.

South from the village of Gevrey, the vineyard road takes you through the heart of these renowned parcels, and in the time it takes to recite their names they are behind you: Chambertin-Clos de Bèze off to your right, with Chapelle and Griotte on your left; literally seconds later Chambertin and Charmes-Chambertin flank you on either side, followed by Latricières. Before you've had time to take it all in, you're over the line and in the commune of Morey-Saint-Denis.

While the great Chambertins are on the slope south of the village, there are other excellent vineyards on the north side as well—Clos Saint-Jacques, Varoilles, Etournelles, Les Cazetiers. Today, most of these are included among the official First Growths and are allowed to add the vineyard name to the name of the commune (selling, for example, as Gevrey-Chambertin Clos Saint-Jacques) or may add the words *Premier Cru* to the name of the commune. Many experts consider it a mistake that, for many years, the vineyards of Varoilles and Clos Saint-Jacques were not included with the finest vineyards of the commune and given Great Growth status. Their excellent wines compare very favorably with the others, except those of Chambertin and the Chambertin-Clos de Bèze.

The communal wines of the village—those that go to market with the words "Gevrey-Chambertin" and no other indication of origin—are less impressive, of course, although some can be very pleasant. Most of them are grown in Gevrey-Chambertin, but some may come from the better vineyards in the neighboring town of Brochon. The amount of wine sold as Gevrey-Chambertin or as Gevrey-Chambertin Premier Cru comes to around 140,000 cases from 200 or so hectares (500 acres).

OUTSTANDING GREAT GROWTH VINEYARDS (*Grands Crus*)

VINEYARD	HECTARES	ACRES
Chambertin	13.5	32.5
Chambertin-Clos de Bèze	15	37.5

GREAT GROWTH VINEYARDS (*Grands Crus*)

Latricières	7	17.5
Mazis (or Mazys)	12.6	31.5
Mazoyères	19.1	47.5
Charmes	12.5	31
Ruchottes and the Clos des Ruchottes	3.1	8.5
Griotte	5.5	13.5
Chapelle	5.1	12.6

PRINCIPAL FIRST GROWTHS (*Premiers Crus*)

Clos Saint-Jacques	7	17.5
Varoilles	6	15
Etournelles	2	5
Les Cazetiers	8	20

LIST OF PRINCIPAL OWNERS OF CHAMBERTIN
AND CHAMBERTIN-CLOS DE BÈZE

Domaine Damoy	J. Drouhin	Consortium Vinicole
Domaine Marion	Peirazeau	Gelin
Louis Latour	Groffier	Tortochot
Philippe Remy	Philippe Duroche	Clair-Daü
L. Camus	André Bart	Mollard-Grivot
Domaine Rebourseau	Elvina	Louis Remy
Domaine Trapet	J. Prieur	Bouchard Père et Fils
Drouhin-Laroze	De Marcilly	Zibetti Frères
Jaboulet-Vercherre	J. and H. Dufouleur	

MOREY-SAINT-DENIS

From Gevrey-Chambertin the Route des Grands Crus leads straight to Morey-Saint-Denis. It is here that the wines of the Côte de Nuits change: the Morey vineyards of Clos de la Roche and Clos Saint-Denis serve as a bridge between the hard sturdiness of the northern part of the commune and the softer, elegant distinction of the Bonnes Mares, Musignys, and other wines from the next commune southward, Chambolle. Hard or soft, sturdy or elegant, one thing is certain: compared to the rest of the Côte de Nuits, these Morey wines are little known.

In bygone days, well before the Appellation Contrôlée laws of the 1930s, although a considerable quantity of Morey wine was made, hardly any was sold as Morey. Most of it was blended with that of its neighbors or sold unblushingly as Gevrey-Chambertin or Chambolle-Musigny. As a result, Morey never achieved star status; and even today relatively few wine lovers are familiar with the commune or its wines—which thus are not in heavy demand and can sometimes be a good value.

The village is unimpressive; few visitors see more from the vineyard road than a main square. However, beside the square—enclosed in a great wall—is the domain of the Clos des Lambrays, one of Morey's better vineyards, and next to it is the Clos de Tart.

In 1860, the best vineyards of Burgundy were rated. By this classification, the finest wines of Morey were considered to be Clos de Tart, Clos des Lambrays, and Bonnes Mares—although Bonnes Mares has only a small foothold in Morey, most of it falling into Chambolle-Musigny. In 1936, the classification was altered, so that the commune's finest wines were now officially listed as: Clos de Tart, Clos de la Roche, Clos Saint-Denis, and Bonnes Mares. Many critics, including myself, felt that the omission of the Clos des Lambrays from this list was a grave mistake, for the wines of Lambrays were made in the traditional manner of long vatting by Mme Cosson and in good years were among the great wines of the slope.

In 1955, I bought from the ebullient Mme Renée Cosson a large part of the 1949 vintage, three cases of which went into my cellar at the Prieuré. I drank one of the remaining bottles in 1977 and without a doubt it was one of the great red wines I had that year. (The 1918 which I had several days later was not in the same class.) In the late sixties Robert Cosson took the operation over from his mother, selling the wines to shippers. In 1980, the Clos des Lambrays was sold, and the new owners, the Saier family, have since rightly succeeded in upgrading this fine vineyard to a Great Growth (*Grand Cru*); and they received an even greater accolade when the I.N.A.O. made Lambrays an Appellation Contrôlée.

Adjoining the Clos des Lambrays is the Clos de Tart, its steep slope held back by a high retaining wall adorned with the vineyard emblem and its owner's name, J. Mommessin, a shipper in Mâcon. Clos de Tart is among the sturdiest of the Morey wines, followed generally by Clos de la Roche.

Bonnes Mares, adjoining Clos de la Roche, straddles the border between Morey-Saint-Denis and Chambolle-Musigny, though (as noted above) it falls mostly in the latter. To the eye there is no distinction between the vines of the two communes. But the soil of the 1.8 hectares (4.6 acres) on the Morey side produces a harder wine than does that of the 13.7 hectares (33.9 acres) within Chambolle-Musigny. Having once owned a small parcel in Bonnes Mares consisting of about fifteen rows of vines, I always marveled at these infinite variations of the soil, which year in year out created consistent differences between my wines on the Chambolle side and those of my neighbors in Morey.

It is worth remembering that until the early sixties some of the important principles of the secondary fermentation, known as the malolactic fermentation, were not properly understood and were often a major problem in Burgundy. Wine samples sent to M. Michel, the oenologist at Beaune, would come back approved as having completed this fermentation and were supposed to be ready for bottling. But the change of temperature after shipment would trigger the latent incomplete malolactic, spoiling the wine. The carbon dioxide that condensed in the bottle as a by-product of the fermentation would make the wine slightly sparkling, or *pétillant,* in addition to spoiling the bouquet. An unattractive deposit of tartrates would form on the sides of the bottle. I recall that this happened to many great estate-bottlings of the 1955 vintage that had been exported, necessitating their return to France. Since then considerable progress has been made in research. Now in all the cellars of Burgundy and Beaujolais and in the *chais* of Bordeaux, wine-makers can be heard discussing their "malo" problem and heaving sighs of relief when competent and dependable laboratory analysis shows that the contents of their vats have truly completed this phase of the magical transformation into wine.

A typical grower's cellar in Burgundy is that of Jacques Seysses, one of the new and younger lights of the Côte de Nuits in Morey-Saint-Denis. An ambitious businessman who worked for his father's Belin biscuit company until it was sold to Nabisco, M. Seysses bottles his wines under the name Domaine Dujac. He inherited his interest in fine wines from his father, who was president of the Club des Cent, without doubt one of the most refined and exclusive food and wine societies in the world. In the late sixties, the older Seysses aided his son in the purchase of parcels of the top vineyards in Morey and the neighboring commune of Chambolle-Musigny. With his holdings in Clos Saint-Denis, Clos de la Roche, Bonnes Mares, and Échézeaux all producing varying amounts of wine, Jacques Seysses needs to have vats of all sizes. "The first fermentation, where the yeasts and enzymes turn the sugar into alcohol, should take place in a vat that's nearly full, so naturally I need different-sized vats to accommodate different holdings," he says. "After the fermentation is complete, I like to heat the cellar up a bit just when I put the wine into the barrel. This way I can be sure that the secondary fermentation—where the malic acid breaks down into lactic acid and carbon dioxide—gets started promptly. This used to be a problem in Burgundy, where the small vats would lose their heat rapidly and the wine would cool off too much. If the temperature stayed too low, then this fermentation might be delayed until after the wine was bottled. But since 1968, when I began here, I haven't had any trouble."

The malolactic fermentation is a vital step in proper vinification. The change from malic acid to lactic acid means a drop in overall acidity in the wines, not only making them more drinkable sooner but also allowing the delicate components of aroma and bouquet to declare themselves. A wine that has not undergone its "malo" will smell strongly of raw green apples, an unpleasant and out-of-place odor in fine red wines.

Apart from the four top-rated growths, there are 102 hectares (251 acres) of vineyard in the commune, producing annually some 35,000 cases of red wine.

GREAT GROWTHS (*Grands Crus*)

VINEYARD	HECTARES	ACRES
Les Bonnes Mares (*see also under Chambolle-Musigny, p. 163*)	1.8	4.6
Clos de la Roche	16.0	40.0
Clos Saint-Denis	6.6	16.5
Clos de Tart	7.5	18.75
Clos des Lambrays	8.7	21.75

FIRST GROWTHS (*Premiers Crus*)

VINEYARD	HECTARES	ACRES
Les Ruchots	2.6	6.5
Les Sorbés	3	7.3
Le Clos Sorbés	3.3	8.2
Les Millandes	4.3	10.6
Le Clos des Ormes (*in part*)	4.8	12
Meix-Rentiers	1.2	2.9
Monts-Luisants	1.5	3.7
Les Bouchots	2	5
Les Blanchards	1.1	4.5
Clos Bussière	3.1	7.4
Aux Charmes	1.2	3.1
Les Charnières	2.4	6
Côte-Rôtie	.4	1.3
Les Mauchamps	2.5	6.2
Les Froichots	0.6	1.6
Les Genevrières	.9	2.2
Les Chaffots	1.25	3
Les Chénevery (*in part*)	3.25	8
La Riotte	2.47	6.1
Clos Baulet	.8	2.1
Les Gruenchers	.6	1.5
Les Façonnières	1.7	4.3

❧

CHAMBOLLE-MUSIGNY

Past the vineyard of Bonnes Mares, the vineyard road swings right into the town of Chambolle, tucked under the highest hill of the Golden Slope. Flanked on the north by a craggy outcrop, the village is a cluster of handsome houses and courtyards of winegrowers. The typical Burgundian houses are made of reddish-brown stone with pretty wooden porches trimmed with geraniums. The linden tree at the southern end of town is said to be the oldest extant in France, planted in the time of Henry IV. Chambolle is the most picturesque of all Côte de Nuits villages, boasting—if that is the word—the most "expensive" cemetery in the world, on land which, if it were a vineyard, would cost more than a million francs a hectare.

Chambolle-Musigny's vineyards cover about 180 hectares (450 acres)—the most expensive of which are Bonnes Mares and Les Musigny, on opposite sides of town—and produce some 90,000 cases of wine, nearly all red. The red wines are full yet delicate, elegant, entrancingly perfumed, and have the fragile yet resolute charm of so-called "feminine" wines. The white Musigny—made in very small quantities—shares some of the greatness of the reds, but tends to lack the finesse of its scarlet sisters.

In addition to Bonnes Mares, scarcer and superior is Les Musigny, the vineyard whose name was added to that of the village in the nineteenth century, as is so often the case with the communes of the Côte d'Or. The wine is noted for its balance of fullness with delicacy, glorious perfume, and lingering bouquet. It is truly one of the great wines of Burgundy. The largest owner is the Comte de Vogüé, related to the Champagne family that owns Moët et Chandon. The other owners are the Domaine Mugnier and Berthaut-Hudelot.

Other superb wines are included among the First Growths (*Premiers Crus*)—wines that have stature and breeding but generally fall just below the topmost two. This status is signified by labels bearing both communal and vineyard name. One of the best is Les Amoureuses, directly below the vineyard of Musigny and lying on the imaginary dividing line that separates Chambolle-Musigny and Vougeot.

Below Les Amoureuses is a steep bank that drops down to a narrow plateau, then plunges another 30 meters to the valley floor, dividing the slope into four levels in all. It is here that the Vouge River chooses to meander out of the mountainside and across the valley. Standing on the plateau above its mouth, you can look southeast and see the whole of the Clos de Vougeot spread out below you. The main valley road bounds the walled vineyard on the east; the vineyard road bounds it on the west. The turrets of the château of the Clos de Vougeot catch the sunlight, while the great vineyards of Musigny slant up the slope behind you. For many, here lies the heart of Burgundy.

GREAT GROWTHS (*Grands Crus*)

VINEYARD	HECTARES	ACRES
Les Musigny	10.7	26.4
Les Bonnes Mares (*in part; see*		
Morey-Saint-Denis for balance)	13.7	33.9

FIRST GROWTHS (*Premiers Crus*)

VINEYARD	HECTARES	ACRES
Les Amoureuses	5.25	13
Les Charmes	5.8	14.4
Les Cras (*in part*)	4.5	10.4
Les Borniques	1.5	3.6
Les Baudes	3.5	8.8
Les Plantes	2.6	6.3
Les Hauts-Doix	1.75	4.3
Les Chatelots	2.6	6.3
Les Gruenchers	3	7.3
Les Groseilles	1.5	3.7
Les Fuées	6.2	15.3
Les Lavrottes	1	2.5
Derrière-la-Grange	0.73	1.8
Les Noirots	2.9	7.1
Les Sentiers	4.8	12.2
Les Fousselottes	4	10
Aux Beaux-Bruns	2.4	6
Les Combottes	0.65	1.6
Aux Combottes	2.27	5.6
Les Carrières	0.7	1.7
Les Chabiots	2.0	5.0
Combe d'Orveau	2.3	5.7
Aux Échanges	1.0	2.5
Les Grands Murs	0.9	2.2

VOUGEOT AND ITS CLOS

Stand on the vineyard road on the bluff to the south of Chambolle-Musigny and you can see the land pitch sharply downwards in front of you, revealing on the plateau below the famous castle of the Clos de Vougeot surrounded by vineyards, the whole enclosed by a weatherbeaten stone wall.

Excepting the Clos—at 50 hectares (124 acres) the largest single vineyard in Burgundy and one of the most famous in the world—there is not a great deal to Vougeot. A tiny settlement nestles to one side of the low wall with its small arched entryways, and outside this wall—the *"clos"*—lie several vineyards. They total about 12 hectares (30 acres) and account for about 4,000 cases of wine. Their wines are sold—if they conform to the proper minimum standards—as Vougeot, followed by the name of the vineyard.

Commune and Clos take their name from the Vouge River, a tiny stream that comes flowing down the hill separating Vougeot from Chambolle-Musigny. The settlement is an ancient one and its vineyards have been in continuous cultivation for centuries, for when the Cistercians arrived at the beginning of the twelfth century these were among the lands given to them by the local squires. Building their monastery downhill from the vines, the monks subsequently pieced together the vineyard which lies within the walls of the Clos, erected the château, and with the wine made the name famous, leaving their stamp on the other vineyards of the area as well. Historians have claimed that no single group in history has done so much for the cause of fine wines as the Cistercian monks, and their crowning achievements are the Clos de Vougeot and Kloster Eberbach in Germany's Rheingau.

The vineyards beyond the Clos are Les Petits-Vougeots, Les Cras, and Clos Blanc de Vougeot, or La Vigne-Blanche (planted in Pinot Chardonnay and producing white wine). The Clos Blanc is very small, less than 2 hectares (5 acres) in all, and most of it is owned by L'Héritier-Guyot, a Dijon shipping firm which is also a maker of cassis.

The Clos de Vougeot vineyard is so famous that it is practically a national monument to France. In the sixteenth century the vineyard was so big that it was felt that a château and a house for the wine-press should be added to the buildings inside the wall. The drawing-up of the plans for this building was entrusted to a young and zealous monk, who went to work with fervor but made the mistake of appending his signature to the completed blueprint. The abbot informed him that he had committed the deadly sin of pride and ordered that his plans should be given to other monks to complete. These new hands made a hopeless botch of the job. Legend has it that the original architect repented of his sin and died of chagrin, following which the Clos was built complete with all its structural faults as a memorial to his fall from grace. It remained in the hands of the clergy until the French Revolution, when the state confiscated Church property.

Since its foundation, the building has undergone repeated additions and renovations, and now it is in the hands of the Confrérie des Chevaliers du Tastevin de Bourgogne, the society which makes sure that the rest of the world does not forget the wines of Burgundy. The members of the order, who are mostly shippers, growers, and visiting dignitaries interested in wines, meet several times a year in the great dining room of the château, and the halls which once resounded with the plainsong of the Church now reverberate with the noise and tumult of the Chevaliers' drinking songs—and loud praises of Burgundy. The great dining hall can seat five hundred, and the towering stone pillars are hung with old leather harvest baskets, each bearing a coat of arms and inscribed with the date of a famous vintage, beginning with 1108.

Since the vineyard was confiscated after the Revolution, it has seldom been under a single ownership. The last sole proprietor lived in the nineteenth century, and his grave lies beside the terraced drive leading up to the forbidding gates of the château. Since his death the ownership has become more and more diverse, and there are now over one hundred growers and shippers within the walls.

Each one of the owners has his own plot of vines of varying ages, the older vines producing the better wine. Those planted along the flat plain bordering N-74 will most likely produce a distinctly inferior wine. As you climb the slope the middle section can be very good, and the top of the vineyard at the level of the château will be the best. Each grower will tend his vines as he sees fit, picking the grapes when he feels that it is time and making wine from them according to his talent, conscience, and ability. Once made, the wines, which total about 20,000 cases or so for the whole 50 hectares, will be sold to different people, some in barrel to shippers and some bottled by the growers. This illustrates the impossibility of generalized comments on vineyards in Burgundy, especially one as big as Clos de Vougeot. In any given vintage, Clos de Vougeot will be sold under hundreds of different labels, some poor, some good, some excellent. I pity the consumer who tries to distinguish from the label the quality of the wine inside, unless he's been able to determine in advance the reliability of the name on the label. Nevertheless, if a summation has to be made, it would be fair to say that in a good year a characteristic Clos de Vougeot is relatively full-bodied and with a big nose. It will not have all the austere majesty of a Chambertin nor the delicate grace of a Musigny or a Romanée-Saint-Vivant but inclines toward the latter. In any case, it is a mouth-filling wine, and the aftertastes can be memorable and lingering. It always manages to preserve a certain delicacy and often has an assertive bouquet all its own.

GREAT GROWTH (*Grand Cru*)

VINEYARD	HECTARES	ACRES
Clos de Vougeot	50	124

FIRST GROWTHS (*Premiers Crus*)

VINEYARD	HECTARES	ACRES
Clos Blanc de Vougeot	1.8	4.6
Les Petits-Vougeots	5.8	14.4
Les Cras	4.2	10.6

LIST OF PRINCIPAL OWNERS
OF CLOS DE VOUGEOT

Amis de Clos-Vougeot	Vougeot
Arnoux-Salbreux	Vosne-Romanée
Beaufour, Noblet, Adrien	Gevrey-Chambertin
Albert Bichot	Beaune
Bocquillon-Liger-Belair	Nuits-Saint-Georges
Roger Capitain	Ladoix-Serrigny
Vve Carrelet de Loisy	Nuits-Saint-Georges
Clair-Daü	Marsannay-La-Côte
Félix Clerger Philibert	Beaune
Christian Confuron	Vougeot
Joseph Confuron	Vosne-Romanée
Vve Jean Confuron	Prémeaux-Prissey
Firmin Coquard	Morey-Saint-Denis
Jean Coquard	Morey-Saint-Denis
Maurice Corbet	Morey-Saint-Denis
Domaine Joseph Drouhin	Beaune
Drouhin-Laroze	Gevrey-Chambertin
Vve Drouhin-Laroze	Gevrey-Chambertin
Jean Dufouleur	Nuits-Saint-Georges
Domaine René Engel et Fils	Vosne-Romanée
André P. Fage	Paris
C. V. V. Faiveley	Nuits-Saint-Georges
Henri Gouroux	Flagey-Échézeaux
Louis Gouroux	Flagey-Échézeaux
Vve Gaston Grivot	Vosne-Romanée
Colette Gros	Vosne-Romanée

François Gros	Vosne-Romanée
Gustave Gros	Vosne-Romanée
Michel-Louis Gros	Vosne-Romanée
Bernard Guyot (Société Viticole Beaujolaise)	Saint Georges-de-Reneins
L'Héritier Guyot	Vougeot
Alfred Haegelen	Vosne-Romanée
Émile Haegelen	Nuits-Saint-Georges
Henri Haegelen	Boulogne-Billancourt
Successeurs Jean Hudelot	Chambolle-Musigny
Noël Hudelot	Vougeot
Paul Indelli	Paris
Jaboulet-Vercherre	Pommard
Jaffelin Frères	Beaune
Geneviève Lamarche	Vosne-Romanée
Henri Lamarche	Vosne-Romanée
Lejay-Lagoutte	Dijon
Leroy	Auxey-Duresses
Leymarie-Coste Vougeot	Eghezee (Belgium)
Jean Méo	Paris
Pierre Merat	Beaune
Misset-Bailly	Dijon
Mongeard Mugneret & Fils	Vosne-Romanée
Jean Morin	Nuits-Saint-Georges
Georges Mugneret	Vosne-Romanée
Étienne Mugnier	Dijon
Charles S. C. Noëllat	Vosne-Romanée
Henri Noëllat	Vosne-Romanée
Jean Nourissat	Dijon
Vve Parfait-Sallot	Chambolle-Musigny
Sté Piat	Mâcon
P. Ponnelle Petits & Fils	Beaune
Ponts et Chaussées	Dijon
Mme H. Pradal	Paris
J. Prieur	Meursault
Vve Rameau (Gendre G. Vadey)	Morey-Saint-Denis
Domaine H. Rebourseau	Gevrey-Chambertin
Raymond Roblot	Vosne-Romanée
Ropiteau-Mignon	Meursault
Alain Roumier	Chambolle-Musigny
Alain Roumier-Quanquin	Chambolle-Musigny
Maria Salbreux	Dijon
Germain Tardy	Morey-Saint-Denis
Jean Thomas	Nuits-Saint-Georges
Clos de Thorey (Thomas)	Nuits-Saint-Georges
Tortochot	Gevrey-Chambertin

Robert Tourlière	Beaune
Mme Wilhem	Fresnes
Domaine des Varoilles	Gevrey-Chambertin

FLAGEY-ÉCHÉZEAUX

Behind the Clos de Vougeot and higher up on the slope are the vineyards of Flagey-Échézeaux. They are in a curious and confusing position because the town of Flagey itself is far down on the plain across the main road, N-74. It is also on the wrong side of the railroad tracks, both literally and figuratively, for there are no vineyards of quality near it on that side of the main road and so far from the slope. Yet the vineyards above the Clos de Vougeot bearing the Échézeaux label are among the finest of the Côte de Nuits. Flagey-Échézeaux as a commune has no *appellation,* hence will not appear on labels except as an address of a grower. If lesser parcels are not sold as Échézeaux or Grand Échézeaux, they can be sold under the label of Vosne-Romanée.

Échézeaux comprises 30 hectares (74 acres) and makes approximately 13,000 cases of wine a year. A much smaller plot, wedged in between Clos de Vougeot and Les Échézeaux, is Les Grands-Échézeaux—"grand" not in size but in its superiority to Échézeaux. The wines of both are excellent *Grands Crus,* bridging the gap between the sturdiness of the better Vougeots and the more delicate wines of Vosne-Romanée, the commune to the south.

The Domaine de la Romanée-Conti is one of the owners of Grands-Échézeaux and Les Échézeaux. Another owner is the son of the late René Engel, who was one of the greatest raconteurs and sources of the wisdom and lore of the entire Côte d'Or. The heirs of Louis Gros are also owners.

For vineyard listing, see under Vosne-Romanée, pages 172–3.

VOSNE-ROMANÉE

Of all the Burgundy wine communes, Vosne-Romanée produces the greatest variety of high-priced wines. In fact, in recent years the prices for some of the rarest ones have shot up so dramatically as to be totally beyond the realm of value. Driving along the Route des Grands Crus, the vineyard road skirts the northern wall of

Clos de Vougeot, cuts between Les Échézeaux and Les Grands-Échézeaux, and in little more than a hundred meters crosses into Vosne-Romanée. The five greatest vineyards of Vosne—Romanée-Conti, La Tâche, Richebourg, La Romanée, and Romanée-Saint-Vivant—are minuscule even by Burgundian standards. Counted together they cover barely 26 hectares (65 acres), with a combined annual output of only about 11,000 cases. The scarcity and the resultant high prices of these wines have made them a status-seeker's emblem. Demand even for the largest of them—Romanée-Saint-Vivant—is so great that the growers could never hope to meet it. The rarity and cost of these wines should make drinking any of them a memorable event.

In spite of its small size—just 1.8 hectares (4.5 acres)—Romanée-Conti is the great vineyard of the commune, and one of the greatest of Burgundies. Its excellence was early recognized and it has always been highly sought after. Romanée-Conti was fed in spoonfuls to Louis XIV to cure his gastric fistula (an intestinal disorder, of which the Sun King had many). Today's doctors might laugh at the prescription, but they would not refuse the medicine.

The vineyard was later fought over by Louis XV's mistress, Mme de Pompadour, and the Prince de Conti, the king's top diplomat. The latter eventually prevailed, adding his name to the property in 1760. A century or so later, it was bought by the ancestors of one of the present owners, Aubert de Villaine, for 330,000 gold francs ($100,000 or $50,000)—cheap today but no mean price for the time.

The wines of Romanée-Conti fall into two distinct categories: the pre-1945 vintages and those thereafter. Until 1945, the owners of the vineyard—unlike all other French growers—managed to keep alive the old, pre-phylloxera French vines on French root-stocks. Over the years the vines had been propagated by the technique called *provinage*—burying the old vine in the ground with only one shoot emerging to become a new one. Thus they were direct descendants of the vines planted by the monks centuries earlier. The devastating phylloxera-bearing vine louse was a constant menace and the vines had to be tended with enormous care. During the war years, manpower was desperately short, and the vines deteriorated until they were yielding only a meager 50 cases a year. In 1945, the owners, then MM de Villaine and Chambon, gave up, tearing up their vineyards and replanting them with vines grafted onto phylloxera-resistant American root-stocks.

In the very great years the wines of the Romanée-Conti vineyard have perfect, rich balance combined with extraordinary breed and finesse, and local experts maintain they are the most "virile" of the wines of Vosne. They have an aftertaste that stays in the mouth an amazingly long time. While quantity is definitely higher than it once was, it is still not considerable, and an average harvest may come to only 700 cases.

* * *

Separated from the other "Greats" by the narrow strip of vineyards called La Grande Rue, owned by Henri Lamarche, is the superb vineyard of La Tâche. It resembles other wines made by the Domaine de la Romanée-Conti, which owns it.

In some vintages La Tâche has come forth with wines more open than Romanée-Conti, though with age the latter will nearly always prevail. The whole world must be satisfied with an annual production of about 1,700 cases of La Tâche.

Bordering both La Romanée-Conti and La Romanée is Richebourg, the second largest of the Vosne vineyards and second only to Romanée-Conti and La Tâche in world prestige and price. Beneath the velvet veneer characteristic of the very best Vosne wines is a robust fullness in both smell and taste. A well-made, well-kept bottle of Richebourg, like many of the Vosne Great Growths, will justify all of the excessively rhapsodic writing on wines which one finds in so many poetic books: truffles, cherries, violets, and a whole cabinet of subtle spices may rise out of the glass to be perceived by the amateur and professional alike. Unlike some of the other Great Growths of Vosne, Richebourg is not a monopoly of any one grower. On the contrary, at the time of this writing it is in the hands of eight different owners, three of whom have sizable holdings: Domaine Louis Gros, Domaine de la Romanée-Conti, and Charles Noëllat. I used to buy the full production of the last-named in the fifties and early sixties, but discontinued the practice when I began finding the wines too light and overpriced, and, on occasion, generally failing to live up to my expectations. Among the eight growers, an average 3,500 cases of the "velvet wine" of Vosne go forth into the world each year.

Just above La Romanée-Conti, divided from it by only a footpath, is the tiny vineyard of La Romanée. Despite the proximity of the vineyards and the similarity between the names, their wines are separate and distinct. La Romanée is perhaps the more robust of the two, making up in fullness and body for what it cedes in finesse. The vineyard is owned entirely by the Abbé Just Liger-Belair, and produces a mere 350 cases.

Just down the slope from La Romanée-Conti and Richebourg, beyond a narrow path, is Romanée-Saint-Vivant, stretching 9.5 hectares (24 acres) up to the back door of the village of Vosne-Romanée itself. The wines from Romanée-Saint-Vivant have a family resemblance to the better wines of the village but are a paler version of them—uniting all the qualities in a slightly minor key. It would be unfair, however, not to mention that they can be, in a good year and when well made, a rhapsody unto themselves.

The most important owner of the great Vosne vineyards today is the Domaine de la Romanée-Conti—a company equally shared by M. Aubert de Villaine and Mme Lalou Bize Leroy—which owns all of the Romanée-Conti and La Tâche vineyards, as well as parts of Richebourg, Grands-Échézeaux, and Échézeaux. The partnership cultivates, vinifies, bottles, and sells approximately half of the Romanée-Saint-Vivant vineyard production, the part formerly owned by the Marey-Monge family. In the late sixties the Domaine purchased a tiny slice of the great Burgundy white-wine vineyard Montrachet, giving them a great and expensive white to match its reds.

Because of the huge demand for the Domaine's top wine, Romanée-Conti, the company has a policy of tie-in sale which obliges its buyers—who are always seeking as much Romanée-Conti as possible—to buy an equal number of bottles or cases from its other vineyard holdings. This fine domaine, which often succeeded in making surprisingly good wines in off vintages, has also sold rather deficient wines from lesser years at prices far beyond their value. Because the wines have been estate-bottled for generations, the only significant collection of older vintages of Romanée-Conti is in the cellars at the Domaine—making a visit a mouth-watering experience. These caves are primitive and modest, but stacked with bottles whose contents have been described by P. Morton Shand, the English wine authority of the early 20th century, as "a mingling of velvet and satin."

These great wines of Vosne-Romanée are, in the opinion of many experts, the supreme examples of great Burgundy. Their balance is magnificent: no one characteristic stands out, but each is superb, and together they form a wine of almost unequaled perfection. All are big, sturdy, and full-bodied, with a satiny richness and the prospect of acquiring a splendid nose with age. Richebourg is perhaps the fullest; Romanée-Conti, La Romanée, and La Tâche being somewhat more delicate, in descending order. The only Burgundian equals of these are the two Chambertins, Les Musigny, Corton, and the best wines of Clos de Vougeot.

The great unifying factor in the wines of Vosne is their softness and finesse. This is true not only of the greatest vineyards but also of those classed just slightly below—such as Grande Rue, Gaudichots, Beaux-Monts (or Beaumonts), and Malconsorts, all of which produce wonderful wines. Some connoisseurs claim that the wines are at times too highly chaptalized, the added sugar making for an occasional over-sweet aftertaste. Nonetheless, the wines of Vosne are among the most glorious in the world.

On the main square of Vosne, shaded around by tall sycamores, is the domain of the Engel family, which was headed by the late René Engel (mentioned previously as a part-owner of Grands-Échézeaux). René Engel was one of the pre-war founders of the Chevaliers du Tastevin and used his considerable literary skills to write about his beloved Burgundy. His son, formerly mayor of Vosne, now dedicates his time to the family holdings at Clos de Vougeot and Grands-Échézeaux.

An example of a less easy transition from one generation to the next is the case of the late Louis Gros. Until his death in the sixties, he was an important grower in Vosne-Romanée, and I selected many top barrels of Richebourg and Clos de Vougeot from his cellars in the years when we were beginning estate-bottlings. Tragically, when he died, a division and rivalry developed among his four children—three sons and a daughter—each of whom inherited part of the family domain and vineyard holdings. His house, begun before his death and in-tended to be one of the largest and most impressive in Vosne, stands unfinished today, with no panes in the frames of the upper-floor windows. One son—Gus-tave—has retired entirely from wine and from the politics that formerly occu-pied him. Disgusted by the family squabbles and fatigued by the extra effort that domain-bottling requires, he has decided (rashly, in my opinion) not to sell his wine under the extremely desirable place-name of Richebourg but to sell it off quickly in barrel to shippers under the generic commune name of Vosne-Romanée.

At Vosne-Romanée the Route des Grand Crus rejoins the main road, N-74.

In Vosne-Romanée:

GREAT GROWTHS (*Grand Crus*)

VINEYARD	HECTARES	ACRES
La Romanée-Conti	1.8	4.5
La Tâche	6	14.9
Le Richebourg	8	19.8
La Romanée	0.83	2
La Romanée-Saint-Vivant	8.5	21.2

FIRST GROWTHS (*Premiers Crus*)

Les Gaudichots	5.8	14.3
Les Malconsorts	5.9	14.7
La Grande Rue	1.3	3.3
Les Beaux-Monts (also Beaumonts)	2.4	6
Les Suchots	13.1	32.4
Clos des Réas	2.1	5.3
Aux Brûlées	3.8	9.6
Les Petits-Monts	3.7	9.2
Aux Reignots	1.7	4.2
Les Chaumes	7.4	17.9

In Flagey-Échézeaux:

GREAT GROWTHS (*Grands Crus*)

VINEYARD	HECTARES	ACRES
Grands-Échézeaux	9.2	23
Échézeaux	30	74

NUITS-SAINT-GEORGES

Nuits-Saint-Georges, with a population of 5,500, is the capital of the Côte de Nuits, largely devoted to the production of wine. Many of the growers of the Côte de Nuits live in Nuits, and many of the shippers and brokers of the region keep their offices here. As a wine town, it presents an image very different from that of bustling, wine-promotion-minded Beaune. In comparison, Nuits seems sober-sided, businesslike, and colorless. Much of its business comes from by-products of wine: Marc de Bourgogne, the fiery brandy distillate made from the pressed skins; Cassis, the black currant liqueur; grape juice; and sparkling Burgundy. Sparkling Burgundy was created by shippers to help them compete with Champagne sales and fame. It is made of small wines that could not normally demand a good price. These are seldom worth drinking and are a poor bargain in countries like the U.S., where the duty is the same as that for Champagne. Now little is found inside or outside France—and so much the better.

The official place-name of Nuits-Saint-Georges covers 376 hectares (940 acres) of vineyards in Nuits and in nearby Prémeaux, a little to the south, these two making up the last of the important communes before the soil changes to emerge as the Côte de Beaune. Actually, the Côte de Nuits extends slightly farther to the south, through the towns of Comblanchien and Corgoloin, whose wines can only be sold as Côtes de Nuits-Villages at best. They are far better known for their limestone and marble quarries, which were the source of the marble for the Paris Opera House.

None of the thirty-odd vineyards in Nuits was included among the thirty-one Great Growths (*Grands Crus*)—the top-rated vineyards of the Côte d'Or, as classified by the I.N.A.O. Nevertheless, some very great vineyards are to be found. They are split nearly evenly between the slope north of Nuits, bordering on Vosne, and the southern slope, which continues to Prémeaux and has ten First Growth vineyards sold as Nuits-Saint-Georges.

After reaching Vosne-Romanée, the vineyard road joins N-74, the main vineyard highway for the Côte d'Or. Anyone who continues on one of the vineyard paths through the First Growths of Vosne will, in less than 200 yards, cross into the beginning of the vineyards of Nuits. Approaching the town from the north, one sees the first of the vineyards on the right and on the lower slope descending from Vosne-Romanée toward the town of Nuits itself. The best vineyard north of town is Aux Boudots. The slope drops gently to a dried-up trickle of a stream and another slope begins on the other side, rising steeply in a great rocky bluff topped with trees and underbrush. Only the lower third of the southern slope is planted in vines, but along it are the best of the vineyards of Nuits: Les Pruliers, Les Porrets (or Porets), Les Cailles, Les Saint-Georges, and, slightly above Saint-Georges, Les Vaucrains. Les Saint-Georges lies along the town line, and to its south are Didiers, Clos des Forêts, and Clos de la Maréchale, the best growths of Prémeaux.

The wines of Nuits are distinguished by their firmness: they are full of texture, or tannin, with so much body that you can actually, so to speak, take bites out of them. They mature slowly, but with age acquire honorable consistency. The firmest is generally Vaucrains, one of the finest of the commune and indeed of the whole Côte de Nuits. Bouquet is also a Nuits characteristic, and the wines are sometimes quite pungent. In most years Les Saint-Georges will, because of its finesse, take the honors in this field, and in addition will be deeper in color and more "winey" than the others. Les Pruliers often starts out with a slightly metallic taste, but this passes and the wine ages wonderfully. Les Porrets and particularly the Clos des Porrets are the fruitiest. Clos des Porrets is a small section of the larger vineyard, and is the best part. It is owned entirely by the sons of Henri Gouges, who was one of the staunchest advocates of authentic Burgundy wines as well as one of Burgundy's most respected growers. Domaine Gouges also makes a good white wine but only in small quantities, and most of it is sold in Paris at Le Taillevent, whose wine list is one of the best in France. Boudots is another good vineyard, and Cailles combines the typical Nuits characteristics with a special velvety quality all its own.

In Nuits-Saint-Georges:

FIRST GROWTHS (*Premiers Crus*)

VINEYARD	HECTARES	ACRES
Les Saint-Georges	7.5	18.6
Les Vaucrains	6.2	15.5
Les Cailles	3.8	9.4
Les Porrets (or Porets)	7.1	17.8
Les Pruliers	7.1	17.8
Aux Boudots	6.3	15.8
Les Hauts-Pruliers (*in part*)	4.5	11.2

Aux Murgers	4.9	12.2
La Richemone	2.2	5.5
Les Chaboeufs	2.8	7.0
La Perrière	3.4	8.5
La Roncière	2.2	5.5
Les Procès	1.9	4.7
Rue-de-Chaux	2.1	5.3
Aux Cras	3.0	7.7
Aux Chaignots	5.9	14.8
Aux Thorey (*in part*)	5.0	12.5
Aux Vignes Rondes	3.8	9.5
Aux Bousselots	4.2	10.5
Les Poulettes	2.1	5.3
Aux Crots (*in part*)	4.5	11.3
Les Vallerots (*in part*)	0.9	2.3
Aux Champs-Perdrix (*in part*)	0.7	1.8
Perrière-Noblet (*in part*)	0.3	0.7
Aux Damodes (*in part*)	8.5	21.3
En La Chaine-Carteau (*in part*)	2.5	6.3
Aux Argillats (*in part*)	1.9	4.8
Clos de la Maréchale	9.5	23.6
Clos-Arlots	6.7	16.8
Clos des Corvées	7.5	18.8
Clos des Forêts	7.1	17.8
Les Didiers	2.5	6.3
Aux Perdrix	3.5	8.8
Les Corvées-Paget	1.6	3.9
Les Clos Saint-Marc	0.9	2.2
Clos des Argilières	4.4	11.0
Clos des Grandes-Vignes (*in part*)	2.2	5.6

The delimited area of *appellation contrôlée* Nuits-Saint-Georges covers a total of 318.2 hectares, of which 151.2 are classified as First Growths.

SOCIÉTÉ CIVILE DU DOMAINE DE LA ROMANÉE-CONTI
PROPRIETAIRE A VOSNE-ROMANÉE (COTE-D'OR)

ROMANÉE-CONTI

APPELLATION ROMANÉE-CONTI CONTROLÉE

7.220 Bouteilles Récoltées

N°   LES ASSOCIÉS-GÉRANTS

ANNÉE 1974

Mise en bouteille au domaine   75 cl
PRODUCE OF FRANCE

☙❧

CÔTE DE NUITS
Hotels and Restaurants

H = *Hotel;* R = *Restaurant*

The visitor to the Côte de Nuits should also consult the "Hotels and Restaurants" sections on pp. 137–39, 145–49, and 203–06, plus Itinerary C, pp. 420–21, Itinerary D, pp. 421–22, Itinerary G, pp. 425–26, and Itinerary J, pp. 427–28.

MARSANNAY-LA-CÔTE (21160—Côte d'Or)
(Paris 331—Dijon 8—Beaune 37)

❧ Village producing the best rosé of Burgundy. From Dijon, take either N-74, the main vineyard road, or D-122 (Avenue J. Jaurès).

H NOVOTEL: On N-74. Tel.: 80.52.14.22. Tlx.: 350728.   122 rooms.
Clean, quiet, and functional rooms. Inexpensive grill for simple snacks. Air-conditioned.

R LES GOURMETS. Tel.: 80.52.16.32.
Good, small, popular restaurant on road leading through the vineyards. Burgundian specialties prepared by Joël Perreaut, the owner since 1979. Try the *jambon persillé,* and *coq au vin,* and if red

Burgundy is your choice for lunch, have some Marsannay rosé as an aperitif. Weather permitting, you may eat in the garden.

GEVREY-CHAMBERTIN (21220—Côte d'Or)
(Paris 309—Beaune 27—Dijon 13—Nuits-Saint-Georges 10)

This famous wine village is the northern gateway to the *Route des Grands Crus* (D-122) and the vineyards of the Côte d'Or. D-122, which runs parallel to N-74, will eventually lead you to Vosne-Romanée.

H HÔTEL LES GRANDS CRUS: Route des Grands Crus. Tel.: 80.34.30.76.   24 decent rooms. Simple, quiet, and clean hotel, opened in 1977, and situated in the midst of the vineyards. No restaurant, but breakfast available.

H LES TERROIRS: 28, route de Dijon, on the N-74. Tel.: 80.34.34.15.   24 soundproofed rooms; no restaurant.

R LA RÔTISSERIE DU CHAMBERTIN: Rue du Chambertin. Tel.: 80.34.33.20. In one of the great red-wine-producing villages of Burgundy, the artistically re-created rooms showing coopers and cellar masters at work—off the hallway to the cellar dining room—are well worth a visit. Taped Burgundian drinking songs add to the atmosphere. Serge Lanoix and Pierre Menneveau, the owners, merit their success. I recommend the restaurant as one of the colorful sights of Burgundy. Expensive. English spoken. One star in Michelin. In my opinion, it deserves two.

R LES MILLESIMES ("The Vintages"): 25, rue de l'Église. Tel.: 80.51.84.24. Small and charming, on the edge of the vineyards, this restaurant was converted from an old vat room. Mother, Monique Sangoy, and daughter attend to the service, and both husbands are responsible for the cooking. One star in Michelin since 1986.

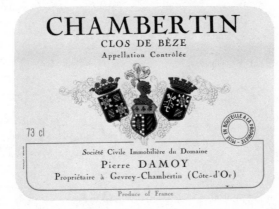

NUITS-SAINT-GEORGES (21700—Côte d'Or)
(Paris 325—Beaune 17—Dijon 22—Chalon-sur-Saône 45)

◖§ Burgundy wine's most important center after Beaune.

HR LA CÔTE D'OR: 1, rue Thurot. Tel.: 80.61.06.10.   7 very comfortable rooms with bath.
A fairly good restaurant, well located in the heart of the Côte de Nuits. Jean Crotet, a very good chef, is responsible for a large, dubious wine list. Two stars in Michelin.

HR LA GENTILHOMMIÈRE: 2 km north-west on route de la Serrée. Tel.: 80.61.12.06. Tlx.: 350401.   20 rooms with bath.
A modernized version of a quiet motel/country inn with good food.

CÔTE DE BEAUNE

The Côte de Beaune is the southern half of the Côte d'Or, winding through the hills from just above Aloxe-Corton to the foothills of Chagny. From its approximately 3,000 hectares (7,500 acres), about twice the area of the Côte de Nuits, come some of Burgundy's best red wines and some of the world's greatest dry whites. Though Beaune is not the first wine town you come to on your trip south along the Côte, it is the most important and is considered Burgundy's wine capital. Beaune glories in the wines that have made its wealth. Bestriding the main north-south autoroute, Beaune does not hide its bottles under a bushel. On the contrary, it almost compels the tourist to stop and dally—and to explore the great wine country that surrounds it. The city is tunneled with wine cellars used by the shipping firms today. Even the old town walls have been turned into storage places for wine.

It is a charming town, with cobbled streets lined by old houses, their steeply pitched roofs colorful with designs in polychrome slate. Everywhere you turn there are wine shops, wine information bureaus, tourist centers, and antique and souvenir shops with wine as their main motif. The town unabashedly exploits wine, but —thanks in part to imaginative architectural controls—its center is not garish or vulgar. Unlike Bordeaux, which seems to have inherited from the English a sense of being above "trade," Beaune cheerfully promotes its wares and in the

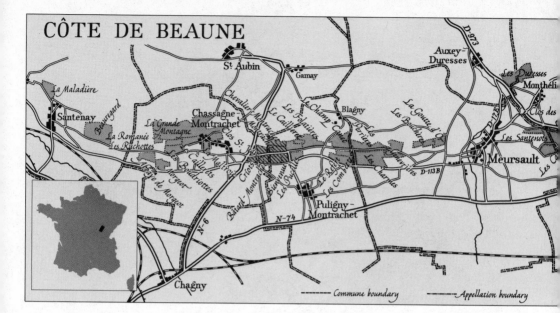

------- *Commune boundary*   ------- *Appellation boundary*

process not only enriches its merchants, restaurateurs, and winegrowing neighbors but also welcomes the novice into the mysteries and rewards of the grape.

As a result of this energy, much of the economy not only of the Côte de Beaune but of the entire Côte d'Or is based on the cellars of Beaune. Wine slogans adorn walls of buildings and restaurants, and billboards lure passing tourists and wine buyers from all over the world into the storerooms of the great firms. Finding these firms is no trouble, but distinguishing the good ones from those less reliable sometimes is. The Beaune telephone directory listed a dozen shippers' "names" under a single telephone number; names of established and dependable firms are imitated by fly-by-nights. Yet behind all this salesmanship lies a genuine love of Burgundian wines, a conviction that there are no others in the world to rival them.

Not that Beaune is simply a show window for its bottles. The town fathers celebrate their historic buildings, through which visitors troop on intelligently guided tours. The city's most notable structure—indeed, one of the most remarkable buildings in all France—is the Hôtel-Dieu, better known as Hospices de Beaune, the fifteenth-century charity hospital whose dazzling Burgundo-Flemish architecture and art collection would be worth a detour if Beaune offered nothing else. Near the Hospices is another fifteenth-century building, once a townhouse for the Dukes of Burgundy, that now serves as the Musée de Vin.

Like many of the other better wine regions, Burgundy exports most of its wine, but many of these "exports" are carried on right in the heart of Burgundy, to tourists who arrive in buses with Swiss, German, and Dutch license plates and who find

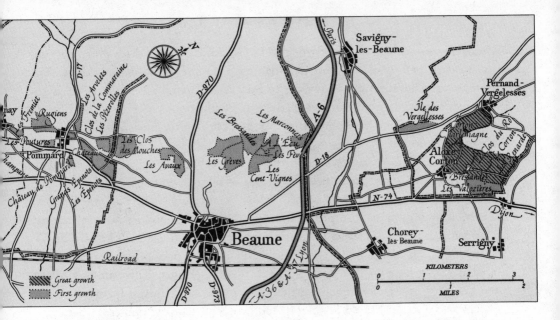

the plethora of place-names part of the local color, a poetry spun by the *négociants*
and shippers to accompany the lusty Burgundian drinking songs—which anyone
will sing at the slightest provocation. Under the influence of all the wine they have
guzzled in the surrounding cellars, the tourists are happy to pay higher prices for
bottles to take home than they would back in New York, London, or Paris.

The great wine event in Beaune each year is the annual auction sale at the Hospices, which provides much of the establishment's revenue. The Hospices was
founded in 1443 by Nicolas Rolin, chancellor to the Duke of Burgundy, and his
wife, Guigone de Salins. Beaune at that time seems to have been almost entirely pop-
ulated by beggars (only twenty-four of its families were considered solvent), and so
it was plainly a promising site for a charity hospital. It has been the custom through
the centuries for peasant and noble growers alike to will parcels of choice vineyard to
the Hospices, the wines from the land being sold to provide for the patients. Since
1851 the sale of these wines has been accomplished at auction. Until 1976 only red
and white wines from the Côte de Beaune were part of the sale, but through a dona-
tion of some Mazis-Chambertin vineyard in 1977, the Côte de Nuits was added to
the list. The auction is held on the third Sunday of each November and is the principal event in a weekend of non-stop wine revelry and general over-indulgence. I
find it more exhausting every year. The prices reach heights justifiable only by the
fact that the proceeds go to charity.

On the day before the auction, hundreds of people gather at a wild free-for-all to
taste the wines to be auctioned on Sunday—all of us drinking from the same few

glasses. That night is held the first of the Trois Glorieuses, the three great Burgundian feasts which have become essential to a proper Hospices weekend. The Confrérie des Chevaliers du Tastevin, the Burgundian wine promotional organization, gives a gala black-tie banquet in the great hall of the château of the Clos de Vougeot. Five hundred Chevaliers appear to the blare of trumpets, all dolled up in their robes, followed by a procession of the new "initiates" ready to be knighted with a vine branch. Status-seekers throughout the world brag of their membership in the Confrérie as if it conferred a degree of prestige and authority; in fact the level of connoisseurship is often painfully low. Nevertheless, there are few who do not exhibit their diploma, complete with the red- and gold-ribboned *tastevin* (the red for red wine and the gold either for white wine or for the sun, I don't know which). The Confrérie has undoubtedly accomplished its purpose of popularizing Burgundy as well as giving impetus to wine societies throughout France. There are now about 8,500 branches of the Confrérie over the globe, with thousands of members.

Sunday's auction has no less pomp and protocol than the dinner on Saturday. With the buyers and spectators assembled in the large Hospices hall, the bidding supposedly continues only as long as the auctioneer's candle remains lighted. This is symbolic more than anything else, because a fresh taper can always be found so long as there are more bidders and more wine to sell. The Hospices auction has served as a fine publicity stunt for years, but in 1977 it was a farce. Two bidders, the Patriarche shipping firm (Burgundy's largest) from Beaune, and the notorious grower-*négociant* Henri Maire from Arbois, conducted a bidding war in front of the world press—photographers, television cameras, and radio microphones—over the first parcel of twenty-one barrels of Corton Cuvée Dr. Peste. One hopes they enjoyed their time in the limelight; Patriarche, at least, certainly paid dearly for it. When the bidding ended, the Corton Cuvée Dr. Peste went to them at eight times the price of a similar wine purchased under normal conditions. However, the quality and type of wine often seem to be secondary considerations at the Hospices auction.

In spite of these exaggerated prices, the Hospices wine sale gives the growers an index to the price that year's market will bear for all Côte d'Or wines. In my opinion, if this ridiculous spiral of bidding and pricing continues, Burgundy's market may collapse. The growers had a taste of poor sales from 1979 through 1984.

After the auction you catch your breath and prepare for the second of the Glorieuses, a splendid candlelight dinner held in the fifteenth-century bastion of the Hôtel-Dieu. Then, if you can make it through Monday morning, Monday lunch is the occasion of La Paulée, the third and final six-hour, six-course banquet where growers bring their wines to be sampled and discussed while the inescapable drinking songs resound through the hall before, during, and after the meal.

If you haven't had enough by then, or if you've nothing to do between courses, between meals, or between songs, you can always pay a visit on Saturday and/or Sunday to the Beaune wine fair, a serious commercial gathering to which growers from every corner of Burgundy bring their wines to be sampled from the barrel.

✦❦✦

ALOXE-CORTON

Aloxe-Corton is a rustic wine village, with all the rough charm you could hope to find in the Côte d'Or and none of Beaune's high-charged atmosphere. It lies at the base of the Mont de Corton, the slope of the great red and white wines. Of the seven Great Growths of the Côte de Beaune, three are situated on the slopes of Aloxe-Corton. The Corton vineyard name will often be found on the label followed by the name of the vineyard parcel from which it comes, the best of them being Le Corton, Corton-Bressandes, and Corton-Clos du Roi. There are about a dozen in all. The rest of the parcels entitled to the *appellation* go to market simply as Corton. The village also produces one of the best white Burgundies, Corton-Charlemagne, a vigorous and perfumed white with a strong character.

A leading grower in Aloxe and president of the Beaune Chamber of Commerce is Daniel Senard, one of the few growers who speak perfect English. In addition to his worries about his fine Corton wines and his duties in Beaune, he has the fascinating *métier* of being a most reliable manufacturer of betting chips used in the chic and famous casinos throughout the world.

While in the wine trade, I tasted and bought M. Senard's wines for over twenty-five years and in that time found him a tireless instructor on the wines of the Corton slope. "Corton is a wine apart," he says. "That may sound commonplace, but it's true. We are on the limit of the Côte de Beaune and the Côte de Nuits and we aren't really part of either. Cortons are naturally hard, with a kind of chewiness, or 'mache,' you do not find elsewhere in the Côte d'Or. As you go from *climat* to *climat* on the Corton slope, you'll discover different shades of character. For the greatest breeding I would have to choose Clos du Roi, but it also takes the longest to develop. To be given a chance, the '78s should not be opened before the late 1980s. The wines from Bressandes are also very fine; they come around sooner and will always show up better in a tasting of recent vintages. They are more tender wines than Clos du Roi, and ultimately lack their stamina once fully mature."

If a photographer asked me to recommend the most dramatic setting for a picture of fine wines in the Côte d'Or, I would pick the Corton slope, which rises out of the plain of the Saône like a well-formed breast. As the vines sweep around the hill into the valley toward Pernand-Vergelesses, the Pinot Noir is suddenly replaced by the Chardonnay grape at the great white-wine vineyard of Corton-Charlemagne. At their best, Corton-Charlemagnes can be deep, assertive, and long-lasting wines, in the class of the illustrious Montrachet. The vineyard is divided into three parts. Two of the principal owners are the estimable shippers Louis Latour and Louis Jadot; the rest belongs to a half-dozen or so growers, the most considerable of them, the Domaine Bonneau de Martray, producing about 2,500 cases, and the smallest producing only about 25. From the road you can see the building that houses the fine firm of Louis Latour, remarkable not least for its multicolored Burgundian roof. The Latour firm sells a fine wine under the trademarked name of Corton-Grancey.

The story of Charlemagne owning a piece of the Corton vineyard named for him has perhaps more truth to it than a lot of the hackneyed tales told about other *climats* to give them some historical pedigree. According to the traditional account, there is a parchment deed to the vineyard in the Basilique of Saint-Andoche in Saulieu, giving young (and not yet emperor) Charlemagne title to the land.

It is no wonder that the Great Growth wines from the Corton slope are expensive: you find the labels on wine lists all over the world, though a year's output of Corton-Charlemagne amounts to only 12,000 cases. The Corton reds from all the Great Growth vineyards total only around 30,000 cases of wine a year—similar to the harvest at a single large Médoc property such as Château Prieuré-Lichine.

Of the Aloxe-Corton First Growths, Valozières, just across the road from Bressandes, makes fine wines, which in better years attain greater breed than the other First Growths.

CLIMATS SOLD AS CORTON

In Aloxe-Corton: red and white

Le Corton	Voirosses	En Pauland (*in part*)
Clos du Roi	Les Fiètres	Les Meix-Lallemant
Les Renardes	Les Perrières	Les Meix
Les Bressandes	La Vigne-au-Saint	Les Combes (*in part*)
Les Languettes (*in part*)	Les Grèves	Le Charlemagne (*in part*)
Les Chaumes (*in part*)	Les Maréchaudes (*in part*)	Les Pougets (*in part*)

In Ladoix-Serrigny: red and white

Les Vergennes	Les Bois de Vergennes
Le Roguet-Corton (*in part*)	Les Carrières
Ladoix-Serrigny (*red only*)	

In Pernand-Vergelesses: white only
Le Charlemagne (*in part*)

FIRST GROWTHS OF ALOXE-CORTON

At Aloxe-Corton:

VINEYARDS	HECTARES	ACRES
Les Chaillots	4.63	11.44
Les Fournières	5.57	13.76
Les Guérets	2.56	6.32
Les Maréchaudes (*in part*)	2.13	5.26
Les Meix (*in part*)	1.90	4.69
En Palaud (*in part*)	1.60	4.00
Les Valozières (*in part*)	6.59	16.28
Les Vercots	4.19	10.35

At Ladoix-Serrigny:

	HECTARES	ACRES
La Coutière	2.52	6.22
Les Grandes Lolières	3.04	7.51
Les Petites Lolières	1.64	4.05
La Toppe-au-Vert	1.84	4.54
Les Maréchaudes	1.72	4.25

PERNAND VERGELESSES

This wine-growing area shares two of its best soils with Aloxe-Corton for the production of the white Charlemagne, and with Savigny-les-Beaune for the red wine of Vergelesses.

First Growths: Ile de Vergelesses (9.3 hectares—23 acres) and Aux Vergelesses (17.8 hectares—44 acres).

Other Growths: (in part) Creux de la Net; En Caradeux Les Fichots.

The First Growths amount to 56.56 hectares (139.75 acres) from a total of 130 hectares of Pernand Vergelesses.

Chorey-les-Beaune has only a small vineyard located on the edge of a plain. The wines are usually sold under the name Côte de Beaune-Villages.

SAVIGNY-LES-BEAUNE

Between Pernand-Vergelesses and Beaune stands the minor wine village of Savigny-les-Beaune. Within its confines there are about 360 hectares (900 acres) of vines, and production in an average year for quantity is about 100,000 cases, nearly all of it red. This wine was greatly appreciated in the distant past (a Duke of Burgundy wanted to elevate one grower to the rank of a demigod for the quality of his wine), but its reputation has diminished since then. It is distinctly light and fragrant, but not a wine to keep for any length of time. Savigny sells its wines either under the commune name or as Savigny-les-Beaune with Côte de Beaune added, but if a wine qualifies for either name it is qualified for both. The firm of Henri de Villamont, owned by the powerful Swiss shipper Pierre Schenk, owns some of the choice parcels in Savigny.

SAVIGNY VINEYARDS

FIRST GROWTHS (*Premiers Crus*)

Aux Vergelesses	Aux Gravains
Bataillère	Les Talmettes
Les Marconnets	Les Charnières
La Dominode	Les Narbantons
Les Jarrons	Les Haut-Marconnets
Basses-Vergelesses	Les Haut-Jarrons
Les Lavières	

And portions of the following vineyards:

Les Perrillets	Les Rouverettes
Les Charnières	Aux Grands-Liards
Aux Fourneaux	Aux Petits-Liards
Aux Serpentières	Petit-Godeaux
Redrescuts	

BEAUNE

The vineyard road from Aloxe-Corton runs directly down to the center of Beaune. The ancient city is more than the hub of the Burgundian wine trade. Beyond the town but still within the limits of the commune of Beaune, more vines are planted than can be found in any other commune of the Côte d'Or, although Pommard and Meursault generally make more wine each year. The best growth of Beaune is generally considered to be that from the vineyard of Grèves, and particularly from the section called L'Enfant Jésus. The famed Burgundian knack for giving everything a colorful twist shows itself in top form here, in the claim that the name was bestowed by early monks and comes from the expression: "It goes down just like little Jesus in velvet trousers." Grèves is one of the fullest and suavest wines of Beaune, while Clos des Mouches is a wine noted for its finesse and considerable body. Slightly behind these is Fèves, a smaller vineyard, whose wines are noted for their fineness and delicate yet pronounced aroma. Beaune Bressandes—not to be confused with Corton-Bressandes in nearby Aloxe-Corton—and Marconnets, Champimonts (or Champ Pimont), and Cras are also highly reputed, and the wines are light but firm with a distinctive bouquet.

In an average year Beaune produces 120,000 cases of red wine and about 5,000 cases of white. It is often excellent wine. In addition to the *appellation* Beaune there are the *appellations* Côte de Beaune and Côte de Beaune-Villages. There will be enormous variation in production from year to year, depending on the wine shippers who do the blending and the amount of wine from the various communes concerned. This can be anything between 5,000 and 10,000 hectoliters, or 60,000 to 110,000 cases.

BEAUNE

FIRST GROWTHS (*Premiers Crus*)

VINEYARD	HECTARES	ACRES
Les Marconnets	8.8	21.8
Les Fèves	4.4	10.9
Les Bressandes	21.8	53.9
Les Grèves	31.7	78.3
Les Clos des Mouches	25.1	62.1
Sur-les-Grèves	4.0	9.9
Aux (or Les) Cras	5.0	12.4
Le Clos de la Mousse	3.4	8.3
Les Teurons	21.5	53.2
Champimonts (or Champ Pimont)	18.1	44.6
En l'Orme	2.1	5.1
En Genêt	4.3	10.7
Les Perrières	3.2	7.9
À L'Écu	5.0	12.4
Les Cent Vignes	23.5	58.1
Les Toussaints	6.4	15.9
Les Chouacheux	5.0	12.4
Les Boucherottes	8.6	21.2
Les Vignes Franches	8.6	21.2
Les Aigrots	22.0	54.4
Pertuisots	5.2	12.7
Tiélandry	2.0	4.9

VINEYARD	HECTARES	ACRES
Les Sizies	8.5	21.0
Les Avaux	13.4	33.1
Les Reversées	5.0	12.3
Le Bas des Teurons	7.3	18.1
Les Seurey	1.2	3.0
La Mignotte	2.4	6.0

And portions of the following:

Clos du Roi	8.4	20.9
Aux Coucherias	9.3	22.9
Les Tuvilains	8.7	21.6
Les Montrevenots	8.3	20.5
Les Blanches Fleurs	1.2	2.9
Les Epenottes	8.1	19.9
Bélissaud	4.9	12.1
Les Beaux Fougets	0.3	0.7

327 hectares of First Growths out of a total area of 521 hectares.

POMMARD

Pommard is one of Burgundy's best-known *appellations,* and not always for the best reasons. Before the Appellation Contrôlée laws came into effect, this easily pronounced name was a label umbrella under which heavy wines of Algeria and Spain and the sunny shores of the Midi were blended with the local red to provide the thick "typical" Burgundies for which the Belgians, Dutch, and English were clamoring. Just as the Greeks' taste in wine was deformed by the resin flavor imparted by the pine barrel, so habitual "Burgundy" drinkers found they did not care for authentic Burgundies, which tend to be light and elegant. Instead, they expected big mucky wines to be produced by the Pinot Noir, which, in Burgundy as everywhere else in the world, makes a lighter wine than the Cabernet Sauvignon. Thus began the misleading cliché that Burgundies are heavy, mouth-filling wines while the Bordeaux wines are light. We can be thankful that the Appellation Contrôlée laws and the Fraud Squad have considerably curbed these abuses.

No commune has suffered more from such prostitution than Pommard. True Pommard deserves better.

The vineyards start just south of Beaune, after N-74 forks, N-74 itself heading for Chagny and the other, smaller road, D-973, swinging into the hills past Volnay, Monthélie, and on to Autun. Curving sharply, the road skirts Pommard village, passing vineyards on either side bordered by the stone walls that often bear the names of local shippers and growers.

The best vineyards are Les Épenots and Les Rugiens. Both can produce excellent wines, characterized by a hardness not found in other Côte de Beaune wines.

In the Château de Pommard the Côte de Beaune has its biggest property. The château and its vineyard, which is classed below the First Growths, are owned by Jean-Louis Laplanche and his vivacious wife. As recently as 1977 the Laplanches were restoring the *caves* of their prerevolutionary domain, and today thousands of visitors are led on tours through the neat cellars as an introduction to the final pitch for sales of their high-priced bottles of wine. There is no way of missing the château because M. Laplanche, a professor of psychology at the Sorbonne, has plastered the countryside with signs advertising direct sales from the vineyard. He has turned the château into a very profitable operation.

Another restored Burgundian domain in Pommard is the twelfth-century Château de la Commaraine. The spacious château and its nearly 4 hectares (10 acres) of vines are owned by Michel Jaboulet-Vercherre, who has a shipping firm in Beaune.

There is less difference among the wines of the various Pommard vineyards than would be found in other Côte d'Or communes, and most of the wine by far is sold without any indication of the particular vineyard parcel on the label.

As for the Pommard village, it is a sleepy place with a bell tower in the main square. Almost before you have entered it, you are out again, in the midst of a sea of vines on your way up the hill to Volnay.

POMMARD

FIRST GROWTHS (*Premiers Crus*)

VINEYARD	HECTARES	ACRES
Les Rugiens-Bas	5.8	14.5
Les Rugiens-Hauts	7.6	18.8
Les Épenots	11.	25.6
Clos des Épenots	3.6	9.0
Les Petits-Épenots	20.2	50.1
Clos de la Commaraine	3.7	9.2
Le Clos Blanc	4.3	10.6
Les Arvelets	8.5	20.9
Les Charmots	3.6	8.9
Les Pézerolles	7.3	15.6
Les Boucherottes	1.7	4.1

VINEYARD	HECTARES	ACRES
Les Saussilles	3.8	9.4
Les Croix-Noires	1.2	3.1
Les Chaponnières	3.3	8.2
Les Fremiers	4.9	12.2
Les Bertins	3.7	9.1
Les Jarollières	3.2	7.9
Les Poutures	4.2	10.9
Le Clos Micot	3.9	9.8
La Refène	2.5	6.1
Clos du Verger	2.55	6.2
Derrière Saint-Jean	1.2	3
La Platière	5.8	14.3
Les Chanlins-Bas	7.1	17.7
Les Combes-Dessus	2.8	6.9
La Chanière	10	24.7

VOLNAY

Leaving the village of Pommard behind, the vineyard road crosses into the Volnay vineyards while a smaller road branches to the right, leading to the village of Volnay, the last important outpost for Côte de Beaune red wine. This charming village of 450 people lies above Pommard and only a stone's throw away from Meursault. The village itself is dominated by the fourteenth-century church, from whose small square one can see across the Burgundian plain clear to the snow-capped Jura.

Volnays are rather delicate wines for Burgundy, quick to mature, with less depth of color than the Beaunes and Pommards, though sometimes with greater elegance. They are suave, rounded, well-balanced, with a particularly fine bouquet. You will find these qualities more often in the better vineyards, such as Les Champans, Les Chevrets, and, probably the best of all, Les Caillerets. In all, Volnay's vineyards cover 215 hectares (530 acres), and the growers make about 90,000 cases annually. All the white wines of Volnay are sold as Meursault.

The Marquis d'Angerville is one of the most respected growers, as was his father before him.

Around the hillside from Volnay is the village of Monthélie. It is one of the most picturesque wine communes of Burgundy, with steep streets and tiny houses, but the wines—both red and white are made—are seldom distinguished.

The Volnay vineyards are as follows:

FIRST GROWTHS (*Premiers Crus*)

VINEYARD	HECTARES	ACRES
Les Caillerets	2.7	6.7
Les Caillerets-dessus	14.7	36.6
Clos des Ducs	2.4	6
Les Brouillards	6.5	16.2
Les Mitans	4	9.9
L'Ormeau	4.3	10.7
Les Angles	3.5	8.7
Les Pointes d'Angles	1.5	3.7
Les Fremiets	6.5	16.2
Les Champans	11.3	28.6
Les Chevrets	6	14.9
Le Clos des Chênes	16.9	42.1
Le Barre	2	4.9
La Bousse d'Or	1.9	4.8

MEURSAULT

Meursault is the Côte d'Or's largest producer of white Burgundies, and the beginning of the great Burgundy white wines. From the village of Meursault south there is a splendid array of vineyards producing wines with distinct personalities. Since the only grape variety for the white wines is the Pinot Chardonnay, the variation and multiplicity of tastes will depend entirely on the different soils in which the vine sinks its roots. To explore fully the various expressions of the single white grape from Meursault to Chassagne would take a lifetime of traveling and tasting pleasure.

Of all the Côte d'Or wine villages, Meursault, with its two thousand inhabitants, gives the greatest appearance of contented prosperity. Its houses are large and even the old stone vineyard complexes reflect a nineteenth-century affluence.

The expensive wines of Meursault are easy to like. Softer certainly than steely Chablis and the harder wines of Puligny, they are straightforward and tend to reach their peak fairly quickly. Meursault's finest wines come from Les Perrières, Les Charmes, and Genevrières—all of which can be great. The vineyard road passes through each in turn and they all look the same, yet any wine with one of these names on its label has an impressive claim to fame. The same cannot be said for a lot of the wine sold under the simple place-name Meursault. Much disappointing wine is made along the broad flatlands bordering N-74 and sold to shippers, who bottle it under the commune name alone. The quality of these wines will vary, depending on how much care the shipper wishes to take and the premium he is willing to pay to make his *cuvée* better than that of his competitors. Some can be a disgrace to a venerable name.

Among the best producers are those with small holdings and small cellars that can be easily controlled by a single family. In 1977, the Patriarche shipping company finished renovating the impressive Château de Meursault, which formerly belonged to the Comte de Moucheron. Patriarche turned the cellars, dating back to the thirteenth century, into a showplace where the wines are sold at retail. Meursault also is the headquarters of the Ropiteau shipping firm, which likewise has large vineyard holdings. They too sell wines at retail in the "Cave de l'Hôpital," a seventeenth-century property which belonged to the Hospices de Beaune.

Close to Meursault are the vineyards of Blagny. Its white is, understandably enough, very close to Meursault in character. If anything, it will be a bit firmer and slightly more assertive than the white Meursault. The place-name of Blagny applies also to certain red wines harvested at an elevation that is fairly high for Pinot Noir. For this reason, the quality of these wines is very good only in the best of years.

If you include the hamlet of Blagny, Meursault has more surface area devoted to vines than any other commune of the Côte d'Or, and it ties with Pommard and Beaune each year for first place in amount of production. The official figures for Meursault are 480 hectares (1,188 acres) of vines, with production averaging 150,000 cases of white—a sizable amount for Burgundy. The best vineyards of the commune are given the designation First Growth (*Premier Cru*) and the right to produce wines that will carry both commune name and vineyard name on the label.

FIRST GROWTHS (*Premiers Crus*)

In Meursault:

VINEYARD	HECTARES	ACRES
Clos des Perrières and Les Perrières	17.8	42.2
Les Charmes-dessus	15.5	38.3
Les Charmes-dessous	12.5	30.8
Les Genevrières-dessus	7.7	19.3
Les Genevrières-dessous	5.25	13
La Goutte d'Or	5.3	13.8
Le Porusot-Dessus	1.8	4.4
Le Porusot	1.6	4
Les Bouchères	4.25	10.5

VINEYARD	HECTARES	ACRES
Les Santenots-Blancs*	2.95	7.3
Les Santenots du Milieu*	7.7	19.8
Les Caillerets*	1.3	3.3
Les Petures*	11	27
Les Cras*	4.8	11.7

* Entitled to the *appellation* Volnay.

In Blagny:

VINEYARD	HECTARES	ACRES
La Jennelotte	4.5	11.9
La Pièce-sous-le-Bois	11.2	27.8
Sous le Dos d'Âne	5.6	13.3
Sous-Blagny	2.0	5.0

AUXEY-DURESSES

Auxey-Duresses is a relatively unknown commune whose vineyards lie adjacent to those of Monthélie. The vineyards have a good southern exposure which compensates for the effects of its elevation. The white wines are certainly of a good quality and can be compared to lesser Meursaults. The red wines have character. The overall place-name of Auxey-Duresses comprises 171 hectares (422 acres), of which 29 hectares (74 acres) are in First Growths. Some of these First Growths have their names mentioned on the label in addition to the place name. They are:

VINEYARD	HECTARES	ACRES
Les Duresses	10.56	26
La Chapelle	1.28	3.2
Climat du Val	8.37	20.7
Les Grands Champs	4.36	11.6
Clos du Val	1.93	4.77

PULIGNY-MONTRACHET

Less than five minutes' drive along the narrow vineyard paths parallel to N-74 takes you from Meursault to Puligny. You reach the village itself before passing any of the vineyards that have made it famous. The great Montrachet and its sister vineyards, Bâtard-Montrachet, Chevalier-Montrachet, Bienvenue-Bâtard-Montrachet, and Criots-Bâtard-Montrachet, are all some 300 meters (330 yards) behind the village on the Puligny-Chassagne border.

In Puligny, everyone makes wine. The mayor is a grower, and he maintains a cordial but deep-rooted rivalry with his genial counterpart in Chassagne. The village priest is another respected grower, and between Masses he is apt to be out in the vineyard, supervising work or just inspecting his vines. At harvest time, the entire village may be found in the vineyards on the slope behind the town.

The four Great Growth vineyards are evenly split between Puligny and Chassagne, justifying the fact that each village followed the established Côte d'Or habit and appended the name of the most famous of the vineyards to its own. From the Montrachet vineyards come the wines that have induced countless ecstasies over the centuries. They began to achieve renown in the mid- and late-eighteenth century and the praise has not stopped since: "divine," "magnificent," "awesome," "gorgeous," "with formal pageantry," and so on, ever more baroque. I still think that Alexandre Dumas' line about Montrachet remains the best—it should be drunk, he said, on one's knees with hat in hand. No public relations man or ad agency could have done better. (Were Dumas alive today, it is true, Montrachet's price alone would stagger him.) Montrachet is a wine of exceptionally full-bodied and sustained elegance, combining breed and great depth with manifold complexities which need time to show.

You can find the great vineyards after leaving the village of Puligny and heading up the slope. The vineyard road cuts abruptly to the left, and at this turn, marked by a large, weathered stone cross, the Great Growth vineyards of Montrachet begin. There above you will be the Montrachet and Chevalier, while below to the left are the Bâtard vineyards: Bâtard, Criots-Bâtard, and Bienvenue-Bâtard (all combined with the Montrachet vineyard name).

The vineyard of Montrachet produces a wine that is as rare as it is magnificent. The average yearly production is variable, usually in the neighborhood of 2,600 cases. In the past, the harvest was often reserved for years in advance and prices were so high as to be almost meaningless. A bottle of authentic Montrachet is still a great rarity, and will always be so. In 1962, the French government expended an extra $1.2 million (£690,000) to divert the new Paris-Lyon motorway, which would otherwise have passed near Puligny and affected the precious 7.5 hectares (18.5 acres) of vines.

In the 1970s a couple of acres of Montrachet were sold for close to $2 million. In the 1980s, the price would be more than tripled. There is no economic justification for such a price. Owning a pocket-handkerchief parcel of what is often considered the greatest dry white-wine vineyard in France (though it does not always live up to this reputation, being dependent on the grower's care) cannot be rationalized—either as a source of ego gratification or as a commercial calling card.

Montrachet was for many years partly in the hands of the Marquis de Laguiche family, which still owns a quarter of the vineyard, making about 600 to 800 cases a year. The Domaine du Baron Thénard also owns a relatively large parcel, while the Domaine de la Romaneé-Conti is a recent owner, making less than 200 cases a year.

Like a crown atop the Montrachet vineyard is its rival in greatness, Chevalier. These wines have the same enveloping richness and the same overwhelming perfume. Chevalier is lighter and not as powerful a wine as Montrachet but, depending upon the skill of the grower, it can sometimes be as great. The Chevalier vineyard splits its 7 hectares (17 acres) among a dozen owners or so. Mme Boillereault de Chauvigné is one, and parcels of the land are in the hands of Bouchard Père et Fils, Leflaive, Jadot and Latour (joint ownership), and Chartron. Among them all, the owners split the ridiculously small amount of 1,700 cases of wine.

Following the vineyard along the slope below Montrachet and Chevalier are the three noble *bâtards* of the Montrachet family. It is only in the last thirty years or so that any distinction has been made among Criots, Bienvenue, and Bâtard; before that they were all sold as Bâtard. Bâtard-Montrachet is walled in from the vineyard road that links Puligny to Chassagne. From within these walls come some 4,000 cases of wine per year—not a great deal for a delicious wine which is in demand all over the world, so it is not surprising that much spurious Montrachet is sold. That is why it is so important to get to know the names of shippers and of those growers who bottle their own good wines at the domain. In its characteristics Bâtard resembles the greater Montrachet, sometimes equaling it. Flanking Bâtard on either side are its near-equals, Criots and Bienvenue. Criots is the smaller of the two, about 1.5 hectares (3.5 acres), averaging annually about 400 cases of wine, little of which is ever seen beyond the region. Bienvenue is very much in the style of Bâtard, and produces approximately 1,000 cases annually—scarcely enough to meet the demand.

Although the Great Growths are accepted as the finest, some of the others are also superb and, in the hands of a talented wine-maker, may turn out equal to the topmost. One of them is Pucelles, on your right as you come to the crossroads just north of Bienvenue-Bâtard-Montrachet; and above Pucelles is Le Cailleret, adjoining the Chevalier. On the opposite side of the village—bordering Meursault—is the excellent Les Combettes.

All of Puligny's white wines share approximately the same characteristics. They are eminently dry, not so soft or so luxurious as Meursaults, and are apt to have a deep, full, rich, flowery, or sometimes fruity, bouquet. The green-gold color takes on different highlights and hues, and the wine has a hardness, strength, and masculinity rare in white wines. I knocked on the cellar doors of the Puligny growers for some forty years, and no matter how bad the weather or how cold and damp the *caves,* the winter rounds of tasting the newly made wines were always a revelation to me. Within the general characteristics that most Puligny whites share—firmness of texture and great body—the range of subtleties of taste, bouquet, and color is nearly infinite. At every grower one begins with the silver *tastevins* at the "lesser" wines and mounts the scale in ascending order of quality from barrel to barrel; though all barrels are from the same parcel, each will have its own strengths and weaknesses. Then, because the grower most often will have bits of vineyard everywhere, we move from parcel to parcel, and each time the pipette draws the wine, a further nuance and subtlety is revealed. This preliminary tasting would take me about two weeks, traveling from grower to grower in one commune after another. It was the fine Puligny *vignerons* who made the cold feet and runny noses of the damp Burgundian winters all worthwhile.

Throughout the commune there are about 234 hectares (580 acres) devoted to vines. The best wines, of course, are those which carry simply the vineyard name (Great Growths) or vineyard name and commune name (First Growths, or *Premiers Crus*). The amount of wine produced in Puligny each year is about 60,000 cases of white and just 3,000 cases of red.

GREAT GROWTHS (*Grands Crus*)

VINEYARD	HECTARES	ACRES
Montrachet (*in part*)	4	9.9
Bâtard-Montrachet (*in part*)	6	14.9
Chevalier-Montrachet	7.1	17.7
Bienvenue-Bâtard-Montrachet	2.3	5.7

FIRST GROWTHS (*Premiers Crus*)

Les Combettes	6.7	16.6
Les Pucelles	6.8	16.8
Les Chalumeaux	7	17.3
Le Cailleret	5.4	13.4
Les Folatières	3.4	8.5
Clovaillon	5.5	13.7
Le Champ-Canet	4.6	11.4
Les Referts	13.2	32.6
Sous le Puits	6.9	17.1
Garenne	0.4	0.9
Hameau de Blagny	4	9.9

CHASSAGNE-MONTRACHET

To discuss all of the Montrachet Great Growth vineyards under Puligny makes Chassagne appear more wine-poor than it is. Of the 30-odd hectares (57 acres) of Great Growth vineyard split between the two communes Puligny has 19 and Chassagne 11 or so. Slightly behind the Great Growths in the legal hierarchy—but sometimes equal in quality, depending on the grower and the shipper—are such Chassagne vineyards as Morgeot, Ruchottes, Caillerets, and La Romanée. Chassagne's whites share many of the characteristics of Puligny: firm but never hard, a bit softer than their neighbor, full, flowery richness, and lingering aftertaste. Montrachet itself has astonishing stamina for a dry white wine, but the others tend to have slightly less longevity. Holding a bottle more than ten years is not recommended, and will be at the owner's risk. They are generally at their best when from three to five years old.

Chassagne also makes some very good red wines, which, because they are little known and are slightly eclipsed by the celebrated whites, are often comparatively inexpensive and sometimes good value. This has not always been the case.

During the eighteenth century, Chassagne was famous for red wines. It is reported that red wine from the vineyard of Morgeot was so highly thought of that the rate of exchange was two bottles of Montrachet for one of red Morgeot.

The reds of Chassagne are generally finer than those of Santenay. They are harder, well-rounded wines, with a *goût du terroir* which is characteristic, and they form a transition between the other reds of the Côte d'Or and those of the southern Burgundy wine districts. Boudriotte is the most masculine at the outset, but it matures into a mellow and not so over-assertive richness; while Clos Saint-Jean reaches its peak rather faster, it is lighter, has more finesse, and develops its bouquet considerably earlier. In general, the red wines of Chassagne are at their peak after about five years but can be drunk younger with considerable enjoyment.

Chassagne has about 356 hectares (860 acres) planted in vines. The wine—when it meets the legal minimum standards—is allowed to use the commune name, and if it comes from a 332-hectare (820-acre) section of this greater whole, may add the designation Côte de Beaune to the common name. Production of the *appellation* Chassagne-Montrachet red wine averages a surprising 55,000 cases a year, whereas the white wines for which the communes are far better known average only 35,000 cases.

GREAT GROWTHS (*Grands Crus*)

White Wines

VINEYARD	HECTARES	ACRES
Montrachet (*in part*)	3.56	8.8
Bâtard-Montrachet (*in part*)	5.82	14.4
Criots-Bâtard-Montrachet	1.42	3.5
(*See* Puligny-Montrachet)		

FIRST GROWTHS (*Premiers Crus*)

Red and White Wines

Les Grandes Ruchottes (*white wines only*)	0.64	1.59
Les Ruchottes (*white wines only*)	1.73	4.26
L'Abbaye de Morgeot	10.92	27.3
La Grande Montagne	8.18	20.45
Morgeot	3.94	9.75
Les Caillerets	5.49	13.6
Clos Saint-Jean	14.36	35.5
Clos de la Boudriotte	2.02	5
Les Boudriottes	17.81	44.3
La Maltroie	8.9	22.8
Champgain	28.35	70.7
La Romanée	3.16	7.86
Les Brussonnes	17.72	43.8
Les Chaumées	10.12	25.1

Les Vergers	9.54	23.6
Les Macherelles	8.01	19.8
Les Champs-Cain	4.24	11.7
Bois de Chassagre	8.79	22

163 hectares of First Growths for an area of 335 hectares in Chassagne-Montrachet.

LIST OF OWNERS OF THE "GREAT GROWTH" VINEYARDS OF MONTRACHET

VINEYARD	OWNER	AREA IN HECTARES, ARES, AND CENTIARES			APPROXIMATE PRODUCTION IN CASES
Montrachet		H.	A.	CA	
	le Marquis de Laguiche	2.	06.	25	635
	Boillereault de Chamigny Lazare	00.	79.	98	245
	A. Ramonet	00.	25.	96	75
	Bouchard Père et Fils	00.	88.	94	275
	Petitjean	00.	05.	42	16
	Colin	00.	09.	10	28
	Amiot	00.	03.	56	11
	Echemann	00.	03.	56	11
	Girard	00.	03.	56	11
	Prieur	00.	58.	36	180
	Domaine de La Romanée-Conti	00.	50.	89	155
	Domaine Thenard	01.	83.	31	560
	Comtes Lafon	00.	31.	82	100
	Gagnard Delagrange	00.	30.	00	100
Chevalier-Montrachet					
	Bouchard Père et Fils	02.	53.	96	790
	Domaine Prieur	00.	13.	65	40
	Clerc	00.	15.	10	45
	Lochardet	00.	19.	31	55
	Bavard	00.	19.	64	60
	Leflaive	01.	83.	48	565
	Niellon	00.	22.	73	70
	G. Deleger	00.	15.	95	45
	R. Deleger	00.	15.	95	45
	Chartron	00.	71.	11	220
	Bellegrand	00.	50.	75	155
	Jadot	00.	52.	00	160

VINEYARD	OWNER	AREA IN HECTARES, ARES, AND CENTIARES			APPROXIMATE PRODUCTION IN CASES
Bâtard-Montrachet					
	André	00.	39.	68	110
	Sauzet	00.	13.	77	45
	Leflaive	01.	24.	94	385
	Bonneau	00.	11.	84	35
	A. Monnot	00.	49.	72	160
	A. Ramonet-J. Bachelet	00.	33.	49	100
	P. Ramonet	00.	26.	49	80
	C. Poirier	00.	97.	03	300
	L. Pernot	00.	38.	36	110
	Bavard	00.	67.	71	190
	Poirier	00.	66.	95	190
	H. Jaquin	00.	32.	23	100
	Domaine de La Romanée-Conti	00.	17.	46	55
	Lequin	00.	24.	33	77
	Paul Jouard	00.	03.	70	11
	Pierre Jouard	00.	12.	70	30
	Delagrange	00.	78.	85	242
	Morey	00.	28.	59	88
	J. Chavy	00.	14.	11	45
	Niellon	00.	11.	90	65
	Picard	00.	08.	26	25
	Clerc	00.	18.	35	55
	Urena	00.	15.	57	50
	Gaillot	00.	29.	07	90
	Lamanthe	00.	26.	08	80
	Prieur	00.	07.	63	25
	Cofinet	00.	26.	07	65
	Gagnard	00.	62.	93	180
	De Marcilly	00.	40.	60	120
	Brenot	00.	37.	44	110
	Bouchard Père et Fils	00.	07.	85	25
	Leflaive	00.	66.	18	200
	Roux	00.	08.	86	30
	G. Colin	00.	09.	22	30
	Pernot	00.	10.	17	30
Bienvenue-Bâtard-Montrachet					
	P. Ramonet-Prudhom	00.	31.	88	100
	A. Ramonet-J. Bachelet	00.	35.	82	110
	Monnot	00.	50.	57	154

VINEYARD	OWNER	AREA IN HECTARES, ARES, AND CENTIARES			APPROXIMATE PRODUCTION IN CASES
	Bonneau	00.	19.	47	56
	Leflaive	01.	15.	80	360
	Carillon	00.	11.	44	35
	Rateau	00.	09.	36	29
	Pernot	00.	18.	18	55
	Sauzet	00.	11.	62	35
	Clerc	00.	64.	46	200
Criots-Bâtard-Montrachet					
	Delagrange	00.	33.	13	100
	de Marcilly	00.	61.	20	190
	E. Delagrange	00.	20.	55	65
	C. Blondeau	00.	05.	04	15
	Perrot	00.	04.	65	14
	Renner	00.	06.	37	16
	Deleger	00.	26.	27	80

SANTENAY AND THE SOUTHERN COMMUNES

Santenay, which always made a claim for its mineral water and its "baths," followed the tradition of some of the great European spas by opening a casino in the early seventies. Here grower, shipper, buyer, and tourist, under the influence of their vineyard tastings, can lay their chips—made locally by the Aloxe-Corton grower Daniel Senard—shoulder to shoulder on the green baize, hoping to come up a winner. In my own days as a buyer and shipper, Santenay was at the end of my tasting and selecting route, and I never felt I could risk anything at the gaming tables. Besides, I'd already spent all my money at the growers' anyway.

Santenay is the last important wine commune of the Côte de Beaune before it trails off into the southernmost Cheilly-les-Maranges, Dezize-les-Maranges, and Sampigny-les-Maranges. The wines—which have equal right to the name of the commune or communal name with "Côte de Beaune" added—are predominantly red and are light, fast-maturing, sometimes pleasantly fruity, and often good if priced below those from some of the other Côte de Beaune wine communes. Authentic red Santenay of a good year from one of the better vineyards such as Maladière and Les Gravières often rivals wines from Chassagne-Montrachet or Volnay, although it never gets into a position to challenge the exceptionally great Burgundies. Some Santenay is blended with the output of the other Côte de Beaune communes and sold as Côte de Beaune-Villages, and some is sold under the more specific commune names. Quantities go to Switzerland and the Netherlands, where, being fairly low in price, the wine is highly appreciated. There are almost 400 hectares (1,000 acres) of vineyards within Santenay's boundaries, and in an average year production amounts to about 90,000 cases of red wine and about 1,300 cases of white.

The other three communes retain their *appellation* status but since their commune names are not widely known, most growers sell under the better-known Côte de Beaune *appellation*. In 1976, only Cheilly-les-Maranges declared any wine under the commune name, and only 2,000 cases at that.

So ends the Côte de Beaune and with it the Côte d'Or, the heart and soul of Burgundy. For me the Côte de Beaune has always been the home of France's greatest dry white wines. Surely the word "dry" alone cannot do justice to their manifold subtleties and great richness. For those who have taken on the pleasant and edifying task of unraveling its wonders, Burgundy will always be more than a place-name and never reducible to a simple "type" of wine, as wine-producing countries outside of France have implied. The striking differences from vineyard to vineyard in the Côte d'Or are remarkable enough, but when these are combined with the human factor of the grower's care, talent, and even philosophy, the number of variables approaches infinity, and no explanation will ever be final or sufficient.

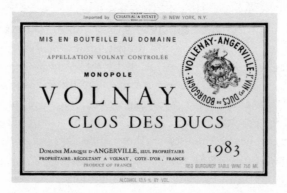

ॐ

CÔTE DE BEAUNE
Hotels and Restaurants
H = *Hotel;* R = *Restaurant*

The visitor to the Côte de Beaune should also consult the "Hotels and Restaurants" sections on pp. 137–39, 145–49, 176–78, and 210–12, plus Itineraries C, D, G, and J on pp. 420–21, 421–22, 425–26, and 427–28, respectively.

BEAUNE (21200—Côte d'Or)
(Paris 315—Dijon 45—Chalon 29—Auxerre 151—Chagny 16)

The capital of Burgundy wines, Beaune harbors dozens of wine merchants who have cellars in this moated town. The wine shops often sell expensive wines of dubious quality. You will be better off buying wines from the growers in the wine villages north and south of the town. These latter will boast *"Vente Directe"* signs and will welcome your purchases.

Do not miss visiting the Hospice de Beaune, with its multicolored tiled roofs overlooking the cobbled courtyard. Across from the entrance to the courtyard is the kitchen, festive with its pots and pans, where nuns for centuries have fed the sick and the poor. The museum houses the painting of the Last Judgment by Roger van der Weyden. Within walking distance is the Musée du Vin on the rue d'Enfer, which, unfortunately, does not have much to offer.

HR CENTRAL: 2, rue V.-Millot. Tel.: 80.24.77.24.   22 rooms (10 with toilet).
Comfortable rooms, reasonably priced; some can be noisy. A good, simple restaurant.

H HÔTEL LE CEP: 27, rue Maufoux. Tel.: 80.22.35.48. Tlx.: 351256.   21 small rooms (19 with toilet).
Luxurious seventeenth-century house with antique furniture. Centrally located, within walking distance of the Hospices de Beaune. English spoken. No restaurant. Breakfast available.

H LA CLOSERIE: 61, route d'Autun (1.5 km south of Beaune on D-973). Tel.: 80.22.15.07. Tlx.: 351213. 30 rooms.
Although slightly beyond the town limits, this clean, modern hotel-motel is very convenient and quiet. It has been appreciated by wine merchants, myself included. Swimming pool. No restaurant; breakfast available.

H SAMOTEL: Route d'Autun (2 km south of Beaune on D-973). Tel.: 80.22.35.55.   Tlx.: 350596. 62 rooms; 4 apartments.
Fair motel comfort. Uninspiring restaurant and snack bar available. If you can't get a room at the Closerie, try here.

HR HÔTEL DE LA POSTE: 1, boulevard Clémenceau. Tel.: 80.22.08.11.   25 comfortable rooms.
Near Musée du Vin, with a good restaurant. The proprietor, Marc Chevillot, who is well known by many American wine-lovers, takes great care to provide the best service. English spoken.

HR RAISIN DE BOURGOGNE: 164, route de Dijon. Tel.: 80.24.69.48.   11 rooms. Walking distance from the center of town.
Charming restaurant. Good value.

HR HOTEL HENRI II: Faubourg Saint-Nicholas. Tel.: 80.22.83.84. Tlx.: 350217.
In the center of town, this new hotel has 48 comfortable rooms. Within walking distance of all parts of the city. Private garage.

HR HÔTEL DE LA CLOCHE: 42, place Madeleine. Tel.: 80.22.22.75.   16 very simple rooms.
Good Burgundian specialties. Perfect for simple, fair-priced lunch or dinner. M. R. Petit, the proprietor, and his wife work hard at making their hotel and restaurant guests welcome and happy.

H HOSTELLERIE DE BRETONNIÈRE: 43, faubourg Bretonnière. Tel.: 80.22.15.77.   20 rooms, some quite decent (12 toilets).
Tranquil, peaceful setting. Breakfast served.

H HOTEL ARCADE: Avenue Charles de Gaulle. 5 minutes' walk from the center of town. Tel.: 80.22.75.67. Tlx.: 351287.   41 rooms with toilet and shower (no bath).
Small, functional rooms in hotel built in 1985. Reasonably priced. There are more comfortable hotels in Beaune.

H BOURGOGNE: Avenue Général-de-Gaulle (2 km southeast of Beaune on D-970). Tel.: 80.22.22.00. Tlx.: 350666.   120 simple rooms.
Modern hotel; restaurant available. It's a good choice if there are no other hotel rooms available in Beaune.

R JACQUES LAINÉ: 10, boulevard Foch, near the Place des Lions. Tel.: 80.24.76.10.
Recently opened, this small, homey place has already received one star in Michelin.

R ROTISSERIE DE LA PAIX: 47, faubourg Madeleine. Tel.: 80.22.33.33.
Good cuisine offered by an enthusiastic, well-trained chef, Jean-Luc Dauphin, and his wife, Marie, who run perhaps one of the best restaurants of Beaune; fairly priced, but next to the busy rail line going from Dijon to the south. One star in Michelin.

R DAME TARTINE: 3, rue Nicolas Rollin (near the Hospice de Beaune). Tel.: 80.22.64.20. Small, good value. Alain Billard ran the Raisin de Bourgogne for eight years, now run by his wife. He seems happy to have moved.

R LE RELAIS DE SAULX: 6, rue Louis Véry. Tel.: 80.22.01.35.
Good menus, whether or not the one star in Michelin is deserved, in this small, pleasant, rather elegant setting.

CHOREY-LES-BEAUNE (21200—Côte d'Or)
(Aloxe-Corton 2—Beaune 4—Dijon 36—Paris 321)

R L'ERMITAGE CORTON: 3 km north of Beaune on N-74. Tel.: 80.22.05.28.   5 very comfortable suites—perhaps the most comfortable in the Beaune area.
Located in the heart of the Burgundy vineyards. This elegant restaurant, managed by André and Monique Parra, is the best in the Beaune area. The good Burgundy wine list is presented by a competent female sommelier. One star in Michelin.

SAVIGNY-LES-BEAUNE (21420—Côte d'Or)
(Paris 320—Beaune 5—Dijon 38—Bouilland 10)
6 km northwest of Beaune; take D-18 to D-2.

HR L'OUVRÉE: Tel.: 80.21.51.52.   22 rooms.
Pleasant hotel with terrace in the midst of vineyards. More than adequate, well-prepared food.

BOUILLAND (21420—Côte d'Or)
(Paris 303—Dijon 44—Beaune 16—Savigny-les-Beaune 10)
From Beaune, take D-2 north.

❧ The winding road from Beaune leads to Bouilland. You can appreciate this small, insignificant village by taking a walk out of the vineyard area and into the countryside.

HR LE VIEUX MOULIN: Tel.: 80.21.51.16.   8 small, quaint rooms (6 with toilet).
A quiet, charming small inn. The host, M. Sylva, has received one star in Michelin.

VIGNOLLES (21200—Côte d'Or)
4 km northeast of Beaune, on D-204.

R AU PETIT TRUC: Tel.: 80.22.01.76.   Garden and terrace.
Edith Remoissenet prepares good, simple, yet imaginative cuisine. Not inexpensive, but full of charm. Reserve in advance. The service can be very slow, especially on weekends, and Mme Remoissenet has been criticized for her sometimes vinegary welcome.

AUXEY-DURESSES (21190—Côte d'Or)
(Beaune 9—Chagny 12—Dijon 48)
From Beaune, take N-74 south.

R LA CRÉMAILLIÈRE: On D-973. Tel.: 80.21.22.60.
This is a good restaurant in the vineyards. It is apt to be full on weekdays and overcrowded on Sundays. If you want to enjoy a reasonably priced restaurant, I'd suggest an early lunch.

MEURSAULT (21190—Côte d'Or)
(Beaune 9—Chagny 10—Dijon 47)
From Beaune, take N-74 south to D-23 and Hôpital de Meursault.

R LE RELAIS DE LA DILIGENCE: Near the station. Tel.: 80.21.21.32.
This good, simple restaurant with reasonably priced menus is a discovery. How long the owner and staff will produce good food remains to be seen.

PULIGNY-MONTRACHET (21190-Meursault)
(Paris 328—Beaune 13—Chalon-sur-Saône 20—Dijon 52—Chagny 5)

❧ In the heart of a village producing some of the greatest white wines in the world.

HR LE MONTRACHET: Place des Marronniers. Tel.: 80.21.30.06.   18 rooms (10 toilets), some acceptable, others small with meager facilities. Another 5 rooms in an annex.
Good cuisine and wine list and good location. One of the best restaurants in the midst of the white Côte de Beaune vineyards.

CHAGNY (71150—Saône-et-Loire)
(Paris 328—Chalon 17—Beaune 16—Mâcon 75—Dijon 83)
At the junction of N-6 and N-74.

HR HÔTEL LAMELOISE: 36, place d'Armes. Tel.: 85.87.08.85.   25 good, old-fashioned rooms.
An old house with pretty Burgundian vaults. Well-located hotel, thanks to its proximity to the great white Burgundy wines of Chassagne-Montrachet, Puligny-Montrachet, and Meursault. Good headquarters for visits to any and all Burgundian vineyards. M. and Mme Lameloise are charming hosts who speak English and run the best restaurant in Burgundy. Very good wine list. Reasonably priced rooms which are in need of refurbishment. Highly rated by top guidebooks, it is a good idea to book ahead. *Relais et Châteaux.* Three stars in Michelin.

HR CHATEAU DE BELLECROIX: On the edge of town, on the N-6. Tel.: 85.87.13.86.   15 rooms.
Madame Gauthier has taken a seventeenth-century château over from the Knights of Malta, in a quiet park of 3 hectares (7½ acres) and, with the help of a good chef, has made this into a good Burgundian hostelry.

SOUTHERN BURGUNDY

The Chalonnais

The Chalonnais is the least-known of the Burgundy wine districts. Until inflated prices for red and white Burgundies became chronic, little was heard of the fresh whites and light reds from the Chalonnais. But since the early seventies these wines have become cheaper alternatives to (if not replacements for) the high-priced Pommards, Meursaults, and Pouilly-Fuissés. For the moment, however, there is not enough Chalonnais wine to make a dent in the demand for these better-known Burgundies: the entire Chalonnais averages only 75,000 cases of white and 350,000 cases of red annually.

Driving south from the Côte d'Or, you can bypass the Chalonnais vineyards by taking N-6 from Chagny and getting on the Autoroute du Soleil, A-6, at the Chalon-sur-Saône-Nord entrance—and in less than an hour you will be at the Mâcon-Sud exit, the doorstep of the Pouilly-Fuissés and the entrance to the Beaujolais. But should you want to visit the vineyards of the Chalonnais, which have many good wine values, then head south from Chagny, on D-981, to the wine village of Rully, the first of the Chalonnais wine towns.

You'll feel as though you've strayed out of wine country. Although often called the "Côte Chalonnaise," there is no definite slope as there was in the Côte d'Or and the landscape is a wilder jumble of hills. The Chalonnais vineyards are sparse and small; the woodland is denser and grows lower down the slope than in the Côte d'Or. Cattle, sheep, and goats graze in great profusion, and, indeed, the sturdy Chalonnais are almost as proud of their hearty beef and pungent goat cheese as they are of their vintages. Or perhaps the winegrowers feel somewhat overshadowed by the great Côte de Beaune to the north, for although the calciferous Chalonnais soil is almost identical in composition to that in the more illustrious slope and the grapes are the same Pinot Noir and Pinot Chardonnay, these wines are country cousins: less distinguished, relatively inexpensive, but often very good.

This is ancient wine country. It was from the great monastic center of Cluny, in the rolling hills northwest of Mâcon, that diligent monks fanned out through medieval Burgundy, founding monasteries and illustrious vineyards wherever they went. From the fourteenth century to the close of the eighteenth, the barrels from the Chalon slope were considered the aristocrats of wine, for the aristocrats of France. The vineyard area was much larger than it is today, and its product was taxed and priced in the same class as the Beaunes, and indeed was often sold as such.

In 1791, when France was divided into administrative departments, the Côte Chalonnaise was excluded from the department of the Côte d'Or, thereby breaking the district's longtime territorial and vinous link to its northern neighbor. Then, in the 1870s, phylloxera struck. The vines of the Chalonnais were more severely affected by this root disease than the plantings in most other areas, and to this day its total cultivated area is below pre-phylloxera levels. Of the four wine-producing areas in the region—Rully, Mercurey, Givry, and Montagny—Mercurey was the least damaged by phylloxera. Because of its quality and abundant quantity, Mercurey still produces the best-known reds of the Chalon slope.

Taking the old vineyard road, D-981, straight south from Chagny, we reach Rully after a drive of 4.5 kilometers (2 miles). There are few vineyards to be seen from the road; they are mostly tucked away on the slopes behind the town. Half a century ago Rully was known as a red-wine area, particularly for *vin mousseux de Bourgogne* (sparkling Burgundy), but little is produced today. In the 1920s, the growers of Rully were refused the right to sell their still red wines as the better-known Mercurey and were forced to produce sparkling reds. This coincided neatly with the repeal of Prohibition in the United States. Sparkling Burgundy caught the Yankee fancy as a sweeter substitute for the more expensive Champagne. But since all sparkling wine is subject to a special high tax in Britain and the United States, these wines, when measured against Champagne, were eventually seen to represent a poor value. As a result, Rully's still-white-wine production has been increasing steadily and now amounts to between 60,000 and 70,000 cases a year—75 percent of its total output—mainly sold in France. Of the white wines, only those made with Chardonnay grapes have the right to the *appellation* Rully. (Those made with Aligoté grapes are still used for *vin mousseux.*) The still white wines are dry, full-bodied, and uncomplicated, and, though they gain from bottle-aging, they should be drunk within three years.

After Rully, the back country roads that take you on a slight detour to Mercurey are just wide enough for one car, and in summer the grass grows up to the windows on either side. Mercurey, as noted, is the largest producer among the four Côte Chalonnaise place-names and its output is almost entirely red, averaging around 250,000 cases per year, or nearly two-thirds of the production of the whole Côte. These red wines, along with the best of Rully, approach the Côte de Beaune in subtlety and depth, although they are a little lighter. Mercurey's whites are surpassed by those of Rully, which are less heavy and less alcoholic.

From Mercurey, we get back on the vineyard road, D-981. Givry, whose wines make the region's boldest claim on history, is 10 kilometers (4 miles) to the south. Even before reaching Givry, one is greeted with signs touting the wines of the local *caveaux,* or tasting cellars, and proclaiming "Givry, the Preferred Wine of Henry IV." Good King Henry is not on record as ever objecting to a glass of anything fermented (he also favored the sparkling wines of Reims and Épernay, eventually to be called Champagne, in addition to the wines of his native Jurançon). The town buildings, despite Henry IV's patronage, are in the Louis XIV style, the open market is a domed roof supported by stone columns, and the streets are noisy with the sound of water splashing from ornate fountains.

Having long supplied the Paris market of the Middle Ages and the Renaissance, Givry boasts large, important cellars as elaborate as any Hollywood set. The biggest *caves* belong to the family of the late Baron Louis Thénard, owner of the fine Givry vineyard Le Cellier aux Moines and part-owner of the great Montrachet, to the north. Givry produces a small red wine, which is fresh and clean, as well as some whites. The reds have less character than those of Mercurey and should be drunk young, certainly within five years, for little is gained by keeping them in the bottle. Some better vineyards include Clos-Saint-Paul and Clos Salomon.

The town of Buxy, to the south on the vineyard road, is a busier, more prosperous-looking place than the village of Montagny, which is perched on the side of the Côte, off to the west. After Mercurey, Montagny is the district's largest producer, making about 25,000 cases of white wine, much of which can be very good. Instead of the golden-honey color of the Côte d'Or, the wines of Montagny possess a green-gold tinge that one looks for in Mâcon Blanc generally, and particularly in Pouilly-Fuissé. To the palate, they begin to have the almond taste one associates with the Mâconnais and Pouilly-Fuissés farther to the south. They should be drunk young, definitely within four years.

The agreeable Chalonnais wines have staged something of a comeback in recent years. But because they are produced only in limited quantities, they are not very easily obtainable.

CHALONNAIS
Hotels and Restaurants

H = *Hotel;* R = *Restaurant*

For other hotels and restaurants in Burgundy, see pp. 137–39, 145–49, 176–78, 203–06, and 218–20, plus Itineraries C, D G, and J, pp. 420–21, 421–22, 425–26, and 427–28, respectively.

CHAGNY (71150—Saône-et-Loire)
(See end of the Côte de Beaune chapter for the HR Lameloise and Château de Bellecroix.)

RULLY (71150—Saône-et-Loire)
(Paris 333—Chalon 15—Chagny 4)

HR HÔTEL DU COMMERCE: Place Sainte-Marie. Tel.: 85.87.20.09.   16 rooms (4 with toilet).
This simple, clean inn, serving regional dishes, is worth mentioning because of the inexpensive
rooms and fair value of its meals.

MERCUREY (71640—Saône-et-Loire)
(Paris 344—Chalon 13—Chagny 12—Beaune 32—Mâcon 72)
From Chagny, take D-981 south to D-978. From Chalon and the Autoroute,
take D-978 west.

HR LE VAL D'OR: On the Grande Rue, D-978. Tel.: 85.47.13.70.   12 rooms (6 with toilet).
An excellent stopover. The food is good, and Jean-Claude Cogny goes far out of his way to welcome his guests, who have high praise for his cooking and moderate prices. It stands to reason
that you should order some of the local Mercurey wine. One star in Michelin.

R LES TEMPLIERS DE MERCURE: at Les Obus. On D-978. Tel.: 85.45.23.63.
Biggish wine-grower's house converted into a tasting room and restaurant. The attractive wine
list features a large assortment of wines bottled by the local growers or estate-bottled.

CHALON-SUR-SAÔNE (71100—Saône-et-Loire)
(Paris 334—Lyon 126—Dijon 67—Mâcon 58—Beaune 33)
Reached directly by both N-6 and the Autoroute. Exit *Sud* when driving north
and exit *Nord* when driving south.

◦§ Chalon-sur-Saône is the northern part of the small farm region of Bresse, which is famous for its
barnyard chickens. Hence restaurants feature *Poulet de Bresse* as their specialty.

HR SAINT-GEORGES: 32, Avenue J. Jaurès, near the railway station. Tel.: 85.48.27.05. Tlx.:
800330.   48 small, functional, air-conditioned rooms. Private garage.
Near the center of the city and the railroad station, the Saint-Georges has modern, quiet rooms.
The restaurant, which is the best in town, is well supervised by M. Choux, with well-chosen and
well-priced menus. One star in Michelin.

GIVRY (71640—Saône-et-Loire)
(Paris 344—Mâcon 67—Chagny 15—Chalon 9—Dijon 78)

◦§ Givry is an example of a small eighteenth-century town, but it dates back even earlier; Givry's
wines once graced Henry IV's supper table.

HR LA HALLE: Tel.: 85.44.32.45.   10 rooms. You can certainly find better rooms elsewhere.
(1 toilet).
Good, simple family cooking at fair prices.

TOURNUS (71700—Saône-et-Loire)
(Paris 360—Chalon-sur-Saône 27—Mâcon 30—Lyon 100—Chagny 27—Geneva 127)

◦§ If you are in Tournus at the end of May or in early June, there is a small fair held by the local
antique dealers. Otherwise, Tournus hasn't much to offer other than its restaurant.

R RESTAURANT GREUZE: (1 km from Autoroute A-6 exit): 4, rue Albert-Thibaudet. Tel.: 85.51.13.52.

The best restaurant of the Côte Chalonnaise. The high-priced menus are a good value and justify the short detour of getting off the Autoroute at Tournus. Good wine list featuring Mâconnais, Beaujolais, and Burgundy wines. Jean Ducloux has achieved a combination of style with informality. *Relais et Châteaux.* Two stars in Michelin.

THE MÂCON WINES

Because of their greatly improved white wines, the vineyards of the Mâcon district have had more attention paid to them in the past twenty years than in the preceding ten hundred. Although the vineyards begin 30 kilometers (18 miles) north of Mâcon at Tournus, the wine that has put the region on the map, Pouilly-Fuissé, is found just beyond Mâcon's southern limit, extending south to overlap with the northern Beaujolais. Though growing steadily in popularity ever since the war, recently Pouilly-Fuissé and its satellites—Pouilly-Vinzelles, Pouilly-Loché, and Saint-Véran—have soared in stature and become major rivals (in both quality and price) of the Meursaults, Chassagnes, and Pulignys of the Côte de Beaune.

Again, if time presses, you can get to the heart of the Mâcon wines by skipping the northern stretch from Tournus to Mâcon, leaving the Autoroute at the Mâcon-Sud exit, in the midst of the Pouilly country. Mâcon is closer to Paris than ever before; a couple of hours on the bulletlike TGV takes you from the center of Paris to the wine capital of Southern Burgundy.

Between Tournus and Mâcon the vineyards are planted on softly rolling hills. Small wine villages abound, as do the cooperatives where most of the growers bring their grapes to be made into wine. Only eight hundred out of more than four thousand growers make and sell their wine independently—often using one of the twenty-five local brokers to handle the sale. Thus the bulk of the 170,000 hectoliters (just under 2 million cases) of white and red Mâcon wine made annually comes from the twenty cooperative cellars.

The cooperative presses the grapes, vats and ferments the juice in large concrete tanks, and sells the finished wine, most of it to shippers who bottle it themselves. Tending the vineyards remains the grower's responsibility. When his grapes are picked, he brings them to the cooperative, where they are weighed. According to the quality of the grapes and the location of the vineyard, the grower will receive so much per kilo from the cooperative's profits after the wine is sold. Some of the better-known cooperatives are in the villages of Azé, Clessé, Lugny, and Viré.

Although their appearance on thousands of wine lists is a recent phenomenon, these whites and reds of Mâcon are hardly newcomers on the wine scene. Back in 1660, or so the story goes, a grower named Claude de Brosse decided that what the area needed was salesmanship. So, with two barrels of his still-fermenting wine he made the heroic 400-kilometer (260-mile) trip to Paris and went on to the court of Louis XIV. It took de Brosse and his ox cart thirty days and God knows how many hazards of highwaymen and mud. A man of gargantuan stature, he immediately caught the king's eye, delivered his pitch . . . and the king sipped. Thereafter, they say, the royal cellars never lacked for wines of Mâcon. Oddly enough, in the entire region there is no memorial to its First Supersalesman.

Today most of the Mâcon white wines, aside from the Pouillys, are either simply "Appellation Mâcon Contrôlée" or, in small quantities, Pinot Chardonnay. This latter name is a recent invention, intended for American consumers in response to their heightened awareness of varietal wines. When well selected, the white Mâcon, and, especially, Mâcon-Villages, a superior classification from specifically designated villages, will be good, round, dry wines, similar in character to Pouilly-Fuissé and less expensive, but lacking the *grain,* or a special depth of taste and extra quality, of the Pouillys and their surrounding vineyards. A certain amount of white wine is also pressed from the lesser Aligoté grapes (wine made from these grapes must be identified as such on the label). Aligoté is of inferior quality and is drunk locally in aperitifs—mostly in Kir, the popular drink made from white wine with a dash of blackcurrant liqueur, *crème de cassis.*

For the wine neophyte and the connoisseur alike, Pouilly-Fuissé is a wine to admire and a place to visit. If any wines of southern Burgundy can be said to have gained a place in the sun today, they are these elegant whites.

Leaving the Autoroute at the Mâcon-Sud exit, we follow signs for Cluny, and turn north onto D-89, which leads to the Patte d'Oie, a tiny intersection of four or five country lanes in the form of a goose's foot that is our gateway to the vineyards.

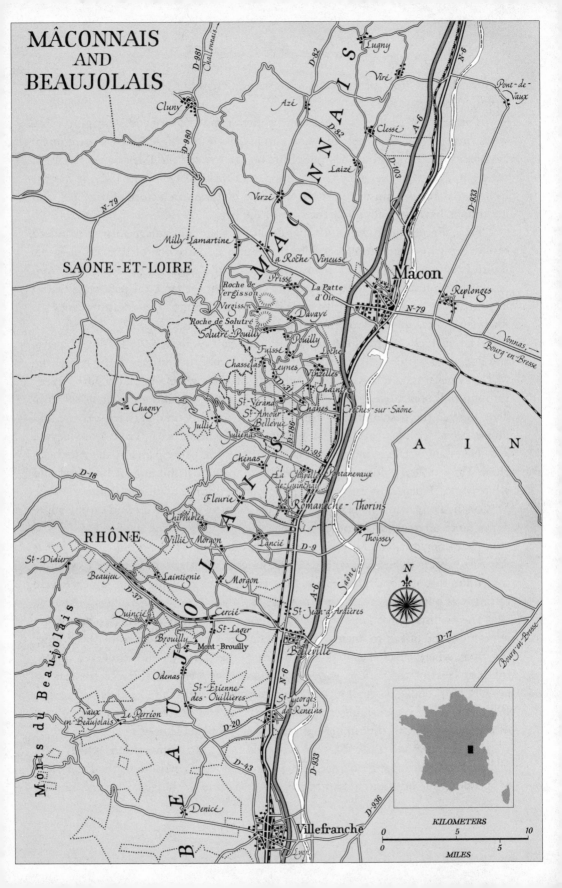

MÂCONNAIS
AND
BEAUJOLAIS

Chalonnais — D-981

Cluny

D-82

Lugny

Viré

Azé

Clessé

Pont-de-Vaux

D-82

D-103

Laizé

A-6

N-6

D-933

Verzé

MÂCONNAIS

Milly-Lamartine

SAÔNE-ET-LOIRE

la Roche-Vineuse

Prissé

Mâcon

Replonges

Roche de Vergisson

La Patte d'Oie

Vergisson

N-79

Roche de Solutré

Davayé

Vonnas,

Solutré-Pouilly

Pouilly

Bourg-en-Bresse

Fuissé

Loché

Chasselas

Leynes

D-31

Vinzelles

Chaintré

A I N

Chagny

St-Vérand

Chânes

Crêches-sur-Saône

St-Amour

Bellevue

D-186

Jullié

Juliénas

D-95

B E A U J O L A I S

Chénas

Fontanevaux

D-18

La Chapelle de-Guinchay

Fleurie

Romanèche - Thorins

Chiroubles

Saône

Villié-Morgon

RHÔNE

Lancié

Thoissey

D-9

A-6

N

Beaujeu

Laintignie

Morgon

St-Jean-d'Ardières

D-37

Quincié

Cercié

D-17

Bourg-en-Bresse

St-Didier

St-Lager

Brouilly

Mont-Brouilly

Belleville

Odenas

Monts du Beaujolais

St-Étienne-des-Ouillières

N-6

St-Georges-de-Reneins

Vaux-en-Beaujolais

Le Perréon

D-20

D-43

D-833

D-936

B E A U J O L A I S

Denicé

Villefranche

Lyon

Each road (each "toe" of the *patte*) leads to a different but equally enchanting drive through the vineyards.

The best way to start is to head in the direction of Davayé and Vergisson. Here, with vineyards off to either side, one climbs gently but steadily toward the main landmarks of the area, the Rock of Solutré on the left and the Rock of Vergisson on the right. From far away they appear to be twin rocks of Gibraltar, and one has the feeling that the sea must be just beyond. The bones of prehistoric horses, elk, and mastodons have been found at the base of Solutré.

Here, among the rolling hills that cradle vineyard and village alike, it is indeed easy to see why some people consider the Pouilly country one of France's most delightful regions. The country roads curl around the sides of the slopes and from nearly any point one can see the swell and contour of the land, the panorama taking in as many as two or three hillsides and valleys at a time. These narrow lanes are intended mostly for the growers and it is easy to lose your way.

The villages that produce the best Pouilly-Fuissés are Solutré-Pouilly, Davayé, and Fuissé, all within walking distance of one another. In contrast to the rest of the Mâcon vineyards, a relatively small amount of their wine, about one-fifth, passes through the cooperative cellars. The individual grower is still the strongest influence here. One of the best is Joseph Corsin, who divides his time between Davayé and Fuissé. Now, with his two sons, M. Corsin tends 60 hectares (150 acres) of vineyard and makes an excellent wine. He was one of the first participants in the Alexis Lichine Tasse d'Or (golden cup) competition, an annual judging of both red and white wines I began in 1960. Before the competition was discontinued in 1973, M. Corsin, along with the *cave coopérative* at Chaintré, won the Tasse d'Or for white wines more often than any other grower.

"The competition," M. Corsin recalls, "took the form of a blind tasting, but it was the growers themselves who were the judges. We'd go from sample to sample, sometimes through one hundred and fifty wines, never knowing if the wine we were tasting was ours. You see, it's not that easy."

The finalists, chosen by the growers as the two best red and the two best white wines from the fifteen to twenty tables of samples, were presented to the head judging table, where I had assembled officials from the I.N.A.O. and the Fraud Squad, the presidents of the various wine associations of the region, some of the leading restaurateurs, and Georges Duboeuf, the main organizer and Beaujolais's moving spirit. It was our responsibility to pick the best red and the best white for the award of the golden Tasse—the runner-ups to be given a silver *tastevin*.

I remember one Tasse d'Or in particular: the 1961 competition, which took place at the Château de Pizay, one of the better red-wine vineyards of the Beaujolais. M. Gaidon, our host and a member of the final panel of judges, who was himself making a fine wine, after tasting a sample which most of us had found to be excellent, stood up and announced: "This wine is excellent, but has not finished its *malo* [the malolactic is the second fermentation]. I don't care how great it is, since it hasn't finished its malolactic fermentation I give it a zero." Well, his zero naturally knocked it out of the competition and another wine won. Poor M. Gaidon! At the end, when the wines were matched up with the growers, he found it was his own wine he had flunked!

The Pouilly-Fuissé villages—Chaintré, Vergisson, Solutré, Pouilly, and Fuissé—produce individually distinctive white wines, although their close relationship is quite evident. As a family, they are full, dry wines, with a body that comes from being relatively high in alcohol. Generally softer and fruitier than Chablis and not as steely, the Pouillys have a slight specific character imparted by the soil, what the growers call *goût du terroir*. They develop within a year and can maintain their freshness for as long as five years.

The wine cooperative at Chaintré runs a pleasant *caveau,* or tasting cellar, with a charming view of the vineyards, where the wines may be sampled. Chaintré and a number of surrounding villages are responsible for a certain amount of Beaujolais Blanc.

There are three other *appellations* in the area, all producing very fine white wines that are generally less expensive than the high-priced Pouilly-Fuissé: Pouilly-Loché, Pouilly-Vinzelles, and Saint-Véran. Pouilly-Loché and Pouilly-Vinzelles have the same *appellation* restrictions as Pouilly-Fuissé, except for location, and are similar in kind to their more illustrious neighbor but with a shade less finesse. In 1971, Saint-Véran became a welcome new *appellation,* named for the village of Saint-Vérand (note the difference in spelling). Villages eligible to contribute to the excellent Saint-Véran wine surround the vineyards of Pouilly-Fuissé, Pouilly-Loché, and

Pouilly-Vinzelles. These villages—Chanes, Saint-Amour, Saint-Vérand, Prissé, Chasselas, Leynes, and Davayé—produce not only good Saint-Véran but also some Beaujolais Blanc as well. Compared to Pouilly-Fuissé, Saint-Véran may be an excellent value, while perhaps not achieving the same high quality. However, if its popularity continues to grow rapidly and prices increase in proportion, its value may become dubious.

ॐ

MÂCONNAIS
Hotels and Restaurants
H = Hotel; R = Restaurant

The visitor to the Mâconnais should also consult the "Hotels and Restaurants" sections on pp. 137–39, 145–49, 176–78, 203–06, 210–12, and 231–37, plus Itineraries C, D, G, and J, pp. 420–21, 421–22, 425–26, and 427–28, respectively.

MÂCON (71000—Saône-et-Loire)
(Paris 404—Lyon 68—Chalon 57)

&❧ A wine fair that is held in mid-May gives one the opportunity to taste a fine gamut of Chalonnais, Maconnais, and Beaujolais wines. The TGV stops here and can take you back to Paris on the world's fastest train in one hour and forty-five minutes. If upon arrival you wish to hire a car: Hertz 85.38.63.22; Europ Car 85.38.64.31; Budget (at the regular train station) 85.38.44.48 and the special TGV station 85.34.62.39.

HR MAPOTEL BELLEVUE: 416, quai Lamartine (close to the Mairie in middle of town). Tel.: 85.38.05.07. Tlx.: 800837.   31 rooms (25 with toilet).
A comfortable hotel-restaurant with soundproofed rooms. Its restaurant, under the direction of André Champagne, is noted for its imaginative and enticing dishes; particularly good are the chicken in *cassis* and the veal knuckle.

HR FRANTEL: 26, rue de Coubertin. Tel.: 85.38.28.06. Tlx.: 800830.   63 rooms.
Comfortable hotel 500 meters north on the road to Paris, not far from the center of town. River-front location with tennis courts. Good overnight stop. The restaurant, called the Saint-Vincent, is unusually good for a hotel.

HR SOFITEL: On A-6 (On the auto route, A-6, 14 km north of Mâcon in Lugny; may also be reached by N-6). Tel.: 85.33.19.00. Tlx.: 800881.   98 rooms.
Air-conditioned, soundproofed. Heated pool. The restaurant, La Bourgogne, is a good stopping place only when in a hurry on the Paris–Lyon Autoroute.

R AUBERGE BRESSANE: 14, rue du 28-juin (just to the right of N-6 as you come from the north near A-6). Tel.: 85.38.07.42.
A large variety of good, reasonably priced menus.

218

SOLUTRÉ-POUILLY (71960—Saône-et-Loire)
(Cluny 25—Mâcon 9—Fuissé 3—Dijon 135)
On D-54, 9 km west of Mâcon.

At the bottom of the Rock of Solutré lie thousands of bones from horses pushed off the cliff by prehistoric man.

HR LE RELAIS DE SOLUTRÉ: Tel.: 85.37.82.67.   30 simple rooms including annex.
The restaurant, centered around a large wood-burning stove, specializes in fish, roasts, and grilled fare. Functional, neat and clean rooms, some with a beautiful view of the hills of Beaujolais and Pouilly-Fuissé, others with a view of the Rock of Solutré.

FUISSÉ (71960—Saône-et-Loire)
(Paris 402—Mâcon 8.5—Villefranche-sur-Saône 45)
On D-172, 86 km west of Mâcon.

R AU POUILLY-FUISSÉ: Tel.: 85.35.60.68.
Spacious simple restaurant with outdoor tables and garden. The proprietor and chef, A. Bonnet, is a personable host and speaks English, having worked for some years as a restaurateur in Cambridge, Massachusetts.

REPLONGES (01750—Ain)
(Paris 410—Bourg-en-Bresse 29—Mâcon 4.5—Tournus 34)

HR LA HUCHETTE: Tel.: 85.31.03.55. Tlx.: 800787. You cross the Saône on N-79, which leads to Bourg-en-Bresse.   10 rooms, 2 suites.
Fine cuisine in a very hospitable restaurant situated in a quiet, charming park. Heated pool.

IGÉ (71960—Saône-et-Loire)

HR HÔTEL DU CHÂTEAU D'IGÉ: 14 km from Mâcon, Sud exit on the A-6, in the village of Igé (500 inhabitants) at the crossroads of D-85 and D-134. Tel.: 85.33.33.99. Tlx.: 351915.
Six comfortable rooms plus 6 suites, large park, relaxing surroundings. You can eat better in the Beaujolais to the south. *Relais et Châteaux.*

BEAUJOLAIS

There is no mistaking the Beaujolais. This rolling land of tight, lush hills and valleys threaded with streams is the wine country of one's fantasies, perhaps France's most scenic vineyard region. Nearly every turn in the narrow, twisting cart roads opens onto new welcoming vistas of vine-covered slopes, each valley centered on its cluster of houses and a church spire. The succession of charming panoramas is practically overwhelming. And the wine reflects the landscape. Beaujolais is one of the most widely drunk red wines in the world, one reason being that it is excellent when young and chilled.

Unless you have a detailed map of the region to guide you, the small roads will lead you in circles. When you get lost—which is inevitable—the cheerful inhabitants will point you in the right direction, and may even offer you a glass to speed you on your way. Indeed, these convivial, round-faced, rosy-cheeked people seem to have been created for the making of wine—or perhaps the making of wine created them? Forget the delicate sniffs and sips, the ruminatory gargles, the suspenseful silences with which we approach the great Burgundies and Bordeaux. The wines of Beaujolais are meant to be swallowed and gulped and unabashedly enjoyed.

In Beaujolais more than in any other winegrowing area of France, I find myself wondering about this almost mystic relationship between the land and the families who cultivate it and the wines they produce. It is not too farfetched to see a connection between the aristocratic vintages of Bordeaux and the great châteaux from which they issue. Burgundy, on the other hand, for all the nobility of its greatest wines, is unmistakably a land of the people of the soil, for whom a hectare or two of well-selected vineyard can be as precious an inheritance as a Picasso. In the Beaujolais one senses a different, closer, kindlier relationship between *Vitis vinifera* and *Homo sapiens,* the generous soil and its diligent cultivators. The wine cries out to be drunk young. Not for the Beaujolais the bottle to be cherished in dusty racks; the wine is for now. And, of course, to be exported throughout the world.

It is hard to imagine this pristinely green and pleasant land as a major economic power. Yet in the world of wine it is. To satisfy the demand for their product, the 9,500 growers of Beaujolais produce an average of more than 1.1 million hectoliters of wine a year—almost 150 million bottles—from 22,000 hectares (55,000 acres). Recently, a succession of short vintages has put annual output below the point where it can meet an ever-increasing demand. The price has skyrocketed. By Easter 1984, after the great '83 vintage, the best since '76, most of the Beaujolais, Beaujo-lais-Villages, and the nine *Crus* (Growths) had already been sold, though most were not yet in bottle. Some of the smaller growths, in fact, like Chiroubles, often sell out in February and March. In the past five years foreign consumption of Beaujolais has climbed 50 percent, while the amount of money spent on Beaujolais in that time has more than doubled. The top six foreign buyers alone—Switzerland, Benelux, Holland, England, the United States, and Germany—consume a third of an average harvest. Fearful that the boom market will not hold, some of Beaujolais's more energetic merchants are doing their best to make sure that their future is now.

There have been signs already that Beaujolais customers will not swallow *any* price for the privilege of drinking the wine. In 1981 there was a large stock of the light 1980 Beaujolais still in the growers' cellars. The *crus* and a number of the Beaujolais-Villages succeeded in making desirable wine, but the public turned away from the simple Beaujolais. It remains to be seen whether the growers and the local shippers heed the warning.

When I began writing about Beaujolais for the first edition of the *Wines of France,* published in 1951, Beaujolais *primeur* or *nouveau,* the very young wine, did not even deserve serious mention. It was young, fruity wine sold in barrels and served in carafes in restaurants in Lyon and in specialized bistros in Paris—strictly the cheap places. In the early 1950s, this *vin nouveau* never saw the inside of a bottle or traveled overseas. But at about that same time, by the strange workings of reverse snobbery, the news spread that it was chic to drink this newly born wine. Smart merchants made it available for both restaurant and home use, and eventually for export. Since then, the taste for *primeur* has become a major fad. At its best, it is light and fresh in color and taste, with a fruity and flowery bouquet that reminds some tasters of peaches and roses. Though an uncomplicated wine, it can move its followers and pushers to exaggerated claims. They bear examination.

Beaujolais *primeur* is the first of any wine to be bottled after the vintage, usually within four to six weeks. One of the early promoters of the region and best shippers of the area, Georges Duboeuf, defends this practice: "It's not as simple as putting young wine in a bottle. First, its taste and chemistry must pass the test. In the two weeks before the earliest shipping date, November 15, we submit samples to the oenological center in Villefranche or Mâcon. There, the wine is tasted by a panel—a grower, a shipper, and a broker—to be sure it has *primeur* character. It then passes automatically to a chemical analysis to verify that the alcoholic content is not more than thirteen percent and that it has less than five grams of acidity and less than two grams of sugar."

Most important is the question of *primeur* character. Not every Beaujolais from every vintage can manage it. The quality of the soil of the particular vineyard and the weather from year to year should determine how much *primeur* should be made there; the excessive fining and filtering involved in the production of a *primeur* fit to be bottled in its infancy also remove most of the wine's personality. For example, in my opinion most of the 1983 vintage should have been aged at least a few months to develop its character, rather than being sold as *primeur*. As *primeur,* much good Beaujolais is nipped in the bud for the sake of current fashion. Which is not to say that all the wines made into *primeur* would gain much if left to mature naturally. In particular, *primeur* has been a great boon for the Bas-Beaujolais. This large expanse of newly planted vines south of Villefranche is a more recent vineyard area, producing huge quantities of rather ordinary wine that benefits little from aging. Sold as *primeur* or *nouveau,* it is no loss to the consumer.

The question of how well *primeur* travels is a real one. My own opinion is that much of it does not travel as well as people think. In any case, more than half of it is exported. Since these wines are sold quickly, the growers get a fast return on their money—no minor matter, given the present outrageously high interest rates.

Whether the shipper waits or not, the period lasting from the vintage in late September or early October until January is the most hectic for the Beaujolais. The *primeur* has to be picked, allowed to ferment, racked, filtered, bottled, labeled, and shipped in the ridiculously short time of four to six weeks. Many weeks later, the other Beaujolais classifications begin their racking, filtering, and bottling, all of which will continue until the next spring. One shipper recalls: "On the first night of the *primeur* market, November 15, there are hundreds and hundreds of trucks and trailers in the Beaujolais to pick up the wine. On every road it is like an army convoy."

Only thirty years ago, Beaujolais was produced almost entirely for the thirsty burghers of Lyon. Hence the old saying: "Three rivers flow into Lyon—the Rhône, the Saône, and the Beaujolais." "In the years following the war," recalls Michel Brun, a Beaujolais salesman, "when our customers were mostly in or around Lyon, and later Paris, people would stop for a glass or two on their way home from work. The café proprietor would always get his wines in the barrel and bottle them himself. For a few *sous,* he'd pour you a glass at the bar. In those days a *pot* of Beaujolais [50 centiliters: 17 fluid ounces] cost 50 centimes, the same as a pack of cigarettes. I'm afraid we've lost that crowd forever."

From a pleasant and cheap bar-wine, served from the barrel, Beaujolais became an inexpensive bottled wine for restaurants and supermarkets. The high price it now fetches has put it beyond the reach of its original clientele. One wonders if the lesser Beaujolais will continue to find an avid market at the prevailing high prices. I personally doubt it. All the same, I hope that Beaujolais' drop in demand and price will be less severe than the precipitous decline of Bordeaux in 1973.

Further evidence of the changing times may be seen in the increasing sophistication of the local growers. Nearly every village of the area posts periodic warnings from the local agricultural advisory board of different vine diseases that may crop up during the growing season, with recommendations on types of treatment. And though most vineyard holdings are small, from 1 to 10 hectares (2.5 to 25 acres), tall stakes coiffed with colored plastic bags may be seen between the vine rows to indicate the areas to be sprayed by helicopter. When I see such technical proficiency, I have to remind myself that even as late as the fifties there was no Autoroute from Paris and only the overburdened National 6 took vacationers past the vineyards on their way to and from the Côte d'Azur. To anyone traveling through the Beaujolais in the old days, it was a poor, yet gay, country. Then, as now, the local pastime was *boules.* For the men, it seems to be the main event on Sundays, when one can drive through the villages and hardly see a woman outdoors. The men play in the public squares, their berets pulled forward into a brim, pausing between rounds to have a swallow of wine.

In those years after the war, the growers, a hospitable lot, were only too happy to show off their little-known wines. It was then that the first *caveaux,* or tasting cellars, were established. Droppers-in could down free samples and buy if they liked. The object was not so much to sell bottles as to promote the wine and broaden the market. Today, dozens of garish *caveaux* painted in bright reds, greens, and yellows dot the countryside; the signs leading to them often make it easier to find the *ca-*

veaux than the local town hall or church. The *dégustation* is still free in most of these cellarettes, but nowadays a contribution is usually requested and rarely withheld. Just as the direct retail sales of Beaujolais have become more intense, so have the mechanics of the wholesale trade. There are now slightly more than 5,000 growers in Beaujolais, two-thirds of whom belong to one of the eighteen cooperatives. Whether sold by individuals or cooperatives, the growers' wine is bought by local shippers, of whom there are about thirty-five today, or by the Beaune shippers, who offer Beaujolais as an inexpensive Burgundy. Usually one of the twenty-five *courtiers,* or brokers, of the area will act as an intermediary in the sale and take a commission on it.

The northern Beaujolais overlaps with southern Pouilly-Fuissé and for a while, as you explore the country around Saint-Amour, these two famous place-names are in fact one. Your best clue to the change in country is to watch for the change in the vines: the Pinot Chardonnay of the Pouillys grows tall, compared to the stubby Gamay used for the Beaujolais. The latter can be recognized by its stunted trunk, barely knee-high, with three to five branches growing more or less vertically from the top, in what is called goblet-pruning, *la taille à gobelet.* The soil of the northern Beaujolais—the Haut-Beaujolais—is rich in manganese and granite and perfectly suited to the Gamay, which otherwise makes rather lackluster wines.

The Haut-Beaujolais runs from Mâcon to the hillsides overlooking Ville-franche, making its way between the plain of the Saône and the mountains farther west. The Haut-Beaujolais contains all of the forty-odd communes of Beaujolais-Villages, all nine Growths (*Crus*), and the heaviest concentration of tasting cellars. South from Villefranche to the Tourdine River, just outside Lyon, is the Bas-Beaujolais, the source of vast amounts of wine with the *appellation* simply of Beaujolais. South of Villefranche, the soil turns chalky again and the Gamay makes a thinner, more common wine.

Among the hundreds of villages in the Haut-Beaujolais, some have made consistently superior wines and so have been given the privilege of either adding their name to the label Beaujolais (as in Beaujolais-Chânes, -Cercié, or -Le Perréon) or selling their wines simply as Beaujolais-Villages.

Beaujolais-Villages and the nine Growths are a fair assurance of basic quality. One of the requirements, in addition to the geographical limits of the *appellation,* is that these wines have an increased minimum percentage of alcohol before chaptalization (10 percent) over simple Beaujolais, which gives them a measure of durability and longevity. In the case of the nine Growths or *Crus*—Saint-Amour, Juliénas, Chénas, Moulin-à-Vent, Fleurie, Chiroubles, Morgon, Brouilly, and Côtes de Brouilly—the minimum percentage is the same, but if the grower wants to add the vineyard name (as does Château de la Chaize in Brouilly), the minimum is raised to 11 percent. In practice, it is not only the minimum that the growers are worried about—it is also the 14 percent maximum. The sins are more often of over-chaptalization than of using under-ripe, sugar-poor grapes.

When it comes to buying Beaujolais, the customer must use his own good sense or his merchant's advice, rather than depending on specific "brands" or vintages. Bargain-priced Beaujolais is usually a poor value. Sometimes they may be fraudulent blends, in which the Beaujolais is drowned by sturdier, more alcoholic, but totally characterless wine from the Rhône, the Midi, or Italy. This kind of blending is illegal in France and, happily, this fraud is often discovered and penalized.

Another source of so-called bargain Beaujolais is much harder to detect from the outside of the bottle: wine from areas of new vine plantings throughout Beaujolais, especially in the Bas-Beaujolais. In the past ten years, the area of the Bas cultivated with vines has increased by 50 percent. The major proportion of new plantings dates from the years of spectacular growth in the Beaujolais market, 1967 to 1972. Grapes may now be found in soil capable of giving only a thin wine in the best of years. The sensationalist press has it that the loaded tank trucks from the Languedoc and Calabria find a ready welcome here.

The first Growth we meet driving south on the N-6 from Mâcon, or on the vineyard road from Chaintré and Saint-Vérand, is the invitingly named Saint-Amour. These wines have a forthright, uncomplicated character and do improve with time in the bottle, but begin to fade after much more than four years. Among the Growths, Saint-Amour is often underrated. In a good vintage, well selected and reasonably priced, its wines can be a pleasant surprise. Since the vineyards have a more eastern than southern exposure, the wines can be a touch acidic after cool summers. The scorching summer of 1976 was perfect for them, and to some palates Saint-Amour came up with the most typically Beaujolais wines of all the *Crus.* At their best, these wines are marked by delicate fruit and perfume, with good firm body. The average annual production is around 140,000 cases.

Two kilometers (1.2 miles) through the vineyards from Saint-Amour is its southern neighbor, perhaps the least known of the nine Growths: Juliénas, named for Julius Caesar. Most of its 488 hectares (1,220 acres) of vines are more favorably exposed to the sun than those of Saint-Amour and, as a result, although the two wines share a similar character, Juliénas is the longer-lived of the two and may profit from a couple of years of bottle age. While in off years it may lack typical Beaujolais charm, it is full and more deeply colored than Saint-Amour. The local *caveau,* along with the one in Villié-Morgon, was the first in Beaujolais and is still located in the cellar of the town church. Château de Juliénas and Les Capitans are two of the best vineyards. The total production averages 300,000 cases.

Heading south from Juliénas, we should join up with what becomes the vineyard road through the Growths. This country lane crosses the stream just south of Juliénas and is the road to follow through most communes of the nine Growths. But our first stop on the way is the village of Chénas.

Chénas the commune and Chénas the wine offer a good illustration of the difference between a place-name (the name of the source of the wine, which you find on a label) and a *commune* (a municipality). *Commune* is a political and legal designation referring to all the hamlets and all the land in a given area around a principal town, in this case Chénas, after which the commune is named. A large part of the commune of Chénas lies within the boundaries of the wine place-name Moulin-à-Vent, and most of its wines are entitled to be sold as Moulin-à-Vent. Those that are sold as Chénas come largely from the 240 hectares (600 acres) of vineyards between the town and the woodland to the west.

Certainly the best place in Chénas to sample its wine is on the terrace of the Robin-Relais des Crus restaurant—known to the locals as Chez Robin—a carefully managed restaurant in the heart of the vineyard. The proprietors serve their Beaujolais slightly chilled, as is the current custom. All Beaujolais, contrary to most red wine, is shown to its best drinking advantage when slightly cool—cellar temperature or the temperature of spring water. Chénas are solid wines—occasionally overly tannic within six months of the vintage—that repay patience for a year or two. They can be big and full, closely approaching in character the Moulin-à-Vent, just to the east, though they may sometimes lack its fruitiness.

On the country road from Chénas to Romanèche-Thorins one can see the windmill of Moulin-à-Vent, high on a hill overlooking the sea of vines of the Growths of the area: Fleurie, Chénas, and Moulin-à-Vent. Moulin-à-Vent has always been worthy of its standing as a ringleader of the Growths, and the old mill itself is a national monument, a symbol of Beaujolais. No one has replaced its broken sails and there is no better spot from which to get a panoramic view of the Haut-Beaujolais vineyards.

Though often considered the king of the Beaujolais, and always the most expensive, Moulin-à-Vent, with its bigness, fullness, and richness in tannin, is quite distinct from the sprightly, flowery lightness that one expects from a "typical" Beaujolais. In great years, such as 1978 or 1983, Moulin-à-Vent matures more slowly than the wine from neighboring villages, being more characteristically Côte de Beaune-like at the end of a couple of years. Two good vineyards are those of Château Portier and Château du Moulin-à-Vent; the latter is run by Mme Cécile Bloud.

The closest contender to Moulin-à-Vent for the crown of Beaujolais is just to the south, in Fleurie. Fleurie has a bit more vineyard than Moulin-à-Vent—700 hectares (1,750 acres) as against about 650 (1,625)—but produces about the same amount of wine—around 300,000 cases a year. Fleurie is perhaps the better known abroad. Flowers, perfume, spring, and elegant, graceful femininity are the first things that come to mind when the name is mentioned, and very often Fleurie does have the fragrant freshness, breeding, and fruitiness to make those comparisons particularly appropriate. It is not as heavy as a Moulin-à-Vent; and from vintage to vintage is quite dependable. Fleurie has one of the most efficiently run *caves coopératives* of the Growths, formerly managed by Mlle Marguerite Chabert, who relinquished the presidency when eighty-five in 1984. Strong and active, she came to personify the charm of her wines. She transferred the reins of her management to François Chabot, her nephew, who is carrying on her tradition of quality.

Just down the street from the Chabert-managed cooperative is the Chabert *charcuterie,* formerly run by Mlle Chabert's late brother and still called by the family name. The three or four times a year that I am in the Beaujolais I always stop off at the shop to stock up on their delicious Beaujolais specialties: *saucisson, cervelas* with truffles or pistachios, and a vast array of other sausages, including my greatest weakness of all, *andouillettes,* which I have them wrap and send to me in the Médoc, at the Prieuré. The essential ingredients of *andouillettes* hardly seem as seductive as the Beaujolais restaurants seem to make them: thin slices of pork tripe bound with a mustardy breading mixture and put in a sausage casing. They are best served hot and crisp from the oven. Nothing flatters a bottle of Fleurie, or even plain Beaujolais, as much as the regional *charcuterie.*

The Cinderella of the Haut-Beaujolais is Chiroubles. Almost unknown beyond the region a decade ago, Chiroubles has become the most popular of all Beaujolais Growths among the French—and it is not easy to find abroad. From its vineyards, just a few kilometers off the vineyard road west of Fleurie, come only 150,000 cases of wine a year. Between the Paris and Lyon clientele, the entire stock could be exhausted three or four times over. It is the shortest-lived Beaujolais, and within a couple of years may have noticeably faded. "I can guarantee it," says Georges Duboeuf, "if you have a tasting of the nine *Crus* from 1977 or 1984, Chiroubles will come out last. But then nobody who enjoys wine would ever think of waiting this long to drink it." It has more of the light fruitiness of a Fleurie than the firmness one used to associate with Morgon, its neighbor to the south. Two Chiroubles vineyards that have had excellent results in recent years are Domaine de Raousset and Marcel Dufoux.

In the town square of Chiroubles stands a monument to one of the great heroes of the region, Victor Pulliat, who, during the phylloxera scourge, was the first to graft native vines onto disease-resistant American root-stock.

No wine in Beaujolais better reflects the caprices of wine fashion than Morgon.

In the days when all Beaujolais was bistro wine *par excellence,* Morgon occupied the place now taken over by Chiroubles as the favorite light tipple of Paris and Lyon. At that time, Morgon was vinified to be light, almost rosé, but with a high degree of alcohol. The customer was invigorated by its pleasing freshness and fortified by its hidden strength. Then, as Beaujolais gained a national and, eventually, an international following, the wines were served less often at the bar from a barrel and more frequently at the dinner table from a bottle. As the serving became more serious, so did the wine. The makers of Morgon gradually vinified it to be harder and longer-lasting, qualities to which it is well suited. These were fat, hard wines that filled the mouth and made up for their lack of floweriness and fruit with depth of character. Now fashion has dictated a trend to the lighter and less complex in all wines, and the growers of Morgon do not intend to be left behind. The distinctive Morgon *goût du terroir,* imparted by the brownish, crumbly slate soil (known locally as *roche pourrie,* or rotten rock), can still be found in the wine, and one can still say *"Ils morgonnent"*—that they repay laying down. However, today they are about as light as most other Growths of Beaujolais.

One of the best growers and a leader in bringing about this change is Jean Descombes, who has won many prizes for his Morgon, including the Alexis Lichine Tasse d'Or. His vines lie on the slope of the Mont de Py, the favored slope of Morgon. Just down the road from M. Descombes's *caves* is the *caveau* of Villié-Morgon. In addition to offering tastings and direct sales of wine, the cellar has a display of wine-making artifacts, including ancient-looking vineyard tools and Roman amphorae.

Brouilly and the Côtes de Brouilly are the last of the Growths on our trip south through the Haut-Beaujolais. Five villages produce Brouilly over an area larger than 1,000 hectares (2,500 acres); three of the villages also produce Côtes de Brouilly, which are the better wines.

Brouilly averages nearly 500,000 cases a year. These are medium-bodied wines with fair balance and quite simple. When served slightly chilled—as most Beaujolais should be—they are delightfully fresh, with a neatly concentrated bouquet. Although they improve in the bottle (up to three years for a good vintage like 1978), they are more likely to be at their best the autumn of the following year.

With a height of only 300 meters or so (1,000 feet), the Mont de Brouilly is not exactly an Alp. However, the chapel on its summit is one of the holier places in the Beaujolais. Notre Dame du Raisin (Our Lady of the Grape) was built more than a century ago by desperate souls who hoped thereby to exorcise the powdery mildew (oïdium) that still attacks the vines of France. Each September 8, before the harvest, a long line of devotees toils up the steep slope to attend a service at which

Our Lady's protection for the crop is invoked. Afterward, the faithful slake their thirsts with, of course, Côtes de Brouilly.

Because of its southern slope, the Côtes de Brouilly produces wines that have more character, longer life, and greater body than those that are labeled merely Brouilly. One of the better vineyards is the pretty Château Thiven, now run by Mme Geoffray, widow of Claude Geoffray, one of my early mentors in the Beaujolais. Over many of M. Geoffray's bottles I learned to appreciate the charms of his beloved Côtes de Brouilly. He felt strongly enough about his wine to become a founder of the Maison du Beaujolais, one of the region's first tasting cellars, easily found on N-6 (which at that time was the only way to reach the Alps or the Côte d'Azur from the north of France).

A local tourist attraction is the Château de la Chaize, which was built by a nephew of the confessor of Louis XIV. Its present owner is the Marquise de Roussy de Sales, whose late husband, the Marquis, was export director of Christian Dior perfumes. As he traveled the world to sell his scents, the Marquis also took time to promote the flowery Beaujolais from his well-known domaine. In nearby Saint-Lager, at the bottom of the slope, there are two tasting cellars where both Brouilly and Côtes de Brouilly may be sampled.

From Odénas south to Villefranche, on D-43, we pass several of the better Beaujolais-Villages, some of which merit a visit, if only to sample the offerings of the *caveaux:* Le Perréon, Saint-Étienne-la-Varenne, Arbuissonnaz, and Saint-Étienne-des-Oullières. From Villefranche, both N-6 and the Autoroute are easily accessible.

Today, I always leave the Beaujolais with mixed feelings—with affection for their past and concern for their future. I'm afraid that Beaujolais's prices may scare the world away. Still it remains France's richest mine of great peasant wine folklore, celebrating the humor, hard work, and *joie de vivre* of its people. The link between the grower and the soil and the wine that issues from it is inescapable. Growers still tell of the not too distant past when the village *lavoir*—where the weekly wash and the yearly (so they say) bleaching of sheets took place—served as the gossip gazette and the center of all local and regional information of any importance. They still remember the arrival of the tractor—only since the war. At the time, the growers felt as if they had broken some secret agreement with the soil and vines that all labor be done by hand. But if they seek a sign of divine forgiveness, they have no further to look than the fame and success that have been their lot in recent years. If ever wine-makers were blessed, it is the growers of Beaujolais.

BEAUJOLAIS-VILLAGES

Appellation Contrôlée

CHATEAU DU BLUIZARD

Jean de Saint-Charles, propriétaire à St-Etienne-la-Varenne

BEAUJOLAIS
Hotels and Restaurants

H = *Hotel;* R = *Restaurant*

The visitor to the Beaujolais should also consult the "Hotels and Restaurants" sections on pp. 137–39, 145–49, 176–78, 203–06, 210–12, 218–20, and 234–37, plus Itinerary G, pp. 425–26.

JULIÉNAS (69840—Rhône)
(Paris 411—Lyon 65—Mâcon 17—Saint-Amour 5)

HR CHEZ LA ROSE: Place du Marché. Tel.: 74.04.41.20.   12 rooms, quite inexpensive. Recommended by the locals as an inexpensive eating spot of good value. Regional cooking.

HR COQ AU VIN: Place du Marché. Tel.: 74.04.41.98.   7 very inexpensive rooms. Restaurant also inexpensive. Good stopover when in the vineyards.

CHÉNAS (69840—Rhône)
(Mâcon 17—Juliénas 5—Lyon 62—Villefranche 35)
From N-6, take D-95 west.

R ROBIN: At Les Deschamps. Tel.: 85.36.72.67.
Run by Daniel Robin and his wife, this restaurant is charmingly situated in the midst of the vineyards. Wines from the nearby vineyard of M. Robin's father are served. M. Robin is a former assistant of Alain Chapel, and the food is excellent, though not inexpensive. Open for lunch only. One star in Michelin.

ROMANÈCHE-THORINS (71570—Saône-et-Loire)
(Mâcon 17—Villefranche 29—Lyon 56)
Exit from Autoroute at Mâcon-Sud, 10 km north of Romanèche,
or exit at Belleville, 6 km to the south.

HR LES MARITONNES: Beyond the train station. Tel.: 85.35.51.70. 19 small, inexpensive rooms (18 with toilet). Swimming pool.
Good, quiet lunch stop when visiting the vineyards. The Beaujolais specialties of M. and Mme Fauvin deserve the one star they have been awarded in Michelin.

R LE COMMERCE: Tel.: 85.35.51.82. 16 rooms (9 with toilet).
A good, simple, inexpensive Beaujolais restaurant, in the heart of the vineyard country.

FLEURIE (69820—Rhône)
(Lyon 57—Villefranche 31—Mâcon 24—Belleville 12)

❦ You can discover the new vintages of Beaujolais at a wine fair held each year in early November.

R AUBERGE DU CEP: Place de l'Église. Tel.: 74.04.10.77.
Gérard Cortembert is a great chef, and you'll receive a warm welcome. High-priced for the area, but many of the dishes are well worth it. For simple fare, consult the *carte établie*. Two stars in Michelin.

THOISSEY (01140—Ain)
(Lyon 56—Mâcon 18—TGV Station 10—Bourg 36—Villefranche 29)
From N-6, 5 km east on D-9. From A-6, exit at Belleville when driving north,
or Mâcon-Sud when driving south.

HR AU CHAPON FIN: Rue du Champ-de-Foire. Tel.: 74.04.04.74. Tlx.: 305728. 25 rooms.
Quiet and pleasant. The best hotel to stay in when visiting the Beaujolais. In the Blanc family you will find charming, solicitous hosts. Comfortable rooms, good food, and an excellent selection of Beaujolais. This is where I prefer to stay when visiting the Beaujolais. English spoken. *Relais et Châteaux.* One star in Michelin.

VONNAS (01540—Ain)
(Mâcon 19—Thoissey 23—Bourg 24—Villefranche 39—Lyon 66)
20 km east of the Beaujolais.

HR GEORGES BLANC (formerly CHEZ LA MÈRE BLANC): Tel.: 74.50.00.10. Tlx.: 380776. 25 rooms. 6 apartments. Swimming pool and tennis.
Very pleasant *relais de campagne,* entirely renovated with luxurious, comfortable rooms. The restaurant has a sensational reputation. Expensive. *Relais et Châteaux.* The chef, Georges Blanc, received his third Michelin star in 1981.

MORGON (69910—Rhône)
(Belleville 8—Villefranche 22—Mâcon 31)

❦ Visit the *cave de dégustation* in Morgon, where you can taste the growers' wines—a whole gamut of them.

BEAUJOLAIS

R LE RELAIS DES CAVEAUX: Located in the village itself. Tel.: 74.04.21.77.
Reasonably priced, good value.

BELLEVILLE (69220—Rhône)
(Villefranche 18—Mâcon 25—Lyon 45—Bourg 40)
Close to the vineyards of Brouilly. This is the exit to take if you are traveling to
or from Paris on Autoroute A-6 and want to visit the Beaujolais vineyards.

HR LE BEAUJOLAIS: 40, rue du Maréchal Foch. Near the Belleville exit from the autoroute. Tel.:
74.66.05.31.   7 small and rather basic rooms.
The wide choice of Beaujolais wines and the carefully prepared regional dishes make this a fairly
satisfying stop when traveling through the Beaujolais vineyards.

SAINT-LAGER (69220—Rhône)
(Belleville 6—Lyon 52—Mâcon 32—Villié-Morgon 10)

R AUBERGE SAINT-LAGER: Tel.: 74.66.16.08.
Inexpensive. New owners, M. and Mme Carrette, offer a variety of good, inexpensive menus in
this vineyard-surrounded restaurant.

SAINT-GEORGES-DE-RENEINS (69830—Rhône)
(Lyon 40—Mâcon 30—Villefranche 9—Bourg 43)

HR HOSTELLERIE DE SAINT-GEORGES: On N-6. Tel.: 74.67.62.78.   5 inexpensive rooms.
Pleasant stop with inexpensive food. Try the soufflé of pike or the *feuilleté* of ham.

BLACERET (69830—Rhône)
(Lyon 42—Mâcon 35—Villefranche 11)

R RESTAURANT DU BEAUJOLAIS: On N-6. Tel.: 74.67.54.75.
Proprietor M. J. Mayançon. Good value for regional specialties. Good selection of wines. Inexpensive.

VILLEFRANCHE-SUR-SAÔNE (69400—Rhône)
(Paris 427—Lyon 32—Mâcon 37)

HR PLAISANCE: 96, Avenue de la Libération. Tel.: 74.65.33.52. Tlx.: 375748.   63 rooms.
Villefranche's nicest hotel. Nice restaurant available: La Fontaine Bleu.

R AUBERGE BRESSANE: At Beauregard, on D-44, 3.5 km east. Tel.: 74.60.93.92.
Good regional cooking by the river. M. Decote, the owner, makes the short trip across the bridge
worthwhile.

HR CHÂTEAU DE CHERVINGES: Chervinges-Gleizé. D-34 or D-38, 3 km from Villefranche-sur-
Saône. Tel.: 74.65.29.76. Tlx.: 380772.   11 rooms, 6 suites. Swimming pool and tennis.
Away from town, another restful, comfortable stop in the southern vineyards of the Beaujolais,
but very difficult to find.

233

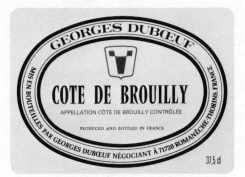

⊹

LYON AND ENVIRONS
Hotels and Restaurants

H = *Hotel;* R = *Restaurant*

Any book that covers the hotels and restaurants of France cannot disregard Lyon, the spiritual hub of French gastronomy. On the other hand, it is not, strictly speaking, in the vineyards: the Beaujolais lies to the north and the Côtes du Rhône wines begin just a short distance to the south, while Lyon occupies the no-man's land in between. But Lyon is the ideal point of departure for your visit to the vineyards of Burgundy, Beaujolais, or the Rhône. It may be hard to believe, but Lyon can be reached by nonstop flights from the following cities: Amsterdam, Athens, Barcelona, Bergen, Bordeaux, Brussels, Copenhagen, Frankfurt, Le Havre, Lille, Limoges, London, Marseille, Milan, Montpellier, Mulhouse, Nantes, Nice, Oran, Paris, Pau, Strasbourg, Tel Aviv, Toulouse, Tunis, and Zurich. Since 1982, through the miracle of the TGV (see the chapter "Suggested Tours"), it has also been easy, fast, and preferable to get there by train.

The list of hotels and restaurants that follows does no more than suggest the abundance of what Lyon and its environs have to offer in the way of dining and accommodations.

LYON (69000—Rhône)
(Paris 462—Bordeaux 550—Marseille 315—Strasbourg 468—Dijon 192—Beaune 154)

⌘ In addition to being the great center of gastronomy. Lyon was also once the great capital of silks and textiles. Therefore, you may wish to visit the Musée Historique des Tissus (cloth museum) at the Hôtel de Villeroy, 34, rue de la Charité; tel.: 78.37.15.05. To nourish the body, try the charcuterie at 12, rue du Plat, called Chorlier's, or Bernachon at 42, cours Franklin-Roosevelt for pastries and chocolate.

Shopping is good in Lyon. Rue de la République is a busy pedestrian street worth investigating. Others worth a stroll are rue Président Edouard Herriot, rue Victor Hugo, rue Auguste Comte, which has a few antique shops, and rue des Archés.

If you want to get to Lyon, or return to Paris, take the train instead of the plane. The Satolas airport is very far out of town (it can take nearly an hour to get there in traffic), and the TGV takes only two hours between the center of Paris and Lyon.

Lyon has many hotels but, unfortunately, few if any that offer real luxury or truly personal service.

HR SOFITEL: 20, quai Gailleton. Tel.: 78.42.72.50. Tlx.: 330225. 200 rooms.
In the center of the city overlooking the Rhône. Considered the best hotel in Lyon, with modern, comfortable, air-conditioned rooms. Deluxe suites available. Expensive for what it is. Restaurant, Les Trois Dômes, on the roof with a panoramic view of the city, has fair service and good food.

H TERMINUS: Perrache Railroad Station, 12, cours de Verdun. Tel.: 78.37.58.11. Tlx.: 330500. 140 rooms (122 with toilet).
Surprisingly quiet hotel, despite proximity to station. Large, good rooms at reasonable prices. Though not central, it is comfortable. No restaurant.

HR GRAND HÔTEL CONCORDE: 11, Rive de Grôlée, on the right bank of the Rhône. Tel.: 78.42.56.21. Tlx.: 330244. 140 air-conditioned rooms.
This hotel, renovated in 1982, lacks personality; but the soundproofed, air-conditioned rooms are comfortable.

HR ROYAL: 20, Place Bellecour, in center of city. Tel.: 78.37.57.31. Tlx.: 310785. 89 rooms.
Good, traditional, comfortable, well located for discovering city by foot. Restaurant available.

HR FRANTEL: 129, rue Servient, in the Crédit Lyonnais bank building. Tel.: 78.62.94.12. Tlx.: 380088. 243 rooms and 2 suites.
The hotel and the good restaurant, called the Arc en Ciel, start on the 32nd floor, granting a high-flying, bird's-eye view of Lyon.

R ORSI: 3, Place Kléber (near the Brotteaux train station). Tel.: 78.89.57.68.
Pierre Orsi, who once had a restaurant in Chicago, has now succeeded in establishing an excellent restaurant on the left bank of the Rhône. Young, long-robed ladies provide the good service in the residential district of one of the city's most popular gastronomic gathering places. Not inexpensive but, considering the quality, a good value. English spoken. *Relais et Châteaux.* Two stars in Michelin.

R DANIEL ET DENISE: 2, rue Tupin, in the center of town. Tel.: 78.37.49.98.
An "in" restaurant among the Lyonnais, where you'll find good food and service. One star in Michelin.

R QUATRE SAISONS: 15, rue Sully. Tel.: 78.93.76.07.
The service of Lucien Bertoli, a former maître d'hôtel at Bocuse, makes the restaurant into a delight, no matter which season you choose to go there. One star in Michelin.

R VETTARD: 7, Place Bellecour. Tel.: 78.42.07.59.
It is difficult to list Lyon's gastronomic highs without including Vettard. Jean Vettard and his wife are traditional hosts. Very centrally located. Two stars in Michelin.

R HENRY: 27, rue de la Martinière. Tel.: 78.28.26.08.
Intimate, elegant, and very good. Prices not excessive, relative to the quality of the food and service. One star in Michelin.

R LÉON DE LYON: 1, rue Pléney. Tel.: 78.28.11.33.
One of the best-known restaurants offering excellent typical Lyon fare. Try the Charolais beef with truffles or the *rognon*. Not inexpensive, but the menus are a good value. The personalized service of the Lacombe family, whom I have known for close to thirty years, and the great gastronomic pleasure provided by the cuisine of Jean-Paul Lacombe, are reflected in the two stars awarded by Michelin.

R NANDRON: 26, quai Jean Moulin. Center of city, along the Saône River. Tel.: 78.42.10.26.
Excellent restaurant with imaginative cooking. Warm family welcome by Odette and Gérard Nandron. *Relais et Châteaux.* Two stars in Michelin.

ON THE OUTSKIRTS OF LYON

HR ALAIN CHAPEL: At Mionnay, 20 km north of Lyon on N-83. Tel.: 78.91.82.02. Tlx.: 30605. 13 rooms.
Claimed by many to be France's greatest chef for imaginative refinement. An experience not to miss if one is anywhere close to Lyon. *Relais et Châteaux.* Three stars in Michelin.

R PAUL BOCUSE: At Collonges-au-Mont d'Or (9 km north on N-433 and D-51): 50, quai de la Plage. Tel.: 78.22.01.40. Tlx.: 375382.
Paul Bocuse is France's greatest gastronomic figure. His restaurant is certainly one of the most famous of France. Traveling incessantly, exporting his talent, he is considered France's "ambassador of gastronomy." Expensive. Reserve far in advance. Three stars in Michelin.

H HOLIDAY INN: On N-6 (10 km from center), close to La Garde exit from A-6. Tel.: 78.35.70.20. Tlx.: 900006. 204 rooms. Comfortable. Covered pool. Cafeteria.

H NOVOTEL-LYON-AEROPORT: 2, rue Lionel-Terray, at Bron (10 km from town by D-406 and N-6, near Bron Airport): Tel.: 78.26.97.48. Tlx.: 340786. Air-conditioned. 200 rooms. Comfortable. Heated pool. Snack yes, dinner no.

HR MÉRIDIEN: Satolas airport (27 km on A-43). Tel.: 7.871.91.61. Tlx.: 380480. Air-conditioned. 120 rooms. Restaurant and bar.

ROANNE (42300—Loire)

(Paris 391—Lyon 88—Villefranche 76—Mâcon 97—Clermont-Ferrand 100—
Chalon-sur-Saône 134—Saint-Étienne 77—Dijon 202)

An ancient city known for its knitwear. When I think of Roanne, I remember fondly how the late Jean Troisgros once took time out from his busy kitchen to help me push my flat-tired Mercedes car down the street to a nearby garage.

HR TROISGROS: 22, cours de la République. Tel.: 77.71.66.97. Tlx.: 307507. 24 comfortable rooms.

This famous temple of gastronomy is not in the vineyards. Pierre Troisgros has achieved a well-deserved reputation for having one of the best restaurants in the world by extracting the delicate tastes from all the seasonal specialties. Although about an hour outside of Lyon, it is well worth a long detour. Pierre, his wife, Olympe, and Michel, their son, in unison contribute to a warm welcome. Reserve well in advance. English spoken. *Relais et Châteaux*. Three stars in Michelin.

CÔTES DU RHÔNE

Although the Côtes du Rhône wines have been around for a millennium and longer, the generic place-name Côtes du Rhône has only recently been recognized. One of the greatest Growths of the Côtes du Rhône, Hermitage, has been discussed by countless wine writers from the eighteenth century onwards—as have, more recently, the wines of Châteauneuf-du-Pape. But even the combined production of these great wines is insignificant in the face of the great ocean of simple *appellation* Côtes du Rhône which is being discovered by those who have come to resent paying ever-higher prices for Beaujolais and Burgundy. However, though there remains some similarity in price between lighter Côtes du Rhône and Beaujolais, there is no similarity in taste. Beaujolais is a light and fruity wine, or should be, whereas the Côtes du Rhône, even if from the lesser villages and vinified to be light, is fuller, deeper in color, and likely to gain from at least some bottle-aging. Unhappily, the trend toward making light Rhône wines has gone so far as to include a Côtes du Rhône *nouveau* in imitation of Beaujolais, which at its best has pleasant and completely distinctive characteristics.

Beginning high in the Swiss Alps, the Rhône flows westward into France, fed along the way by mountain streams and melting glaciers, and emerging on the plain east

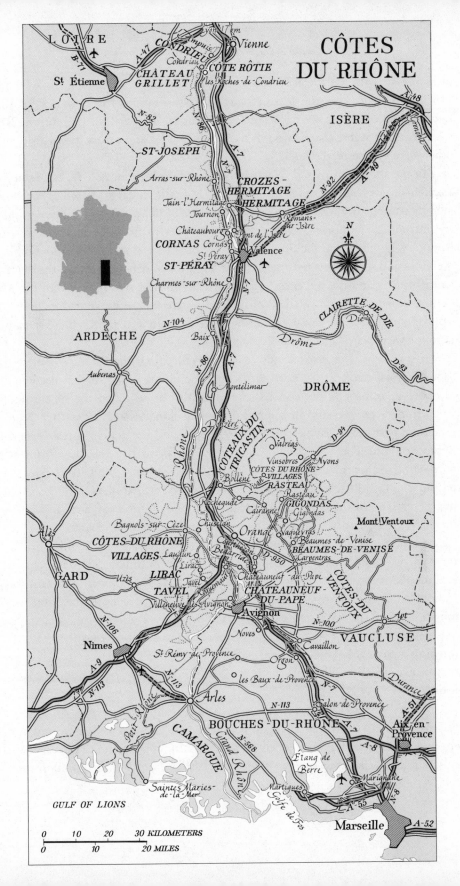

CÔTES DU RHÔNE

LOIRE

ISÈRE

ARDÈCHE

DRÔME

GARD

VAUCLUSE

BOUCHES-DU-RHÔNE

St. Étienne

CONDRIEU
Ampuis
Condrieu
CÔTE RÔTIE
CHÂTEAU GRILLET
les Roches-de-Condrieu
Vienne

ST-JOSEPH
Arras-sur-Rhône
CROZES-HERMITAGE
HERMITAGE
Tain-l'Hermitage
Tournon
Châteaubourg
Romans-sur-Isère
Pont de l'Isère
CORNAS
Cornas
St Péray
Valence
ST-PÉRAY
Charmes-sur-Rhône

CLAIRETTE DE DIE
Die

Baix
Drôme

Aubenas
Montélimar
DRÔME

Donzère
COTEAUX DU TRICASTIN
Valréas
Vinsobres
Nyons
CÔTES DU RHÔNE VILLAGES
Bollène
RASTEAU
Rasteau
GIGONDAS
Rochegude
Cairanne
Gigondas
Mont Ventoux
Bagnols-sur-Cèze
Chusclan
Orange
Vacqueyras
Beaumes-de-Venise
CÔTES-DU-RHÔNE VILLAGES
Courthézon
BEAUMES-DE-VENISE
Carpentras
Alès
Laudun
Bédarrides
CÔTES DU VENTOUX
Uzès
LIRAC
Lirac
Tavel
Châteauneuf-du-Pape
TAVEL
Roquemaure
CHÂTEAUNEUF-DU-PAPE
Villeneuve-lès-Avignon
Avignon
Apt
Nîmes
Noves
Cavaillon
St-Rémy-de-Provence
Orgon
les Baux-de-Provence
Arles
Salon-de-Provence
Aix-en-Provence
CAMARGUE
Étang de Berre
Marignane
Saintes-Maries-de-la-Mer
Martigues
Golfe de Fos
Marseille

GULF OF LIONS

0   10   20   30 KILOMETERS
0   10   20 MILES

of Lyon. At Lyon the Rhône meets the Saône and turns south for its 315-kilometer (190-mile) journey to the Mediterranean. Physically it is the mightiest of all the rivers in France, and in spring when the melting snows swell the current, the Rhône tumbles more water faster through mountain gorges and across the plain than any other watercourse in the land.

In the sixth century B.C., Phocaean sailors, Greeks from Asia Minor, established a settlement at the mouth of the Rhône at Massalia, today's Marseille. Arch-trades-men by nature, they lost no time bartering their local produce up and down the valley, including amphorae of wine made from vines planted along the banks of the Rhône. Whether it was the Phocaeans or the native Celts and Ligurians who planted the vines and first cultivated them is still a matter of debate. Braving the fierce current of spring and the merciless wind called the mistral that blows from the Massif Central down the Rhône Valley to the Mediterranean, the hearty sailors poled their flatboats up to what are now the cities of Arles, Avignon, and Orange, spreading a taste for their wares and their wine along the way.

It is at Lyon, the gastronomic center of France, that the Rhône is joined by the Saône. From Bresse, to the northeast, come the plump chickens that become *poulet en vessie*—a young chicken cooked in a pig's bladder to retain the succulence—or, when thin slices of truffle are slipped under the skin, *poulet en demi-deuil*. From the mountain pastures of Savoie come butter, cream, and the perfect cheeses for wine—Reblochon and Tome de Savoie. From the cool depths of the Lac d'Annecy and mountain streams come crayfish, trout, and *homble-chevalier*, while to the northwest, on the rolling hills just above Roanne, creamy white Charollais cattle graze, fattening themselves for the tables of the great restaurants of the Lyon area. In addition to the starred restaurants within the city itself, such as Léon de Lyon, run by the Lacombe family, there is a galaxy just at the city's door. Arguably the most brilliant of them all is Alain Chapel's three-star restaurant in Mionnay, La Mère Charles. In Roanne Pierre Troisgros, his wife, Olympe, and their son, Michel, maintain the gastronomic institution that Troisgros has become; in the suburbs of Lyon, in Collonges, one of the most famous and flamboyant in France, Paul Bocuse; and at Vienne, La Pyramide, where the late Fernand Point held court until the late fifties, teaching many of the men who are today the great chefs of France. The Point tradition of excellence in all things culinary is mightily upheld by the aging Mado, his widow.

Vienne, just 30 kilometers (18 miles) south from Lyon on A-7, is still a perfect place to begin a visit to the Côtes du Rhône wines. The vineyards split into a northern and a southern region divided by a vineless no-man's land. The northern half closely follows the steep sides of the Rhône Valley from Vienne 60 kilometers (36 miles) to Valence, while the southern half stretches from the Donzère River, north of Orange, 60 kilometers (36 miles) down to Avignon, the capital of the southern Côtes du Rhône.

NORTHERN CÔTES DU RHÔNE

Côte Rôtie

About 8 kilometers (5 miles) south of Vienne on the vineyard road, N-86, is the village of Ampuis, famous for little save its renowned rare red wine, Côte Rôtie. The 60 or so hectares (150 acres) of the terraced vineyards zigzag up the steep slope facing south and southeast so the vines of the Syrah, the noble grape that is the source of the northern Côtes du Rhône wines, get the full benefit of the summer sun. With such a small vineyard and limited output, averaging around 20,000 cases a year, the great wines from the "Roasted Slope" will never produce a world-famous wine simply because there is not enough to go around. The entire *appellation* makes less wine than my Château Prieuré-Lichine and less than any one of a number of my Margaux neighbors. Besides, most of the 20,000 cases are consumed in the top restaurants of the Rhône Valley.

On the Côte Rôtie slope itself, a traditional distinction used to be made between the wines grown on two parts of the slope: the Côte Brune and the Côte Blonde, "brunette" and "blond." Coming from the richer soil, the Côte Brune wines take longer to show themselves, while the Blondes develop more quickly and fade earlier. Some growers and shippers still indicate Côte Brune and Côte Blonde on the label, though this is less frequently met with now than in the past. Two growers who do are Pierre Barge and Marcel Guigal.

In recent years the vineyards have been shrinking because of the steepness of the slope and the backbreaking labor needed to maintain the terraces, some of which are only wide enough for three or four rows of vines. Today, about ninety growers remain, and every year they and their vineyard workers must lug up tons of soil washed down by the rains. Mechanization of this work is nearly impossible.

Côte Rôtie wines, whether Brune or Blonde, were traditionally full and often hard, high in tannin and alcohol. They benefited from and even required long barrel-aging, up to five years at times. Nowadays, because of the great expense of interest charges and ullage (evaporation), the practice is dying out. The wines still gain enormously with age, and it is a great mistake to drink them too young. I have admired many a bottle of these strong wines, but I would find it difficult to make them part of my daily fare. Because of its concentrated character, Côte Rôtie is a wine of richness and contrast. Charm and easy drinkability are not among its attributes, however, and it is capable of overpowering other wines served with it.

The largest of the Côte Rôtie holdings is owned by Étienne Guigal, who a few years ago bought the vineyards of the rival firm Vidal-Fleury and who gives a good example of rigorous selection of vats. Maurice Gentaz, Albert Dervieux-Thaize, and René Rostaing, all in Ampuis, are other good growers.

❧ *Condrieu and Château Grillet* ☙

Following in quick succession beyond the Côte Rôtie on N-86 are the two smallest vineyard place-names of the entire Côtes du Rhône—indeed, among the smallest of France: Condrieu, whose heavily scented white wines are grown on 10 hectares (25 acres), and Château Grillet, France's smallest Appellation Contrôlée white wine, with less than 3 hectares (7.5 acres) of vines. Both wines are made from the Viognier grape, a white-wine grape of small yield with a full, spiced, and lingering aftertaste. Of the two, the wines of Condrieu will be the more dependable, having, at their best, a smell of Muscat and violet. But both of these wines, with their tiny production, are distinguished perhaps more for their rarity and consequent snob-appeal than anything else.

There was a time when nearly the only place to find any of Château Grillet's 700-odd-case production of white wine was the restaurant La Pyramide in Vienne. Château Grillet remains in the hands of a single proprietor, the Canet family, who extract such a high price for their wine that it is a dubious value. Condrieu is only a few drops more plentiful, with an annual production of around 1,400 cases. Unlike the great classic white wines of Hermitage made with Marsanne and Roussanne grapes, the Viognier-based wines of Condrieu and Château Grillet gain little after three years in bottle, and may have an occasional taste of greenness in certain vintages. Earlier picking and bottling have done much to make fresher wines. In addition to being blessed with these rare and expensive wines, Condrieu is the home of a fine two-star restaurant-hotel, the Beau Rivage, whose terraces overlook the Rhône.

South of Château Grillet there are no great vineyards until you reach the bridge over the Rhône at Tournon and Tain, less than an hour's scenic drive away. Here the slopes of the red and white wines of Hermitage on the left bank stare across the valley at those of Saint-Joseph on the right. If you make the trip in summer, as I often have, you may be held up by the heavy southbound traffic of truckers, tourists, and vacationers on their way to the sun.

❧ *Hermitage* ❧

Hermitage, only after Châteauneuf-du-Pape and the lesser *appellation* Côtes du Rhône, is the most renowned of Rhône wines and is esteemed as the oldest vineyard in France.

As the story goes, Gaspard de Stérimberg, a valiant knight in Pope Innocent III's crusade against the Albigensian heretics (1208–1213), repented his violent life and retired to the wilderness and the steep slopes above the Rhône to build a small retreat—"his hermitage"—and cultivate his garden of grapes. As adept at wielding a plow as a sword, Gaspard soon covered the hillside of thin, meager soil with vines and began making the wine which has given the slope its fame. The 123 hectares (307 acres) of vineyard are now divided into three valleys: Les Murets for the white wines and Les Bessards and Greffieux for the red, producing in all around 30,000 cases of red and 12,000 cases of white a year. The red-wine grape, the Syrah (sometimes and in some countries referred to as Petite Syrah), is the same grape used in the Côte Rôtie. It is thought to have been brought back from the eastern Crusades as the *Shiraz* (named for the Persian city), some say by Stérimberg himself, though I can find no record that his travels took him that far east. The white-wine grapes, Marsanne and, to a small extent, Roussanne, are cultivated on the middle slope. Both white and red wines are inclined to be harsh in their youth. After eight years or so, red Hermitage begins to reach maturity as a soft and velvety wine, big and generous to the nose and palate.

In the days when long aging of wines was traditional and did not involve huge interest rates, the slow-maturing Hermitages were highly esteemed and sought after in France and abroad. But today's Hermitage suffers from the current tendency to drink most wine young. A well-made Hermitage does not begin to emerge until after at least four years in the bottle. Although many wine drinkers today will gladly pay a high price for the fine and famous Bordeaux and Burgundies and show patience for keeping them until they mature and develop, they are unwilling to make this sacrifice for wines of borderline fame such as Hermitage. Partly in response to the trend toward youth and lightness in wines, Hermitage growers are vinifying their wines to be less robust. Traditional vinification saw to it that red Hermitages were vatted for weeks at a time after the fermentation was completed (often with stems on for added tannin) and then aged in oak barrels three or four years before bottling.

The white wines of Hermitage also had long barrel-aging and bottles often waited a decade or so to be ready for drinking. When made this way the white wines are dry, though lacking in acidity (and therefore freshness), with a big, heavy body, which made them particular favorites in the nineteenth century, especially in England. For many growers on the slope, these traditional white-wine vinification methods are a thing of the past, though a rare few vintners continue them.

Chante-Alouette, one of the most celebrated of the white Hermitages, is both the name of a vineyard and the trademark of the firm of Chapoutier. The wine is usually a blend from good vineyards. Chapoutier owns 70 hectares (175 acres). Some of the growers, like their Burgundian neighbors to the north, have painted their names in whitewash on the dividing walls, or *mas,* between their plots. Chapoutier and Paul Jaboulet Aîné, the two most prominent, are shippers as well as important growers.

The excellent firm of Paul Jaboulet Aîné owns 66 hectares (165 acres) divided between Hermitage and Crozes-Hermitages. They are also respected shippers of other Rhône wines. J. L. Chave is another excellent producer.

⤙ *Crozes-Hermitages* ⤚

The vineyards of Crozes-Hermitages, a source of Syrah-based red and a bit of white wine, are just to the north after crossing the bridge to Tain l'Hermitage. These lesser wines are pleasant and quicker to mature than Hermitage, but they cannot be compared to the wines of Hermitage. They will be seen more often on wine lists because they produce five times what Hermitage does.

⤙ *Saint-Joseph* ⤚

Recently many good growers have improved the quality of Saint-Joseph. Among the best one can count Bernard Gripa, who makes both red and white wines, Jean-Louis Grippat, Jean Marsanne, Georges Charve, and Robert Trolat. The reason for a decline of the quality of Saint-Joseph has been that the 250 hectares (625 acres) have been spread over twenty-six communes and that terraced hillsides from which the best wines came have been abandoned. The indifferent red wine and the less frequently met white wine of Saint-Joseph, across the river, have become somewhat known in the last decade or two. Saint-Joseph whites often taste "green" because of the early picking, which the growers hope will give them the characteristic of freshness. The red is made from the Syrah and the white from the Marsanne and Roussanne grape varieties.

⤳ Saint-Péray and Cornas ⤶

Just south of Tournon on the Rhône's right bank, opposite Hermitage and Valence, are the small districts and small wines of Saint-Péray and Cornas. Together they cover about 100 hectares (240 acres), which are nearly evenly split between the whites of Saint-Péray and the reds of Cornas. The red wines of Cornas typically can be hard, rough, and austere when young, maturing fairly well but never attaining any kind of a peak. The small *appellation* of Cornas, amounting to 70 hectares, producing some 35,000 cases annually, nearly disappeared as the city folk of Valence and other places came to build houses in the vineyards. Six or seven growers have stuck to making better wines, and Auguste Clape, Guy de Barjac, Marcel Juge, and Noel Verset, among others, will continue to make their rather rough red wines from 100 percent Syrah grapes which make this dark red wine hard, tannic, and perhaps rustic when young. At the end of seven or eight years one is pleasantly surprised to see that this strength is coupled with good personality. Saint-Péray, like the whites of Hermitage, is made from Marsanne and Roussanne grapes. Since 1825, when a grower named Louis-André Fauré brought in a cellar master from Champagne, over half of the Saint-Péray production has been made into sparkling wine, or *mousseux*.

Another sparkling wine of the region, though not officially part of the Côtes du Rhône, comes from the vineyards of Clairette de Die. The vineyards follow a horseshoe bend in the Drôme River about 40 kilometers (24 miles) east of the Rhône. The Clairette grape, used to make white wines in the Languedoc-Roussillon area, here makes a sparkling wine full in flavor and color—although (as I have observed in my *Encyclopedia of Wines & Spirits*) for those used to Champagne, Clairette de Die is an acquired taste.

With these vineyards the northern Côtes du Rhône comes to an end just across the Rhône from Valence. Aside from a few backyard plots, there are no vines for 70 kilometers (43 miles). A-7 will take you quickly through this region of fruit trees and melon fields, leaving you at Bollène or Orange in the heart of the southern half of the Côtes du Rhône.

SOUTHERN CÔTES DU RHÔNE

These meridional vineyards are different in every way from their illustrious cousins in the north. In the first place, the vines are not confined to the Rhône banks, as in the northern Côtes du Rhône, but cover an area nearly as wide as it is long, in all about 35,000 hectares (86,500 acres)—compared to the 5,000 hectares (12,500 acres) in the northern half—and accounting for more than 85 percent of all Côtes du Rhône wine. Nearly three-quarters of the wine from the southern Côtes du Rhône is vinified by one of the fifty-five communal wine cooperatives—some of which sell their wine in bottle directly to consumers, although most of it is shipped in tank-trucks to *négociants,* who assemble or blend it for their own bottling. In the more individualistic northern Côtes du Rhône, on the other hand, scarcely a fifth of the wine sees the inside of the one cooperative at Tain-l'Hermitage. Finally, rather than basing each of their wines on one or two grape varieties, as is done in the northern Côtes du Rhône (as well as most of France), the growers of the southern Côtes find that a combination of a number of different grapes allows them to finish with a more rounded and balanced product. Châteauneuf-du-Pape alone may have as many as thirteen authorized grape varieties, although most growers manage quite well with six or seven. Since 1960, the wine production of the southern Côtes du Rhône has doubled—sometimes at the expense of quality, especially in the southernmost part of the meridional Côtes, toward Nîmes.

Whatever land is not planted in vines is covered in olive, almond, and pear trees, fields of lavender, and potatoes that, when dug fresh from the earth, have a smell of iris; south from Orange is the melon country of Carpentras. Staunchly rooted everywhere are the hedgelike rows of cypress trees, protecting the vines and everything else from the mistral—which, for reasons only known to nature, blows with increasing vengeance as you descend the Rhône. On the lower-lying areas along the highway, fields are planted in reeds. Once sufficiently tall, they are cut, dried, and bound together to make windbreaks around the houses in an effort to keep out the wind and the red-clay dust that is borne along with it.

Out of the great sweep of southern Côtes du Rhône vineyards, sixteen villages have been granted permission to add their name or the word "Villages" to the words "Côtes du Rhône" on the label. They now account for about 20,000 cases of white and about 700,000 cases of red wine. Wine labeled simply "Côtes du Rhône-Villages" will be a blend of the different village wines. Two of the better villages whose wine is likely to be seen sold with their own names on the label are Chusclan, which I've found produces a distinctively spiced wine, and Laudun, which makes the best of Côtes du Rhône-Villages white wines. Other good Côtes du Rhône come from Vinsobres, Cairanne, Vacqueyras, and Visan. With the exception of Laudun, they are nearly all devoted to red wine made from the Grenache, Mourvèdre, and Cinsault grapes, with a sprinkling of other grape varieties.

Virtually all these villages have cooperative cellars, usually large and factory-like in appearance. In many instances they have helped improve the overall quality of regional wines. Usually there is a reception area where the wines may be tasted—most often without charge—and bought.

Just north of Bollène is the Tricastin. Not officially part of the Côtes du Rhône as yet, the Coteaux du Tricastin was recently made an Appellation Contrôlée on its own. The 1,350 hectares (3,375 acres) of vineyard around the town of Saint-Paul-Trois-Châteaux had fallen into nearly complete disuse from the time the phylloxera hit in the late nineteenth century until the repatriation of the winegrowing French from Algeria beginning in 1962. Light reds and rosés are made from the usual Rhône grape varieties, and most wine is sold in barrel to shippers. Some plantings of Gamay, Merlot, and Cabernet Sauvignon grape varieties, which come from outside the Rhône, have been tried successfully in this department known as Ardèche.

The ideal fantasy image of a romantic castle, moat and all, has been baptized and transformed into a wine university with tasting rooms, library, and meeting rooms which hold classes in oenology and marketing, thus elevating wine to the highly civilized level it deserves. It was opened in 1978 at Château de Suze.

As you follow the wine villages south from Bollène on D-8, the thick, guttural accent of French Provence becomes stronger and the sales pitch increases in volume. Two villages along the better slopes in the foothills of the Mont Ventoux have been elevated to Appellation Contrôlée status: Gigondas and Beaumes-de-Venise. Gigondas makes red wine, largely with Grenache grapes, though Syrah and Cinsault have been planted in the past decade to give more staying power and color, yielding a wine similar to Châteauneuf-du-Pape. Beaumes-de-Venise, a very good *vin doux naturel,* is a fortified sweet wine made from the muscat grape in the style of the muscats from Languedoc-Roussillon. It is more delicate than its southern counterparts and usually less fortified. Nearly all of its annual production of 50,000 cases remains in France and the Common Market countries. Slightly to the north of Beaumes-de-Venise is another *vin doux naturel,* though less successful, that of Rasteau.

Lying to the south of Rasteau and Beaumes-de-Venise, and southeast of the whole of the Côtes du Rhône-Villages region are the extensive vineyards of the Côtes du Ventoux. Most of the wines from the 5,000-hectare (12,500-acre) area are rosés and light reds, called *vins de café* or *vins d'une nuit* for the fact that the wines used to be vatted only one night. A small amount of white wine is also made—in all, production comes to the equivalent of about 2 million cases per year.

Châteauneuf-du-Pape, perhaps the best known of all better Rhône wines, is 30 kilometers (19 miles) from Beaumes-de-Venise across the plain between the Ventoux and the Vaucluse hills. To get there directly from Beaumes, head for Courthézon and follow signs for Châteauneuf-du-Pape, or preferably treat yourself to a visit to Avignon, on D-942, the city of the French popes and the uncontested chef-d'oeuvre of the southern wine region. It makes no difference whether you travel and tipple your way through the reds and whites of Châteauneuf, the rosés of Tavel, and the reds and rosés of Lirac before visiting Avignon or afterwards, but there is no avoiding one of the most enchanting cities of France.

Avignon, along with Aix-en-Provence, is not only a gateway to Provence but stands on its own as the center for a summer festival of drama and music. Since the festival was created in 1962 by Jean Vilar, it has grown steadily in popularity, attracting huge numbers of tourists who fill the city's grand hotels and youth hostels, often overflowing into the city parks and squares. The 93,000 Avignonais show signs of chafing under this yearly flood of tourists, and talk is frequently heard of suspending the summer festival in order to give the town back to its inhabitants.

Until the early fourteenth century, Avignon lived in the commercial and military shadow of its mightier neighboring cities, Aix-en-Provence, Nîmes, Arles, and Marseille. But in 1305, the College of Cardinals in Rome—dominated by Philippe IV, King of France, who had maneuvered a French majority in the College—elected the archbishop of Bordeaux, Bertrand de Goth, as Pope. Crowned in Perugia as Clement V, he moved the Papacy to Avignon in 1309, where it remained until 1377. In the sixty-eight years of the "Second Babylonian Captivity," as the Roman chroniclers called it, seven French popes occupied the fortress-like Palais des Papes, one of the largest feudal castles in the world.

Although impressively austere and relatively unadorned on the outside, inside the palace's great succession of halls and chambers reflects the florid temperament and lavish hand of Clement VI, who, during his reign from 1342 to 1352, embellished the work already begun by Benedict XII. Today one can still see the grape vines that are part of the wall decoration in Clement VI's bedroom. It is no idle flourish, for in fact it was the popes in Avignon who began the vineyards at the summer residence they established just up the river at Châteauneuf-du-Pape (called "New Castle of the Pope" to distinguish it from the older edifice in Avignon), 25 kilometers (15 miles) from Avignon.

Châteauneuf's vineyards now cover 3,000 hectares (7,500 acres) stretching out along D-17, and each year produce the equivalent of a million cases of red wine and about 10,000 cases of white. Fragments of the castle still remain, with one lone tower and a few crumbling walls overlooking the vineyards.

As with many other of the rich, long-lived reds of the Côtes du Rhône, Châteauneuf-du-Pape has changed its vinification method in the last thirty years or so to produce wines that are lighter and easier to drink when young, that is, within three years. Perhaps Châteauneuf's best grower until his retirement in 1977 was the late Philippe Dufays, an ex-doctor who gave up medicine for viticulture. A quick-witted chain smoker, he was the source I always counted on for information on the southern Côtes du Rhône. A man of means and leisure, he devoted his time to the study of the myriad grape varieties of Châteauneuf, trying to determine just what it was that each grape contributed to the wine. "An ampelographer [the proper term for someone who studies grapes] could go on forever here in Châteauneuf," he used to say. Thirteen grape varieties can go into a single bottle of red, but most reliable growers concentrate on perhaps six or seven. Grenache, Dufays pointed out, gives mellowness and alcohol; Mourvèdre, Syrah, Muscardin, and Vaccarese add body, color, and firmness; Counoise, Picpoule, and Cinsault lend vinosity, bouquet, and freshness; and Clairette and Bourboulenc donate finesse and warmth. Terret Noir, Picardan, and Roussanne are also allowed, but are seen less and less.

The vines in Châteauneuf grow farther apart than elsewhere in France, with often as much as 1.5 to 2 meters (5 to 7 feet) between rows. About a third of the Châteauneuf vineyards is covered with the famous "rolled stones," about the size of small, flattish coconuts. Eons ago, the Rhône pushed and tumbled the stones from the Alps, and even though they cover only a relatively small part of the Châteauneuf vineyard area, they have come to symbolize the warmth and generosity of the climate and the wine. The grapes mature, caught between the scorching heat of the sun and the reflected warmth from the stones. As a result of this roasting and of new, shorter vatting methods, the wines often surpass the required 12.5 percent of alcohol (a legal minimum matched by few French red wines and exceeded by none without chaptalization), sometimes reaching 13 or even 14 percent.

Châteauneuf is characteristically deep in color and full-bodied, but softer than either a Hermitage or a Côte Rôtie, and is quicker to mature than other top Rhône wines. It is often ready after three or four years. The wine has a good bouquet (though not so intense as in the Côte Rôtie) and a special grapey taste termed "vinosity." Some of the more important properties in Châteauneuf include Domaine de Beaucastel, Domaine de Beaurenard, Domaine des Fines Roches, Château Fortia, Château de la Gardine, Domaine de Mont Redon, Domaine de Nalys, Domaine des Sénéchaux, Domaine de la Solitude, Château de Vaudieu, and Domaine de la Terre.

One cannot leave the region of Châteauneuf-du-Pape—or even the Rhône, for that matter—without saying a word about the great work done for this area and indeed all of France by the late Baron Le Roy de Boiseaumarié, the man instrumental in the establishment of the laws governing the Appellation Contrôlée in France. After the First World War, fraud was rampant throughout the vineyards of France, and Châteauneuf-du-Pape was the first region to mount an attack against misleading labeling and downright lies. At the head of this movement toward strict controls—which subsequently made France a model for the rest of the wine world—was the Baron Le Roy, who for his untiring efforts was honored with a statue in his lifetime.

One of my last memories of Baron Le Roy is of a special occasion when we opened the oldest bottle of wine either of us had ever drunk. It was an amphora retrieved by Jacques Cousteau from the floor of the Mediterranean, and presented to the Baron with the seal still intact after what M. Cousteau judged to be close to two thousand years. Having removed the top of the vessel with some difficulty, we poured a sample of the ancient liquid into our small glasses. It had no color, bouquet, or taste; all of the tannins, tartrates, pectins, and other elements of flavor and aroma had long since precipitated to the bottom of the amphora. The wine had returned to the water and minerals from which it had had its genesis. After eyeing it thoughtfully for a minute and giving it an occasional swirl in the glass, the Baron pronounced his verdict: "Some bad Burgundian shipper, no doubt."

Tavel, with its vineyards of the world's best rosé, is just down the road (D-976) from Châteauneuf-du-Pape and is the home of another fine grower, Armand Maby, former mayor of Tavel. A fine rosé is just as dependent as a red wine on a proper choice of grape varieties, and M. Maby feels strongly that both a good balance and proper vinification are necessary to make truly noble rosé. "Too much Grenache makes a light wine with no staying power," he says, "so it's best to add Syrah for color and Mourvèdre for depth. Otherwise the Grenache will turn that awful orange *rancio* color most people associate with bad rosés—and rightly so. We let the grapes macerate for a week or so, kept cold to prevent fermentation. Once the skins have imparted the proper color and the important pectins and proteins to the juice, giving it body and longevity, we remove the skins and allow the fermentation to begin." The cheap shortcut, which makes poor, thin rosés, is to press the grapes right away, crushing the skins to extract only the color from them without getting any of the other beneficial elements. Little wonder rosés have a doubtful reputation among wine lovers.

In Lirac, next door, both reds and rosés are made. Though they are not as well known, the rosés are the equal of those of Tavel. Vintage years, which mean less along the Rhône than they do in other wine regions of France, mean least of all for the rosés of Tavel and Lirac. Most years the grapes reach 12 percent alcohol and beyond, giving these particular rosés a longer life than most. Still, the wines should be drunk as young as possible, with an upper limit of four years. The main producer of Tavel, besides Monsieur Maby, is the local cooperative, Les Vignerons de Tavel. It accounts for much of the yearly production of 250,000 cases. M. de Bez, a third important grower, sells part of his output as Château d'Aquéria.

The lesser vineyard areas of the *appellation* Côtes du Rhône continue south past Avignon in the direction of Nîmes. From these broad, flat vineyards comes the great quantity of simple, rather ordinary *appellation* Côtes du Rhône.

RHÔNE VINTAGES

1959   The sun-drenched southern valley of the Rhône got an overabundance of heat, which scorched the vines. The grapes from the other Rhône districts enjoyed the same healthy ripeness as the other districts of France.

1960   A good vintage. The only region in France that produced high-quality wines that year. Favored by good weather, both during the development of the grape and the harvest. One of the better vintages for the past fifteen years, though now declined.

1961   With the other regions of France, the Rhône Valley produced a very good vintage.

1962   A small vintage which produced flat wines lacking in character, but with some isolated successes.

1963   A very small, very poor, vintage. Wine completely lacking in color. Very clearly inferior to the disappointing '62s.

1964   An average vintage.

1965 A fair vintage. The Côtes du Rhône region, unlike other parts of France, did not lack sunshine. The harvest weather was nearly ideal.

1966 A top vintage. The best since the very good 1960, which was exceptional in the Rhône. The great '66s even surpassed it.

1967 The Rhône, which is blessed with more good vintages than any other wine district in France, outdid itself in 1967 as in 1966.

1968 A few quite pleasant wines were produced. Now gone.

1969 Small in quantity and fair in quality—disappointing color. The main exceptions were in the Côte Rôtie, where good wines were produced.

1970 A very good vintage in quantity and quality.

1971 Fair to good.

1972 Most of the Rhône wines were disappointing, but a few were good.

1973 One of the largest harvests on record since the Second World War. But the quality was only average, since the wines lacked both acidity and fruit. Generally mediocre wines. Hail struck at Hermitage, but those wines which escaped turned out to be very good, an exception to the rest of the Rhône.

1974 A good vintage in general, with, unfortunately, many exceptions. Good color, good fruit, and character, and in some cases an excellent lasting ability.

1975 Average quality at best, with a few highs and lows, more of the latter than the former. Châteauneuf-du-Pape was particularly disappointing.

1976 Rather good. Thirty percent of the wine, generally from Condrieu, Côte Rôtie, and Hermitage, was of very good quality. Twenty-five percent or so was very acceptable, and the remaining 45 percent—from Châteauneuf-du-Pape and other southern Côtes du Rhône—was mediocre. Late-summer rains lasted through the harvest in the south, swelling the grapes and producing some weak wines.

1977 The Côtes du Rhône was unquestionably one of the most favored regions in France in 1977. The sun and warm weather prevailed, producing an abundant crop of full, round, well-balanced wines which will be long-lasting both on the palate and in the cellar. This excellent quality applies to much of the vintage, and full-pleasing wines will be easy to find. Both Châteauneuf-du-Pape and Tavel had very good vintages.

1978 An exceptionally excellent vintage. Châteauneuf-du-Pape and the pink wines of Tavel were exceptionally favored.

1979 Very good quality, though less even than 1978. The wines were well balanced, with good color. The Tavels were on a par with those of 1978.

1980 A good year, somewhat similar to 1978, but less consistent.

1981 Good quality. Good, full-bodied wines were produced. The spring frost did not spare the Rhône, which nevertheless suffered less than the Beaujolais.

1982 Generally, 1982 was a rather fair year except for the Côtes du Rhône, which were consistently good. The northern Rhône produced particularly outstanding wines in the Côte Rôtie and Hermitage vineyards.

1983 Brokers and growers are categorical that the Côtes du Rhône are bigger, better, and darker wines than the 1982s. There is more good, harder wine available with finer, delicate aromas. This also applies to the Châteauneuf-du-Pape.

In the northern district, including Hermitage, Crozes, and the Côte Rotie, the wines are of an exceptional quality rarely seen since World War II.

1984   A good vintage.

1985   A very great vintage according to the Rhône's best authorities. "Very exceptional" describes the high quality.

RHÔNE
Hotels and Restaurants

H = *Hotel*; R = *Restaurant*

VIENNE (38200—Isère)
(Paris 492—Lyon 31—Roanne 126—Valence 70)
The Autoroute A-7 leads directly through the center of town.

❧ The old city is worth seeing for the harmonious blend of its Gothic cathedral with its Roman temple and theater.

H MERCURE: At Chasse-sur-Rhône, 8 km north of Vienne on A-7, exit at Chasse-Givors. Tel.: 78.73.13.94.   108 air-conditioned rooms.
A convenient place to sleep when driving to and from the Riviera.

H LA RÉSIDENCE DE LA PYRAMIDE: 41, quai Riondet. Tel.: 74.53.16.46.   15 rooms (11 with toilet).
If you don't feel like traveling after your dinner at the Pyramide, this hotel in the midst of a garden—a three-minute drive from the restaurant—is comfortable and quiet, with a view of the Rhône. No restaurant. Breakfast available.

HR CHÂTEAU DES SEPT FONTAINES: at Seyssuel, 38200 Vienne. 3 km northwest on N-7 and then on D-4. Tel.: 74.85.25.70. 15 rooms. Restaurant available.
Nice, quiet rooms in the midst of a small park. Tennis.

R LA PYRAMIDE: Boulevard Fernand Point. Tel.: 74.53.01.96.
One of the original bastions of gastronomy. Fernand Point was the first of the gastronomic stars to whom the world paid reverence. His aging widow continues the tradition, and a great tradition it is, knit by teamwork, which makes La Pyramide a traditional example of gastronomic quality. If Michelin gives its three stars perennially to La Pyramide, it is not only through deference to this great contributor to the fine cuisine of France; it is also well deserved by those who daily contribute. Reservations are mandatory. Expensive.

R CHEZ RENÉ: At Saint-Romain-en-Gal, exit auto route at Vienne, on the right bank of the Rhône, less than 1 km west of Vienne; take the Pont Saint-Louis and N-86. Tel.: 74.53.19.72. If you decide to deny yourself the experience of the Pyramide, then compromise at Chez René. You'll find a good meal at more down-to-earth prices. Try one of the well-priced menus.

CONDRIEU (69420—Rhône)
(Lyon 41—Lyon-Satolas airport 65—Vienne 11)
Across the Rhône from Vienne on the left bank.

The town has been famous for its tough, leather-breeched bargemen. To this day, they take part each Bastille Day (July 14) in championship contests on the Rhône River.

HR BEAU RIVAGE: 2, rue du Beau-Rivage. Tel.: 74.59.52.24. Tlx.: 308946. 24 rooms.
Comfortable rooms overlooking the Rhône, with garden and terrace. A gracious welcome. The wine cellar has a good assortment of Rhône Valley wines, especially the local Condrieu. *Relais et Châteaux.* Madame Castaing, for all her 75 years, runs one of the best-recommended restaurants in the Northern Rhône and well deserves her two stars in Michelin.

LES ROCHES-DE-CONDRIEU (38370—Isère)
(Paris 504—Vienne 12—Lyon 41—Grenoble 104—Tournon 72)
Across the Rhône and south from Vienne on the left bank, 1 km from Condrieu on D-4.

HR BELLEVUE: 1, quai du Rhône. Tel.: 74.56.41.42. 19 simple rooms (17 with toilet).
Good restaurant overlooking the Rhône. Fair prices. One star in Michelin.

TAIN-L'HERMITAGE (26600—Drôme)
(Paris 548—Lyon 90—Valence 15—Vienne 56—Grenoble 99—
Le Puy 106—Saint-Étienne 75)

HR LE COMMERCE: 69, Ave Jean-Jaures/1 Ave du Docteur Paul-Durand (near the church and the train station). Tel.: 75.08.65.00. Tlx.: 345573. 48 small rooms (all with toilet). Swimming pool.
Recent remodeling has made this a comfortable hotel in this famous wine village. Reasonable restaurant available.

R RESTAURANT REYNAUD: 82, Avenue, President Roosevelt. Tel: 75.07.22.10.
Jean-Marc Reynaud and his charming wife, Danielle, have moved from their former bastion, the Château de Chateaubourg, to open the best restaurant in Tain-l'Hermitage.

PONT-DE-L'ISÈRE (26600—Drôme)
(Châteaubourg 17—Valence 9—Tournon 9—Tain l'Hermitage 9)
Off Autoroute A-7 at Tain or Valence-Nord.

HR CHABRAN 45E PARALLÈLE: 29, Avenue du 45è Parallèle (in front of the town hall). Tel.: 75.84.60.09. 12 comfortable, small, modern, soundproofed rooms.
Owner-chef Michel Chabran, who was formerly at Pic in nearby Valence, has established a high standard. Fine local wine list. Expensive. *Relais et Châteaux.* Two stars in Michelin.

VALENCE (26000—Drôme)
(Paris 561—Lyon 100—Nîmes 149—Avignon 126—Marseille 215—
Grenoble 97—Roanne 185)

Picturesque old streets. Don't leave without taking a stroll along the esplanades of the Champs de Mars. At sunset the view is spectacular.

HR PIC: 285, Avenue Victor-Hugo. Tel.: 75.44.15.32. 1 air-conditioned suite and 4 comfortable, modest rooms.
One of the famous, expensive, but excellent-value three-star restaurants. The welcome is discreet and warm, and one is immediately aware of the refinement in décor and place settings. If weather permits, lunch or dinner on the garden terrace is delightful. Jacques Pic is a superb master chef. *Relais et Châteaux.*

HR CHÂTEAU DU BESSET: At Saint-Romain-de-Lerps, 13 km northwest of Valence and 9 km northwest of Saint-Péray on D-287. Tel.: 75.58.52.22. Tlx.: 345261. 4 suites, 6 luxurious, spacious rooms. Heated swimming pool; tennis.
This medieval manor is situated within a 50-hectare park. The owner, M. Gozlan, spent a fortune restoring this sumptuous château-inn. Among the most comfortable rooms you'll find between Paris and the Riviera. "His and hers" joint bathtubs are a worthwhile if expensive experience. The present chef is good. *Relais et Châteaux.* A star in Michelin.

H HOTEL 2000: Avenue de Romans on N-532, Route de Grenoble, 2 km east of the autoroute exit. Tel.: 75.43.73.01. Tlx.: 345873. 30 smallish rooms.
Moderately priced, comfortable, functional hotel. No restaurant; breakfast available.

H NOVOTEL-VALENCE-SUD: 217, Avenue de Provence, near Valence-Sud, exit from A-7. Tel.: 75.42.20.15. Tlx.: 345823. 107 soundproofed rooms.
No restaurant, breakfast available, snack bar.

R AUBERGE DES TROIS CANARDS: at Granges-les-Valence, 3 km from Valence on the other side of the Rhône. 565, Avenue République. Tel.: 75.44.43.24.
Good food at reasonable prices.

CHARMES-SUR-RHÔNE (07800—Ardèche)
(Valence 11—Montélimar 38—Crest 25—Privas 28—Saint-Péray 11)
On the west bank of the Rhône, on N-86.

HR LA VIEILLE AUBERGE: Rue Bertois. Tel.: 75.60.80.10. 7 air-conditioned and inexpensive rooms.
A charming small hotel-restaurant at the very top of the village overlooking the Rhône—a good value.

BAIX (07210—Ardèche)
(Montélimar 25—Valence 33—Rochemaure 15—Tournon 45)
On N-86, 8 km south of the Loriol exit from A-7.

HR LA CARDINALE ET SA RÉSIDENCE: Located on the Rhône. Tel.: 75.85.80.40. Tlx.: 346143. 10 good, smallish rooms, with good bathrooms, in the hotel and 5 excellent suites in its luxurious annex, La Résidence de la Cardinale, set in a park 3 km away, with a swimming pool.
A converted lordly manor in a park, in a charming, memorable site on the right bank of the Rhône, with a good restaurant. I recommend this as a comfortable stopover. The Motte family are charming hosts. *Relais et Châteaux.*

MONTÉLIMAR (26200—Drôme)
(Avignon 81—Aix-en-Provence 152—Marseille 182—Nîmes 100—
Valence 45—Orange 53—Lyon 195)

ᲝჇ Known earlier for its medieval fortress, Montélimar is now famous for its almond-studded nougat. The leading factory, Chabert et Guillot, at 1, rue André-Ducater, produces five hundred tons of nougat each year.

HR LE RELAIS DE L'EMPÉREUR: 1, Place Marx-Dormoy. Tel.: 75.01.29.00. Tlx.: 345537. 40 rooms (36 with toilet).
Comfortable, Empire-style rooms. (Napoleon slept here.) Pretty Liliane Latry, daughter of the owners, runs a good hotel and restaurant with a fine Rhône Valley wine list.

HR LE PARC CHABAUD: 16, avenue d'Aygu. Tel.: 75.01.65.66. Tlx.: 345324. 22 rooms.
Situated in a park in the center of town. Restaurant available.

ROCHEGUDE (26130—Drôme)
(Avignon 51—Bollène 8—Orange 15—Valence 96—Montélimar 55—Carpentras 23—Alés 85)
From A-7 exit at Bollène if driving south, or at Orange if driving north.

ᲝჇ The grandiose Château de Suze, 4 km north at Suze-la-Rousse, has been transformed into the Université du Vin. The tasting rooms and classrooms of this wine university take students from all over the world. Information can be had by writing to the Château de Suze, 26790 Suze-la-Rousse. Tel.: 75.04.86.09.

HR CHÂTEAU DE ROCHEGUDE: Tel.: 75.04.81.88. Tlx.: 345661. 25 luxurious, air-conditioned rooms and 4 suites.
Elegant, comfortable, expensive; pretentious old castle, yet unforgettable, if only for its display of questionable taste in decoration. Tennis court and heated swimming pool. Restaurant. *Relais et Châteaux.*

CÔTE DE RHÔNE

VAISON-LA-ROMAINE (SEGURET) (84110—Vaucluse)
(Avignon 47—Carpentras 28—Montélimar 65—Pont-Saint-Esprit 41—
Bollène 22—Châteauneuf-du-Pape 27—Vaison 9—Cairanne 6—
Vacqueyras 6—Gigondas 4—Beaumes 7—Sainte-Cécile 12)

HR LA TABLE DU COMTAT: Tel.: 90.36.91.49.   8 rooms.
At the top of the village of Séguret, enjoying a superb view of tens of thousands of acres of the Côtes du Rhône vineyards. Some of the 8 small, comfortable rooms also enjoy this memorable view. Franck Gomez has a well-deserved Michelin star for his air-conditioned restaurant.

ORANGE (84100—Vaucluse)
(Avignon 29—Aix-en-Provence 96—Montélimar 55—Valence 99—
Nîmes 55—Bollène 25—Carpentras 23)

Now you really find yourself in sun-drenched Provence. While in Orange, see the great Roman theater, built under the reign of the Emperor Augustus. If you have more time, the Arc de Triomphe is one of the best-preserved relics of the Gallo-Roman period. A concert festival is held at the end of July and a wine fair in September and February.

HR EUROMOTEL: On D-17, 80, Route de Caderousse. Tel.: 90.34.24.10. Tlx.: 431550.   98 rooms. Swimming pool.
Motel of quiet, modern comfort. Restaurant has simple menus.

HR ARÈNE: Place de Langes (center of town). Tel.: 90.34.10.95. Tlx.: 431195. Swimming pool.   30 rooms.
Remodeled hotel. Recommended for price rather than quality. Separate restaurant.

BAGNOLS-SUR-CÈZE (30200—Gard)
(Pont-Saint-Esprit 11—Avignon 33—Nîmes 48—Orange 29)
Across the Rhône from Orange.

The museum houses a collection of modern paintings assembled with the help of Renoir, whose work figures here, along with that of Matisse and Bonnard.

HR LE MAS DE VENTADOUS: 69, Route d'Avignon or N-580. Tel.: 66.89.61.26. Tlx.: 490949.   22 modern rooms in small bungalows around a swimming pool, in a large park. Tennis.

R MAÎTRE ITIER: At Connaux, 8 km south of Bagnols on N-86. Tel.: 66.82.00.24.
Well-prepared, classical family cooking served in an attractive, air-conditioned dining room. It is not only for Maître Itier's closeness to the Tavel, Lirac, and Châteauneuf-du-Pape vineyards that it is included in this listing. The food is really good. One star in Michelin.

ROQUEMAURE (30150—Gard)
(Avignon 14—Bagnols-sur-Cèze 19—Nîmes 45—Orange 11—Pont-Saint-Esprit 30)

HR CHÂTEAU DE CUBIÈRES: On the road to Avignon, D-980. Tel.: 66.50.14.28.   19 rooms.
Inexpensive hotel, considering the pretty setting in the midst of a park amongst the Côtes du Rhône vineyards. Warm welcome. The food could be improved. Good wine list.

CHÂTEAUNEUF-DU-PAPE (84230—Vaucluse)
(Avignon 17—Orange 13—Carpentras 24—Roquemaure 10)

❧ The fortress of the popes is now crumbling, but the vineyards they planted still flourish with a vengeance.

HR HOSTELLERIE DU CHÂTEAU DES FINES ROCHES: On D-17, 2 km south of the center of town in the direction of Avignon. Very comfortable stopover. Tel.: 90.83.70.23.   7 luxurious rooms. Warm welcome by the Estevenin family. You will enjoy the splendid view over the Châteauneuf-du-Pape vineyards and the entire Rhône Valley. An exceptionally good assortment of Châteauneuf-du-Pape wines. English spoken. One star in Michelin.

R LE PISTOU: Rue de l'Église. Tel.: 90.83.71.75.
A good, simple family restaurant.

HR LA MÈRE GERMAINE: Place de la Fontaine. Tel.: 90.39.70.72.   6 small rooms.
Marc Beutheret is a good chef. Beautiful view overlooking the Rhône Valley.

HR LOGIS D'ARNAVEL: Route de Roquemaure. Tel.: 90.83.73.22. Tlx.: 431625.   15 rooms.
Old country house on the crossroads of the two autoroutes: the one going to the Riviera and the other leading to Spain. Swimming pool. Park.

R LA MULE DU PAPE: Place de la Fontaine in the center of the village. Tel.: 90.83.73.30.
A competent restaurant in the midst of a very famous vineyard countryside. Fair food. Reasonably priced menus. English spoken.

TAVEL (30126—Gard)
(Paris 680—Nîmes 39—Avignon 14—Orange 20—Roquemaure 8.5—Arles 50—Uzès 32)
The capital of rosé.

HR AUBERGE DE TAVEL: Tel.: 66.50.03.41.   11 rooms, 10 toilets. Small swimming pool.
Good service and reasonable prices. The food is good. The rooms are basic. M. Bonneraux offers an interesting tasting of five different estate-bottled Tavels during the meal, which is recommended. One star in Michelin.

HR HOSTELLERIE DU SEIGNEUR: Place du Tavel. Tel.: 66.50.04.26.   7 reasonably priced rooms.
In the village producing one of the best rosés of France, M. Ange Bodo offers a good menu at a very reasonable price; *à la carte* prices are steeper.

VILLENEUVE-LÈS-AVIGNON (30400—Gard)
(Avignon 2.5—Marseille 103—Nimes 44—Orange 22)

HR LE PRIEURÉ: 7, Place du Chapître (behind the church). Tel.: 90.25.18.20. Tlx.: 431042.   30 rooms and apartments. Swimming pool and tennis.
Beautiful site in an old priory, within a pleasant park. Good food and wine list. Expensive. *Relais et Châteaux.* One star in Michelin.

HR LA MAGNANERAIE: 37, rue du Camp de Bataille. Tel.: 90.25.11.11.   21 air-conditioned rooms (18 with toilet).
Charming fifteenth-century manor with restaurant overlooking the town. Rather expensive—not so if you consider the impressive view.

AVIGNON (84000—Vaucluse)
(Paris 686—Aix-en-Provence 80—Marseille 100—Valence 124—Arles 36—
Nîmes 43—Lyon 224—Toulon 156—Nice 255)

❧ The vineyards of Châteauneuf-du-Pape are this Roman-built city's chief claim to wine fame. This moated city is insufficiently recognized for its dramatic beauty and is worth a detour. The palace of the popes is a striking specimen of fourteenth-century Gothic architecture. (See chapter on Côtes du Rhône.) An antique salon is held in February, and a very good drama festival in July and August.

HR SOFITEL: Pont d'Avignon, rue de la Balance, facing the Palace of the Popes in the center of the old, historic quarter of the Balance. Tel.: 90.85.91.23. Tlx.: 431215. 86 air-conditioned rooms plus 3 suites.
Small-scale restaurant and coffee shop available.

HR EUROPE: 12, Place Crillon. Tel.: 90.82.66.92. Tlx.: 431965. 65 air-conditioned rooms, 6 suites. Garden.
Retains the grand style of a private sixteenth-century house of a well-known local nobleman. I find this to be the pleasantest hotel in the city itself. Good meals available at La Vieille Fontaine restaurant.

R HIÉLY LUCULLUS: 5, rue de la République. Tel.: 90.86.17.07. Near the Palace of the Popes. Parking is difficult. Leave your car either at the hotel or on the Place du Palais des Papes. Wherever you park, a long walk is well worthwhile.
By far the best restaurant in Avignon, without exorbitant prices. A good Châteauneuf-du-Pape is offered in carafes. Tables are limited, so reserve in advance. Air-conditioned. *Relais et Châteaux.* Two stars in Michelin.

H NOVOTEL AVIGNON-SUD: On N-7, 5 km south of town. Tel.: 90.87.62.36. Tlx.: 432878. 79 rooms.
Functional, air-conditioned rooms. Snacks available. Heated swimming pool.

HR LES FRÊNES: At 84140 Montfavet, avenue des Vertes-Rives. 5 km southeast, take D-53. 20 quiet, air-conditioned rooms on the luxury side. Tel.: 90.31.17.93. Tlx.: 431164.
The restaurant is run like an elegant, private home by Jacques Biancone, a former architect, now a convert to the cause of fine cuisine. *Relais et Châteaux.*

HR MERCURE: 2, rue Marie de Médicis, on N-7, route de Marseille. Tel.: 90.88.91.10. Tlx.: 431994. 103 functional rooms.
Air-conditioned, adequate. Simple cuisine. Discothèque, heated pool.

R AUBERGE DE FRANCE: 28, Place de l'Horloge (close to the Palace of the Popes). Tel.: 90.82.58.86.
Redecorated. Good cuisine, good wine list. Reasonably priced. Reserve in advance. One star in Michelin.

LE PONTET (84130—Vaucluse)
Suburb of Avignon.

HR AUBERGE DE CASSAGNE: Route de Vedène (5 km east on N-7 or at the Avignon-Nord exit on A-7). Tel.: 90.31.04.18. Tlx.: 432997. 14 pretty, comfortable rooms.

With modern Provençal décor. Surrounded by cypress and olive trees and graced with a beautiful view. Swimming pool and tennis available. Moderate prices. Good chef. One star in Michelin.

LES ANGLES (30400—Gard)
Villeneuve-les-Avignon, on opposite side of the Rhône, 4 km from Avignon.

HR ERMITAGE MEISSONNIER: 32, avenue de Verdun, route de Nîmes (4 km west of Avignon on the other side of the Rhône on N-100). Hotel tel.: 90.25.41.02. Restaurant tel.: 90.25.41.68. Tlx.: 490715. 16 so-called air-conditioned rooms in a nearby annex.
Quiet, pleasant terrace and garden. Father, Paul-Louis, and son, Michel Meissonnier. run an excellent restaurant. Recently, some visitors have criticized the service and the rooms. One star in Michelin.

UZÈS (30700—Gard)
(Paris 706—Avignon 38—Alès 33—Nimes 25—Arles 54—Bagnols-sur-Cèze 28)

HR CHÂTEAU D'ARPAILLARGUES, HÔTEL D'AGOULT: At Arpaillargues, Route d'Anduze, 4 km west on D-982. Tel.: 66.22.14.48. Tlx.: 490415.
Luxurious, elegant restaurant. Reports have it that the exceptionally beautiful house, setting, and 28 rooms may be better than the food and service. Militating against these reports is the reputation of Gérard Savry and his brother, who own many successful restored châteaux and monasteries, of which l'Abbaye de Villeneuve, south of Nantes, is one.

NOVES (13550—Bouches-du-Rhône)
(Paris 692—Marseille 91—Orange 36—Avignon 13—Carpentras 29—
Saint Rémy-de-Provence 16—Cavaillon 16—Arles 36)

HR AUBERGE DE NOVES: At the Avignon-Sud exit from A-7, 2 km northwest from Noves on D-28. Tel.: 90.94.19.21. Tlx.: 431312. 19 comfortable, elegant rooms. Park, swimming pool, tennis.
M. Lalleman is the ideal host in this delightful, highly recommended country inn. English spoken. *Relais et Châteaux.* The refined food has earned him one star in Michelin.

CASTILLON-DU-GARD (30—Gard)
(Pont-du-Gard 4—Uzès 14—Alès 47—Nîmes 25—Avignon 27—
Orange 37—Arles 40—Lyon 229)

HR LE VIEUX CASTILLON: At 30210 Remoulins, 4 km northwest on D-981 and D-22. Tel.: 66.37.00.77. Tlx.: 490946. 33 good rooms and 2 suites.
An old village abandoned for centuries has been carefully reconstructed to form a unique hotel complex. A swimming pool on the third floor above the rooms, with a beautiful view, makes this a memorable, comfortable stopover. René Traversac who owns the Château d'Artigny and other luxurious *Relais et Châteaux* along the Loire, was the artisan of this newly opened super-inn near the Pont-du-Gard, the Roman bridge built in 20 B.C. The perfect condition of the 2,000-year-old stones makes this a famous tourist attraction.

CÔTE DE RHÔNE

SAINT-RÉMY-DE-PROVENCE (13210—Bouches-du-Rhône)
(Paris 708—Marseille 91—Nîmes 41—Arles 24—Avignon 21)
Charming Roman town with beautifully preserved remains. Worth a detour.
From Avignon, take N-570 south.

H HOSTELLERIE DU VALLON DE VALRUGUES: Chemin de Canto Cigalo from D-99. Tel.:
90.92.04.40. Tlx.: 431677. 24 rooms and 10 suites.
Attractive hotel with a garden. Heated pool. Tennis. No restaurant.

HR AUBERGE DE LA GRAÏO: 12, boulevard Mirabeau. Tel.: 90.92.15.33. 10 rooms.
Reasonably priced restaurant and rooms. Attractive location.

HR LE CASTELET DES ALPILLES: 6, Place Mireille. Tel.: 90.92.07.21. 19 rooms (13 toilets).
Large, comfortable house in a garden. Reasonably priced menus. Good, unpretentious.

H LE CHÂTEAU DES ALPILLES: On D-31. Tel.: 90.92.03.33. Tlx.: 431487.
In a park with tennis and swimming pool, 1 suite and 15 comfortable rooms make up this attractive hotel in this charming village. Breakfast available. No restaurant.

LES BAUX-DE-PROVENCE (13520—Bouches-du-Rhône)
(Marseille 86—Nîmes 44—Avignon 31—Arles 19—Saint-Rémy-de-Provence 9—
Aix-en-Provence 65—Salon-de-Provence 32)

◖ A geological quirk and a turbulent past conspire to make this the most haunting site in the
Bouches-du-Rhône. In the now ruined castle, great lords once vied at the medieval courts of love
for a lady's favors.

HR OUSTAÙ DE BAUMANIÈRE: Tel.: 90.54.33.07. Tlx.: 420203. 15 air-conditioned rooms and 11
suites.
M. Raymond Thuilier and Jean-André Charial have made this charming, elegant inn into one of
France's chapels of gastronomy. Although expensive, it is most deserving of its three stars in
Michelin. In a dramatic setting. Swimming pool, park, and tennis. Excellent wine list. *Relais et
Châteaux.*

HR LA CABRO D'OR: Tel.: 90.54.33.21. Tlx.: 401810. 22 rooms. Swimming pool. Tennis.
Same management as Oustaù de Baumanière, but less pretentious and less expensive. Redone in
1984. *Relais et Châteaux.* One star in Michelin.

R LA RIBOTO DE TAVEN: Tel.: 90.97.34.23. At Val d'Enfer on D-27.
Good restaurant, enhanced by the warm welcome and pleasant surroundings. One star in
Michelin.

ARLES (13200—Bouches-du-Rhône)
(Paris 722—Marseille 92—Aix-en-Provence 76—Avignon 36—Nîmes 31)

◖ Ancient Roman provincial capital. Not to be missed are the arena, the Roman theater, the Avenue des Alyscamps, the cloisters of St. Trophime, and, outside the town, the Abbey of Mont-
majour: Van Gogh made many drawings of it.

HR HÔTEL JULES CÉSAR—RESTAURANT LOU MARQUÈS: 7, boulevard des Lices, near post office. Tel.: 90.93.43.20. Tlx.: 400239. 57 rooms and 3 suites. Good, comfortable rooms and bathrooms. Modernized cloister. The Lou Marquès is a good restaurant. Very charming setting. *Relais et Châteaux.*

FONTVIEILLE *(13900—Bouches-du-Rhône)*
(Avignon 30—Marseille 92—Nîmes 42—Salon-de-Provence 37—
Saint-Remy-de-Provence 18)

HR AUBERGE LA REGALIDO: Rue Frédéric Mistral (9.5 km north from Arles on N-510). Tel.: 90.97.60.22 and 90.97.62.01. 12 rooms and 1 suite.
A small auberge in an old oil mill. Good, charming. *Relais et Châteaux.* One star in Michelin.

NÎMES *(30000—Gard)*
(Lyon 250—Aix-en-Provence 105—Marseille 123—Montpellier 51—Avignon 43—
Arles 31—Saint-Étienne 245—Toulouse 290—Perpignan 195—Bordeaux 535—
Paris 711—Clermont-Ferrand 391—Grenoble 250—Nice 280)

❦ The Maison Carrée is a gem and considered the most perfectly intact of the Roman temples that remain. The big Roman arena has bullfights in summer. In Vergèze, southwest of Nîmes, is the source of that most fashionable of sparkling waters, Perrier. Tel.: 66.84.60.27.

HR IMPERATOR: Place Aristide Briand. Tel.: 66.21.90.30. Tlx.: 490635. 65 acceptable, air-conditioned (when it works) rooms.
New management as of 1985 has improved the chances of this old restored house and good hotel becoming the best combination HR in town. The restaurant with its garden, Enclos de la Fontaine, has one star in Michelin.

LOIRE

France's longest and most famous river begins in the hills southwest of Lyon, far from the mighty castles and wine that have made its name throughout the world. It flows northward, parallel to the Rhône and the Saône, for half of its 1,000-kilometer length, before reaching the first vineyards at Sancerre and Pouilly-Fumé. At Orléans the river turns westward and passes through Blois, Tours, Saumur, Angers, and Nantes before finally reaching the Atlantic Ocean.

Any travelers interested in wine will find in the Loire a fantastic offering—even Burgundy, with its dozens of *appellations,* cannot match the Loire for diversity. A few of the wines are great—the wonderful and increasingly rare sweet wines from the Anjou and Touraine—but almost all are seductively pleasant, a vinous mirror image of their country.

It is the countryside along this westward-flowing leg of the river from Sancerre to Nantes that is known as the *pays de Loire* and, indeed, "Loire" takes in far more than the river alone: the name evokes a fertile countryside of orchards in flower, the luminously blue sky of spring, a calm manner, and an easygoing way of life. As all wine can be a reflection of the country and character of those who make it, one can easily see why the wines of the Loire are commonly called the most charming of France.

The famed historic castles of the Loire dot the countryside by the dozens, from the greatest residences of kings like Charles VIII and François I to the homes of courtiers and financiers of the seventeenth and eighteenth centuries. They stretch from east of Orléans to west of Angers, extending into the countryside, and adorn the Loire's many tributaries—the Cher, bridged by the magnificent Château de Chenonceaux; the Cosson, bordered by the largest of the Loire châteaux, Chambord; and the Indre, graced by the enchanting Azay-le-Rideau. Once in the *val de Loire* you are never far from one of these stately homes set in the midst of immaculate parks and gardens.

Despite its charm, the Loire is a fickle river. In summer (the drought of 1976 will be long remembered), the river shrinks to a web of shallow streams known as *luisettes,* which weave between the sandbars and river islands called *grèves.* When the river gets this low the farmers can walk their cows to the grassy islands in the middle Loire to graze. When the autumn rains come the river swells, sometimes flooding the banks and breaking through the levees.

Undaunted by the stream's unpredictability, Dutch traders familiar with its seasonal changes used the Loire from the earliest times as an artery of travel and transport, right up until the nineteenth century, when it was superseded by the railroad. Small flat boats called *péniches* plied the Loire as far as Tours, carrying their cargoes upstream from Nantes. From the fifteenth to the eighteenth century, Parisians en route to their favorite country retreats traveled by coach as far as Orléans and there embarked, coach and all, aboard river rafts which took them the next leg of their journey downstream. Madame de Sévigné writes of a pleasant six-day trip past the poplar- and willow-lined banks from Orléans 300 kilometers (180 miles) to Nantes.

MUSCADET

It is from the vineyards around Nantes region today that one of the wines of France most rapidly growing in popularity is found—Muscadet. From the Loire's mouth on the Atlantic, the vineyards cover 120 kilometers (72 miles) of the river's length and spread out over three *appellations,* Muscadet making half a million cases a year, Muscadet des Coteaux de la Loire making half that amount from the lesser areas, and finally, most abundant of all, Muscadet de Sèvre-et-Maine—named for the Sèvre and Maine rivers south of Nantes and the Loire. It is here that the best Muscadets are made: over four million cases annually.

Only within the last thirty years have these young, fresh wines achieved great popularity, not only in France but abroad. Until well into the First World War, all of them were consumed in Nantes and Saint-Nazaire. Between the wars, Muscadet became a favorite carafe wine of the small restaurants and bistros. Before the Appellation Contrôlée laws came into effect in the 1930s, Muscadets were openly blended with Chablis to stretch the supply of that scarce and famous wine. Now, with the continual price increases in white Burgundies coupled with greatly improved wine-making methods in the Muscadet district, this large region of inexpensive wine not only is now famous throughout France, but has justifiably begun to enjoy a world vogue as well.

The name "Muscadet" is taken from the name of the vine, originally called the Muscadet de Bourgogne, or Melon de Bourgogne. Also planted within the region is a certain amount of Gros Plant, also known as Folle Blanche, and formerly used in Cognac. "To be made properly," says one of the region's better shippers, "the juice from the Muscadet grapes should ferment slowly to retain the fruitiness of the wine. Many growers have cellars deeply cut into the hillsides, which are cool and keep the fermentation steady and slow. For the fermentation, aging, and storing of the wine, we use large concrete vats. Contrary to the practice in many other regions, our wine never sees any wood from vat or barrel. To taste it we draw directly from the top of the vat, using a long pipette. After the fermentation is complete, some wine is filtered and bottled directly; the wine left *sur lie* ["on the lees"] is bottled shortly afterward—in the early spring months—hence adding character to the wine."

The lees are the precipitates that result from fermentation, composed mostly of dead yeasts. By remaining in the vat in contact with the lees, the wine gains an extra measure of fruit and body, the same way Champagne gains in character by remaining in contact with sediment in the bottle before disgorgement. By not racking the wine, the grower allows it also to retain a bit of carbon dioxide from the fermentation, giving a refreshing liveliness to the palate.

The term *sur lie* has been defined. Many of the cheaper Muscadets have had the carbon dioxide added artificially and may also contain a trace of unfermented sugar, which covers the natural acidity of the wine.

Sur lie or not, Muscadet is a light, fresh wine with distinctive fruit, which gains nothing by being aged. The Muscadet grape is not naturally acidic and must be harvested early to make a wine of characteristic freshness. The picking often begins in the first week of September, although in the unprecedentedly hot summers of 1976 and 1982 the harvest should have begun in late August. As it was, the grapes were too ripe and the growers had to prevent the malolactic fermentation (the secondary fermentation breaking down acids) from taking place for the wine to retain sufficient acidity.

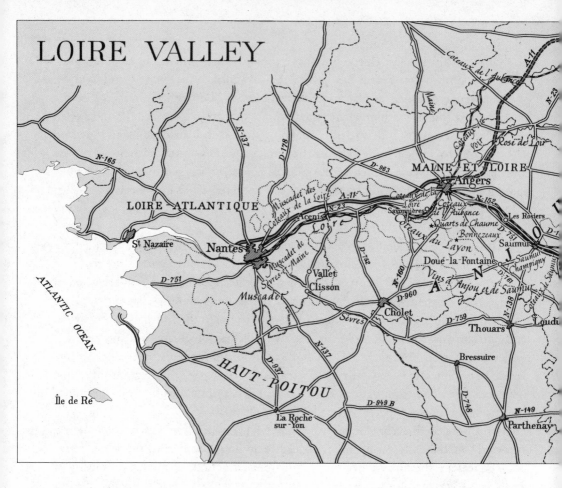

LOIRE VALLEY

Even with such exceptions as 1976, vintage years in Muscadet are not of great importance beyond indicating the age of the wine in the bottle. A Muscadet over two or three years in the bottle may well have lost whatever charm it once had.

Since the Muscadet region does not classify the production of the separate communes surrounding the Loire from the Sèvre-et-Maine to the Coteaux de la Loire, the seeker of top-quality wines from this area is still severely handicapped. At present, there is no system that distinguishes between the individual vineyards of Saint-Fiacre, La Haie Fouassière, or Le Pallet in the same way that Beaujolais differentiates between the place-name Beaujolais and Beaujolais-Villages, or between the production of the top villages of Fleurie, Brouilly, or Morgon, for instance. Noteworthy vineyard areas surround the villages of Vallet (the unofficial capital of Muscadet), Mouzillon, Le Pallet, Saint-Fiacre, La Haie Fouassière, Vertou, Monnières, and Gorges, and Haute-Goulaine. The V.D.Q.S. of the region (Vins Délimités de Qualité Supérieure, another category of wines of less distinction than the Appellation

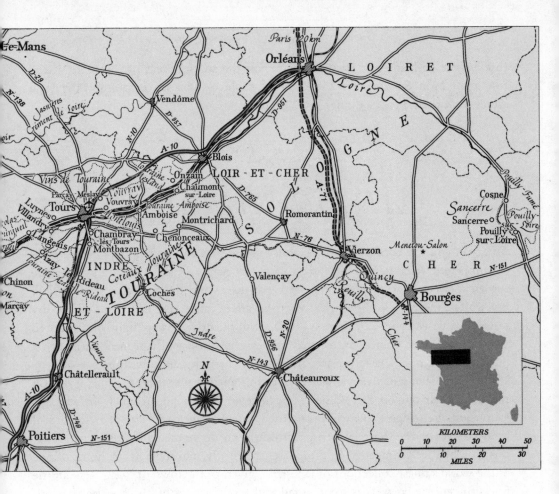

Contrôlée) is Gros Plant, the name of the secondary white-wine grape, which produces a more acid, heavy common wine.

COTEAUX D'ANCENIS

Upstream from Nantes 40 kilometers (24 miles) is the pretty town of Ancenis, whose vineyards on either side of the Loire also make some of the more pleasant red and white V.D.Q.S. wines, which you will often find on menus in the restaurants of the Muscadet region. The "Coteaux d'Ancenis" on the label will be followed necessarily by the name of the grape used to make it. If you don't get as far as Ancenis, just outside of Nantes at Basse-Goulaine, on the south shores of the Loire, is the restaurant Mon Rêve, where the knowledgeable Nantais drive to enjoy the local wines with their Sunday dinner.

❧

ANJOU-SAUMUR

Muscadet country continues beyond Ancenis another 20 kilometers (12 miles) upstream before we cross into the complex array of Anjou wines. Among its whites are the great sweet wines made along the Layon River and the agreeable semi-dry and dry whites; the rosés come in the sweetish variety called rosé d'Anjou and the dry called rosé de la Loire, and there is also a small quantity of fine, lightish, fruity red wine. Nowhere in France, or, for that matter, the world will you meet with such a profusion of types of tastes, nearly all of them charming and inviting.

The noble city of Angers, which gives this ancient province its name, is not on the Loire itself but on the Maine, 8 kilometers (5 miles) upstream from where it joins the Loire. Angers today is a contented, broad-boulevarded city of 135,000, still brooded over by the stern, immense thirteenth-century semicircular castle-fortress. It was used by the Plantagenets in the sixteenth century, and today is the home of one of the world's finest collections of tapestries, given to the town of King René in the fifteenth century, as well as some wonderful modern ones by the late Jean Lurçat. Within the fortress walls are well-manicured gardens and lawns, with a small chapel looking out onto the Maine River.

The Anjou vineyards fan out west from Angers along the Loire, toward Muscadet and eastward along the southern bank of the river, beyond Saumur, the other parent-wine town of the region. Though a multitude of grape varieties are planted, the Anjou growers favor the Chenin Blanc for the white wines and the Cabernet Franc for the reds. They also grow Groslot and Gamay for rosé, as well as Chardonnay, Sauvignon, and Cabernet-Sauvignon. Whether sweet or dry, sparkling or still, the grapes remain the same; it is the vinification that changes.

Before the Second World War, apart from some light red wines the growers made for their home use, Anjou was a country known only for its white wines, either the semi-sweet ones, sold in cafés and bistros from Nantes to Paris in slender half bottles called *fillettes,* or the sweet dessert wines which, like the few that remain today, could last to a great age and graced all the finest tables of the region. After the war, tastes turned to the drier wines, and the Muscadets, Sancerres, Pouilly-Fumés, and wines of Alsace took over the Paris clientele. So growers turned to their rosé wines, which found an eager market in Belgium, Switzerland, Holland, England, and the United States.

Although Groslot and Gamay grapes can go into a rosé, along with the Cabernet Franc, the best rosé wine is made with Cabernet Franc alone. One of the best sources has been the village of Tigné, south of the Layon River.

In deference to the sweet-toothed foreign market, all rosé from the Anjou used to be semi-sweet, but, to accommodate drier tastes, a new *appellation* was created. Sold under the label Rosé de la Loire, it now accounts for the equivalent of about 250,000 cases and is sure to grow in popularity in the future.

Anjou's best white wines—and some would say the region's best of any type—come from the 5,000 hectares (12,500 acres) of vineyard south of Angers, along the Layon River. A trip through the Coteaux du Layon villages is an enchanting drive from Angers, on N-161 to Beaulieu-sur-Layon, and south along the river through the vineyard towns. Anjou is also increasing its production of red wines, with nearly 90,000 hectoliters produced in 1981. These wines are light, fresh, fruity, a bit tannic, but very agreeable on the whole.

❧ Coteaux du Layon ☙

Coteaux du Layon is a general name for the region's sweet white wines; some of the better villages within the *appellation* are Beaulieu-sur-Layon, Rablay-sur-Layon, Rochefort, and Faye d'Anjou. The wines are sweet and high in alcohol, and the best vineyards only pick after all the Chenin Blanc grapes have been affected by the *pourriture noble, Botrytis cinerea*. The two best *appellations* from the Coteaux are Quart de Chaumes and Bonnezeaux. They are the sweetest wines of the Coteaux, and their fruit and lingering acidity give them great elegance and finesse. Originally, all the vineyards of the village Chaumes were owned by one man, who rented them out to workers in return for a quarter share of each vintage. The lord reserved the right to choose which section of the vineyards his quarter should come from, and it came to be called Quart de Chaumes. Nature has its marvelous quirks: this area, 50 hectares in size (125 acres), has its own microclimate. It is better protected from cold winds from the north and west than its neighbors, and the grapes mature sooner. Between them, Bonnezeaux and Quart de Chaumes make less than the equivalent of 20,000 cases a year.

The best of the Coteaux du Layon will equal these two rarities in finesse and staying power. The Chenin grape is naturally hard and slow to mature, so the wines should age in bottle to allow the bouquet and distinction to emerge—about ten years is generally agreed on as a minimum. This is one of the few wine regions where the growers prefer to keep their wines in their cellars to take on the patina of age before selling them. Unfortunately, only one grower in ten can afford to hold wines that long, so many must content themselves with making lighter, younger-drinking, sweet white wine. These will be pleasant, especially as aperitif wines, but lacking the majesty of the best.

Without a doubt, the region's most dazzling collection of Coteaux du Layon wines lies in the labyrinthine cellars of Joseph Touchais, grower at Doué-la-Fontaine and president of the Anjou-Saumur growers' association. "These are the great unknown wines of France," he says. "Those who've had a fine bottle of twenty-year-old Quart de Chaumes, Bonnezeaux, or Coteaux du Layon won't forget the great balance of sweetness and fruit that make them even longer-lived than Sauternes. We pay our bills by selling our rosé d'Anjou abroad (3 million cases a year) and do our best to continue with the sweet wines." A walk through M. Touchais's hewn limestone cellars is mind-boggling—he estimates his stock to be over 2 million bottles, some vintages going as far back as 1870, probably the largest collection of old white wine in France.

The Layon region is not all sweet white and rosé. At Brissac, Anjou's best red wine is made, sold simply as Anjou. After sampling some of Brissac's better-than-average red wine, you can stop off at the fine early-seventeenth-century Château de Brissac. It was built by Charles de Cossé, Maréchal of France, whose family lives there to this day.

There are also the semi-sweet white wines and rosés of the Coteaux de l'Aubance, making the small amount of thirty-odd thousand cases a year, generally less fruity than the better Coteaux du Layon wines.

❧ *Savennières* ❧

Although there is not a plentiful supply of good Anjou still, dry white wine even in good years, some of the best comes from the small pocket of vineyards south of Angers around the town of Savennières. The sun-poor vintages of Chenin Blanc tend to be hard and unfriendly, but they are dry wines that improve with age. Two of the best communes may add their names to the Savennières *appellation:* Coulée-de-Sérrant (Mme Joly) and Roches-aux-Moines. These can be excellent. They are good for many years and are definitely among the very best dry white wines of the Loire.

◦◦ *Saumur* ◦◦

Upriver from Angers is the old town of Saumur, a pleasant, sleepy place, over-shadowed by its prominent neighbors, Tours on the east and Angers on the west. The town is split into three parts: the north bank and the south bank of the river and the island in between, all connected by a long bridge with an impressive view of the Loire.

Saumur's glory lies in the past. On a limestone outcropping high above the river and the town's typical blue-slate-roofed houses stand the jagged towers of the Château de Saumur, built at the end of the fourteenth century by Louis I, duke of Anjou. In more recent times, Saumur has been known for its famed Cadre Noir riding school. The Black Brigade, so named for the black uniforms they wore, was the training school for the French cavalry until 1969, and continues today as the national riding school, the École Nationale d'Équitation.

Besides providing a sturdy foundation for many of the châteaux along the Loire, the ubiquitous limestone bedrock has been used by wine-makers and shippers who, over the centuries, built their houses and warehouses right up the cliff face. At the rear of the buildings, they carved cool, dark cellars, literally caves, out of the chalky rock, where they make and store their wine to this day.

Equally practical use of the cliff face has been made by mushroom farmers, who flourish in and around Saumur. The cool obscurity of the caves is perfectly suited to the cultivation of the so-called *champignon de Paris* for dining tables all over France. But the cliffs above the Loire were occupied long before the triumphs of the grape and fungus were generally practiced. In prehistoric times, the cliffs' cave dwellers carved homes out of the rock. You can see their former habitations high above you as you drive along the northern bank of the Loire from Saumur to Tours and Vouvray. Residents of these early high-rises preferred the northern bank of the Loire for its southern exposure. Many of these cliff-face homes have been enlarged and fitted out for living in today, their large, square windows looking out over the river. Since the vineyards begin where cliffs leave off, the chimneys of these troglodyte houses, which have been pierced through the rock, emerge at the edge of the vineyard above.

Unlike the rest of the rosé-rich region, Saumur is still largely white-wine country and makes five times as much dry and semi-sweet still white wine as red and rosé. The Cabernet Franc–based red wine, made at Champigny, is known for being one of the best of the Loire, equal to and nearly indistinguishable from the fine reds of nearby Chinon and Bourgueil.

Saumur *mousseux,* the region's sparkling white and rosé, is nearly as important a product as the rest of the Saumur *appellations* combined. As Champagne prices climbed through the seventies and early eighties, the *mousseux* gained popularity in France as a cheaper alternative. At its best, it has all the pleasant charm of the better Loire sparkling wines, but more often than not it will leave you hankering for the real thing.

TOURAINE

"I was born and raised in the garden of France—Touraine." So proclaimed François Rabelais, the sixteenth-century satirist and gourmand from Chinon, in the heart of Touraine country. Perhaps nowhere in the Loire Valley are the praises of the soft climate and lush endowment of fruits, flowers, and vegetables more deserved than in the Touraine; since Rabelais, hardly a generation has passed without a writer or poet singing its praises.

The high and mighty of French history graced the Touraine with greater attention than any other wine region and left behind the grandest of the Loire châteaux. Azay-le-Rideau, Amboise, Blois, Chenonceaux, Chambord, Villandry, Chaumont, and dozens more dot the countryside and draw hundreds of thousands of visitors every year.

Driving from Saumur, the Touraine and its vineyards begin with Chinon and Bourgueil and sweep up the Loire to Blois, with Tours itself nearly in the middle. Most of the 6,000 hectares (15,000 acres) of A.O.C. vines are south of the river, extending to the great hunting ground of Sologne, source of the region's best game.

In typical Loire Valley style, the Touraine has nearly a dozen or more *appellations,* but four of these are truly noble in the eyes of local growers: Chinon and Bourgueil (including Saint-Nicolas-de-Bourgueil) for red wines, and Vouvray and Montlouis for whites.

Chinon and Bourgueil, along with Saumur-Champigny, are the Loire's best red wines. Local connoisseurs like to go on about Chinon smelling of violets and Bourgueil of raspberries, but even local experts confuse the two regularly. They are closer to the truth maintaining that Bourgueil takes bottle age better than Chinon. The main difference between the two wines is their origin: Bourgueil is north of the river and Chinon is south. The beguiling and subtle differences among these red wines can be more accurately traced to the particular vineyard and particular slope. The best of the Chinon, they say, comes from the vineyards along the Vienne River, particularly around Cravant and Saint-Louans, just west of Chinon.

Next door to the village of Bourgueil is Saint-Nicolas-de-Bourgueil, making wine of the same quality or slightly superior; its separate *appellation* is explained by the fact that, when the National Institute of Place-names was codifying the *appellations* of the Touraine, the mayor of Saint-Nicolas-de-Bourgueil was the largest vineyard holder and successfully lobbied for his own communal *appellation*. Although Saint-Nicolas-de-Bourgueil sells for slightly more than Bourgueil, there is little to choose between them. Most Saint-Nicolas-de-Bourgueil is sold directly to private consumers.

There is a trend among the growers generally to sell their Gamay wines *en primeur,* like Beaujolais, just after the wine is made. The growers like *primeur* business because it gives them some quick money—even though *primeur* wines are not their vocation and the Cabernet Franc–based wines are not truly fit for this treatment.

Between Chinon-Bourgueil and Tours there is little wine of importance but a number of magnificent châteaux to visit. Close by to Chinon (take D-16 north to D-7) is Château d'Ussé, the seemingly enchanted, towered, and gabled affair said to have inspired Charles Perrault when he wrote "Sleeping Beauty." A short drive down D-7 from Ussé is Château de Villandry, the last of the great Loire castles to be built. Only a part of the castle remains, but the formal, symmetrical sixteenth-century gardens are unique in France for their intricacy. Midway between Chinon and Tours on D-751 is the architectural jewel of Azay-le-Rideau (take D-751) on the Indre River. For its pure Renaissance style, which harmonizes so well with its riverside setting, the castle, along with Chenonceaux, has always been one of the most-visited of the Loire châteaux.

Twenty kilometers (12 miles) along the north bank of the river from Bourgueil is the château at Langeais, unusual for a Loire château in being located right in town.

For a city of its historic importance, it seems surprising that Tours does not have a castle-fort as do Saumur, Chinon, and Angers. To compensate, there is the cathedral of Saint-Gatien, a monument to the diverse periods of Gothic style.

VOUVRAY

Drive upstream from Tours 10 km on N-152 to reach the town of Vouvray, the site of Touraine's best-known vineyard, which produces one of the Loire's finest wines. As Bourgueil has Chinon on the southern bank to balance out the reds, Vouvray has its counterpart in Montlouis, home also of a fine, but lesser, white wine. As with the white Anjou wine from the Coteaux du Layon, the Vouvray growers consider that their greatest achievement is to make the rare sweet, fruity wines from the super-mature *Botrytis*-affected Chenin grapes. Most of the time, though, Vouvray ranges from dry to semi-sweet and, increasingly, the growers have turned to making the better-selling dry wines. Also gaining in popularity is sparkling Vouvray. Like the Anjou growers who make and market a popular rosé while their hearts are more in their fine sweet white wines, the growers of Vouvray produce a popular *mousseux* to be able to continue with their small production of dry and sweet wines. Also increasing in the Touraine, for the same reason, is the production of Gamay-based rosés. These are no substitute for the best Gamay-made wine, Beaujolais. In the Touraine the Gamay makes a slightly acid wine lacking the fruit of the average Beaujolais.

One of Vouvray's best growers, making both sparkling and sweet wines, is Gaston Huet, Mayor of Vouvray and local historian. "Our customers want the sparkling Vouvray, and it accounts for nearly half of our production," he says. "Vouvray *mousseux* can be excellent if it is bottle-fermented, Champagne-style, to retain the character of the Chenin grape. Yet too often the growers try to imitate the inimitable Champagne because customers expect all sparkling wine to be Champagne." Since the French appetite for *mousseux* knows no limit, nearly all sparkling Vouvray is popped open in France, while about half of the still Vouvray is shipped abroad. In addition to sparkling (*mousseux*) Vouvray, there are the *pétillant,* or slightly "crackling," Vouvrays, although they are less common now than in the past.

When vinified dry, Vouvray is a full and fruity wine, but in hotter vintages the growers set aside certain parcels for the grapes to be affected by *Botrytis cinerea,* the same "noble rot" of Sauternes. The sweeter the Vouvray, the longer it will last and the longer you should wait before opening it. Compared to the great sweet wine rivals from the Coteaux du Layon, the Vouvray wines tend to age better and retain their great fruit and freshness longer. However, like the Layon wines, the sweet Vouvrays, because of their underlying acidity, age better and retain their fruit longer than Sauternes and Barsacs, most of which have lost their fruit after fifteen years.

One of Vouvray's important producers is Dr. Bernard Avignon, the new owner of the Domaine de Bidaudière, whose cellars and château have a fine view overlooking the Loire. The cellars are true *caves,* carved into the limestone hillside behind the château. Above the cliffs are the vineyards, where the most elevated land produces the best wine. The best Vouvray comes from M. Gaston Huet, mayor, and proprietor of the Clos du Bourg and of the Clos Le Mont. Other good producers include M. Allias, Prince Philippe Poniatowski, Clos Naudin of Foreau in Vouvray, and the firm of Marc Bredif at Rochecorbon. While many growers, large and small, put their backs and souls into their wine and bottle their own production, there is a growers' cooperative at Vouvray which has become increasingly important.

Before leaving the Touraine, find time to stop off at Château d'Amboise at Amboise, high on the cliff overlooking the Loire. In 1516, at the age of sixty-five, Leonardo da Vinci came there upon the invitation of the young King François I. In his brief time in France, Leonardo's genius helped to introduce the arts of the Italian Renaissance, reshaping the whole of French architecture. He died at Amboise in 1519 and was buried in the chapel of the château.

❧ *Montlouis* ☙

The Montlouis vineyards are just across the Loire from Vouvray, covering 300 hectares (750 acres) on the southern bank. Montlouis distinguishes itself from Vouvray by being more supple and by possessing much less character than the Vouvrays, and is therefore meant for earlier drinking. It should be clearly distinguished from its better neighbors. Dry Montlouis is often vinified in a slightly less dry manner than a Vouvray of the same vintage. The small amount of residual sugar compensates for character. The output is small—around 125,000 cases—but it can be found outside France, occasionally sold as "Chenin Blanc Appellation Montlouis."

The *appellation* Touraine covers whites, rosés, and red wines, which can offer pleasant surprises. Three Touraine villages have been distinguished which may append their name after "Touraine" on the label. They are Touraine-Azay-le-Rideau, which makes white and rosé wine; Touraine-Mesland, making mostly Gamay-based rosés and red wines, the latter being poor substitutes for Beaujolais; and Touraine-Amboise, making both red and white wine. Since they are made in the heart of Loire châteaux country, most of these wines are drunk on the spot with the local specialties of potted pork called *rillons* and *rillettes,* white sausage called *boudin blanc,* or the fine freshwater fish, pike, bream, shad, eel, and mullet.

The Touraine vineyards officially end at Blois. North of Tours are the minor wine regions of Coteaux du Loir, a small tributary of the Loire (notice the different spelling) and Jasnières along the Loir River. Jasnières's dry and sweet wines are the better of the two, and its sweet white wines can occasionally rival the Vouvrays, but, at the rate of only 6,000 cases a year, it is not likely you'll find it outside the local restaurants.

THE EASTERN LOIRE: SANCERRE AND POUILLY-FUMÉ

As you retrace the Loire from Blois, the river heads north to Orléans and then curves south through the last of the important Loire wines: Sancerre and Pouilly-Fumé and the satellites to the west, Quincy and Reuilly, from the towns of those names south of Vierzon. Though largely white-wine country, this region is an exception to the rest of the Loire because the wines are not made from the favored Chenin Blanc, but from the Sauvignon Blanc. The white Sauvignon is normally at home in Bordeaux, where it is one of the grape varieties used to make dry white Graves and the sweet wines from Sauternes. The reds and the ever-increasing rosés come from the Cabernet Franc grape variety.

Sancerre

Lovers of the Beaujolais countryside would feel at home in the rolling hills of Sancerre. The vine-covered slopes planted in Sauvignon surrounding the hilltop village of Sancerre face in all directions and, driving along the winding narrow roads from one small wine commune to the next, it is more than likely the uninitiated will lose his way.

The Sancerre soil is equally confusing, composed of mixing and overlapping distinct layers of limestone and clay that significantly alter the character of the wine from vine plot to vine plot. The wines of greatest finesse are found where there is most limestone. The poorer slopes are left open for grazing goats.

In the past couple of decades or so, the white wines of Sancerre have achieved great popularity in France, mainly in Paris, and have recently caught on abroad in much the same way as its lesser but more productive rival, Muscadet. "Sancerre is not a complex wine," says René Laporte, grower at Saint-Satur. "It's not a wine that demands a lot of brow-wrinkling and introspection—its simplicity gives it immediate appeal." Slightly bland, with a good balance of acidity, Sancerre epitomizes a carefree white wine, as average Beaujolais once did for red wines. Like Beaujolais,

Sancerre should be drunk young and fresh with the bloom of youth. This may explain why many Paris restaurants offer their customers a Beaujolais for their red wine and a Sancerre for their white. Seafood of all kinds—from oysters to striped bass—find the perfect mate in a cool glass of Sancerre or Pouilly-Fumé.

In the past decade, Sancerre's output has doubled and the area under vines has spread out to cover large stretches of formerly abandoned vineyard on the steeper slopes, where cultivation was too difficult. Quite a bit has been planted in Cabernet Franc for the rosés, with red Sancerres gaining somewhat in favor. It is a wonder that a mere 1,600 hectares (4,250 acres) can satisfy the huge demand.

Six hundred families in fourteen communes divide up these sixteen hundred hectares. The Sancerre growers have responded to the steadily increasing popularity of Sancerre by petitioning the I.N.A.O. to approve the use of district place-names to designate wines from certain distinct areas within Sancerre. Sancerre is enough in demand, the growers feel, for the customers to cope with the confusion that will result.

Overlooking all the vineyards is the charming hilltop village of Sancerre, one of the most picturesque wine towns of the Loire Valley. It is criss-crossed by tiny, alley-like streets that open onto small squares, usually decked out in geraniums. From the base of the château, at the plateau's edge, you have a splendid view across the Loire, over to the vineyards of Pouilly-Fumé; off in the opposite direction is Chavignol, one of the best Sancerre communes and site of the *chèvrerie,* the goat co-operative where nearly a thousand *chèvres* contribute to the making of the Appellation Contrôlée local specialty, *crottin de Chavignol,* a piquant goat cheese that goes well with all the local wines.

❧ *Pouilly-Fumé* ☙

Sancerre's neighbor across the Loire, Pouilly-Fumé, makes half the wine Sancerre does. The difference between the wines, generally speaking, is not remarkable, but when at its best Pouilly-Fumé can be a more complex, more flowery wine, and with great depth of taste, which emerges after a year or two in the bottle. Its slightly nobler quality and relative rarity compared to Sancerre have pushed the price for Pouilly-Fumé beyond reasonable limits in many cases.

Getting any of the growers from either side of the river to testify on these differences is frustrating at best. Says Paul Figeat, grower at the Pouilly-Fumé village Les Loges, "Why, Sancerre and Pouilly-Fumé are as different as two different people—no description could do them justice." When pressed, Figeat will admit that maybe his wine has more "notes" or taste than the initially more charming wines across the river at Sancerre.

Pouilly's 600 or so hectares (1,500 acres) of wines begin nearly at the river's edge. The terrain rises sharply from the river bank—after climbing the steep main street of the wine village of Les Loges, the road then levels off to a plateau of rolling hills, where most of the Pouilly-Fumé vineyards are found. The main wine village is not Pouilly-sur-Loire, the region's largest town, but Saint-Andelain, where the greatest concentration of good vineyards lies. Pouilly-sur-Loire is also the name of the lesser *appellation* wine made from a blend of Sauvignon and Chasselas.

Because of the lay of the land downstream across the river in Sancerre and the configuration of hills there, the hail-bearing winds from the west usually only skirt Sancerre, but can devastate Pouilly. Says Jean-Pierre Renaud, grower and broker at Saint-Andelain, "It seems to hail practically every year, but we haven't had a major storm since 1971. Even in a light storm, the hailstones bruise the vines and cripple anything they don't knock off—a bad storm is as bad as phylloxera. In 1977, we got badly frozen in March and then in the summer hail came—there wasn't much, but it only hit the unfrozen vines! We were lucky to have a third of our normal harvest." The region was hit with hail again in 1978—if the weather behaved like this all the time, Pouilly-Fumé would not have the international fame it enjoys today.

The largest property of the region, around 50 hectares (125 acres), is the Château de Nozet of the Ladoucette family, now run by Baron Patrick Ladoucette. As a shipper, he uses his 45 hectares of vines to form a base for the large quantity of Pouilly-Fumé he sells. Although many growers may vie to surpass Ladoucette's quality, Ladoucette dominates the area.

⋈ *Quincy and Reuilly* ⋊

About 60 kilometers (36 miles) southwest of Sancerre are the twin white-wine vineyards of Quincy and Reuilly. These small vineyards of Sauvignon Blanc were once prominent, but they have now fallen into eclipse. Quincy has 115 hectares (288 acres) and Reuilly has 40 hectares (100 acres). Together, they produce only about 40,000 cases of wine a year. The wines are nearly identical in character—fruity, but in cooler years tending to lack the characteristic charm of Sancerre, which they otherwise resemble. One of the best growers was the late Gaston Lapha, in Quincy, who made a special effort to spread the name of his wine and vineyard region.

Midway between Sancerre and Quincy-Reuilly is the ancient city of Bourges, where Vercingetorix, the Gallic warrior and hero to every French schoolchild, fought off the assault of Caesar's armies. In the fifteenth century it was home to Jacques Coeur, part-time financial adviser to King Charles VII and full-time trader-entrepreneur. Coeur's huge network of traders in furs, spices, and precious stones stretched from France to India and made him the wealthiest man in Europe. His financial genius helped Charles win back Normandy from the English in 1450. Unfortunately, all the historic glamour of Jacques Coeur will not bring the wines of Reuilly and Quincy back into the world arena of wine. Menetou Salon white has 82 hectares (205 acres), and the red has 53 hectares (132 acres).

Beyond the Appellation Contrôlée wines covered in this chapter, there are a few lesser *appellations* and fairly dozens of pleasant V.D.Q.S. wines dotting the Loire countryside and worth a visit, if only for the eye appeal of the vineyards. North of Sancerre, around the town of Gien, is the Coteaux Giennois, home of light reds and whites. Surrounding Orléans is a region which produced huge quantities of wine for the gullets of thirsty Renaissance Parisians. Now that transportation of wine is not the major problem it was until the advent of the railroad in the first half of the nineteenth century, the Orléanais is strictly a minor region, better known for its vinegar. On either side of the Jasnières vineyards, north of Tours, are the Coteaux du Vendomois and Coteaux du Loir, the first a source of minor white rosé, the second a nearly extinct region of reds and whites. Far to the south from the Anjou, on the edge of Cognac country, are the wines, now gaining in fame, of the Haut-Poitou, making some very noteworthy white wines and indifferent reds.

I mention these only because the valley of the Loire offers so much to the traveler-historian-sightseer-wine-lover that perhaps in your wanderings through the valley they call the "Garden of France" you will run across these wines at the inns and restaurants you visit.

LOIRE VINTAGES

1969 A good vintage for all the wines of the Loire. With the exception of sweet wines, the quality of the whites is a thing of the past.

1970 The large quantity prevented any high peaks of quality. A fairly good vintage.

1971 Good, excellent in Muscadet, now faded.

1972 Not a good vintage. The wines were light and without character.

1973 The quality was only good and nothing more. With the exception of sweet wines, no longer of interest.

1974 Fruity, well-balanced wines were produced, flat in that they lacked character and acidity. These wines were fine when drunk very young. Fine sweet wines.

1975   Very good vintage. Many excellent Muscadets were produced, but some were harvested a bit too late and the grapes were thus overripe, lacking their characteristic greenness.

An exceptionally good vintage in the Anjou, Vouvray, exceptionally good in Pouilly-Fumé and Sancerre.

1976   Very good in Muscadet, Vouvray, Sancerre, and Pouilly-Fumé, especially for the Vouvray.

1977   The late March frost did not spare the Loire. Muscadet was the worst hit, with an estimated loss of 60 percent. Otherwise quite good.

1978   A good vintage for Muscadet, somewhat resembling the 1975s. The rest of the Loire produced wines of very good quality. Regrettably for Sancerre, their vineyards were badly hit by hail.

1979   A good year for Muscadet since the harvest ended before the rains began. Despite their acidity the wines are fairly well-balanced and fruity. The quality grape for Anjou rosés, Cabernet Franc, was harvested under rainy conditions; hence the wines are disappointing. Good yields of Vouvray, in fact double the yield of 1978, but lacking in quality. Most of the 1979 vintage was used for sparkling wines.

1980   The Muscadets, a bit acid, are of lesser quality than the 1979s. In Anjou the wines were superior to those of 1979. Vouvray yielded good, fruity wines.

1981   The Muscadets produced a good vintage, perfumed, lighter than the previous vintages.

Dry Vouvrays and demi-sec Vouvrays were produced in limited quantities: a spring frost and poor flowering caused a 50 percent loss. However, unlike the 1979 and 1980 vintages, 1981 is a quality vintage of well-balanced wines. Very little sweet Vouvray was produced because late rains prevented the development of *botrytis,* or noble rot. By contrast with 1979, sparkling Vouvray was produced in small quantities, as most of the wine was made into good dry wines. Pouilly-Fumé and Sancerre made a good vintage.

1982   Muscadet produced some very good fine wines, well balanced and harmonious, with an unusually low acidity but good aroma owing to the inherent richness of the musts.

In Anjou and Saumur, the abundant harvests resulted in wines of varying quality, as was the case in Touraine. The crop for sweet wines was vastly reduced by late rains, while the reds had a successful year, producing fruity, elegant wines.

The dry Vouvrays were generally good, but the late rains prevented any production of sweet botrycized wines.

Sancerre and Pouilly produced fine, balanced wines with a rich bouquet, far superior to those of previous years.

1983   Growers making dry wines at both ends of the Loire, from Muscadet at one to Pouilly-Fumé and Sancerre at the other, were elated. Some feel that despite the huge quantities, the 1983 vintage was superior to 1982.

In Anjou and Vouvray, the dry wines were good, but the producers made very little—if any—sweet wine, as botrytis did not develop.

1984   Muscadet was the most favored area of·the Loire. Other wines were nevertheless in good balance, if a little on the acid side, and enjoyed more character than the overly soft 1983s. In Vouvray the quality was fair, and again, as in 1979, a large amount had to be made into sparkling wine. As to the other areas, one could rate them as fair to good, but on the hard side.

1985   From one end of the Loire to the other, the growers were elated. Muscadet is round, full, and pleasant. *Botrytis* developed, to make marvelous sweet wines in the Coteaux du Layon, which had not been produced for a few years. These successful results include the red wines of Bourgeuil and Chinon. The January 1985 freeze did not spare Sancerre and Pouilly-Fumé. Some problems with frozen vines arose during the harvest, more in regard to a lack of quantity than to quality.

LOIRE
Hotels and Restaurants

H = *Hotel;* R = *Restaurant*

Listed from west to east, or upstream.

MUSCADET

NANTES (44000—Loire-Atlantique)
(La Baule 78—La Rochelle 148—Rennes 106—Saint-Nazaire 61—Angers 87—Bordeaux 333
—La Roche-sur-Yon 67—Saumur 127—Lorient 154—Le Mans 178—Poitiers 176)

The city of Nantes, the capital of Brittany, is a port and a gastronomic haven for such seafood and shellfish as sole, bass, turbot, mackerel, mullet, and scallops. These are often prepared with *beurre blanc,* a Nantes specialty made of lightly salted butter, shallots, and vinegar. *Andouille* and *andouillette, boudin,* mutton, and hams are other regional dishes, as is the Breton crêpe, which can be eaten plain or with jam, cheese, eggs, ham, or salad. Other than Muscadet, the *biscuits* of Nantes are its best-known export industry.

Once in the center of Nantes, you may wish to stroll to the château of the Ducs de Bretagne, right next to the cathedral.

. . . .

HR FRANTEL: 3, rue Dr. Zamenhof (Île de Beaulieu). Tel.: 40.47.10.58. Tlx.: 711440. 150 rooms. If you are lucky, your room may have a view of the Loire.
The restaurant, Le Tillac, has improved in quality and is now up to the level of its modern, comfortable rooms.

HR SOFITEL: Rue Alexandre Millerand (Île de Beaulieu). Tel.: 40.47.61.03. Tlx.: 710990. 98 rooms. Air-conditioned.
Comfortable, warm welcome. Its restaurant, La Pêcherie, specializes in "fruit of the sea" and fish. Some enthusiasts consider it one of the best seafood restaurants in town.

R LES MARAICHERS: 21, rue Fouré. Tel.: 40.47.06.51.
Very good, small, expensive seafood restaurant, where reservations are suggested. One star in Michelin.

R LA CIGOGNE: 16, rue J.-J. Rousseau. Tel.: 40.89.12.64.
One of the best bistros of Nantes, with a commendable menu at reasonable prices.

OUTSIDE NANTES

HR DOMAINE D'ORVAULT: At Orvault, Chemin des-Marais'-du-Cens. 7 km northwest on N-137, the road to Rennes. Tel.: 40.76.84.02. Tlx.: 700454. 30 rooms.
Charming for an overnight stay, with a good restaurant. Unfortunately, this quiet, comfortable, luxurious spot is in the northern suburbs of Nantes and outside of the Muscadet vineyards. One star in Michelin.

HR LA LANDE-SAINT-MARTIN: At Haute-Goulaine Route de Clisson (11 km southeast on N-149 bis). Tel.: 40.80.00.80. Tlx.: 700520. 40 rooms (34 with toilet).
Considered suitable by some, this hotel-restaurant's main recommendation is its proximity to the vineyards.

HR ABBAYE DE VILLENEUVE: 1 km south of Sorinières (10 km south of Nantes, at the entrance or exit of the Nantes autoroute, A-801, which leads south). 44, route des Sables d'Olonne. Tel.: 40.04.40.25. Tlx.: 710451.
Old abbey with cloisters dating from the fourteenth to seventeenth century. Great refinement in the décor of its 14 rooms, which I found to be very comfortable. Good food, good selection of wines. Very recommendable. My preferred overnight stop in Nantes has become much more accessible to the center of the city, now that the new expressway has an exit and entrance at Sorinières, a few yards from the entrance to the Abbaye de Villeneuve. *Relais et Châteaux*.

R MON RÊVE: At Basse-Goulaine (8 km east by N-751 and south on D-119)—La Divatte. Tel.: 40.54.57.11 and 40.03.55.50.
Very good, pleasant restaurant in a large villa close to the river, specializes in local dishes. Expensive. The owner and chef, M. Ryngel, established the reputation of the Domaine de la Berthelotière (Domaine d'Orvault, above) when he was chef there.

R DELPHIN: At Pontbellevue (9 km east by D-68 and D-337 or by A-11). Tel.: 40.49.04.13.
Very good restaurant along the Loire River. The imaginative dishes of Joseph Delphin help to make this elegant restaurant one of the very best of Nantes. Good wine list. Two stars in Michelin.

R MANOIR DE LA COMÈTE: At Saint-Sebastien-sur-Loire (6 km from the center of town, on the road to Clisson). 21, avenue de la Libération. Tel.: 40.34.15.93.
Christian Thomas is a young chef who has attracted well-deserved attention. Good service in the atmosphere of a private residence, with a good cellar. Warm welcome.

CLISSON (44190—Loire-Atlantique)
(Paris 374—Les Sables-d'Olonne 85—Nantes 28)
· Right in the heart of the Muscadet vineyards.

HR LA CASCADE: At Gervaux. Tel.: 40.78.02.41. 10 rooms. (5 toilets.)
Beautiful house on the Sèvre River, south of the Muscadet vineyards. Simple, inexpensive, well-assorted menus.

R LA BONNE AUBERGE: Tel.: 40.78.01.90.
The up-and-coming restaurant of this pretty town, located in the heart of the Muscadet vineyards, received one star in Michelin in 1986.

Anjou-Saumur
ANGERS (49000—Maine-et-Loire)
(Paris 284—Le Mans 89—Nantes 90—Poitiers 138—Tours 110—Saumur 52)
An Autoroute now connects Angers and Nantes.

Once the capital of the old province of Anjou, Angers was a battleground from the time of the Romans to the Normans, and during the Hundred Years War it was the scene of conflict between the English and the French. Now the thirteenth-century château, overlooking the Maine River, contains a rare collection of medieval tapestries. Those also interested in modern tapestries should visit the old Hospital of Saint-Jean, built in the twelfth century. It is now a museum devoted to the works of Jean Lurçat, a man who in the twentieth century revived the art of tapestry making.

Angers is the birthplace of the liqueur Cointreau. The surrounding area is also renowned for its peaches, pears, plums, and the harvest of its other fruit trees.

The Anjou wine fair, held in the second half of January, is more colorful than Angers' claim to being the capital for umbrellas and parasols.

HR CONCORDE: 18, boulevard Foch. Tel.: 41.87.37.20. Tlx.: 720923. 70 centrally located rooms.
Modern, comfortable rooms. Food available until midnight. The wine list could stand some improvement.

R LE TOUSSAINT: 7, rue Toussaint (near the cathedral). Tel.: 41.87.46.20.
This small, intimate restaurant, run by Michel Bignon, features fish in *beurre blanc,* Loire shad (alone), duck *foie gras*—all of which justified a star in Michelin.

R LE GUÉRÉ: 9, Place du Railliement. Tel.: 41.87.64.94.
Paul Le Guéré is a very good chef and, with his wife, Martine, who handles the wine, will provide you with the best meal in Angers.

R LE LOGIS: 17, rue Saint-Laud. Tel.: 41.87.44.15.
There is no question but that its fish specialties make this one of the best small restaurants in town, despite the rather cool welcome. One star in Michelin.

LES ROSIERS-SUR-LOIRE (49350—Maine-et-Loire)
(Paris 284—Angers 30—Saumur 16)

ᛊᏻ This gentle countryside of the Coteaux du Layon vineyards produces white wines that age well. The largest cellars can be found at Doué-la-Fontaine, 25 km south of Les Rosiers. Otherwise, the Jeanne de Laval restaurant and its comfortable annex are reasons enough to stop in Les Rosiers.

HR JEANNE DE LAVAL: Place de l'Église. Tel.: 41.51.80.17.   4 rooms.
The Augereau family also own a nearby annex, the Duc d'Anjou, an old house of 9 comfortable and more desirable rooms. It is worth not only the detour, but a journey. I have always been very partial to this excellent restaurant, located on the Loire. The food is not inexpensive, but it is good value. Superb wine cellar. In fine weather you may eat in the garden. A much-deserved star in Michelin.

SAUMUR (49400—Maine-et-Loire)
(Paris 301—Angers 52—Tours 66—Nantes 139)

ᛊᏻ For some, Saumur is synonymous with its riding school; for others, with its many sparkling-wine firms. The castle is impressive when seen from afar, but in this land, competitive with medieval and Renaissance châteaux, Saumur lies fairly low on my list. Instead of a trip to the Museum of Decorative Arts, equine fanciers might find their time better spent at the Musée du Cheval.

HR LE PRIEURÉ: At Chênehutte-Les-Tuffeaux (8 km northwest on D-751 and 9 km on D-161). Tel.: 41.50.15.31. Tlx.: 720379.   35 rooms.
A beautiful manor house in the midst of a park overlooking the Loire Valley. The very comfortable rooms, decorated with great taste, are recommended. Large heated swimming pool. Good restaurant. The warmth of the welcome could stand some reheating. *Relais et Châteaux.* One star in Michelin.

Touraine

AZAY-LE-RIDEAU (37190—Indre-et-Loire)
(Paris 262—Tours 26—Chinon 21—Saumur 46)

ᛊᏻ The fairy-tale château of Azay-le-Rideau is perhaps the most graceful of all the Loire's châteaux, where the architecture of France meets the Renaissance of Italy. The turrets, intended not for defense but for decoration, are reflected in the waters of the Indre. The paintings, furniture, and tapestries vividly evoke the Renaissance, and an inspection of the old kitchen is also worthwhile. From the end of March through the middle of August, the *son et lumière* takes the form of a promenade around the château by actors adorned in Renaissance costume.

HR LE GRAND MONARQUE: Place de la République, in front of the château. Tel.: 47.45.40.08.   30 rooms (only 9 toilets).
Quiet, reasonably priced rooms in this town with one of the Loire's most beautiful châteaux. The hotel and the food are just barely adequate.

R AUBERGE DU XII SIÈCLE: At Saché, 7 km southeast on D-17. Tel.: 47.26.86.58.
Its claim to being medieval is justified. So is its star in Michelin.

CHINON (37500—Indre-et-Loire)
(Paris 285—Angers 80—Tours 49—Saumur 29)

◖ This is the town where Joan of Arc first sought out and recognized the irresolute dauphin who then became Charles VII. Each summer night she is brought to life during the *son et lumière* spectacle held at the château. In August, you can visit the medieval market which recalls the days of Rabelais.

An antique show is held here in mid-July.

HR CHÂTEAU DE MARÇAY: At Marçay (7 km south on D-116). Tel.: 47.93.03.47. Tlx.: 751475. A total of 40 rooms of various sizes. Tennis. Swimming pool.
Why stay in Chinon if you can afford to stay at the Château de Marçay, owned by Philippe Mollard, with its exceptionally beautiful, very comfortable rooms in an authentic fifteenth-century château? A beautiful park surrounds this very memorable hotel, which has good food and excellent service, but is unfortunately expensive. Highly recommended as an ideal place to stay during your visit to the Loire. *Relais et Châteaux.* One star in Michelin.

LANGEAIS (37130—Indre-et-Loire)
(Tours 24—Angers 83—Saumur 41—Chinon 31)

◖ When driving in this countryside, you will see why so many kings of France were torn between establishing their thrones in Paris or in the Loire. Louis XI and Charles VIII opted for the latter.

HR HOTEL HOSTEN RESTAURANT LE LANGEAIS: 2, rue Gambetta. Tel.: *Hotel:* 47.96.82.12. *Restaurant:* 47.96.70.63. 11 rooms.
Fairly comfortable hotel; convenient for visiting the lovely château in the heart of town. The restaurant is now run by M. Jean-Jacques Hosten and was awarded one Michelin star in 1983.

VILLANDRY (37300—Indre-et-Loire)
(Paris 254—Azay-le-Rideau 10—Langeais 13—Chinon 31—
Tours 16—Saumur 51—Luynes 9)

◖ It is not so much the Château de Villandry that has made this place famous as the ultra-pruned and -clipped, symmetrical gardens. With their canals and fountains, they are the perfect incarnation of *jardins à la française,* and most beautiful.

HR LE CHEVAL ROUGE: Tel.: 47.50.02.07. 20 rooms (13 with toilet).
The best restaurant when visiting the superb Renaissance château of Azay-le-Rideau. The fine gardens of the Château de Villandry are nearby. One star in Michelin.

SAVONNIÈRES (37300—Indre-et-Loire)
(Tours 13—Chinon 34—Saumur 56—Chenonceaux 44—Langeais 15—
Villandry 3—Azay-le-Rideau 17—Luynes 6)

◖ Human hands once carved the portals of the château with charming animals and doves. In the nearby grotto nature has carved, and continues to carve, stalagmites, stalactites, and other petrified wonders.

H LES CÈDRES: Route from Tours to Villandry (3 km on D-7 before Savonnières). Tel.: 47.53.00.28. Tlx.: 752074. 35 rooms.
Rustic, comfortable hotel, pool. Fairly good adjoining restaurant (Tel.: 47.53.37.58) under separate management.

LUYNES (37230—Indre-et-Loire)
(Tours 13—Saumur 55—Angers 97—Langeais 14—Chinon 45)

◖§ The privately owned feudal château, which dominates the village, is imposing. Regrettably, the old Gallo-Roman aqueduct is poorly maintained.

HR DOMAINE DE BEAUVOIS: At Saint-Étienne-de-Chigny (4 km by D-49 or 3 km by D-76). Tel.: 47.55.50.11. Tlx.: 750204. 41 very comfortable rooms (39 with toilet).
Magnificent old residence in the midst of a superb forest. Good, honest food. Although the prices are rather high, this is a very recommendable stopover. Swimming pool. *Relais et Châteaux.* One star in Michelin.

TOURS (37000—Indre-et-Loire)
(Paris 234—Poitiers 103—Blois 59—Bordeaux 332—Chartres 139—Angers 106)

◖§ The Autoroute makes Tours a few hours' drive from Paris. While you are there, let a visit to Barrier become part of your trip through the châteaux country.
    Along with Nantes, Tours is the largest city along the Loire. You may wish to visit the Musée des Vins de Touraine, 16, rue Nationale, tel.: 47.61.07.93. One of the local specialties, stuffed prunes, can be had from Sabat, 76, rue Nationale, or from Poirault, 31, rue Nationale. Try to sample the other regional specialty, *rillettes de Tours.*
    In July there is a fair of garlic and basil.
    You can rent bicycles from M. Barat, 156, rue Giraudeau, tel.: 47.61.03.58, or from Grammont Motorcycles, 93, avenue de Grammont, tel.: 47.66.62.83, and then cycle on the flat, pretty roads along the Loire.

HR BORDEAUX: 3, place Maréchal Leclerc. Tel.: 47.05.40.32. Tlx.: 750414. 54 rooms (45 with toilets).
Centrally located near station. The best hotel-restaurant food in town.

HR MÉRIDIEN: 292, avenue de Grammont. Tel.: 47.28.00.80. Tlx.: 750922. 120 small, air-conditioned rooms.
Modern, in the midst of a formal garden with swimming pool and tennis. The hotel service has been criticized. Competent restaurant.

R RÔTISSERIE TOURANGELLE: 23, rue du Commerce. Tel.: 47.05.71.21.
Good restaurant, which has progressed favorably.

R LES TUFFEAUX: 19, rue Lavoisier. In the old district, on the same street as the cathedral. Tel.: 47.47.19.89.
Considered to have the best food in Tours, which is not saying much. One star in Michelin.

HR CHÂTEAU DE BEAULIEU: At Joué-les-Tours, 5 km southwest on Route de Villandry by D-86 and D-207. Tel.: 47.53.20.26. 17 rooms (9 toilets).
In the midst of a park. Comfort and quiet make this a worthwhile stopover.

South of Tours and of the Cher

MONTBAZON (37250—Indre-et-Loire)
(Chinon 41—Tours 13—Montrichard 41—Saumur 66—Chatellerault 60—
Loches 32—Chenonceaux 32—Paris 247)

❧ The castle park is a good excuse for a long walk if you are staying in Montbazon.
Oenology courses are held intermittently at Château d'Artigny.

HR CHÂTEAU D'ARTIGNY: 2 km by D-17 on road to Azay-le-Rideau. Tel.: 47.26.24.24. Tlx.: 750900. 55 rooms. Heated pool. 2 tennis courts. Golf.
Sumptuous castle towering over the Indre Valley. Best hotel in center of Loire Valley. Luxurious, expensive, well worth the cost for visiting famous Loire châteaux and vineyards. The perfume king François Coty built this palatial château in the prewar days, and it is now enjoyed by discriminating, well-heeled guests. Dinner service when crowded could be improved. English spoken. *Relais et Châteaux.* The food is very good and worth the star in Michelin.

HR DOMAINE DE LA TORTINIÈRE: 1.5 km to the north of Montbazon on N-10 and D-287. Tel.: 47.26.00.19. Tlx.: 750806. 21 rooms (11 in the château, 10 in a pavilion).
Beautiful and quite luxurious nineteenth-century château, overlooking the valley in the midst of a quiet park. Good small restaurant. Expensive. One star in Michelin.

ROCHECORBON (37210—Indre-et-Loire)
(Tours 5—Vouvray 5—Blois 49)
On the road to Vouvray.

❧ Rochecorbon lies at the foot of cliffs harboring dozens of troglodyte houses. You may wish to visit the shipping firm of Marc Bredif.

R L'OUBLIETTE: 34, rue des Clouets, near Vouvray. Tel.: 47.52.50.49.
Good cooking prepared with quality ingredients.

VOUVRAY (37210—Indre-et-Loire)
(Tours 10—Amboise 16—Blois 49—Paris 234)

❧ More troglodyte houses and wine and mushroom cellars hidden in the chalky cliffs.
I would recommend that unhurried picnickers stop off for provisions at Hardouin, 9, rue du Commerce. Many a time I have passed the tempting windows of this charcutier where I would buy pâtés, *rillettes,* sausages, and other Touraine specialties. Then I would chase it all down in the wine cellars of Vouvray, which are the ideal place to taste, free of charge, the Vouvray wines. Cellars include Vallée Coquette, tel.: 47.52.60.20., La Caillerie, tel.: 47.52.60.20., and Vallée de Vaux, tel.: 47.52.93.22. Others worth visiting are those of Mayor Gaston Huet, Prince Philippe Poniatowski, Foreau, and Dr. Avignon's Domaine de Bidaudières.

HR LE GRAND VATEL: 8, rue Brulé. Tel.: 47.52.70.32. 7 small rooms.
A decent restaurant in the center of a famous wine village.

AMBOISE (37400—Indre-et-Loire)
(Paris 223—Blois 35—Tours 24—Chenonceaux 11—
Chaumont 17—Loches 33—Chambord 50)

ᕽᎶ Francis I summoned a noted Italian painter to his court at Amboise. Leonardo da Vinci brought the Mona Lisa with him in his luggage, but his mind carried weightier material: the creative conception of the Renaissance.

Da Vinci's mortal remains are buried at Amboise.

. . .

HR LE CHOISEUIL: Facing the Loire. Tel.: 47.30.45.45. Tlx.: 752068.   18 rooms, including 3 suites. Totally and very well redone in 1985, this historic stopover was one of the first comfortable, luxurious inns along the Loire. I used to recommend it in the fifties and early sixties. I had lunch here at the end of 1985. The restaurant needs further testing before being suggested as one's headquarters along the Loire. René Traversac, with his numerous *Relais et Châteaux,* such as Château d'Artigny, the Domaine de Beauvois, and others, is the owner.

HR CHÂTEAU DE PRAY: 2 km northeast on D-751, the road to Chargé. Tel.: 47.57.23.67.   16 rooms, only 8 toilets.
Small, attractive eighteenth-century château, comfortable, with a restaurant beautifully situated on a terrace in the midst of a park overlooking the Loire Valley.

HR AUBERGE DU MAIL: 32, quai du Général-de-Gaulle. Tel.: 47.57.60.39.   13 small, inexpensive rooms.
Considered to be a very good restaurant in Amboise. On the Loire River. Large assortment of local Loire wines.

CHENONCEAUX (37150—Indre-et-Loire)
(Paris 224—Tours 35—Blois 42—Amboise 12—Montrichard 9)

ᕽᎶ Gracefully straddling the River Cher, Chenonceaux is one of the most harmoniously beautiful châteaux of the Loire. France owes this well-preserved château to Catherine Briçonnet, the first of six women who left their imprint here. Briçonnet was followed by Diane de Poitiers, who, twenty years older than King Henri II, nonetheless seduced him with her charm and beauty. At Henri's death, his wife, Catherine de' Medici, forced her to retreat, brokenhearted, to the nearby Château de Chaumont. Medici then hosted picnics, masquerades, and fireworks displays of utter decadence. The château is now owned by the Meunier family, whose fortune was made from chocolate.

The *son et lumière,* held nightly at 10:00 P.M. during the summer months, is worth a stopover. If you visit by day, a brief look at the wax museum will conjure forth four centuries' worth of history.

. . .

HR LE BON LABOUREUR ET CHÂTEAU: 6, rue Dr. Bretonneau (on N-76). Tel.: 47.23.90.02.   29 rooms (21 with toilets).
Good restaurant when visiting one of the most beautiful châteaux of the Loire. Not overpriced.

CHAUMONT-SUR-LOIRE (41150—Loir-et-Cher)
(Paris 200—Blois 17—Tours 41—Amboise 17—Montrichard 18)

ᕽᎶ In an area so rich with châteaux, this feudal fortress may be worth a photograph or two, but, in my opinion, it does not need a visit.

. . .

HR HOSTELLERIE DU CHÂTEAU: 2, rue de Lattre-de-Tassigny. Tel.: 54.20.98.04.   15 rooms of varying standards (14 toilets).
Halfway between Blois and Amboise on the Loire River. Charming, pretty inn, swimming pool. Unfortunately on the main road along the Loire.

ONZAIN (41150—Loir-et-Cher)
(Paris 197—Blois 16—Amboise 21—Tours 45—Montrichard 21)

HR DOMAINE DES HAUTS-DE-LOIRE: 4 km on the D-1, Route de Mesland. Tel.: 54.20.72.57. Tlx.: 751547.   30 rooms.
On the right bank of the river, in a large park on the other side of the Loire from the Château de Chaumont, the Bonnigal family operates this pleasant manor, which has style, taste, and charm. Excellent service; you are made to feel super-welcome. *Relais et Châteaux.* One star in Michelin.

CHAMBORD (41250—Loir-et-Cher)
(Paris 175—Blois 18—Châteaurouxɪoo—Orléans 45—
Romorantin-Lanthenay 40—Tours 79)

Francis I was not a man of simple tastes. The grandiose 441-room castle was a display of megalomania which could barely be justified by his hunting of deer and boar, and of the Countess de Thoury, who owned a neighboring château. This vast, overdecorated habitat knew no rival until Louis XIV decided to build Versailles. Until the invention of the skyscraper, everything in height and grandeur went downhill after that.

HR ST-MICHEL: 103, Place Saint-Michel. Tel.: 54.20.31.31.   37 smallish, fair rooms, 2 suites (22 toilets). Tennis.
Facing the château, it is noisy and touristy. Not having traveled with a dog, in checking this hotel later I found Michelin saying that dogs are not accepted and Le Bottin Gourmand saying that they are. Take your pick. However, a stay is justified by its location across from the famous and impressive château. For lunch, or to see the *son et lumière* spectacle.

BRACIEUX (41250—Loir-et-Cher)
(Chambord 9—Cheverney 9—Blois 15—Paris 183)

The Loire is overabundantly rich in regal châteaux. They stretch for over a couple of hundred kms from Orléans to Angers. Bracieux is a gastronomic hub for several important châteaux which are all within a few kilometers of Le Relais.

R LE RELAIS: 1, avenue de Chambord. Tel.: 54.46.41.22.
Bernard Robin has, as a great chef, gained the plaudits of France's gastronomic community. His artistry has earned him a second Michelin star, and you can walk off your succulent lunch visiting the local château and museums.

BLOIS (41000—Loir-et-Cher)
(Paris 181—Bourges 117—Chartres 128—Le Mans 109—Poitiers 149—
Orléans 60—Tours 63—Angers 162)

At the imposing Château of Blois, one can trace the evolution of French architecture from feudal times to High Renaissance, this last epitomized in the grand staircase commissioned by Francis I. It is in the center of town—difficult to get to. Why not see some of the other Loire châteaux?

Chocolate lovers may wish to visit the headquarters of a leading chocolate manufacturer, Poulain.

If you happen to be in Blois on the first or third Sunday of any month, you can hear a concert of bells at the Basilica of Nôtre-Dame-de-la-Trinité.

This is also riding country.

HR NOVOTEL: At La Chaussée-Saint-Victor, 4 km away on the D-152, 20, rue des Pontières. Tel.: 54.78.33.57. Tlx.: 750232. 116 functional rooms, in calm surroundings.
It has certainly not been inspired by the grandiose château, 5 km away.

R LA PENICHE: Promenade du Mail, moored between two bridges on the right bank. Tel.: 54.74.37.23.
A bit out of the ordinary. Although this restaurant on a fixed-up barge does not live up to the grandeur of the château, one can eat fairly well in fun surroundings.

HR RELAIS DES LANDES: At Ouchamps, 41120 Les Montils, 15 km south of Blois on D-751 and D-764 and D-7. Tel.: 54.44.03.33. Tlx.: 751454. 16 comfortable rooms, 2 suites. Tennis.
This very quiet seventeenth-century house in the midst of a 10-hectare park has been newly redecorated by Gérard Badénier, which makes it, one may hope and trust, recommendable for those on their way to visit the Loire châteaux. The restaurant does not have a long enough record to permit evaluation one way or the other. It does have a good wine list.

MONTRICHARD (41400—Loir-et-Cher)
(Paris 215—Chenonceaux 9—Blois 32—Tours 44—Romorantin 50—
Loches 31—Chatellerault 85)

Starting from Tours east, one should not confuse the banks of the Loire with those of the River Cher to the south, eventually forming a vast triangle. For instance: Chenonceaux, close to Tours, is not on the Loire but is close enough not to form a separation worth mentioning.

Some of the houses date back to the fifteenth and sixteenth centuries. The town's main attraction is its castle, now in ruins, overlooking the River Cher, but I prefer the scooped-out, chalk cliff troglodyte dwellings and the damp hillside cellars that store mushrooms and sparkling wines. Montrichard has several firms that sell Vouvray and the wines of the Loire.

HR LE BELLEVUE: Quai du Cher. Tel.: 54.32.06.17. 30 functional rooms.
Basic, comfortable, recently remodeled rooms, fair restaurant, not expensive, on the Cher close to Chenonceaux.

HR CHÂTEAU DE LA MENAUDIÈRE: 3 km northwest from Montrichard, on the road to Amboise. Tel.: 54.32.02.44. Tlx.: 751246.
A fifteenth-century château, restored in the eighteenth century, under the supervision of Colette Moulard. 25 comfortable rooms in the midst of a charming park. Tennis. Fair food.

VALENÇAY (36600—Indre)
(Paris 237—Blois 55—Bourges 73—Chambord 56—Loches 48—Romorantin 32)

An impressive château which was acquired in 1803 by Talleyrand, who entertained royally, irrespective of which king or emperor he served—or double-crossed.

HR ESPAGNE: 9, rue du Château. Tel.: 54.00.00.02. Tlx.: 751675.   18 quiet rooms.
Run by the Fourré family, who give their best. Quiet, charming, traditional old house with good service and good food. Reservations suggested. Comfortable rooms. *Relais et Châteaux.* One star in Michelin.

South of the Loire and North of the Cher

ROMORANTIN-LANTHENAY (41200—Loir-et-Cher)
(Paris 200—Blois 41—Tours 93—Orléans 68)

☙ Romorantin is on the road to the châteaux of the Loire if you are driving from Pouilly-sur-Loire and Sancerre or going shooting in the Sologne, France's hunting country. A few old buildings here should be glanced at before taking off. A new autoroute will bring Romorantin within two hours of Paris as of the end of 1986. Exit at Salbris.

HR LE GRAND HÔTEL LION D'OR: 69, rue Georges Clemenceau. Tel.: 54.76.00.28. Tlx.: 750990.   10 renovated rooms. Old stagecoach inn.
Excellent restaurant run by Alain Barrat and his son-in-law chef, Didier Clément, and the family, who are devotees of light refined cuisine and excel in service and the search for quality. A great deal of effort goes into refinement, and a great deal of thought goes daily into the creative menus. *Relais et Châteaux.* Two stars in Michelin.

Eastern Loire

SANCERRE (18300—Cher)
(Paris 203—Bourges 46—La Charité-sur-Loire 26—Nevers 50)

☙ A beautiful panorama, winding streets, wine, and goat cheese are the chief attributes of this famous old wine town.

HR LE PANORAMIC: Rempart des Augustins. Tel.: 48.54.22.44.
A newly constructed hotel with 56 functional rooms. Mr Sivet also owns the adjoining Tasse d'Argent restaurant.

R LA TASSE D'ARGENT: 18, Rempart des Augustins. Tel.: 48.54.01.44.
Inexpensive restaurant in this famous wine village. Beautiful view over the vineyards. Try one of the good menus.

HR L'ÉTOILE: 2, quai de Loire, at Saint-Thibault (5 km east of Sancerre on D-4). Tel.: 48.54.12.15.   11 simple rooms.
Close to Sancerre vineyards. The large, tempting menu offers many dishes at a fair value, to be enjoyed along with a view of the Loire River.

POUILLY-SUR-LOIRE (58150—Nièvre)
(Nevers 37—Bourges 63—Sancerre 17—Château Chinon 89—
Cosne 15—La Charité-sur-Loire 13—Paris 202)

HR L'ESPÉRANCE: 17, rue René-Couard. Tel.: 86.39.10.68.   4 inexpensive rooms, only 2 toilets.
This good restaurant specializes in regional cooking, has a good well-priced "regional menu."

You are in the heart of the Pouilly-Fumé district and you can take the advice of Jacques Raveau, who has a well-deserved star in Michelin.

POUGUES-LES-EAUX (58320—Nièvre)
(Nevers 11—Bourges 63—Pouilly-sur-Loire 26)

H CHÂTEAU DE MIMONT: 3 km from Nevers. Tel.: 86.68.81.44.   7 rooms, some very well furnished, respecting the eighteenth- and nineteenth-century periods.
In a large park. Swimming pool, tennis. No restaurant.

NEVERS (58000—Nièvre)
(Dijon 188—Montluçon 99—Roanne 152—Pouilly-sur-Loire 37—Sancerre 49)

Though many consider it a part of the province of Burgundy, Nevers really belongs to the Loire. One can still find some old Nevers plates, but most of the local pottery and enamels have seen better days.

HR P.L.M. LOIRE: Quai Médiné. Tel.: 86.61.50.92. Tlx.: 801112.   60 functional rooms.
Restaurant overlooking the river.

HR MAPOTEL DIANE: 38, rue du Midi. Tel.: 86.57.28.10 or 86.57.25.88. Tlx.: 801021.   30 comfortable rooms.
The best hotel in town, but not worth a detour.

HR LA RENAISSANCE: Magny-Cours, 12 km south on the road to Moulins. Tel.: 86.58.10.40
9 rooms.
The rooms have recently been renovated. The excellent restaurant offers menus, suggested by Jean-Claude Dray, which are an outstanding value and highly recommended. Two stars in Michelin.

HR LA PORTE DU CROUX: 17, rue Porte du Croux. Tel.: 86.57.12.71.
Close to railway station. A good restaurant at prices far from excessive.

LES BEZARDS (45290—Nogent-sur-Vernisson)
(Paris 137—Auxerre 76—Orléans 70—Gien 16—Montargis 23—Orly airport 132)

HR AUBERGE DES TEMPLIERS: Tel.: 38.31.80.01. Tlx.: 780998.   Take autoroute A-6, exit Dordives and take N-7 in the direction of Montargis and Nevers. 31 very good, comfortable rooms; 6 suites. Heated swimming pool. Tennis.
Luxurious, expensive gastronomic stopover, expertly run by Pierre and Françoise Depée. During the hunting season, game from the Sologne hunting reserves is one of the specialties. Roast turbot and a galaxy of other tempting goodies may be offered, along with a great wine list. Warm welcome. Excellent service. English spoken. *Relais et Châteaux.* Two stars in Michelin.

HR CHÂTEAU DES BEZARDS: Tel.: 38.31.80.03. Tlx.: 780335.   38 rooms and 5 suites. Tennis.
Enclosed swimming pool.
This nice, relatively expensive inn should not be confused with the Auberge. On its own it is very good, but it does not match up to its neighbor.

Outside of the vineyards proper, there are a few restaurants on any visitor's itinerary that cannot be omitted:

VÉZELAY (89450—Yonne)
(Paris 224—Auxerre 52—Avallon 15)

Almost in the midst of Burgundy, Vézelay boasts the Basilica of Sainte-Madeleine. Founded in the ninth century, this masterpiece of Romanesque architecture was a stopover in 1146 for pilgrims on their way to Santiago de Compostela.

What a great combination—the abbey and one of the great restaurants of France, L'Espérance, which has been recognized with a top rating of three stars by Michelin.

HR L'ESPÉRANCE: At Saint-Père (3 km by D-957 and 2 km by N-458). Tel.: 86.33.20.45. Tlx.: 800005.   20 rooms.

Marc Meneau has on several occasions provided meals which I have found utterly exquisite. Finesse and imagination are the keynotes of this marvelous restaurant. If Vézelay, with one of the greatest of Romanesque churches, is not worth a detour, then be sure to be tempted by this restaurant. *Relais et Châteaux.* Three stars in Michelin.

BOURGES (18000—Cher)
(Paris 226—Tours 148—Orléans 105—Nevers 68—Dijon 244)

It is worth visiting the palace of Jacques Coeur, the native son of Bourges and an adventurer and economist who financed the king. False accusations of jealousy sent him to prison, and he later died fighting the Turks while in the service of the pope.

R JACQUES COEUR: 3, place Jacques-Coeur. Tel.: 48.70.12.72.

The best restaurant in this medieval town.

ALSACE

Dressed in autumn glory, Alsace is one of the most beautiful of the world's vine-yards. As the picking begins, in the early weeks of October, the leaves of the vines of Riesling, Gewürztraminer, Pinot Gris, and Sylvaner, as well as of the maple, ash, and beech in the forests above the vines, turn to pale yellow and burnt amber, and the entire vineyard on the slopes of the Vosges is a blaze of color, activity, and rustic charm.

Of all the vineyards of France, only Champagne lies farther north than Alsace. The province is set slightly apart from the rest of France by the Vosges Mountains, which look across the Rhine into the Black Forest of Germany. Resolutely and staunchly French by nationality, in the past one hundred years the people of Alsace have spent nearly half their time under the German flag. Among themselves the Alsatians still speak their dialect, and their French comes out slowly and broadly with a "foreign" (though not German) lilt. The most striking feature of the region, set-ting it off from France and Germany alike, is the great Alsatian cuisine—like the wine, a sublime combination of German raw materials and French know-how. In the twenty-minute drive from Germany into Alsace you travel from the desert of so-called "continental" cuisine (no better than American "continental" or Swiss "con-tinental") to a true haven of gastronomy. Sauerkraut, a German staple, becomes

Oberhai 23 km, Strasbourg 43 km, Paris by A-35 570 km

Lièpre
Sélestat
Châtenois
N-59
Sté-Croix-aux-Mines
D-159
Ht. Koenigsbourg
Kintzheim
N-83

BAS-RHIN

St Hippolyte

Bergheim
D-416
Ribeauvillé
Ill
Guémar
Illhaeusern
D-106
Riquewihr
Ostheim
Marckolsheim
Mittelwihr
N-415
Bennwihr
Kaysersberg
Kientzheim
D-4
Lapoutroie 6 km.
Ammerschwihr
Houssen
D-10
Artzenheim
Les Trois Épis
Niedermorschwihr
Canal de Colmar
D-11
Ingersheim
Turckheim
D-468
Colmar
Horbourg-Wihr
GERMANY
Wettolsheim
N-415
Eguisheim
Breisach
D-41
HAUT-RHIN
Neuf-Brisach
Ste-Croix-en-Plaine
N-83
Railroad
N
N-422
Canal du Rhône au Rhin
Rouffach
Rhin
Autobahn
Route des Vins
Freiburg im Breisgau 20 km.
Baden-Baden 170 km, Frankfurt 270 km.
Guebwiller
Basel 35 km.
Réguisheim
Ill

KILOMETERS

ALSACE

0   5   10
0   6
MILES

Mulhouse 15 km.

choucroute garnie à l'alsacienne, marinated cabbage cooked slowly with three or four different kinds of sausage, pig's knuckles, salted and smoked pork, with the occasional surprise of a drumstick of goose or partridge. This is a country famous for its *foie gras,* the liver of a fatted goose or duck, served nakedly *mi-cuit,* or wrapped around a fresh Périgord truffle and encased in light brioche dough, or used to form the heart of one of the forty-odd different kinds of Alsatian *pâtés* and *terrines.*

All of these certainly and more in the (now passé) *nouvelle cuisine* vein can be had at the great eating outposts of Aux Armes de France in Ammerschwihr, whose kitchen is presided over by Pierre and Philippe Gaertner, and L'Auberge de L'Ill at Illhaeusern, the perennial three-star restaurant which has become the favorite of tourists from all over the world, and especially Germany.

The fish dishes range from the elegantly simple *truite au bleu,* trout quickly poached in a *court bouillon* with herbs and a dash of Riesling, to the formidable Alsatian version of freshwater bouillabaisse, *matelote de poissons au Riesling,* in which pieces of perch, trout, pike, and eel swim in a rich sauce of cream and mushrooms.

The vineyards begin at the doorstep of Strasbourg, 460 kilometers (285 miles) from Paris and 20 kilometers (12 miles) from the Rhine. The Rhine is the "winiest" river in the world, beginning with the Alsatian vineyards in the south, where the banks are shared by the Germans and the French. Just across the river here are the wines of Baden, and as one drives north downstream mists bathe the vineyards of the Palatinate north of Worms and eventually the Rheinhessen and the Rheingau.

Despite the immense Gothic cathedral, its rich history, and its rich cuisine, Strasbourg is not the wine capital of the region. That honor goes to Colmar, 70 kilometers (43 miles) to the south. The vines follow the slope of the Vosges range, parallel to the Rhine from Molsheim to Thann—110 kilometers (70 miles)—but always upland from the river plain, usually between 150 and 400 meters (490 to 1,322 feet), in much the same way that the Burgundy vineyards follow the Golden Slope, the Côte d'Or hills parallel to the Saône. The dividing line for quality in Alsatian wines coincides more or less with the departmental boundary. The wines of the Haut-Rhin, the Upper (in fact the southern) Rhine, particularly those surrounding Colmar, are on the average superior in quality to those of the northern half from Sélestat to Strasbourg, known as Bas-Rhin, or lower Rhine.

There are notable exceptions to this axiom—the fine Bas-Rhin vineyards of Barr being one—but, as an introductory rule of thumb, it holds true. The northern half is generally cooler and produces shorter, more acidic wines, and is planted largely in Sylvaner, a lesser grape which gives an abundant yield.

The harvest scene continues today largely as it was a century ago. Carts, now pulled by tractor, line the road, waiting for the first full *hottes,* the pickers' wooden cone-shaped carrying baskets, of grapes. The carrier still pours his grapes into larger wooden (or now often brightly colored plastic) tubs lined up neatly in the wagon, while another vineyard hand pushes them down with a long wooden-handled pestle.

Although the notion of different growths based on different soils and microclimates, such as prevails in Burgundy, is beginning to take effect in Alsace, the guiding principle that distinguishes the wines is the difference in grape variety. There are five "noble" varieties entitled to Appellation Contrôlée status. The name is usually printed on the label below the shipper's name. A grape variety indicated thus will mean that all of the wine, 100 percent of it, comes from the specified grape: Sylvaner, Pinot Gris (previously called Tokay d'Alsace), Muscat, Gewürztraminer, or Riesling. Each variety, when brought to maturity in the vineyard and well vinified in the cellar, will have an unmistakable individuality.

Planted in a quarter of the total vineyard area, the Sylvaner predominates and gives the highest yield, producing close to a third of all the wines. Because the yield is high and the wine straightforward and easy to drink, it will usually be a good value. The Muscat makes a wine totally different from the sweet Muscats of the Midi. Under the guiding hand of Alsatian growers the wine is full in the nose, and yet refreshingly dry. The last decade has seen its decline in popularity, and it now represents less than 5 percent of all the wines and is most often used in shippers' blends.

The fancifully named Tokay d'Alsace had nothing to do with the Hungarian Tokay. In 1984 the use of the name Tokay d'Alsace was forbidden and the grape variety must now only be called Pinot Gris. This grape gives a full, golden wine with a marked bouquet and lingering aftertaste on the palate. Like the Gewürztraminer and Riesling, it can improve with age in the bottle for up to three to five years.

Gewürztraminer and Riesling are the two grape varieties clearly head and shoulders above the rest. *Gewürz* in German means "spice" and the wines that come from this small reddish grape are true to the name. The bold, assertive spiciness and often complex bouquet and the lingering echoes of taste have made the Gewürztraminer a wine novice's favorite. After the Sylvaner, and ahead of the Riesling, it is the most widely planted grape in Alsace. In the great years with hot summers—like 1976 and especially 1983 and 1985—some growers vinify their Gewürztraminers to be slightly sweet; the sugar content the grapes have when picked is high, and the vinification methods arrest fermentation, leaving residual sugars behind. When such rare superripeness is achieved, the wine can reach 14 percent alcohol, combining acidity, fruitiness, and its own individual character in an admirable balance: a perfect accompaniment to strong, spicy dishes, which leave Gewürztraminer undaunted. For many connoisseurs, though, its pronounced taste and bouquet may be too unrefined and overpowering.

Which brings us to the Riesling. It has always been one of the world's noblest grape varieties, and it produces Germany's greatest wines. "Comparing the Riesling to the Gewürztraminer," said the late René Kuehn, shipper and grower at Ammerschwihr, "is like comparing the *grande dame* of a nineteenth-century novel to her counterpart of easier virtue, the *demi-mondaine*. The *grande dame,* the Riesling, takes a while to get to know, demanding, subtle and elegant, and ultimately more profound than the Gewürztraminer. The Gewürztraminer is the *demi-mondaine,* smiling and busty, the appeal and *éclat* all on the surface. It is often easier to make a good Gewürztraminer than a good Riesling, because the mistakes in the vinification will be covered up by its rather domineering character."

This difficulty, and the relatively small yield, have kept the plantings of Riesling down to 15 percent of the Alsace vineyard area, the equivalent of about 1.4 million cases being produced annually. The major centers for it are around Barr, in northern Alsace, 35 kilometers (21 miles) from Strasbourg; Ribeauvillé; and Kaysersberg, 12 kilometers (7 miles) to the south, in the heart of the best vineyard area. One out of every five vines planted is a Gewürztraminer, most of them concentrated in southern Alsace, along the gentle slopes from Ribeauvillé to Guebwiller, 25 kilometers or so (15 miles) from Colmar.

These proportions will no doubt change in the coming years with the new government policy of forbidding new plantings of non-noble grapes, such as Chasselas, Müller-Thurgau (a cross between Sylvaner and Riesling), Knipperlé, and Goldriesling. These grapes are used for the making of the simple Vin d'Alsace *appellation,* with no grape listed, or may be sold as Zwicker. Edelzwicker is a blend of exclusively noble grape varieties.

In the past decade the total Alsatian vineyard area has grown by 1,700 hectares (4,250 acres) and now stands at 12,500 hectares, with a possibility of another 1,000 being added in the near future. This will make it approximately the size of the Haut-Médoc, Graves, Sauternes, and Barsac districts together, and close to twice the size of the Napa Valley in California. The increased plantation rights may bring about a consolidation of the vineyard holdings. There are now some 10,000 growers, with an average holding of just over 1 hectare apiece (about 2½ acres), who produce an average of 800,000 hectoliters of wine, the equivalent of 9 million cases per year. As it stands now, 30 percent of the owners hold 80 percent of the land. Most of the small growers with 1 hectare or less raise the lesser grape varieties, part of the wine from which is for personal consumption.

This great expansion of vines, while it is clearly justified by the surging demand for the wine in France and abroad, is beginning to cause concern among the better growers and wine officials of the region. Not all of the wines from the new vineyards are going to be of top quality, and rather than group them under the same umbrella of *Vins d'Alsace* with all the others, a two-class division is being contemplated, with place-names indicated in each. It is not known how many years it will be before this plan takes effect. More certain is the tendency for more of the wine to be sold directly to consumers traveling on holiday or buying by mail. Already 15 percent of the harvest is sold directly to the customer without a local retailer or the shipper as an intermediary. French, Belgian, Dutch, and German tourists who flock to the area, attracted by the old stones, picturesque countryside, good food, and colorful villages, are also drawn to the signs of *"Propre Récolte"*—indicating a grower selling his own harvest, and making both a producer's and a wholesaler's profit. Given the hard work and thrift for which Alsatian growers are so renowned, this is the trend of the future, as it will be for the rest of France.

But the world has not always stood in line for Alsatian wine. In the early nineteenth century, Alsace had the reputation for planting common, high-yield vines, like the Chasselas. When Alsace was annexed by Germany with Lorraine after the Franco-Prussian War in 1871, the situation was aggravated by the German wine industry, of which the Alsatians became part. The German shippers considered Alsace a "southern" vineyard, as the French look on their own Languedoc-Roussillon today, and therefore capable of producing great quantities of wine with a high degree of alcohol for blending with the lighter German wines. Matters continued in this way until 1918 brought Alsace back into the French fold once again. In spite of the fact that there were no customers in France after nearly half a century of absence, and that the Germans were in no mood to buy, the Alsatian growers took the courageous and costly step of replanting much of the vineyard area with noble grape varieties. However, just as the newly planted vines began to bear their best grapes, and the customers were returning to the joys of the Riesling and the Gewürz, Alsace and Lorraine once again, in 1940, fell under German rule. The Second World War brought tremendous destruction to the vineyards and towns of Alsace, which found itself a battleground of intense fighting in the final months of the war. Towns such as Ammerschwihr and others along the main road in the plain were 90 percent destroyed by the end of 1944. Yet today the reconstruction has safeguarded the essential Alsatian style and none of the destruction is apparent.

The one positive thing coming out of the war's devastation was the creation after V-E Day in 1945 of the communal wine cooperatives, which were formed to bring that year's great vintage into the press rooms. It is since the war that Alsatian wine has taken its place little by little on the wine lists throughout France. Today, the eighteen cooperatives have an overall total of nearly 2,000 members, who account for nearly a third of all of Alsace's wine.

From Paris, an easy five-hour drive on the Autoroute through Champagne country, or less than an hour's plane flight, brings you to Strasbourg. From there it is just a short, pretty drive south on N-422 along the base of the Vosges to discover the colorful vineyards. Continue along N-422 until you reach Sélestat.

The serious vineyard tour should begin when you get off the highway at Sélestat and take N-59 to Chatenois toward the vine slopes, where the Route des Vins goes south. Overlooking Saint-Hippolyte just south of Chatenois is the feudal castle of Haut-Königsberg, dominating the entire plain of the Rhine. It was once the seat of a line of Swiss counts and saw hard use as a fortress through the centuries. Its most impressive feature today is the panoramic view it offers of the entire plain of the Rhine, with Germany beyond, and of the string of castles along the Vosges hilltops. A visit to the eagles' aerie is practically a must.

The vineyard road is strung together from the small local meandering roads that follow the Vosges slope, where the high-staked vines yield the best wine. Most of the villages in the valley were destroyed during the Second World War, but a number along the Route des Vins fortunately escaped destruction and today remain Alsace's main tourist drawing card. The most picturesque of them all is the sixteenth-century village of Riquewihr. Challenged only by Saint-Émilion and Chinon, it is one of France's most charming wine villages. The narrow cobbled streets weave through the village, hemmed in by half-timbered houses with porches decked with flowers. Some houses open onto inner courts ringed by balconies with carefully wrought wooden trim and window boxes of geraniums.

Jean Hugel, whose family has been making and shipping wine in Riquewihr since the eighteenth century, points out that there are no great houses of the château type, such as those found in the Bordeaux region. "At the end of the Middle Ages you judged the wealth of a town and its houses not by their size, but by the quality of the stone with which they were built. They had five grades, according to hardness, and Riquewihr has the hardest and the best of all stone." Whether by solid construction or blind luck, Riquewihr has survived successive centuries of war.

A number of shipping firms in addition to Hugel's, such as Dopff, Dopff-Irion, and Preiss-Zimmer, are based in Riquewihr, with offices in the upper stories and retail stores at street level, where ambling tourists, seduced by the quaintness of the town, part with their francs, pounds, guilders, and deutschmarks for a sampling of the local wares. "The wine lovers come and discover the old stone and timber houses, and the sightseeing tourists discover our wine," says Hugel. "Not a bad arrangement." Riquewihriens in both the tourist and the wine trade have capitalized on the appeal of their architecture and occasionally must be forgiven for excessive cuteness, such as the fake storks—the local good-luck symbol—and the models of various other animals perching on the rooftops.

Less gussied up and more of a growers' town is Kaysersberg, still one of the prettiest in Alsace after Riquewihr. Its name means "Emperor's Mountain," and it was in fact an emperor's property—bought outright in the thirteenth century by Frederick II of Prussia, who went about rebuilding and fortifying the town and the castle which overlooks it. Of the castle, only the ruins of a lone tower and the ramparts remain.

The castle lends its name to the slope of vineyards shared by Kaysersberg and Kientzheim (not to be confused with Kintzheim, the village just south of Chatenois), a little way down the road (D-28). The 26 hectares (64 acres) of the Schlossberg, literally "Castle Mountain," are rich in granite and are the perfect site for Riesling vines, making the Kientzheim cooperative one of the best sources of good Riesling. Good soils and slopes were recognized in 1984 by the I.N.A.O. in Alsace. Schlossberg was among the first to feature its name on labels. It has already been used for some time as an uncontrolled place-name on several growers' bottles. Beyond Schlossberg, there are about 400 hectares (1,000 acres) of vines on the Kaysersberg-Kientzheim slope, containing Alsace's largest area of Gewürztraminer, and accounting for a substantial portion of all Gewürztraminer produced.

Kaysersberg, a town of good *choucroute* in an area of good wine, is the home of Marcel Blanck, one of Kaysersberg's better growers, and the former local inspector for the I.N.A.O. A big, ruddy man with a round face, he can be found at harvest time in the courtyard of his wine-making installation wearing a leather apron over his well-fed body, and the typical *vigneron*'s rubber boots—his being green.

His operation is typical of the area in its combination of old principles with new techniques. "We still crush the grapes with the stems on," he says, pointing over to the row of modern horizontal presses. "Some growers don't, but we feel that it gives the wine an extra shot of tannin, helping it to live longer in the bottle." From the presses, the juice flows into vats, sealed from all contact with air to prevent fermentation. "Then we centrifuge the juice to take out the lees, return the juice to the vat, and let the fermentation begin. We like to bottle the wine early to capture the characteristic fruit, usually beginning in March."

Vats these days are made of concrete and stainless steel, and are increasingly replacing the typical long, oval wooden vats with the ornately carved fronts, an influence of traditional German wine-making, which remained in use through the sixties and early seventies. The old vats that still remain in use have long since lost their tannin, but are still used by shippers and growers on the doubtful contention that the wine from previous vintages now impregnating the wood is somehow beneficial to the newly made wine.

Coming from the quaint charm of Kaysersberg to the dull modern village of

Ammerschwihr is a shock and makes clear how total the destruction of war can be—hardly a house was left standing here. But Ammerschwihr still is an important wine village.

Not far to the southeast on N-415 is the bustling city of Colmar, a commercial and tourist center, ready to satisfy the needs of sightseer, art lover, and wine buyer alike. Luckily, Colmar still retains many of the picturesque features of the smaller villages. The old city at the center of town has been banned to cars and has the same winding streets and half-timbered houses seen in Riquewihr and Kaysersberg.

Colmar's importance to the regional wines goes back centuries, to the time of the local drinking clubs, or *poêles* (the name literally means "stoves"). The *poêles* were private clubs, and just as the tradesmen of the town competed to be admitted, so the *poêles* themselves would compete to get the best wines for their members. This system was encouraged by the fact that most growers at the time were tradesmen who tended their vines in their spare time—a custom still in existence today. The growers were privileged members of the *poêles* and happy to be so, for they were always assured of an eager audience for their wine. Part of the function of the *poêles* is continued today by La Confrérie de Saint-Étienne, the organization for the promotion of the wines of Alsace, which like its counterparts in Burgundy and Bordeaux holds dinners where much eating, drinking, and singing take place. New members are thus inducted into this newly formed "old" order.

No one with the slightest interest in German Renaissance art can leave Colmar without a visit to the Unterlinden Museum to see the gruesome but breathtaking triptych altarpiece painted by Matthias Grünewald.

The villages producing fine wines continue south from Colmar a short distance, coming to a halt at Éguisheim, another fine tourist center that escaped the major part of the war's destruction. It is also the shipping home of Léon Beyer. The vineyards continue south beyond Éguisheim and Guebwiller to Thann, but from Éguisheim, the vineyard road runs into the highway, so this is where a vineyard tour should end. The wines at this end of the Haut-Rhin will usually be of good quality, though lacking somewhat in distinction. All Alsatian wine with the right to the *appellation* must now be bottled within the confines of Alsace, thus assuring authenticity if not some degree of quality. Gone are the long-distance tank trucks to shippers elsewhere—and, consequently, the blending procedures too often associated with them.

Many different white *eaux-de-vie* or brandies are made in Alsace, and these are very popular in France and more and more throughout Europe. Right in among the vineyards are great raspberry and strawberry patches and orchards which yield the fruit distilled to make these strong colorless spirits. Some four kilos of raspberries are needed to make a bottle of *eau-de-vie de framboise,* which makes it fabulously expensive and almost impossible to find. While the production of genuine *framboise* is dying out on account of its prohibitive cost, other brandies have come to take its place: *mûre* from blackberries; *fraise,* made from strawberries; *myrtille,* from bilberries; *mirabelle,* from yellow plums; *reine-claude,* nearly as rare as *framboise,* made from greengage plums; *quetsch,* from blue plums grown down on the Rhine plain; *kirsch* from cherries; and *houx* from holly, the last two being specialties from Les Trois Épis above Ammerschwihr. Even these are expensive, and as often as not the commercial brands are mixed with alcohol and synthetic flavors. Served in glasses chilled by swirling an ice cube around the inside, these *alcools blancs* give off an intense fruit bouquet, which, when the brandies are well made, can capture the very essence of the fruit. In the good ones, which will be bone-dry, the fruit taste lingers on the palate long after the brandy has been swallowed.

Great comfort lies ahead for those who nostalgically look back at luxurious trains. A new super first-class train is a forerunner of many lines; its main feature is the gastronomic event of a three-star restaurant under the supervision of Joël Robuchon, owner of the Paris restaurant Jamin. The train daily leaves Strasbourg in the morning, arrives in Paris in less than four hours, and returns in the evening to Strasbourg, the capital of Alsace.

⚜

ALSACE VINTAGES

1969 A good vintage—good character, slightly acid, not great, now faded.

1970 Only fair in quality owing to the tremendous quantity produced—the largest in this century. Now faded.

1971 Fair to good, ranging upward in quality from wines very high in alcoholic content, thus destroying the light, sprightly, easy-to-drink characteristics of good Alsatian wines. But many small producers successful in their endeavors will look back at '71 as a highly prestigious vintage. Today it is only of academic interest.

1972 Though pleasant and typically Alsatian, most of the wines lacked depth and were slightly acid.

1973 The most abundant year in Alsace since the war. Most wines showed a certain lack of acidity, so they did not last long in bottle and should have been drunk young.

1974 Well balanced, fresh despite rains throughout harvest, these should be drunk when very young.

1975 A good vintage; the wines are characteristically fruity and harmonious.

1976 One of the greatest vintages in decades. Owing to the drought, a considerable amount of sweet wine was made.

1977 Generally good vintage. Fairly good balance of fruit and acidity. The Gewürztraminer was better than the Rieslings.

1978 Instead of the usual 800,000–900,000 hectoliters of wine, only 600,000 was produced. Much of the shortfall in quantity occurred in the Gewürztraminer. The Rieslings, however, were more plentiful, ripe and good.

1979 Good vintage, and of abundant quantity. These wines were very well balanced.

1980 Quite good, but the quality was irregular and the quantity small. Almost nonexistent harvest of Gewürztraminer.

1981 The quality was excellent, with a relatively strong character of the grape variety. The balance of acidity was laudable. However, there was a problem of quantity: the Sylvaners produced only 50 percent of a normal crop, and the Gewürztraminer was also below normal (as in 1980). Those Rieslings which were not prematurely harvested were excellent.

1982 A very good vintage, for both quantity and quality; the wines had great personality and bold aroma.

1983 A great vintage. The Riesling and Gewürztraminer growers were overjoyed with the hot harvest weather, which produced late-harvest sweet wines of a quality not seen since 1976 or 1921, and even surpassing the former.

1984 After the great 1983s, 1984 was a big disappointment. A few fair dry wines will be found.

1985 A great vintage. Some growers claim it is better than the great '83s. The Gewürztraminers have more character than the preceding vintages, and the "late harvest" wines produced beautiful results.

Alsatian wines taste best when drunk young, not over five years old, freshness being one of their main attractions, which they lose with age. Like most dry white wines, those from Alsace also have a tendency to maderize.

ALSACE GRAND CRU

Riesling Schlossberg

APPELLATION ALSACE GRAND CRU CONTRÔLÉE

BLANCK

Domaine des Comtes de Lupfen   0,70 ℓ

Mise en Bouteilles au Domaine des Comtes de Lupfen.
Propriété de Paul Blanck et ses fils à Kientzheim (Kaysersberg)
Haut-Rhin · France

⚓

ALSACE
Hotels and Restaurants
H = *Hotel;* R = *Restaurant*

MARLENHEIM (67520—Bas-Rhin)
(Paris 467—Molsheim 12—Strasbourg 20)

HR HOSTELLERIE DU CERF: 30, avenue du Général-de-Gaulle. Tel.: 88.87.73.73.   18 rooms. (13 toilets.)
Old coach inn, restored tastefully by the owner, Robert Husser, in this rather sad environment of the suburbs of Strasbourg. Specializing in Alsatian cuisine and seafood. Average prices. Two stars in Michelin.

STRASBOURG (67000—Bas-Rhin)
(Paris 488—Lyon 468—Colmar 69)
Direct air connection with Paris; A-35 Autoroute takes you there in about 5 hours.

❧ This was already an old city when Gutenberg was devising his printing press here in 1439. In the past one hundred years this capital of Alsace has changed hands between France and Germany three times, making it to some extent a hybrid of both cultures. The cathedral and its beautiful spire overlook the old streets and taverns, which are well worth a walking visit. Alsatian cuisine is notable too, and you should not leave before tasting some *choucroute.* You can purchase the famous local *foie gras* at La Boutique du Foie Gras, 6, rue Friesé, tel.: 88.32.28.42, or at La Toque Blanche, 36, rue Hallerbardes, tel.: 88.32.47.13.

HR HILTON STRASBOURG: Avenue Herrenschmidt, fairly close to the center of town, in front of the Palais de la Musique et des Congrès. Tel.: 88.37.10.10. Tlx.: 890363.   247 rooms.
The newest hotel in eastern France. Luxurious, air-conditioned. The Maison du Boeuf is a good restaurant. One star in Michelin.

HR HOLIDAY INN: 20, place de Bordeaux. Tel.: 88.35.70.00. Tlx.: 890515.   164 air-conditioned rooms.
Fairly large rooms with baths; functionally comfortable. Limited restaurant, swimming pool, and sauna available.

HR SOFITEL: Place Saint-Pierre-le-Jeune. Tel.: 88.32.99.30. Tlx.: 870894.   180 air-conditioned rooms plus 5 suites.
Quiet hotel with good service and indoor garden. Restaurant called the Châteaubriand.

HR TERMINUS-GRUBER: 10, place de la Gare. Tel.: 88.32.87.00. Tlx.: 870998.   64 rooms and 6 suites.
Large, comfortable hotel in front of the train station. Good food and wine list. Reasonable prices. Restaurant called Cour de Rosemont.

HR NOVOTEL STRASBOURG SUD: At Illkirch-Graffenstaden (10 km south of Strasbourg on N-83 leading to Colmar). Tel.: 88.66.21.56. Tlx.: 890142. 76 air-conditioned rooms. Functional. Good service. Snack-restaurant and swimming pool available.

R AU CROCODILE: 10, rue de l'Outre, near the Place Kléber. Tel.: 88.32.13.02. Luxurious restaurant, inspired by Émile Jüng, whose wife is a charming hostess. Excellent wine list, excelling in regional wines. The food is not typically Alsatian. Two stars in Michelin.

R MAISON KAMMERZELL: 16, Place de la Cathédrale. Tel.: 88.32.42.14. Tlx.: 890221. This centrally located restaurant is very popular, located in a half-timbered house near the cathedral. Cuisine is not only traditionally Alsatian, but reasonably priced as well. Here, as elsewhere in Alsace, *choucroute* is a must for any traveler. One star in Michelin.

R VALENTIN-SORG: 6, place de l'Homme de Fer. Tel.: 88.32.12.16. M. Schmitt produces excellent food in this fourteenth-floor restaurant with the backdrop of a great panorama of Strasbourg. The prices are high, but so is the quality. One star in Michelin.

R ZIMMER-SENGEL: 8, rue Temple-Neuf, near the cathedral. Tel.: 88.32.35.01. Centrally located, affording good food if you want a departure from Alsatian specialties. If you're on a *choucroute* or *foie gras* hunt, go to the other Zimmer outside of town, in Wantzenau.

R ZIMMER AT LA WANTZENAU: 23, rue des Héros (13 km northeast). Tel.: 88.96.62.08. Cuisine and wine list of good quality. Alsatian specialties. One star in Michelin.

R BUEREHIESEL: 4, parc de l'Orangerie, in front of European Council Hall. Tel.: 88.61.62.24. Old seventeenth-century farm in the middle of the Orangerie Park, with a terrace by the lake. Excellent cuisine and wine list. In addition to the *foie gras,* try the *poularde à la vapeur.* High quality, but not typically Alsatian. Rather expensive. Two stars in Michelin.

R MAISON DES TANNEURS: 42, rue du Bain aux Plantes. Tel.: 88.32.79.70. Pleasant and picturesque, typically Alsatian setting, along the Ill stream in the Petite France quarter. Good cooking and wine list accompanied by a warm welcome to large array of Alsatian specialties; I had one of the best *choucroutes* of Alsace here.

BLAESHEIM (67113—Bas-Rhin)
(Paris 491—Molsheim 15—Obernai 14—Strasbourg 19—Sélestat 34)

R AU BOEUF: 183, rue du Maréchal Foch. Tel.: 88.68.81.31. Georges Voegtling is a good chef. Appetizing dishes from smoked goose to saddle of hare and fresh salmon with sorrel sauce are presented in rustic surroundings. Good assortment of Alsatian wines. One star in Michelin.

OBERNAI (67210—Bas-Rhin)
(Strasbourg 30—Sélestat 23—Colmar 45—Molsheim 10)

HR LE PARC: 169, rue Général-Gouraud. Tel.: 88.95.50.08. Tlx.: 870615. 33 comfortable rooms. An Alsatian hostelry with pigeon nests and lavish window flowerpots. Good menus. Fits well into this town with typical Alsatian setting.

HR BEAU SITE: 1, rue Général-de-Gaulle, at Ottrott-le-Haut, 4 km west on N-426 from Obernai. Tel.: 88.95.80.61. Tlx.: 870445. 14 inexpensive rooms (12 with toilet).
Recognition of M. Schreiber's *menus de dégustation* resulted in one star in Michelin. This new au-berge-inn has added nice, modern rooms. Another stopping place while you are in Alsace.

BALDENHEIM (67600—Bas-Rhin)
(Colmar 30—Strasbourg 47—Sélestat 8)
Off the vineyard road.

R LA COURONNE: 45, rue Sélestat. Tel.: 88.85.32.22.
Good restaurant with reasonable prices in a typical Alsatian setting. One star in Michelin.

RIBEAUVILLÉ (68150—Haut-Rhin)
(Paris 431—Colmar 18—Strasbourg 60—Mulhouse 59—Saint-Dié 41—Sélestat 15)

⌘ Its Riesling and Traminer wines have put this small but charming village on the map. If you are in the area on the first Sunday in September, there is an old Alsatian folk festival which includes a procession of fiddlers and the chance to drink from a fountain of wine in the village square.

HR LE CLOS SAINT-VINCENT: Route de Bergheim. Tel.: 89.73.67.65. 11 rooms.
Beautiful inn atop a vineyard hillside, this pleasant, small hotel-restaurant overlooks the plain below and into Germany. Bertrand Chapotin is an intelligent chef who could improve his wel-come by acquiring some of the charm of Marie-Laure, his wife. You should reserve ahead, as the restaurant is small. Rooms are comfortable and quiet. One of Alsace's most beautiful stopovers. Expensive. *Relais et Châteaux.* One star in Michelin.

ILLHAEUSERN (68150—Haut-Rhin)
(Paris 438—Colmar 17—Strasbourg 60—Bâle 91—
Fribourg 53—Sélestat 13—Ribeauvillé 9)

R AUBERGE DE L'ILL: Rue de Collonges. Tel.: 89.71.83.23.
From all over the world, people gravitate to this inn, which is considered the best restaurant in Alsace and one of France's gastronomic meccas. The Gault & Millau guide joins with the three stars of Michelin and the four stars of the Bottin Gourmand to applaud the efforts of the Hae-berlin brothers for their great restaurant and great value. Reserve ahead. Well worth the price. *Traditions et Qualité.*

RIQUEWIHR (68340—Haut-Rhin)
(Paris 434—Colmar 13—Ribeauville 4.5)
One of the most picturesque wine villages of France.

⌘ The quaintest of all the Alsatian vineyard towns, Riquewihr swarms with tourists from the sum-mer through to the harvest. The village miraculously escaped the ravages of war. Wine fanciers should pop in on the winery of Jean Hugel.

H LE RIQUEWIHR: Route Ribeauvillé. Tel.: 89.47.83.13. 49 small, pleasant, functional rooms. At the entrance of the village, in the midst of vines. No restaurant.

R AUBERGE DE SCHOENENBOURG: 2, rue de la Piscine. Tel.: 89.47.92.28.   25 rooms.
This good restaurant, in the vineyards just outside of town, is often crowded with tourists who come to Riquewihr having heard of its charm. The food is competently prepared and reasonably priced, and, as in all Alsatian restaurants in summer, the service is apt to be slow. English spoken.

KAYSERSBERG (68240—Haut-Rhin)
(Paris 434—Colmar 10)
Old village, hometown of Albert Schweitzer.

HR CHAMBARD: 9, rue du Général-de-Gaulle. Tel.: 89.47.10.17. Tlx.: 880272.   20 comfortable rooms and 2 suites.
Among the best food in the area. Its cuisine and wine list of great quality make it one of the best of the region. It is usually crowded in summer and through harvest time. Reservations suggested. The limited menus are reasonable; ordering *à la carte* is expensive. One star in Michelin.

HR LE CHÂTEAU: Rue du Général-de-Gaulle. Tel.: 89.78.24.33.   12 small rooms.
Big, noisy in summer and fall, but fair meals. Inexpensive.

H LES REMPARTS: 4, rue de la Flieh. Tel.: 89.47.12.12.   28 rooms.
A quiet and comfortable, reasonably priced hotel. No restaurant; breakfast available.

R CHÂTEAU DE REICHENSTEIN: 68, Grand Rue, Kientzheim, which belongs to the commune of Kientzheim. 1 km north of Kaysersberg, south of Riquewihr. Tel.: 89.47.15.88.
Another practical stopover in the middle of the vineyards where you can have *choucroute*.

AMMERSCHWIHR (68770—Haut-Rhin)
(Paris 438—Colmar 8—Ribeauville 18—Sélestat 25—Mulhouse 49)

HR AUX ARMES DE FRANCE: 1, Grand Rue. Tel.: 89.47.10.12.   9 rooms.
Under the direction of its owner, Pierre Gaertner—a former student of Fernand Point—and his son Philippe, this restaurant has become one of the best in Alsace. Two stars in Michelin.

LES TROIS-ÉPIS (68410—Haut-Rhin)
(Paris 448—Colmar 12—Ammerschwihr 8)

A fifteenth-century miracle accounts for the charming name of this town: The Three Ears of Corn. This is a wonderful place for short walks or long hikes into the mountains.

HR GRAND HÔTEL: Place de l'Église. Tel.: 89.49.80.65. Tlx.: 880229.   49 rooms.
If you like a large, old-fashioned spa hotel (now modernized), which can revive you with an indoor pool, a sauna, and a grand view of the Vosges Mountains from the terrace, then this comfortable place claims to be the answer. You can get a variety of inexpensive menus at the adjoining Alsatian tavern—the Auberge. The restaurant is called the Hohlandsbourg.

HR MARCHAL: Tel.: 89.49.81.61.   40 rooms.
A modern, comfortable hotel set in a pine forest. Menus are reasonable. Exceptional view from the dining room and a warm welcome from the Marchal family.

LAPOUTROIE (68650—Haut-Rhin)
(Paris 444—Colmar 19—Kaysersberg 9)

HR LE FAUDÉ: 28, rue du Général-Duffieux. Tel.: 89.47.50.35.   28 rooms (25 with toilet).
This clean, modern, small hotel is well run and deserves a mention because the menus are reasonably priced.

COLMAR (68000—Haut-Rhin)
(Paris 445—Strasbourg 69—Bâle 74—Belfort 71—Fribourg 48—Mulhouse 41—Sélestat 22)
Direct air connection with Paris.

This is the wine capital of Alsace. The center of town is a haven for pedestrians, who, undisturbed by traffic, can fully enjoy meandering past the old houses. Historians claim that the Musée d'Unterlinden is one of the most-visited museums in France, since it houses the great fifteenth-century Issenheim altarpiece by Matthias Grünewald.

To get to Colmar from Paris or Champagne, take the autoroute to Strasbourg and drive south through the vineyards, sipping and nibbling your way to Colmar. If in a rented car, you can fly back to Paris from the airport at Colmar.

HR LE CHAMPS DE MARS: 2, avenue de la Marne. Tel.: 89.41.54.54. Tlx.: 880928.   75 rooms.
On the central garden of the Champs de Mars. Modern hotel with a reasonably priced restaurant. Nothing to write home about.

HR TERMINUS-BRISTOL: 7, place de la Gare. Tel.: 89.23.59.59. Tlx.: 880248.   70 rooms.
Richard Riehm owns this hotel (with flashy furniture), which is quiet and centrally located, but its main claim to fame is its restaurant, called the Rendezvous de Chasse. One star in Michelin.

R MAISON DES TÊTES: 19, rue des Têtes. Tel.: 89.24.43.43.
Fair prices for a *brasserie*. A beautiful seventeenth-century house is the setting for good, abundant food, which accents the Alsatian in all things: *choucroute,* hare in cream sauce, and an array of terrines and pâtés.

R AU FER ROUGE: 52, Grande-Rue. Tel.: 89.41.37.24.
In an old Alsatian quarter. The cuisine is of high quality, and rates its star in Michelin.

R SCHILLINGER: 16, rue Stanislas. Tel.: 89.41.43.17.
A beautiful, luxurious restaurant. The best in Colmar, for its cuisine and extensive wine list. Book ahead. Received its second Michelin star in 1986.

WETTOLSHEIM (68920—Haut-Rhin)
(Colmar 4.5 km in direction of Munster, by D-1 bis)

HR LE PÈRE FLORANC: 9, rue Herzog. Tel.: 89.41.39.14.   31 rooms (22 toilets).
Comfortable rooms and a warm welcome. The restaurant has a rich cuisine sparked by great imagination; an ideal stopover. One star in Michelin.

ÉGUISHEIM (68420—Haut-Rhin)
(Belfort 65—Colmar 7—Mulhouse 38—Rouffach 10—Sélestat 31)

R CAVEAU D'ÉGUISHEIM: 3, place du Château Saint-Léon. Tel.: 89.41.08.89.
In a very colorful Alsatian village, this restaurant, although it is highly recommended by the

guidebooks, left me unimpressed. A qualified former staff member of L'Auberge de l'Ill took over the restaurant in 1983. One star in Michelin.

ARTZENHEIM (68320—Haut-Rhin)
(In the direction of Germany.)
(Paris 460—Colmar 17—Mulhouse 48—Sélestat 20—Strasbourg 67)

HR AUBERGE D'ARTZENHEIM: 30, rue du Sponeck. Tel.: 89.71.60.51. 10 rooms (6 with toilet).

The Husser-Schmidt management offers you inexpensive rooms in the hotel and well-priced menus in the restaurant. Although disdained by Michelin, this inn has been highly touted by Gault & Millau, which loves to criticize the Michelin awards and to bill as discoveries those restaurants and hotels which have been shunned by the other guides.

ANDOLSHEIM (68600—Haut-Rhin)
(Colmar—5 km by N-415)

HR LE SOLEIL: 1, rue de Colmar. Tel.: 89.71.40.53. 17 rooms (12 with toilet).

Here is an inn with mixed but good menus. A house specialty (in autumn and winter) is pheasant with red cabbage. For this and many other dishes they have an attractively assorted wine list.

ROUFFACH (68250—Haut-Rhin)
(Paris 458—Colmar 15—Mulhouse 28—Bâle airport 40—Guebwiller 10—Belfort 60)

HR CHÂTEAU D'ISENBOURG: Tel.: 89.49.63.53. Tlx.: 880819. Tennis and swimming pool in a small park. 40 rooms.

From this nineteenth-century castle, in the midst of vines, the view is unique. For sheer comfort and atmosphere, this is one of the highly recommended places for visits to the Alsatian vineyards. Heated swimming pool. Good cuisine and wine list. *Relais et Châteaux.*

MULHOUSE (68100—Haut-Rhin)
(Paris 468—Bâle 34—Belfort 44—Colmar 41—Sélestat 63—Fribourg 58—
Strasbourg 110—Dijon 229—Reims 358)

◎§ Lovers of vintage cars might care to visit the Musée de l'Automobile at 192, avenue de Colmar (tel.: 89.42.29.17), which contains 420 vintage automobiles. Mulhouse is now mainly an industrial city, producing textile looms and Peugeot cars.

HR FRANTEL: 4, place Charles-de-Gaulle. Tel.: 89.46.01.23. Tlx.: 881807.   96 rooms.
Across from the station. Comfortable, quiet setting. A good menu and the comfort of the rooms make this the best hotel in town.

STEINBRUNN-LE-BAS (68440—Haut-Rhin)
(Mulhouse—8 km southeast)

R LE MOULIN DU KAEGY: Tel.: 89.81.30.34.
A charming restaurant set in a mill outside of town offers good food and a well-selected wine list; excellent quality throughout, and rather expensive. One star in Michelin.

LANGUEDOC-ROUSSILLON

The Heart of the Midi

Cradle of French viniculture, the region called the Midi stretches from the mouth of the Rhône just west of Marseille down to the Spanish border south of Perpignan, varying in width from 20 to 100 kilometers (12 to 60 miles). Although no two Frenchmen will agree on the exact boundaries, there is no disagreement on the connotations of the word: the Midi is the south of deep blue skies contrasted against the ocher-red rock and the subtle shades of silvery grays and greens of the scrubby pine-like vegetation along the Mediterranean the locals call the *garrigue*. It is a land of nearly flat terracotta-tiled roofs on yellow stucco houses; of wine-steeped stews, called *civets* and *daubes,* and of the celebrated *cassoulet* (whose spiritual capital is Toulouse)—as much an experience as a dish—a casserole of white haricot beans cooked with pork and mutton, or goose, or duck, bacon, and garlic sausage. And it is the land of copious cheap, mediocre wine.

The Languedoc-Roussillon vineyards are to wine what the Middle East is to oil. They occupy 435,000 hectares (1,075,000 acres), 35 percent of France's entire vineyard area—that is, six times the size of the Bordelais, seventy times the size of the Côte d'Or—the biggest, most intensively cultivated wine area in the world. Out of that immense sweep of green come almost a billion gallons of wine a year—some 370 million cases—which amounts to a case and then some for every man, woman, and child in France, England, and the United States. If France's wine belt is little known to the world, it is because a great majority of the Languedoc-Roussillon wines have no Appellation d'Origine Contrôlée, meaning that they are not controlled by the National Institute of Place-names (I.N.A.O.), and are sold as table wine with no indication of origin on the label. They are the *vins ordinaires* of France. This ocean of non-A.O.C. wine falls into three categories.

First, there are the V.D.Q.S., *Vins Délimités de Qualité Supérieure,* wines from a precisely defined area with specific regulations regarding cultivation of the vine and the making of the wine, with specified grape varieties, limited yields, minimum alcoholic content, and other controlled characteristics. However, the rules for V.D.Q.S. wines are of the same type as for A.O.C. (specifying area of production, grape variety, and production methods) and are controlled by the I.N.A.O. but are less stringent. All V.D.Q.S. wines must be "labeled," that is, they must pass a taste test before they are analyzed and accepted as V.D.Q.S. They are, thus, a steppingstone to Appellation Contrôlée. The V.D.Q.S. wines in the Languedoc-Roussillon account for only 3 percent of the region's total wine production, but amount to more than half of all the V.D.Q.S. produced in France and among them, certainly, are some of France's best. For a complete list see Appendix VIII.

Second, but far below the V.D.Q.S. in quality, are the *vins de pays*—"country wines." The simple country vintage has, of course, existed since the first grapes were planted and fermented, but it is only since World War II that there has been any attempt to regulate it. There are around forty-five *vins de pays* in the Languedoc-Roussillon, usually named for the valley or the slope where they are grown, such as the Coteaux du Thaux, in the department of the Hérault, or the Vallée du Paradis and Côtes de Perpignan in the Aude. The regulation of these wines is left to the local associations that limit the area of the particular *pays,* ruling on exactly where the named valley or hillside begins and ends. *Vins de pays* must be made with certain grape varieties, usually Grenache, Cinsault, Mourvèdre, Syrah, and others, and are limited in yield to the relatively large amount of 100 hectoliters per hectare (1,093 gallons per acre). (Nearly three times the 35 hectoliters per hectare [400 gallons per acre] limit in the Côte d'Or.) Minimum alcoholic content of the wines must be 10 percent or more, depending on where they are produced. Their usually mediocre quality is always directly related to the standards of the local governing board that accepts them, the final criteria being a chemical analysis and the tasters' judgment of the wine's character, which is supposed to reflect the particular terrain

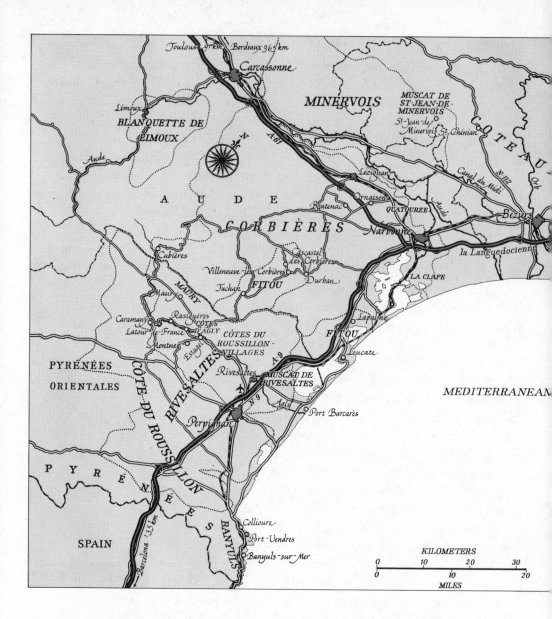

and microclimate of its origin. However, the *vin de pays* designation is no guarantee whatever of quality, because nearly any "country" can have its wine. Whether it is grown on the better hillsides far inland or on the sands along the Mediterranean coast, in areas as small as a Burgundy vineyard or as large as a Texas ranch, it can all be entitled to the *vin de pays* designation. Furthermore, the control of grape variety, yield per hectare, and vinification methods is inconsistent and sometimes lax.

Vin de pays accounts for around 15 percent of the total Languedoc-Roussillon output, but this will no doubt rise in the coming years as more and more growers

314

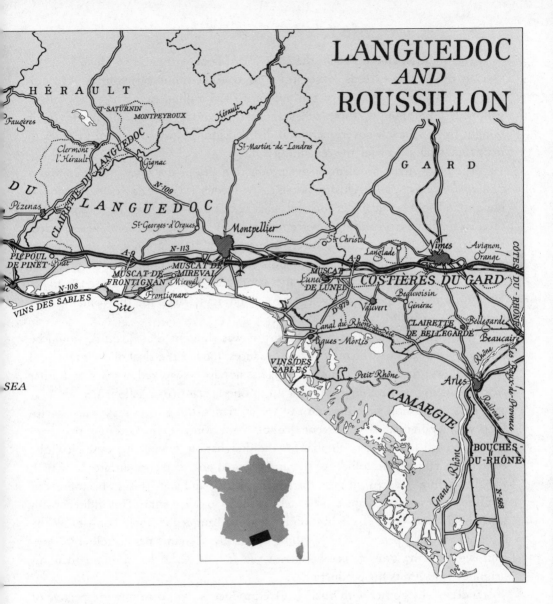

try to free themselves from the anonymity of the barrel-bottom classification, *vin de table,* officially known as *vin de consommation courante.* The daily French swill, the backbone, heart, and basic economic incentive of the Languedoc-Roussillon wine industry, accounts for nine out of ten bottles produced in the Midi, an average of 345 million of the 370 million cases the area produces annually. These are the wines that come to mind when *vin du Midi* is mentioned. "There is no getting around it," says an official in the Ministry of Agriculture in Montpellier, "France has the worst table wine in Europe." Why is it so bad and why is there so much?

The question answers itself: the wine is bad because there is so much of it. Invariably production exceeds consumption by 10 to 20 million hectoliters (520 million gallons), the equivalent of 110 million to 220 million cases (or 3 to 5 billion gallons). That amount, three times the annual production of all Bordeaux, is bought by the French government and distilled into industrial alcohol in order to maintain stable prices for the remaining wine.

The crux of the problem of overproduction lies in the often-cited expression *"La qualité ne paie pas"*—Quality doesn't pay. French *vin ordinaire,* or table wine, is bought and sold by alcoholic content, what is called in the trade the hectoliter/degree, each degree representing 1 percent of alcohol by volume. The higher the alcoholic content, the bigger the grower's return per hectare of vines. A hectoliter of wine (about 130 bottles) bought by a bulk shipper from a cooperative at 10 percent alcohol content might be worth 18 francs per degree, meaning in this case 180 francs for the hectoliter, or the equivalent of around 1.35 francs for the contents of a bottle.

When this system came into practice it was thought that quantity would be limited by the fact that the more a vine produces, the less the alcoholic content, and thus the lower the value of the wine. This has not always worked in practice. Rather than producing 80 hectoliters of wine from one hectare (650 gallons per acre), at 11.5 percent alcohol, which would pay 16,560 francs, the grower makes 200 hectoliters with a potential of 7.5 percent alcohol, that is, only slightly stronger than beer and by French law scarcely eligible for the designation "wine." To raise alcoholic content, he takes 80 hectoliters of the unfermented juice and concentrates it by half, literally boiling it down, to raise the sugar content, and adds this 40 hectoliters of syrup to the rest of the grape must to ferment into so-called wine. This indirect form of chaptalization—true chaptalization is illegal in Languedoc-Roussillon—raises the alcohol to about 9 percent, which will be worth, say, 18 francs per hectoliter/degree. This will pay the grower, per hectare, 1,380 francs—5,210 francs more than his neighbor who limits his production.

Indeed, why bother with quality? Overproduction will continue irrespective of the government in power, because over half the voters of the region make wine on a full- or part-time basis. They are a vociferous group, mostly leftist, and active in promoting their cause. "For the time being," as one high government official put it, "there is no easy solution."

It is not simply a question of the growers producing too much and too bad; the shipper, the consumer, and the government are equally at fault. The grower is to blame for his failure to replant vineyards with "noble" grape varieties that produce less wine but of better quality, and that ultimately would return a higher profit. The shippers are to blame for being interested only in the cheapest wine that they can lay their hands on, and for an almost total lack of interest in quality. They buy the wines from the cooperatives in the departments of the Gard, Hérault, Aude, and Pyrénées-Orientales, placing orders by phone for so many thousand hectoliters of wine at, say, 10 percent alcoholic content, and so much at 11 percent. These are then shipped by tank truck and railroad car to Paris and other metropolitan centers, where they are bottled and sold under the well-known brand names throughout France. Some brokers claim that most shippers rarely even bother to taste the wine before buying—and with reason; it is all the same, and it is nearly all what the English call "plonk." Anytime the cooperative wines get too expensive and too light, the shippers may import cheaper wines to fortify the mix. This is perfectly legal, if the wine is sold as a brand-name wine and not as specifically French. At the end of the line there is the consumer, who is unwilling to pay for decent wine.

So the vicious circle continues, the government buying up the excess in over-abundant years for fear that the growers will revolt against the low prices paid for their wines; and revolt they do. Dozens of times from 1960 to 1984 roadblocks and barricades have been thrown up against the tanktrucks and train cars arriving from Italy with the cheap, deeply colored, and highly alcoholic *vin médecin* the shippers use to doctor the wines of the Midi. In March 1976 at the Montredon bridge outside Narbonne, growers clashed with police in a bloody confrontation that left two dead.

In 1975 and 1976 the Languedoc-Roussillon had two bumper crops back to back and as a result the stocks of wine at the cooperatives and the shippers grew enormously. Prices, which were already low to begin with, fell even further and the producers had to go begging for customers. The government was obliged to buy up excess wine for distillation at high prices. Once the word got out that the government was there to take up the slack, the problem of overproduction became even more acute, for anyone who had limited their production in order to produce a better wine was, so to speak, financially penalized.

The incentives to overproduce remain; none of the conditions that produced the tragedy at Montredon has been resolved. If another abundant harvest comes along, the French government will probably step in to buy up the excess again.

But there are signs of a change in the Midi. Better vine varieties are appearing; the cooperatives are calling upon trained oenologists; a certain amount of competitive pride is noticeable; and not everyone shares in the sins that have made the Midi such an infamous wine region. The main source of poor-quality wine is the fertile plain between the low hillsides, where the better wines are made, and the Mediterranean. The combination of rich, humid soil, poor grape varieties, such as Aramon, and a thick application of fertilizer to push production is a guarantee of making poor ordinary wine. Until the mid-seventies, when fertilizer was still relatively cheap, it was not unusual to find some of the plain vineyards producing close to 250 hectoliters per hectare (2,186 gallons per acre)—in some cases the equivalent of six bottles of wine per vine. Since then fertilizer prices have more than tripled, so the huge yields so often cited by the sensationalist press in France are no longer as common. Still, it remains to be seen whether decent wines can be made in these broad plains, which after all make up close to two-thirds of the Languedoc-Roussillon vineyard area. In regions where irrigation is possible, such as the department of the Gard, for instance, grapevines have been ripped up and replaced by fruit trees. The French government has made desultory attempts to provide financial incentives to convert vineyards, but many regions of the plain are far from the sources of irrigation necessary to make fruits and vegetables a surer bet than vines.

For a few producers, particularly in the Aude and the Pyrénées-Orientales, the making of fine wine is a matter of pride. Two groups which are making a great effort to produce full, fruity, characterful wines that would honor any wine region of France are the Vignerons de Val d'Orbieu in Narbonne and the Vignerons Catalans in Perpignan. Marc Dubernet, a Bordeaux-trained oenologist who advises both groups, moved to Narbonne after working with many of Bordeaux's châteaux. He looks at his switch from the aristocracy of Bordeaux's wines to those of the proletarian Midi this way: "When I came to the Midi I felt the way the American pioneers must have felt in the 1800's. Wines have been made in the Midi since before the Romans, but the history of the search for quality is scarcely more than a decade old. In the Aude and Pyrénées-Orientales great progress has been made, but we still have at least a decade to go before the concepts of limited yield and noble grape variety are appreciated, understood, and generalized. That will happen only when better prices are paid for the wines. We already supervise the production of a fifth of all the Corbières wine made, but we'll soon be supervising a quarter or better. There are many wines in the region that deserve better treatment from the growers than they receive." It is largely through the efforts of those like Dubernet that the wines of Côtes du Roussillon were elevated in status and given the accolade of their own Appellation Contrôlée. If Dubernet and his colleagues have anything to do with it, the wines of Corbières (recently awarded an A.O.C.), Minervois (also an A.O.C.), and other Midi regions are likely to gain in prestige and quality. For all that, it bears repeating that although the well-made Midi wine is very much of a rarity, it exists and it is worth seeking out.

Partly at fault for the delay in improving the quality of the Midi wine have been forces beyond anyone's control. As one *négociant* put it, "We haven't really recovered from the loss of Algeria." He refers, of course, to the highly alcoholic—13 to 14 percent—deeply colored, "fat" wines from Oran and Algiers that were traditionally used to mix with the lighter Midi wines and sold under brand names, helping the Midi to find a ready market. Although blends are frowned upon in better wines because they adulterate any inner personality, it so happened that the rich, dark, heavy Algerian wines were the perfect complement for the unfortunate *vin du Midi*. For some years after Algerian independence in 1962, wines continued to cross the Mediterranean to become part of the Frenchman's daily *pinard*. But after the radical government of Houari Boumedienne confiscated the newly developed oil wells in the Sahara, France slapped an embargo on Algerian wine, which now is exported almost entirely to Russia.

It has not been easy to find a replacement for that great fatness of the Algerian blend. It is about time the Midi growers looked to their own vineyards rather than to Italy, Sicily, and Sardinia. Until they do, it is likely that the consumption of V.D.Q.S., *vin de pays,* and *vin de table* will continue to drop, as it has since 1972.

Although it is still the source of France's least flattering wine, for its heritage alone the Midi deserves better. It was the Midi that first nurtured the vines of France. The first people to make a permanent impression on the region were the Phocaean sailors, Greeks from Asia Minor, who landed in the sixth century B.C. at present-day Marseille, then called Massalia. Whether they cultivated the indigenous vines or brought their own is uncertain, but it was not long before wine was bought and bartered in the Phocaean trading centers of Massalia and Agathe-Tyche, present-day Agde (reached overland by caravans of donkeys, brought to France for the first time) and Arles (reached by flat boats poled up the Rhône), and a dozen other towns. Within a century the vines had spread with the traders west from Massalia down to Narbonne and beyond. By the second century B.C. wines from the entire Languedoc vineyard were sold as Béziers wine, named for the town that supplied the wooden casks used for transport. But the Phocaeans were tradesmen rather than empire builders or colonizers, and it took the Romans, with whom the Phocaeans were allied commercially and militarily, to bring a structure and dynamism that few regions beyond Rome had at the time. Threatened by Celtic tribes from the north, the Phocaeans called on Rome for help, and in 123 B.C. troops arrived and the Greco-Roman influence was implanted in the Midi to stay.

By the time of Christ, Marseille, Nîmes, Arles, and Narbonne were important Roman military and commercial centers, as the stunning architecture of their Roman buildings from that time testifies. Narbonne supplanted Marseille as the main garrison headquarters and trade center between Rome and Spain. The entire region, *la Gaule narbonnaise,* became an exporter of olive oil, wood, flax, hemp, and, of course, wine. This boulevard of Latindom, as Cicero called it, corresponded more or less to the outlines of the Languedoc-Roussillon today.

Languedoc was first of all a language, literally the *langue d'oc,* spoken until this century in various dialects in nearly all of France south of Saint-Étienne. It was distinguished from the *langue d'oïl* spoken in the northern half of France: "oc" and "oïl" being the manner in which each, respectively, said "yes." The language is more often referred to now as *occitan* and in recent years it has come back into popularity throughout local French *lycées* and universities. As a province of wine, however, the Languedoc now begins where the River Gard meets the Rhône, about 15 kilometers (9 miles) south of Avignon, the first A.O.C. vineyards lying on the rolling plain between Nîmes and Arles: the region of Clairette de Bellegarde, and a large area of V.D.Q.S. wine called the Costières du Gard. Clairette de Bellegarde is a dry white wine made from the Clairette grape, and, like most white wines of the region, it suffers from a certain flatness and an exaggerated degree of alcohol. This is due to the intense heat and sun of the Midi summers, which lower the acidity in the grapes, making them coarse and depriving them of freshness. The immense cooperative of Bellegarde is the main producer. Costières du Gard makes the equivalent of roughly a million cases a year, from the hills south of Nîmes that look out to the Camargue and the sea beyond. The dry red, white, and rosé wines are vinified for the most part in the large cooperatives of Vauvert, Générac, and Beauvoisin. Nîmes, Arles, and the Camargue make up three-star tourist attractions and do much to provide romantic backdrop for the wines of the area.

As you approach Nîmes from the north on Expressway A-9, signs announce it as *la ville romaine,* and indeed this is no idle boast. Before Nîmes, between Remoulins and Uzès, is the Pont du Gard, which has two claims: first, that it is the best-preserved Roman bridge in existence; and second, that it is one of the most-visited historic attractions of France.

Of the seventy-odd Roman amphitheaters left in the world, the Nîmes arena, built two thousand years ago, is the most perfectly preserved. There, in the first decades after Christ, gladiators fought bears, bulls, wild boars, and each other before more than 20,000 spectators. Between acts, to clear the air, usherettes would burn bundles of aromatic herbs gathered from the hillsides outside of town and sprinkle red powder over the arena floor so the bloodstains would not show.

Along the Boulevard Victor-Hugo, down from the arena, is the Maison Carrée, the Square House, in fact a Roman temple built in the last century B.C. with Corinthian pillars and an inner sanctum for pagan religious ceremonies. Today, when the week-long fête, the famous Nîmes *Féria,* begins at Pentecost, the streets are jammed with celebrants who carry on far into the night, and as might be expected the Nîmes arena becomes the center of activity, featuring bullfights that continue throughout the summer season. These *corridas* are truly Spanish to the most discerning *aficionado,* since the bulls and matadors and their *cuadrillas* come up from Spain for the occasion. The local spectators have even learned to cheer with resounding *"Olés."*

Just 30 kilometers (18 miles) away on N-113, which takes you through the heart of Clairette de Bellegarde, is the other Roman jewel of the Midi, Arles, the ancient Roman regional capital. It too has an amphitheater, less well preserved than the one in Nîmes, but intact enough to hold its own *corridas,* and a theater, of which only fragments now remain. In the epoch of Roman Gaul, Arles was the center of commerce while Nîmes was more a center of culture. Just south of Arles, the Rhône splits in two, and in the delta lies the 56,000-hectare marshy expanse (138,-000 acres) known as the Camargue, a series of inland salt marshes where bulls and wild horses roam free. Much is still made of the cowboyness of it all, although the roundup into specific herds, called *manades,* is a custom on the wane.

The sandy, salt-rich soil does not prevent the cultivation of the vine along the coast between the marshes and the sea. From the sullen and impressive fortified city of Aigues-Mortes, along the sandy littoral to Montpellier on road D-62, thousands of hectares of vineyard are planted, producing a table wine called *vin de sable,* wine from sand. The most important producer of this strange wine is the Salins du Midi Company. The largest single vineyard owner in all of France, with 1,650 hectares (4,125 acres) of vines, les Salins runs one of the most fully automated and mechanized wine operations in France. Weeding, trimming, spraying, plowing, and even picking of the dozen or so grape varieties are all fully mechanized. This impressive agricultural operation, run by a former student of the School of Agronomy at Montpellier, has a modern installation and a great technological advantage over other large-scale producers.

In contrast, dilapidated equipment dating from between the wars, as well as lackadaisical control of the wine-making, is commonplace in many of the regional communal cooperatives. So, for all the facelessness of the Salins du Midi product, they at least put out a clean wine. Much of their wine is sold in large quantities to the tens of thousands of summer vacationers who invade the newly developed range of beaches, small ports, and condominiums—in many of which the French government is the major stockholder.

After following the shoreline, the road from Aigues-Mortes heads inland to the old town of Montpellier. The home of France's oldest university, located in its oldest vineyard region, Montpellier is the capital of French—therefore, world—viticulture. Viticulture is the study of the cultivation of the vine, from the selection of special clones and hybrids in the laboratory to the planting, grafting, and tending in the vineyard. (Viniculture, whose French capital is Bordeaux, takes up where viticulture leaves off, being a study of the transformation and elaboration of the grape juice into the wine itself.) Professor Jean Branas, one of the guiding lights of the École Nationale Supérieure Agronomique of Montpellier, was a world-renowned authority on growth patterns of vines and the development and refinement of root stocks for grafting.

Montpellier has been a wine town for centuries, and many of the houses in the old sections of the city still have cellars and the vestiges of old wine-making equipment. Montpellier by the fifteenth century had become a leading producer of liqueurs, thanks to recipes brought from Italy by Catherine de Medici. A local potable favored by Louis XIV is said to have contained amber, aniseed, cinnamon, and musk. In the 1530s, when Rabelais was struggling to finish medical school, not the least of his distractions were the products of nearby Mireval and Frontignan, homes today of sweet, fortified white wines known as Muscat. The Muscat vines, named for a port in Arabia, were probably introduced by returning Crusaders. Wine-making was permanently influenced by Dr. Jean-Antoine Chaptal, professor at the Montpellier School of Medicine, whose work in the early nineteenth century did much to elucidate the direct relationship between sugar and the alcoholic content in wine. He found that sugar—he encouraged the use of beet sugar—added in limited amounts to the must (the fermenting juice, never to the finished wine), along with the natural sugars in the grape, would be transformed by the enzymes and yeasts into alcohol, to bring it into better balance with the other constituents of the wine. Though the practice is abused in many cases, chaptalization, as it has come to be called, has salvaged billions of bottles that would otherwise have been thin and weak. Ironically, the growers of Languedoc-Roussillon, except those in the great place names, are forbidden to chaptalize their wines. The Ministry of Agriculture and the I.N.A.O. feel that, under the hot Midi sun, grapes should be able to attain a high sugar content naturally. If sensible yields were maintained, this would be true. Too often, though, the vines are pushed to produce ridiculously high quantities of grapes, which inevitably lack the sugar content of those in vineyards where production is sensibly limited.

South from Montpellier you have the choice of heading back toward the sea, on N-108 through the Muscat grape region of Minerval and Frontignan to the coastal towns of Sète and Agde, or into the hills of the Coteaux du Languedoc on N-109, where some of the better V.D.Q.S. wines are made. If you venture into the region, you might try the fine restaurant at Gignac, known by the owners' name—Capion. The pattern for quality is the same for the entire region: the closer to the ocean, the richer and more humid the soil and the more common and characterless the wine. The broad plain from Montpellier to Narbonne on either side of Autoroute A-9 is the heart of this high-yield area. The Coteaux, the slopes of Languedoc 20 or 30 kilometers (12 to 18 miles) inland, can produce some fair wines, and as a V.D.Q.S. *appellation* the Coteaux du Languedoc has had a dozen villages or so selected by the I.N.A.O. as being particularly good. Worth noting are Saint-Saturnin, Saint-Chinian, Faugères, and La Clape.

Then, we come to an oasis of Appellation Contrôlée: Clairette de Languedoc, along the better slopes of the Black Mountain, the romantic, rugged range that slants south to the Corbières. The vineyards consist of about 1,100 hectares (2,750 acres). The wine is dry and full (at least 13 percent alcohol). The tiny back roads that travel through the Coteaux du Languedoc villages of Faugères and Saint-Chinian, skirting the hills, take one through beautiful countryside to the Minervois, a region of a recent Appellation Contrôlée of red, white, and rosé wine, and one of the better Muscat wines, the Muscat de Saint-Jean-de-Minervois. Like the muscat wines of Lunel, Frontignan, and Mireval, the Saint-Jean-de-Minervois are rich, sweet, fortified amber-colored wines made from the Muscat grape. The grapes are allowed to ripen to supermaturity on the vine; when the sweet must is fermenting, before all the sugar turns to alcohol, pure alcohol is added, killing the yeasts and leaving behind unfermented sugar and a final alcoholic content approaching 18 percent.

In the eyes of the wine law-makers, these do not qualify as true wines, but rather as "natural sweet wines," *vins doux naturels,* or V.D.N. A good V.D.N. from the Muscat grape will be a heady wine, with a pleasant bouquet and fruitiness imparted by the grape. For those who like sweet aperitifs, the better V.D.N.'s served cool can be quite pleasant—they certainly have a devoted following in France.

The Minervois in 1984 became an Appellation Contrôlée wine. The entire region was previously classified as V.D.Q.S. The wines are actively promoted by the growers' association, and the tourists who flock to the newly developed beaches along the coast near Narbonne are beginning to appreciate the rugged beauty of the inland countryside, as well as the wines that are grown there. These are mainly red, and when well made are strong in character and alcohol and will improve with a few years in the bottle. When well made so their true character emerges, Minervois combines tannin with a certain acidity. Like the wines made in Corbières, their neighbor to the south, Minervois is often sold in the typical *occitan* bottle, which looks like a cross between a Burgundy bottle and a squat Champagne bottle. Most of the time there is no vintage listed.

The best of the Corbières vineyards lie south of the Narbonne-Carcassonne Autoroute, stretching west from the Mediterranean. They produce the equivalent of more than 5 million cases of wine a year, 95 percent red, 4 percent rosé, and 1 percent white. Corbières was the largest V.D.Q.S. region of France, accounting for more than 40 percent of all French V.D.Q.S. wine. The 33,000 hectares of vines (81,500 acres) cover the Corbières range of hills and extend 70 kilometers (42 miles) to Fitou, near the sea. The uncultivated landscape has a wild, romantic allure. Toward the sea, the *garrigue* and *maquis,* the scrubby pine-type vegetation, mix with thyme, lavender, and jasmine; while further west into the hill country the terrain is rough and deeply valleyed. The climate can be mercilessly hot and dry in the summer. As the local wisdom has it, Corbières was born under the Fire Sign.

The well-made wine of Corbières, having recently achieved an I.N.A.O. (A.O.C.) status, is just as sturdy as the country that produces it. Most of it is vinified by the sixty communal cooperative cellars. Some of the better wines, for reasons of soil or technique, are Cascastel, Castelmaure, and Baziolles. The popularity of Corbières, which can be good, would be much greater if the life-span of this fat, round, pleasant-when-young wine were able to last beyond its three- or four-year limit. Much beyond this time it oxidizes, losing its color and its sturdy round character, becoming faded and thin. Wines with a higher alcoholic content are sturdier and may qualify for the designation of Corbières-Supérieure. This early fading can be circumvented by the judicious planting of noble grape varieties and clones as has been admirably shown by a number of the region's producers—both individual growers and such cooperative efforts as the Vignerons de Val d'Orbieu mentioned above. When in this corner of the Languedoc be sure to try the incomparable *civet de langouste,* a highly spiced local lobster stew, and *coq à la Tuchanaise,* a chicken fricassee made with the local Corbières wine.

A number of domaines in Corbières—some smaller than many Bordeaux "châteaux"—estate-bottle their wines. These include such excellent values as Domaine de Villemajou and Domaine de la Voûte in Boutenac, Domaine Saint-Maurice in Bizanet, and Domaine de Montjoie in Saint-Laurent de Cabrerisse.

On the Corbières-Minervois border, beside the River Aude, is Carcassonne, still overlooked by the great fortified Cité on the hill above it. The unsuspecting tourist driving through the town at night will be met by a breathtaking, seemingly endless display of towered and crenellated ramparts—one of Europe's architectural wonders. The hilltop site was built on by the Romans in the first century B.C.; the inner ramparts were constructed by the Visigoths in the fifth century A.D.; the outer fortresses by Louis IX, better known as Saint Louis, in the thirteenth century. With every improvement in ballistics and assault tactics through the ages, succeeding feudal regimes improved and strengthened the fortifications. By the time of Philip the Bold in the mid-fourteenth century, three rings of stone walls, ditches, and obstacles surrounded the city as protection against everything from catapults and battering rams to flaming arrows and assault towers. After the province of Roussillon was annexed to France in 1659, the fortress lost its usefulness and gradually crumbled into near-ruin. And so the Cité would have remained if not for the dedicated work of Eugène Emmanuel Viollet-le-Duc, the great nineteenth-century architect and author who also restored many other great edifices, notably the cathedrals of Chartres, Amiens, and Reims. In 1844, thanks to his efforts, the French government began to restore the ramparts and interior of the Cité, continuing the work to this day. Despite the grumblings of purist detractors, who would have left the old stones untouched, Carcassonne stands witness to twenty-one centuries of European history.

You can cross the wine region from Nîmes to Carcassonne by autoroute, but you won't see any vines to speak of along the way. The broad plain on either side of the highway bears no resemblance to the hill towns and vineyards you'll find on the side roads, such as D-610 and D-18.

Around the town of Limoux, due south of Carcassonne on the Aude, are the vineyards of Blanquette de Limoux, a sparkling wine, made mostly from a white grape called the Mauzac, and some Chardonnay. A non-sparkling variety is also made under the name Vin de Blanquette, and nearly all of the vinification for the region is handled by the cooperative in Limoux. From my recent experience with it, the sparkling Blanquette is well made, though without a great deal of character—at its best resembling a lesser non-vintage Champagne. Since it suffers the same tax as Champagne in many importing countries, including the United States and Britain, it has not been a particularly good value, although a steep rise in Champagne prices a few years ago temporarily made it a better one.

The last A.O.C. wines of the Languedoc can be found by driving south from Narbonne on the road that leads to Spain. To the west you can see the beginning of the Pyrénées. The entire area from Toulouse to Narbonne to the Spanish border is subjected to the wind from the Pyrénées called the *tramontane.* On its most ferocious days the trailer-hauling vacationers on their way to and from Spain have to pull over to the side of the road and wait for the winds to subside so they are not overturned. The red wine Fitou is grown in two areas: on the coast between Lapalme and the town of Fitou, and a bit west from there between Cascastel and Paziols and taking in the towns of Villeneuve-les-Corbières and Tuchan. It is a picturesque region that does much to flatter its sturdy wine. The vine types are Carignan and Grenache, which must—singly or together—make up three-quarters of any wine carrying the name Fitou. The remaining quarter may be made of other varieties, usually Cinsault and Mourvèdre. In the past, growers tended to make pungent, deeply colored wines high in alcoholic content and with a thick, concentrated taste to them. However, new oenological methods, pioneered largely by the Vignerons Catalans in Perpignan, have shown that Fitous can be wines of great pleasure. Annual production is the equivalent of around 600,000 cases.

The Corbières vineyard area, with its islands of A.O.C. wines, Corbières itself, Blanquette de Limoux and Fitou, is the last wine area of the Languedoc before crossing south into the Roussillon.

The Roussillon vineyards produce the full gamut of wines: dry reds, rosés, and whites, all made from the area's standard grape varieties (Carignan, Cinsault, Grenache, Mourvèdre) and a large assortment of fortified sweet aperitif wines—*vins doux naturels.* But it is the relatively unknown wines of the Côtes du Roussillon that hold high the banner of Languedoc-Roussillon. Like Beaujolais and Côtes du Rhone, the

Côtes du Roussillon have a number of hillside villages with distinctive microclimates, which may label their wines as Côtes du Roussillon-Villages. Worth noting are Montner, Caramany, Latour-de-France, Estagel, and Planèzes. In all, Côtes du Roussillon plus the Villages make the equivalent of about 3 million cases a year. Again, it is the Vignerons Catalans who have taken the lead in producing the region's finest wines and therefore perhaps the best of Languedoc-Roussillon.

The Roussillon is also a huge producer of several *vins doux naturels:* Rivesaltes, red, white, and rosé-colored fortified sweet wines from four different grapes planted in the entire Roussillon area; Muscat de Rivesaltes, a V.D.N. made only from the Muscat grape; Banyuls and Maury, both red V.D.N.s made from the Grenache. The popularity of sweet fortified wines cannot be doubted: 500,000 hectoliters of the stuff—that's 75 million bottles—most of it drunk in France. But in the mid-eighties sales in France slowed down considerably. In addition to its *vin doux naturel,* Banyuls also produces a dry red wine and a rosé, both called "Grenache" after the dominant grape variety. They have won some renown in their home country, but are rarely found elsewhere in France and are almost never exported. About four-fifths of the production—total output averages 30,000 hectoliters, the equivalent of around 330,-000 cases, each year—is vinified at one of nine cooperative cellars.

The center of Roussillon and the animating force of this corner of France is the colorful city of Perpignan, where French is spoken with a bouncing lilt inherited from Catalonian ancestors. Perpignan through the centuries has switched nationalities even more often than Alsace-Lorraine. Until the fourteenth century Perpignan was the capital of Spanish Catalonia. Then, from the 1340s to the 1640s, a three-way pulling match went on between the Aragonese, the French, and the Perpignanais, who were never quite sure whose side they were on. In 1642, Louis XIII, with the help of the swashbuckling Musketeers, laid siege to the Spanish-held city, starving the population along with the Aragonese army, which capitulated on September 9 of that year. Finally, in 1659, the treaty of the Pyrénées was signed, bringing Perpignan and the Roussillon back into the French fold for good. South of Perpignan, in Collioure, a charming port and beach town next to Banyuls near the Spanish border, you can still see the Château Royal of the kings of Majorca, as you quaff some of the local, rather hot-blooded red wine that bespeaks its Hispanic ancestry.

In the early 1960s, President de Gaulle instituted an overall development plan to open up the more popular sandy beaches on the sunny Mediterranean coast from the Camargue to the Spanish border. Hundreds of kilometers of unoccupied beach were turned into ports and resorts for low-income French vacationers and tourists from abroad. The A-9 Autoroute, the Languedocienne (which south of Narbonne becomes La Catalanne), leading to Spain, makes these resorts just as accessible to Parisians as the overcrowded Riviera. Every summer, beginning with the first days of

June, thousands of sailing and motor boats ply the waves along the coast while overloaded cars and packed buses bring still more vacationers through the vineyard area to the sandy beaches. The tourist trade boom in this southern corner of Mediterranean France has helped to promote the local wines and give identity to the millions of labels on the shelves of supermarkets throughout France.

LANGUEDOC-ROUSSILLON
Hotels and Restaurants

H = *Hotel;* R = *Restaurant*

This large, bulk-wine-producing vineyard area of France begins around Nîmes on the border of the less important sections of the Côtes du Rhône and continues south to Spain.

The autoroute at Nîmes is A-9, called the Languedocienne. Depending on the areas you wish to visit, see map on page 315 for the exits from the autoroute.

NÎMES (30000—Gard)
(Lyon 249—Aix-en-Provence 105—Marseille 123—Montpellier 51—Avignon 43—Arles 31)

For city description see "Côtes du Rhône" chapter, page 262.

MONTPELLIER (34000—Hérault)
(Paris 760—Nice 324—Toulouse 240—Marseille 164—Nîmes 51—Arles 74—
Avignon 96—Carcassonne 193—Millau 115—Perpignan 152)

The town really isn't worth much of a detour. The university, one of the oldest in France, was the birthplace of ampelography (the study of the grapevine); considerable research was and is still done there.

. . .

HR HOTEL FRANTEL: 218, rue du Bastion-Ventadour, in the center of town in the *quartier* Polygone. Tel.: 67.64.65.66. Tlx.: 480362. 116 air-conditioned rooms.
The hotel, like most of the Frantel chain, is modern and well run.

HR MÉTROPOLE: 3, rue Clos-René, in the center of town. Tel.: 67.58.11.22. Tlx.: 480410.   92 very comfortable rooms, including 4 air-conditioned suites.
Pleasant, old-fashioned look, with exotic garden. The restaurant, La Closerie, offers well-prepared and recently improved food. Refined surroundings. A bit difficult to find because of the one-way streets, it is well worth the effort, as the management "tries harder," especially Bernard Jourdan.

R LA RÉSERVE RIMBAUD: 820, avenue de Saint-Maur, quartier des Aubes. Tel.: 67.72.52.53.
Weather permitting, the fine cuisine may be enjoyed on a terrace overlooking Le Lez River. If you are forced indoors, the dining room is comfortable but regrettably expensive.

R LE CHANDELIER: 3, rue Leenhardt. Tel.: 67.92.61.62.
Gilbert Furlan and his partner run a good restaurant—perhaps the best in town. One star in Michelin.

R AYAME: 20, place des Martyrs-de-la-Résistance, near the Préfecture. Tel.: 67.60.40.51.
Japanese cooking. If you are looking for a change, the sashimi and tempura are good. In the best culinary tradition of old Japan. Small, limited seating. Preferable to reserve.

SAINT-MARTIN-DE-LONDRES (34380—Hérault)
(Paris 770—Béziers 75—Nîmes 62—Montpellier 25)
Take D-986 north from Montpellier.

HR LA CRÈCHE: Route Frouzet (5 km northwest by D-122). Tel.: 67.55.00.04.   7 rooms.
A quiet oasis of solitude where the food is good and the few rooms are comfortable; set in extensive parkland.

SÈTE (34200—Hérault)
(Paris 781—Béziers 63—Montpellier 29)

R LA PALANGROTTE: 1, rampe Paul-Valéry. Tel.: 67.74.80.35.
Fish specialties.

BÉZIERS (34500—Hérault)
(Paris 835—Marseille 227—Perpignan 93—Montpellier 67—Narbonne 27)

☙ Béziers is a wine town of ordinary bulk wine. It was discovered and recognized by Julius Caesar and his Roman legions.

R L'OLIVIER: 12, rue Boïeldieu. Tel.: 67.28.86.64.
Small restaurant with very good cuisine, carefully prepared. Reservations suggested.

SAINT-PONS-DE-THOMIÈRES (34220—Hérault)
(Béziers 51—Carcassonne 65—Montpellier 120—Narbonne 60—Toulouse 120—Albi 90)

HR CHÂTEAU DE PONDERACH: 1 km on the road to Narbonne. Inland, way off the autoroute. Tel.: 67.97.02.57.   11 rooms.
Old, comfortable private domaine, transformed into a charming inn, in the midst of beautiful mountainous country. *Relais et Châteaux.*

NARBONNE (11100—Aude)
(Paris 850—Montpellier 92—Perpignan 62—Carcassonne 56—Béziers 27)

HR MAPOTEL DU LANGUEDOC: 22, boulevard Gambetta. Tel.: 68.65.14.74. Tlx.: 505167. 45 rooms (29 toilets).
This old hotel has been somewhat modernized. Centrally located, so it can be noisy. Smallish rooms. Restaurant offers reasonably priced, straightforward menus. If you must stay here, remember the old saying that in the world of the blind, the one-eyed man is king.

H NOVOTEL: 3 km outside of town, near Narbonne-Sud autoroute exit. Tel.: 68.41.59.52. Tlx.: 500480. 96 air-conditioned rooms.
Functionally comfortable, clean, modern rooms. Snack bar. Swimming pool.

R LE RÉVERBÈRE: 4, place des Jacobins. Tel.: 68.32.29.18.
Good, large portions, beautifully prepared by a sincere, dedicated chef, Claude Giraud, who will go far. Take the *ménu dégustation,* which is very reasonably priced, and a Corbières coming from the nearby vineyards. One star in Michelin.

R LE FLORIDE: 66, boulevard Frédéric Mistral, near railroad station. Tel.: 68.32.05.52.
Although the restaurant is disregarded by guidebooks, I have had *cassoulet* here unsurpassed by any, and matchless *perdreaux au choux*—all prepared by the wife of the host. The owner's independent attitude may have antagonized many (and may have cost him some stars), but I'd be delighted to make a detour to enjoy such cooking at reasonable prices.

R ALSACE: 2, avenue P. Semard, facing the railroad station. Tel.: 68.65.10.24.
My choice would be Le Floride or Le Réverbère (see above), but if there is no room at either, you'll do nicely (for a higher price) with the Alsace and its fish specialties.

HR RELAIS DU VAL D'ORBIEU: At Ornaisons (14 km on D-24). Tel.: 68.27.10.27. 17 rooms.
Quiet setting, elegant, comfortable in a park with swimming pool. This converted mill is quite out of the way. One would hope that the restaurant measures up to the hotel.

PORT-BARCARÈS (66420—Pyrénées-Orientales)
(Paris 915—Narbonne 60—Perpignan 20)
Perpignan-Nord exit from Autoroute.

H HÔTEL LYDIA-PLAYA: 4 km south on D-90. Tel.: 68.86.25.25. Tlx.: 500837. 192 air-conditioned rooms. Swimming pool. Tennis.
A large beach complex facing the ocean on one side and the inlet on the other. Two-thirds of the rooms have been sold as condominiums, but a number may be rented. Generally comfortable and functional. Nearby is the casino, built on a marooned ship called the *Lydia.* Fairly expensive.

PERPIGNAN (66000—Pyrénées-Orientales)
(Barcelona 186—Carcassonne 107—Béziers 93—Narbonne 62—
Montpellier 152—Toulouse 204)

HR PARC HÔTEL and RESTAURANT CHAPON FIN: 18, boulevard Jean Bourrat. Tel.: 68.35.14.14. 67 air-conditioned rooms.
Reasonably priced rooms and a fairly good restaurant.

HR LE MAS DES ARCADES: Avenue d'Espagne, Route du Perthus. Tel.: 68.85.11.11. Tlx.: 500176. 128 air-conditioned rooms.
South of town. Modern hotel with comfortable rooms around a swimming pool. Just-adequate restaurant.

H NOVOTEL: 10 km north of Perpignan, at intersection N-9 and N-9E. Tel.: 68.64.02.22 or 68.35.36.22. Tlx.: 500851. 85 air-conditioned rooms.
Snack bar. Swimming pool. The usual standard modern comfort of a Novotel hotel.

R FESTIN DE PIERRE: 7, rue du Théâtre. Tel.: 68.51.28.74.
Some claim this conservatively decorated restaurant to be the best in town.

R FRANÇOIS VILLON: 1, rue du Four-Saint-Jean (near cathedral). Tel.: 68.51.18.43.
In the authentic setting of an old house, this is a fairly good restaurant with reasonable prices.

R LES ANTIQUAIRES: Place Depres. Tel.: 68.34.06.58.
Good cooking, reasonably priced.

CARCASSONNE (11000—Aude)
(Perpignan 110—Toulouse 91—Béziers 78—Narbonne 56)

This fortified town, with its ramparts, crenellated walls, and towers, is a great tourist site. (See page 324.)

H TERMINUS: 2, avenue Maréchal Joffre. Tel.: 68.25.25.00. Tlx.: 500198. 110 rooms (88 with toilet).
Near station. No restaurant. You can find better in Carcassonne, especially at the Domaine d'Auriac.

HR CITÉ: Place Église. Tel.: 68.25.03.34. Tlx.: 500829. 54 rooms.
Medieval-style hotel with comfortable rooms, many of which command a view of the ramparts; beautifully located in the very heart of the old city.

HR DOMAINE D'AURIAC: 4 km southeast by D-104 Saint-Hilaire road to Auriac. Tel.: 68.25.72.22. Tlx.: 500385. 23 rooms, including 2 suites.
Beautiful nineteenth-century house with comfortable rooms. Reasonably priced. Large park with swimming pool and tennis. Good restaurant. If you can get one of the better rooms, this is the best stopover. *Relais et Châteaux.*

HR LOGIS DE TRENCAVEL: 290, avenue du Général Leclerc. Tel.: 68.71.09.53. 12 simple rooms.
Although criticized by some, Trencavel has a good restaurant. Try the *cassoulet,* the dish considered a specialty from Toulouse to Narbonne.

R AUBERGE DU PONT-LEVIS: Near La Porte Narbonnaise. Tel.: 68.25.55.23.
Fair restaurant with a view of the old city from the terrace.

HR MONTSÉGUR: 1, avenue Bunau-Varilla. Tel.: 68.25.31.41. 21 rooms.

R LE LANGUEDOC: 32, allée d'Iena. Tel.: 68.25.22.17.
Nineteenth-century house, well furnished. The Languedoc offers meals at decent prices.

PROVENCE

Over the centuries, across customs and cultures, few places in the world have had the magic appeal of Provence. For generations it has sparked the imagination as the land of sunlit pastel water and sky, towering cliff-top villages and red clay soil. Long before the days of the paid vacation and the paved highway, Frenchman and foreigner alike journeyed in body and spirit to the beaches of the Riviera or the hill towns behind Saint-Tropez and Nice to restore themselves. Only a few generations ago, the Riviera was a winter rather than a summer resort, and in the thin rays of the November sun Russian grand dukes and the other international nobility sought relief from the colder north. Even then, there was an element of snobbery in the Côte d'Azur vacation.

The appeal remains today, for the Riviera is still the world's playground, enticing vacationers with the image of beaches famous for their carefree toplessness, casinos, and discothèques of every description. As a wine region, for all its 25,000 hectares of vines (63,100 acres), there is not much to it. Three-quarters of the wines of Provence are rosé, most from the newly created *appellation contrôlée,* Côtes de Provence. Though Provence is more a state of mind than an identifiable region, for the purposes of wine geography it has been confined to the rough triangle formed by Aix-en-Provence, Toulon, and Cannes. Even though the "Côtes de Provence" name might have you believe that the vine grows everywhere from Marseille to Italy, in fact, the better wines end just beyond Saint-Raphaël, scarcely halfway to the border.

From whatever corner they come, the wines of Provence, with a few rare exceptions, are meant to complement the beauty of the country, not rival it. The abundant rosés, when well made, should be dry and with no orangish cast. Drunk in the first year after the harvest, they are pleasing to behold and eminently unserious but, unfortunately for some, too alcoholic. A chilled bottle of Provençal rosé is at its best when served at an early evening meal on the restaurant terrace in Saint-Tropez or at a picnic in the foothills beyond Grasse. With the Niçoise onion tart called *pissaladière,* the Marseillais *bouillabaisse* found throughout Provence, the garlic-and-herb soup called *aigo bouïdo,* whose curative powers have passed into legend, or the garlic-laced vegetable fantasy *ratatouille,* any wines with more pretensions than those from Provence would be overwhelmed.

For the traveler, the wine drinker, or anyone else interested in the culture and history of Provence, it all begins at Aix, the ancient capital of the province. The city was established as Aquae Sextiae a century before Christ by the Roman consul Sextius, who was attracted to the health-giving warm springs he found there—still the source of the fountains in the Cours Mirabeau. The Cours is one of France's great boulevards, lined in cathedral-like perfection with immense plane trees that shade the sidewalk cafés and the summer strollers who pass by. Since being overtaken commercially by Marseille in the nineteenth century, Aix has made its mark in the arts, and now holds a yearly summer music festival. The town's artistic connection dates from long before the festival. Just east from Aix, scarcely 10 kilometers (6 miles) on D-17, is Mont Sainte-Victoire, where Aix's great son Paul Cézanne made his home and studio in his later years and where, in the stark, hilly countryside, he found the landscapes of his final works. This hill country of Provence is as beautiful today as it was in Cézanne's time. It has the barren and austere beauty of chalky white escarpments that break out of the reddish earth terrain. The character and aspect of the country change constantly with the movement of the sun and the mood of the season.

This country also happens to be a vast region of wine. The former V.D.Q.S. *appellations* (*Vins Délimités de Qualité Supérieure*) of Coteaux d'Aix-en-Provence and Coteaux des Baux-de-Provence, now A.O.C.'s, stretch along thousands of hectares from the village of Baux to beyond Aix. The wines are mostly simple rosés, with a few unexceptional whites and reds. The hilltop village of Les Baux-de-Provence is better known for its three-star restaurant, Oustaù de Baumanière, run by Raymond Thuilier and his nephew, who are pillars of French gastronomy. Nevertheless, the Coteaux des Baux received, in 1986, the accolade of becoming an *appellation contrôlée* for twelve growths.

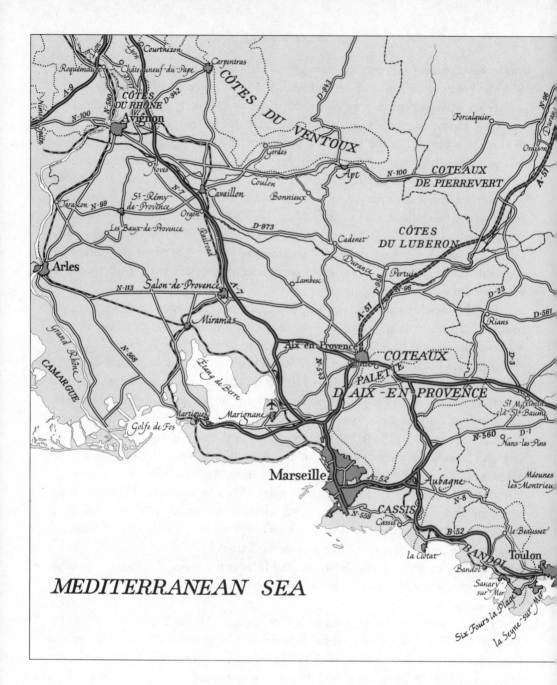

One property that has emerged from the Coteaux d'Aix-en-Provence in the past decade is Château Vignelaure, 32 kilometers (19 miles) northeast of Aix, in Rians. Vignelaure's 55 hectares (135 acres) of vines are run by the ex-realtor George Brunet, who first came on the wine scene in the fifties when he built the Haut-Médoc

334

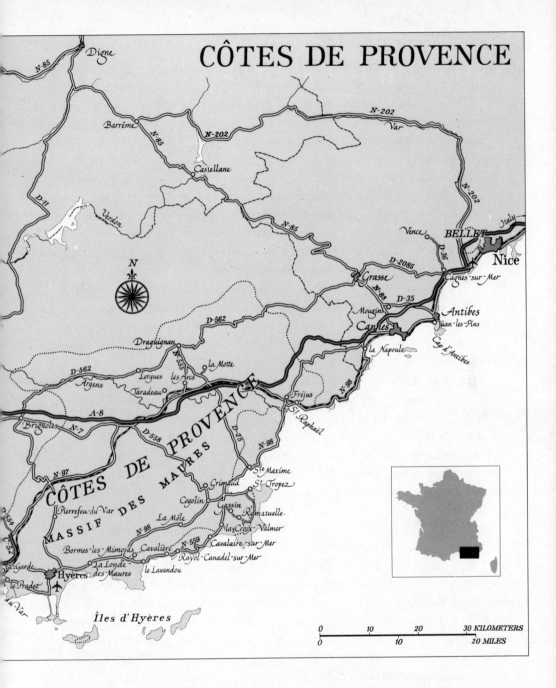

CÔTES DE PROVENCE

vineyard La Lagune into a top growth. Once La Lagune was back on its feet, he sold it and moved to Provence, armed with some Cabernet Sauvignon vines and good business know-how. Now his 20,000-case production of red wine, made from a blend of Cabernet Sauvignon and the preferred local grapes, Grenache and Syrah, can be

335

found in some of the best restaurants of the region and elsewhere in France. Unfortunately for M. Brunet, the I.N.A.O.'s 1976 decision to upgrade the Côtes de Provence from a V.D.Q.S. to an *Appellation Contrôlée* did not improve the standing of Château Vignelaure, which lies outside the Côtes de Provence. But, through great expenditure and hard work, Brunet's vineyard has acquired a standing of its own, and in 1986 became itself an *appellation contrôlée*.

Nearly as extensive as the Coteaux d'Aix-en-Provence are the bordering Coteaux du Lubéron, which specialize more in hearty reds in the style of the Côtes du Rhône, and the Coteaux de Pierrevert. Most of these wines are sold through the local grocery stores or as the house wine in moderately priced restaurants.

To the south of Aix, not far from Cézanne's hillside retreat, is the tiny *appellation* of Palette. There are only two growers to divide the 12 hectares (30 acres) of vines and 4,000 cases of wine between them. The larger and better known of the two is Château Simone, whose scarce bottles may be found in the better restaurants of the area, but not far beyond. Already the autoroute that sweeps down from Paris to the seaside resorts has cut into the Palette vineyards considerably, and the suburbanization of the countryside from Aix continues seemingly unabated.

After skirting Palette, the Autoroute du Soleil quickly takes you the 30 kilometers or so (18 miles south) to Marseille, world capital of *pastis* and *bouillabaisse*. It is this latter gift to the world that is really worth investigating. No two restaurateurs will agree about what goes into a *bouillabaisse* to make it authentic. The local rockfish called *rascasse*, garlic, saffron, and other herbs are essential, but beyond that all is individual finesse and genius. Every other restaurant around the city's Old Port offers its own genuine *bouillabaisse*, which, when well made, can be the best seafood soup in the world.

Though Marseille is not in the vineyards, the vineyards of Cassis and Bandol —homes, respectively, of the best whites and the best reds of Provence—are not far to the east down N-559. They are not typical wine towns because their activity is still concentrated on their seaports and fishing. In Cassis, for instance, the locals are more interested in the connoisseurship of their fine fish and shellfish than in the nuances of their white, red, and rosé wines. A visitor to Cassis finds it hard to imagine that there are 150 hectares (375 acres) of vineyard on the hillsides just outside of town. Like so many of the better Provence vineyards, those of Cassis are protected from the cold, dry winds of the mistral by a screen of hills. Here it happens to be the great Cap Canaille cliff, just to the east of town (on D-41a). It not only helps to shield the vineyard, but also offers an impressive view of the surrounding hills and the bay.

A half-hour's pretty drive along the coast road through La Ciotat brings you to

Bandol, the best-known specific Appellation Contrôlée wine of Provence. Bandol is better known than Palette, Cassis, and Bellet simply because there is more of it than the other three A.O.C. wines put together. Compared to any other wine region in France, however, the output is minuscule: 200 growers scattered throughout the craggy hills behind the port town make about 60,000 cases of red wine a year, and a bit more rosé—only 30 or 40 of the growers bother to vinify and bottle their wines themselves. Three of the better known of the region are Domaine Tempier, Château des Pradeaux, and Domaine de Val d'Arenc, all specializing in Bandol red wine. Of all the Provence reds, the Bandols are the hardiest; they can take from three to six years in bottle before they are ready to drink.

But Bandol, Cassis, Palette, and Bellet (from the hills of Nice), though A.O.C. wines, are not typical of the wine picture of Provence. Much more typical by their vineyard area and the amount they produce are the wines of the new *appellation,* Côtes de Provence. The heart of the best of these wines begins not far beyond Bandol, at Toulon, and stretches 80 kilometers (48 miles) like a half-moon across the rugged Maures vineyard plateau to Saint-Raphaël, with Saint-Tropez nearly in the middle.

If you ask any grower from the wine villages in the Maures why his wines are better than those in other regions, he'll probably tell you it is because his vines are planted on the seaward slope, protected from the mistral winds that blow from the north. To travel through this country you can choose the high road past Draguignan, the commercial wine capital of the region, or the low road along the coast, through the seaside resort towns. Draguignan is in the midst of some of the better wine villages, such as les Arcs, which has the Château Sainte-Roseline; Taradeau, with Château de Selle and Domaine de Saint-Martin; and Lorgues, with Castel-Roubin and Clos du Relais.

The low road is definitely the one to take if you're interested in color, scenery, and fun, because it takes you to Saint-Tropez.

Who would have thought that a resort town as colorfully pleasure-bound as Saint-Tropez would be "capital" to some of the best Côtes de Provence wines? Long before Brigitte Bardot and others put it on the map, Saint-Tropez was cited by wine writers as the center for the best Provence reds and rosés. Practically within hearing distance of the discothèques and motorboats of the Saint-Tropez gulf, vines are cultivated along the hills, producing some surprisingly good wine, most of it rosé. These are supple, extremely drinkable, uncomplicated wines, a shade less alcoholic than some of the other wines of Provence. There is a combination of grape varieties—Mourvèdre, Cinsault, and Grenache, which are the basic grape varieties, with limited quantities of Carignan, Syrah, Tibouren, and a grape called Pecoui-Touar.

The Mourvèdre usually contributes body in Bandol; here its earmarks are harmony and elegance. A stone's throw behind Saint-Tropez is one of the better *domaines,* the Château de Minuty, on the road that climbs from Saint-Tropez to Gassin.

Saint-Tropez itself, traffic-bound in summer, remains for all its touristy glitter, an unusually charming and busy town filled with cafés, boutiques from the Parisian *couturiers,* and enough night life to satisfy any appetite. Saint-Tropez's Pampelone and Tahiti beaches have made topless bathing a fixture of the summer scene for more than a decade.

After you find space in the huge parking lots near the waterfront, where thousands of showy yachts are moored, you can stroll uphill to Place Carnot to watch the *boules* players in their nightly tournaments.

In addition to Château Sainte-Roseline, Château de Selle, Domaine de Saint-Martin, Castel-Roubin, and Clos du Relais, other well-known *domaines* of the region are Domaine de Saint-Maur at Cogolin; Domaine de l'Aumerade, Domaine de la Grande Loube, and Domaine de la Clapière at Hyères; Clos Mireille, Domaine du Galoupet, and Domaine de la Source at La Londe-les-Maures; Domaine Rimaurescq at Pignan; Domaine de la Croix at la Croix-Valmer; Coteau-du-Ferrage at Pierrefeu-du-Var; Domaine de Moulières at la Valette-du-Var; Clos Cibonne at Le Pradet; Domaine de Brégançon and Domaine de Noyer at Bormes; Clos de la Bastide-Verte at La Garde; Domaine-du-Jas-d'Esclans at La Motte; and Domaine de Mauvanne at Les Salins d'Hyères. One of the best cooperatives is at Saint-Tropez, selling its wine under the name Les Maîtres Vignerons de la Presqu'île de Saint-Tropez. The well-known broker M. Bagnis, at Pierrefeu, sells under the name L'Estadon.

The attractions and seductions of this coastline continue through Sainte-Maxime, and Saint-Raphaël, up to La Napoule (with its three-star restaurant, l'Oasis), where the Côtes de Provence officially ends, and on through Cannes, Antibes, Nice, and Monte Carlo. From the hills behind these famous beach towns there are no noteworthy wines, with the possible exception of tiny Bellet, near Nice—for all the distinction of being one of Provence's five Appellation Contrôlée wines, Bellet's five thousand cases of reds, whites, and rosés are overpriced and not all that distinctive. For the most part, the hill country behind these glamorous resort towns produces rather poor and short-lived rosés.

Of far greater attraction are the innumerable restaurants and bistros that dot the coastline and the inland hill country as well. To attempt a complete list of any kind would be impossible but, just the same, mention should be made of Roger Vergé's Moulin de Mougins, at Mougins. In addition to charming restaurants, this rolling countryside above Nice, around Grasse, is filled with lavender and other flowers which provide the essential oils used in perfumes. More than two dozen perfume manufacturers have their factories here. In nearby Nice and Antibes, flowers are put to a more immediate use at the colorful and sweet-scented flower market, where cut flowers from the hothouses of Antibes and the surrounding countryside are sold.

✑

PROVENCE
Hotels and Restaurants

H = *Hotel;* R = *Restaurant*

Decades of intense tourism have provided Provence with innumerable hotels and restaurants— out of proportion, certainly, with the stature of its wines. Because vacationers to this corner of France are often more interested in beaches, scenery, and night life than in their accommodations or meals—and because they are a captive clientele—the general gastronomic standard of the area has suffered in comparison to that in other regions of France.

Besides covering the Côtes de Provence vineyard area, this hotel-restaurant list offers a small selection from beyond the vineyard area. In additon to these, there are many to choose from in Cannes, Antibes, Nice, Èze, Beaulieu, and Monte Carlo. For the region around Avignon, see also the hotel-restaurant list of the Côtes du Rhone. For the area surrounding Nîmes, consult the listings for Languedoc-Roussillon.

There is excellent air service to Nice, which has the most important airport in France after Paris. Start your visit either from the Nice airport or from Marignane, the airport at Marseille.

GORDES (84220—Vaucluse)
(Apt 20—Avignon 38—Carpentras 34)

R LES BORIES: Route de l'Abbaye de Sénanque (2 km northwest by D-177). Tel.: 90.72.00.51.   3 rooms, 2 luxurious.

A charming restaurant at the foot of the Mont Ventoux hills. Close to the old Château de Gordes with its fabulous collection of paintings by Vasarely, considered to be one of France's best modern artists. You will regret neither the food nor the view, nor the visit to the Château de Gordes museum. Rather expensive. One star in Michelin.

SAINT-RÉMY-DE-PROVENCE (13210—Bouches-du-Rhône)
(Paris 708—Marseille 91—Nîmes 41—Arles 24—Avignon 21—Salon-de-Provence 37)
From Avignon take N-570 south. On A-7, exit Castillon, then D-99.

🙚 Charming Roman town. Beautifully preserved Roman ruins. Worth a detour.

HR HOSTELLERIE DU VALLON DE VALRUGUES: Chemin de Cante Cigalo by D-99. Tel.: 90.92.04.40. Tlx.: 431677.   24 rooms and 10 suites.
Agreeable hotel in garden, with heated swimming pool. Tennis.

HR AUBERGE DE LA REINE JEANNE: 12, boulevard Mirabeau. Tel.: 90.92.15.33.   10 rooms.
Reasonably priced restaurant and reasonable rooms in a pleasant setting.

HR LE CASTELET DES ALPILLES: 6, place Mireille. Tel.: 90.92.07.21.   19 rooms (13 toilets).
Charming and good without pretense. Restaurant available.

HR CHÂTEAU DES ALPILLES: on D-31. Tel.: 90.92.03.33. Tlx.: 431487.   21 good rooms (15 toilets) plus 1 suite. Pool. Tennis.
Transformed nineteenth-century château in the midst of a park. No restaurant, but in summer a short broiled menu can be had around the swimming pool.

LES BAUX-DE-PROVENCE (13520—Bouches-du-Rhône)
(Marseille 86—Nîmes 44—Avignon 31—Arles 19—Saint-Rémy-de-Provence 9—
Aix-en-Provence 65—Salon-de-Provence 32)
Exit at Cavaillon on A-7.

🙚 Strange, beautiful site. This village contributed bauxite, which was discovered nearby at the beginning of the nineteenth century and which started the aluminum industry throughout the world. The quarries surrounding the village also contributed a softish stone liked by sculptors, but this nest of tranquillity is mainly known today for its hub of gastronomy.

HR OUSTAÙ DE BAUMANIÈRE. Tel.: 90.54.33.07. Tlx.: 420203.   15 air-conditioned, comfortable rooms, 11 suites. Pool, park, and tennis.
Expensive. Raymond Thuilier has made this charming, elegant inn into one of France's chapels of gastronomy. Were L'Oustaù de Baumanière to disappear, the fame of Les Baux-de-Provence, charming as it is, would evaporate. Fine wine list. *Relais et Châteaux.* It is most deserving of its three stars in Michelin.

HR LA CABRO D'OR: Tel.: 90.54.33.21. Tlx.: 401810.   22 rooms. Pool. Tennis.
Same management as Oustaù de Baumanière, but less pretentious and less expensive.

340

R LA RIBOTO DE TAVEN: Tel.: 90.97.34.23.
Good, reasonably priced restaurant, which offers a warm welcome and pleasant surroundings.
One star in Michelin.

SALON-DE-PROVENCE (13300—Bouches-du-Rhône)
(Aix-en-Provence 36—Avignon 46—Marseille 55—Arles 42—Nîmes 71)

❧ In the midst of olive groves, Salon boasts of many medieval curiosities, not the least of which is that Michel Nostradamus lived and died here in the sixteenth century as a healer whose successful secret medicines during the epidemics in Aix and Lyon brought him the jealousy of his colleagues. During his retirement he switched from medicine to astrology, which brought him new fame. Catherine de' Medici requested him to make horoscopes for Charles IX, as well as for most of her entourage.

HR ABBAYE DE SAINTE CROIX: 5 km northeast from Salon-de-Provence, exit from A-7 by D-16, on road to Val-de-Cuech. Tel.: 90.56.24.55. Tlx.: 401247.   22 rooms and 4 suites.
Well-restored old abbey with agreeable, well-decorated rooms. Swimming pool. Simple food at high prices. Marvelous view of rolling hills. *Relais et Châteaux.*

HR MERCURE: 9 km south off A-7 after Lançon. Tel.: 90.53.90.70. Tlx.: 440183.   100 air-conditioned rooms. 20 minutes from the Marignane Airport of Marseille. Heated pool.
On the expensive side. Restaurant available for dinner only.

AIX-EN-PROVENCE (13100—Bouches-du-Rhône)
(Avignon 80—Marseille 31—Nîmes 105—Manosque 53—Toulon 81—Apt 55—
Aubagne 36—Arles 76—Brignoles 57—Nice 175)

❧ For a description of this colorful town, see page 333.

HR NOVOTEL AIX-SUD: 3 km on the Aix-Est exit of A-8 on the périphérique sud, avenue Arc-de-Meyran. Tel.: 42.27.90.49. Tlx.: 420517.   80 functional, comfortable, air-conditioned rooms.
Snacks and simple menus. Pool.

HR NOVOTEL AIX-EST: Résidence Beaumanoir; off Aix-Est exit from A-8. Tel.: 42.27.47.50. Tlx.: 400244.   100 air-conditioned rooms.
Snacks and simple menus. A functional stopover.

HR MAS D'ENTREMONT: At Celony (3 km from Aix, northwest on N-7). Tel.: 42.23.45.32. 9 rooms and 7 bungalows.
An old manor-house in the midst of a beautiful park. Well-furnished, with pool and tennis. The food is well served but average.

H LE NÈGRE COSTE: 33, cours Mirabeau. Tel.: 42.27.74.22. Tlx.: 440184.   36 rooms (30 with toilet).
A centrally located hotel, very comfortable and reasonably priced. No restaurant.

R CAVES HENRI IV: Le Clos de la Violette, 10, avenue de la Violette, Tel.: 42.23.30.71.
Reasonably priced menus are conceived by young Jean-Pierre Banzo and Brigitte, his smiling wife. This air-conditioned cellar restaurant has been given one star in Michelin and is said to be the best in town.

341

NANS-LES-PINS (83860—Var)
(Aix-en-Provence 42—Brignoles 26—Toulon 65—Marseille 41)

HR DOMAINE DE CHÂTEAUNEUF: 3.5 km north by D-80 and N-560. Tel.: 94.78.90.06. Tlx.: 400747. 30 very comfortable rooms, plus 4 suites. Tennis.
Charming eighteenth-century *gentilhommière provençale*. In the midst of a huge park, surrounded by vineyards. Fairly good food, served on a terrace if weather permits. Heated swimming pool. *Relais et Châteaux.*

COTIGNAC (83570—Var)
(North of Toulon 70—north of Brignoles 24—west of Draguignan 36—
Saint-Raphaël 66—Sainte-Maxime 68)
Exit A-8 at Brignoles.

HR LOU CALEN: 1, cours Gambetta. Tel.: 94.04.60.40. 8 rooms. 8 small suites.
Lovely Provençal-style building. Park and swimming pool. Quite good meals, in comfortable setting, and at good prices. With all of the attractive places in Provence, this seems like a very big detour off the autoroute.

BRIGNOLES (83170—Var)
(Aix-en-Provence 57—Cannes 98—Draguignan 53—Toulon 50—
Marseille 64—Aubagne 47—Barjols 22—Le Luc 22)
On A-8.

HR L'ABBAYE DE LA CELLE: At La Celle, 2 km south of Brignoles, taking the D-554 and D-405 on the road to Toulon. (This is a small detour.) Tel.: 94.69.08.44. 33 rooms.
In the midst of a quiet park, this old abbey with well-furnished rooms is a charming stopover. Good service. The rooms are better than the food.

BANDOL (83150—Var)
(Draguignan 98—Aix-en-Provence 74—Marseille 51—Toulon 17)
When traveling on A-8, exit at Toulon-le-Canet going south and Gardanne when going north.
When on A-50 between Marseilles and Toulon, exit at Bandol.

Bandol claims to have 320 sunny days a year. Perhaps this is why the surrounding hills yield the best red wines of Provence.

HR PLM ÎLE ROUSSE: 17, boulevard Louis-Lumière. Tel.: 94.29.46.86. Tlx.: 400372. 53 very comfortable air-conditioned rooms and 2 suites.
Pleasant, expensive, with private beach in the port. Excellent service and seafood. The lobster is as expensive as the best room.

R AUBERGE DU PORT: 9, allées Jean-Moulin. Tel.: 94.29.42.63.
Intimate, pleasant restaurant. Good seafood but high prices.

HR SOUKANA: Île de Bendor. 8 minutes by special craft. Pool. Tennis.
Soukana and the Delos are two small hotels, the first having 50 rooms, the second 55. Supposedly

built by the King of Pastis, the strong aperitif so popular in southern France, Soukana claims to be a great center for scuba-diving. I cannot recommend either place, as I have never been to the island of Bendor.

LE LAVANDOU (83980—Var)
(Cannes 104—Draguignan 78—Sainte-Maxime 43—Toulon 49—
Hyères 23—Saint-Tropez 38)

HR ROCHES FLEURIES: At Aiguebelle-Plage (5.5 km northeast). Tel.: 94.71.05.07. Tlx.: 403997. 48 air-conditioned rooms. Pool.
Good food on a terrace overlooking the beach.

H L'ORANGERAIE: At Saint-Clair (3 km by N-559). Tel.: 94.71.04.25. 19 air-conditioned rooms and 3 suites.
No restaurant. Modern and functional hotel owned by Mme Marcellin.

R AU VIEUX PORT: Quai Gabriel-Péri. Tel.: 94.71.00.21.
If you like fish, bouillabaisse, lobster, and good desserts, this good, rather expensive seafood restaurant is recommended. One star in Michelin.

CAVALIÈRE (83980—Var)
(Draguignan 71—Le Lavandou 8—Hyères 30—Cannes 92—
Sainte-Maxime 35—Toulon 48—Saint-Tropez 31)
Not to be confused with Cavalaire-sur-mer further east

HR LE CLUB: Plage de Cavalière. Entrance by D-559. Tel.: 94.05.80.14. Tlx.: 420317. 26 air-conditioned rooms and 6 suites.
A luxurious hotel. The demi-pension is mandatory in season. Private beach. Expensive, but the comfort of the rooms and the good food are well worth it. Beautiful pool. Tennis. One star in Michelin.

LE RAYOL (83240—Var)
(Cavalaire 7—Le Lavandou 14—Saint-Tropez 25—Sainte-Maxime 29—
Toulon 54—Hyères 36—Draguignan 65)

HR BAILLI DE SUFFREN: Plage du Rayol. Tel.: 94.71.35.77. Tlx.: 420535. 50 very comfortable rooms.
Facing the sea, on the beach. Beautiful sea views. Hospitable.

RAMATUELLE (83350—Var)
(Brignoles 66—Draguignan 53—Hyères 54—Le Lavandou 37—
Sainte-Maxime 17—Saint-Tropez 10—Toulon 79)

H HOSTELLERIE DU BAOU. Tel.: 94.79.20.48. Tlx.: 461516. 20 air-conditioned rooms.
Pretty Provençal house, comfortable rooms with a good view over a village full of charm. Terrace and garden overlooking the sea.

SAINT-TROPEZ (83990—Var)
(Draguignan 50—Toulon 69—Sainte-Maxime 14—Aix-en-Provence 120—
Brignoles 63—Cannes 75—Saint-Raphaël 37—Marseille 133)

HR BYBLOS: Avenue Paul-Signac. Tel.: 94.97.00.04. Tlx.: 470235.   70 air-conditioned rooms.
The rooms and suites are in a group of houses forming a village which is fashionable, swinging,
and expensive. One star in Michelin.

HR RÉSIDENCE DE LA PINÈDE. Tel.: 94.97.04.21. Tlx.: 470489.   35 large air-conditioned rooms,
5 suites.
On the beach that calls itself the Bouillabaisse (1 km from town): luxurious, expensive.

R LES MAURES: 4, rue Docteur Boutin. Tel.: 94.97.01.50.
When it specialized in seafood it was more popular than today. Still a meeting place, may be the
best restaurant in town. Good but expensive.

R LEÏ MOUSCARDINS: 16, rue Portalet. Tel.: 94.97.01.53. At the end of the harbor.
Fairly good, expensive, uneven food.

GRIMAUD (83310—Var)
(Brignoles 53—Draguignan 46—Hyères 45—Le Lavandou 33—
Sainte-Maxime 13—Saint-Tropez 10—Toulon 63)

R LES SANTONS: Route Nationale. Tel.: 94.43.21.02.
Very good and expensive. Was the best restaurant in Saint-Tropez area. During the season you
must reserve days ahead and fight the Saint-Tropez traffic to enjoy Claude Girard's imaginative
innovations, which are served in a beautiful house decorated in a typically Provençal manner.
One star in Michelin. *Traditions et Qualité.*

SAINTE-MAXIME (83120—Var)
(Aix-en-Provence 127—Saint-Tropez 14—Cannes 61—Toulon 73—
Draguignan 36—Saint-Raphaël 23—Fréjus 21)

R LA GRUPPI: Avenue Charles-de-Gaulle. Tel.: 94.96.03.61.
Seafood specialties.

DRAGUIGNAN (83300—Var)
(Aix-en-Provence 106—Antibes 72—Cannes 65—Fréjus 29—Grasse 56—
Nice 90—Toulon 81—Marseille 118—Saint-Raphaël 33)

R LA CALÈCHE: 7, boulevard Gabriel-Péri, near the railway station. Tel.: 94.68.13.97.
If you take the regular menu, both the quality and the price will please.

FRÉJUS (83600—Var)
(Brignoles 63—Sainte-Maxime 21—Marseille 130—Cannes 40—Draguignan 29—
Hyères 76—Saint-Raphaël 4—Grasse 53—Saint-Tropez 35)

HR LE VIEUX FOUR: 57, rue Grisolle. Tel.: 94.51.56.38.   8 rooms.
Reasonably priced menus.

SAINT-RAPHAËL (83700—Var)
(Draguignan 33—Marseille 134—Toulon 96—Aix-en-Provence 119—Cannes 43)

HR LA RIVIERA: 12, rue Charabois. Tel.: 94.95.23.18. 7 rooms.
Young chef prepares reasonably priced menus.

An exception must be made on the insistence of many who, having visited the vineyards of France, also wish to enjoy the Riviera. I have therefore added these pages for the sake of completing the guide section, rather than adding them to the wine section.

LA NAPOULE (06210—Alpes-Maritimes)
(Cannes 8—Grasse 28—Saint-Raphaël 34—Nice 40—Paris 900)

R L'OASIS: Rue Honoré Carle. Tel.: 93.49.95.52.
The imaginative and creative Louis Outhier, called a classic by some, is so used to a complete array of stars in *all* the guidebooks that it seems redundant to mention the three stars awarded his expensive restaurant by Michelin.

CANNES (06400—Alpes Maritimes)
(Grasse 17—Nice 33—Fréjus 40—Monte Carlo 58—Draguignan 61—
Toulon 123—Marseille 155—Grenoble 316—Paris 901)

Whatever the distance, millions gravitate to this playground of the Riviera. Irrespective of where you stay during the film festival, it is a madhouse, but in quieter periods you can enjoy good accommodations, good food, and a bizarre array of characters.

HR LE MAJESTIC: 6, La Croisette. Tel.: 93.68.91.00. Tlx.: 470787. 250 air-conditioned rooms, 12 suites. Pool.
Large, comfortable rooms, some with balconies facing the sea. It has its private beach and a pool with heated seawater. It combines expense with elegance. Whichever currency you may have, it is very expensive.

HR LE CARLTON: 58, La Croisette. Tel.: 93.68.91.68. Tlx.: 470720. 295 air-conditioned rooms, 30 suites.
Totally modernized, in the middle of the beach. Has been the standard of elegant living in this pleasure-oriented town for decades.

HR GRAY D'ALBION: 38, rue des Serbes. Tel.: 93.68.54.54. Tlx.: 470744. 200 air-conditioned rooms, 14 suites.
Luxurious, elegant, comfortable, modern hotel. The Royal Gray is the best restaurant in town and has been awarded two stars in Michelin. Its coffee shop, with Lebanese and Italian dishes, is open 24 hours a day.

HR MARTINEZ CONCORDE: 73, La Croisette. Tel.: 93.68.91.91. Tlx.: 470708. 385 air-conditioned rooms, 18 suites. Pool.
Luxurious, soundproofed rooms. Its restaurant, La Palme d'Or, has one star in Michelin.

JUAN-LES-PINS (06160—Alpes Maritimes)
(Antibes 2—Cannes 9—Nice 24—Aix-en-Provence 160—Paris 918)

HR JUANA: La Pinède, avenue Gallice. Tel.: 93.61.08.70. Tlx.: 470778.   42 air-conditioned rooms, 5 suites. Heated pool.

Luxurious rooms in a large villa. The Barrache brothers can be rightly proud of the reputation they have earned among Riviera gastronomes. Their restaurant, La Terrasse, has been awarded two stars in Michelin.

ANTIBES (06600—Alpes Maritimes)
(Cannes 11—Grasse 18—Nice 23—Aix-en-Provence 158—Paris 916)

❦ Originally Greek, then Roman. In the twelfth century the Château Grimaldi, a fortified, crenellated castle, was built. It now houses some of the works of Picasso, who in the period of one year in 1946 filled it with paintings, lithographs, drawings, and ceramics. A marineland has recently been built and can be visited 4 km outside of town, on the corner of N-7 and D-4.

HR HÔTEL DU CAP: Boulevard Kennedy. Cap d'Antibes. Tel.: 93.61.39.01. Tlx.: 470763.   100 beautiful, air-conditioned rooms, 10 suites. Pool. Tennis.

Chic luxury, coupled with excellent service under the professional eye of M. Hirondelle. In a park overlooking the Mediterranean. The greatly sought-after Eden Roc on the beach, and its swimming pool for lunch, make this combination the name one could drop, provided one can get in.

R LA BONNE AUBERGE: 5 km north on the N-7 at La Brague. Tel.: 93.33.36.65. Tlx.: 470989.

The Rostang family has gravitated between two and three Michelin stars, some years making the ultimate rating, other years being penalized. La Bonne Auberge now has two stars; perhaps next year they might return to their three-star status. They are one of the top restaurants of the Riviera.

R CHEZ FÉLIX: 50, boulevard Aguillon. Tel.: 93.34.01.64.

This fish specialist, known as Félix au Port, is a colorful place to dine, inside or on the terrace, and to watch bicycle clowns and other street entertainers.

MOUGINS (06250—Alpes Maritimes)
(Vallauris 8—Cannes 7—Grasse 11—Antibes 12—Nice 32—Paris 908)

HR LE MOULIN DE MOUGINS: 424, chemin du Moulin, quartier Notre-Dame-de-Vie. Tel.: 93.75.78.24. Tlx.: 970732.   3 rooms, 2 suites.

From far and near, gastronomic pilgrims come to pay homage to the talents of Roger Vergé. Many also come to be seen and to gawk at the international celebrities who have helped foster the reputation of this marvelous restaurant, featuring a superb wine list. If reservations weeks ahead are necessary for accommodations, it is wise to reserve days ahead for the restaurant. *Traditions et Qualité.* Three stars in Michelin.

R LE RELAIS À MOUGINS: Place de la Mairie, in the old village. Tel.: 93.90.03.47.

The imaginative creativity of André Surmain made him many friends at Lutèce in New York. This charming restaurant is daily making him many admirers in this competitive, sunny world of gastronomy. Relais Gourmand of *Relais et Châteaux.* One star in Michelin.

SAINT-PAUL-DE-VENCE—below Vence (06570—Alpes Maritimes)
(Vence 4—Cagnes-sur-Mer 7—Nice 20—Grasse 22—Cannes 27—Paris 930)

HR LE MAS D'ARTIGNY: Chemin des Salettes. Tel.: 93.32.84.54. Tlx.: 470601.   52 air-conditioned rooms, 29 suites. Pool. Tennis.
On top of a hill, enjoying superb views. René Traversac, owner of Château d'Artigny and other luxuriously restored châteaux transformed into hotels, has received plaudits from his following in bringing this complex, offering apartments with private patio, garden, and pool, to the Riviera. *Relais et Châteaux.* One star in Michelin.

H LA COLOMBE D'OR: 1, place du Général-de-Gaulle. Tel.: 93.32.80.02. Tlx.: 970607.   14 rooms, 8 suites. Pool.
This pretty sight is internationally known for its clientele of French movie celebrities and its collection of Impressionist paintings, stolen and retrieved several times.

VENCE (06140—Alpes Maritimes)
(Antibes 19—Nice 22—Grasse 25—Cannes 30—Paris 930)

HR CHÂTEAU SAINT-MARTIN: Route de Coursegoules. Tel.: 93.58.02.02. Tlx.: 470282.   15 rooms. Pool. Tennis.
Comfortable, quiet site. Service and good food have brought people to seek out the Château Saint-Martin, despite the distance from the sea, as their headquarters on the Riviera.

NICE (06000—Alpes Maritimes)
(Cannes 32—San Remo 66—Aix-en-Provence 176—Marseille 187—
Genoa 194—Turin 220—Lyon 470—Paris 931)

HR NEGRESCO: 37, promenade des Anglais. Tel.: 93.88.39.51. Tlx.: 460040.   140 air-conditioned rooms, 10 suites.
In the past this hotel made news as the most palatial hotel of the Côte d'Azur. It still maintains very high standards today. Its restaurant, the Chantecler, is making gastronomic news. The Gault Millau guide considers it tops in France, awarding it a rating of 19.5 out of 20. Le Bottin Gourmand gives it four stars, its highest rating. And Michelin gives it two stars, which means "excellent cooking, worth a detour."

SAINT-JEAN-CAP-FERRAT (06230—Alpes Maritimes)
(Villefranche 2.5—Nice 11—Monte Carlo 13—Menton 23—Paris 944)

HR GRAND HOTEL DU CAP: Boulevard du Général-de-Gaulle. Tel.: 93.01.04.54. Tlx.: 470184.   58 air-conditioned rooms, 7 suites. Pool. Tennis.
One of the well-known, luxurious hotels along the coast. Its restaurant is very good, with one star in Michelin. I have preferred the Voile d'Or, within walking distance.

HR LA VOILE D'OR: 31, avenue Jean-Mermoz. Tel.: 93.01.13.13. Tlx.: 470317.   46 air-conditioned rooms, 5 suites. Pool.
There is a sense of a relaxed atmosphere in this beautiful site of refined elegance. Good service makes the Voile d'Or not only sought after but also remembered.

BEAULIEU-SUR-MER (06310—Alpes Maritimes)
(Nice 10—Menton 20—Monte Carlo 21—Paris 944)

HR LE MÉTROPOLE: 15, boulevard du Maréchal-Leclerc. Tel.: 93.01.00.08. Tlx.: 470304. 50 air-conditioned rooms, 3 suites. Saltwater pool.
Has always been a cornerstone of quality, but recently has achieved a standing ovation from critics and a long list of customers alike. Previously I would have given an edge vote to La Réserve. Today I would reverse my decision. *Relais et Châteaux*. One star in Michelin.

HR LA RÉSERVE DE BEAULIEU: 5, boulevard du Maréchal-Leclerc. Tel.: 93.01.00.01. Tlx.: 470301. 50 air-conditioned rooms, 3 suites. Pool.
There was a time when I considered this tops of any hotel in existence in food and service on the sea-front. Still very good, La Réserve de Beaulieu has lost a bit of its superb veneer; perhaps some to its neighbor, the Métropole. *Traditions et Qualité*. One star in Michelin.

ÈZE-BORD-DE-MER (06360—Alpes Maritimes)
On the lower Corniche.

(Beaulieu 3—Cap d'Ail 5—Monte Carlo 7—Nice 12—Menton 18—Paris 947)

HR CAP ESTEL: Tel.: 93.01.50.44. Tlx.: 470305. 37 rooms, 9 suites. Pool. Private beach.
Set in a park that juts out to sea, this luxurious hotel in the midst of a flower garden is peaceful and super-comfortable.

ÈZE (06360—Alpes Maritimes)
On the Moyenne Corniche.

(Monte Carlo 8—Nice 12—Menton 18—Paris 946)

HR LA CHÈVRE D'OR: Rue du Barri. Tel.: 93.41.12.12. Tlx.: 970839. 6 rooms, 3 suites. Small pool.
To reach the Chèvre d'Or in this village which is like a medieval eagle's nest, is the epitome of charm. The view from the restaurant is extraordinary, perhaps capturing better than most other places the beauty of the coast and its various levels. *Relais et Châteaux*.

HR LE CHÂTEAU ÈZA: Tel.: 93.41.12.24. Tlx.: 470382. 7 rooms, 2 suites.
If you can stand the climb you get a great memorable view.

MONACO (Principality of)
(Menton 9—Nice 18—San Remo 45—Cannes 51—Marseille 206—Paris 958)

HR HOTEL DE PARIS: Place du Casino, Monte Carlo. Tel.: 93.50.80.80. Tlx.: 469925. 220 rooms, 34 suites. Pool.
A very demanding world clientele has always approved of the comfort of the rooms, many of which overlook the small yachting port of Monte Carlo and the palace beyond. In summer the two restaurants are filled with legendary and larger-than-life characters. The expensive downstairs restaurant is situated in a sumptuous, Empire-style dining room; the grill upstairs, a bit less expensive, enjoys a magnificent view like so many fabulous places along the Riviera. The bar is for

those who want to be seen jabbering in at least five languages and who wish to contemplate mostly aging characters under layers of makeup. One star in Michelin.

ROQUEBRUNE-CAP-MARTIN (06190—Alpes Maritimes)
(Menton 5—Monte Carlo 7—Nice 26—Paris 958)

R LE ROQUEBRUNE: 100, avenue Jean-Jaurès, Corniche Inférieure. Tel.: 93.35.00.16.
It is a pleasant diversion, in August, to enjoy the various fish dishes created by Marine and Laurence Marinovich, served on a beautiful terrace overlooking Cap Martin, to get away from crowded Monte Carlo. One star in Michelin.

THE LESSER WINES
OF FRANCE

The Southwest; the Mountain Country; Corsica

Of the ninety-five departments, including Corsica, that make up France, over eighty produce wine. In the fifty years I've spent traveling the vineyards, buying wines and looking for new ones, I've had the pleasure of rediscovering many of the lesser-known regions that make their own wines. Not all French wines are good and not every *vin de pays* is a good glass of wine, but France does produce more good wine in a greater variety than any other country in the world. Among these lesser wines, I have selected what I feel are the best, in the same way that I selected the best and the most interesting in their class in Bordeaux, Burgundy, and the other main wine regions of France. Most of the wines in this chapter are not exported, many do not even reach Paris, but all the wines discussed can be found in and around the countryside where they are made. It is in the small inns and restaurants of the Savoie that Apremont is truly meant to be appreciated; it is in the mountain cafés of the western Pyrénées southeast of Biarritz that the red wines of Irouléguy will taste their best. Whether they are available in your neighborhood shop or not, these wines will be worth remembering for the day you find yourself on the back roads of the Basque country or in the mountains west of Chamonix.

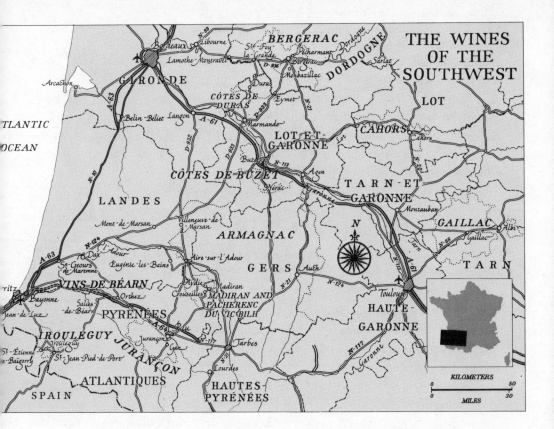

The map labels (part of the image):

THE WINES OF THE SOUTHWEST

What all these regional wines share, whether from the Alps, the Pyrénées, the Jura or the Dordogne, is their "typicalness." When they are well made, they will be what the French would call *typé,* meaning that their character is a distinct and unique expression of the climate, soil, grape variety, and viticultural and vinicultural methods particular to the region in which they are made. It is because these four variables that determine the quality of a wine have become "constant and loyal," as the governing body, the National Institute of Place-names (the I.N.A.O.), puts it, that the wine region will have been granted its own place-name. Among the most recent examples here discussed are Cahors, which moved from V.D.Q.S. classification to a controlled place-name in 1971; Côtes de Buzet, which was granted the same accolade in 1973; and the Minervois, in 1984, and several others in 1985 and 1986.

Because they are so individual, not all of these wines will appeal to all palates. A well-made Cahors, vinified in the method traditional to the region, is a forceful, dark, and rich wine, unmistakably Cahors-like. Though it may not be ambrosia to some, it will deserve respect for its integrity, the way any well-made art object would, whether or not we happen to like the particular period or style. The new

351

methods of vinification throughout France, however, have tended to produce lighter red wines and Cahors is no exception in bending to this new trend.

Whether made by the new methods or the old, the wines from these regions should be less expensive than similar wines from Bordeaux, Burgundy, and the Rhône. If the price and quality are right they will be a good value—a truism perhaps, but value remains the final consideration when buying wine, whether in thousand-case lots or a single bottle at the neighborhood store.

THE SOUTHWEST

The great wine region of the French southwest is, of course, Bordeaux. For its diversity of high-quality wines it is unequaled in the world. Yet the southwest is more than simply the Gironde department. In the Dordogne and Périgord not far to the east are the wines of Bergerac and Cahors. Southeast from Bordeaux are the wines of the Côtes de Duras, then Gaillac; farther south towards Armagnac is Madiran; and in the foothills of the Pyrénées are the wines of the Jurançon, Irouléguy, and Béarn. Lumping these wines together is more a matter of geographical coincidence than deep vinous relationship. What they all share is the recognition from the National Institute of Place-names (I.N.A.O.) that their wines are worthy of individual attention, because they are pure expressions of the soil, microclimate, and grape.

Among these southwestern wines the reds range from the light Madirans to the deep richness of Cahors; the whites can be fruity and dry, such as the unusually good Montravel, or full and sweet, such as the Jurançons and Monbazillacs. Even sparkling wines are represented by the Gaillac *mousseux.* I would argue in fact that in some cases the selection of wines is too broad—very often the dry whites did lack freshness, which spoiled the reputation they are now regaining, the reds age poorly, and the sparkling wines are merely curios. All the regions, however, in all their diversity of character and countryside, are in the process of improving their wine-making and wine-marketing. It is probable, therefore, that as they improve we shall hear more from them in the near future.*

If one were to list the main wines of the Southwest in some order of quality, the list might well start with . . .

---

* A number of restaurants and hotels located in the southwest may be found listed under "Armagnac Hotels and Restaurants," page 406, and in the hotel and restaurant listings in the chapter "Suggested Tours."

CAHORS

When driving westward across France from Bordeaux or Biarritz to the Mediterranean, one usually takes the Toulouse-Carcassonne road (N-113) or the Autoroute A-61. However, one misses a great deal of the beauty of France by not taking the more scenic northerly route through the truffle- and *foie gras*-rich hills around the scenic town of Cahors, the regional capital of viticulture. Like so much of southwestern France after the fall of Roman Gaul, Cahors fell first to the sword of the Visigoths and then, three hundred years later, to Moorish invaders. But whatever its history, since 1971 Cahors has been known to the outside world for its Appellation Contrôlée.

The principal Cahors grape is the Malbec or Cot, known locally as the Auxerrois, formerly widely planted in the Bordeaux area. Alone, it makes a rather inky, dark-looking, full, hard wine, so Merlot, which gives tender, faster-maturing wines, and Jurançon are also planted. The 1,300 hectares (3,250 acres) of vines grow in the old alluvial soils which have formed terraces and little hills inside the steeply banked bends of the scenic River Lot. Cahors's limestone pebbles so cover the fine red earth that the vines, in many places, seem to be growing out of broken stones. These vines produce a wine that is deservedly becoming better known; it is robust and flavorsome, and has a pronounced bouquet. By dedication and hard work one grower, Georges Vigouroux, has done much to enhance the reputation of Cahors wines. Years ago he cleared a stony field and planted his vines, setting about to make the best wine possible from what was available to him. The resulting wines from the 62 stony hectares of the Château de Haute-Serre, 7 km south of Cahors, are not cheap, but Vigouroux deserves special recognition for his enterprise, and for showing the importance of the human element in the making of good wine. Another grower of Cahors, Jean Jouffreau of the Clos de Gamot and the Château de Cayrou, has gained a wide reputation for his collection of old wine stocks. His barrels and bottles of Cahors wine date back fifty years and more, so the claim goes. Since everyone has been tasting from the same barrel for years now, one wonders what he's been topping it up with. A good restaurant at Cahors is Le Balandre. Since 1985 Georges Vigouroux has reopened the luxurious Château de Mercuès at Mercuès, 8 kilometers northeast of Cahors, making Cahors that much more attractive. The main cooperative is in Parnac, 20 km from Cahors, and farther still along the Lot is the fortfied village of Puy l'Evêque, which is another wine center. Other growers and shippers to look for are L. E. Reutenauer, Durou et Fils, and the Château de Chambert.

☙

MADIRAN AND PACHERENC DU VIC BILH

The gentle slopes of the Adour River lead south to the vineyards of Madiran and Pacherenc du Vic Bilh not fifteen minutes' drive from the town of Aire-sur-l'Adour. Also close at hand is the much-talked-about and many-starred hotel-restaurant-spa at Eugénie-les-Bains of Michel and Christine Guérard, who have been credited with inventing the so-called *cuisine minceur,* the gastronomy high in quality but low in calories. How slimming the new cuisine is is debatable, but Les Prés d'Eugénie remains a spot of pilgrimage for those interested in the finesse of the most *haute* of cuisines. It's a little strange that this great bastion of thinness should be in the middle of one of the great *foie gras* centers of France, where the geese and ducks of the Landes line up for their twice and thrice daily *gavage,* or "forced" feeding of corn. (In fact, the geese come running at mealtime.) After months of *gavage,* their overgrown livers become one of the great luxury delicacies, along with caviar and truffles.

Madiran, the red wine of the country, is full-bodied, short to the taste, and one of the best reds of the Pyrénées, which is a limited endorsement. In 1984, the production of Madiran was 400,000 cases. Its pronounced bouquet is due to the local grapes: Tannat, Courbu, Bouchy, and Pinenc. To give the wine a bit of breed, growers have recently been planting Cabernet Sauvignon. Two of the better Madiran producers, who have found the proper balance of these grapes, are Château de Peyros and M. Laplace at Aydie. Pacherenc du Vic Bilh is the white wine from the Madiran region, but it is hard to find today. Both wines, along with the regional *appellation,* Vin de Pays Basque, are to a large extent produced at the cooperatives at Madiran itself on D-43, at Crouseilles just south from Madiran on D-139, and at Diusse on D-13.

☙

CÔTES DE BUZET

The vineyards of Buzet, an Appellation Contrôlée since 1973, are scattered over some 40 km of hillsides to the east of Agen. These red, rosé, and white wines are well vinified by the cooperative of Buzet at Espiens, consisting of 200 growers.

The red grape varieties account for 95 percent of the total production and consist of 50 percent Merlot; the remaining 50 percent is divided between Cabernet Franc and Cabernet Sauvignon. The white wines are made from Sémillon, Sauvignon, and Muscadelle grape varieties. The average production amounts to approximately 40,000 cases a year.

⚓

BERGERAC

Ninety kilometers (54 miles) nearly due east from Bordeaux on the Dordogne is the city of Bergerac, more famous for the legendary character of Cyrano than for its five place-names of red and white wine. The proximity of the Bergerac vineyards to those of Bordeaux and the fact that both regions use the same vines have led to unfortunate comparisons between the two, and even the best of the Bergerac wines find it difficult to lure customers away from Bordeaux. With the possible exception of the sweet white wine of Monbazillac, the wines of the region—sold under the controlled place-names of Montravel, Pécharmant, Rosette, and Bergerac—rarely achieve great distinction.

Monbazillac is grown around the town of the same tongue-twisting name 7 kilometers (4 miles) south of Bergerac. As a sweetish white table wine, Monbazillac never attains the quality or complexities of the better Barsac and Sauternes, but it may be compared to the minor sweet wines of Bordeaux, such as Cérons and Sainte-Croix-du-Mont. Still, Monbazillac has its devotees, and growers find a market for their inexpensive 700,000-case annual production. In France, it remains popular in the home as a sweet aperitif as well as at thousands of town and country fairs, where it is given away as a prize to sharpshooters and ring-tossers.

The city of Bergerac, though dull and quiet today, had a tormented history during the period of English rule in Guyenne (1154–1453). It passed back and forth between French and English hands over the three centuries of occupation and during the Hundred Years' War (1337–1453). The taking of Bergerac in 1450 marked the beginning of the end of the English presence in the southwest of France.

Forty kilometers downstream from Bergerac toward Bordeaux on the northern bank of the Dordogne are the vineyards of Montravel, making about 150,000 cases of white wine a year. In the past decade or so a pleasant dry white wine has been made here, much superior to the semi-sweet variety that had been traditional. The controlled *appellations* are Montravel, Côtes de Montravel, and Haut-Montravel. Other wines from the Bergerac region include Rosette, a white wine from just north of Bergerac often said to have a taste the French call *pierre à fusil* or flinty, and

Pécharmant, a full, hard red wine whose 40,000-case yearly output, produced from 200 hectares of land, has been falling recently as the suburbs of Bergerac expand into the vineyards.

Forty-five kilometers (27 miles) south of Bergerac (take D-936 to Saint-Foy-la-Grande and D-708) is the small town of Duras, northwest of Marmande, surrounded by 1,000-odd hectares (approximately 2,470 acres) of Côtes de Duras vineyards, home of about 400,000 cases of wine a year, two-thirds of it white. Another 60 kilometers (36 miles) south of Duras on the Garonne River is the Côtes de Buzet, a new *appellation* since 1973, with the equivalent of about 250,000 cases of wine per year, nearly all red. While I have nothing against the wines of Buzet, this recently created *appellation* is another example of the pointless spread of controlled placenames, which only adds to the confusion of wine buyers both in France and abroad.

Bergerac wines are inexpensive, fresh, and pleasingly fruity, and may be found easily in restaurants throughout the beautiful and historically colorful province of the Dordogne, some 50 kilometers (30 miles) northeast of Bergerac. For me the Dordogne has always been one of France's most enchanting provinces, and for a pleasant drive from Bergerac I'd recommend a trip to Les Eyzies and Sarlat. As it happens, the countryside has more appeal to the eye than the wines do to the palate.

GAILLAC

Ninety kilometers (54 miles) southeast of Cahors is the town of Gaillac on the River Tarn—not a big river but one of the most beautiful in France, a sparkling trout stream cutting through the towering, majestic cliffs above. In the hills near Gaillac, 5,000 sloping hectares (12,300 acres) are planted in Duras, Gamay, Syrah, and Negrette for the reds and rosés and largely Mauzac, with some Muscadelle, Sémillon, and the special local grape Len de l'El for the white wines. This last grape takes its catchy name from the Provençal for "out of sight" (in French, *loin de l'oeil*). Both still and sparkling white wines are made, and both tend to be sweet—in all, the equivalent of about 200,000 cases. The sparkling wines must be made according to the Champagne method of secondary fermentation in the bottle, or by the Gaillac method—a slight variation in which the wines are bottled while they still hold unresolved sugar, causing imprisoned fermentation and often a fairly heavy bottle sediment as well. The reds and rosés account for just over 100,000 cases of rather uninspired wine. The town of Cordes is worth a detour, and you can taste Gaillac in medieval surroundings.

JURANÇON

As the story goes, on the 15th of December, 1533, no sooner had the future King Henry IV come into the world than a clove of garlic was passed over his lips, followed by a few beneficial drops of the heavy, sweet white wine of Jurançon. From this auspicious beginning, Henry went on to become one of France's most popular kings, an appropriate fate for the man who coined the phrase "a chicken in every pot."

Sweet Jurançon, about half of the 200,000-case annual production, has often been described in elaborate and flowery terms, with particular reference to carnations, although I suspect this is more an example of local chauvinism than of critical taste. The wine is sweet, spicy, and unique. The dry Jurançon, which does little credit to the *appellation,* is sold as *blanc de blanc,* apeing the Champagne terminology, which simply means white wine made from white grapes. One of the main sources for both the sweet and dry is the cooperative cellar at Gan, an establishment that has done much to improve the local wine, though only occasionally achieving quality that would attract good King Henry today.

IROULÉGUY

Still farther south and west, in the dramatic valleys of the Pyrénées at the heart of the Basque country, are the towns of Saint-Jean-Pied-de-Port and Saint-Étienne-de-Baïgorry, bordering on either side the tiny scattered vineyards of Irouléguy. This small *appellation* (125 hectares), a cooperative, one of the least-known wine place-names of France, makes about 20,000 cases of red and rosé a year, the reds being rather light but with a good if small, limited flavor.

The Basque country is shared by France and Spain and inhabited by a people fiercely unto themselves. As the seemingly ageless whitewashed houses perched in the hillside villages testify, the rugged, hilly country of the Pyrénées has been their home for centuries. The hardy individualism of the Basque extends even to his language, which has no known roots and remains a philological enigma. It is a land from another era. Through the steep and winding roads you still run into carts pulled by white oxen yoked at the horns. Another ancient mainstay of the Basque culture is the patriarch's hold on the family and womenfolk: not only do the men rule the home during the week, but at church on Sundays they sit in the upper galleries alone while their wives and daughters remain below. Though untouched by changing times, their contributions to Europe and the world have had a surprisingly long reach. The *beret* Basque, the *espadrille* (the rope-soled canvas shoe), *jai alai* (known there as *pelote basque*), and the world's best shepherds are all originally from this tiny mountain region. Of the beret they say that a Basque countryman removes it only when climbing the steps of church and climbing into bed, while the *espadrille* is a staple for any Mediterranean vacationer from Gibraltar to Greece. Sheep-herding has been in Basque blood as long as their tough stubbornness, and the expertise and renown of Basque shepherds have taken them to flocks all over the globe, from Canada to Argentina and Australia. For all that, the Basque remains an autonomist at heart, and has only reluctantly accepted integration into France. His Spanish brother to the south still resists rule from Madrid, and the independence movement continues to have great popular support there.

Just to the north of the Basque country, east of the city of Pau, is the region of Béarn, traditionally thought of as the heartland of Henry IV. In recent years it has distinguished itself in a small way by producing the Appellation Contrôlée wines of Béarn, three-quarters of it red and rosé, 90 percent of it coming from the growers' cooperative at Bellocq. Other Béarn-labeled wines come from the entire Pyrénées area, notably Madiran.

THE MOUNTAIN COUNTRY

JURA

On the Franco-Swiss border in eastern France are the Jura Mountains. They rise out of the plain between Lyon and Grenoble and curve northeastward in a 375-kilometer (230-mile) arc to just south of Basel. Geologically speaking, as mountains go, they are young—younger than the Alps—and on the low side, averaging less than 1,000 meters (3,280 feet). Along their western slopes, facing across the plain of Bresse to Burgundy, between the small towns of Saint-Amour (no relation to the Beaujolais town of that name) and Arbois, are the vineyards of the Côtes du Jura. The Jura themselves are probably better known to the world as the final home of the renegade

Madiran

Appellation Madiran Contrôlée

Mise en bouteilles
au Domaine

Vignobles LAPLACE
AYDIE
(Pyrénées-Atlantiques)

0,73 l

philosopher Voltaire, at Ferney on the Swiss border, and as the birthplace and boyhood home of Louis Pasteur, than for the small amount of their distinctively made white, light red, rosé, and "yellow" wines.

Pasteur's connection with the Jura dates from his birth in 1822 in Dôle in the western Jura, near the wine town of Arbois, where he was brought up from the age of five. While in Lille as dean of the faculty of sciences, Pasteur was asked by a brewer to investigate the causes of fermentation. He postulated correctly that fermentation is due to tiny microorganisms, yeasts in fact, which convert sugar into alcohol. In pursuit of the mysteries of bacteria, Pasteur returned to his native province in the late 1850s to conduct experiments which led to the discovery of the way bacteria could spoil milk. He showed that the "germs" causing spoilage were not spontaneously generated by the liquids themselves, but were introduced, owing to poor standards of cleanliness and exposure to air. The foreign microbes identified as the *Acetobacter* type could be killed by heating the liquid to near boiling. Pasteurization has helped dairy farmers more than winegrowers, but there is still use for the procedure in wine-making when the level of volatile acidity is too high in the wine, condemning it to turn eventually to vinegar. Most oenologists today agree that Pasteur's work marked the beginning of modern oenology, whose first postulate is that the old wives' tales and country cures are no longer enough to assure a cleanly made and well-vinified wine.

The wine village of Arbois, Pasteur's boyhood home, is surrounded by some of the best of the Jura vineyards, making white, rosé, and the most distinctive wine of the Jura, the *vin jaune,* or yellow wine. This comes exclusively from the grape variety known as the Savagnin, and drinkable bottles of *vin jaune,* aged fifty years or more, are by no means rare. The wine takes on a deep golden color and a completely maderized or oxidized bouquet. It is thus one of the few wines of France (or the world, with the exception of those of the Sherry region of Spain) in which maderization is desired.

To obtain *vin jaune,* the grapes are harvested late and pressed in the same manner as for white wine. The juice is put in barrels and remains there six to ten years—six years is the legal minimum. Once the wine is in the barrel, a film forms on top, similar to the Sherry *flor,* and remains there until bottling. In the Jura, the yeasts live on oxygen from the air and contribute the peculiar yellow color and nutty fragrance that mark *vin jaune.* Two of the better Arbois producers are Christian Rolet and Émile Rousseau, while one of the biggest, almost to the point of holding a monopoly on the production, is Henri Maire. In this tiny area, M. Maire has fostered the fame of his wine as well as his own glory. His super-commercialization of the local wine is a success story certainly, although his product sometimes reflects the lack of competition from the rest of the region.

Arbois also makes rosé and light red wines—in all, the equivalent of about 150,-000 cases per year. Local vintners will try to convince you that the rosé is one of the best in France, on a par with Tavel, although more objective opinion ranks it lower. The white wines of Arbois are particularly well liked in Bourg-en-Bresse in the Bresse country, that marvelously rich farm region famous for its Appellation Contrôlée chickens—the *poulets de Bresse*—and the smooth and elegant *bleu de Bresse* cheese.

Below Arbois is the tiny *appellation* of Château-Chalon, also famous for *vin jaune,* making the equivalent of just under 10,000 cases per year. It also produces another typical Jura wine called *vin de paille,* or "straw wine," not merely because it is the color of straw, but because traditionally the grapes are laid on straw mats after picking and allowed to dry in the sun for a time to make them richer in sugar. Actually, *vin de paille* is usually made today by hanging the grapes up in well-ventilated rooms. The drying process, which by law requires at least two months, results in a wine of richness and longevity. Because of the expense of making it, *vin de paille* may cease to exist. Some bottles of it are splendid after more than sixty years, lighter in body and fresher than Sauternes. I have tasted a few of these interesting curios, but I don't believe it would be a devastating blow should they disappear.

Southwest of Château-Chalon, the tiny district of L'Étoile produces the best white wine of the Côtes du Jura in three variations: *vin de paille, vin jaune,* and sparkling wines—in all, the small equivalent of about 15,000 cases per year. I do not recall having seen these wines outside the district. By tasting them locally I feel that I've taken a step toward completing my own education in the wines of France, but they left no lasting impression.

৵৯

SAVOIE

The Jura Mountains give way to the Alps and the province of Savoie to the south, most famous for its alpine ski resorts Val d'Isère, Courchevel, and Chamonix, site of Europe's highest peak, Mont Blanc at 4,807 meters (15,771 feet). From the lower alpine slopes, called *préalpes,* come the white, rosé, and light red wines of Savoie and the three place-names of Seyssell, Crépy, and Roussette. Dividing this small region into three is really just so much hairsplitting, necessitated by local chauvinism, and confuses the wine drinker more than it enlightens him. In addition to Seyssell, Crépy, and Roussette, there is the general Vin de Savoie *appellation,* covering some sixty communes scattered throughout the mountain country, fifteen of which have been singled out as eligible to place their name after or below the words *"Vin de Savoie."* Among the better wine-making communes are Apremont, Ayze, Abymes, and Chignin; they have much or little to recommend them, according to the means and dedication of the individual grower. Nearly all of the wine is white, with 100,-000 cases or so of an indifferent Gamay-based red.

The three controlled place-names account for some 50,000 cases of wine out of the 650,000 cases that the entire region produces annually. Perhaps the most beautifully situated of the three are the 100 hectares (247 acres) of Crépy vineyard, stretching along the French shores of Lake Léman between Geneva and the resort spa of Évian-les-Bains, source of one of France's most distributed and best-known mineral waters. Crépy makes the equivalent of about 40,000 cases annually of dry, light, and fresh white wine from Chasselas grapes; there is no red.

From farther to the south, on the road to Aix-les-Bains, D-991, come the still and sparkling white wines of Seyssell, a small wine town on the Rhône. These wines, rarely shipped beyond the mountain region, are made from a mix of the local grape varieties Altesse and Molette. Seyssell is often *pétillant,* slightly crackling, owing to uncompleted fermentation at the time of bottling. The last Savoie *appellation* is Roussette de Savoie, a white wine made from a mix of Altesse and Mondeuse grapes grown largely along the slopes overlooking the Lac de Bourget, France's largest lake. Although a purification program is now under way, in recent years the lake has been too polluted to support many of the fish for which alpine lakes have been famous. Its neighbor just to the northeast, the Lac d'Annecy, is not only blessed with fish, but on its banks at the small town of Talloires is the site of one of France's great restaurants, L'Auberge de Père Bise.

CORSICA

Corsica, the *belle île,* birthplace of Napoleon, the institution of vendetta, and the term *maquis,* is France's most dramatic department, combining stunning beaches along the west coast with snow-capped mountains in the center. It has great beauty, but I'll always remember it as a singularly frustrating place. As an American army captain, I was assigned as aide-de-camp to the newly appointed commanding general there during the Second World War. Our orders, from Allied Forces Headquarters in Algiers, were to construct an air and army base on Corsica for landings in southern France as well as for the provision of air support for the Allies' Italian campaign. We were to find thirty thousand civilian laborers to undertake the construction of the base, and to get it done, they made clear, in record time. In Ajaccio, we proceeded to beat the bushes for recruits. Fifty turned up. Slowly the number swelled to a hundred or so, whereupon we gave up and imported thousands of Yugoslavs who had served as labor troops for the Italians.

When officials from Allied Command came to the island for a weekend's inspection tour, they expected to find us in the trenches eating C rations. Far from it. Although the Corsicans had little interest in building airfields, they had no objection to cooking. It was a pleasure to see the surprise on the command officers' faces when they sat down in the general's mess. It featured such local specialties as *figatelli,* the distinctive spicy sausage made from the free-roaming, chestnut-eating pigs, and the local goat cheese, which, besides having a strong whiff of the goat about it, featured a rind infested with worms that jumped out as you cut into it. I don't imagine that our guests have forgotten it either.

As with so many wine regions, the more beautiful the countryside, the more ordinary the wine. This holds true in Corsica as it does on the mainland, in such areas as the Languedoc-Roussillon and the Riviera. The Corsican climate is almost ideal for growing vines in quantity, the varieties being mostly Spanish or Madeiran in origin: Malvoisie, Mellucio, Sciaccarello, as well as vines common in the Côtes du Rhône and Midi, such as Grenache, Cinsault, and Carignan. When I was stationed there, it was a sleepy island without much good wine to be found. Now, with the demands of tourism and the improved viticultural techniques imported by the *pieds noirs* who settled here *en masse* after Algerian independence, Corsica makes some pleasant bottles. Chauvinistic, Napoleonistic, Corsicans have by certain terrorist acts discouraged these North African settlers from continuing their wine and vine activities, and most of their wineries are for sale. Formerly drunk only by local residents and summer tourists, they are now being shipped to continental France. Assertive, cheap, and alcoholic, they seem to be finding favor.

The seven Appellation Contrôlée place-names of Corsica make the hefty equivalent of about a million cases a year, nearly all red or rosé. Probably ten times that much is made under no *appellation*. Those million cases are rarely enough to satisfy the island's needs, especially with the hot summer sun that parches the one million throats—three-quarters of them vacationing tourists and the rest staunch and easy-living locals. The wines produced are not of any high degree of quality, with the exception of a very few grown around the principal city of Ajaccio, and those from the hills overlooking Calvi, and a few more around Sartène, the self-styled "most Corsican of all towns" in the southern mountains. Figari is a full-bodied red from the southern tip of the island. Many Corsican wines are still rough and common, but some of the better *appellations* are emerging with some good wine. One of the best is the powerfully alcoholic rosé of Patrimonio, grown in the north of the island near Bastia. Others of notable quality are the dry white from the Cap Corse in the north, the rosé and red from Porto-Vecchio, from around the tourist town in the southeast, the aforementioned Sartène. The general regional *appellation* wine, which can vary from very pleasant to poor, is Vin de Corse.

Through the mountains, plains, hills, and valleys of the rest of France, pleasant and agreeable wines can be found. They do not often leave the regions where they are made, which in a way is just as well; they can be a delightful surprise when one is taking a tour through the vineyards, but they do not travel well. Some of the better local wines have been classified as *Vins Délimités de Qualité Supérieure,* or V.D.Q.S. This is a less stringent sort of Appellation Contrôlée than the actual A.O.C. The biggest producer of V.D.Q.S. wine is the Languedoc-Roussillon, and a fuller description of the wines may be found in that chapter. Below the V.D.Q.S. wines there are the *vins de pays,* the *vins de table,* and the wines which have no official name at all but are just blends of wines meant for sale in supermarkets throughout France under brand names. A fuller description of these may be found in the chapter on Languedoc-Roussillon, again the biggest producer by far. A list of the V.D.Q.S. wines appears on page 505.

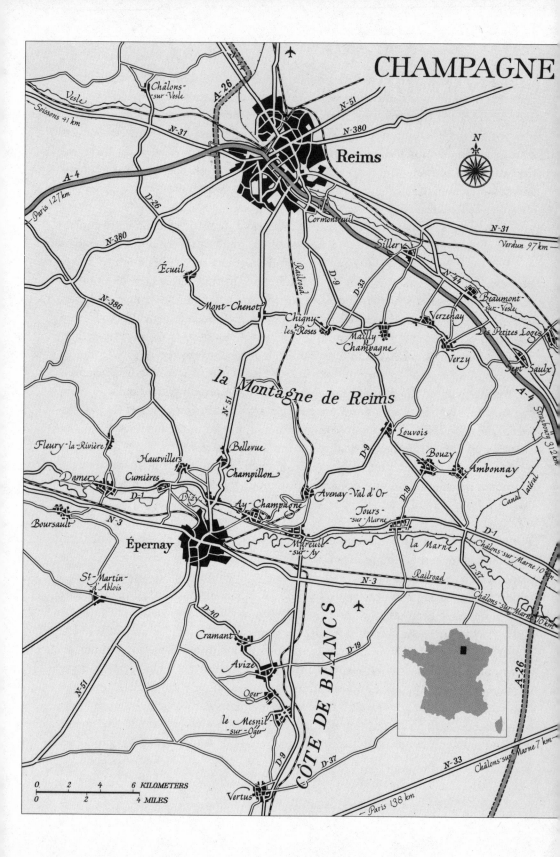

CHAMPAGNE

CHAMPAGNE

Less than an hour's drive east from Paris begin the vineyards of the world's best-known wine name—Champagne.

Nearly from the day of its "discovery" Champagne has worked its spell on the world as has no other wine. In fact, even though the best of it is made from the fermented juice of the noble Burgundy grapes, the Pinot Noir, Pinot Chardonnay, and Meunier, many people do not even think of it as a wine; Champagne is in a class by itself and obeys its own laws of time, place, and mood.

Much of the romance of wine is built on the notoriety of Champagne. From its very beginnings in the court and high society of eighteenth-century Versailles and Paris, Champagne was the drink of celebration and seduction. Freed from the sobering restraint of Louis XIV with his death in 1715, the high-living aristocracy under the regent, Philippe Duc d'Orléans, set out on a decade of carefree debauchery while they waited for the child-king Louis XV to assume his full royal powers. In this notorious court of licentiousness and promiscuity, where food and sex held center stage, Champagne was an accompaniment to all.

In a short time Champagne seduced the rest of Paris beyond the court and the rest of the courts of Europe as well. Wherever matters of taste and style were being set, there you would find a salesman of Champagne. These early shippers were the most dashing and extravagant tradesmen of their day. They traversed western Europe, Russia, and America, always in grand style, convincing the world that no festivity was worthy of the name without the popping of corks. They were masters of publicity and the publicity stunt as no other wine salesmen have ever been. Among the adventures of the Heidsieck family, there are those of Charles-Henri, who traveled to Moscow and beyond on a white stallion, and impressed his hosts enough to pick up the business of the Tsar. Claude Moët, one of the founders of Moët et Chandon, convinced Mme de Pompadour that Champagne was indispensable to any successful *soirée*. A century and a half later the Moët et Chandon salesman in America, with the irreverence typical of Champagne, sent a train car full of the house brand to the victims of the San Francisco earthquake. To hear it told, the Gay Nineties were an unending party at Maxim's and every *salon privé* in Europe and the New World, and throughout it all Champagne never stopped flowing.

Times may have calmed down somewhat, but our appreciation of Champagne has not. For the world beyond France, Champagne remains the only wine worthy of festivity: to baptize babies and christen ocean liners, to honor Christmas and ring in the New Year, to celebrate weddings and engagements, to toast felicitations on jobs well done and friends and lovers remet. The French, on the other hand, who consume 65 percent of all the Champagne produced, are happy to use all these excuses, but are just as content with no excuse at all. Rather than popping a cork only to honor a grand occasion, they are more likely to turn an everyday event into something special by opening a bottle of their most famous product.

The French are also devoted to the all-Champagne meal—that is, one with all courses accompanied by Champagnes—which is surprising in a people reputedly so sensitive to their palates and stomachs. The *repas au Champagne* is meant to be taken as a sign of largess and good living. More often it is a sign that the host is less informed about, or has less confidence in, his taste in wines than in food, and so chooses the safe way out with Champagne—the theory being that Champagne goes with everything. In this capacity as the luxury safety valve, Champagne has become something of the rich man's brand-name wine. The fact is, however, that Champagne does *not* go with everything. By its very nature and typical acidity, it calls too much attention to itself to work truly well with food. More accurately put, Champagne is a wine of occasion rather than a wine of cuisine. For my part, I prefer my bubbles before the meal. As wine lists improve, offering wider selections of fine Bordeaux, Burgundies, and local wines, and customers gain knowledge and confidence, Champagne is less of a favorite for a businessman's lunch than before.

Champagne's vineyard country stretches along 32,000 hectares (80,000 acres) of forest and hill country, although nowadays only 26,500 hectares (66,250 acres) are planted. The rolling swells of land—scarcely hills—are covered in vines along with maple, elm, and pine in the higher reaches. Narrow roads wind through the vineyard and forest land from village to village, and at the heart of Champagne nearly everyone is occupied with the making of wine. The best villages begin just south of Reims along the base and slope of the Montagne de Reims, the hill-plateau south of the city. The best vineyards follow the slope around to Épernay. Driving from one village to the next on the small, tractor-sized roads, you pass through Sillery, Mailly, Verzenay, Bouzy, and Ay (pronounced Ah-ee), arriving finally at Épernay, Champagne's other main city, on the banks of the Marne. From Épernay the best vineyards continue along the south-facing slope of the Marne Valley, with Cumières and Hautvillers, then south of Épernay, through the villages of Cramant, Avize, Oger, and Vertus, along what they call the Côte des Blancs. "The Slope of the Whites" is where the ethereal lightness of the best Champagne originates; it takes its name from the fact that the main grape planted is the Chardonnay, as opposed to the red wine grape, the Pinot Noir. Most of the best Champagne is a blend of wines from both red and white grapes. A small amount—coveted by its *amateurs*—is made solely from white grapes, and so is called *blanc de blanc,* meaning white wine from white grapes. A tiny amount of pink Champagne is made from red and white grapes, although the best houses maintain it more as a novelty than anything else.

These three districts in the department of the Marne—la Montagne de Reims, the valley of the Marne, and the Côte des Blancs—are the core territory of the most noble Champagne.

Like any wine, sparkling or still, Champagne owes its unique character to the subtle interplay between microclimate, soil, grape variety, and the expertise and care of the maker. To begin with, Champagne is France's most northerly vineyard, lying at a latitude above even the best slopes of Alsace, on the Rhine to the east. Of Europe's vineyards, only the Rheingau and Mosel, in Germany, lie further north. At such a latitude, the vines risk frosts in the spring and poor ripening in the fall. Although they are made with the same grapes as the wines of the Côte d'Or, the still reds of the region—Bouzy for instance—and the still whites, called Coteaux Champenois, never have the depth and complexity of their Côte d'Or cousins. The difference lies mainly in the cooler climate.

The next, and perhaps primary, ingredient in Champagne's individuality is its soil, the famed Kimmeridgian clay—a limestone-clay mixture that stretches through the best of the Champagne villages and southward to Chablis, also home of great Pinot Chardonnay–based wines. In Champagne and Chablis alike, the limestone-rich soil makes a perfect base for this white grape, as well as for the Pinot Noir. Kimmeridgian clay accounts for about half of the Champagne vineyard area. Regions poor in limestone, especially those in the department of the Aube, are planted in the more ordinary grape, the Pinot Meunier.

After the soil, the grape, and the climate, there remains only the Champagne-maker himself. There are two types: the 150 shippers (*négociants-manipulants*), who manufacture their own wines (most of them without vineyards of their own), of whom perhaps a dozen or so do an important volume of business; and the 4,600 *récoltants-manipulants*—vineyard growers who make, bottle, and sell their own Champagne, made from their own grapes. They are among the 15,000 or so growers in all who grow grapes to sell to the Champagne shippers.

By far the more important, in terms of quality and prestige, are the shippers, who sell 70 percent of all the Champagne sold and do over 95 percent of the export business. It is on the shoulders of these Champagne houses and a number of the smaller prestige firms that the great fame of Champagne has been built. Even today, the top thirteen—Moët et Chandon, Mumm, Veuve Clicquot-Ponsardin, Marne & Champagne, Mercier, Pommery & Greno, Laurent-Perrier, Lanson, Taittinger, Perrier-Jouët, Piper-Heidsieck, Charles Heidsieck, Pol Roger—do close to half of the Champagne business. Also important for their traditional excellence are Krug, Bollinger, Louis Roederer, Ruinart, Jacquesson, and Heidsieck Monopole.

The houses are divided between Reims and Épernay, with a few distributed in the other vineyard towns. Two of relative importance, Bollinger and Deutz & Geldermann, are located in Ay, just north of Épernay, and Jacquesson is located in Dizy. Between the wars a snobbish attitude held that Reims was superior to Épernay as a Champagne source. As far as the wine is concerned, the only difference between the two cities is that Reims has better-known houses and exports more than Épernay, which, on its side, is home of the Comité Interprofessionel du Vin de Champagne. The C.I.V.C., as it is called, is the governing body strictly controlling all aspects of the Champagne trade. Both cities ship an equal amount of wine.

The history of the Champagne families, many of them descended from the first shipper-salesmen, follows that of Champagne the wine and Champagne the region. Before the wine became the region's business, Reims was a center for woolen goods. A number of firms, notably Pommery & Greno, Veuve Clicquot-Ponsardin, and Ruinart, owe their founding to the renegade sons of the textile barons.

The institution of the Champagne shipper began in the eighteenth century with the buying and selling of the wine between the vineyards and Paris and Versailles, and little thought was given at the time to vine-growing and wine-making. In the early decades of the eighteenth century, the rudiments of the Champagne method—inducing a second fermentation in the bottle—were just being understood and applied with increasing success. A mixture of fact and folklore has it that Dom Pérignon, a monk at the abbey in the vineyard town of Hautvillers, was responsible for this discovery, and for other advances in Champagne-making. The precise extent of his contribution will never be known, but it is likely that he was the first to apply a rational method to the problems of blending different wines and among the first to cork the bottles properly with the typical mushroom-shaped Champagne cork. In any event, the sparkling wine caught on in no time with the Paris and Versailles of the *Régence,* and the rest of the world was not far behind. The shippers catered to the aristocratic fad and bought their Champagnes directly from the growers to ship to their clients.

Champagne in bottle was an even greater luxury in the eighteenth century than it is today. The hand-blown bottles always had imperfections, and the sugar addition necessary to cause the second fermentation in bottle was done largely by guesswork. The result was that pressure from the fermentation in the bottle was often too strong and caused a ruinous number of breakages. With this sort of imposed scarcity, Champagne could not help but be reserved for the wealthy. But the party-givers under Louis XV seemed in no way daunted by the price. Champagne historian Patrick Forbes tells of a masked ball in 1739 where no fewer than 1,800 bottles were uncorked.

As business boomed, the shippers had to assure themselves a more reliable supply of wine than the growers offered and so they themselves bought grapes to vinify and, in some cases, bought vineyards of their own. At the same time a few of the more enterprising growers, by now envious of the *négociants'* business, began to seek customers on their own. Once they had succeeded in branching out, they found that their own vineyards were inadequate to meet the demand, so they too began to buy and vinify grapes from other growers. And so was born the *négociant-manipulant,* or shipper-manufacturer, of today.

The pattern of expanding enterprise continues now more than ever. On average, in the past decade three new firms have formed every year. For the most part these are growers whose profits in Champagne's boom years of the late sixties and early seventies encouraged them to branch out into the business of manufacturing and selling their own wines.

Until the 1950s, many of the top firms mentioned above were staunch family dynasties of long-standing reputation. Like many Bordeaux shipping firms, many in Champagne were founded by foreign entrepreneurs, who rightly saw the future there. Jacques Bollinger, Joseph Krug, P. A. Mumm, and Florenz-Louis Heidsieck came from Germany in the late eighteenth and early nineteenth centuries to found the companies that bear their names today. After the Second World War, however, much of the vitality of the founding families had drained away, and many firms found it necessary either to merge or to go public and sell stock.

The result is that Champagne is now big business: in addition to extensive vineyard holdings in Brazil and Argentina, an import business in New York, and a sparkling-wine firm in California, the giant company of Moët-Hennessy controls the three Champagne firms of Moët et Chandon, Mercier, and Ruinart Père et Fils, the Hennessy Cognac firm, and Christian Dior perfumes. Seagrams, of the United States and Canada, now owns Mumm and Heidsieck Monopole as well as Perrier-Jouët. Majority control of Krug Champagne has passed from the Krug family into the hands of the Cognac firm of Rémy-Martin, which has also acquired Charles Heidsieck. There have been a number of mergers and associations of larger firms with smaller ones, such as Charles Heidsieck with Henriot, Veuve Clicquot with Canard-Duchêne and Taittinger with Irroy. Taittinger's other holdings include the Paris luxury hotel the Crillon. The venturesome Gardinier brothers achieved control of both Lanson and Pommery, but in 1983 resold them to a large French group, BSN, whose major interest was Danone yogurt. Félix Chatellier, who owns Château Dauzac in Margaux, has grouped together the three small Champagne firms of Abel Lepitre, Georges Goulet, and Saint-Marceaux. Four firms now sell stock to the public to bring in cash and are quoted on the Paris Stock Exchange: Moët-Hennessy, Piper-Heidsieck, Taittinger, and Veuve Clicquot-Ponsardin.

Like any commodity, Champagne is at the mercy of its market. The C.I.V.C. has done an admirable job in curbing the wilder swings in price and supply and demand, and, without its governance, Champagne's boom-and-bust period of the early seventies would have been far more disastrous than it was. In those years, Champagne, along with the rest of French wines, went through a period of euphoria and prices shot up dramatically. Demand was so feverish that even the poorer grapes were snatched up by the shippers in a minute. In ten years' time the area cultivated in vines doubled and the new vines were quickly pushed into production—this despite viticulture's first law, that young vines make an acid wine.

Then, in 1974, the French wine market collapsed and the Champagne houses were left sitting on stocks of bottles that numbered into the millions. Since then, business has improved, but the glitter of profits is still greatly diminished. The C.I.V.C. looks ahead optimistically, but their forecasts have had to be adjusted downward because of a series of short crops. It is hoped this problem was solved in the mid-1980s. Years of very small production during the early 1980s created a serious shortage of Champagne. The great quantity of high-quality wines harvested in 1982, together with a large quantity in 1983, has restored the balance.

All of this concern with high finance and the cost of bottle stocks is necessary because Champagne is a difficult and expensive product to make. Champagne of the best quality takes at least three to four years in the bottle in the firm's cellar before it matures enough to be drunk. The legal minimum is only a year, but the best firms may age some of their bottles up to six years before putting them on the market. A

Champagne

BRUNO PAILLARD

Reims-France

BRUT   CHAMPAGNE CRÉMANT
BLANC DE BLANCS   75cl

PRODUCE OF FRANCE

Champagne firm selling 5 million bottles a year (there are four or five of this size) needs at least three times that many (15 million or so) in stock at any one time for aging. The price of stocking the wine over this aging period is Champagne's greatest expense. The money spent on producing Champagne today, with all that that entails, as we'll see, only begins to be paid back after three or four years.

In the meantime, the interest charged on the loans taken out to pay for new equipment and upkeep of the old, and for the production of the wine itself, is at least 15 percent compounded yearly. When it is finally added up, the financing of the maturing stocks of wine accounts for over a third of the price of the bottle of Champagne. A Champagne firm that ages its wine an average of two and a half years can sell its bottles for considerably less than a firm that ages it for four years.

The other main expense in the making of the Champagne—averaging about 35 percent of the total cost—is buying the grapes. Most of the big firms mentioned already own vineyards, but, of the total 26,500 hectares (66,250 acres) planted, the shippers own only 3,500 (8,750 acres), and no one firm has enough vineyard to satisfy its needs. The rest of the grapes must be bought from the growers. Although there is no hierarchy of *crus* in Champagne, as there is in Bordeaux or in Burgundy, the different vineyard villages have been rated according to the excellence of the wines they produce. The classification is done by percentages, 100 percent being the best grade, with the scale descending to 77 percent for the outlying regions. The percentage rating of the villages has changed considerably over the years and is still reviewed periodically. For the time being, there are fifteen villages rated 99 percent or better, all of them found in the three main growing regions around Épernay and Reims. The growers' grapes are sold by the kilo (1 kilogram equals 2.2 pounds) at a price set by the Growers' Association, the Shippers' Association, and the C.I.V.C., based on a calculation of the average market price of a bottle of Champagne. The departmental prefect makes this price official and hears appeals in case of protest on anyone's part. The price the grower gets for his grapes will be a simple computation based on both the percentage rating of the village where his vineyards are and the price ratified by the prefect. If he lives in Vertus, say, where the vineyards are rated 95 percent and the established price is (in 1981) 20 francs per kilo of grapes, he will get 19 francs per kilo. In 1983, the price per kilo was set at 15.5 francs, and in 1984 it was established at 18 francs per kilo. Obviously, the better firms buy better grapes, which further adds to the per-bottle cost.

The next great expense is the manufacture of the Champagne. "Manufacture" is indeed the word, for the making of Champagne is a complicated process involving many steps. Unlike wine made by one grower from his vines, the Champagne made by a firm is a product assembled from the wines of grapes from many different villages and, in the case of non-vintage Champagne, a number of different years. As in Cognac, much of the finesse and artistry of Champagne-making is in the proper blending to attain a rounded, balanced, consistent product. It is worth keeping in mind that, even though a vineyard may be rated 100 percent or 99 percent, it does not follow that the wine from those grapes alone would be the ideal Champagne. Over two-and-a-half centuries of tasting the different village wines has given the Champagne-makers a fair idea of what characteristics can be found in the wines of each village. For instance, Prince Edmond de Polignac, who was in charge of Pommery & Greno's vinification, had a special preference for the wines of Oger. "It's a complete, full, and round wine and will marry well with everything when we make our blend. Avize I would call a characterful wine, while Ambonnay is softer, with more perfume; Bouzy and Verzenay have distinctive tastes that stand out." Also, in the generations or centuries that the firms have been making their brands, they have developed house "styles" that are often as distinctive as the *Grands Crus* of the Côte d'Or.

The miracle of Champagne begins with the *ban de vendange,* the decree by the local prefect that the harvest may begin. This custom, formerly shared by other wine regions, is a holdover from the days when the growers were sometimes tempted to harvest their grapes early and, therefore, unripe. Since the date is decided by the vineyard owners anyway and passed along to the prefect, today the *ban* is a matter of ceremony. Once the harvest begins, the picked grapes are quickly brought to the various firms' *vendangeoirs* (pressing houses) in the vineyard villages to be pressed. Speed is essential because the longer the grapes wait in the picking baskets the greater is the risk that they will begin to ferment and oxidize. Greater too is the risk that the color of the Pinot Noir and the Pinot Meunier skins will bleed into the clear juice. Care must also be taken to avoid any rotted grapes, since Champagne is a delicate wine and the bubbles carry the whiff of poor vinification straight to the drinker's nose. In the days of the horse and cart, a Champagne house with scattered vineyards needed to have a pressing house in every vineyard village. Today's speedier transportation methods have permitted them to reduce the number of these costly installations.

At the *vendangeoirs* the grapes are pressed in the broad, flat wooden presses, designed to free the juice quickly from the skins and so permit the making of a white wine from dark-skinned grapes. The grapes are pressed five or six times, but only the first two pressings are of truly high quality. From the press, the juice goes directly into barrels, which are transported to the firm's main cellar in Reims or Épernay, or, as is more likely now, pumped into tank trucks and emptied into vats at the firm's cellars to be fermented.

The picking and pressing continue until November, and by that time it is cold in the north of France. This makes for an ideal temperature for a slow fermentation, though in late-picked vintages care must be taken that the temperature not drop so low as to stop the process altogether.

After racking the wine, or pumping it from one barrel or vat to another to clear it of sediment and rid it of some of its carbon dioxide, the firm takes samples of all vats, or barrels, and prepares a blend. In good vintages, much of the Champagne may be blended to make a "vintage Champagne," composed only of the wines of the year. In non-vintage years, vats of wine are assembled from different years to make the house non-vintage Champagne. A good non-vintage blend is possible only with large inventories of wines from previous vintages, all with different taste characteristics. Such a northerly vineyard region as Champagne tends to make slightly acidic wines in the off-years, but during storage these wines will gradually lose their acidity and be suitable for blending with newer wines. It is this flexibility that gives the large firm the advantage over the small grower-producer, who cannot hope to equal the firm's consistent standard.

Once the blending is finished in early spring, bottling may begin—and with it the beginning of *la méthode champenoise*. Until now, the wine has been simple, rather dry, white wine. But just before bottling there is added to the vatted wine a mixture of cane sugar dissolved in the same wine and specially selected yeasts. The wine is then bottled and capped with a plastic "cork" and stored on its side on wooden slats.

By now it is April, and aboveground, far from the cool Champagne cellars, the sap is beginning to rise in the vines. As it does, the wine in bottle mysteriously begins its second fermentation. The residual yeasts in the still wine, along with those added before bottling, convert the added sugar into alcohol and carbon dioxide, which is trapped in the bottle and develops the natural sparkle of Champagne. The addition of sugar and yeast is rigorously controlled to keep the bubble pressure at the right level. Scientific exactitude dates only from the turn of the century. Before that, it was not unusual for a Champagne firm to lose over half its bottles from the pressure of excessive bottle fermentation. When properly done, the bubble pressure should amount to five or six times the atmospheric pressure.

This bottle fermentation is usually finished in three months, but the wines in bottle are left lying on their sides for at least a year (by law) or up to four or five, so that the Champagne (as it can now be called) can age. As it remains in contact with the sediment in the bottle, composed mostly of dead yeasts and tartrates, it gains in depth of taste.

At the end of this aging period the bottles are ready for the *remuage* and *dégorgement*. The *remuage* is the riddling or shaking of the bottles. Bottles of Champagne must be shaken in a particular manner (known technically as riddling) so the sediment will free itself from the side of the bottle and lodge in the neck. The first step is the gradual *mise sur pointe,* turning the bottles upside down in special racks or *pupitres. Pupitres* are made from two hinged, sloping boards, much like artists' easels, with holes cut on both sides in such a way that they will hold a bottle firmly when it is inserted neck first. The bottles are put in at a very slight angle and over a period of time are slowly elevated until they are literally upside down. Each day a trained man, a *remueur,* goes through and carefully shakes each bottle, putting it back at a slightly more elevated angle, and turning it about a quarter turn each time. This slightly shakes the sediment and slowly, as the bottle is raised, it slides down to the neck, where it rests against the cork. The *remueur* works at top speed, using both hands, and is capable of turning 32,000 bottles a day. The entire process takes six weeks to three months to complete. When he has finished, the bottles are standing on their heads in the racks, the sediment is next to the cork, and the wine is ready for the *dégorgement.*

The trick in disgorging a highly pressurized bottle of Champagne is to lose as little of it as possible while removing all of the sediment. In the days before absolutely clear Champagne was achieved, Champagne glasses were made of frosted, or milky, glass to mask any of the residual sediment that had not been removed.

Slowly, the cork is pried off, and the sediment is allowed to shoot out, propelled by the pressure in the bottle. The job has been simplified by nearly all Champagne houses with the modern method of freezing the necks of the bottles. The sediment and a small amount of wine become frozen, and, again, the pressure that has been built up shoots it out in a solid lump. The wine is then brought back to its original level with a little of the same wine from another bottle and is ready for *dosage* and the final cork.

The *dosage* of a Champagne depends on the taste of the market for which it is destined. It is a matter of sophistication now to prefer one's Champagne as dry as possible—that is, *brut.* Other grades of sweetness in Champagne are achieved by increasing the amount of sugar in the *dosage. Brut,* being the lowest, is 0–2 percent sugar by volume; *extra-sec* (extra dry) is 2–3 percent; *sec* (dry) is 3–6 percent; *demi-sec* (semi-sweet) is 6–8 percent; and *doux* (sweet) is 8–10 percent. Sweeter Champagnes are still served with desserts, but otherwise they are not as popular as they were a century ago. Generally only the best-quality wines are used for *brut* Champagne, since any defects, which in the others will be masked by the added sugar, will here be apparent. However, virtually all Champagne, even *brut,* has a sugar *dosage.* After the *dosage,* the bottle goes to its final corking with the specially wired cap and is then stored to await shipment.

In addition to the shippers of the traditional type, who make their brands of wine and sell them under their own labels, there are also firms that deal in "buyer's own brands" or private labels. Companies such as Marne et Champagne, Henriot, and Trouillard sell a large quantity of Champagne already in bottle to other firms that have run short of Champagne. The needy firms affix their own labels to the bottles and sell them as their own. These above-mentioned B.O.B. firms, as they are called, also supply a large number of the famous French restaurateurs with Champagne to be sold with the house or the chef's brand.

No visit to the Champagne district is complete without a tour of the cellars of at least one of the famous firms. Many of them boast huge *caves,* gallery after gallery carved through the chalky rock thirty meters below ground. In the long arched corridors you can see the thousands of bottles lying on their sides ready to begin the *mise sur pointe;* in others you'll find thousands upon thousands of bottles standing neck down, waiting for the *dégorgement. Dégorgeurs* will be at work over their long machines, inserting the bottles neck first into freezing brine, while at the other end of the line men remove the bottles, pop the corks, and remove the frozen wad of sediment. Some of the most impressive cellars are those of Pommery & Greno in Reims, with 18 kilometers (11 miles) of cellars, and those of Moët et Chandon and Mercier in Épernay. Pommery's long limestone galleries are of particular interest because of the friezes depicting vineyard scenes carved high on the walls. Also stuck into a nook along one of the corridors at Pommery is the twelfth-century stone statue of Notre-Dame-des-Crayères, studded with semiprecious stones.

Whichever cellars you visit, the guides will certainly tell you how the townspeople of Reims or Épernay retreated to the cellars during both world wars. Between 1914 and 1918, 80 percent of Reims was destroyed by German shells; even the majestic Gothic cathedral was badly hit. But because of the safe haven of the Champagne cellars, casualties among the population were relatively low.

Here is a partial list of the houses that carry the banner of Champagne throughout the world:

FIRM	CITY
Ayala	Ay
Besserat de Bellefont	Reims
Bollinger	Ay
Canard-Duchêne	Ludes
Charbaut	Mareuil-sur-Ay
de Cazanove	Avize
Veuve Clicquot-Ponsardin	Reims
Deutz et Geldermann	Ay
Heidsieck Monopole	Reims
Charles Heidsieck	Reims
Henriot	Reims
Irroy	Reims
Jacquesson	Dizy
Krug	Reims
Lanson	Reims
Laurent-Perrier	Reims
Mercier	Épernay
Moët et Chandon	Épernay
G. H. Mumm	Reims
Joseph Perrier	Châlons-sur-Marne
Perrier-Jouët	Épernay
Philipponnat	Mareuil-sur-Ay
Piper-Heidsieck	Reims
Pol Roger	Épernay
Pommery & Greno	Reims
Louis Roederer	Reims
Ruinart	Reims
Salon	Le Mesnil-sur-Oger
Taittinger	Reims

CHAMPAGNE VINTAGES

Like all white wines, sparkling or not, Champagne should be drunk fairly young, say at the most within ten years of its delivery to the consumer. This in spite of the fact that some connoisseurs like to talk about bottles decades old. Like all white wines, Champagne has a tendency to maderize with age, turning brown and musty.

1964 A very good vintage, plentiful in quantity. Wines were round and full. 93 million bottles produced.

1965 A non-vintage year.

1966 Magnificent wines. Excellent bouquet with great finesse. Well balanced. Some 80 million bottles produced.

1967 What could have been an exceptional vintage was diminished by pouring rains between the fifth and twenty-first of September, just one week before the harvest. Rot developed in grapes that lacked maturity. Non-vintage.

1968 Disastrous vintage.

1969 A good vintage, well-balanced and full-bodied. Small quantity produced.

1970 The most abundant vintage on record. The quality was good to fair.

1971 Good vintage. The small quantity produced caused high prices.

1972 Not a vintage year.

1973 A good and very plentiful vintage year.

1974 Fairly good vintage; wines without too much depth of character.

1975 A vintage year. Wines of a good quality, with a tendency toward lack of acidity.

1976 The 1976 vintage was one of significant quantity and good quality. A vintage year.

1977 Although this will not be a vintage year, the Champagne producers were happy with the wines they made.

1978 A harvest of good wine, although poor early summer weather limited the crop to 550,000 hectoliters, the equivalent of approximately 70 million bottles, far below what is needed to meet the demand. Limited yield has pushed opening grape prices up 20 percent from 1977. Many houses made a vintage.

1979 Abundant harvest of good quality. Certain firms made vintage wines.

1980 Exceptionally low quantity drove prices up to the highest level on record. Champagne firms suffering from diminishing inventories needed a large vintage, and could only look forward with hopeful anticipation to subsequent harvests.

1981 Quality was good, with less acidity than 1980. This will be a vintage year. Owing to late spring frosts, however, quantity was even more disastrous than in 1980. Only 350,000 barrels were produced in 1981 (as compared with a far-from-sufficient 420,000 in 1980, and 800,000 in 1979).

1982 The Champagne region was one of the most favored this year, producing a fine vintage in sufficient quantities (300 million bottles) to make up for the serious shortfalls of the 1980 and '81 harvests.

1983 As in 1982, a tremendously large quantity, over 300 million bottles, was produced. However, the quality was not as good as in 1982, hence this will not be a vintage year.

1984 The poor summer and autumn weather did not contribute to a good wine. 728,000 *pièces,* or barrels, were produced, which will amount to 196 million bottles. At best it will make a fair non-vintage.

1985 "Extraordinary" is the word applied by many to this harmoniously well-balanced vintage, which is high in quality but suffers from a lack of quantity. 120 million bottles were produced, which did not replace the 190 million bottles sold by the shippers in 1985. The shortfall in quantity was due to the January freezing weather, which hit Champagne more than any other region of France and resulted in a loss of some 30–40 millions of its vines.

⚜

CHAMPAGNE
Hotels and Restaurants

H *= Hotel;* R *= Restaurant*

On the road to Reims:

LA FERTÉ-SOUS-JOUARRE (77260—Seine-et-Marne)
(Paris 68—Châlons-sur-Marne 97—Melun 63—Reims 82—Meaux 20—Troyes 117—Épernay 73)
Exit on A-4—Saint-Jean La Ferté.

R AUBERGE DE CONDÉ: 1, avenue Montmirail. Tel.: 60.22.00.07.
Rich food superbly served. Expensive. Alexis Tingaud, the owner-chef, has sixty years' experience. *Relais et Châteaux. Traditions et Qualité; Relais Gourmand.* Two stars in Michelin.

FÈRE-EN-TARDENOIS (02130—Aisne)
(Soissons 26—Reims 46—Châlons-sur-Marne 84—Paris 112—Château-Thierry 22—Laon 54)
Exit at Montreuil-aux-Lions, coming from Paris, or Saint-Jean La Ferté going to Paris.

❧ One hour's drive from Paris. The old fortress of Fère is a very impressive ruin. It claims to be the
prototype for the Château of Chenonceaux.

HR HOSTELLERIE DU CHÂTEAU: 3 km north by D-967, Route de Fismes. Tel.: 23.82.21.13. Tlx.:
145526. 19 rooms, including 7 suites. Tennis.

378

Warm welcome in a beautiful setting of an old manor house in midst of park. Very comfortable rooms. Excellent food, but expensive. *Relais et Châteaux.* One star in Michelin.

BERRY-AU-BAC (02190—Aisne)
(Paris 163—Laon 27—Reims 20—Soissons 47—Fère-en-Tardenois 48—
Rethel 46—Vouziers 64)

R LA CÔTE 108 (Chez Courville): On N-44, the road to Laon. Tel.: 23.79.95.04.
Good cooking. Nice welcome in a pleasant setting. One star in Michelin.

REIMS (51100—Marne)
(Verdun 118—Metz 182—Laon 48—Châlons-sur-Marne 42—Paris 150—
Charleville 83—Lille 205—Luxembourg 232—Brussels 214)

There are three attractions to Reims, each equally alluring: the Champagne cellars, the restaurant of Boyer-Crayères (one of the great tables of gastronomy in France), and the cathedral where Joan of Arc crowned Charles VII. The miracle of this cathedral is that in the midst of battlefields it withstood two wars. The Champagne cellars of Veuve-Clicquot, tel.: 26.85.00.68; Krug, tel.: 26.47.28.15; Louis Roederer, tel.: 26.40.42.11.; G. H. Mumm, tel.: 26.40.22.73.; Pommery et Greno, tel.: 26.05.05.01.; and Taittinger, tel.: 26.85.45.35 are a few of the many that are located here.

H LA PAIX: 9, rue Buirette. Tel.: 26.40.04.08. Tlx.: 830974.   100 rooms.
Modern hotel. Sleep here, but eat at Boyer-Crayères or Le Chardonnay or Le Florence (all listed below). Despite its central location, there are more exciting and interesting places to stay in the region.

HR FRANTEL and Restaurant LES OMBRAGES: 31, boulevard Paul-Doumer, near the cathedral. Tel.: 26.88.53.54. Tlx.: 830629.   120 air-conditioned rooms.
Les Ombrages is a good, standardized modern hotel.

H BRISTOL: 76, place Drouet-d'Erlon. Tel.: 26.40.52.25. Tlx.: 830600.   38 rooms.
No restaurant. Central, close to the station. Comfortable, inexpensive rooms.

H CRYSTAL: 86, place Drouet-d'Erlon. Tel.: 26.88.44.44.   31 rooms, 25 toilets.
Close to the station. No restaurant. Basic, quiet rooms. Inexpensive.

HR NOVOTEL REIMS TINQUEUX: West exit on N-31, 3 km outside of Reims on the road to Soissons. Tel.: 26.08.11.61. Tlx.: 830034.   125 rooms.
Snacks available. Comfortable modern standard, without charm. Menus at reasonable prices, and Champagne at very attractive prices.

HR MERCURE: East exit on N-44, the road to Châlons-sur-Marne. Tel.: 26.05.00.08. Tlx.: 830782.   98 rooms.
Modern motel. Swimming pool. Restaurant available.

HR BOYER-CRAYÈRES: 64, boulevard Henri Vasnier. Tel.: 26.82.80.80. Tlx.: 830959.   16 large, luxurious rooms.
Since 1983, Gérard Boyer shines with his wonderful cuisine in the former château of the Princes de Polignac of Pommery. Not only one of the best restaurants of Champagne but one of the best

of France. Elyane Boyer, with her charming, welcoming smile, is an additional pearl to a necklace of quality. This temple of gastronomy was transformed without regard to price by a recent Champagne lord. Reserve way ahead. *Relais et Châteaux.* Three stars in Michelin. Good wine list.

R LE CHARDONNAY (formerly BOYER): 184, avenue d'Épernay, near the hippodrome. Tel.: 26.06.08.60.
The restaurant started by Papa Boyer in the center of town, which Gérard still oversees from his suburban palace, has become good value and offers the widest array of finest Champagnes at most reasonable prices. One star in Michelin.

R LE FLORENCE: 43, boulevard Foch, in front of the station. Tel.: 26.47.12.70.
Quiet, elegant restaurant. Menus are good value, with irreproachable service. Denise Maillot is very friendly. One star in Michelin.

R BRASSERIE LE BOULINGRIN: 48, rue de Mars. Tel.: 26.40.63.44.
Popular *brasserie*-restaurant with large turnover. The food is good and the prices reasonable.

R LE VIGNERON: Place Paul Janot. Tel.: 26.47.00.71.
Assorted menus at reasonable prices. Remarkable Champagne list, and a good cellar for Coteaux Champenois *rouge,* if you like it. Amusing Champagne memorabilia.

CHÂLONS-SUR-VESLE (51140—Marne)
8 km from Reims, west on N-31, then on D-26, the road to Soissons.

R L'ASSIETTE CHAMPENOISE: Tel.: 26.49.34.94.
Good quality. Very quiet. Luxurious atmosphere and in good taste, in the midst of a tiny village, close to Reims. Expensive. One star in Michelin.

MONT-CHENOT (51500—Marne)
(Reims 11—Épernay 16—Paris 154—Châlons-sur-Marne 40)

HR AUBERGE DU GRAND CERF: On N-51, halfway between Reims and Épernay, in the Rilly-la-Montagne vineyards. Tel.: 26.97.60.07. 10 rooms, 2 with toilet (inexpensive). I suggest you sleep elsewhere.
Since M. and Mme Guichaoua became the new proprietors, this has become one of the best restaurants in the region. All three menus offered in the completely redecorated restaurant are good values as is the excellent Champagne wine list. One star in Michelin.

BEAUMONT-SUR-VESLE (51400—Marne)
(Paris 161—Châlons-sur-Marne 28—Épernay 54—Reims 18)

HR LA MAISON DU CHAMPAGNE: 2, rue du Port. Tel.: 26.61.62.45. 10 rooms (6 with toilet).
A welcoming dining room with large fireplace. Reasonable prices.

SEPT-SAULX (51400—Marne)
(Reims 25—Châlons-sur-Marne 25—Épernay 32)

HR LE CHEVAL BLANC: 2, rue du Moulin. Tel.: 26.61.60.27 and 26.61.60.27. Tlx.: 830885. 22 rooms. Tennis.

Pretty inn. Very quiet in the midst of a park. Good cuisine. A large fireplace (where the food is broiled) gives atmosphere in a luxurious dining room. One star in Michelin.

CHERVILLE (51150—Marne)
(Épernay 15—Reims 29—Châlons-sur-Marne 16)

R RELAIS DE CHERVILLE: 1, rue de l'Église, D-3, between Épernay and Châlons-sur-Marne. Tel.: 26.69.52.76.
One of the newer restaurants in the region. Pleasant decor, good cuisine.

ÉPERNAY (51200—Marne)
(Paris 138—Reims 27—Châlons-sur-Marne 32)

After Reims, this is the second Champagne capital of France. Visit the cellars of Moët et Chandon at 18, avenue de Champagne, tel.: 26.54.71.11; Pol Roger at 1, rue Henri-Lelarge, tel.: 26.51.41.95; or Perrier-Jouët at 26, avenue de Champagne, tel.: 26.51.20.53.

HR ROYAL CHAMPAGNE: 6 km from Épernay on N-51 to Champillon. 1 km to Bellevue. Tel.: 26.51.11.51. Tlx.: 830111. 23 rooms.
Charming eighteenth-century inn with a very good restaurant. Very comfortable rooms overlooking the vineyards. Beautiful view over the Marne Valley and Épernay. *Relais et Châteaux*. One star in Michelin.

HR LA BRIQUETERIE: At Vinay (7 km from Épernay, south, by D-51, on the road to Sézanne). Tel.: 26.54.11.22. Tlx.: 842007. 42 rooms.
Charming hotel in a big garden. Good food in pleasant setting, although somewhat expensive. One star in Michelin.

H CHAMPAGNE: 30, rue Eugène-Mercier, near the main Champagne cellars. Tel.: 26.55.30.22. 30 rooms.
Modern, small, in center of town. No restaurant; breakfast available.

HR LE CHAPON FIN: 2, place Mendès-France. Tel.: 26.55.40.03.
Taken over by the former director at Berceaux. Newly redecorated. In front of the railroad station. Inexpensive. Good value.

R LE PALMIER: 2, place Carnot. Tel.: 26.53.07.29.
This restaurant is run by native Moroccans who offer an excellent couscous at a low price. Good for a change of pace.

VERTUS (51130—Marne)
(Épernay 20 km to the north—Châlons-sur-Marne 32—Paris 138—Reims 47)

HR HOSTELLERIE DE LA REINE BLANCHE: 18, avenue Louis-Lenoir, near the post office. Tel.: 26.52.20.76. 23 air-conditioned and comfortable rooms.
Modern structure in the midst of the white-wine-producing district of Champagne.

LE-MESNIL-SUR-OGER (51190—Marne)
(Paris 155—Épernay 15—Reims 35—Châlons-sur-Marne 42—Vertus 6)

R LE MESNIL: 2, rue Pasteur. Tel.: 26.57.95.57.
In the heart of the white-wine vineyards. Good restaurant, fairly priced.

MONTMORT-LUCY (51270—Marne)
(Paris 130—Épernay 18)
On the Épernay-Sézanne road.

HR LE CHEVAL BLANC: Route de Sézanne. Tel.: 26.59.10.03.   12 rooms (14 toilets).
Good meals in generous portions. Very reasonable. Rooms inexpensive.

CHÂLONS-SUR-MARNE (51000—Marne)
(Paris 188—Reims 45—Épernay 32—Verdun 87)

HR AUX ARMES DE LA CHAMPAGNE: At L'Épine, 8 km east by N-3. Tel.: 26.68.10.43. Tlx.:
830998.   38 rooms, 24 toilets.
Good food and wine list. Comfortable, modern rooms. One star in Michelin.

HR HOTEL D'ANGLETERRE: 19, place Monseigneur Tissier. Tel: 26.68.21.51.   18 rooms (13 with
toilet).
Not expensive, with a good restaurant.

COGNAC,
ARMAGNAC,
CALVADOS

COGNAC

In the southwest corner of France, scarcely 100 kilometers (60 miles) north of the great vineyards of Bordeaux, is the town of Cognac. It is a small contented place on the edge of the Charente River, surrounded by a countryside of slightly rolling hills and vineyard land. The river is as peaceful and as slow-moving as the country and the towns it travels through. Just upstream from Cognac is the other brandy town, Jarnac, where a number of the famous firms, such as Bisquit-Dubouché, Hine, Delamain, and Courvoisier are located. But the main center for Cognac has been and ever shall be Cognac itself; its 29,000 people work and live for practically nothing beyond the splendid liquid to which it gives its name. Cognac's only other claim to fame is that it was the birthplace of François I, the French Renaissance king who fought and ruled valorously until he ended his days not along the Charente, but at the Château d'Amboise upon the Loire.

The life of the town of Cognac seems split. Up the hill from the riverside is the Cognac where the normal commerce of everyday life takes place, where on Thursdays and Saturdays the produce market opens, and where the swans paddle slowly in the Parc François Ier in front of the château where that king was born. Even this fifteenth-century landmark has been taken over as headquarters for one of the Cognac firms. But in the lower town along the Charente dockside, on the *quais,* the world moves to a different rhythm. As you travel along the narrow streets between the huge, grim-looking sheds or *chais,* where the Cognac firms age their brandy, time takes on a special meaning.

The *chais* are long stone and concrete warehouses with shallow-pitched tile roofs; in their dark interiors, row upon row of barrels are lined up, stacked on racks up to eight high. The head barrel in each row is adorned with cryptic markings indicating the age of the Cognac inside and its source. In other wings of the *chai* there are probably huge oaken vats, where broad, flat wooden paddles blend different Cognacs to make the firms' different types, such as Three-Star, V.S.O.P., and Special Reserve. If you visit here on an early summer morning, you will be met by the woody alcoholic aroma of thousands of barrels of Cognac evaporating into the air as they age. The tile roofs and outside walls of the *chais* are blackened by a fungus named *Torula cognaciensis,* which feeds on the alcohol in the air. Every year the equivalent of more than 8 million bottles of Cognac disappears into the air, 3 percent of all Cognac in barrel—they call it the "angels' share."

Just as Burgundy growers like having their vineyard parcels scattered as an insurance against hail damage, the Cognac shippers scatter their *chais* through the Charente countryside to lower the risk (and the insurance cost) of fire. The aging spirit is so volatile (as anyone who has *flambéed* a crêpe knows) that the towns of Jarnac and Cognac now prohibit the building of any new *chais* within the town limits. Bisquit Dubouché, forced to expand, moved their offices and cellars to their vineyard estate, Château de Lignères, just outside of Rouillac, north of Jarnac.

Brandy is nothing more than distilled wine. Anyone can make a brandy. Concentration of spirits by distillation is nearly as old as civilization itself, dating back to the Arab discovery of the process in the early Middle Ages. The word *alcohol* itself derives from the Arabic word for the black powder that was processed to make eye paint called *koh'l* for the harem beauties. When the spirit of wine was first distilled, it was given this name—*al-kohl*—because of the similarity of the process.

It is not known when alcohol distillation first came to France, but the man given the credit today for first describing the process in detail is a thirteenth-century alchemist named Arnaud de Villeneuve. A student of his, Raimond Lulle, wrote later of his master's work, saying, "This *eau-de-vie,* this water of life, was the emana-

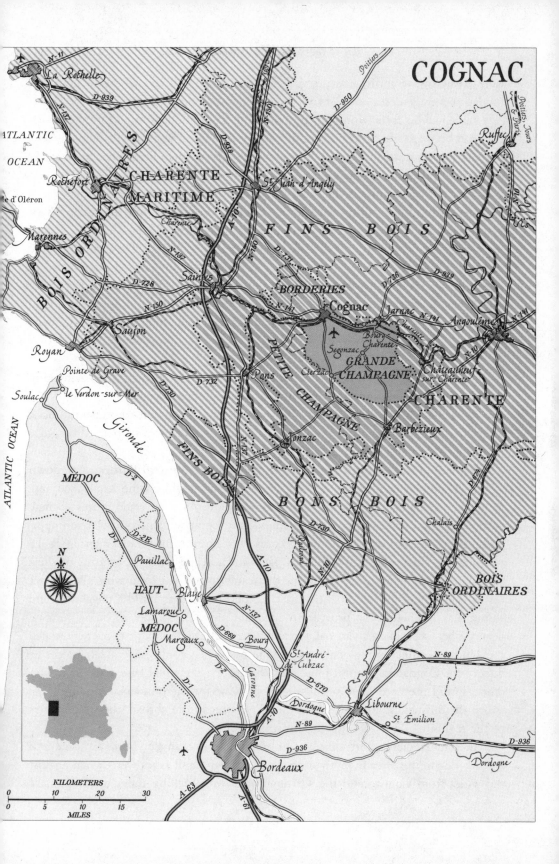

COGNAC

tion of the divine spirit, newly revealed because man was too young to need this modern beverage destined to revive the energies of modern decrepitude."

Lulle had his facts wrong on the first point: distillation through forced evaporation had been around for centuries. But as to the magical water of life being a tonic to flagging spirits, of that there can be no doubt. Since then France has made it her business to produce the finest *eaux-de-vie* of them all.

Many other regions in France and many other countries in the world make brandies, either by distilling wine as for Cognac, or by distilling the rendering of grape skins and other fruit after the juice has been pressed from them. In France these latter *eaux-de-vie* are called *marc*, known in Italy as *grappa*. They vary from the fine and rare *eau-de-vie de marc de Champagne*, made from the pressed grapes used to make the sparkling wine, to the leathery but distinguished brandy from Burgundy called *marc de Bourgogne*, to the very rawest *marcs* made in the hills and plains of France by wandering distillers in their alembics. But as anyone who has tasted the real thing can tell you, there is only one Cognac.

Although *eaux-de-vie* in France go back to the fifteenth century, Cognac-making began in earnest only at the beginning of the eighteenth century, and aged Cognac—a redundancy today, because all Cognac is aged—began to appear only about a century later. Even so the Cognac region wine-makers had to be pushed by grave necessity to distill their wines.

Beginning in the thirteenth century, traders from northern Europe came down to the Charente region to buy salt and wheat. The local white wine was loaded only to fill the hold after the salt and wheat were aboard. As more trade routes opened, other sources for salt and wheat were found and the wine gained in relative importance. By 1666, Jean-Baptiste Colbert, Louis XIV's new Minister of Finance, was lamenting the sorry state of the French navy as compared with the swarms of ships from Holland, England, and Denmark that came to buy the local wine. To protect his flank on the southern Atlantic coast, Colbert decided to build a naval port and shipyard at Rochefort. To provide an adequate supply of timber to build the new fleet, Colbert set aside the vast oak forest region to the east of Cognac country, called the Limousin after its regional capital Limoges. This would have a fateful consequence for Cognac in the not-too-distant future. As the naval base grew in importance, so did the need for a steady supply of wine for the builders and sailors. Between the business at Rochefort and the thirsty ships from abroad, the wine-makers of the region could hardly fill the demand.

In a remarkably short time the entire situation changed, both at home and abroad. Beginning already in 1630 or so, special per-barrel taxes were levied against the wines from Cognac and the surrounding towns, making them uncompetitive with the wines produced closer to the coast. To outwit the tax collector and offer a different product, the growers turned to distilling their vintages. This cut down on the number of barrels taxed and produced a spirit that would not spoil and go sour during the long journey north. The Dutch and English merchants were delighted; less space was taken on board their ships, and the wines could be diluted with water to a normal drinking strength once they arrived in London or Amsterdam.

For all its excellence, Cognac was still rough stuff. After being twice distilled, as is done now, it was put in barrel at about 70 percent alcohol, close to twice the strength of today's, and shipped for immediate consumption. Not intended for the genteel, it was sold in the taverns and on the street corners of Paris, London, and Amsterdam. Scruffy salesmen, carrying trays hung around their necks, sold the small earthenware bottles to laborers on their way to and from work. In the London pubs of the day "brandy-wine" (from the Dutch *brandewijn,* or "burned wine") became as popular as workingman's beer.

Those who could afford them preferred *liqueurs.* The mixture and recipe for these varied according to the current state of the herbal art. Aging of young Cognacs with the specific intention of mellowing them to improve their color and bouquet by prolonged contact with the oak of the barrel, and to soften the harshness by evaporation, became popularly practiced in the 1780s and 1790s. Here is where the Limousin oak so carefully set aside by Minister Colbert a century before became all-important. Oak of all descriptions and origins was tried in the making of the Cognac but nothing had the same beneficial result on the brandy as that from the Limousin forest. The so-called Limousin oak is wide-grained enough to impart sufficient tannin and woodiness to the Cognac as it ages. A tighter-grained oak, called Tronçais, from the forests north of Vichy, is much harder and ages the Cognac much more slowly, and so is especially sought after to make the wooden staves for Cognac blending vats. Although Colbert is known today as Louis XIV's crafty Minister of Finance, whose juggling kept the extravagant court of the Sun King afloat, in Cognac he is forever remembered as the man who preserved the forests for the making of France's greatest brandy.

The Cognac region today is a strictly defined spread over 100,000 hectares (250,000 acres) and four departments: Charente and Charente Maritime, which have the majority of the vineyards, and the Dordogne and Deux-Sèvres, where two very small areas are found.

The secret of Cognac's greatness lies in the chalk-rich soil. The entire Cognac-producing region is divided into six geographic areas, called *crus* or growths, according to the composition of the soil. Although the best regions have been known from the time that Cognac began to be distilled, the *crus* were outlined scientifically for the first time in 1860, when a French geologist named Coquand took samples of the soil, while a Cognac-tasting colleague sampled the local brandy. From test to test, when they compared notes, the results were the same: the more chalk Coquand found in a given area, the better his friend found the Cognac.

The best of these regions is called Grande Champagne. The name has nothing to do with the famous sparkling wine made in the north of France, but refers to the chalky plain of the best area, which is similar to that of the other region. Grande Champagne is thought of as a sort of *Premier Cru* of the region, covering about 13,000 hectares (32,500 acres) south of the Charente River, bordering on the town of Cognac itself. Only a small step down in excellence is Petite Champagne, circling Grande Champagne on the south and a bit larger, at 16,200 hectares (40,500 acres). Grande and Petite Champagne Cognacs complement each other perfectly: Grande Champagne being much heavier and more robust, and when taken straight, too pungent; while Petite Champagne is lighter and more elegant than Grande Champagne, making up with finesse for lack of power. It ages more quickly than Grande Champagne. When the two are blended together they strike a perfect balance and— provided at least 50 percent Grande Champagne is used—may be sold with the special *appellation* of Fine Champagne or Grande Fine Champagne.

Borderies, northeast of the town of Cognac, is the smallest of the six *crus* with only 4,000 hectares of vines (10,000 acres). Although it makes only about 5 percent of the Cognac of the region, Borderies has always been prized for its pronounced earthy character. For this reason it has often been used to fill out paler blends.

Surrounding these inner three entirely is the 40,000 hectares (100,000 acres) of Fins Bois, source of 40 percent of all the Cognac made, as much as the first three *crus* combined. Though slightly less fine, Fins Bois does have delicacy and ages comparatively quickly. In V.S.O.P. Cognac the youngest Cognac in the blend will be a Fins Bois, the proportion depending on the style of the firm and the price of the Cognac.

Beyond Fins Bois are Bons Bois and Bois Ordinaires, stretching all the way to the Île de Ré, off the coast from La Rochelle. The soil in both is more fertile than in the other areas, and as a result the wine and the Cognac made from it are more common than in the other four.

Although the most chalk-rich soils will provide the best wine for distillation into the best Cognac, the method of distillation is all-important if the best of the wine is to be extracted and its more acrid elements left behind. Even the best wine for making Cognac is a poor drink. The vine used nearly exclusively is the Saint-Émilion (no relation to the district in Bordeaux), a variety of the Mediterranean grape the Ugni Blanc. Without the hot sun of the Riviera to ripen it fully, the Saint-Émilion makes a thin, light, acid wine, low in alcohol (7 to 9 percent). It is only the miracle of the "Charente still," as the old-fashioned pot still is called, that makes possible the greatness of Cognac and the distinction of the different *crus*.

The design of the Charente pot still is basically the same today as it was in the time of Arnaud de Villeneuve. Distillation of wine into brandy is possible because the alcohol in wine turns to vapor at a lower temperature than does water. So the relatively gentle heat of distillation can draw off the alcohol and concentrate it—the condensation of this vapor becomes the essence of Cognac.

Brandy-making in the Charente still requires two distillations. The first brings the wine to 28 percent alcohol and the second brings it to about 70 percent. Most other stills in the world, such as those to make most whiskey (malt whiskeys being an exception), are called continuous stills; they require only one step to attain the proper degree of alcohol. While the pot still is slower certainly, it allows the distiller greater control, permitting him to remove certain portions of the distillate and re-distill them for further refinement. In the making of Cognac, the distillation is the most delicate step of all.

Beginning sometime in late October or early November, the grower brings his wine into his distillery (most growers have their own) and fills the copper heating pot, which is set atop a brick furnace. The exposed portion looks like the cupola of a Russian cathedral and is called the *chapiteau*. From its top, where the spire should be, there is a long pipe bent into an elegant curve which disappears into a large round condensing tank where the pipe spirals through cool water which condenses the vapor. The curved portion is given the apt name of "swan's neck" and the spiral is called the *serpentin*. The *serpentin* emerges from the condensing tank as a spigot. It is here that a new Cognac will see the light of day before disappearing into a barrel. The grower carefully tends the fire, bringing the temperature of the wine to boiling, usually around 93°C. (199°F.), depending on the original alcoholic content.

The first parts to vaporize are in fact non-alcoholic, such as important esters and aldehydes which are essential to the development of a Cognac's bouquet. Then the alcohols themselves vaporize. Before passing through the swan's neck into the con-denser, all vapors gather in the *chapiteau;* and there, in the enlarged space above the heating wine, some of the heavier elements and alcohols condense on the sides and fall back into the wine to be boiled again. This process ensures a proper sequence of evaporation of the different components in the wine. The vapor moves slowly through the swan's neck to the *serpentin,* where it is condensed. This first distillation is followed by the second, which further concentrates the brandy.

The miracle of aging in wood depends on the fact that wooden barrels are wa-tertight without being airtight. Both the water and the alcohol in Cognac seep into the pores of the wood and are slowly evaporated on contact with the air. At the same time the Cognac is also extracting important elements from the inside of the cask, such as tannins and lignins that gradually deepen the color and add a woody taste. A 350-liter barrel of 25-year-old Cognac (the equivalent of 460 75-centiliter bottles) will contain 500 grams (1.1 pounds) of wood material extracted from the barrel.

If the climate is humid, as the Cognac region tends to be, less water will be lost in proportion to alcohol.

This explains in part the superiority of the humid London climate for Cognac aging. London shippers used to buy their vintage Cognacs in barrel and age them in bonded warehouses, which in effect were guarded cellars in which no blending was permitted. If any of these London-bottled-in-excise-bond Cognacs can be found, they can be among the finest and rarest of Cognacs.

The young Cognac fresh from the still is as raw and harsh as the wine was thin and acid. Its official age is designated *compte* 00. On April 1st after the distillation officially ends, only a couple of months later, the age becomes *compte* 0, and thereafter it changes every year at April 1. As of now the minimum age of three-star Cognac or its equivalent is *compte* 2, for V.S.O.P. or its equivalent it is *compte* 4, and for old Cognacs the minimum is *compte* 6. Because of the huge stocks of Cognac the producing firms have on hand, and the enormous sales volume (110–120 million bottles a year), the Bureau National du Cognac, the local regulatory agency, can keep track of Cognacs only through *compte* 6. After that, all regulation and maintenance of quality and integrity in the aging become the firm's responsibility and a matter of prestige and pride. (About 65 percent of all Cognac is sold before it reaches V.S.O.P. age anyway, so the bureau does in fact oversee the bulk of the business.)

By law, no Cognac may be labeled with a vintage date. Therefore, the designations of V.S.O.P., Extra, Special Reserve, and so forth have no precise meaning but represent simply general gradations of age. The term "Napoleon" may be used only for Cognac *compte* 6 or older, but beyond that has no specific meaning as far as age is concerned, and can be used by any firm on any Cognac.

Although many firms have their own vineyards and distill their own wines, the famous firms distill only a small amount of the Cognac themselves. It is more common for a firm to distill wines bought either at the cooperatives or from the individual growers. Most Cognac, however, around 90 percent of it, arrives at the Cognac firm already distilled, either by professional distillers or by the individual growers themselves, who make their wine, distill it, and sell it to the Cognac firms. When you consider that it takes seven liters of wine to make one liter of Cognac, it is clear that a huge amount of wine and, therefore, a huge amount of vineyard are necessary to maintain an adequate supply of brandy. For instance, Bisquit, located near Rouillac, has about 300 hectares (750 acres) of vineyard, which supplies less than 10 percent of its needs. The firm does distill about half of its brandy from wine bought from growers. Courvoisier, on the other hand, with neither vineyards nor distillery, prefers instead to make its 8 million bottles sold yearly with *eaux-de-vie* bought from growers and professional distillers. Hine, the fine firm just across the street from Courvoisier in Jarnac, also has no vineyards or stills and buys young Cognacs already distilled for aging, blending, bottling, and selling. Hennessy Cognac has distilling facilities and about 500 hectares of vines (1,250 acres) which supply less than 10 percent of their *eaux-de-vie*. The remainder comes from the wines bought to distill (around 65 percent) and from the purchase of *eaux-de-vie* already distilled by the 600–700 local distillers (accounting for a bit less than 30 percent). Martell and Otard, also in Cognac, both have vines and stills, but they too must buy the bulk of their brandies.

The growers who make their own wine, distill it, and sell it to the Cognac firms are called *bouilleurs de cru,* and there are over seven thousand of them, supplying the firms with close to a third of all the Cognac that is made. The typical Charentais farmhouse, called a *logis,* incorporates all the grower needs to tend his vines, make his wine, and distill it into *eau-de-vie.* The house is generally made up of four wings drawn up into a square with a courtyard in the middle. To enter the house one must pass through a gated stone archway into the court and from there into the house itself. More often than not the *logis* gates are closed, making the establishment look more like a fortress than a farmhouse.

Despite the importance of the *bouilleurs de cru,* there are two facets of Cognac-making in which they cannot compete with the great firms: aging and blending. These two are inextricably linked. Aging great stocks of Cognac can be extremely expensive, simply because the money spent today to make the Cognac will only begin to be paid back in three or four years, at the least. It is essential to maintain stocks of Cognac if the best possible blends are sought. Because no date is placed on a Cognac bottle, vintages have no importance to the consumer; but they are quite important to the Cognac blender. The fine shades of depth of taste, earthiness, finesse, and so on, vary greatly from Cognac to Cognac, and each firm likes to maintain a house style or type, just as the Champagne firms do.

For all French wines but Champagne, the blending of wines of different vintages and different regions is considered a last resort, and it is always looked on as a little suspect. But in Cognac, blending is raised to the highest of arts. Jean Beneteau of Hine likens it to the mixing and juxtaposition of colors: "We take what by themselves are disparate elements, all excellent in their way but incomplete, and, as if they were colors on a painter's palette, we bring different Cognacs together to make a statement of grace and harmony on the taster's palate."

I have always likened Cognac blending to the blending of Champagne, Sherry, and Port. In all cases the total blend is a better product than any one of the components. The blending of the Cognac of different *crus* and different vintages is always done after they have been bought or distilled by the shippers. The barrels are emptied into gutters running into the blending vats, where great wooden paddles slowly turn and agitate them. Properly done, blending is a slow and exacting task. Cognacs may be blended at any time in their development in the cask, but a year or two of age at least is required before the young *eaux-de-vie* show their character with sufficient clarity to be judged. Although aging a Cognac in barrel does result in alcohol evaporation, the loss amounts on the average to less than 1 percent alcohol per year. It would take 40 to 50 years of aging and evaporation to reduce a new Cognac of 70 percent alcohol to the suitable drinking strength of around 40 percent. "If you aged the contents of a 75-centiliter bottle in wood, after forty years of aging," says Bernard Hine, "the Cognac you'd have would be the proper strength for drinking, but there would be only 6 centiliters of it left—just enough for two of the ounce-sized miniature bottles!" Obviously, it is not financially possible to let nature take its course. So a necessary part of Cognac blending involves using distilled water to reduce the high alcoholic content of the fiery spirit.

In addition to the time-honored technique of "speeding up" the aging of a Cognac by adding distilled water, there are other (perhaps less traditional) techniques used to enhance the apparent age of a Cognac. None of the techniques is harmful in any way, but they are deviations just the same from the naturally slow process of aging a spirit in wood. To enhance the woody taste and deepen color, wooden chips or a wood concentrate are sometimes added while the Cognac is in barrel; for deeper color (as well as added sweetness), caramel (burnt sugar) is added, while to soften and further sweeten, vanilla, which is strictly forbidden, is sometimes used.

More than any other French product of the vine, Cognac has suffered from its image of luxury. Its market is the world, and since around 85 percent of all Cognac is sold abroad, whenever an importing country wants to raise its tax revenues, it is goods considered luxuries, such as perfumes, Champagnes, and Cognacs, that are hit with heavy import duties. And Cognac is often especially singled out. Consequently, in the wine slump of the early seventies, Cognac suffered greater setbacks in sales than any other wine or brandy region. Toward the end of the 1960s it had seemed that demand for Cognac would continue to grow from 8 to 10 percent a year, as it had all through the decade. New vineyards were planted in anticipation of increased demand; and record high yields of wine were recorded in nearly every harvest. But, just when the Cognac firms were set to loose this great quantity of Cognac on the world, the world turned its back. Britain, the largest importer at the time, devalued its currency, making French goods more expensive. In retaliation against the duties imposed on American chickens going into France, the U.S. Treasury placed higher duties on the finer Cognacs. In the "American Chicken War," as the French came to call it, the big losers were the American Cognac drinker and the French Cognac firms: the chickens stayed in the warehouses and the high-priced Cognacs remained on the shelves. And there were many more instances of trade interference. In 1977 alone there were more than forty restrictive measures instituted against the importation of Cognac, involving more than thirty different countries throughout the world. Countries that already taxed it raised the taxes higher; a few that did not, imposed them for the first time. During this period some countries banned Cognac outright, among them Brazil, Ghana, and Peru. The result of all this was a drop in 1974 of 20 percent in Cognac sales. Although it took over three years for the market to rebound from the slump, by 1978 sales attained the levels of the record-breaking year of 1971–72. The 10 to 15 percent growth per year of the pre-slump days may seem overoptimistic but a 4 to 5 percent growth seems likely, and the shippers, for the time being at least, remain sanguine about the future.

In spite of these nagging problems, Cognac's international sales and reputation (one can hardly imagine a world without it) have had the beneficial effect of attracting large investors—mostly in the form of other wine and spirit companies that wish to diversify. Many companies from France and abroad have purchased controlling or minority interest in over a dozen Cognac shipping firms. Without the capital from these new parent companies to tide them over the lean years of the mid-1970s, a number of these smaller firms might well have folded.

One of Cognac's healthiest firms, owing largely to its diversity of interests, is Hennessy Cognac, officially known as Moët-Hennessy. Hennessy has formed its own publicly owned multinational company combining the interests of Moët & Chandon Champagne, Christian Dior perfumes, and Domaine Chandon sparkling wines in the Napa Valley of California. Courvoisier, the largest firm in Jarnac, and Salignac in Cognac are now owned by the Canadian spirit company Hiram Walker, while the small firm of Augier is owned by Seagrams of the United States and Canada. Distillers Company Limited of England—whose Johnnie Walker, Dewar's, White Horse, and Vat 69, among many others, give them control of the Scotch whisky business—added yet another jewel to their crown with the purchase of Hine Cognac in Jarnac.

Three well-known French aperitif companies have nailed down a sizable corner of the Cognac market: Ricard, makers of France's best-selling *pastis,* owns Bisquit Cognac; Berger, also making a popular *pastis,* owns Gauthier Frères; and Saint-Raphaël, makers of the aperitif of the same name, holds a minority share of Otard Cognac, which in turn owns the fine, small Bordeaux-based firm of Exshaw. The list of ownerships and intermarriages goes on, with more and more French, Italians, and Germans counting out their money for a share in the world's most elegant spirit.

It isn't just the shippers who have banded together for financial security; the growers and distillers have done so as well, grouping themselves under the banner of Unicoop, the region's largest wine-distilling cooperative. Unicoop sells its Cognacs under the label of Prince de Polignac (no relation to the venerable Champagne family that had a major interest in Pommery until 1979).

The vicissitudes of international trade and finance being what they are, it is all the more remarkable that two of Cognac's largest firms should still be family-owned and -run. Martell, the largest seller in the town of Cognac, put up 25 percent of its equity for sale on the Paris Bourse, but then apparently thought better of it and bought the shares back. Since then, a younger brother of René Martell, the current president, has sold his 12 percent share of the company to the Elf-Gabon oil company. Rémy-Martin, Cognac's third- or fourth-largest seller, is still in the hands of the descendants of André Renaud, who bought the company in 1924. Much later, in the 1970s, Rémy-Martin took over the Champagne firm of Krug.

Added to the global financial and political handicaps that Cognac faces, there is also the dreaded problem of fashion. With the turn against long, heavy meals, fewer people have the time or the inclination to cap their meals with a snifter of Cognac, no matter how rare. The result of all of this is a huge backlog of maturing Cognacs—there is now about an eight-year supply, just under a billion bottles.

However, it is not all gloom on the Charente *quai*-sides. After the disastrous sales year of 1974, business, as mentioned above, has picked up steadily. The Bureau National de Cognac, the local regulatory agency, has been active in restricting the output of the growers to under 100 hectoliters per hectare (1,060 gallons per acre, which is a Common Market regulation), and the producers of the major firms have reacted with their customary zeal to the challenge of selling Cognac to a world of new dining and drinking habits and the *nouvelle cuisine*. The retail customer is also being catered to in this way. Whereas in the past the bottles used to be frosted or opaque and squat, the trend now is to clear, svelte ones. The Cognacs also tend to be drier, to have less sweetening added to them, and to be a bit lighter in color for this reason also. The blenders have moved away from using Borderies in the better blends because of its rather overpowering personality. In all, it is safe to say that Cognac will not only survive but prosper, for it has been proved time and again that the world's taste for Cognac can withstand the momentary obstacles of fashion and taxes far better than that for any other brandy.

Cognac, like Champagne, is one of the wine regions best prepared to receive tourists. The well-known shipping firms give tours of their aging *chais* and distilleries (if they have any). In Cognac itself you may visit Hennessy, Martell, Otard, and Rémy-Martin, among others; in Jarnac there are Courvoisier and Hine; and in nearby Rouillac there is Bisquit. In season (June to October), tours are given from 8:00 to 11:30 and from 2:00 to 4:30, and are conducted in all languages.

Outside the two principal towns, hundreds of signs dot the Charente country-side indicating the locations of small producers of the Pineau des Charentes, a sweet-ish aperitif wine made from the wines of the Charente region with an addition of *eau-de-vie*. It has an alcoholic strength of up to 18 percent. Also numerous are signs for *vente directe* (direct sale) of the Cognac of local producers.

ARMAGNAC

It says something about Armagnac that its first appearance in world history should be as a land of warriors. Nine Gascon tribes occupied the large area southwest of Bordeaux bounded on the west by the sandy pine barrens of the Landes, on the east by the Gers River, on the south by the Pyrénées, and on the north by the Garonne River. Intertribal warfare was fierce—the only time the Gascons stopped fighting one another was when they did battle against the invading armies of Rome. In suc-ceeding centuries, Gascon horsemen and swordsmen played a leading role, often as mercenaries, in the power struggles of medieval France. Their finest moment was to come under Louis XIII, who created, around the personage of d'Artagnan, the famed King's Musketeers.

If Gascons had been only warriors and knights, however, we would have heard no more about them than what was immortalized by Alexandre Dumas. But from the time of the Romans Gascony has cultivated vines and the art of wine-making; and one part of it especially renowned for this noble enterprise has always been Ar-magnac. Here, as the science of distillation moved slowly north from Moorish Spain, brandy-making was begun—probably even before the white wines of the Charente ever became Cognac.

Of all the French wine regions, Armagnac has remained the least touched by the march of time and civilization. Knotty black oak and pine still cover the rolling hills, and the swarthy Gascon is as hot-blooded and individualistic as ever—and still likely to believe in the witches of Armagnac, who are said to bring luck to their friends and inflict curses on their enemies. Armagnac brandy, a match for the coun-try and the people who make it, is full-bodied, pungent, and strong. Much of it goes to market in a flat, nearly circular, long-necked flagon called the *basquaise*. The best Armagnac is made in Bas-Armagnac, which is the westernmost of the region's three component districts and is called locally by the forbidding name of Armagnac Noir. The best of the Bas-Armagnac was known as Grand-Bas. (Here, as elsewhere in

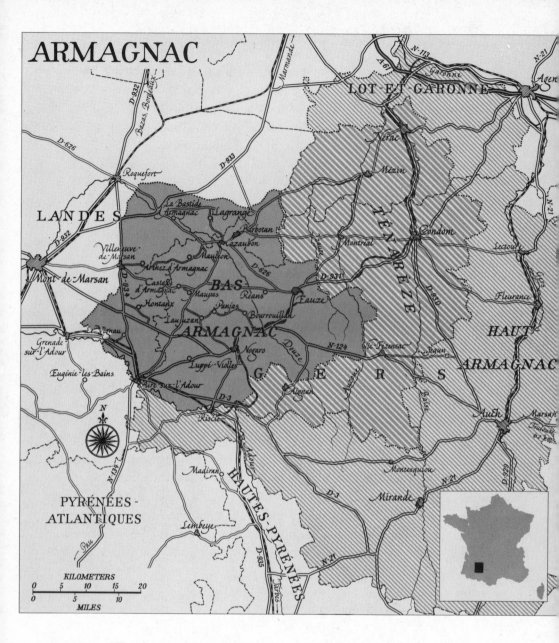

French nomenclature, the designation *bas*—"lower"—had nothing to do with quality but was used in a strictly geographical sense.) Bas-Armagnac commonly appears under its own label, whereas the production of the other two districts, Ténarèze and Haut-Armagnac, is most often used in blends which are sold under the simple generic label "Armagnac."

Armagnac's power is not one of alcohol, but of earthiness, and every step of the

Armagnac process is undertaken to enhance the unique nature of the spirit. The main grape for the Bas-Armagnac is the Baco, which is especially suited to the sandy soil there; sand is for Armagnac what chalk is for Cognac—the sandier the soil, the finer the spirit. In the chalkier regions of Armagnac the Cognac grape, the Ugni Blanc, is used.

Under the hot southern sun, the Baco, Ugni Blanc, and Colombard ripen slowly and make a wine of low alcoholic content. This is one of the reasons the *alembic Armagnaçais*, the traditional still, can be used with such success. As soon as the white wine has stopped fermenting, it is taken from the vat, with the lees—the precipitated material—and distilled in the special Armagnac still. Rather than using the double distillation method described for Cognac, the Armagnac still has five or eight pots on top of one another, and as the spirit moves from each successive pot, vaporizing and condensing at each stage, it becomes stronger and stronger in alcohol. Above the succession of pots, where the *chapiteau* on a Cognac still would normally be, there is a straight pipe leading to the *serpentin* and the condenser. This direct feed-in prevents any rectification from taking place, and so all of the rougher flavor-enhancing elements pass directly into the brandy.

Georges Samalens, one of Armagnac's most distinguished producers and shippers, contrasts Armagnac and Cognac in this fashion: "Cognac gains its distinction by finesse, while Armagnac gains its by power. We are a bit rougher, but we are closer to the soil, and as a result we need more age." However, the double distillation technique used in Cognac has found some adoption in Armagnac since 1972, by the houses of Janneau and Samalens.

Armagnac distilled in the traditional manner is 50-55 percent alcohol when it comes from the still. This compares with a fresh Cognac at about 70 percent alcohol. So when Armagnac growers insist that their brandy needs more time in barrel than Cognac, they are not referring to the simple evaporation of alcohol but to the harmonizing, marrying, and taming of the harsher elements in the spirit. For this, aging in the 400-liter coarse-grained Armagnac oak is essential. The local oak is a sappier, darker wood than the Limousin oak used in Cognac. As a result, an Armagnac aged ten years will be as dark as a Cognac twice that age.

Color notwithstanding, however, Armagnac needs much more aging in wood to attain a finesse comparable to that of Cognac. Because the local oak is becoming scarce, many firms now use Limousin or Tronçais oak. The question of Armagnac age and vintages, though officially regulated, is still a matter of some dispute. The Armagnac producers and the Bureau National Interprofessionel d'Armagnac (B.N.I.A.) use the same system to date their spirits as is used in Cognac. In late September or October the wine is made and distilled almost immediately, and its age is designated as *compte* oo. On the thirtieth of April all distillation must stop and all brandy distilled since the vintage becomes *compte* o. Every year on April 1 the brandy officially gains another year, although in fact it may be a number of months older. The minimum age at which Armagnac may be sold as Armagnac is *compte* 1, which may be sold in casks but never in bottles; for Three Star or its equivalent, *compte* 2; for V.S.O.P., *compte* 4; and for Hors d'Age, "Napoléon," or Extra, the Armagnac must be at least *compte* 5, whereas in Cognac it would be *compte* 6. Unlike Cognac, Armagnacs are still permitted to indicate specific vintage years and specific ages—except when imported into the United States. For an Armagnac house to export specific vintage years to the States it must have the agreement of the Bureau of Alcohol, Tobacco and Firearms of the U.S. Treasury. Armagnac used to be labeled as "ten years old," but because of abuses this practice has been stopped.

Determining the age of an Armagnac has not always been such a straightforward proposition. It is only since the 1960s that the wildly exaggerated claims of fantastic vintages have been stopped. For a while it seemed that venerable Armagnacs from the middle of the nineteenth century were as common as today's V.S.O.P. Such abuses were not easy to monitor, much less control. Then as now, Armagnac sales were spread out over the entire Armagnac region, each of the hundreds and hundreds of small producers and dozens of shippers selling as retailers directly to passing Armagnac amateurs. This is in marked contrast to Cognac sales, over three-quarters of which are made from either Cognac or Jarnac, from shippers selling wholesale, of which 80 percent is exported. Only 40 percent of bottled Armagnac leaves the region. Not only did this geographical handicap to controlling Armagnac ages need to be overcome, but the very nature of the Gascon producer as well. By tradition the Gascon is secretive and not easily given to cooperation, but by the 1950s it was clear even to them that the unreliability of Armagnac vintages and ages was hurting business. The Bureau National Interprofessionel d'Armagnac then took inventory of the volume and age of all Armagnacs, and since then it has slowly been able to stem the flow of fantasy brandy. On average, an Armagnac is likely to be older than a comparable Cognac, both because the age is needed for smoothness and because sales are slower.

All the vagaries of vintage notwithstanding, a well-aged Bas-Armagnac is an incomparable experience. "Half the tasting is in the nose, rather than on the palate," says Georges Samalens. Especially when judging fiery young Armagnacs, Samalens rubs a few drops between his palms and sniffs the bouquet. This gentle heating releases whatever is distinctive in the bouquet which will emerge more prominently as the spirit ages. "In a fine old Bas-Armagnac," says Samalens, "you might smell peaches, the pines of the Landes forest, pears and flowers. The very best of the old Bas-Armagnacs have the unmistakable aroma of plum and violets."

Unfortunately, these Armagnacs are available in few places outside the region, for it has remained frustratingly true that the best Armagnacs are to be had at the homes of the growers. A haphazard approach to marketing, the result of the local people's staunch individualism, has been Armagnac's biggest obstacle to gaining the international reputation and acceptance it will need to prosper as Cognac has. Gustave Ledun, a former director of the Armagnac growers' association, sums it up: "Armagnac is less well known than Cognac, stuck in an unknown, out-of-the-way place; commercially it's a newcomer, even though it's the oldest brandy of France." The only recourse for the unfulfilled Armagnac enthusiast, it would seem, is to go directly to the source—to take in the savage beauty of the countryside and sample and select among hundreds and hundreds of Armagnacs that are made there.

At last count, there were fifteen thousand Armagnac growers cultivating about 10,000 hectares (25,000 acres) of vines used for making Armagnac. There is another 20,000 hectares (50,000 acres) which could be used to make the brandy, but for the present the demand is not there, so the cheap white and red *vin de table*, called Vin de Gers, is made instead. Of the three local appellations, Bas-Armagnac is (as already noted) the only one normally sold under its own label; it accounts for about a third of the Armagnac sold. Less than 5 percent is labeled as Ténarèze and practically none at all as Haut-Armagnac, for, truth to tell, it's nothing to brag about. This leaves slightly over 60 percent of all Armagnac to be sold under the generic appellation "Armagnac." This may be a blend of all three districts, although Ténarèze and Bas-Armagnac make up the usual combination. Of the 15,000 growers, there are about 1,400 who have stocks of old Armagnac for sale; this number includes both shippers and growers. The rest of the growers sell their produce to shippers or to one of the twelve cooperatives—either as wines to be distilled or as young Armagnacs for aging and blending. In the Bas-Armagnac, some of the better growers—often called *domaines*—and shippers, who are usually growers themselves, include Domaine de Gayrosse, Domaine de Boignières, and Claude Lacourtoisie, all in the picturesque town of La Bastide d'Armagnac; in Laujazan, along with the Samalens brothers' shipping firm is the Domaine de Lacave Barregeat, run by their cousins; in Le Frêche, there is the largest retail seller of the Bas-Armagnac at Domaine de Boignières; and in Castex d'Armagnac there is the stately Château de Castex d'Armagnac of the Baron de Saint-Pastou. Also worthy of mention are the Domaine de Lassaubatju in Hontanx, Domaine de l'Arépic in Le Vignau, Domaine de Cavaillon in Lagrange, Domaine de Jouanda in Arthez d'Armagnac, Domaine de Maupas in Mauléon d'Armagnac, and Domaine de Pérrin Bourrouillan and Château de Ravignan in Perquie in the Landes. I must mention that much of my knowledge and affection for the region was gained at the side of one of its champions, the late

Duc Pierre de Montesquiou-Fézenzac. Armagnac is still made under his name by Pernod. M. de Montesquiou's daughter, Victoire, and her husband, Patrick de Montal, are carrying on the quality Armagnac tradition with pride.

Before leaving Armagnac, at one time you could have made a visit to the Thursday afternoon market at Eauze. Winter and summer, rain or shine, farmers and small tradesmen from all over the region assembled in the main square to display their produce and wares. Along with their ducks and geese, live and killed—and of course the fattened liver of each—the Armagnac farmer found room in the *camionnette* for samples of his brandy. The local sacrament could be seen: he would pull a sample flask from his pocket; uncorking it with his teeth, he would pour a few drops on the hands of the buyer, who rubbed his palms together and sniffed. A brief discussion of age, quantity, and price followed, and the purchase was made. Sadly, this scene has disappeared from the drama of the Eauze market day. Progress, if you may call it that, has now restricted these market meetings to once a year, at the time of the annual fair held in late spring or early summer. The revitalization of Armagnac sales, dependent as it is on the centralization of production and publicity efforts, has diverted the growers from the Eauze market to the cooperatives and to the many shippers in Condom. The commercial reach of Armagnac is far greater, but hardly as picturesque.

Another vanishing feature of Armagnac may be the *alembic ambulant*, the traveling still. In the old days there were many more stills than the present twenty—drawn by the placid Pyrénées oxen, creaking from village to village to distill the local wine. Today the oxen are replaced by flat-bed trucks, although this has not made the *alembics* any less infernal. In the 150 farmyards where they stop, they light up the night with dancing flames and hissing steam as logs are tossed into the furnace mouth and Armagnac's thin white wine is transformed into the manliest of French brandies.

CALVADOS

In Normandy, on the wedge of land that juts into the Atlantic above Brittany, is the English Channel country of Calvados, home of the world's finest apple brandy. Normandy in springtime is one of France's most beautiful sights. Hill and vale from Rennes to the Atlantic Ocean are covered with blossoming apple trees, and the air is fresh from the scent. Besides for its apple trees and the local specialty, *tripes à la mode de Caen,* this tongue of land is best known as the site of the Allied landings on June 6, 1944. Certainly since then the words "Normandy beach" have never been the same.

Calvados is made from the fermented juice of apples in the same way that Cognac is made from grapes. The apples must be crushed according to traditional methods and left to macerate for a month. The juice is then distilled twice in a pot still and has about the same percentage of alcohol as Cognac. Like both Cognac and Armagnac, it is a fiery spirit when young, attaining a proper fullness with age.

Like Armagnac, Calvados has had great difficulty organizing itself to expand its clientele. Significant stocks have been built up in recent years to make possible more long-range commitments to buyers, and sales have generally been up since 1976. The Bureau National du Calvados has taken over much of the research and planning necessary for increasing the market that the small, family-run operation could not have hoped to undertake.

Calvados has suffered a bit from its reputation as a heady peasant spirit—its dryness (for no sugar is added) often makes it seem stronger than it really is. At its best, a well-aged "Calva" will combine the fleeting sappiness and tang of apples with a dry oakiness gained from the barrel. It is not for the faint-hearted, but in nuance and depth of taste it is surpassed only by the best of Cognac and Armagnac. Unlike his colleagues in Cognac, the Calvados shipper was allowed to put a vintage on the bottle label. In the past, controls were lax to say the least, and young Calvados would be passed off as fantastically ancient. Now the industry recognizes that, in the long run, it loses more than it gains by such petty deception, and strict controls are enforced. If age is mentioned on the label, it usually follows this system: three stars or three apples indicate a Calvados at least two years old; Vieux or Réserve is three years old; Very Old or Vieille Réserve is four years old; and V.S.O.P. is five. In essence this is identical to Cognac labeling, except that the stars or apples indicate specific ages, not just descriptions of types of spirit. The professionals of the region like to point out that, on average, Calvados is older than any other French brandy. The best Calvados region is that of Vallée d'Auge, which is the only Calvados place-name permitted. One sometimes finds very old Vallée d'Auge which can be excellent. Alas, these are very rare.

A *marc,* called Eau-de-Vie de Marc de Cidre, is also made from the apple pressings left over after the fermentation, but—fortunately—it is not often found outside of France.

If you come to Calvados and have your fill of the spirited brandy they make, be sure to try the *cidre de la Vallée d'Auge.* It is a sparkling, alcoholic cider and thoroughly refreshing when served cool from stone pitchers at the local restaurants.

⚜

COGNAC
Hotels and Restaurants

H = *Hotel;* R = *Restaurant*

The easiest access to Cognac is by rail from Paris or Spain to Angoulême, or by autoroute through Poitiers to Saintes. Cognac is less than 100 kilometers northwest of Bordeaux. This list uses Cognac as the center point. All other towns are indicated as approaches to Cognac.

The main Cognac distillers have visiting hours and tours. While in Cognac visit the distilleries of Hennessey, Martell, Otard, and Rémy-Martin; the latter receives visitors only by appointment. For more information, see pp. 383–95, plus Itinerary K, pp. 428–29.

COGNAC (16100—Charente)
(Angoulême 42—Bordeaux 113—Saintes 26—Jarnac 14—La Rochelle 114)

H LE FRANÇOIS Ier: Place François-Ier, in center of town. Tel.: 45.32.07.18.   29 rooms (24 with toilets).
No restaurant, breakfast available. Medium comfort. Inexpensive.

HR LE VALOIS: 35, rue du 14 juillet. Tel.: 45.82.76.00. Tlx.: 790987.   27 smallish, comfortable, functional, air-conditioned rooms.
Convenient, central location. No restaurant.

H LE MODERNE: 24, rue Élysée-Mousnier. Tel.: 45.82.19.53. 36 rooms.
No restaurant, breakfast available. Fair comfort. Inexpensive.

HR LES PIGEONS BLANCS: 110, rue Jules-Brisson, on road to Saint-Jean-d'Angély, just outside of
Cognac. Tel.: 45.82.16.36. Six rooms with toilet.
Good.

SAINT-LAURENT-DE-COGNAC (16100—Charente)
6 km on N-141 toward Saintes

HR LE LOGIS DE BEAULIEU. Tel.: 45.82.30.50. Tlx.: 791020. 20 quiet rooms (13 with toilet).
Pleasant setting in a park, close to main roads. Good food and fairly reasonable. Its proximity to
Cognac makes this one of the favorite restaurants of the Cognac shippers.

CIERZAC (16660—Charente)
(Angoulême 49—Poitiers 141)
13 km south of Cognac on D-731, road to Barbezieux, at Saint-Fort-sur-le-Né

HR LE MOULIN DE CIERZAC. Tel.: 45.83.01.32. 10 rooms (only 5 with toilet).
Good food, in a park overlooking a river.

JARNAC (16200—Charente)
(Cognac 14—Bordeaux 112—Angoulême 28—Barbezieux 27—Poitiers 119)
In Jarnac visit the distilleries of Courvoisier and Hine.

HR LE DOMAINE DE FLEURAC: At Fleurac (9 km east on N-141 and D-384 or 10 km by D-66 or
D-158). Tel.: 45.81.78.22. 10 rooms in the main house, another 7, which are small, in the annex
(15 with toilets).
Quiet, pleasant nineteenth-century château in the midst of beautiful parkland. Fair food. Reasonable. English spoken.

R RESTAURANT DU CHÂTEAU: Place du Château. Tel.: 45.81.07.17.
M. Destrieux, the owner, is a very welcoming host. Good food.

R LA RIBAUDIÈRE: 6 km from Jarnac on N-541 at Bourg Charente. Tel.: 45.81.30.54.
Simple, inexpensive inn on the Charente River.

SAINTES (17100—Charente-Maritime)
(Cognac 27—Jarnac 41—Angoulême 70—Royan 37—Rochefort 39—
Bordeaux 118—Poitiers 126)

HR COMMERCE MANCINI: Rue des Messageries. Tel.: 46.93.06.61. Tlx.: 791012. 34 rooms, 6
suites.
Close to post office. Pleasant, comfortable. Best hotel and restaurant in Saintes. Reasonable food,
but not worth a detour.

BARBEZIEUX (16300—Charente)
(Angoulême 33—Bordeaux 85—Cognac 33—Jarnac 40—Saintes 54—
Libourne 66—Saint-Émilion 73)

HR LA BOULE D'OR: 9, boulevard Gambetta. Tel.: 45.78.22.72. 28 rooms (14 with toilet).
Simple, good, inexpensive menus. Comfortable. South of Cognac, Jarnac, and Angoulême.

ANGOULÊME (16000—Charente)
(Jarnac 28—Cognac 42—La Rochelle 126—Poitiers 110—Bordeaux 118—Périgueux 85)

HR HOSTELLERIE DU MOULIN DU MAINE-BRUN: At Asnières-sur-Nouère (across town and 8 km from Angoulême on N-141, road to Cognac). Tel.: 45.96.92.62. Tlx.: 791053. 16 luxurious rooms and 2 suites. The restaurant is now called Le Moulin Gourmand. Swimming pool. Elegant, in the midst of a park, quiet. May be the best hotel-restaurant of the Cognac region. Rather expensive, but good value. Good food and wine list. The restaurant is tastefully decorated with period furniture. M. Menager distills his own Cognac and is only too eager to show off his small distillery. The management is now supervised by Irene and Raymond Menager. English spoken. *Relais et Châteaux.* One star in Michelin.

HR GRAND HÔTEL DE FRANCE: 1, place des Halles (in center of town). Tel.: 45.95.47.95. Tlx.: 791020. 61 fairly comfortable rooms (44 with toilet).
Good restaurant available, fair prices.

H NOVOTEL: At Champniers (6 km north on N-10). Tel.: 45.68.53.22. Tlx.: 790153. 100 air-conditioned and soundproofed rooms.
Snacks available. Swimming pool.

R LA CHAMADE: 13, rampe d'Aguesseau. Tel.: 45.38.41.33.
Philippe Lafforgue in 1985 filled a need for a good restaurant in the center of town. It has become a small gastronomic attraction in Angoulême.

MARENNES (17320—Charente-Maritime)
(Cognac 70—Jarnac 84—Bordeaux 160—Saintes 40—Rochefort 20—
La Rochelle 50—Royan 31)

One of the world capitals for oysters. Don't be dissuaded by the general belief that oysters should only be eaten during months with an "r" in the name. These luscious bivalves can be had fresh from the Marennes oyster beds at any time of the year. However, finicky gourmets may not wish to enjoy them during the summer months; though fresh, the oysters will be milky, which detracts somewhat from their usual salty and tangy taste of the sea.

R LA FRANCE: 8, rue de la République. Tel.: 46.85.00.37.
Fair, inexpensive restaurant.

HR LES CLAIRES: At Bourcefranc-le-Chapus (5 km). Tel.: 46.85.08.01. Tlx.: 792055. 20 rooms. Quiet, comfortable. Good food at moderate prices. Surrounded by oyster beds from which fresh oysters are served year round. There is a large assortment of other fresh fish as well. Warm welcome. One star in Michelin.

LA ROCHELLE (17000—Charente-Maritime)
(Cognac 96—Bordeaux 188—Angoulême 126—Niort 63—Nantes 146—Rochefort 30)

A colorful medieval fortified fishing port with small streets bordered by arcades, this city was the center of the religious wars during the sixteenth century. Historically inclined citizens still fulminate over the Italian architect/traitor who constructed the fortified ramparts for the Protestants. Having done so, he switched sides and headed the assault by the Catholics on what he knew to be the strategically weak sections of the ramparts. Seafood is the local specialty. This town is worth a detour.

H LES BRISES: Avenue Philippe Vincent, on the Digue Richelieu. Tel.: 46.43.89.37. 46 quiet rooms of which 35 overlook the ocean bay.
Appropriate in fine weather. No restaurant.

HR LE YACHTMAN: 23, quai Valin. Tel.: 46.41.26.91.   40 rooms.
Modern hotel with swimming pool. A young chef has taken on the burden of following Le Divellec, now in Paris, who was La Rochelle's gastronomic hero.

HR FRANCE-ANGLETERRE and R LE RICHELIEU: 22, rue Gargoulleau. Tel.: 46.41.34.66. Tlx.: 790717.   76 rooms.
Quiet, modern hotel within a garden in the center of town. Good restaurant. The most convenient for discovering this historic town.

HR ST-JEAN D'ACRE and AU VIEUX PORT: 4, Place de la Chaîne. Tel.: 46.41.73.03. Tlx.: 790913.   49 small, inexpensive modern rooms.
A small seafood bistro.

R RICHARD COUTANCEAU: Plage de la Concurrence. Tel.: 46.41.48.19.
At the entrance of the port, specializing in fish and seafood. May be the best restaurant in La Rochelle. Two stars in Michelin.

R LA MARMITE: 14, rue Saint Jean-du-Perot, near the port. Tel.: 46.41.17.03.
Louis Marzin knows how to deal with the produce of the sea. One star in Michelin.

R SERGE: 46, cours des Dames. Tel.: 46.41.18.80.
In the port. Good food, but expensive relative to value. Prices made up for by a charming terrace where you can taste good oysters and good Muscadet. One star in Michelin.

NIEUIL (16270—Charente)
(Angoulême 42—Limoges 65—Ruffec 36)

HR CHÂTEAU DE NIEUIL: Tel.: 45.71.36.38. Tlx.: 791230.   10 rooms, 3 suites. Swimming pool and tennis.
Impressive château, large rooms in a large park. *Relais & Châteaux.* One star in Michelin.

&

ARMAGNAC
Hotels and Restaurants
H = *Hotel;* R = *Restaurant*

There are excellent restaurants (listed alphabetically) scattered throughout the Armagnac region. Many of them carry extensive selections of old Armagnacs which can be ordered by the glass.

AIRE-SUR-L'ADOUR (40800—Landes)
(Paris 721—Auch 82—Dax 76—Tarbes 69—Condom 67—Orthez 59—
Pau 49—Mont-de-Marsan 31—Segos 9)

HR DOMAINE DE BASSIBÉ: In Segos (Gers), 9 km southwest on N-134 and D-260. Tel.: 62.09.46.71 or 62.09.43.55. Tlx.: 531918. 6 comfortable rooms and 3 suites.
Jean-Pierre Capelle studied kitchen artistry under Michel Guérard, and with pride he runs this *Relais & Châteaux* which has one star in Michelin.

AUCH (32000—Gers)
(Agen 73—Bordeaux 181—Toulouse 77—Condom 43)

◖ This is the ancient capital of Armagnac and Gascony where the musketeer D'Artagnan first took up fencing. The cathedral with its dark wood pews is the masterpiece here. However, the pilgrims of today beat a path to a different altar, in search of Monsieur Daguin's *foie gras* creations.

HR HÔTEL DE FRANCE: Place de la Libération. Tel.: 62.05.00.44. Tlx.: 520474.   30 air-conditioned rooms.

M. André Daguin has done much to promote the specialties of Gascony, which include *foie gras* and Armagnac brandy. Some rooms are comfortable, some luxurious. The good food is worth more than a detour. A new bar, called Le Neuvième, has recently been opened, offering simple, fast service at reasonable prices until 1:00 A.M. Les Caves de l'Hôtel de France, next to the hotel, offer a good assortment of fine Armagnacs and *foie gras*. *Relais et Châteaux*. Two stars in Michelin.

BARBOTAN-LES-THERMES (32150—Gers)
(Auch 73—Mont-de-Marsan 43—Condom 37—Eauze 20—Aire-sur-l'Adour 35—Agen 77)

HR THERMALE BASTIDE GASCONNE: Tel.: 62.69.52.09. Tlx.: 521009.   50 rooms.
Christine and Michel Guérard recommended this fine hotel-restaurant-spa formerly owned by Mme Guérard's father. Michel periodically oversees the restaurant, while his wife is responsible for the décor. The hotel is comfortable, and the food, understandably, is very good. Pool and tennis court.

BIARRITZ (64200—Pyrénées-Atlantiques)
(Bordeaux 190—Dax 57—Hendaye 28—Bayonne 8—Pau 115—San Sebastian, Spain 50)

If you are thirsting for a couple of days in a comfortable seaside resort, why not spend at least a weekend in Biarritz?

A very easily driven road through the flat forest of the Landes leads from Bordeaux to Biarritz and takes less than two hours. If you are contemplating going to Armagnac, Biarritz is again an easy detour.

HR LE PALAIS: 1, avenue de l'Impératrice. Tel.: 59.24.09.40. Tlx.: 570000.   140 rooms, 20 apartments.
I consider this to be one of the most comfortable, luxurious resort hotels in France.

HR MIRAMAR: avenue de l'Impératrice. Tel.: 59.24.85.20. Tlx.: 540831.   105 modern comfortable rooms, 17 suites. Swimming pool.
The main feature of this very well run establishment is its rest and slimming cure, known as the saltwater center of Thalassotherapie. I have lost kilos there in a short period and have enjoyed the well-thought-out and well-prepared meals consisting of 850 calories a day. The Relais du Miramar was given one star in 1985 by Michelin, and Mr Daniel Broch, the manager, and his team deserve applause.

HR LE CHÂTEAU DE BRINDOS: 5 km from Biarritz. Tel.: 59.23.17.68. Tlx.: 541428.
In a small park close to the airport. 16 comfortable rooms. *Relais et Châteaux*. One star in Michelin.

R LE CAFÉ DE PARIS: 5, place Bellevue, close to the Casino. Tel.: 59.24.19.53.
Elegant and refined gastronomy. This excellent restaurant deserves its star in Michelin. Pierre Laporte is the most deserving great chef in the Basque country.

CONDOM (32100—Gers)
(Bordeaux 124—Toulouse 110—Agen 40—Auch 43—Mont-de-Marsan 80)

HR LE LOGIS DES CORDELIERS and RESTAURANT LA TABLE: Rue des Cordeliers. Tel.: 62.28.03.68. 21 rooms.
Fair food in this setting of the chapel of a fourteenth-century monastery. The menus are expensive, but their quality makes them a good value. The wine list is unimaginative; unless one feels in the mood for a great bottle, the relatively inexpensive Côtes de Buzet or Madiran might be preferred. Since Jean-Louis Palladin, the chef, left for the Watergate in Washington, D.C., the restaurant has lost its Michelin stars.

EAUZE (32800—Gers)
(Bordeaux 145—Auch 52—Aire-sur-l'Adour 38—Condom 29—Mont-de-Marsan 52)
This is the capital of Armagnac.

HR DE L'ARMAGNAC: 1, rue Blançat. Tel.: 62.09.88.11. 14 rooms (only 2 with toilets), to avoid. Small, simple, and inexpensive, with country food cooked by the *patronne*.

R MOULIN DU POUY: Tel.: 62.09.82.58.
The young Jean-Luc Arnaud, a native Gascon, studied under great chefs and has returned to make a name for himself, which he is doing by having Master André Daguin recommend him as being the best in the area.

EUGÉNIE-LES-BAINS (40320—Landes)
(Aire-sur l'Adour 13—Mont-de-Marsan 25—Pau 54—
Villeneuve-de-Marsan 34—Bordeaux 145—Biarritz 127—Eauze 50)

HR LES PRÉS D'EUGÉNIE and Restaurant MICHEL GUÉRARD. Tel.: 58.51.19.01. Tlx.: 540470. 38 rooms (super-comfortable). Tennis. Swimming pool.
The search for the finest quality in food, wines, service, and décor is the heartbeat of the Guérards' achievement, and it gives one a sense of elation to experience it. The warm humanity of Michel Guérard matches the artistry of his imaginative approach to cooking, which has not only revolutionized French cuisine but influenced that of the world. *Relais et Châteaux*. Three stars in Michelin.

FLEURANCE (32500—Gers)
(Condom 29—Toulouse 85—Lourdes 120—Bordeaux 180)

HR LE FLEURANCE: on the Route d'Agen, 2 km outside of town on the road between Auch and Agen. Tel.: 62.06.07.70. 25 rooms (19 toilets).
The restaurant, separately run by Bernard Cusinato, with his wife Nicole serving the dishes, has been recommended as being good by André Daguin.

GIMONT (32200—Gers)
(Auch 27—Toulouse-Blagnac airport 40—Toulouse 50—Montauban 70—
Tarbes 100—Lourdes 120—Bordeaux 220)

HR CHATEAU DE LARROQUE: Route Toulouse. Tel.: 62.67.77.44. Tlx.: 531135. 15 rooms, including 7 large ones. Tennis.

Located in a 20-hectare park. A large, converted Second Empire house which is a *Relais et Châteaux.*

LUPPÉ-VIOLLES (32110—Gers)
(Roquefort 43—Condom 55—Aire-sur-l'Adour 12—Auch 69—Pau 62—
Mont-de-Marsan 37—Tarbes 66—Bordeaux 170)

HR RELAIS DE L'ARMAGNAC: On N-124. Tel.: 62.09.04.54. 10 basic rooms.
Although the new light cuisine is the theme, Roger and Martine Duffour also offer succulent regional goose and game dishes at fairly reasonable prices.

MAGESCQ (40990—Landes)
(Dax 17—Bordeaux 132—Biarritz 50—Bayonne 42—Mont-de-Marsan 65—
Eugénie-Les-Bains 91)

HR LE RELAIS DE LA POSTE: rue de la Poste, on N-10. Tel.: 58.47.70.25. 15 agreeable rooms.
The marvelous food of Bernard and Jean Coussau is superior to the rooms. One of the best restaurants offering specialties of the Landes. Good wine list. Tennis, swimming pool. Two stars in Michelin. An excellent stopover is driving to Biarritz or Spain.

PLAISANCE-DU-GERS (32160—Gers)
(Auch 54—Aire-sur-l'Adour 30—Tarbes 48—Eauze 59—Tarbes 44—Mirande 24)

HR LA RIPA-ALTA: Place de l'Église. Tel.: 62.69.30.43. 15 rooms (6 with toilet).
Regional cooking at its best in this delightful small restaurant on the church square. One star in Michelin.

POUDENAS (47170—Lot-et-Garonne)
(Bordeaux 140—Agen 49—Condom 19—Nérac 15—Mont-de-Marsan 66)

R LA BELLE GASCONNE: on D-656 facing an old water mill. Tel.: 58.65.71.58.
M. and Mme Gracia-Soubiran, both of whom trained at Raymond Thuilier's Oustaù de Baumanière, carefully prepare meals featuring fresh regional specialties. The *foie gras* is excellent. Well-appointed wine-cellar with good local wine. One star in Michelin.

VILLENEUVE-DE-MARSAN (40190—Landes)
(Aire-sur-l'Adour 21—Auch 87—Condom 64—Mont-de-Marsan 17—Bordeaux 123)

HR DARROZE: Grand' Rue. Tel.: 58.45.20.07.   35 rooms, of which 12 are comfortable, 20 a bit less so, and 3 whose price would be attractive to anyone on a budget.
Since 1983, Francis Darroze, with his successful brother, Claude (in Langon), has strongly revived the restaurant built by their late father, Jean, which had achieved a national reputation. Being in the heart of the Landes, naturally their specialties are geese and ducks, their livers as well as all their other attributes. Excellent selection of Armagnacs. One star in Michelin.

HR L'EUROPE: Place de La Boiterie. Tel.: 58.45.20.08.   15 simple rooms.
M. Garrapit, the gracious host at this small hotel, presents light Gascony cooking. Honest prices. One star in Michelin. Swimming pool. I prefer Darroze.

SUGGESTED
TOURS

There is scarcely a corner of France that is not touched by vineyards and the life of wine. Even in the heart of Paris, vines climb up the hill of Montmartre and are good for a few cases of wine each year.

Taken by themselves, the main French vineyards are oases of pleasure, even to the traveler on a short visit. Certainly there is a lifetime of traveling and tasting pleasure in France for anyone interested solely in appreciating its vintages.

However, the vineyard countryside offers other delights to the non-oenophile side of every wine-lover. Over the past two thousand years, the history and culture of France have been inextricably bound up with the vineyards. And to discover them, one does not go only to Paris, but into the French countryside. The growing of vines and the making of wine have always been one of the most civilizing of man's enterprises. Therefore it is not surprising that the vineyard roads should follow the earliest veins of French civilization.

A number of France's most fascinating and charming towns are vineyard villages that offer their own flavorful bouquets of wine and history. There are Saint-Émilion, with all its medieval stone and the ruined archway at its center, and Riquewihr, with its typically Alsatian, timber-laced houses. Chinon lies in the midst of Renaissance pageantry; here art history, gastronomy, and viticultural expression echo the lives of many of the kings of France.

Haute cuisine also has a way of following the *Routes des Vins,* because food and wine go together. Every vineyard region in France boasts one or more restaurants awarded high honors in the world of gastronomy; many of the greatest French chefs prefer the provinces to the cities, and the wine provinces in particular. In Burgundy, Alain Chapel reigns in Mionnay, Paul Bocuse in Collonges, Lameloise in Chagny. And in Roanne, one comes upon the gustatorial treasures of Jean Troisgros. There are others: Bernard Loiseau in Saulieu, Gérard Boyer in Reims, Georges Blanc in Vonnas, and Marc Meneau in Vézelay. The Haeberlin brothers and Gaertner help make Alsace memorable. Michel Augereau in Les Rosiers sets tables that are among the finest in the Loire. And in Bordeaux, chefs Amat, Darroze, Garcia, Gauthier, and Male have helped push the *haute* in *haute cuisine* still higher.

As for lodging, many luxurious hotels will be found in the remoter corners of France. The Relais et Châteaux Association includes many hotels that were once stately private castles, converted now to receive guests in great style and comfort in spacious rooms, invariably on the expensive side. The Relais et Châteaux Association also has its own, rather costly, illustrated guide to its member hotels. In this book I point out the restaurants picked by Michelin, and show the accolade of the stars received, as well as those currently members of the *Relais et Châteaux* configuration. But please, please remember that three-star restaurants are an essentially filling experience, and don't try to pop them into a rapid succession but give yourself time for digestion, reflection, and perspective. You will often find many Michelin two-star restaurants memorable experiences, as they may be trying all the harder to achieve the supreme glory of that third star.

Not that expensive meals and accommodations are obligatory when traveling through France. Country inns and restaurants offer respectable rooms (often too small for my taste) and good hearty fare at very affordable prices, especially in the vineyard regions. In addition, there are many moderately priced modern hotels which boast less charm, but do provide cleanliness, comfort, and convenience. All told, there are food and lodging in France to satisfy any traveler's budget.

In the fifteen itineraries that follow I have restricted myself to the vineyard regions and the country that lies between. Using Paris as the starting point, the traveler may strike off in several directions—all of them distinct and all of them exciting. To the east lie Champagne and Alsace, to the south Burgundy and the Rhône, to the southwest the Loire, Cognac, Bordeaux, and the Dordogne. These itineraries attempt to unite France's cultural heritage and varied vineyard landscapes with the world of wonderful wines and high gastronomy. And, as anyone who has visited France can tell you, there is an embarrassment of riches. It is perhaps best to state forthrightly that it is impossible to be comprehensive; the itineraries inevitably represent compromises forced upon the average traveler by lack of time. If you are able to follow them in a more leisurely fashion, you are certain to gain in enjoyment and treasured memories.

VINEYARD TRAVEL IN FRANCE

First-time travelers to the vineyard country—even the French themselves—are often unaware that no introduction is needed to visit many of the Bordeaux wine châteaux or Burgundy cellars. It should be remembered that most wine-makers do not speak English, although in certain areas you will occasionally find male and female guides who lead tours in two or three languages at once. Generally speaking, Bordeaux, Cognac, and Champagne are the best organized in this respect.

As a matter of Gallic perversity, most wine establishments—whether an acre plot in Pouilly-Fuissé or a large Bordeaux château—will not be open on weekends or during July and August. They also close from 12 noon to 2:30 for that moment of high holiness in France: lunch.

In Burgundy—and particularly in the Beaujolais—rather than visiting the *vignerons* themselves (who sometimes are available and sometimes not), you may find it more rewarding to stop in at the *caveaux de dégustation* found along the vineyard roads and in villages. These tasting rooms, maintained by the growers' associations of various wine-making communities, offer a wide selection of the local wines at modest prices.

Transportation

PLANE TRAVEL

There are a number of airlines that fly directly from the United States to France—TWA, Pan Am, Aeromexico, Pakistan International Airlines, and Air France.

Although many tourists are under the illusion that they receive better food and wine on Air France, this has not always been my own experience. I personally prefer TWA or Pan Am, the latter being the more wine-minded.

Domestic flights take off from Orly Ouest, and a few from Charles de Gaulle. Some of the vineyard towns and cities with airports are Bordeaux, Nice, Strasbourg, Colmar, Lyon, Marseille, Tours, and Nantes. A word of caution: The domestic flights are expensive. Air Inter, however, along with several other domestic airlines, has offered certain reductions to small children, students and the young, newlyweds, large families, and passengers 60 or 65 and over. So check ahead with Air France or Air Inter to see what's available.

⚘

TRAIN TRAVEL

French trains are fast, clean, comfortable, and almost always exactly on time. For all train travel in the high season and on weekends, it is wise to have a seat reserved ahead of time.

Paris to Bordeaux: Many daily direct trains take four and a half hours from the Gare d'Austerlitz to the Gare Saint-Jean in Bordeaux. For an extra fee, you may make the journey in only four hours aboard the Trans-Europe Express. (Either way, the train may be preferable to the Paris-to-Bordeaux plane which, with Paris-to-airport connections and the inevitable wait, takes almost three hours. And the plane fare is probably also less attractive unless you fall into the "newlywed student over 65" category.)

Paris to Champagne: Reims, the capital of Champagne, is an hour and a half from Paris.

Paris to the Loire: Two hours brings you to the Tours station of Saint-Pierre-des-Corps, a short drive from the city of Tours and the charms of the Touraine.

Paris to Burgundy: Train travel to Burgundy is now speedier than to the rest of France, thanks to the advent of the new TGV, the *Train à Grande Vitesse,* literally translated as "Very Fast Train." It cruises comfortably at 280 kilometers (160 miles) per hour. Most interesting for the wine traveler is that lines are now open, with a two-hour service between Paris and Lyon, some with a stop at Mâcon, only a bicycle ride away from the Mâconnais vineyards of Pouilly-Fuissé. Travel time between Mâcon and Paris is one hour and forty minutes. The other convenient stop on the TGV Paris-to-Lyon route is Creusot-Montchanin, an otherwise ugly industrial center that is 32 kilometers from Chagny itself, and 47 kilometers from Beaune. (Whatever your destination, reservations are necessary to board a TGV.) Additional straight, bullet-like tracks have now been laid toward various cities in the south of France, and they will carry this new "Concorde" of trains.

Strasbourg to Paris: Four hours, or less, brings you from Strasbourg to Paris in luxury, as the new super-first-class train, featuring a three-star restaurant under the supervision of Joël Robuchon, owner of the Paris Jamin restaurant, is now in operation. The train returns to Strasbourg, capital of Alsace, in the evening.

NOTE: There is one important train connection which France has *not* as yet mastered, and that is the trip from Bordeaux to Burgundy. The Dordogne and the Massif Central mountains lie between, making even the most direct trip—Bordeaux to Lyon—a nine-hour affair. The Dordogne itineraries given below will make the journey by car into a most desirable and very recommendable vacation in itself.

AUTOMOBILE TRAVEL

Until fairly recently in France, the slow "scenic route" was the only way to get anywhere by car. In the last half-decade, the face of France has drastically changed. From a country of back roads, it has become a land of four-lane superhighways known as *autoroutes*. In the past, the charm of the countryside compensated for the slowness of getting there; now the monotony of the autoroute is compensated for by ease and speed and the precious time that is gained. In the itineraries that follow, I have tried to combine the advantages and comforts of the autoroutes with the pleasures of detours onto scenic roads in the famous vineyard areas. Knowing when to use the autoroutes can, in fact, make all the difference in your enjoyment of travel through France.

• Since some new autoroutes are still being built, you may occasionally find yourself "deviated" on and off the highway at various points.

• *When* you travel in France makes a great difference in the time needed to drive from one region to another. It has always been my belief that the national religion in France is not Catholicism, but *les Vacances*. They begin with ritualistic fervor at the beginning of July and don't let up until the end of August. If at all possible, avoid traveling on either the first or last days of the summer months.

• Most cities and many towns have car rental agencies, either in the center of town, at the train station, or at the airport. While you can easily travel by train or plane to and from the various winegrowing regions, a car is absolutely necessary once you are within the vineyard area.

• The traveling time indicated in the itineraries is based on average traffic and weather conditions. If contending with *les Vacances,* adjust your schedule accordingly.

• On standard French road maps, *A* (and *B*) indicates a four-lane autoroute, and *N* stands for *route nationale. D* represents the *routes départementales*—roads that are small but beautifully kept up, rarely have potholes, and are often scenic.

⌁ *Hotels and Restaurants* ℰ

Despite the high quality and dependability of the ratings given in many guidebooks, including Michelin, I find their judgment wanting in their assessment of hotel rooms. They often fail to note spaciousness or comfort, which—rightly or wrongly—I consider to be of prime importance. In evaluating the rooms of hotels in the vineyard regions, I have made a point of doing so.

It should also be remembered that hotel and restaurant reservations may be very difficult to make between the beginning of June and early October. In the main resorts of France, rooms are booked weeks in advance. Reservations are doubly difficult in the Relais et Châteaux hotels, which are often sumptuous but with a relatively small number of rooms. In addition, many of the large hotels in the French countryside close down for a couple of months in the winter. So if your visit is planned from November to March, check ahead for the seasonal closing dates.

The hotels and restaurants at the end of this chapter are a selection of establishments that are actually outside the confines of the vineyard regions but that nonetheless play an important role in a number of itineraries.

A general and final word of advice: As I have already said, the following itineraries exist in order to give you some suggestions about the places you might wish to visit and where you might wish to eat and stay. But they are only guidelines. Often when I ask American visitors to France about their travel plans, they breathlessly respond: "We're going to all the three-star restaurants." That's all very well, but do not forget that the three-star restaurants of today were once one- and two-star restaurants, and that the apprentices of today may well be making gastronomic headlines tomorrow. A refined palate and refined taste recognize excellence in any form.

This same approach applies to your choice and appreciation of wines. The top, top wines are not necessarily the only ones capable of giving wine drinkers the greatest possible enjoyment. And a blind adherence to the 1855 classification of Bordeaux is not necessarily a guarantee of pleasure. One must not shun standards, but quality cannot be judged solely by snobbery or by past performance, nor by the raves of so-called expert oracles. Labels, on wine as much as on anything else, often serve as little more than a crutch for those who do not trust their own instincts or who do not have the imagination or the desire to look further.

So listen to others with more experience, who can help guide you, but build up your own knowledge and preferences on suggestions such as those that follow. You'll find that you will return again to the places you discovered with enthusiasm, and in time will be able to guide others in discovering the wines and vineyards of France.

The fifteen itineraries below have been organized to accommodate the traveler who is in a hurry; they represent a regrettable race against time. Consider them at best a framework within which you can see—in a limited amount of time—the regions of France that I have been admiring for a whole lifetime.

The New Telephone System in France

France has had many upheavals. One of the most recent ones occurred at the end of October 1985, when the entire French telephone system was updated. The previous six- or seven-figure numbers have now incorporated the previous area codes of either one or two figures as part of the telephone number.

The exceptions to this rule are Paris and the Hauts-de-Seine, Seine-Saint-Denis, and the Val-de-Marne areas. In the case of these regions the digit 4 was added as a first number to the existing seven-figure number.

The other Greater Paris areas, or outer rim, of Val-d'Oise, Yvelines, Essonne, and Seine-et-Marne followed the general rule in incorporating their area code of either 3 for the first two or 6 for the last two into the existing seven-figure number.

To simplify:

From province to province or locally:
Dial the eight-figure number (*without* the previous 16).

From Paris/Greater Paris region to within the region:
Dial only the eight-figure number.

From Paris/Greater Paris region to the provinces:
Dial 16, wait for the tone, and then dial the eight-figure number. (This is, in fact, no different from the previous system.)

From the provinces to Paris/Greater Paris region:
Dial 16, wait for the tone, dial 1 and then the eight-figure number.

From abroad to the provinces:
Dial the international access code, the country code for France, followed by the eight-figure number.

From abroad to Paris/Greater Paris region:
Dial the international access code, the country code for France followed by 1, and then the eight-figure number.

THE ITINERARIES

Itinerary A

CHAMPAGNE: ONE DAY

Champagne, whose bottles contain the world's most elegant bubbles, is a sparkling and feasible destination for a one-day trip from the French capital.

On whatever day you choose—except Saturdays and Sundays—depart quite early in the morning from the Porte de Bercy in Paris. Drive on speedy Autoroute A-4 for 130 kilometers (one and a half hours, depending on traffic), when you will arrive in Reims. This notable city is the focal point for the wines of Champagne.

Spend the morning touring the chalk cellars where millions of bottles lie, row upon row, for miles underground. Most worth visiting among these catacomb-cellars are Pommery & Greno, Roederer, and Taittinger. They, like the other Champagne firms, have visiting hours and guided tours.

A walk through the cellars of Reims should certainly work up an appetite for lunch. I would suggest that you try Boyer la Crayère, one of the very great restaurants of France, or else one of the other numerous good restaurants in the area (see pages 379–80).

If you are still in Reims after lunch, either stay for a leisurely visit to the cathedral, or proceed to Épernay and its cellars. For a scenic drive, take the Vineyard Route D-9 from Reims to Mailly-Champagne, then to Verzenay and Verzy via D-26, and finally to Épernay by way of Louvois, Avenay-Val d'Or, and Ay-Champagne.

Only a half-hour from Reims even via this more circuitous route, Épernay is the second city of fine Champagnes. It contains a number of important cellars, notably Pol Roger and the much larger Moët et Chandon, both of which are well worth a visit.

If you wish to return to Paris the same day, you may take N-3 west from Épernay, joining

Autoroute A-4 at Château-Thierry for a speedy return to Paris. If you can afford to take a bit more time, continue on N-3 to La Ferté-sous-Jouarre. This small town is the home of the marvelous Auberge de Condé (two stars in Michelin), an appropriate gastronomic finale to your Champagne excursion. The return from La Ferté-sous-Jouarre is short: you can be back in Paris for the night almost before the last bubbles stop rising in your Champagne glass.

⚜

Itinerary B

LOIRE: TWO DAYS

The Loire valley is a spectacular vision of vineyards and of Renaissance châteaux rising out of the morning mist in the greenest and most elegant of all French countrysides. And a two-day itinerary will provide you with at least a glimpse of this valley, quite properly known as "The Garden of France."

After an early breakfast of coffee and *croissants,* leave Paris by car on N-118 (by the Porte de Saint-Cloud) or on Autoroute A-10 (by the Porte d'Italie). Follow A-10, and then A-11, to Chartres, which is certainly the most inspirational gateway to the Loire. The town of Chartres is synonymous with its splendid thirteenth-century cathedral, now even more beautiful with its recently restored stained-glass windows.

By late morning you should be driving south on N-154. A half-hour's trip will bring you to the A-10 at Allaines; continue in the direction of Orléans. Bypass the city of Orléans and before long you will be gazing at the famous staircase of Château de Blois, built by François I. Although this is the true birthplace of the French Renaissance, a thoroughgoing visit to the château might well be delayed until a subsequent visit.

At Blois, cross the Loire and you can choose either Chambord or Cheverny, with lunch at Bracieux between both these architectural marvels, and then join D-751, a perfect little road that runs west for miles along the river and sidles up to several splendid castles. Drive slowly as you approach Chaumont, and glance up; the château is perched on a hill and casts its centuries-old shadow over the little town.

The next architectural wonder en route, at left, is Château d'Amboise. It is worth a serious look—if only because the tomb of Leonardo da Vinci is here.

If you wish to spend the night in a good but small hotel in the château country, I suggest that you make reservations well in advance. This advice especially applies to the Relais et Châteaux. As a perusal of the listings on pages 281–93 will make clear, these hotels have a very limited number of rooms, in the Loire just as in the rest of France.

Whether or not you are staying there overnight, with the approach of dusk head toward Chenonceaux. There, on certain nights from June to mid-September, you may witness a *son et lumière* ("sound and light") show that lasts an hour and a half. The French are truly expert at this kind of thing: the spotlights, music, and narrative reenact the story of Chenonceaux's past with near-fairytale splendor.

As an eye-opener on the following morning, make a short pilgrimage to Azay-le-Rideau—to

419

my mind the most harmonious and graceful of all the Renaissance châteaux of the Loire. Also on D-751, continuing west, is Chinon. And when you reach Saumur, you should visit the wine cellars built into the cold recesses of its limestone cliffs.

Just past Saumur is Gennes, where you may cross the Loire to the town of Les Rosiers. (An alternate route would be to cross the river at Saumur, and take D-952 to Les Rosiers.) Depending on the pace of the châteaux-philes accompanying you (who, it is hoped, will encourage you to stay an extra day), you will arrive at Les Rosiers in time for a late lunch, certainly in time for dinner. M. Augereau, at the Auberge de Jeanne de Laval, is one of my favorite chef-hosts in the Loire valley.

After dinner, or early the next morning if you sleep over, drive to Le Mans. From this car-racing capital, Autoroute A-11 will scoot you back to Paris in record-breaking time—certainly less than two hours.

If you can possibly arrange to have a third day at your disposal, linger in the Loire countryside. After visiting Amboise, for example, you can cross the river again in order to visit the vineyards and chalk cellars in the hillsides of Vouvray.

Here is an interesting alternative that will help reduce the effects of jet lag if you are arriving on a morning plane from the U.S. at Charles de Gaulle Airport. Instead of facing up to Paris, hire a car at the airport and drive directly to one of the many luxurious hotels in the Loire countryside. By the time you return to Paris you should be refreshed and well rested.

⚭

Itinerary C

BURGUNDY: TWO DAYS

Most American travelers are surprised to learn that distances within France are not great. The heart of Burgundy begins in Beaune, 315 kilometers from Paris and a drive of only three hours by car. Once in Burgundy, travelers are further surprised to find out that the "vast" wine-producing region of Burgundy stretches only from Gevrey-Chambertin (12 kilometers south of Dijon) to Chassagne-Montrachet, near Chagny—a total distance of 42 kilometers. This represents no more than a fast half-hour's drive, yet the area may take days to see properly.

It is thus feasible to cover Burgundy in a short two-day trip, though it makes sense to concentrate on a single portion, the Côte d'Or. This Golden Slope encompasses the great vineyards of the Côte de Nuits and the Côte de Beaune.

Start fresh on the morning of your first day, and drive from Paris on Autoroute A-6 directly to Beaune. Have lunch either in Beaune or in the region. Either have lunch in Beaune, or in the region where you will pass the afternoon: the Côte de Nuits.

To get to the Côte de Nuits, leave Beaune on N-74, traveling north a few kilometers to the village of Vosne-Romanée. Exit at Vosne and take the well-paved country road known as the *Route des Grands Crus*. This vineyard road will pass the famous vineyards of the Romanée-Conti, and lead you to Chambolle-Musigny via the Clos de Vougeot. Other recognizable place names beyond there include Morey-Saint-Denis and eventually Gevrey-Chambertin. At this last village you can regain N-74 and return south to Beaune in a matter of minutes.

Have dinner and spend the night in Beaune, or in any one of the good hotels and restaurants in the surroundings. (For hotels and restaurants see pages 137–39, 176–78, and 203–06.)

The following morning, if you have not had time to do so before, explore Beaune, the wine capital of Burgundy. You may walk through the cobblestone streets to the Hospices de Beaune, with its colorful tiled roof; it is a superb example of Burgundian architecture. If you are inclined, the Musée de Vin is almost next door.

Your next destination, either in the last morning or early afternoon, should be the Côte de Beaune. Begin by driving south from Beaune on N-74. After one kilometer, take the right-hand fork, which is D-973 leading to Pommard. This will once again put you on the vinous *Route des Grands Crus*. The vineyard road goes to Volnay, and in another few minutes reaches Meursault. But this is a place to linger and to taste, visiting the growers as you go. Sooner or later, depending on your pace, you will arrive in Puligny-Montrachet. Here, to your right, you will see Montrachet's tiny nineteen-acre expanse—source of the precious liquid that is in constant demand worldwide. Just before Montrachet, note a small old stone cross beside the road; it may be thought of as an *arc de triomphe* for French white wine, since it casts its shadow on several of the greatest white-wine vineyards of the world. After this thought-provoking sight, you may wish to ruminate on what you have seen with a delectable lunch at Lameloise, in Chagny, or at the Montrachet Restaurant in Puligny-Montrachet.

That night, regain Autoroute A-6 at Beaune, for an easy, speedy return to Paris. It is much faster to drive back, but if you have rented a car, do not wish to drive, and have the extra time, you may choose to take a fast, two-hour train from Dijon to Paris.

ஃ

Itinerary D

BURGUNDY INCLUDING CHABLIS: THREE DAYS

If you have an extra day in which to discover Burgundy, you may consider a stop on your way down at the vineyards of Chablis. Otherwise use that third day to explore the Côte d'Or more thoroughly. Following are my suggestions for how to proceed.

Leave Paris by car from the Porte d'Orléans or the Porte d'Italie, driving south on Autoroute A-6. After about an hour and a half, exit at Auxerre-Sud. Take D-965 east, which will quickly bring you to your first stop: the village of Chablis. (You may wish to leave A-6 earlier at Joigny for a gastronomic experience at La Côte Saint-Jacques. Happily satiated, you can then proceed to Chablis, using two smaller roads, D-943 and D-91.)

In Chablis, I suggest you visit a few of the growers—say, Fèvre, Dauvissat, Servin, or Jean Durup. They will be glad to point out and name the vineyards of platinum-colored grapes that produce the best-known white wines in the world.

Once you have visited Chablis, drive on to dinner and the night in either Avallon or Saulieu, or go as far as the Côte d'Or. (For hotels and restaurants see pages 176–78 and 203–06.)

The following morning, continue to Beaune, a city very much worth exploring. After lunch,

421

drive north from the city to see the vineyards of the Côte de Nuits. On your third day you will have the leisure time to visit the Côte de Beaune, which is the southern half of the Côte d'Or. Have lunch in one of the good restaurants located in the vineyard area (see pages 203–06). For suggestions about how to spend your time in the Côte d'Or and Beaune, consult Itinerary C.

In the evening, drive back from Beaune on A-6 to Paris. But if you have some extra time, are tired of driving, and history and mustard are on your shopping list, leave your rented car and take the train back from Dijon.

The only frustration you should have felt about this trip is having to return home so soon. There are so many vineyards, growers, and shipping firms, and so many fine restaurants, that three days is hardly enough time for all the vinous joys of the Golden Slope.

NOTE: If you have come to Burgundy by car at the end of your stay in France, avoid Paris traffic on your return, and drive directly to Orly or Charles de Gaulle Airport for a flight home, or to your next destination.

Itinerary E

BORDEAUX: THREE DAYS

Bordeaux is the name of a beautiful city, and the name of an even more spectacular wine, and I consider that your trip to France would be incomplete without experiencing both.

Moreover, travel to Bordeaux is not the problem it once was. For example, the trip from Paris to Mérignac airport takes only one hour by plane, not including the usual hotel-to-airport connections. In a taxi, plan on forty-five minutes from Paris to Charles de Gaulle Airport (barring excessive traffic) and thirty to forty minutes from midtown to Orly Ouest. Mérignac, Bordeaux's modern air terminal, is a half-hour west of the city.

The domestic airline, Air Inter, offers frequent and regularly scheduled service from Paris to Bordeaux on their "red flights" at the regular full fare. It also has economical "blue flights," offering a 50 percent savings, and the "white flights" a 30 percent savings, to passengers under 26 and those of 60–65 or over. (Since publication, this offer may have been altered, so have your travel agent check with Air France or Air Inter.) Bordeaux is also only an hour from Nice or Marseille on Air Inter, an hour from Geneva and Madrid on Air France, and only an hour and twenty minutes from London.

There are also trains. They are modern, clean, and efficient, and they run frequently from the Gare d'Austerlitz to the Gare Saint-Jean in Bordeaux. The additional time spent (the train takes four and a half hours) is made up for by the beauty of the scenery.

Another alternative is to drive, since this allows you the possibility of stopovers. Going straight through, Autoroute A-10 will take you all the way from Paris to Bordeaux in less than six easy hours.

If you arrive in Bordeaux by one o'clock, you might plan to spend the rest of the afternoon in the Médoc (Haut-Médoc). If you did not bring your own car, rent one either at the airport or at the train station. Avis has an office within walking distance from the Gare Saint-Jean.

For reasons best known to local chauvinistic politicians, signs indicating directions to the Médoc are dismally lacking. However, the Médoc may be reached from Bordeaux by paying close attention to the following directions: Watch for signs indicating directions to Pauillac and to Soulac, a small resort at the mouth of the Gironde River. After leaving the outskirts of Bordeaux at a distance of 4 kilometers or so, you will reach the Rocade, an autoroute that makes a quarter-circle on the western edge of Bordeaux. Cross over the Rocade and proceed a couple of kilometers. Now you must watch for an inconspicuous sign indicating Blanquefort and Pauillac, which is set beside a barely visible fork to the right. This, *mesdames, messieurs,* is the small gateway to the famous vineyard road of the Médoc, a road I have always liked to refer to as the Fifth Avenue, Bond Street, or Rue de la Paix of the great red wines of the world. Known prosaically enough as D-2, this *Circuit Touristique du Médoc* meanders through the villages and Appellations Controlées of Margaux, Saint-Julien, Pauillac, and Saint-Estèphe. Many of the châteaux welcome visitors. Except for Château Prieuré-Lichine in Margaux, which is open seven days a week, most of the châteaux close on Saturdays and Sundays. During the summer, go to Saint-Estèphe, where you will find Cos d'Estournel open to visitors on weekends. Nevertheless, just driving past the vineyards on weekends will give you the sensation of driving through a most distinguished wine list. Before you leave the Médoc, you might visit the Wine Museum of Château Mouton-Rothschild, in Pauillac. (Appointments are recommended.) Telephone: 56.59.22.22.

If you wish, have lunch on the way (for restaurants, see pages 62–65) but keep in mind that the Médoc provides very few decent places to sleep. There is, in fact, only one hotel to be recommended: the Relais de Margaux, a newly opened (1985), luxuriously comfortable inn. For dinner in Bordeaux there are a number of mouthwatering choices available, since Bordeaux has lately become a gastronomic mecca. (For hotels and restaurants, see pages 33–38.)

With its elegant eighteenth-century classical lines, Bordeaux is a city worth exploring. And *Vieux* Bordeaux has been restored to include attractive pedestrian malls that will prompt you to browse and window-shop.

In late morning or early afternoon, set out for the vineyards of Saint-Émilion. Take N-89 to Libourne, and then follow the signs.

Stroll about the town before lunch. If you have lunch there, conclude your Bordeaux-bedecked meal with Saint-Émilion's other specialty—macaroons. Among the vineyards in Saint-Émilion, those most worth visiting are Châteaux Cheval-Blanc, Figeac, and Canon. Continuing into Pomerol, note Château Pétrus; you will be startled by the unassuming appearance of this château that produces one of the most expensive great red wines of France.

On your third and last day in Bordeaux, you should consider a visit to Sauternes, Barsac, and Graves. Take Autoroute A-61 south to Langon. (When leaving Bordeaux, follow the familiar blue-and-white autoroute signs in the direction of Toulouse. Once you are on A-61 you will have an easy twenty minutes on the autoroute before reaching the exit at Langon.) Have lunch at Claude Darroze in Langon, or in the village of Sauternes, which is easily reached from the exit ramp at Langon. (See pages 109–11.)

Take the vineyard road, called the *Circuit du Sauternais,* to visit Château d'Yquem and Château Guiraud, among other châteaux. However, be forewarned: Château d'Yquem is a bit difficult to find without a map, and an appointment is necessary to see the *chais.* In Barsac you may wish to visit Château Coutet and possibly Château Nairac, where Tom Heeter, an American, makes a small quantity of excellent wine.

If the Sauternes–Barsac excursion does not allow you enough time to see the city of Bordeaux, you might instead consider a shorter visit to Château Haut-Brion, only fifteen minutes from the center of town. Watch for signs indicating the road to Arcachon and Pessac; that will put you on N-650 going west. (Do not, however, take Autoroute A-63, which also goes to Arcachon.) Five minutes on N-650 will bring you to Château Haut-Brion, on the right just before Pessac. Haut-Brion is an appropriate note on which to end your three-day trip, since the château is the historical birthplace of the fame of the great red wines of Bordeaux.

If you have the resources for a fourth day, you will be that much more fortunate, because it is my own chauvinistic belief that the enhanced understanding and enjoyment of this fine region and this fine wine are proportional to the amount of extra time spent in Bordeaux.

⚜

Itinerary F

CHAMPAGNE–ALSACE: THREE DAYS

In this brief journey you will have a chance to discover two entirely different wines: Champagne—traditionally the greatest of all sparkling wines—and the French Rhine wines of Alsace.

The best way to begin is to take Autoroute A-4 east for one and a half hours till you arrive in the city of Reims. Spend the morning visiting one of the Champagne cellars of Pommery & Greno, Roederer, Taittinger, and others if you have time.

After lunch (see pages 379–80) in Reims—perhaps Boyer La Crayère if you can afford it (otherwise see pages 378–82)—you may wish to proceed on the scenic vineyard route, D-9 to Mailly-Champagne. From there, D-26 leads you to Verzy, whence you can go south to Épernay. After visits to such *caves* as Pol Roger and Moët et Chandon, have dinner and spend the night in Épernay, or in any one of the many good hotels and restaurants in the Champagne area.

Alsace will be your destination on the following day. Take Autoroute A-4 east once again, till you join A-32 and then A-34 for three hours of easy driving to Strasbourg. Have lunch in this city whose unique French-and-German temperament is at once quaint and hearty (see pages 303–6). A perfect introduction to Alsace would be a meal that includes a *choucroute*, washed down with a good young Riesling or Gewürztraminer.

The afternoon might be used for walking about the old town of Strasbourg and visiting the cathedral. Either spend the night in Strasbourg, or drive out to the vineyards, famous not only for their wines but for the large number of charming, cozy inns and château-hotels. (For hotels, see pages 305–11.)

Sunrise to sundown the following day is best devoted to a thorough visit of the colorful hillside vineyards on D-10, better known as the *Route des Vins*. Put on your walking shoes as you approach Riquewihr; this utterly charming village deserves a short exploration on foot.

The food is good in all of Alsace. But if you want a really extraordinary meal, try to reserve a table for lunch or dinner at the Haeberlin brothers' Auberge de l'Ill in Illhaeusern, 55 kilometers south of Strasbourg. (Incidentally, I wouldn't wait to have your *choucroute* here; this popular specialty might be too plebeian for the Auberge de l'Ill.) Or you might plan a meal at another very good restaurant, Aux Armes de France in Ammerschwihr. If you have driven on to Colmar, Schillinger would be the ideal restaurant for dinner. And since your hourglass might have run out by

424

that time, you are right beside the Colmar airport, from which an evening plane will whisk you back to Paris for the night.

⁂

Itinerary G

BEAUJOLAIS–BURGUNDY: FOUR OR FIVE DAYS

Four to five days will give you ample time to ramble through the bountiful vineyard countryside of Burgundy and the Beaujolais.

Start in the morning by taking the TGV from Paris to the city of Mâcon. The world's fastest train will have you there in less than two hours—traveling at the high speed of 280 kilometers (175 miles) per hour. If you prefer, take the evening TGV to Mâcon, which arrives just in time for you to book into a Mâconnais or Beaujolais hotel for the night.

Make arrangements beforehand to rent a car in Mâcon, then drive directly to the distinguished white-wine vineyards of Pouilly-Fuissé. Just beyond Pouilly-Fuissé, you will find yourself in the Beaujolais.

Here you will recognize many familiar names from wine bottles. The villages you will drive through may include Juliénas, Chénas, and Fleurie, separated by Moulin-à-Vent, where you can see the old windmill still standing. Farther south lie the villages of Villié-Morgon and Brouilly. (In Burgundy, remember, what I mean by "farther south" is a distance of only a few kilometers.)

Scattered throughout these vineyards, and in almost every Beaujolais village, the flamboyant *caveaux de dégustation* welcome you. Here, for a nominal fee, you may sample glasses poured and proudly offered by local growers. These colorful *caveaux* are set against a landscape so charming that it has tempted the palette quite as often as the palate.

Either sleep in the Beaujolais (see hotels and restaurants, pages 231–37) or drive from Brouilly on D-37 east to Belleville, where you will see signs ushering you onto A-6 going north to Beaune.

You might devote your second day in Burgundy to the white-wine vineyards of Chassagne-Montrachet, Puligny-Montrachet, and Meursault in the Côte de Beaune. Have dinner and spend the night either in the city of Beaune or in the surrounding vineyards of the Côte de Beaune. (See listings on pages 203–06.)

On your third day, tour the city of Beaune, and then drive up into the vineyards of the Côte de Nuits. Along the *Route des Grands Crus,* some of the villages you will pass through include Vosne-Romanée, Chambolle-Musigny (via the Clos de Vougeot), Morey-Saint-Denis, and Gevrey-Chambertin. That evening have dinner in the Côte de Beaune or Côte de Nuits, and spend the night in Dijon, Nuits-Saint-Georges, Beaune, or Chagny. (See pages 176–78 and 203–06.)

Devote most of your fourth day to driving slowly back to Paris. If you take the A-6, exit for lunch or dinner at Saulieu or Avallon, and if you have the time or inclination, briefly visit the vineyards of Chablis. (See hotels and restaurants on pages 137–39 and 145–49.) Then, on to Paris.

NOTE: Here is a "quickie" Paris–Burgundy version of the above itinerary.

Take the TGV to Mâcon in the evening, have dinner, and spend the night in the Beaujolais.

The following morning, tour the Beaujolais. After an early lunch, drive up and spend the afternoon in the Côte de Beaune, and the night somewhere in the neighborhood. On your second day visit the Côte de Nuits, have lunch, and return via Chablis to Paris. This is a trip that can be accomplished in only two nights and two days.

Itinerary H

BORDEAUX–ARMAGNAC: FOUR OR FIVE DAYS

Southeast of Bordeaux lies Armagnac, the wild and untamed brandy-producing district of Old Gascony. This short trip will enable you to sample its treasures—goose, duck, *foie gras* and Armagnac's own brandy. These specialties are revered now just as they were in the days when they graced the great tables of the king's musketeers.

Start with a morning flight from Paris to Bordeaux. Spend that afternoon touring the Médoc, with dinner and the night spent in Bordeaux. On the second day visit Saint-Émilion after a morning shopping in Bordeaux. Devote an hour or two on the morning of your third day to visiting Château Haut-Brion in the Bordeaux suburb of Pessac. And in the afternoon discover the wine district of Sauternes. (For details about Bordeaux, consult Itinerary E.)

Instead of returning to Bordeaux that evening, proceed south to Mont-de-Marsan either on D-932, south of Langon, or on one of the smaller roads. From there drive to Aire-sur-l'Adour, the town closest to your destination for the night, Eugénie-les-Bains. In this town, so small you can scarcely find it on the map, is one of France's great gastronomic treasures: Les Prés d'Eugénie, the establishment of Michel Guérard, who invented *Cuisine Minceur.* The accommodations, with spa facilities in the midst of tranquillity, are as elegant as the cuisine that will appear at your table.

Penetrate the uncombed countryside of Armagnac the following day. You should try to include a visit to the market town of Eauze. Signs all along the road will coax you to buy not only Armagnac, but *foie gras* as well. Since the Armagnac region encompasses part of the Landes, it is here that you may discover the vast difference between good *foie gras,* a whole, unadulterated duck or goose liver, and *pâté de foie gras.* The *pâté,* a cheap imitation, is goose or duck liver diluted with pork, fat, and other very decent but cheaper materials. *Foie gras* in its entirety rises to the heights of caviar, truffles, and Belons or Marennes oysters.

After stopping to buy a bottle or two of Armagnac from some of the respectable producers (mentioned in the chapter on Armagnac), head towards Auch. Lunch at the Hôtel de France in Auch will let you experience the best of Gascon cooking.

From Auch continue your trip on N-124 to Toulouse, where you will find frequent flights to Paris in the afternoon or early evening.

If, however, you have some time to spare, proceed on the morning of your fourth day from Eugénie-les-Bains to the town of Luppé-Violles. Have lunch at the Relais de l'Armagnac, or at one of the other good restaurants in Armagnac (see pages 406-10). Then have dinner and spend the night at the Hôtel de France in Auch.

An hour's drive the following morning will bring you to the city of Toulouse, which you do not need to visit. If you do, check to see if the excellent family-run restaurant Darroze is open and avail yourself of a meal. The capital of *cassoulet* offers the traveler its regional dish, and the airport where you may leave your rented car and take one of the frequent Air Inter planes back to Paris.

⚜

Itinerary I

BORDEAUX–BIARRITZ–ARMAGNAC: FIVE OR SIX DAYS

You may wish to cool off between visits to Bordeaux and Armagnac in the course of Itinerary H, especially if you are traveling in hot summer weather, so include the following detour for a splash in the ocean at Biarritz.

After your visit to Sauternes on the third day of your trip, take the fast, straight N-10 highway going south. Drive for about 175 kilometers until you reach Magescq, just south of Castets. You may decide to have lunch at the Relais de la Poste (two stars in Michelin) in Magescq. (See the listing in the section on Armagnac, page 409.) After what should be a resplendent meal, proceed again on N-10, bypassing Bayonne, to the fabled seaside resort at Biarritz. (If it is very hot or a particularly busy weekend with heavy traffic, you may join Autoroute A-63 south from Saint-Geours-de-Maremne. Then exit at Biarritz.) I can recommend the Hôtel de Palais in Biarritz, one of the most luxurious and comfortable resort hotels in France.

After a couple of days and an adequate dose of surf and sun in Biarritz, you can continue on to Eugénie-les-Bains, and take up the Armagnac itinerary once again. With this detour you will have included two variants on the theme of *eau-de-vie:* Armagnac itself, and the life-giving ocean in the Basque country.

⚜

Itinerary J

CHAMPAGNE–ALSACE–BURGUNDY: FIVE DAYS

If you were planning a dinner party, you might start with Champagne as an aperitif, introduce the first course with an Alsatian Riesling, and conclude the meal with a distinctive red Burgundy. This same sequence suggests a very interesting and well-balanced five-day itinerary.

Spark your appetite first with a day's visit to Champagne, only an hour-and-a-half from Paris. You may have dinner and spend the night in either Reims or Épernay.

Champagne elegantly paves the way to Alsace the following day, by taking A-4, the Autoroute de l'Est, to Strasbourg. Spend the afternoon visiting the cathedral and the old town, and then satiate yourself with *choucroute*. The following morning you should set out to see the vineyards of Alsace. You will drive through a large number of very charming villages, where storks on the rooftops are the local emblem. The village of Riquewihr and the town of Colmar both deserve more than a cursory glance. (For details on how to spend your time in Champagne and Alsace, refer to Itinerary F.)

Instead of rushing on a plane back to Paris at the end of your third day, stay in a hotel at Colmar or drive down N-422 and use the new autoroute that connects with Mulhouse. (For hotels and restaurants, see pages 309-11.) Then, after a night in Colmar or Mulhouse, take the fast Autoroute A-36 to Beaune. The distance of 250 kilometers can be covered in a little over two hours.

Beaune lies in the center of the Côte d'Or, the name for two famous vineyard slopes, the Côte de Nuits and the Côte de Beaune. Both of them deserve scrutiny. If you have a bit more time, you can dip down to see the Beaujolais and take the TGV from Mâcon back to Paris. Otherwise drive back to Paris on A-6 from Beaune.

⚜

Itinerary K

BORDEAUX–COGNAC–LOIRE: SIX OR SEVEN DAYS

In the course of six days you will have the chance to observe three separate landscapes, each with its very own cultural and vinicultural heritage.

Begin by taking a morning plane from Paris to Mérignac airport in Bordeaux. Once there, rent a car and spend the rest of the afternoon visiting the vineyards of the Médoc. Spend the night in Margaux at the Relais de Margaux or in Bordeaux, and on the following morning, after visiting *Vieux* Bordeaux, drive out to see Saint-Émilion. Again spend the night in Margaux or in Bordeaux, and on your third day plan to visit Haut-Brion, and the sweet-white-wine vineyards of Barsac and Sauternes. For historical, architectural, and literary (but not vinicultural) enlightenment, stop at Montesquieu's moated fourteenth-century château at Labrède. (For more details about how to spend your time in the Bordeaux region, see Itinerary E.)

On the morning of the fourth day, bid *au revoir* to Bordeaux and take the new Autoroute A-10 north to Saintes, a drive of less than one hour. Exit at Saintes to visit one of the name-brand firms at nearby Cognac; they include Hennessy, Martell, and Rémy-Martin. If you have time and still feel inquisitive, you may proceed 15 kilometers to Jarnac, to call at such firms as Courvoisier or Hine. In the long stone *chais,* sniff the woody aroma of the air; your nose should capture a hint of the "angels' share" (see page 384).

After this detour, which will have distilled in your mind the long process of making Cognac, retreat to Saintes. From there, N-137 north will take you to the beautiful and historic seaport of La Rochelle. You can spend the remainder of the afternoon and night there (for hotels and restaurants, see pages 404-05); in the surrounding area there are a number of good restaurants featuring fresh seafood. Otherwise, continue north via La Roche-sur-Yon to Nantes. Spend the night at the Abbaye de Villeneuve, provided you are able to make a reservation in one of the few rooms at this

428

delightful and comfortable hotel located in Les Sorinières, just south of Nantes. It is worth a detour. There are also several attractive hotels in the city of Nantes itself (see pages 251–52).

The Muscadet vineyards should be your objective on the following day. Then take Autoroute A-11 to Angers, forty-five minutes away. You may visit the museum of tapestries at the château of Angers. It's my belief, though, that you can skip the conducted tour of the château. If I were with you, we would stay at the Auberge de Jeanne de Laval in Les-Rosiers-sur-Loire, where I would leave the menu in the hands of M. Augereau, the chef. Or I would suggest pushing on to Château de Marçay, beyond Chinon. This hotel has the spacious, comfortable rooms that we would all like to believe represent our minimum requirement. (For hotels and restaurants, see pages 284–85.)

On your sixth day, assuming you have to return to Paris by nightfall, examine at least the exteriors of the Loire châteaux of Chinon, Villandry, and Azay-le-Rideau, and try to visit Chenonceaux. The latter, seen from the outside, is a must. Autoroute A-10 from Tours is your speediest way back to Paris.

If you are blessed with a little more time, linger a bit longer in the Loire. Stay that extra night either at the Domaine de Beauvois in Luynes, at the Domaine des Hauts de Loire in Onzain, or at the Choiseuil in Amboise; all three are marvelous châteaux-hotels.

On your seventh day, plan to tour the wine cellars of Vouvray, and include in your castle-hunt the châteaux of Amboise and Chambord.

In the late afternoon, head north by way of Chartres, a minor detour considering the great beauty of the cathedral. Then bounce back to the twentieth century with a fast one-hour trip back on the A-11 to Paris.

Itinerary L

BORDEAUX–DORDOGNE–BURGUNDY EIGHT OR NINE DAYS

This is a wine book and a guide. And I would feel very poor if I had never visited the Bordeaux region and the vineyards of Burgundy. I have traveled hundred of times from one region to the other—mostly by plane or straight through by car. Yet the beauty that lies on the way I have, in my haste, too often overlooked. For between the two precious jewels of Bordeaux and Burgundy lie the golden links of the Dordogne/Périgord. (Details about accommodations in the Dordogne/Périgord region itself appear after Itinerary O.)

Whether known by the ancient provincial name of Périgord, or by the modern departmental name of Dordogne, the region you are about to encounter is, in my estimation, the most beautiful and tranquil of all French countrysides—a jumble of scenic, well-paved, and winding country lanes that look like a kitschy painter's dream. One recurring scene is a château perched on a hill flanked on either side by trees, with cows grazing on the sloping pastures below. Through this pastoral setting meanders the Dordogne River, where willow trees dip their branches into the shimmering and slow-moving waters.

A bonus for the wine-conscious traveler lies in the fact that this exquisite landscape is between the two important wine-producing regions of Bordeaux and Burgundy. And while the wines of the Dordogne hold only local interest, the Périgord specialties of truffles and *foie gras* perfectly complement the scenery.

Begin your eight- or nine-day trip by flying in the morning to Bordeaux. You should spend the following two-and-a-half days visiting the Bordeaux vineyards of the Haut-Médoc, Sauternes, and Saint-Émilion. Be sure to try the finer Bordeaux restaurants, and take time to admire the classical eighteenth-century elegance of the city itself. (For details on this first section of your trip, refer to Itinerary E.)

Then to the Dordogne. In this circuitous, meandering region, full of caves (many once occupied by prehistoric man) and other nooks and crannies, it is difficult and unnecessary to plot strict, linear itineraries. And it hardly does justice to the countryside. Where you go and the amount of time you take really depend only on how much you appreciate beauty and the number of days you can afford to spare. On the map on page 432 I have tried to indicate the roads that provide the easiest routes from one town to another, and those small, incredibly beautiful country roads where signs should really read (in French): "Slow! Drivers sightseeing."

To give you an idea of what to visit, the following itinerary should be helpful. Its loose construction will allow you time and space to pursue travel plans in the Dordogne as you see fit.

If you have spent the morning or the afternoon of your third day in Saint-Émilion, take fast and functional D-936 from Saint-Émilion east to Bergerac, a trip of little more than an hour. From Bergerac you may drive on D-660 to Lalinde and to Mauzac, where I suggest you take small D-31, which snuggles beside the river, to Tremolat and Le Bugue. Farther east lies Les Eyzies, and even if you don't care to rub elbows with Cro-Magnon man, you might use this archaeological outpost as a base of operations for a day or two.

Sarlat is readily reached directly from Les Eyzies, or you can drive through Saint-Cyprien and Beynac in order to see the cliff-hanging Château de Beynac, which dominates the Dordogne. Once in Sarlat, leave your car at least momentarily for a walk about this restored and bustling medieval town full of small trees and old merchant houses. Sarlat is also the ancient capital of Périgord Noir, so named in early times from the dark foliage of the surrounding oak forests.

After Sarlat, you might choose to drive east to Souillac, crossing the Dordogne River at La Treyne for a spectacular view. After the bridge, you have the choice of two roads: D-247 or D-673. Either one will bring you to a plateau that must make shareholders in Kodak jump for joy. Here you can view a town built vertically on the face of a cliff and known as Rocamadour.

(Incidentally, when exploring the Dordogne, you will be wise to invest in the Michelin map No. 75. The scale of 1 : 200,000 gives good detail and has the advantage of including tiny blue sunbursts that indicate particularly noteworthy panoramas en route.)

After a good long gaze at Rocamadour and a stroll through the village itself, you might stay into the evening to enjoy their nightly *son et lumière*. (For an explanation of *son et lumière*, see pages 419–20.)

Only 15 kilometers east of Rocamadour lies the *gouffre* (chasm) of Padirac, and this too is worth a visit. These subterranean galleries, hollowed out by an underground river, provide an exploration à la Jules Verne into the bowels of the earth. If you have time for only one cavern or grotto, Padirac's is the one to see.

It is unrealistic to tell you how much time it will take to travel from Bergerac, for example, to Rocamadour, since you will be stopping frequently along the way. But the distance between these two towns, in technical terms, is only 140 kilometers.

After visiting Rocamadour or Padirac, you can either drive south to Cahors (see Itinerary N) and join the autoroute of Toulouse to head east with easy driving, or drive north via N-140 to Brive-la-Gaillarde. In Varetz, which is only 10 kilometers from Brive, you will find a hotel that should satisfy most expectations: the romantic Château de Castel-Novel, and its two-star restaurant. Depending on how much time you have spent wandering the various byways, this hotel is a fine destination for your first, second, or even third night in the Dordogne countryside. (For other hotels and restaurants in the Dordogne, see the listings below on pages 437–49.)

You can proceed the following morning from Brive-la-Gaillarde via N-89 to Tulle and the large industrial city of Clermont-Ferrand. There are certainly better roads and more attractive places at which to dillydally; but the reason I suggest this route is that from Clermont-Ferrand you will find relief, during your drive east, in the form of B-71. This is the fast, straight autoroute that runs to Saint-Étienne.

If you wish to reward yourself with an unsurpassable gastronomic experience, leave the autoroute at Chabreloche and head toward Roanne through the eastern part of the Massif Central. The long ascent (and subsequent descent) through the mountains is an appropriate premonition of the metaphorical heights to which you will climb when, after reserving, you taste the menus at the Frères Troisgros.

If such a detour holds no charm for your blighted soul, do not exit the autoroute at Chabreloche, but continue southeast to Saint-Étienne. Here the autoroute becomes A-47 and continues to Lyon. Though on the map these autoroutes do not appear to shorten the distance between you and Burgundy, you will see that the fast, easy driving quickly compensates for the apparent detour.

Assuming you have arrived in Burgundy on the sixth or seventh day of this itinerary, you still have plenty of time for a drive through the Beaujolais. Continue north and tour the city of Beaune and the vineyards of the Côte de Beaune and the Côte de Nuits. (For details on how to spend your time in Burgundy, consult itineraries C, D, G, and J.)

On your way back to Paris thereafter, you can also stop at Chablis. However, if exhausted by your trip (as you may well be) and tired of the steering wheel, leave your rented car at Dijon and take one of the fast, frequent trains back to Paris.

For another route between Bordeaux and Burgundy, see the following two itineraries.

⚭

Itinerary M

BORDEAUX–DORDOGNE–BURGUNDY (NORTHERN CIRCUIT): EIGHT DAYS

This second Dordogne itinerary may be undertaken as an alternative cross-country trip from Bordeaux to Burgundy. I need hardly say that sections from this plan and from Itinerary L may be fitted together to map out a journey particularly suited to your own inclinations and time schedule.

The first two-and-a-half-to-three days will again be spent in Bordeaux, visiting the city and the vineyards that surround it. (For details, see Itinerary E.) However, in order to use your time

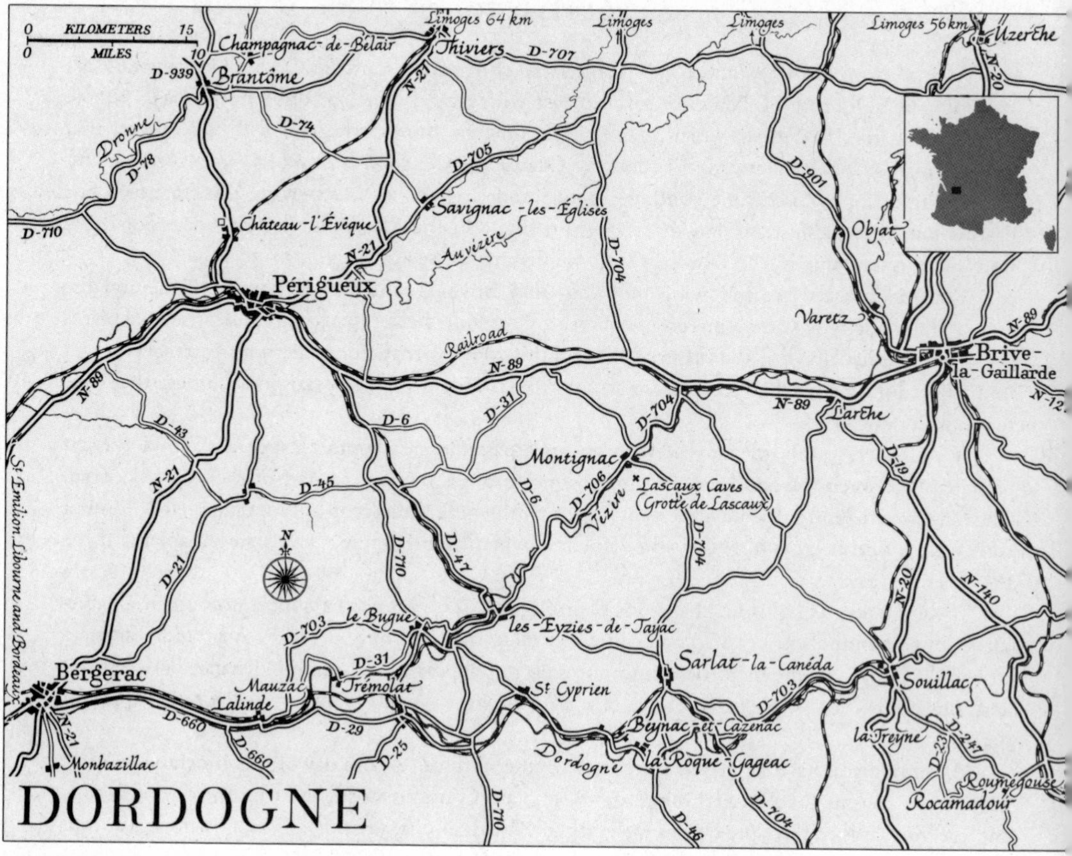
DORDOGNE
0 KILOMETERS 15
0 MILES 10
Limoges 64 km
Limoges
Limoges
Limoges 56 km
Uzerche
Champagnac-de-Bélair
Thiviers
D-707
D-939
Brantôme
N-21
N-20
D-74
Dronne
D-78
D-705
D-901
Savignac-les-Églises
Château-l'Évêque
Objat
D-710
N-21
Auvézère
D-704
Périgueux
Varetz
N-89
Railroad
Brive-la-Gaillarde
N-89
N-89
N-89
N-12
D-31
D-6
Larche
D-43
D-704
N-21
Montignac
D-19
D-45
D-706
Lascaux Caves (Grotte de Lascaux)
D-6
Vézère
St Emilion, Libourne and Bordeaux
N
D-710
D-47
D-704
D-21
N-20
N-140
D-703
le Bugue
les-Eyzies-de-Tayac
Bergerac
D-31
Sarlat-la-Canéda
Mauzac
Trémolat
St Cyprien
D-703
Souillac
Lalinde
D-660
D-29
Beynac-et-Cazenac
la Treyne
N-21
D-660
D-25
Dordogne
la Roque-Gageac
D-23
D-247
Monbazillac
Roumégouse
Rocamadour
D-710
D-704
D-46

economically, you may decide to use your third morning in Bordeaux for an excursion to Saint-Émilion.

From nearby Libourne take N-89 to Périgueux, a fitting place to start your journey: this town is the ancient capital of Périgord. You can then proceed on D-705 northeast for about half an hour to Savignac-les-Églises. At the Hotel du Parc you will find an excellent dinner, since you are in the heartland of Périgord gastronomy. In at least one restaurant during your trip you should sample what Périgord is famous for: *foie gras* (and all the food related to geese and ducks) and, especially, expensive truffles. These "black diamonds" are found close to certain oak trees, just below the surface of the ground and hence invisible. Their perfume is so delicate that they can be discovered only with the help of the long, sensitive snout of an inquisitive and specially trained pig or dog.

At some point in the early part of your trip, call at Brantôme, a town that really does deserve its flattering characterization as the "Venice of Périgord." It is an enchanted town, through which flows the glistening Dronne River. Brantôme also boasts a couple of exquisite hotels with one- or two-star restaurants.

From Brantôme go north to Limoges, not a pretty city, but a place where you might wish to inspect—and buy from—such world-famous porcelain factories as Haviland, Bernardaud, Fontanille and Marraud, and Ancienne Manufacture Royale.

A little over an hour away on D-941, via Borganeuf, lies Aubusson. Handsome modern tapestries are still to be found (examples are the works of Jean Lurçat and Picard le Doux) amid the bulk of crass, touristy designs. So be prepared to come as a discriminating buyer or admirer.

From Aubusson drive to Montluçon. (If coming directly from Limoges, drive via Guéret, the least winding though least scenic route.) From there you can make a short detour to Moulins to have dinner and spend the night at the two-star Hôtel de Paris. A series of fairly good roads that night, or the following day, will finally bring you via Digoin to Mâcon, the gateway to your destination: Beaujolais. Depending on the time spent in the Dordogne, you should have at least a day or two to explore this colorful wine region of France. (For a detailed account of how to spend this last portion of your trip, see Itinerary G.)

NOTE: Good as the French railways are, do not attempt to travel by train from Bordeaux to Burgundy. The route is long and circuitous. Instead, if you do not wish to drive, it is more feasible to fly from Mérignac airport in Bordeaux to the Lyon–Satolas airport. But this method of transportation is recommended only for those who are in a desperate hurry.

⚜

Itinerary N

BORDEAUX-SOUTHERN DORDOGNE— CAHORS—ALBI—ROQUEFORT— LES GORGES DU TARN—NÎMES— RIVIERA

It must now be obvious that in Bordeaux I can't stay long away from the Dordogne. If speed were the only object, one could reach Provence and the Mediterranean coast in record time by sticking to the autoroutes and major routes. But if you would like to turn the clock back—to tour lazily through a most beautiful part of the country, the old France, not greatly changed in the last twenty years—then take this way. From Cahors to Avignon you will be out of this world.

We all like to go at our own pace, spending longer in one place than another; but, to strike a fair average, I have worked out the journey, day by day, to take a week.

DAY 1 Begin by taking a plane to Bordeaux, and arrange to spend two nights there. Itinerary: hire your car at the airport and, in the afternoon, make a tour of the Médoc, following the Route des Vins through Cantenac, where you can visit Château Prieuré-Lichine—open with English-speaking guides every day, including holidays and weekends—Margaux, Saint-Julien, and Pauillac to Saint-Estèphe.

The names of the great vineyards on the way will dazzle the eyes of wine lovers who have never been here before. You will be back in Margaux or Bordeaux in plenty of time for a good night's rest.

DAY 2   Drive out to Saint-Émilion and Pomerol, on the far side of the Dordogne River. There is plenty to see in Saint-Émilion, in my opinion the prettiest wine town in France: the ninth-century Église Monolithe forms the foundation of one of the restaurants. You may wish to taste at luncheon the Bordeaux specialty, lamprey in red wine sauce.

Back in Bordeaux that afternoon, stroll around the old town: the Allées des Piétons (narrow streets paved for pedestrians), the gorgeous seventeenth-century buildings of the Place du Parlement and the fascinating shops which have sprung up there.

DAY 3   Check out of your hotel early, to leave Bordeaux by way of Graves, Barsac, and Sauternes, taking Autoroute A-62, which starts beyond the quai of the Garonne River in Bordeaux. Follow the signs for Agen-Toulouse; this is an expressway, gobbling up the kilometers and halving your time. But if you can spare a little of that time for non-vinous sightseeing, leave the autoroute at Labrède for a look at the romantic castle there, once home to Montesquieu, one of France's most revered writers.

On to the charming Sauternes-Barsac region, where the luscious dessert wines are made—look for the signs Circuit du Sauternais, which will take you along winding roads in a countryside punctuated by châteaux. You might end up at hospitable Château Guiraud, in Sauternes, open every day to visitors; and before leaving the area, try to catch a glimpse of the majestic Château d'Yquem on top of its vineyard mound—just the outside —it can be visited only by appointment.

After that, I suggest lunch either at the little inn in Sauternes or, for serious eaters, at the marvelous Claude Darroze restaurant in Langon, some 8 km farther on, tel.: 56.63.00.48. You might like to make a reservation on your way; and let me remind you that any good restaurant will turn you down after 2:00 p.m., so don't be late.

From there, take the fast Autoroute A-62. About half an hour later, turn off at Agen to head toward Cahors. You may prefer to spend the night at Château Saint-Marcel in Bon-Encontre, 4 km beyond Agen, rather than press on this evening.

Committed gourmets who have lunched lightly, or have worked off a big meal in the park of Saint-Marcel, may think it worthwile to drive northeast to Puymirol, 14 km east of Agen, for dinner before turning in at Bon-Encontre.

On the other hand, travelers in a hurry to get to Cahors could disregard the Agen exit and push on to Montauban, barely more than an hour from Langon by A-62—an additional 75 km southeast, but such an easy drive. The speed limit is 130 kph; I would probably navigate the distance in over a half-hour, making the approach to Cahors that much faster. At Montauban one moves onto the N-20.

Don't forget that distances are short between the many "beauty spots" in this district. From Cahors to Rocamadour or vice versa is only about 65 km north; the villages of Beynac, Saint-Cyprien, and Les Eyzies are not more than 100 km away. These are the heart of the lovely Dordogne; or from Cahors drive along the impressive canyons along the Lot River to Cabrerets. An alternative itinerary takes you from the beauty of the Dordogne River south by Cahors and Albi, joining A-62 at Toulouse and continuing on to Carcassonne.

Cahors itself, the traditional center for robust red wines, is not to be missed. Visit the town; you may also wish to include a visit to the newly planted vineyards of Georges Vigouroux and the older vineyards of his neighbors, Château Chambert and Domaine des Quatre. You will want to stay the night at Cahors, and you can do so in luxury, and swim at the now reopened Château de Mercuès, or at La Pescalerie, 2 km from Cabrerets, some 33 km from Cahors.

DAY 4 With the wines of Cahors behind you and those of the Côtes du Rhône to look forward to, give yourself the treat of a lifetime and set out for the fabulous Gorges du Tarn. Start early. Drive south from Cahors, 37 km on N-20 to Caussade, where, if in a hurry and aching for the easy speed of a straight expressway, then go south to Montauban and join Autoroute A-62, via Toulouse. Or turn off east on D-926, a road heading for Villefranche-de-Rouergue; after 8 km you arrive at Sept-fonds, and, just beyond, slow down to turn right on D-115 for Saint-Antonin, where he twisting road and, eventually, D-600 will take you to Cordes—a small historic medieval town that must be seen and will not be forgotten. The road is delightful, winding but wide enough.

Lunch at Cordes and continue 25 km south on the D-60 to Albi. You may decide to sleep here after visiting the Toulouse-Lautrec Museum and the red, fortresslike cathedral. But should you have the strength, courage, and patience for another 115 km along a narrow, pretty road (D-999), you can reach Millau via Roquefort and its cheeses in time to dine and spend the night at the cozy, comfortable La Musardière.

DAY 5 Now you are in the area of Les Grandes Causses: high, chalky plains, arid and stony, split here and there into steep gorges, threaded by clear trout streams. The most spectacular of these clefts, Les Gorges du Tarn, are watered by the sparkling Tarn River, which snakes between Millau to Sainte-Énimie—I think it is the most sensationally dramatic waterway in France.

To start with, leave Millau early in the morning. You will have a rather routine half-hour drive to Aguessac, then to La Gresse and Le Rozier and Les Vignes at the very beginning of the Gorges du Tarn. Now drive slowly to take in the beauty around you, which grows lovelier all the way to La Malène. Check in at the Château de la Caze, 5 km on beyond the town, and a little later backtrack to La Malène, park your car, and take a boat.

From May 1 to September 30, one can enjoy river trips lasting a little over half an hour and some 8 km in length. At the finish, aptly named La Sublime, a taxi will be waiting to take you back to your point of embarkation and the return to Château de la Caze for the night; while at the end of the day, the boats will be hoisted on long trucks and restored to their point of departure. You will have a memorable outing—the flat-bottomed boats carry a man in the back, a small outboard en-gine, and a man in the front with a long pole to push the craft over the shallow bends into the deeper swirls of the river and point out the big fish. When the season ends, your Tarn gondolier returns to his trade of bookbinding.

If you are lucky at the Château de la Caze, you will have a room with a marvelous view over the Gorges and dinner on the terrace. Enjoy the hotel and its park and allow yourself a rather later start in the morning.

DAY 6 Setting out in a fairly leisurely way on the short drive to Sainte-Énimie, 8 km on the D-907, you should still have time to absorb the final, magnificent sights of the Gorges du Tarn—steep canyons overshadowed by bizarre rocks and grottoes, a population consisting largely of sheep. With no particularly good stopovers on the stretch to Nîmes, and the better to enjoy the beauty of the drive, a picnic is definitely indicated; I took one last time I went this fantastic way.

At Sainte-Énimie, call in on the pleasant grocer/charcutier, André Paulet, tel.: 66.48.50.11, to collect the mouth-watering ingredients of the picnic. His shop will have more than you need in the way of pâtés, cold chicken, sausages, ham, prepared eggs, and the mutton tripe which is a specialty of the region. He sometimes closes at 12:30, so don't be late. Be sure to buy your wine in advance, however—or stick to beer: the local wines are some of the worst for miles around.

Next door to the grocery, you can buy bread; while on the other side of Paulet, there is an interesting little antique shop which was recommended to me by the owners of Château de la Caze. At Sainte-Énimie, your next stop is Florac; and before that little town tucked under the cliffs, you will find lovely places for picnicking. After this *déjeuner sur l'herbe* you will be crossing the arid landscape of the Causses and the Corniche des Cevennes (D-907), a famous road over a series of slate and granite plateaux, with tremendous panoramas over the ravines and torrents that look toward the Mediterranean coast. Lower down, the slopes are green and wooded, the streams rich in trout, olive groves stand among vineyards, all of which signals that you are really in the Midi, en route (still on D-907) for Nîmes, with its splendid Roman amphitheater and Maison Carrée.

At the Hôtel Imperator you could eat fairly well on the terrace or, now that you have reached Les Côtes du Rhône (qv), you may prefer to go on to Tavel, Avignon, Noves, or Aix-en-Provence—and so to the relaxations of the Riviera.

DAY 7 At the end of the holiday, wine buffs may choose to drive back north through the Côtes du Rhône, Beaujolais, and Burgundy—a long stint. Lazier spirits will give up the car at Nice and dawdle a day or two in the sun before flying home.

⤮

Itinerary O

CHAMPAGNE–ALSACE–SWITZERLAND–BURGUNDY: EIGHT DAYS

This eight-day tour of France's major eastern wine-producing regions is a more elaborate version of Itinerary J. The alternate use of the Swiss autoroutes is not so much a detour as a change of pace, one you might not naturally think of when touring the French vineyards.

On the fourth day of your trip in Alsace (see Itinerary J), instead of driving from Mulhouse to Beaune, take Autoroute A-35 south to Basel (Bâle) in Switzerland. Then continue on the Swiss autoroutes to Bern and drive south through Switzerland to the Lake of Geneva (Lac Léman). Stop, if you can, at Crissier, just 6 kilometers from Lausanne; Girardet's at Crissier is probably the world's greatest restaurant *outside* of France.

From Lausanne to Geneva takes little more than half an hour past the Cointrin Geneva airport on speedy Autoroute N-1. As an alternate route, follow the old road around the lake, and tour the hillside vineyards overlooking the water. Be sure to taste the characteristic Vaudois wines; they are to be found in various inns and restaurants along the water. Being a convention center, Geneva has many good restaurants and hotels where you can spend the night—or nights, since Geneva is a pretty city and shouldn't be passed over lightly.

Plan to spend your fifth night in Geneva, and on the next day proceed 50 kilometers on A-41 to Annecy. From Annecy continue briefly on D-909 round the east side of the lake to Talloires. If you did not feast at Girardet's in Crissier, this is where you might recoup with a lunch at the Auberge du Père Bise—yet another memorable chapel of high gastronomy.

Lyon, which epitomizes the theme of *Haute Cuisine,* is only an hour-and-a-half by autoroute from Lac d'Annecy. You might well reach it for dinner and the night (see pages 234–37).

The following day you should have time to explore the Beaujolais region, just north of Lyon, spending the night there (see pages 231–37). Or push farther north and sleep in the environs of Beaune (see pages 203–06).

The Côte d'Or is the very heart of Burgundy and should be explored. (For details on both Beaujolais and the Côte d'Or, refer to itineraries C and G.) From Beaune, take A-6 back to Paris.

Although this expedition sounds very long, the total mileage, eased by eight days of soft beds and fine meals, is only 1,500 kilometers. And 90 percent of it is fast, easy driving on autoroutes where a speed of 120 kilometers (75 miles) per hour should be considered comfortable. As I have noted, by making good use of the autoroutes, and avoiding smaller roads except where they are a charming asset to your trip, you will save time, effort, and energy that is better devoted to the enjoyment of your stay in France.

PLACES TO EAT AND STAY

Even the most dedicated wine tourist in France may sometimes find himself having to eat and sleep outside the wine districts. What follows is a selection of fine hotels and restaurants in areas not covered in the earlier chapters of this book, alphabetically listed. All are on or near the routes of the itineraries.

DORDOGNE, PERIGORD, AND GORGES DU TARN

It is worth taking a few days off to discover what may be the most beautiful and scenic countryside of France. It separates Bordeaux from the Côtes du Rhône, Beaujolais, and Burgundy. The local wines are Bergerac, Côtes de Duras, and Cahors. The towns are listed alphabetically in small type.

H = *Hotel;* R = *Restaurant*

AGEN (47000—Lot-et-Garonne)
(Auch 71—Montauban 74—Cahors 87—Toulouse 116—Bordeaux 140—
Albi 147—Pau 157—Paris 642)

Not all its 35,000 inhabitants spend their time putting up jars of *pruneaux* (prunes) and watching rugby—its two main pursuits. Its specialties in the realm of food are *foie gras*, truffles, walnuts, and *cèpes*.

. . .

HR CHÂTEAU SAINT-MARCEL: 4 km from Agen at Bon-Encontre. Tel.: 53.96.61.30.   12 rooms.
If sleepy and tired from tasting too many Sauternes, or if driving on to Toulouse or feeling too fatigued to push on to Bordeaux, this good, small, inexpensive inn with some charm will assure you of a quiet night, as it is in the midst of a park. Prices are reasonable. English spoken.

R L'AUBERGADE: At Puymirol, 14 km southeast of Agen, 52, rue Royale. Tel.: 53.95.31.46.
A small, old mansion house, the best of this area's restaurants. In the medieval village of Puymirol, Michel Trama offers imaginative, excellent cuisine—naturally, leeks, truffles, duck, and various fruit sauces are his specialties. The local wines are offered at reasonable prices. A beautiful stopover. Two stars in Michelin.

ALBI (81000—Tarn)
(Toulouse 76—Rodez 78—Carcassonne 107—Millau 113—Béziers 144— Montpellier 208—Bordeaux 275—Paris 699)

Cross the old bridge over the Tarn River to get the best view of Albi, known as the "Red Town" for the blank red brick of its cathedral walls. For many, the main attraction is the museum dedicated to the paintings of Toulouse-Lautrec, a native son of Albi. The six hundred works by him are housed in the former archbishop's palace, the Palais de la Berbie, which was built at the same time as the cathedral and in the same red brick, fortresslike style. It is regrettable that this, one of the most heavily visited of France's provincial museums, is so badly lit and that many of the paintings are exposed to sunlight. Gaillac, the local wine, is not of much interest, but it is worth going through Albi to reach the Gorges du Tarn, a spectacular visual experience.

6HR LA RÉSERVE: 3 km northwest of Albi at Fonvialane, on the road to Cordes. Tel.: 63.60.79.79. Tlx.: 520850.   20 fairly small, comfortable rooms. Tennis, park, heated swimming pool.
This *Relais et Châteaux* hotel overlooks the Tarn River. It is run by the Rieux family, who also own the Hostellerie Saint-Antoine in Albi.

HR HOSTELLERIE SAINT-ANTOINE: 17, rue Saint-Antoine. Tel.: 63.54.04.04. Tlx.: 520850.   56 comfortable rooms. 20 air-conditioned.
The two places together (including above) have contributed to a father, mother, and daughter team of very hospitable professionals. Good, reasonable menus.

AUBUSSON (23000—Creuse)
(Guéret 42—Montluçon 63—Limoges 90—Clermont-Ferrand 93— Tulle 108—Brive-la-Gaillarde 137)

Here in the lovely valley of the Creuse, tapestries were first woven five hundred years ago. They are still being woven today, although a rather corny taste prevails among the recent tapestry designs.

HR LE FRANCE: 6, rue des Déportés. Tel.: 55.66.10.22.   25 rooms (13 with toilet).
If modern tapestries interest you sufficiently to make you stay the night in Aubusson, you'll find a few decent rooms in this not much more than adequate hotel. Otherwise, drive on.

BEAULIEU-SUR-DORDOGNE (19120—Corrèze)
(Tulle 40—Brive-la-Gaillarde 47—Sarlat 75—Les Eyzies 83—Trémolat 118— Bordeaux 240—Toulouse 240)

❧ See the impressive Romanesque church of Saint-Pierre.

HR MAPOTEL LE TURENNE: Boulevard Saint-Rodolphe de Turenne. Tel.: 55.91.10.16.   21 inexpensive rooms.
A fair inn in the Dordogne countryside.

BERGERAC (24100—Dordogne)
(Lalinde 19—Le Bugue 43—Périgueux 47—Les Eyzies 60—Sarlat 75— Agen 90—Bordeaux 92—Angoulême 109)

❧ The town found its fame in the long-nosed image of Edmond Rostand's ugly but sincere hero, Cyrano. Bergerac also possesses France's only Musée de Tabac, which traces the development of tobacco from the time it was discovered among the American Indians.

HR LE CYRANO: 2, boulevard Montaigne. Tel.: 53.57.02.76. Behind the Nôtre-Dame church.   10 small rooms.
The restaurant here is a good place to stop if you are hungry. For sleeping accommodations I would recommend you go elsewhere. One star in Michelin.

HR CHÂTEAU DE MONVIEL: 36 km south of Bergerac. (See Monviel.)

BESSE-EN-CHANDESSE (63610—Puy-de-Dôme)
(Le Mont Doré 27—Issoire 35—Clermont-Ferrand 50—Le Puy 129— Saint-Étienne 176—Valence 294)

HR LES MOUFLONS: Route Super-Besse (D-978). Tel.: 73.79.51.31.   50 rooms (all with toilets). Reasonable prices. In a shady park. One star in Michelin.

BEYNAC ET CAZENAC (24220—Dordogne)
(Sarlat 11—Les Eyzies 21—Gaillarde 52—Cahors 55—Périgueux 64— Bergerac 70—Bordeaux 162)

❧ Beynac is a romantic village situated in one of the most beautiful stretches of the Dordogne River. It nestles beneath a fortified castle that is still quite well preserved.

H MANOIR DE ROCHECOURBE: In Vézac, 2 km southeast of Beynac. Take D-703 and D-57. Tel.: 53.29.50.79.   7 rooms.
This delightful small manor has really large, charmingly furnished rooms. Large, modern bathrooms. Unfortunately, it has no restaurant, but good meals are available in medium-priced establishments in the surrounding area. Breakfast is served. Tranquillity and good value. No elevator for second and third floors.

BRANTÔME (24310—Dordogne)
(Nontron 22—Périgueux 27—Angoulême 58—Les Eyzies 72—Bergerac 74—
Limoges 90—Libourne 117—Bordeaux 120—Clermont-Ferrand 284)

❧ The tourist office refers to Brantôme as "the Venice of the Périgord," but despite this corny epithet, it is indeed the loveliest of the Périgord/Dordogne towns. Islanded in the Dronne River, Brantôme grew up around the abbey founded by Charlemagne.

HR LES FRÈRES CHARBONNEL or HÔTEL CHABROL: Rue Gambetta. Tel.: 53.05.70.15. 20 rooms (19 with toilet).
Small decent rooms, reasonably priced. Good restaurant with intelligent wine list and good view of the Dronne. If the place is not overly luxurious, there is luxury in the warm welcome given by M. Charbonnel, who is conscientious in the management of his hotel. One star in Michelin.

HR LE MOULIN DE L'ABBAYE: Route de Bourdeilles. Tel.: 53.05.80.22. Tlx.: 560570. 9 rooms and 3 suites.
This pretty mill, converted into a luxurious hotel, is surrounded on three sides by tiny waterfalls of the Dronne. Exquisite terrace for delightful eating in good weather, and superb view of the mill-wheel and the sixteenth-century stone bridge that gracefully links both sides of the village. The rooms, though not large, are ultra-comfortable and tastefully done. Reserve ahead. Competent wine list; good restaurant. Walking distance from grottoes and the center of town. *Relais et Châteaux.* One star in Michelin.

HR HOSTELLERIE MOULIN DU ROC: at Champagnac-de-Belair, 6 km northeast from Brantôme on D-78 and D-83. Tel.: 53.54.80.36 Tlx.: 571555. 5 rooms, 1 suite.
A small walnut-oil mill nestled near the Dronne has been transformed into one of the most charming and intimate inns in the Dordogne. This pastoral nook, lovingly run by Solange and Lucien Gardillou, approached through a tumble of flowers, has small but perfect rooms which show great warmth and delicacy of taste. The salon downstairs is a curiosity since it has ingeniously incorporated the mill's nineteenth-century machinery into the décor of the room. *Relais et Châteaux.* Good wine list, and a good restaurant which has been highly praised by Gault and Millau and the Bottin Gourmand, and has two stars in Michelin.

BRIVE-LA-GAILLARDE (19100—Corrèze)
(Tulle 29—Les Eyzies 62—Périgueux 73—Limoges 93—Aubusson 137—
Clermont-Ferrand 180—Bordeaux 193—Albi 212—Toulouse 213)

❧ This charming old town owes its name to the gallantry with which its inhabitants survived the sieges of many wars.

HR LA TRUFFE NOIRE: 22, boulevard Anatole France. Tel.: 55.74.35.32. 35 rooms (32 with toilet).
Decent hotel in the center of town. The place to stay if you can't get into nearby Château de Castel-Novel, or find your budget is strained. Reasonably priced restaurant.

H HÔTEL URBIS: 32, rue Marcelin Roche. Tel.: 55.74.34.70. Tlx.: 590195. 55 rooms (all with bathrooms).
In the center of town, a more modern and more impersonal hotel. Recently remodeled. Not as good as La Truffe Noire. No restaurant, but breakfast available.

HR CHÂTEAU DE CASTEL-NOVEL: On the road to Objat, 10 km northwest of Brive-la-Gaillarde. In Varetz. Tel.: 55.85.00.01. Tlx.: 590065. 25 rooms and 5 suites.
A spectacular fourteenth-century renovated château perched on the top of a mountain overlooking the valley. Imaginatively renovated, retaining the old style and adding every conceivable modern comfort. The owners, Albert Parveau and his wife, speak English and are dedicated to providing excellent service. A place to reserve ahead of time and not to miss. Swimming pool and tennis courts. *Relais et Châteaux*. The restaurant has achieved two stars in Michelin.

LE BUGUE (24260—Dordogne)
(Les Eyzies 10—Sarlat 33—Périgueux 41—Bergerac 43—Libourne 70—
Brive-la-Gaillarde 73—Cahors 87—Bordeaux 120)

HR MAPOTEL ROYAL VÉZÈRE: Place de l'Hôtel de Ville. Tel.: 53.06.20.01. Tlx.: 540710. 51 rooms, 4 apartments.
Newly redecorated hotel that is so twentieth-century-modern the rest of the Dordogne looks like an anachronism beside it. Comfortable rooms. Terrace and small swimming pool on roof-patio over-looking the peaceful Vézère River. The best hotel of its kind in the area. English spoken. The Al-busca Restaurant offers a variety of good menus. Fair-to-good wine list.

CAHORS (46000—Lot)
(Montauban 60—Rocamadour 61—Cordes 86—Gaillac 89—Agen 92—Les Eyzies 94—
Brive-la-Gaillarde 102—Bergerac 105—Albi 111—Toulouse 112—Rodez 118—
Périgueux 137—Aurillac 136—Libourne 166—Bordeaux 212)

☙ Beautiful Cahors is a place whose many old surviving monuments reflect its importance in the Middle Ages, when it was a major commercial and university town. Cahors became the banking center of Europe, lending to the papacy and royalty alike, and its commercial influence extended from Norway to the Middle East.
See the unusual Pont Valentré, a remarkable fortified bridge with three imposing towers.
If visiting Cahors out of season (November to March), be sure to load up with truffles. Every Saturday, the **foie gras** and truffle market is a gastronomic event, but all year round it is the dark, full-bodied wines of Cahors which carry high the banner of this medieval city.
The drive along the valley of the Lot River from Fumel on D-911, passing the Château de Mercuès, on to Cahors or continuing still on to Cabrerets to reach the Pescalerie, is dramatically impressive. The overhanging cliffs and canyons are in contrast to the Cahors vineyard scenery between Fumel and Cahors.

H HÔTEL DE FRANCE: 252, avenue Jean Jaurès. Tel.: 65.35.16.76. Tlx.: 520394. 77 rooms.
Near railway station. No restaurant.

R LE BALANDRE: 5, ave Charles de Freycinet (near the railway station). Tel.: 65.30.01.97. Gilles Marc, an able chef, recently opened what promises to be the best restaurant in town.

R LA TAVERNE: 41, rue Delpech (very central). Tel.: 65.35.28.66. Good, simple.
One star in Michelin.

HR CHÂTEAU DE MERCUÈS: 8 km northwest of Cahors on N-20, then the D-911. Tel.: 65.20.00.01. Tlx.: 521307. 40 rooms, including 2 suites. Large swimming pool. 2 tennis courts. Heliport.

The large rooms are very comfortable, but rather expensive. The great medieval castle, with a superb view overlooking a bend in the River Lot, makes this a memorable site. The late Mr Hereil, the father of the Caravelle and a vice-president of Chrysler, modernized this old castle as a meeting place for top executives, and it became one of the first *Relais et Châteaux*. Closed in the late seventies and early eighties, it was purchased by Georges Vigouroux, one of the most important vineyard growers and shippers in Cahors. Now luxuriously refurbished, it will do a great deal to lift the image of the wine region of Cahors. Well managed by Yves Buchin.

HR LA PESCALERIE: 2.5 km from Cabrerets, on the road to Figeac. 33 km from Cahors. Tel.: 65.31.22.55.   10 comfortable rooms (7 large, 3 small).
A charming seventeenth-century manor, set in a park which, at night, is difficult to find along the badly signposted roads. The proprietors, husband and wife (Hélène Combette), have now restored this family property which used to be a fishery on the banks of the Célé River. I recommend a detour to the Pescalerie if you wish to find unforgettable charm in an out-of-the-way countryside, far removed from the bustle of everyday life. A short wine list featuring the wines of Cahors. *Relais et Châteaux*.

Do not miss a visit to one of the Dordogne's most beautiful villages, a photographer's delight: St-Cirq-Lapopie, 8 km from the Pescalerie. The prehistoric grottoes of Pech-Merle add still another justification for a detour to Cabrerets.

CLERMONT-FERRAND (63000—Puy-de-Dôme)
(Montluçon 90—Aubusson 93—Moulins 96—Roanne 100—Saint-Étienne 149—
Limoges 184—Lyon 176—Bordeaux 368)

This busy modern city, the center of the Michelin tire business, is also the historic capital of Auvergne, where old buildings survive in the midst of twentieth-century bustle. From here you can take the autoroute to Lyon, then go north to Beaujolais or Burgundy or south along the Rhône to the Riviera.

HR FRANTEL: 83, boulevard Gergovia. Tel.: 73.93.05.75. Tlx.: 392658.   124 air-conditioned rooms. In the center of town. Comfortable, functional. La Rétirade restaurant is one of the most competent in town.

HR PLM ARVERNE: 16, Place Delille. Tel.: 73.91.92.06. Tlx.: 392741.   57 rooms.
Comfortable rooms that Gault et Millau overoptimistically consider luxurious.

R BUFFET GARE ROUTIÈRE: 69, boulevard Gergovia. Tel.: 73.93.13.32 or 73.91.36.42.
Inexpensive and decent restaurant one flight up. Simple, good snacks on street floor.

HR HOTEL RADIO: at Chamalière, 3 kilometers west of Clermont. Many claim this to be the best restaurant in Clermont, a claim that cannot be made for the rooms.

LA COQUILLE (24450—Dordogne)
(Nontron 31—Brantôme 42—Limoges 48—Périgueux 53—Brive-la-Gaillarde 98)

HR CHÂTEAU DE MAVALEIX: 5 km south of Coquille on N-21, 10 km north of Thiviers. Tel.: 53.52.82.01. Tlx.: 540131.   30 rooms (all with toilet).

A so-called thirteenth-century château, converted in 1967 into a hotel which lies on the way to Limoges, in the middle of a huge park. The rooms are sizable. Inexpensive, but the château itself is fraying a bit at the seams. Restaurant has passable meals.

CORDES (81170—Tarn)
(Gaillac 24—Albi 25—Villefranche-de-Rouergue 47—Montauban 71—
Toulouse 78—Rodez 85—Paris 681)

The fortified village, built in the thirteenth century, is dramatically situated on top of a very steep hill. Its quiet, cobbled streets are lined with souvenir shops, many of which are located in Gothic houses of the thirteenth and fourteenth centuries. Being reminiscent of the Middle Ages, it is somewhat akin to Carcassone, Mont Saint-Michel, or the Palace of the Popes in Avignon.

Music festival, July–August.

From Cordes it is only a short drive to Gaillac (25 km), whose not-too-interesting wines (the whites better than the reds), can anyway be tasted in Cordes.

HR LE GRAND ECUYER: Rue Voltaire. Tel.: 63.56.01.03.   16 well-decorated, comfortable rooms. Excellent value. Beautiful view.
Mr Thuries is a pastry chef with experience acquired in the kitchen of Paul Bocuse. One star in Michelin. Good sommelier.

LALINDE (24150—Dordogne)
(Trémolat 20—Bergerac 22—Les Eyzies 37—Périgueux 59—Sarlat 60—Brive-la-Gaillarde 99—
Bordeaux 111—Tulle 127—Clermont-Ferrand 273)

HR LA METAIRIE: 2 km north from at Mauzac, 9 km from Lalinde. Tel.: 53.22.50.47.   11 rooms, 1 suite.
Swimming pool. Each room has a separate patio, overlooking surrounding fields. Quiet and tranquil. Respectable rooms. If traveling toward Bergerac, this is the last outpost of real beauty in the Dordogne. Better-than-competent food. Like so many others, wine list could be improved.

LACAVE (46200—Souillac)
(See Souillac.)

The underground grottoes offer a marvelous spectacle.

LES EYZIES-DE-TAYAC (24620—Dordogne)
A center of excavations dealing with prehistoric Cro-Magnon man.

(Le Bugue 10—Sarlat 21—Trémolat 24—Lalinde 37—Périgueux 45—Bergerac 59—
Brive-la-Gaillarde 62—Cahors 87—Libourne 121—Bordeaux 152)

Les Eyzies is the most comfortable and gastronomically recommendable place to stay overnight. It is also recommendable as your headquarters for the caves of Lascaux, near Montignac, some 25 km away. The real cave, the capital of prehistory, was discovered in 1940. This Sistine Chapel of prehistory, as it has been called, has been closed to the public for twenty years. For the last decade, artists have been at work to re-create the cave and its 1,500 drawings at a site located fifteen minutes away by foot. I had the good fortune to see the original Lascaux and then Lascaux II, its

443

facsimile reproduction, the same afternoon. The replica is really worth a visit. It faithfully conveys the wonder of the original caves.

If you must have the real thing, even if on a much smaller scale, plan to visit the nearby Grotte de Font-de-Gaume with its multicolored prehistoric drawings. Because the number of visitors allowed is limited, be sure that your hotel is booked to cover any delay you may have in visiting the Font-de-Gaume. Otherwise, you may want to tour the National Museum of Prehistory in town, which houses a large collection of Cro-Magnon artifacts.

HR LE CENTENAIRE: Tel.: 53.06.97.18. Tlx.: 541921.   29 comfortable rooms and 3 apartments. Roland Mazère, the owners' son, is the chef. His training, in some of the outstanding restaurants of France, gave him the dexterity to acquire a second Michelin star in 1981. Alain Scholly oversees the excellent service and will be a reliable adviser for the continuation of your trip through the Dordogne.

HR MAPOTEL CRO-MAGNON: Tel.: 53.06.97.06. Tlx.: 570637.   25 smallish rooms, 1 apartment. Small park, swimming pool. English spoken. Run by the owners, M. and Mme Leyssales, who are hospitable and charming hosts. One star in Michelin.

LEZOUX (63190—Puy-de-Dôme)
(Thiers 10—Clermont-Ferrand 27—Vichy 42—Roanne 75—Lyon 150)

HR CHÂTEAU DE CODIGNAT: In Bort-l'Etang, 8 km from Lezoux, southeast on D-223 and D-115. Tel.: 73.68.43.03.   11 rooms and 3 apartments.
Imposing, pretentious château (called fifteenth-century), which offers modern, quiet, sizable rooms. Rather expensive. Swimming pool. The hotel is worth a small detour; the restaurant is not. *Relais et Châteaux.*

LIMOGES (87000—Haute-Vienne)
(Aubusson 88—Brantôme 90—Brive-la-Gaillarde 93—Périgueux 100—Poitiers 118—
Montluçon 145—Clermont-Ferrand 184—Bordeaux 215—Toulouse 304)

*In this rather dull capital of great porcelains, manufacturers abound. But those who "cook" the most artistically beautiful designs are de Haviland and Bernardaud. Many shops sell a wide assortment of Limoges porcelain.

HR FRANTEL: Place de la République. Tel.: 55.34.65.30. Tlx.: 580771.   75 modern, functional rooms.
The restaurant, Le Renoir, was considered one of the the best in town.

HR LUK HÔTEL: 29, place Jourdan. Tel.: 55.33.44.00. Tlx.: 580704.   56 rooms.
A good, modern hotel, completely renovated, in the center of the city.

HR LE MAS CERISE: Tel.: 55.00.26.28. 5 km from Limoges on the road to Eymoutiers.   15 functional rooms.
A good effort at cooking in town.

HR LA CHAPELLE SAINT-MARTIN: Nieul—87510 on D-35 from N-147, 11 km from Limoges. Tel.: 55.75.80.17.   9 rooms.
A pleasant, old nineteenth-century house in a park. *Relais et Châteaux.* One star in Michelin.

LA MALÈNE (48000—Lozère)

(Meyrueis 23—Florac 41—Mende 41—Séverac-le-Château 32—
Millau 42—Le Vigan 81—Paris 601)

❧ In the heart of the Gorges du Tarn, the superb display of natural beauty as the river winds its way through the bottom of a canyon is an unforgettable sight. If in a hurry, you can drive and stop every so often at specially designated sites, but it is worth taking a boat ride. The price includes a taxi which takes one back to the point of departure.

HR CHÂTEAU DE LA CAZE: 5 km northeast of La Malène on the D-907 bis. Tel.: 66.48.51.01.   14 rooms. 6 apartments in farm annex which lacks the charm of the château but is very comfortable. If you are lucky, you will get a room with an unforgettable view, overlooking the Gorges du Tarn, such as you will not have from the rooms in the annex, known as the farm. The château is set in the midst of a large park. The dining room is built in the former chapel of the château, and you can also dine on the terrace. One star in Michelin. This is an extraordinarily beautiful site, definitely recommended and worth a memorable detour.

HR MANOIR DE MONTESQUIOU: Tel.: 66.48.51.12.   10 rooms, 2 suites. Open seasonally. Nicely furnished, medium-sized rooms with modern plumbing. Reasonably priced. Terrace. English spoken.

MILLAU (12000—Aveyron)

(Rodez 71—Mende 97—Albi 113—Montpellier 115—
Béziers 125—Nîmes 166—Paris 640)

❧ Aside from its historical background and its factory for treating leather for gloves, clothes, bags, and shoes (Alric, 11, rue de la Saunerie, tel.: 65.60.53.12), Millau's main virtue is that it is at one end of the glorious, unforgettable Gorges du Tarn and 30 km from Roquefort, where the cheese manufacturers' caves are well worth visiting.

HR LA MUSARDIÈRE: In the center, on the road to Rodez, 34, avenue de la République. Tel.: 65.60.20.63.
12 quiet, reasonably priced rooms, each with a different personality and décor. Comfortable. This luxurious private mansion, run by Giselle Canac, provides good food. English spoken. *Relais et Châteaux.* One star in Michelin.

HR INTERNATIONAL HOTEL: 1, place de la Tine. Tel.: 65.60.20.66.   118 air-conditioned rooms. Centrally located. Michelin generously gave it one star.

MONTIGNAC (24290—Dordogne)

(Brive 38—Perigueux 47—Sarlat 25—Cahors 98—Bergerac 83—
Limoges 102—Paris 496)

HR CHÂTEAU DE PUY ROBERT: 3 km on D-65. Tel.: 53.51.89.24.   15 rooms.
This small, picturesque nineteenth-century château was totally refurbished in 1985 by Albert Parveaux, the quality-minded owner of the Château de Castel-Novel in Varetz, near Brive, to make your stay in close proximity to the Caves of Lascaux still more comfortable.

MONTLUÇON (03100—Allier)
(Aubusson 63—Moulins 67—Clermont-Ferrand 90—Bourges 93—
Roanne 140—Limoges 145—Poitiers 200—Lyon 227)

HR HOSTELLERIE DU CHÂTEAU SAINT-JEAN: Route Clermont-Ferrand, close to the hippodrome. Tel.: 70.05.04.65. 8 rooms.
Comfortable rooms in a park. Restaurant in a twelfth-century chapel.

MONTRAND-LES-BAINS (42210—Loire)
(Saint-Étienne 27—Roanne 50—Lyon 68—Thiers 80—Clermont-Ferrand 122)

HR HOSTELLERIE LA POULARDE: 2, rue Saint-Étienne. Tel.: 77.54.40.06. 20 rooms.
Newly redecorated, not inexpensive. *Relais et Châteaux.* Two stars in Michelin.

MONVIEL (47290—Lot-et-Garonne)
(Duras 30—Bergerac 36 [on N-21]—Marmande 38—Agen 57—Buzet 60—Bordeaux 125)

Coming from Bordeaux, exit on autoroute at Marmande; take the direction of Périgueux and then D-124 to Monbahus. If coming from Toulouse, exit at Agen then take N-21 until Cancon.

HR CHÂTEAU DE MONVIEL: 10.5 km from Cancon. Tel.: 53.01.71.64. Tlx.: 560800 (specify Château de Monviel). 8 rooms. Heated swimming pool.
A two-hundred-year-old nobleman's residence. 8 spacious, well-decorated rooms showing a combination of taste and comfort. M. and Mme Leroy have shown the same taste in their daily kitchen as they have in the decoration of some of their spacious and comfortable rooms, of which six are in the château and two close by. It is regrettable that they don't have more. Although outside the Bordeaux vineyards, you have the Côtes de Duras, which are the local wines, to the west and the Bergeracs to the north. Good local wine list. *Relais et Châteaux.*

MOULINS (03000—Allier)
(Nevers 54—Guéret 65—Montluçon 67—Clermont-Ferrand 96—Roanne 98—
Mâcon 135—Châlons-sur-Saône 135—Lyon 184—Bordeaux 473)

HR HÔTEL DE PARIS: 21, rue de Paris. Tel.: 70.44.00.58. Tlx.: 394853. 20 pleasant rooms and 9 apartments.
In the old district close to the cathedral. François Laustriat runs an exceptionally good restaurant. The menus are a good value. *Relais et Châteaux.* One star in Michelin.

PÉRIGUEUX (24000—Dordogne)
(Le Bugue 41—Les Eyzies 45—Bergerac 47—Sarlat 66—Brive-la-Gaillarde 73—
Limoges 100—Bordeaux 121)

HR DOMINO: 21, place Francheville. Tel.: 53.08.25.80. Tlx.: 570230. 38 rooms.
In the center of town. If you haven't seen enough of this old Roman city, and want to spend the night, this is the place to stay. Otherwise try Savignac-les-Églises, Brantôme, or Champagnac-de-Belair.

ROANNE (42300—Loire)
(Saint-Étienne 77—Lyon 86—Moulins 98—Clermont-Ferrand 100—Chalons-sur-Saône 132—
Montluçon 140—Valence 195—Dijon 200—Paris 391)

HR TROISGROS: Place de la Gare. Tel.: 77.71.66.97. Tlx.: 307507.   18 comfortable rooms and 6 suites.
This is worth the steep, winding, and seemingly endless descent through the hills from Clermont-Ferrand to Roanne. It is even worth a detour from Paris, or from wherever you happen to be. The very personable Pierre Troisgros offers highly imaginative menus, which are expensive but worth every franc. Well-selected wines and excellent wine cellar. The rooms are modern, plush, and the right place to sleep after an all-absorbing meal. *Relais et Châteaux.* Three stars in Michelin.

HR GRAND HÔTEL: 18, cours de la République. Tel.: 77.71.48.82. Tlx.: 300573.   48 rooms (3 toilets).
If you cannot sleep at Troisgros, try this hotel as a compromise. It's located near the train station. Reasonably priced. The adjoining restaurant is called L'Astrée.

ROCAMADOUR (46500—Lot)
(Gramat 9—Padirac 16—Brive-la-Gaillarde 54—Cahors 64—Sarlat 65—Tulle 80—
Les Eyzies 87—Bergerac 140—Bordeaux 232—Clermont-Ferrand 235)

One of France's great sights. The château and fourteenth-century ramparts are built of the rock that juts out of the valley 150 meters below. *Son et lumière* every night from Easter to mid-October.

HR BEAU SITE ET NOTRE DAME: Tel.: 65.33.63.08. Tlx.: 520421.   55 rooms (48 with toilet).
Located in the middle of the one-street village that lies in the shadow of the château fortifications above. Good view. Decent rooms and bathrooms. Respectable restaurant and wine list featuring local Cahors wines.

HR HÔTEL DE L'ASCENSEUR: Tel.: 65.33.62.44 or 65.33.62.43.   55 rooms.
Located near the Beau Site, with comparable view of the valley. Charmless, small, but clean and reasonably priced rooms. Restaurant available.

HR CHÂTEAU DE ROUMEGOUSE: 4 km southeast of Rocamadour on the way to Gramat. Tel.: 65.33.63.81.   10 rooms, 2 suites.
This château-hotel has large, comfortable rooms, and is the place to stay while in Rocamadour. Balustraded stone terrace overlooking the Gramat valley. Fun/pretentious baronial-style dining room. *Relais et Châteaux.*

ROQUEFORT-SUR-SOULZON (12000—Aveyron)
(Millau 24—Lodève 65—Rodez 82—Le Vigan 76—Toulouse 172—Paris 655)

The detour to visit this automated manufacturer of one of the world's best-known cheeses is well worthwhile, but patience is needed, for the highly recommended tours are conducted on an hourly basis during the summer.

H LE GRAND HÔTEL: Rue de Lauras. Tel.: 65.59.90.20.   16 rooms (10 toilets).
From fair to middling. I stayed overnight in this hotel, owned by Patrick Lenfant, with Alfred Knopf, my publisher, in 1951. I was not impressed by their rooms then, and, unfortunately, not much has been done to make me change my mind 35 years later.

SAINT-CYPRIEN (24220—Dordogne)
(Le Bugue 13—Les Eyzies 16—Sarlat 21—Bergerac 53—Périgueux 54)

HR L'ABBAYE: Tel.: 53.29.20.48.   20 rooms (18 with toilet).
Beautifully located in Dordogne, this simple, respectable hotel has decent rooms, and a restaurant featuring reasonable menus. Warm welcome.

SAINT-ÉTIENNE (42000—Loire)
(Lyon 59—Roanne 77—Valence 118—Clermont-Ferrand 149—Nice 490)

R PIERRE GAGNAIRE: 3, rue Georges-Teissier, in the center of town. Tel.: 77.37.57.93.
Pierre and Françoise Gagnaire's small establishment has evoked rapturous praise from *Gault et Millau*. In 1986 Michelin gave it two stars.

HR NOVOTEL: Andrézieux-Bouthéon, 16 km from Saint-Étienne, near the airport. Tel.: 77.36.55.63. Tlx.: 900722.   98 air-conditioned rooms.
A limited snack bar–restaurant. Small swimming pool.

HR LE GRAND HÔTEL: 10, avenue de la Libération. Tel.: 77.32.99.77. Tlx.: 300811.   66 rooms.
A new restaurant, the "Chantegril" has recently opened.

R LE CLOS FLEURI: Saint-Priest-en-Jarez, 76, avenue A. Raimond, 4 km north of town on D-11. Tel.: 77.74.63.24.
A good restaurant, with a pleasant garden for dining when weather permits.

SAINT-YRIEIX-LA-PERCHE (87500—Haute-Vienne)
(Limoges 41—Rochechouart 52—Périgueux 62—Brive 62—Tulle 74)

HR MOULIN DE LA GORCE: 2 km south of La Roche-L'Abeille on D-17. Tel.: 55.00.70.66.   9 very unstandard rooms in a sixteenth-century mill on a romantic stream. The food and comfort are worth a detour. Jean Bertranet, the owner, is justifiably proud of his two-star rating in Michelin.

SARLAT-LA-CANEDA (24200—Dordogne)
(Trémolat 13—Les Eyzies 21—Le Bugue 33—Brive-la-Gaillarde 50—Périgueux 66—
Rocamadour 65—Cahors 71—Bergerac 75—Bordeaux 150—Clermont-Ferrand 237)

HR HÔTEL DE LA MADELEINE: 1, Place de la Petite Rigaudie. Tel.: 53.59.12.40 and 53.59.10.41. Tlx.: 550689.   19 rooms and 3 suites.
The best hotel in town. The usual small rooms, at decent prices, but it can be noisy at night. Decent menus, and one of the better wine lists.

HR HOSTELLERIE DE MEYSSET: Argentouleau, 2 km northwest of Sarlat on the road to Les Eyzies. Tel.: 53.59.08.29. 20 rooms, 6 suites (all with toilet).
Quiet, in the center of a park, this is the hotel to stay at if you don't want to be right in Sarlat. The food, however, is not what one would expect in gastronomically inclined Sarlat.

SOUILLAC—LACAVE (46200—Lot)
(Cahors 60—Toulouse 170)

H CHÂTEAU DE LA TREYNE: 3 km west of Lacave on D-43 overlooking the Dordogne at a very beautiful site. Tel.: 65.32.66.66.   10 rooms (only 5 toilets) and 2 suites. Pool. Tennis.

TRÉMOLAT (24510—Dordogne)
(Sarlat 13—Le Bugue 14—Lalinde 20—Les Eyzies 24—Périgueux 54—
Bergerac 42—Brive-la-Gaillarde 86—Clermont-Ferrand 274)

HR LE VIEUX LOGIS: Tel.: 53.22.80.06. Tlx.: 541025.   19 rooms, 3 apartments.
An attractive country-style inn which has been in M. Bernard Giraudel's family for a couple of centuries, set on the edge of the village. The rooms are not palatial but are very comfortable, tasteful, and attractive. Good restaurant with excellent service, in a dining room that is supposed to be a reminder of a coach-and-horses era. Pretty outdoor terrace. *Relais et Châteaux.*

❧

ELSEWHERE IN FRANCE

On the Road to Chartres and the Loire:

ABLIS (78600—Yvelines)
(Rambouillet 15—Chartres 30—Étampes 30—Versailles 45—Orly airport 45—
Paris 63—Orléans 76—Roissy airport [Charles-de-Gaulle] 80)

HR CHÂTEAU D'ESCLIMONT: (28700 Auneau), 6 km west of Ablis on D-168, just off the autoroute A-11 which takes you to Chartres. Tel.: 37.31.15.15. Tlx.: 780560.   48 beautifully decorated rooms and 8 suites. Heated pool. Tennis.
This is the new *Relais et Châteaux* of René Traversac who has set his high-standard mark in transforming beautiful châteaux, which this is, into comfortable hotels and good restaurants such as Château d'Artigny and Le Prieuré at Chènehutte-les-Tuffeaux in the Loire and Castillon-du-Gard in the Rhône. This may be an easy drive or your first stop on your way to visit the châteaux of the Loire and Bordeaux.

❧

EAST OF FRANCE

On the Road from Lyon to Geneva and the Wines of Seyssel and Savoie:

ANNECY (74000—Haute-Savoie)
(Talloires 13—Aix-les-Bains 34—Geneva 43—Chambéry 49—Thonon 72—
Bourg-en-Bresse 122—Lyon 140—Paris 548)

R AUBERGE DE SAVOIE: 1, place Saint-François. Tel.: 50.45.03.05.
Try one of the menus and you should not be disappointed. You will always remember the scenic lake. One star in Michelin.

LE BOURGET-DU-LAC (73370—Savoie)
(Aix-les-Bains 9—Chambéry 11—Belley 25—Annecy 42—La Tour-du-Pin 48—
Geneva 86—Lyon 103)

HR OMBREMONT: 2 km north on N-504. Tel.: 79.25.00.23. Tlx.: 980832.   18 rooms.
The rooms, the food, the views, and the comfort are quite outstanding. *Relais et Châteaux*. One star in Michelin.

R LE BATEAU IVRE: Close to the lake. Tel.: 79.25.02.66.
Refined and elegant decoration. The young Jean-Pierre Jacob has acquired two stars in Michelin and makes this perhaps the best restaurant between the Lake of Annecy and Lyon.

450

CHAMBÉRY (73000—Savoie)
(Annecy 47—Grenoble 55—Geneva 79—Lyon 98—Bourg-en-Bresse 108—
Valence 124—Vienne 165—Turin 202)

HR GRAND HÔTEL—LA VANOISE: 6, place de la Gare, facing the station. Tel.: 79.69.54.54. Tlx.: 320910. 50 nice, air-conditioned rooms and 5 suites.
La Vanoise is quite a good independent restaurant. Tel.: 79.69.02.78.

R ROUBATCHEFF: 6, rue du Théâtre. Tel.: 79.33.24.91.
I like the Russian dishes and hope that the tendency will be to add more of them rather than less. Unfortunately, the latter is the case. One star in Michelin.

FAVERGES-DE-LA-TOUR (38110—Isère)
(La Tour-du-Pin 10—Morestel 13—Chambéry 40—Vienne 53—Lyon 65—
Bourg-en-Bresse 76—Geneva 113—Paris 563)

HR LE CHÂTEAU DE FAVERGES: Autoroute A-43, exit La Tour-du-Pin. Tel.: 74.97.42.52. Tlx.: 300372. 40 comfortable rooms.
A beautiful, elegant château in the midst of a 15-hectare park. Heated pool. Tennis courts. The rooms in the annex are of lesser interest. For its leisurely comfort it is worth making a detour from, or to, Lyon. *Relais et Châteaux.* One star in Michelin.

GRENOBLE (38000—Isère)
(Chambéry 55—Valence 94—Annecy 99—Lyon 104—Vienne 106—Briançon 114—
Bourg-en-Bresse 142—Geneva 144—Marseille 281—Nice 334—Paris 568)

H PARK HÔTEL: 10, place Paul-Mistral. Tel.: 76.87.29.11. Tlx.: 320767. 59 air-conditioned rooms, 2 suites.
Well-equipped, modern rooms, some with beautiful mountain views. The Taverne serves simple dishes till midnight.

R LA POULARDE BRESSANE: 12, place Paul-Mistral. Tel.: 76.87.08.90.
Jean-Charles Piccinini is a good chef. One star in Michelin.

R AUBERGE BRESSANE: 38 ter, rue Beaublache. Tel.: 76.87.64.29.
Simple yet warm décor is the background for Roger Décher, an excellent chef. One star in Michelin.

SAINT-JULIEN-EN-GENEVOIS (74160—Haute-Savoie)
(Geneva 9—Annecy 35—Nantua 55—Chambéry 84—Lyon 168)

R LA DILIGENCE ET TAVERNE DU POSTILLON: Avenue de Genève, in the center of town. Tel.: 50.49.07.55.
Behind the church. A good restaurant on the French side of the frontier when leaving Switzerland. Very good, imaginative menus. *Relais et Châteaux.* One star in Michelin.

R ABBAYE DE POMMIER: 8 km south on N-201 at Presilly. Tel.: 50.04.40.64.
Another good restaurant close to Geneva, which is handy for the Swiss who appreciate good food. One star in Michelin.

TALLOIRES (74290—Haute-Savoie)
Exit on Annecy Nord.
(Annecy 13—Faverges 15—Thônes 17—Aix-les-Bains 47—Megève 48—
Geneva 56—Lyon 153—Paris 545)

HR L'AUBERGE DU PÈRE BISE: On Lac Annecy. Tel.: 50.60.72.01. Tlx.: 385812.   22 rooms and 10 suites.
Overlooking the lake, this luxurious inn has for several decades been a gastronomic mecca. Those fond of desserts will be super-delighted. Bise has always been a gastronomic highlight, having been one of the first three-star Michelin restaurants in the provinces. Recently it lost one star, but in 1985, bravo!—it regained it. Charlyne Bise and Sophie, her daughter, run a dependable highlight.

HR LE COTTAGE: Tel.: 50.60.71.10.   34 nice rooms overlooking the lake or the mountains.
The restaurant is simpler than at the Auberge but, on the whole, more than competent, with a very good wine list.

HR L'ABBAYE: Route du Port. Tel.: 50.67.40.88. Tlx.: 385307.   31 rooms, 2 suites.
Luxurious rooms in a seventeenth-century Benedictine abbey. Enjoyable food can be served on the terrace overlooking the lake. *Relais et Châteaux.*

CENTRAL FRANCE

AUTUN (71400—Saône-et-Loire)
(Chalon-sur-Saône 53—Beaune 56—Avallon 80—Dijon 85—Nevers 103—Lyon 186)

HR HOSTELLERIE DU VIEUX MOULIN: Porte d'Arroux. Tel.: 85.52.10.90.   18 rooms. (13 toilets)
Pretty garden. Rather small rooms. The restaurant is considered to be better than the hotel.

BESSE-EN-CHANDESSE (63610—Puy-de-Dôme)
(Le Mont Dore 27—Issoire 35—Clermont-Ferrand 50—Le Puy 129—
Saint-Étienne 176—Valence 294)

HR LES MOUFLONS: Route Super-Besse. Tel.: 73.79.51.31.   50 rooms.
Reasonable prices. In a shady park. One star in Michelin.

CHATEAUROUX (36000—Indre)
(Vierzon 58—Bourges 67—Blois 80—Tours 109—Poitiers 120—
Limoges 126—Nevers 134—Paris 260)

HR ÉLYSÉE HÔTEL: Tel.: 54.22.33.66. 17 rooms, and JEAN BARDET RESTAURANT: 1, rue Jean-Jacques Rousseau. Tel.: 54.34.88.69.
If not much can be said regarding the hotel, which is in the center of town, and its modern, functional rooms, one can praise Jean Bardet's marvelous cuisine, which has been applauded by all the guidebooks, including Michelin with its two stars.

MONTROND-LES-BAINS (42210—Loire)
(Feurs 11—Montbrison 14—Saint-Étienne 27—Roanne 50—Lyon 68—
Thiers 80—Clermont-Ferrand 122—Paris 497)

HR HOSTELLERIE LA POULARDE: 2, rue Saint-Étienne. Tel.: 77.54.40.06. 15 rooms.
A delightful stopover to eat, sleep, and drink. Well worth exiting off the autoroute for at least a meal. *Relais et Châteaux.* Two stars in Michelin.

CASTELNAUDARY (11400—Aude)
(Carcassonne 36—Toulouse 55—Albi 88—Narbonne 92—Bordeaux 303)

⌖ The reputed birthplace of cassoulet, the legendary bean-sausage-goose dish.

HR MAPOTEL DES PALMES ET INDUSTRIES: 10, rue du Maréchal Foch. Tel.: 68.23.03.10 and 68.23.17.10. Tlx.: 500372.
Not worth a detour. Stopping at this hotel with its 20 functional, modern rooms (15 toilets) is justified if you feel sleepy driving on the autoroute between Toulouse and Carcassonne.

TOULOUSE (31000—Haute Garonne)
(Auch 78—Béziers 90—Carcassonne 92—Albi 107—Montpellier 107—Cahors 113—
Agen 114—Rodez 154—Bordeaux 253—Bayonne 279—Nîmes 290)

⌖ This large, rather dull city's claim to fame is as the headquarters where the Concorde and the Airbus were built.

Although it originated in Castelnaudary, cassoulet is gastronomically associated with Toulouse.

HR GRAND HÔTEL DE L'OPÉRA: 1, place du Capitole. Tel.: 61.21.82.66. Tlx.: 521998. 46 rooms, 2 suites.

A quiet, centrally located, air-conditioned hotel. Good rooms. Some overlook a patio with a swimming pool. The restaurant, called Les Jardins de l'Opéra, is elegant, and Dominique Toulousy is an excellent chef and well deserves his star in Michelin. Pretty Michèle Douin is the manager.

H FRANTEL-WILSON: 7, rue Labéda. Tel.: 61.21.21.75. Tlx.: 530550. 91 air-conditioned rooms. No restaurant.
In center of business district. Recently remodeled.

HR DIANE-SAINT-SIMON: 3, rue de Saint-Simon. Tel.: 61.07.59.52. Tlx.: 530518. 33 rooms.
Northwest on the road to the airport, take the rocade (surrounding expressway) to Foix. Coming from Bordeaux, take the autoroute to Montpellier, exit at Toulouse-Mirail-Cugnaux.
A small house, dating from the turn of the century, set in a park with some bungalows. Tennis. Swimming pool. The Saint-Simon restaurant is good. Beautiful view. The distance from the center of town makes this slightly difficult to find and perhaps rather unnecessary.

R VANEL: 22, rue Maurice-Fontvieille, close to the Place Wilson. Tel.: 61.21.51.82.
Unanimously considered the best restaurant in Toulouse. Good wine list. Father Vanel, in his seventies, goes from classical tradition to exotic subtlety. Two stars in Michelin.

453

R DARROZE: 19, rue Castellane, near the Place Wilson (walking distance from the Grand Hôtel de l'Opéra). Tel.: 61.62.34.70.

I like the cuisine of Pierre Darroze and Viviane, his daughter-in-law. The entire family contributes to your gastronomic welfare. The mother is at the register; Henri, the son, as the sommelier will offer you a very good assortment of wines; Françoise, his sister, oversees the service. Henri is proud of some fifty Bas-Armagnacs which he can offer you. They have been awarded one star in Michelin and I would be happy to see them get another.

R LA BELLE ÉPOQUE: 3, rue Pargaminières. Tel.: 61.23.22.12.

One of the better restaurants of the town. One star in Michelin.

R ORSI BOUCHON LYONNAIS: 13, rue de l'Industrie. Tel.: 61.62.97.43.

Laurent Orsi trained under Bocuse and now specializes in fish dishes.

SOUTHWEST FRANCE AND SOUTH OF ARMAGNAC

(also see end of Armagnac chapter)

SAINT-JEAN-PIED-DE-PORT (64220—Pyrénées-Atlantiques)
(Bayonne 52—Saint-Jean-de-Luz 65—Dax 88—Pau 102—San Sebastian 97)

HR PYRÉNÉES: 19, place Général-de-Gaulle. Tel.: 59.37.01.01.   31 rooms (24 toilets).

In contrast to the rather basic rooms, Mr Firmin Arrambide has created a high version of Basque cuisine. The entire family contributes to the service in this large village at the foot of the Pyrénées. This is one of the very recent gastronomic discoveries in this beautiful, out-of-the-way countryside, as exemplified by the two stars in Michelin.

CENTRAL/WESTERN FRANCE

The Loire, on the Road to Cognac and Bordeaux:

POITIERS (86000—Vienne)
(Saumur 90—Tours 100—Angoulême 110—Limoges 119—Châteauroux 120—
Angers 134—La Rochelle 138—Nantes 180—Bordeaux 227—Paris 333)

❦ It is worth a visit for those deeply interested in old churches. Otherwise it can claim to be a good stopover on the way to or from Bordeaux.

H LE FRANCE: 28, rue Carnot. Tel.: 49.41.32.01. Tlx.: 790526.   87 rooms.

This hotel and its restaurant are not worth much of a detour.

R CHEZ VLADIMIR: 10, rue Jean Macé. Tel.: 49.41.69.72.
Russian cooking in a Russian atomosphere and with Russian music. Open for dinner only.

HR DOMAINE DE PERIGNY: (86190 Vouillé) 17 km south from Poitiers, just outside of Vouillée on
N-149. Tel.: 49.51.80.43. Tlx: 791400. 38 nice rooms. Pool. 3 tennis courts.
Set in a beautiful large park. The food is good. If stopping off in Poitiers it is worth coming here.
Georges Brossard has made an effort to make this quiet, comfortable stopover inviting.

SWITZERLAND

We are not attempting to make a complete list of hotels and restaurants in Switzerland. But because one of my favorite eastern itineraries suggests using the new direct autoroute through Switzerland to connect Alsace and Burgundy, I have included a sampling of the best Swiss hotels and
restaurants along the way.

BASEL (in French: "Bâle")
(Belfort 67—Mulhouse 32—Bern 91—Freiburg 71—Lyon 67—
Strasbourg 145—Colmar 80—Paris 551)

HR HÔTEL DES TROIS ROIS: Blumenrain 8. Tel.: (61)25.52.52. Tlx.: 962937. 90 air-conditioned
rooms.
Switzerland has always prided itself on the caliber and professionalism of its hoteliers. This hotel
claims to be the oldest in Switzerland, supposedly founded in 1026. Professionalism is found in the

excellent service, which has been appreciated by an international Who's Who for years. The rooms are large and ultra-comfortable and enjoy a beautiful view of the Rhine. The restaurant, Rôtisserie des Rois, is also good, with excellent service and interesting menus.

HR HILTON: Aeschengraben 31. Tel.: (61)22.66.22. Tlx.: 962055.   217 air-conditioned rooms and 10 suites. Heated pool.
Close to the station and 15 minutes from the Bâle-Mulhouse airport. Beautiful views from the top rooms on to the Vosges and Black Forest mountains.

HR HÔTEL INTERNATIONAL: Steinentorstrasse 25. Tel.: (61)22.18.70. Tlx.: 962370.   205 air-conditioned rooms and 5 suites. Pool.
The usual high standard. Good food, if not the best.

HR EULER: Centralhahnplatz 14. Tel.: (61)23.45.00. Tlx.: 962215.   58 air-conditioned rooms and 8 suites.
Luxurious, large rooms, just like the Hôtel des Trois Rois. Has the advantage of being close to the station and to the airport.

R BRUDERHOLZ "STUCKI": Bruderholzallee 42. Tel.: (61)35.82.22.
One of the best restaurants in Switzerland. As a chef, Hans Stucki is considered practically on a par with Freddy Girardet. Here you can taste Swiss food at its best, accompanied by very good wines which you can select from an immense wine list, giving you a chance to drink good Swiss wine such as Aigle. *Relais et Châteaux.* Two stars in Michelin.

BERN
(Geneva 152—Zurich 121—Basel 90—Belfort 140)

HR HÔTEL SCHWEIZERHOF: Bahnhofplatz 11. Tel.: (31)22.45.01. 10 rooms.
Large rooms, as often previously found in Switzerland. The Gauers have been running this hotel in the center of town for a couple of generations. They can provide you with the best food in Bern, at the restaurant known as the Schultheissenstube. They even have a night club in this rather dull capital of Switzerland.

LAUSANNE
(Bern 94—Geneva 62)

HR HÔTEL BEAU RIVAGE: Place du Général Guisan, Ouchy. Tel.: (21)26.38.31.   220 rooms.
In lower Lausanne, on the lake in Ouchy. Luxurious rooms in a superbly modernized, old-fashioned Swiss hotel-palace. Huge, super-comfortable rooms with balconies facing the lake and the French Alps beyond. This hotel is rightly proud of its separate restaurant, Wellingtonia, which has an excellent wine cellar.

HR LAUSANNE PALACE: 7, 9 Grand Chêne. Tel.: (21)20.37.11.   200 rooms.
An excellent hotel, in the heart of town, with comfortable rooms and a good restaurant called Le Relais-Grill.

HR CARLTON: 4, avenue de Cour. Tel.: (21)26.32.35.
Out of the heart of the city, this charming hotel has the advantage of being quiet. The restaurant, Le Richelieu, is especially good.

R GIRARDET: 1, route d'Yverdon, Crissier, 6 km from Lausanne. Tel.: (21)34.15.14.
Much ink has been spilled in praising the qualities of Freddy Girardet, who is considered by some
to be the greatest chef running the greatest restaurant in the world. Unquestionably, his cooking
can be superb, embodying Swiss cuisine at its best. Gault-Millau, who have been known at times to
overrate a restaurant, have given Girardet 19.5 out of a possible 20 and have vacillated between
calling him the gastronomic equivalent of Johann Sebastian Bach and of Mozart. He is unquestionably, in any event, one of the greatest gastronomic artists whose food I have had the privilege
of tasting. Reserve ahead of time. Three stars in Michelin.

COPPET
(Geneva 13—Lausanne 47)

HR HÔTEL DU LAC: Tel.: (22)76.15.21.   11 rooms, 5 suites.
Both the hotel and the restaurant are outstanding. Rather expensive. *Relais et Châteaux.*

GENEVA
(Lyon 156—Bern 154—Turin 255—Paris 513—Bourg-en-Bresse 118—Lausanne 63)

Dozens of good hotels are to be found in Geneva. Most of the top ones have good restaurants. In
addition, there are some 20 very good hotels within easy driving distance in the suburbs. Your *con-
cierge* will be happy to suggest restaurants in or outside Geneva where you will be sure to eat well.

TASTING WINE

The best time to taste wines seriously is when your senses are sharpest and your powers of concentration are at their highest. For most people that time is just before lunch or dinner, although most professional tastings take place in the morning. If a meal is to accompany the tasting, the simpler the food the better. Food of some kind can be an aid; the proteins and carbohydrates in bread and cheese, for example, help to clear the palate and tongue of the lingering acids of the wine and prepare the mouth for the next sip. However, tasting professionally as a buyer or grower, I don't want to flatter the wine by having anything to eat between one sample and another.

Smoking during a tasting or during the meal between courses is considered impolite to others when fine wines are being served and appreciated. Generally speaking, habitual smoking may impair the tasting ability of the palate, but professional tasters who smoke have learned to compensate for this dulling and still perform their job with acute sensitivity.

Good taste in wines is more easily recognized than defined. Unless one takes the trouble to formulate and use a consistent, descriptive vocabulary, with terms that someone else can understand, one will be handicapped in communicating the description of a wine. Descriptions of wine, however, are not essential to the enjoyment of wine. If overdone, they can be merely pompous.

It is a challenge to describe a wine so that someone else can understand and imagine the taste of it. Important to the accurate and understandable communication of wine taste—in addition to a finely tuned sense of smell and taste—is a psychological affinity with whomever you are tasting and matching impressions. I had a wine-buying associate in the Rhine named Karl Ress with whom I developed this relationship to a remarkable degree. Even though I was far from fluent in German and Ress spoke no French or English, we had a common language in wine. From his descriptions of wines by letter or telephone, I could practically taste them. This sort of nearly instinctive agreement is rare, though generally easier to find among white wines than red, the white wines being less complex.

Describing tastes has another practical application. If you note down your reactions to the wine in front of you, you will be able to refer to the notes at a later date when the wines will have developed further. By recording both taste reactions and price, you will be able to make intelligent decisions on future purchases. Keeping a notebook with comments or a card file also serves as a pleasant reminder of fine bottles and enjoyable dinners.

Critical tasting demands practice, concentration, and memory. What you are attempting to do is separate and distinguish between the many smell and taste sensations that characterize the wine. When tasting a wine professionally or as a serious amateur, one relies on the memory of the evolution of similar wines previously encountered, which if red may have tasted raw, tannic, and unappealing at the time, though later attaining softness, roundness, and elegance. When tasting, one tries to perceive the hidden notes that will develop as it matures.

The first question to ask is: what does the wine look like? Lift the glass, filled to one-third, by the stem and tilt it against a light background. Whether white or red, wines should be limpid and untroubled to the eye. Young white wines range from the nearly colorless silvery-greenish tint of the Muscadets to the yellow-green of Chablis to the straw-colored white Burgundies. Dry whites from Graves will more often be light straw in hue, with little or no green to them. Sauternes and Barsacs should be a frank yellow, turning to gold and amber as they age. Young white wines from the Loire, which should be dry, such as Muscadet, Sancerre, and Pouilly-Fumé, should not appear too yellow, as this will be a sign of premature oxidation due to a lack of acidity, late picking, overripe grapes, or late bottling.

The variations in red wine are nearly infinite. Young red wines are lighter and more purplish in color than those with even eighteen months of bottle age. Beaujolais, red wine from the Loire, and some of the lighter Côtes du Rhône wines will still have "vegetal" purplishness to the eye, which indicates youth and minimal or no barrel aging.

As red wine ages, these traces of purple disappear and the color develops into deep red, a color referred to as "bordeaux" in France and "burgundy" in America. A mature claret or Burgundy will be brick red on the edges.

Signs of brownishness around the edges of red wines (best seen when tilting the glass in front of a light background) may indicate age. Rosés should be pink with no tinge of yellow or orange, as is sometimes found in two- or three-year-old Provence rosés that are over the hill.

The next question is: what does the wine smell like? Swirl the wine slowly three or four times in the glass and smell it.

The first thing to notice, surprising as it may sound, is whether the wine smells like wine. Are there any "off" or non-wine odors? The smell of apples in white wines will mean an excess of malic acid, usually due to an early bottling. White wines are sometimes bottled before the malolactic fermentation is finished in order to preserve an extra measure of acidity and freshness. In most good wines, however, this is not desirable. The smell of old leaves in a red wine will indicate that it is in decline. The smell is initially sweetish and can be mistaken for richness; closer examination will reveal it for what it is: fatigue. A smell resembling Sherry or dry Madeira in white wines is the smell of an oxidized wine, one literally "maderized."

Other off smells of every possible description can be found in wine, all indicating poor, sloppy, careless, or unlucky vinification. Fermentation or storage in vats or barrels corroded by decades of wine tartrates or grapes picked when overly mature with a touch of rot will result in a wine that is unclean in smell and, therefore, unpleasant. The presence of carbon dioxide in red wine (felt especially by a slight prickle on the tongue) will indicate that the wine finished its malolactic fermentation in the bottle. Red wines thus afflicted may have a cloudy deposit around the shoulders of the bottle and a peculiar smell, which disappears if the wine is poured several times from glass to glass.

These are all faults we hope no wine will suffer from.

What are the attributes to look for? Above all, freshness and a harmonious vinosity which characterizes a wine whose elements have subtly integrated themselves. This should be true especially for the older bottles. As the saying goes, the wine that ages best is the one that stays young longest. This is where a great vintage triumphs.

The woody taste and smell of a wine drawn from new oak barrels should be barely perceptible to the nose and palate, although it will tend to be more noticeable in young wines with little or no bottle age. This brings us to the difference between "aroma" and "bouquet," words which are often used interchangeably in wine talk. Properly speaking, aroma is the smell of the wine when it is new, usually from the barrel or vat. Bouquet is the smell or "nose" a wine acquires in the course of being aged in bottle. Therefore one speaks of a wine having a fine bouquet, meaning that the finer notes and nuances of smell have emerged in bottle.

The positive features of smell are those you'd look for in taste: freshness and fruitiness in youth, which may seem like rawness in fine reds when young and harmonious balance and richness in maturity. Roughly speaking, a wine, whether red or white, is "balanced" when there is an equal amount of alcohol, fruitiness, and acidity. Over the long haul, it is the acidity of the wine that carries the fruit. On the other hand, lack of fruit or over-acidity will make the wine uncommonly hard and ungiving. The 1969 red Bordeaux, for instance, suffered from smallness of fruit, compared to their acidity. This question of acidity is also very pertinent to white wines, especially Alsatian wines, in which their grapiness is harmonized by the acidity that keeps the wines from being flabby. This will be revealed in the nose and palate.

A cool temperature (around 16° C. or 60° F.) may also help some red wines, such as Beaujolais, whose typical floweriness tends to dissipate slightly more quickly at room temperature. Cool temperatures will help to concentrate a wine's fruit, and it is interesting to note its development in the glass as the temperature rises. Some châteaux in Bordeaux do not serve their wines at room temperature, preferring to bring them directly from cellar to table so the guests can enjoy the wine as it gradually reveals all of its character. Professor Peynaud aptly states that the cells sensitive to taste, the papillae, are only found on the rough part of the tongue and are equipped with several hundred taste buds. The saliva that lubricates the papillae is as important in tasting wine as in our perception of food flavors. Only four basic tastes can be distinguished by the tongue's papillae: sour, sweet, salt and bitter. Not everyone is equally attuned to the detection of these tastes.

The tip of the tongue is most sensitive to the sweet taste, which is provided by the wine's alcohol and sugar. The sides of the tongue taste the salts. The bitter taste from the wine's phenolic components called tannins, are detected when swallowing at the back of the tongue.

To taste for the maximum pleasure requires nothing out of the ordinary. Take a small amount of wine (more than a sip, but less than a gulp) on the tongue and, before swallowing it, let it rest on the tongue, purse your lips, and draw some air in over it, making a gurgling sound. This is an optional step, but the aeration does expose many other dimensions of the wine. What it specifically consists of is impossible to define—this alone is reason to keep pulling corks. The olfactory area is situated in the upper part of the nose.

To describe the taste of wine is at the same time the easiest and the hardest of the three steps of wine appreciation: the object is pleasure, not brow wrinkling. Still, identifying and "naming" tastes is a game that all people who drink wine with enjoyment can play. Descriptions of wines in terms of violets, carnations, currants, truffles, and any other fruit or tuber known to man may sound needlessly esoteric, but it can have a special accuracy. Oenologists have demonstrated that all flowers and fruits are composed of the same molecules, and it is not unusual that they should arrange themselves in similar patterns when they strike the nose or palate. This "poetic" vocabulary is fine as long as it does not inhibit enjoyment or make anyone feel left out. When you serve more than one wine of the same type, your vocabulary will tend to be a little more technical. Comparing red Bordeaux, you may say that one is lighter and more elegant than another, which may have more tannin (betrayed by the wine's hardness) and seem more complex. Comparing wines is the most instructive way to learn about them, and the best way of testing yourself as a taster. The difficulty and demands on you are of course increased when you taste a wine blindly. And, happily, the best way to deepen your knowledge of wines is to "teach" and taste with friends. You may know more about wine, but they will bring their own curiosity and enthusiasm, impelling you into new regions of knowledge and expertise.

FOOD AND WINE

The harmonious combination of food and wine at the dinner table helps to cement family bonds and acts as a catalyst to new friendships. In some cases, the greater the bottle, the stronger the bond created or renewed. Great wine deserves discussion and can help to resolve temporarily the most divergent opinions and politics.

Food does not, and should not, simply sate the appetite. A meal poorly prepared or thoughtlessly composed is a desecration to body and soul, and could be a sign of contempt for your guests and yourself. This does not imply that you must have *grande cuisine* every time you sit down, or that every bottle you uncork should be a great one. It means simply that, however humble or simple, the meal should be a reflection of the care and concern felt for those who partake of it.

The foods and wines should fit one another, as well as the occasion and your mood. Most of the time, this happens naturally. A Montrachet with a chicken sandwich may indeed be great, but it would be even greater if you gave it the ceremony of a poached bass with a delicate sauce. Save your chicken sandwich for a Mâcon white.

In the same way, the exigencies of occasion, place, and climate logically shape our choice of food and wine. A weekday evening after a hard day is not the best time to sit down to a great banquet with fine wines. Fatigued, we are apt to want respite and simplicity more than anything else. Great Bordeaux and Burgundies are not shown to their best advantage in the heat of a summer resort. This is more than a simple matter of temperature. The demands made by a great wine and complex food can often be out of place on a summer holiday. This explains why the well-heeled resorts of the Côte d'Azur stock relatively few Burgundies and Bordeaux, compared with the Bandols, the Côtes de Provence, and rosés of all kinds.

There are wines to be drunk away from food at any time of the day, such as Rhines, Moselles, Ports, and Sherries. In France, Champagnes, Alsatian wines, Barsacs, Sauternes, sweet Vouvrays, and Coteaux du Layon can be enjoyed by themselves any time. But, essentially, French wines are meant to accompany food. Good wine can make any food taste better and turn a humdrum plate into a memorable meal.

In England and America, cocktails and highballs are popular before-dinner drinks. Americans are now less abusive of the practice than in the past, and moderation (as exemplified by the white-wine fashion) has gained a strong foothold. On the other hand, the French in recent years have become infatuated with the mixed drink; in better homes it is often considered chic to offer a whiskey before the meal. Or else, before sitting down to a good meal, a Frenchman may sip a sweet and syrupy concoction, such as *pastis* or a cheap, sweet Port, then drink acid wine with his food, and top it off with a liqueur. How you insult your stomach depends on where you were brought up. There's no doubt that a strongly alcoholic drink with a pronounced and often sweet flavor confuses your taste buds and makes it difficult to savor wines. A glass of white wine, a chilled dry Sherry or a dry Champagne—all derived from grapes—serves to prepare the palate for wine, rather than numbing it.

Enjoy yourself, but remain aware that if you restrict your drinking to one cocktail or Scotch, rather than several, the wine and food that follow will be that much more perceptively enjoyed.

As for smoking, the French are much less strict than wine lovers in England and America. Many of the best tasters I know smoke, and many winegrowers smoke while drinking wines, *but never during meals.*

Through the centuries, certain ideas about matching wines to foods have been formulated to help you get the most from a bottle, but the "rules" themselves are little more than tested preferences. It is a matter of instinct and common sense that certain wines taste better than others with specific dishes. If rules inhibit your enjoyment of wines, there should be no rules. As you learn about wines by tasting, you will invent your own guidelines. No rules about wine fall into the realm of etiquette; they merely indicate the most pleasing combinations of food and drink and help you to avoid unpleasant ones. What tastes right to your palate is likely to please another's.

In France, a dinner consists of a number of courses accompanied by two or three different wines. Soup is served, for it acts as an alkalizer; the main course will determine the choice of wine; and the vegetables are served separately, for few taste good with wines. A cheese course is added before the dessert because cheese brings out the taste especially of red wine better than anything else. And the whole meal is planned so that the light and simple dishes and wines precede the heavier, more complex ones.

Confining yourself to one wine, the wine you like best, can give much satisfaction. On special occasions when two or more wines are served with a variety of courses, you will be able to compare simple wines with more complex ones, noting the virtues of one against the particular strong points of the other, and so on.

Since they are matched with the food in complexity and richness, the wines are generally served in order of greatness, the lesser wines preparing the palate for the greater wines to come. This translates into two principles. The first is to serve the white wines before the reds. Dry whites are generally more acidic and less complex, and would taste insignificant and unpleasantly sharp if drunk after the fullness of reds. The only exception to this is the serving of dessert wines such as Barsac and Sauternes at the end of the meal with dessert. The second principle is to serve the younger wine before the older wine. This goes for white wines as well as reds, but is especially important for the latter. In most cases the older bottle of red wine will have expanded into more notes of taste, finesse, and depth than the younger red. Exceptions to this rule abound, however, with regard to specific vintages. It bears repeating that the relative "greatness" of a wine is rarely totally dependent on the greatness of the vintage. If you served two comparable Bordeaux reds, one from 1981 and the other from 1980, you might be tempted to serve the 1981 after the 1980 on the theory that the "greater" vintage should follow the lesser, but for drinking now the 1980 is superior to the 1981. It should also be noted that if red Burgundies and red Bordeaux come together at the same meal, the Bordeaux should come first. This combination should be avoided, however.

There is no limit to the appropriate combinations of food and wine. The following is a list of suggested affinities, and latitude must be allowed for, depending on the time, place, mood, and company.

TO BEGIN THE MEAL

ARTICHOKES AND ASPARAGUS   When served with vinaigrette, avoid fine wine, if possible, as vinegar makes any wine taste sour. If wine is a must, opt instead for melted butter with the vegetable, and have a young, minor Bordeaux, a dry white, or any wine, knowing it will not be enhanced by the artichokes or asparagus.

AVOCADO   When served stuffed with shrimp, crab, or lobster, it may be accompanied by those wines mentioned as going well with fish.

CAVIAR   Champagne; otherwise take the traditional vodka.

CRUDITÉS   Pre-dinner raw vegetables will be well or poorly accompanied by wines, depending on the character of the dressing or dip—if any—served with them: simple dry white wine is recommended.

EGGS   Eggs alone do not help the taste of wines, whether white or red. Mâcon whites and Beaujolais are as good as any.

ESCARGOTS   Full-bodied reds, though not the most elegant. Beaujolais, Côtes du Rhône are recommended. Also red Burgundies, young red Bordeaux, Bourgueil, Chinon, Cahors, or other strong red.

FOIE GRAS   A fine Barsac or Sauternes; late-harvest Alsatian wines and Champagnes can be substituted. The sweet wines of late harvest are the best choice.

CURED HAM, SAUSAGES, AND OTHER COLD CUTS   Beaujolais-Villages, Brouilly, Fleurie, Chiroubles, Côte de Beaune reds, a young Bordeaux, or, if white is wanted, take a Côte de Beaune.

PASTA   A full wine, either red or white, depending on the dish and sauce: a rough-and-ready Rhône red or a Bordeaux château or red Provence. Sauces of clams, mussels, or other seafood take well to a straightforward dry white, such as Sancerre, Pouilly-Fumé, or a moderately priced white Burgundy; sauces that accent cheese, cream, and eggs are better with the above-mentioned reds.

PÂTÉ   A well-made country *pâté* goes well with either dry red or white wine; good *crus* of Beaujolais with a game *pâté*, or red Burgundy. The whites often favored over the reds are those of Alsace, land of *pâtés* and *terrines par excellence*.

PIZZA   Straightforward red wine or a full-bodied white.

QUICHES, ONION AND LEEK TARTS   Because the filling can be eggy, open-faced tarts can be a problem. Try a full and fruity white wine such as a Mâcon-Villages or white Rhône, if young and fresh. Onion tart and Riesling, Gewürztraminer, or Sylvaner are classic combinations.

RATATOUILLE   Uncomplicated red wine or rosé, such as Bandol, Rhône, Tavel or Lirac rosé, Beaujolais, Bordeaux of a recent light vintage; Loire red.

SALADS   Green salads (lettuce, watercress, chicory, endive, etc.). Salads do as little for wines as wines do for salads. Vinegary dressings hamper the wines. Dressings made with brandy or wine rather than vinegar or the fresh mayonnaise-based dressing used in composed salads can be a good alternative at a simple lunch, at which a dry and fruity white may be served, e.g., Saint-Véran, Pouilly-Fuissé, Coteaux Champenois, Riesling, Sylvaner, and young dry white Graves.

SOUFFLÉS   Cheese: fine with red wine. Fish: dry white.

SOUPS   Historically, Sherry has been honored both as an ingredient of soup and as the proper drink to accompany it. I prefer to *faire chabrol*, that is, stir a couple of spoonfuls of wine into my soupplate at the table. If it is a cream-based soup, try white wine. With heartier, thicker soups, reds are good; for bisques, with large chunks of lobster, crab, or other shellfish, serve a dry white. For chowders, try dry whites normally associated with fish, e.g., white Burgundies (not the greatest) with communal *appellations,* Mâcon white, Muscadet, or Sancerre, dry Vouvray, or white Graves.

FISH AND SHELLFISH

SHELLFISH   Not to drink wine with fish and shellfish is inconceivable to me. With raw oysters and clams take Chablis, Muscadet, Sancerre, Pouilly-Fumé, Saint-Véran, Pouilly-Fuissé, Champagne, or a fresh dry Alsatian. Lobster and crab need a bit more fruitiness to stand up to them, so choose a fine white château-bottled Graves from a recent vintage or a young white Burgundy from a commune *appellation,* e.g., Meursault, Chassagne, and Puligny. The more elaborately the shellfish is prepared and sauced, the fruitier and more august the bottle can be.

FISH   With a few exceptions, nearly any good, young, dry white wine will go well with fish in virtually any form. Oilier fish, such as mackerel and salmon, need a more pronounced wine: a Muscadet or Gros Plant for the first, and a fuller, more refined white for the second. In the Bordeaux, fresh salmon can be served with Sauternes. At Prieuré-Lichine, where I like to serve my own wine, I use the local fish recipes intended for red-wine drinkers: *lamproie à la bordelaise* or bass or mullet poached in a red wine sauce. For these red-wine-poached fish dishes, a light red, such as a good Médoc, Saint-Émilion, or Pomerol from a light year, are other particular favorites. For bouillabaisse, the Marseillais maintain that the dry wine of nearby Cassis is the best, though any young and fresh dry white will do well. Try particularly Sancerre, Muscadet, dry Alsatian, or dry white Graves. Other preparations which result in a "fishier" character, such as smoked herring (kippers), haddock (as in finnan haddie), sardines and mackerel, and smoked eel and salmon (Nova Scotia, Scotch, Norwegian, etc.), demand white wine of a pronounced and fresh acidity, e.g., Muscadet, even a Gewürztraminer or Coteaux Champenois, or a white wine from Savoie or Alsace.

Fish whose character is determined by the sauce they are served with—cod, sole, haddock, flounder—will demand wine that complements their sauce. A poached bass or shad with a cream or *velouté* sauce will do well with a fine white Burgundy, such as a Corton-Charlemagne, a Meursault, a good Puligny or Chassagne-Montrachet, a fine white Hermitage, Saint-Véran, Pouilly-Fumé, Sancerre, Pouilly-Fuissé, or a château-bottled Graves from a better vineyard, such as Carbonnieux. A red snapper quickly broiled and served only with melted butter and oil and herbs will do well with a regional Mâcon or Graves white wine, but a rare and fine white Burgundy would also be excellent.

MEATS, GAME, AND POULTRY

BEEF   Boiled: a red from Bordeaux or one of the lesser regions, such as Bourg, Blaye, Fronsac, and Côtes-de-Castillon. Steaks, whether tournedos or minute steaks, all take red wines. Roast beef is an excuse for the finest bottle of red, a fine Bordeaux château, mature red Hermitage, fine Burgundy. The finer the bottle, the finer the match.

DUCK OR GOOSE   Any good red, preferably full rather than fruity, e.g., good Bordeaux, Châteauneuf-du-Pape, a fine, big red Burgundy.

OTHER GAME BIRDS   such as quail, grouse, and pheasant, take any fine red.

CHICKEN AND TURKEY   Depending on their method of preparation, these are probably the two most versatile food choices for wine drinkers. Nearly any bottle of good dry white or red wine will do justice, although I prefer red. Beaujolais—Brouilly, Moulin-à-Vent, Chiroubles, etc.—Burgundies, Côtes du Rhône and good châteaux of Bordeaux; fine, dry Graves whites, Rhône whites, Burgundy whites from the Mâconnais, Chalonnais, or Côte d'Or.

HAM   Ham has a particular affinity for young Burgundies, such as Côte de Beaune, and Beaujolais. If the ham is broiled, choose a full white, such as Meursault.

HOT DOGS, HAMBURGERS, AND SANDWICHES   Nearly anything dry, simple, and direct. Beaujolais, Chinon, Bourgueil, Corbières or, if it is handy, a Mâcon *blanc*.

KIDNEYS   Young lamb and veal kidneys go well with full and fine reds or, if white is preferred, an Alsatian Riesling, or a Saint-Véran, Pouilly-Fuissé, or Puligny-Montrachet.   Gamier kidneys from older animals or the younger ones grilled with mustard might do better with a Beaujolais or a lighter Rhône red.

LAMB   Since roasting results in a finer, more delicate flavor than grilling and broiling of chops, I'd reserve the better bottles for the roasts. Great red Bordeaux are traditional, but any fine, full red wine will be perfect. Cutlets do well with less exalted wines from the Côtes du Rhône, Volnays, Pommards, Santenay, Rully, as well as Bordeaux.

LIVER   As for kidneys, err on the side of assertive character, e.g., red Bordeaux, Beaujolais, or a hearty Rhône.

PORK   White wines, provided they aren't too dry, and reds.

RABBIT   As with chicken, it will depend on its method of preparation. Fruity, light reds, such as Beaujolais, young Rhône wines, good red Bordeaux and Burgundies. When cooked in a light or spicy sauce, it may call for an Alsatian white or white Graves.

SWEETBREADS   Sweetbreads can be a delicate and grand dish calling for a fine red or white, e.g., Margaux or Saint-Julien, Pomerol or Saint-Émilion, Volnay, Côte de Nuits from the better vineyards, or, among the whites, Meursault, Chassagne and Puligny-Montrachet, Pouilly-Fuissé, Pouilly-Fumé, or fine, château-bottled Graves. If the sauce is sweetish, a good Riesling or Gewürztraminer would be good.

TONGUE   Like any cold meat, depending on its garnish, it will go especially well with a dry white, such as Mâcon-Villages or Saint-Véran, or a red of any description, with the possible exception of a Muscadet, which is assertively acid and dry.

TRIPE   Hearty peasant fare calling for a simple, dry red or rosé. Madiran, Irouléguy, Fitou, Cahors, Côtes du Roussillon, or Tavel or Lirac rosé.

VEAL   Roast veal has always been a favorite of mine to show off a fine bottle of red. Its neutral character leaves the stage to any wine. If the roast is slightly sweetly sauced, it can also flatter the greatest bottle of red or white château-bottled Graves, or a full, young white Burgundy. For veal Scaloppini: red Bordeaux, Côtes du Rhône, a *cru* of Beaujolais, or, if white is preferred, Saint-Véran or other Mâcon white.

VENISON   Red Burgundy, preferably a fine, great Médoc of power, red Graves, Saint-Émilion, or Pomerol, mature Hermitage or Côte Rôtie, or a great bottle of Pinot Gris d'Alsace or Riesling.

STEWS, CASSEROLES, AND OTHER COMPOSITIONS   These can range from the heartiest, most forthright fare, such as a *cassoulet,* to the richest and most elegant, such as *boeuf bourguignon, coq au vin, civet de lapin,* or preferably *civet de lièvre* calling for a red Burgundy, Chambertin, Richebourg, or a great red Bordeaux. If it is red-wine-based stew, the quality of the wine and the cut of meat, game, or poultry will determine the quality of wine to serve. A spicy *goulash* or *chili con carne,* depending on the fieriness, would also take a white wine, or perhaps beer. *Paella:* an uncomplicated red or fullish white. *Cassoulet:* one of the heartier reds, such as Cahors, Côtes du Roussillon, Madiran, or Fitou. Among the whites, Gewürztraminer and Riesling could be used. *Curries:* depending on how hot you like them, serve (in order of spiciness) white Hermitage or Gewürztraminer. For a red, choose among those suggested for *cassoulet. Meat Loaf:* the same as suggested for *cassoulet. Choucroute garnie:* for this Alsatian specialty of sauerkraut with sausages, most dry Alsatian wines do well. Usually the dish is not so refined as to demand the greatest wine: the pervading brininess of the sauerkraut needs a rather strong foil. Red wines are not flattered by the dish. A very dry Champagne would not be amiss.

CHEESES France, the land of 430 cheeses; any one of them can help you finish the bottle and the meal. Nearly any cheese will make any wine taste better. For the great bottles, serve blander cheeses, such as mild Cheddars, Gruyères, Tome de Savoie, Reblochon, Camembert, and Port-Salut. Blue cheeses, such as Bleu de Bresse and Roquefort, can overpower the delicate elegance of a fine wine, although the Sauternais drink their wines with Roquefort.

DESSERTS

Fine desserts take Barsac and Sauternes, Quart de Chaumes and Coteaux du Layon, and vintage Champagne. I do not believe that chocolate desserts spoil all sweet wine, but, for my part, I would not choose a very sweet or very chocolaty dessert to highlight a very old bottle—a strawberry mousse or some other mild custard-based dish would do well. Unless Champagne is sweet, desserts bring out their acidity.

APPLE PIES, TARTS, ETC. Sweet Alsatian wines, Monbazillac, Coteaux du Layon, Quart de Chaumes, a lesser Sauternes or a *vin doux naturel* such as a fine Banyuls.

CAKES Because of their sweetness, many filled cakes are not suitable to dessert wines. The French find that lightly iced and unfilled types—Genoises, *reine de saba,* and some of the other unadorned recipes—flatter good wines, such as Sauternes and late-picked Alsatian wine. Sweet Vouvrays and Monbazillacs are good alternatives.

CHEESECAKE This could be accompanied by a dessert wine, though not the best.

CRÈME BRÛLÉE Mild and unctuous enough to flatter the best Barsac, Sauternes, Coteaux du Layon, sweet Vouvray, Quart de Chaumes.

CRÊPES Depending on the sweetness of the filling and sauce, a sweet Loire, Monbazillac, Cérons, or château-bottled Sauternes.

FRUIT

Fruits high in acid are not friendly to most wines, although Champagne can be a good choice. For very sweet fruits, as for sweet desserts, Champagne is too acidic. Ripe peaches and strawberries go well with red wine.

TROPICAL FRUITS   Mango and papaya, for instance, go well with Coteaux du Layon, sweet Vouvray, and sweet Sauternes. Melon goes with them equally well; try also *vins doux naturels,* such as Beaumes-des-Venise or Rivesaltes and the fortified Muscat wines, such as Muscat de Lunel, Muscat de Frontignan, Muscat de Saint-Jean de Minervois, etc.

FRUIT COMPOTES   If sweet and not overly acidic, they go well with sweet Loire and Barsac, as well as Sauternes.

FRUIT PUDDINGS AND FLANS, ETC.   Depending on your purse, a Cérons, Monbazillac, Barsac, Sauternes, or Vouvray.

ICES   Champagne, or a small glass of Barsac or Sauternes.

ZABAGLIONE   A fortified Muscat wine (Beaumes-de-Venise, Muscat de Frontignan, or Banyuls, etc.) or a Monbazillac.

WINE AND HEALTH

When medicine was in its infancy—and wine already a high art—wine was often prescribed to treat various ailments: gallstones, heart problems, all manner of chills and fevers, and always to quell the pain of childbirth and primitive surgery.

I am not a physician and wouldn't presume to suggest that wine might be prescribed for specific maladies or disorders. But I am happy to find that my beliefs about the benefits of wine to health, developed during an observant lifetime, are also held by many eminent physicians and scientists.

At the age of eight or nine, when living in Paris, I was given half a glass of red Bordeaux every morning at eleven o'clock, because I was skinny and believed to be anemic. I don't know whether it was the wine or not, but I'm certainly neither skinny nor anemic today!

Much later I learned that the alcohol in wine is accompanied by a rich store of nutrients—vitamins, minerals, sugars from the grapes themselves, and yeasts which are a by-product of the fermentation process. Red wine has more of these elements than white, because many of them are incorporated during the maceration of grape skins and juice. Red wines are especially rich in the B vitamins, and the deep color of red wine helps to preserve vitamins which are easily destroyed by exposure to light.

Both red and white wines contain important amounts of easily assimilable iron, and the high nutrient content of wine distinguishes it from beer and spirits.

People cherish countless misconceptions about wine: that white wine is "purer" than red; that red wine causes headaches and white wine doesn't; that red wine puts on weight but white wine has fewer calories; and that all wine is calorie-laden and spells disaster for dieters. It is important to understand that such ideas are silly and wrong.

The calorie count of any wine is determined, simply enough, by the concentrations of sugar and alcohol. A bottle of dry red or white wine contains about 525 calories. This is fewer than many people believe.

One of Europe's foremost authorities on wine and health states that wine can be used to replace 500 calories of fat or sugar in the daily diet: "These calories will be completely consumed and will not add an ounce of body weight. So employed, wine is very useful in reducing." These 500 calories add up to about one-fifth of the average daily requirement; so wine can be part of even the most conscientious weight-loss plan. By replacing carbohydrate calories it cuts down on cravings for starchy or sugary foods.

While rich in potassium (a mineral that is helpful in weight reduction), wine has a low sodium content and poses no problems for most people on low-salt diets. The extremely low sugar content of dry wines—no more than about 1 percent—makes them safe for most diabetics to drink. Some physicians believe too that the regular use of wine helps to reduce susceptibility to arteriosclerosis by lowering the level of cholesterol in the body.

Throughout history, when wars were incessant, the wounded after battle—especially during the Napoleonic conflicts—were given red wine, not only to deaden pain and bolster courage, but because it was believed to help in the healing of wounds and in keeping infection at bay. Science has now shown that the acids in wine—independently of alcohol—slow the growth of bacteria. Some red wines, in fact, actually enhance the effects of antibiotics.

Wine is very rarely forbidden by doctors, who, in my experience, are the largest single occupational group in the ever-proliferating wine-appreciation societies.

Wine soothes, relaxes, and refreshes. It stimulates the appetite and the blood flow. Of course, the reasons we drink wine are as much spiritual as physical. Wine's greatest virtue is its ability to induce serenity and a sense of well-being. And most of the attributes for which a lover of wine praises his favorite vintages are ineffable—they live in the imagination and the memory, not in the test tube.

BUYING WINE

Until recently, it was actually easier to buy great Burgundies and château-bottled Bordeaux in New York, London, or Los Angeles than in Paris. But, although most experts believe that the ocean voyage adds a year or two to the age of a wine, this is of slight importance when buying a wine that may not mature for another decade or so. Moreover, improved wine-making technique has become commonplace in the past two decades, resulting in fresher, sturdier, "younger" wines—particularly among the whites, which now retain their freshness much better than in the past.

In the United States, the customer in the restaurant often knows much more about wine than the captain. When he orders a bottle, he usually has an idea of what he's looking for, but the waiter usually knows little more than the price and where to find it on the shelf.

At the retail level in England, this has not been the case. The London wine merchants, some of whom opened shop in the early eighteenth century, not only sold wine, but imported it from France in barrel and bottled it. This practice continued until the sixties in wines and until the early seventies for Ports. Such handling of the wine required great expertise.

An informed merchant or headwaiter can be an invaluable help in the enjoyment of wines. One can only judge the value of their advice by trial and error, and the merchant or wine waiter can only judge his customer by his reactions and requirements. When a bottle in the restaurant or store does not live up to your expectations (assuming they are reasonable), tell the waiter or merchant. The more you speak up, the more readily a wine can be matched to your needs and the better the service you will get.

Getting value for your money in a restaurant is rather different from doing the same thing in a shop. The choice in a restaurant is often limited. Specific shippers, growers, and vintages are often not indicated. Not to ascertain this information before ordering is to risk disappointment. Choices critically made and advice critically given are the two best ways of avoiding poor bottles and poor values due to overpricing. If you do find a faulty or overpriced bottle, complain, complain, complain.

A number of restaurants have built up good cellars and excellent wine lists. In restaurants which have ignored their wine lists, the manager may know very little about wine but, if tactfully handled, may be willing to learn. It cannot be repeated too insistently that in a restaurant or a shop the regular customer gets the service he deserves.

VINTAGE CHARTS

Too much wine buying and drinking is done from vintage charts. Wines from a district such as Burgundy or Bordeaux vary enormously in a single year, and a good vintage will have its own highs and lows from vineyard to vineyard.

It is perhaps easiest to think of vintage charts as a table of generalities, full of exceptions. Nineteen seventy-five was rightly hailed as a great year for red Bordeaux, and yet 1975 Burgundies, with very few exceptions, were light and disappointingly poor. Just as the microclimate can vary as much as this from region to region, the microclimates from place-name to place-name can also vary: Saint-Émilion vintages are not automatically similar to those of the Haut-Médoc. Late-harvested wines such as Sauternes and sweet Loires may be positively influenced by a beautifully sunny late October or spoiled by late rains—by which time Burgundies and Bordeaux will be happily fermenting in the vats.

In Burgundy, if you buy other than estate-bottled wines, depending on the shipper, the year on the label may not be the same as that of the wine in the bottle. Many shippers stretch good vintages with bad ones or will label poor vintages as good ones. There is no such difficulty, of course, when buying château-bottled Bordeaux, where the entire output from any given vintage at any property is identical from bottle to bottle.

It is no wonder that shippers are tempted to put false vintage labels on bottles. Many wine lovers are slaves to their charts, and if a year is not lauded in the tables they will not consider the wine. Perfect examples are the 1965, 1969, 1972, 1974, 1977, 1980, and 1984 vintages of Bordeaux, which when selected with care had some very enjoyable bottles, especially in their younger years, and often proved to be outstanding values. When young they are more enjoyable than great vintages, which require many years to mature and acquire a satisfying softness and roundness. Yet they remained hard to sell because they were poorly rated on unknowledgeable charts. Great vintages are rated according to the excellence they will achieve only when fully mature. The 1975s from classified Bordeaux châteaux can be great, but only beginning in the middle 1980s. A '73 or a '74, or even a 1980 in 1985, although rated lower on the charts, gave far greater pleasure through the early '80s. The excellent 1976 Bordeaux was enjoyable before the 1975s, which will be rated higher, and the same is true for the rounder '79s vis-à-vis the harder '78s. Vintage charts, being essentially simplistic, may rate some Bordeaux years misleadingly low, ignoring the pleasure that they offer when well selected. Sometimes it also happens that the potential excellence of certain vintages is not appreciated or noticed in the year these wines were made. Nineteen sixty-six for red Bordeaux was a superb vintage, though it was not fully appreciated at the time; many of them took a decade to show their greatness. Lastly, certain merchants and shippers with their eyes on their inventories will play up vintages to clear their shelves and warehouses.

A vintage chart can be of help when buying wines, but it is as much a mistake to assume that the entire glorious gamut of wines can be reduced to a series of pat formulas on a tiny card as it is to think that nations or people can be rated on a score of one to twenty. To understand wine, one must be sensitive to shades and nuances; nothing is all black or all white. Shaded grays express not only the reality of differences in wine, but the nuances of vintages. The slave to vintage charts will miss the pleasures of good wines produced in "average" years, because he will be too insensitive to discover them. Scientific wine-making methods have recently improved so substantially that, in the Médoc district of Bordeaux, for instance, where a light year used to turn out a poor wine for lack of proper knowledge of vinification, the wines may now be of good quality, the difference from those of better years being merely that they mature more quickly. In sum, a chart is helpful only when its limitations are appreciated.

⚜

HALF BOTTLES

Half bottles are good for trying out young whites and for red wines. Great wines suffer a bit from being in half bottles. They age more quickly and often differently than they would in full bottles or magnums. A Great Growth Médoc of the '70 or '75 vintage may have reached its peak in half bottle (and will stay there awhile), whereas the full bottle of the same wine would only just be coming around, and the magnum would still be noticeably "younger" and better. Half bottles are a wise buy in Barsacs and Sauternes, which, because of their sweetness, are sipping wines and usually consumed in small quantities.

VINTAGE CHART FOR ALL FRENCH WINES
1931–1985

No vintage chart is a sure guide to the wines rated, for great wines cannot be standardized. Wines are a product of inconstant nature and fallible man. There will be enough enjoyable bottles in any one district in any off year to make exceptions invalidating anything so dogmatic as a vintage chart. Often overlooked, nevertheless a major factor in the purchase of wines, is the proper selection of wines that are sufficiently mature for present-day consumption. Very great years are often slow in maturing, hence your consideration of whether the wines will be consumed immediately or laid away for future consumption should be a determining factor in your selections.

EXPLANATION OF RATINGS

20, 19—exceptionally great	14, 13, 12—very good	7, 6—low average
18, 17—very great	11, 10—good	5, 4—poor
16, 15—great	9, 8—fair	3, 2, 1—very poor

N.B.: Many dry white wines as well as many reds may be too old for present-day consumption. All such wines are indicated by *italic figures*. All white Bordeaux older than 1975 which are not Sauternes, Barsac, or Sainte-Croix-du-Mont should be considered as possibly being maderized.

Vintage	Red Bordeaux	Sweet White Bordeaux	Red Burgundy (Côte d'Or)	White Burgundy	Red Burgundy (Beaujolais)	Rhône	Loire	Alsace	Champagne
1931	*3*	*2*	*4*	*4*	*3*	*10*	*7*	*5*	*6*
1932	*1*	*1*	*3*	*4*	*5*	*11*	*7*	*5*	*6*
1933	*10*	*6*	*17*	*16*	*17*	*14*	*14*	*12*	*15*

Vintage	Red Bordeaux	Sweet White Bordeaux	Red Burgundy (Côte d'Or)	White Burgundy	Red Burgundy (Beaujolais)	Rhône	Loire	Alsace	Champagne
1934	17	15	17	16	17	16	15	16	15
1935	5	6	12	13	12	9	12	14	11
1936	8	8	8	6	9	14	9	10	10
1937	15	18	15	15	13	14	14	17	14
1938	9	8	14	13	10	13	9	10	12
1939	5	6	3	3	8	10	8	4	8
1940	8	9	9	9	8	9	8	11	8
1941	2	1	4	4	5	9	7	8	12
1942	12	15	12	15	14	15	11	13	15
1943	14	15	14	15	12	15	16	15	13
1944	11	9	4	5	7	9	7	5	9
1945	19	19	19	14	17	17	18	17	17
1946	8	7	12	9	10	15	10	10	11
1947	19	18	18	17	17	16	19	17	19
1948	15	16	13	10	10	8	10	12	14
1949	18	18	19	16	17	17	16	17	17
1950	14	15	12	18	12	15	10	8	9
1951	9	6	8	8	7	9	7	9	7
1952	15	15	16	16	16	17	14	15	17
1953	19	16	15	14	18	13	17	17	17
1954	12	9	10	11	10	16	10	11	10
1955	18	17	17	18	17	16	16	17	18
1956	12	10	10	14	9	14	12	13	12
1957	13	13	13	15	15	17	13	14	13
1958	11	13	9	17	13	16	15	16	12
1959	17	16	18	16	16	16	17	19	18
1960	13	13	8	14	10	16	14	13	14
1961	20	19	19	18	19	18	17	17	18
1962	17	18	15	16	16	15	16	15	16
1963	8	6	9	11	9	11	9	11	7
1964	16	12	16	15	17	15	15	15	16
1965	11	10	10	11	11	15	10	10	6
1966	18	19	15	16	16	17	15	14	18
1967	15	19	13	15	14	16	14	14	15
1968	9	7	5	6	11	10	10	11	9
1969	12	12	18.5	16	15	13	15	14	14
1970	18	17	14	16	14	18	15	14	16
1971	17	18	16	16	16	16	18	17	17
1972	13	11	15	11	12	12	10	12	12
1973	15.5	13	14	16	13	11	13	13	15
1974	15	9	14	15	13	13	14	13	13.5
1975	18.5	18.5	11	12	11	12	13	15	14

478

Vintage	Red Bordeaux	Sweet White Bordeaux	Red Burgundy (Côte d'Or)	White Burgundy	Red Burgundy (Beaujolais)	Rhône	Loire	Alsace	Champagne
1976	17.5	17	17	15.5	19	16	16	17	14.5
1977	14	13	13	11	12	15	13	13.5	15
1978	18.5	16	18	17	17	17	16	16	16.5
1979	17.5	16	15.5	17	14	15	14	14	14
1980	15	16	13.5	16	12	14	13	13	13
1981	17.5	17.5	14.5	15	17	15	15	15	14
1982	19.5	17.5	16	17	13	15	15	15	16
1983	19	19.5	17	17.5	18	14	14	19	14
1984	15.5	16	15	16	14	16	14	15	13
1985	19	17	17	16	19	18	15.5	19	14

STORING AND SERVING WINE

STORING WINE

For those with ready cash and patience, the ideal wine-buying strategy is to make purchases as soon as the wines have demonstrated their quality, before the costs of long storage and increased demand are added to the price. Old bottles are always expensive and the wine drinker can save enormously by buying the good and great vintages when they are young. The matter of patience is important, because the great wine's value will only be fully realized once the wine is mature. No matter how good a bargain you make when buying a fine vintage, you will have wasted your money if you drink the wine before it has been given a chance to develop. Another consideration is the storage itself. When you buy wines to keep, you reduce the risk of improper storage by poorly equipped merchants or warehouses. Wine advertised for quick sale can be poor or badly stored, and value for your money may be slight. Reputable merchants who know their business, however, can, through judicious purchasing, offer good wines at reasonable prices.

There's a delight in owning a cellar, for you then have within your own home a bottled treasure of taste sensations, as full of potential pleasure as a fine library or a collection of records, and you can always select a bottle according to your mood.

Small wine cellars are easily made in a cool corner of a storage closet, away from steam pipes and light. They should be properly ventilated, and any nearby pipes should be wrapped with insulation.

The main problem in wine storage is sudden change of temperature. Wines can stand extremes of temperature if they reach such extremes gradually. For this reason, summer is usually easier on wines than winter, when steam heating warms up a storage space each day, while the temperature drops quickly during the night. If this continues for a short time, it will age the wine prematurely. Over a longer period the wine may spoil.

White wines should be kept in the coolest spot practicable, usually nearest the floor, for they can spoil in a matter of months. Red Bordeaux and Burgundies can be placed above them, on top, while the fortified wines can stand upright on the shelf beside your brandies and spirits. All natural wines should be laid on their sides, so that the wine wets the cork, keeping it from drying and shrinking. For this reason, places for storing wine should not be too dry.

Three compartmented shelves will hold several dozen bottles in an area only a meter long. The compartments or bins need not be large for a small cellar, and a bin will hold almost a case. The best bins are diamond-shaped, for bottles piled in a flat bin may have a tendency to roll when one is removed, unless the bottles are braced. A thermometer should be hung nearby so that you can check to see that temperature remains constant, constancy being more important than degree, although 13°C. (55°F.) is considered ideal. The simplest arrangement is to transfer wine to whiskey cases, standing the cases on edge in a closet.

The size of a wine cellar depends on how often you serve wines, your budget, and available space. The cellar should be replenished periodically by new stocks, both bottles for current serving and others for laying down. A cellar gives most pleasure when there is a well-balanced stock to choose from. A cellar book, in which you keep a record of your wines, with notes of your preferences, is a help when restocking, as well as being a diary for the pleasures you get from wines. If prices of wines are listed in a cellar book, it is easier to replace wines of the same price category (taking into consideration the inflation factor), without insisting on the identical wine, so that you may drink several wines in a certain range over a period of time, rather than one wine, which may rise in price or deteriorate.

SERVING WINES

For most wines we drink every day, no special treatment or precaution is necessary. However, special occasions calling for special bottles may, for one reason or another, require particular attention.

Whatever you do, *do not wrap the bottle in a napkin* like a baby in swaddling clothes. You and your guests should be able to see the label; there is nothing shameful about it. After removing a bottle of white wine or Champagne from an ice bucket, use a napkin to catch the cold water dripping from the bottom of the bottle.

Red Wines

If you have bought an old red wine which may have sediment, it should rest for two or three weeks to allow it to recompose itself. Before serving it, the wine should be stood upright for at least half a day, so that the sediment falls to the bottom of the bottle.

OPENING WINES

When you open a bottle of wine, cut the lead-foil capsule below the lip with a knife; use a clean, damp cloth to remove the mold which usually forms under the capsule.

To remove the cork, any corkscrew that can be manipulated smoothly is fine. In choosing an old-fashioned T-screw, look for one with a long stem (great wines have long corks) which is rounded—not sharp enough to cut through the cork as you pull. If the cork should break or turn out to be old and powdery, it can be removed by leverage: insert the screw delicately, slightly sideways; set the bottle on its side, then turn the screw gently, using some leverage to lift the bottom of the corkscrew toward the upper side of the bottle.

The best corkscrew of all is the new Screw-pull, marketed by a Texan throughout the world since 1980. It has a clever plastic lever, and a very long rounded screw which does not cut through the cork—and it is thus suitable for young and old wines alike.

❧ *Corky Bottles* ❧

One occasionally finds a defect in even the finest of corks—sometimes an invisible vein which, with age, is liable to deteriorate and turn moldy. This is not the fault of the wine-maker and may happen to the best bottles. The wine will then have an unpleasant corky taste and smell—and the cork will smell of itself and not of the wine. In a restaurant, the waiter should smell the cork and then bring it to you; and the reason why a little wine is poured first into the glass of the host is that he may make sure the wine is not corky before it is offered to his guests. Sometimes the infection is so slight that only the first glassful is spoiled; therefore, when you open the wine at home and believe it is bad, pour out a glass, and then taste another to see whether the whole bottle is affected. In a restaurant, it must, of course, be sent back at once.

DECANTING

Stand the bottle upright for at least a few hours before decanting so the sediment may fall to the bottom. Remove the cork gently, peel away the whole lead foil, and wipe the neck clean with a damp cloth. For the decanting itself the bottle should be taken up gently, held steady in the position in which you first grasp it, and poured very slowly in one continuous movement into a clean decanter until the deposit begins to rise to the neck of the bottle—then stop at once. So that you may keep an eye on the sediment, hold the neck of the bottle in front of a light or candle as you pour. Since the process of decanting enables the wine to breathe, there is little need to leave the decanter stopper out. Here again, the age of the wine will determine how long it should be exposed to air before drinking; the younger the wine is, the longer it should breathe. The purpose of a wine basket is to hold steady a bottle which may contain sediment; since in restaurants many waiters pour the wine in jerks and wave these baskets about, they are usually superfluous. There is no good reason to use them.

For a young red wine, decanting can be used as an efficient way to allow the wine to breathe, and decanting an hour or so ahead will bring out many of its virtues. In a restaurant, order the wine as soon as you sit down. Many a wine drinker has noticed that it is only when the bottle is nearly finished that the wine seems to come into its own, simply because it takes time for a wine to open up in contact with the air. The swirling of wine in a large glass hastens this action, and that is why wineglasses are only one-third filled, and why they should be large. Even in modest Burgundian restaurants, glasses like large brandy snifters are used for all wines.

White wines should be served cool, the sweeter the cooler, but they lose their flavor when iced too much. A couple of hours in the refrigerator is usually sufficient, or a much shorter time in an ice bucket will do the trick. In a restaurant, if your white wine sits too long in the bucket, see that the bottle is put on the table to remedy the overchilling. Rosé wines are also served chilled, and slight chilling helps red Beaujolais. In hot climates, any red wine, including Bordeaux, should be brought down to a temperature of 17° or 18° Celsius (63–64° Fahrenheit).

GLASSES

Most people prefer clear crystal stemmed glasses for wine, unadorned, so that the sparkle of light on the wine is easily seen. The larger the glass, the better. A water glass is usually better than most small wineglasses, for two-thirds of the space can be left so that the wine can be swirled around.

Wine is shown off by its glass, just as a woman's beauty is shown off by her dress. Great wines can be ruined in small glasses, for the air cannot get at the surface of the wine to release its bouquet. Wineglasses, like fine wines, have always been a symbol of civilized living. The finest glasses are large and tulip-shaped, clear and thin, without markings, the bowl the size of a large orange or an apple. When less than half filled, such a glass permits the full enjoyment of the color, bouquet, and taste of a fine wine. France has made an art of clear crystal glasses, as exemplified by Baccarat.

Although there are many different shapes of glasses for different wines, a single glass, large, thin, and clear, can serve for all, making service and replacement simpler.

APPENDICES
AND INDEX

I

BOTTLE SIZES AND
COOPERAGE IN FRANCE

A. CONTAINERS AND MEASURES

Until 1978, French bottle sizes were not standardized—some regions preferred 75 centiliters, some 73, and some even 70. Beginning with the 1978 vintage, however, it has been mandatory that all regular bottles contain 75 centiliters (= 750 milliliters) and state this on the label. Half-bottles, magnums, and so forth are based on this standard measure.

BOTTLE SIZES

WINE	BOTTLES	MANUFACTURER'S NAME	METRIC CAPACITY	U.S. OUNCES
ALSACE	½ bottle		37.50 cl.	12.17
	bottle		75.00 cl.	25.36
ANJOU	½ bottle		37.50 cl.	12.68
	bottle		75.00 cl.	25.36
BEAUJOLAIS	½ bottle		37.50 cl.	12.68
"Pot"	⅔ bottle		50.00 cl.	16.90
	bottle		75.00 cl.	25.36
BORDEAUX				
Fillette (old term)	½ bottle	Bordelaise ⅜	37.50 cl.	12.17
Bottle	bottle	Bordelaise ¾	75.00 cl.	25.36
Magnum	2 bottles	Magnum	1.50 l.	50.71
Marie-Jeanne	3 bottles (approx.)	No longer available		
Double Magnum	4 bottles	Bordelaise 3 l.	3.00 l.	101.42
Jeroboam	6 bottles	Bordelaise 4.5 l.	4.50 l.	152.13
Impériale	8 bottles	Bordelaise 6 l.	6.00 l.	202.85
BURGUNDY	½ bottle		37.50 cl.	12.68
	bottle		75.00 cl.	25.36
Magnum	2 bottles		1.50 l.	50.71

WINE	BOTTLES	METRIC CAPACITY	U.S. OUNCES
CHAMPAGNE			
Split	¼ bottle	18.75 cl.	6.34/9.25
Pint	½ bottle	37.50 cl.	12.68
Fifth	bottle	75.00 cl.	25.36
Magnum	2 bottles	1.50 l.	50.71
Jeroboam	4 bottles	3.00 l.	101.42
Rehoboam	6 bottles	4.50 l.	152.13
Methuselah	8 bottles	6.00 l.	202.84
Salmanazar	12 bottles	9.00 l.	304.26
Balthazar	16 bottles	12.00 l.	405.68
Nebuchadnezzar	20 bottles	15.00 l.	507.10

B. COOPERAGE

CASK OR BARREL	DESCRIPTION	METRIC CAPACITY LITERS	U.S. EQUIVALENT U.S. GALLONS	BRITISH EQUIVALENT IMP. GALLONS
Alsace				
Foudre	As in Germany, a huge barrel for sales and storage purposes	1,000 liters or any other size. No standard size is adhered to	264.2	220.0
Aume	Used principally for shipping. Same size as Burgundy *feuillette*		30.1	25.1
Beaujolais				
Pièce		216	57.1	47.5
Feuillette	One-half *pièce*	108	28.5	23.7
Quartaut	One-quarter *pièce*	54	14.3	11.9
Bordeaux				
Barrique	*Hogshead*—so-called. Most common Bordeaux cask. Yields 24/25 cases of 12 75-centiliter bottles each	225	59.4	49.5
Tonneau	*A measure equal to 4 barriques.* No actual barrel this size. Château production and price quotations are stated in *tonneaux*. Yields 96/100 cases of 12 75-centiliter bottles each	900	237.8	197.9
Demi-Barrique or Feuillette	One-half *barrique*	112	29.6	24.6
Quartaut	One-quarter *barrique*	56	14.8	12.3
Burgundy				
Pièce	Regular Burgundy barrel. When bottled, yields 24/25 cases of 12 bottles each	228	60.2	50.1

Region	Barrel	Description			
	Queue	Old French measure consisting of 2 pièces. No actual cask this size. Sales by Hospices de Beaune made in terms of queue	456	120.5	100.3
Chablis	Feuillette	One-half pièce	114	30.1	25.1
	Quartaut	One-quarter pièce	57	15.1	12.6
	Feuillette	Standard Chablis barrel. Larger than feuillette of Côte d'Or	132	34.9	29.0
Champagne	Queue	Regular Champagne cask. Also called a pièce	205	54.2	45.1
	Demi-Queue	One-half queue	108	28.5	23.7
Loire Valley Anjou Layon Saumur	Pièce	Capacity variable	220	58.1	48.4
Vouvray	Pièce	Capacity same as Bordeaux hogshead	225	59.4	49.5
Mâconnais	Pièce	Nearly the same size as the Beaujolais pièce	215	56.8	47.3
The Midi	Demi-Muid	Storage barrel	600–700 (approx.)	171.7 (approx.)	143.0 (approx.)
Rhône Valley	Pièce	Standard barrel in the area of Châteauneuf-du-Pape. Slightly smaller than the pièce of the Côte d'Or	225	59.4	49.5

II

FRENCH AND AMERICAN MEASURES AND CONVERSION TABLES

UNITS OF CAPACITY—LIQUID MEASURE

METRIC SYSTEM

Unit	Comparison	U.S. Equivalent
Milliliter (ml.)	.001 l.	.0338 fluid ounce
Centiliter (cl.)	.01 l.	.3381 fluid ounce
Liter (l.)	100 cl.	1.0567 quarts, or 33.81 fluid ounces
Hectoliter (hl.)	100 l.	26.4178 gallons

One hectoliter is equal to slightly more than the volume of 133 75-centiliter (750 milliliter) bottles; i.e., 1 hectoliter = approximately 11 cases (of 12 bottles each) plus one bottle.

LIQUID MEASURES—U.S.

Unit	Comparison	Metric Equivalent
Fluid ounce (fl. oz.)	————	29.5729 ml.
Pint (pt.)	16 fl. oz.	.4732 l.
Quart (qt.)	32 fl. oz. 2 pt.	.9463 l.
Gallon (gal.)	8 pt. 4 qt.	3.7853 l.

As of 1979 the following bottle sizes became mandatory in the United States and in the countries of the European Economic Community:

COMPARING THE NEW WITH THE OLD BOTTLE SIZES

New Metric Sizes	Approx. Fluid Ounces	Old U.S. Sizes	Approx. Fluid Ounces
100 ml.	3.4	Miniature	2, 3, or 4
187 ml.	6.3	2/5 pint	6.4
375 ml.	12.7	4/5 pint	12.8
750 ml.	25.4	4/5 quart	25.6

APPENDIX II

New Metric Sizes	Approx. Fluid Ounces	Old U.S. Sizes	Approx. Fluid Ounces
1 l.	33.8	1 quart	32.0
1.5 l.	50.7	2/5 gallon	51.2
3 l.	101	4/5 gallon	102.4

USEFUL FRENCH-AMERICAN MEASURES

Kilometers	Miles	Miles	Kilometers
1	0.621	1	1.609
2	1.243	2	3.219
3	1.864	3	4.828
10	6.214	10	16.093
20	12.427	20	32.187
30	18.641	30	48.280
40	24.855	40	64.374
50	31.069	50	80.467
60	37.282	60	96.561
70	43.496	70	112.654
80	49.710	80	128.748
90	55.923	90	144.841
100	62.137	100	160.934

UNITS OF AREA, OR SQUARE MEASURES

METRIC SYSTEM

Unit	Comparison	U.S. Equivalent
Square meter (m.)	centiare	10.7639 sq. ft.
Are (a.)	100 sq. meters	3.9537 sq. rd.
Hectare (ha.)	10,000 sq. meters	2.471 acres
Square kilometer (km.)	1,000,000 sq. meters	.3861 sq. mi.

Hectares	Acres	Acres	Hectares
1	2.471	1	0.405
2	4.942	2	0.809
3	7.413	3	1.214
4	9.884	4	1.619
5	12.355	5	2.023
6	14.826	6	2.428
7	17.297	7	2.833
8	19.768	8	3.238
9	22.239	9	3.642
10	24.711	10	4.047

APPENDIX II

Hectares	Acres		Acres	Hectares
20	49.421		20	8.094
30	74.132		30	12.141
40	98.842		40	16.187
50	123.553		50	20.234
60	148.263		60	24.281
70	172.974		70	28.328
80	197.684		80	32.375
90	222.395		90	36.422
100	247.105		100	40.469

10,000 square meters = 1 hectare   9 square feet = 1 square yard
100 hectares = 1 square kilometer   4,840 square yards = 1 acre
144 square inches = 1 square foot   640 acres = 1 square mile

TEMPERATURE

Centigrade degrees	Fahrenheit degrees	Centigrade degrees	Fahrenheit degrees
40.0	104.0	13.9	57.0
38.9	102.0	11.1	52.0
36.1	97.0	10.0	50.0
35.0	95.0	8.3	47.0
33.3	92.0	5.5	42.0
30.5	87.0	5.0	41.0
30.0	86.0	2.8	37.0
27.8	82.0	0.0	32.0
25.0	77.0	−2.8	27.0
22.2	72.0	−5.0	23.0
20.0	68.0	−5.5	22.0
19.4	67.0	−8.3	17.0
16.7	62.0	−10.0	14.0
15.0	59.0	−11.1	12.0

FAHRENHEIT AND CENTIGRADE CONVERSIONS

To convert Fahrenheit to Centigrade, subtract 32 degrees and multiply by 5/9; to convert Centigrade to Fahrenheit, multiply by 9/5 and add 32 degrees.

III

BORDEAUX WINE:
CLASSIFICATION OF 1855

THE OFFICIAL CLASSIFICATION
OF THE GREAT GROWTHS OF THE GIRONDE

The official production is given in tons (*tonneaux*), the Bordeaux standard measure, consisting of 4 barrels. A *tonneau* used to average around 96 cases when bottled; since 1978 a *tonneau* consists of 100 cases, or 1200 bottles of 75 centiliters (750 milliliters) each.

The following figures of production are approximate, varying from year to year, and an estimate has been attempted by deducting the ullage, or evaporation, which usually consists of 15 percent.

HAUT-MÉDOC WINES

FIRST GROWTHS (*Premiers Crus*)

	COMMUNE	HECTARES	ACRES	AVERAGE PRODUCTION, TONNEAUX	AVERAGE PRODUCTION, CASES (*12 bottles*)
Château Lafite-Rothschild	*Pauillac*	88	220	250	22,000
Château Latour	*Pauillac*	60	150	220	20,000
Château Margaux	*Margaux*	75	187.5	250	23,000
Château Haut-Brion*	*Pessac, Graves*	40	100	140	13,000

* This wine, although a Graves, is universally recognized and classified as one of the four First Growths of the Médoc.

SECOND GROWTHS (*Deuxièmes Crus*)

	COMMUNE	HECTARES	ACRES	AVERAGE PRODUCTION, TONNEAUX	AVERAGE PRODUCTION, CASES
Château Mouton-Rothschild	*Pauillac*	70	175	250	22,000
Château Rausan-Ségla	*Margaux*			140	11,000
Château Rauzan-Gassies	*Margaux*	29	72.5	120	11,000

	COMMUNE	HECTARES	ACRES	AVERAGE PRODUCTION, TONNEAUX	AVERAGE PRODUCTION, CASES (12 bottles)
Château Léoville-Las-Cases	Saint-Julien	80	200	260	25,000
Château Léoville-Poyferré	Saint-Julien	60	150	220	22,000
Château Léoville-Barton	Saint-Julien	45	112.5	150	14,000
Château Durfort-Vivens	Margaux	31	75	90	7,000
Château Lascombes	Margaux	92	230	275	25,000
Château Gruaud-Larose	Saint-Julien	82	205	320	30,000
Château Brane-Cantenac	Cantenac-Margaux	115	287.5	375	35,000
Château Pichon-Longueville (Baron)	Pauillac	30	75	110	11,000
Château Pichon-Lalande	Pauillac	70	175	250	24,000
Château Ducru-Beaucaillou	Saint-Julien	50	125	220	20,000
Château Cos d'Estournel	Saint-Estèphe	60	160	275	25,000
Château Montrose	Saint-Estèphe	70	175	320	30,000

* Decreed a First Growth in 1973.

THIRD GROWTHS (*Troisièmes Crus*)

	COMMUNE	HECTARES	ACRES	AVERAGE PRODUCTION, TONNEAUX	AVERAGE PRODUCTION, CASES (12 bottles)
Château Giscours	Labarde-Margaux	78	195	350	25,000
Château Kirwan	Cantenac-Margaux	35	80	175	15,000
Château d'Issan	Cantenac-Margaux	35	87.5	130	11,000
Château Lagrange	Saint-Julien	107	267.5	400	40,000
Château Langoa-Barton	Saint-Julien	17	42.5	60	5,000
Château Malescot-Saint-Exupéry	Margaux	30	75	130	12,000
Château Cantenac-Brown	Cantenac-Margaux	32	80	140	13,000
Château Palmer	Cantenac-Margaux	40	100	140	12,500
Château La Lagune	Ludon-Haut-Médoc	70	175	250	24,000

	COMMUNE	HECTARES	ACRES	AVERAGE PRODUCTION, TONNEAUX	AVERAGE PRODUCTION, CASES (*12 bottles*)
Château Desmirail	*Margaux*	—	—	—	—
Château Calon-Ségur	*Saint-Estèphe*	50	125	220	20,000
Château Ferrière	*Margaux*	—	—	10	900
Château Marquis d'Alesme-Becker	*Margaux*	15	375	75	7,000
Château Boyd-Cantenac	*Cantenac-Margaux*	18	45	80	7,000

FOURTH GROWTHS (*Quatrièmes Crus*)

	COMMUNE	HECTARES	ACRES	AVERAGE PRODUCTION, TONNEAUX	AVERAGE PRODUCTION, CASES (*12 bottles*)
Château Saint-Pierre	*Saint-Julien*	17	42.5	60	4,500
Château Branaire	*Saint-Julien*	49	122.5	200	19,000
Château Talbot	*Saint-Julien*	100	250	375	35,000
Château Duhart-Milon-Rothschild	*Pauillac*	58	145	220	20,000
Château Pouget	*Cantenac-Margaux*	12	30	70	6,000
Château La Tour-Carnet	*Saint-Laurent-Haut-Médoc*	30	75	120	11,000
Château Lafon-Rochet	*Saint-Estèphe*	45	112.5	130	12,000
Château Beychevelle	*Saint-Julien*	70	175	350	32,000
Château Prieuré-Lichine	*Cantenac-Margaux*	60	150	260	18,000
Château Marquis-de-Terme	*Margaux*	38	95	170	15,500

FIFTH GROWTHS (*Cinquièmes Crus*)

	COMMUNE	HECTARES	ACRES	AVERAGE PRODUCTION, TONNEAUX	AVERAGE PRODUCTION, CASES (*12 bottles*)
Château Pontet-Canet	*Pauillac*	76	190	400	40,000
Château Batailley	*Pauillac*	55	137.5	270	25,000
Château Grand-Puy-Lacoste	*Pauillac*	45	112.5	180	12,000
Château Grand-Puy-Ducasse	*Pauillac*	33	82.5	150	14,000
Château Haut-Batailley	*Pauillac*	22	55	60	10,000
Château Lynch-Bages	*Pauillac*	65	162.5	250	24,000
Château Lynch-Moussas	*Pauillac*	40	100	175	17,000

	COMMUNE	HECTARES	ACRES	AVERAGE PRODUCTION, TONNEAUX	AVERAGE PRODUCTION, CASES (12 bottles)
Château Dauzac	Labarde-Margaux	55	125	270	25,000
Château Mouton-Baronne-Philippe (formerly known as Mouton Baron Philippe)	Pauillac	55	137.5	230	21,000
Château du Tertre	Arsac-Margaux	50	125	200	18,000
Château Haut-Bages-Libéral	Pauillac	23	57.5	100	8,000
Château Pédesclaux	Pauillac			100	8,000
Château Belgrave	Saint-Laurent-Haut-Médoc	35	87.5	100	9,000
Château de Camensac	Saint-Laurent-Haut-Médoc	62	155	260	25,000
Château Cos Labory	Saint-Estèphe	15	37.5	60	5,000
Château Clerc-Milon-Rothschild	Pauillac	25	62.5	100	8,000
Château Croizet-Bages	Pauillac	25	62.5	100	8,000
Château Cantemerle	Macau-Haut-Médoc	57	142.5	250	25,000

According to the French Government's decree of June 21, 1973, granting a new official and legal Classification to the First Growths of the Médoc wines, the listing and presentation of the Classification should read as follows:

MÉDOC
1973 CLASSIFICATION
FIRST GROWTHS
(in alphabetical order)

Château Lafite-Rothschild
Château Latour
Château Margaux
Château Mouton-Rothschild
Graves: Château Haut-Brion

1855 CLASSIFICATION

Second, Third, Fourth, and Fifth Growths*

* Not modified by the governmental decree.

IV

SAINT-ÉMILION:
SUGGESTED 1985 OFFICIAL
CLASSIFICATION

In 1985 the best Saint-Émilion wines were again, for the third time, classified by the Institut National des Appellations d'Origine as First Great Growths and Great Growths. This classification was open to revision and has since been appealed by some of those who were demoted in the change. To be decreed into law, this suggested classification requires the signatures of the Minister of Agriculture and the Minister of Consommation (Consumption). These signatures have not been forthcoming, one year after the I.N.A.O. proposed this new ranking.

The following figures of production are approximate and indicate average annual output, as given by the communes and taken from their Déclarations de Récoltes records, minus approx. 15 percent in ullage.

FIRST GREAT GROWTHS (*Saint-Émilion—Premiers Grands Crus Classés*)

		HECTARES	ACRES	TONNEAUX	CASES
A)	Château Ausone	7	17.5	35	2,800
	Château Cheval-Blanc	35	88	160	14,000
B)	Château Beauséjour-				
	Duffau-Lagarrosse	6	15	25	2,000
	Château Belair	13	32	50	4,000
	Château Canon	20	50	100	9,000
	Clos Fourtet	20	50	80	6,700
	Château Figeac	34	85	180	15,000
	Château La Gaffelière	20	50	110	9,400
	Château Magdelaine	11	27	40	3,700
	Château Pavie	35	88	200	16,200
	Château Trottevieille	9	22	50	4,000

GREAT GROWTHS (*Saint-Émilion—Grands Crus Classés*)

	HECTARES	ACRES	TONNEAUX
Château l'Angélus	25	62.5	150
Château l'Arrosée	9	22.5	35
Château Balestard-la-Tonnelle	8	20	40

APPENDIX IV

	HECTARES	ACRES	TONNEAUX	CASES
Château Beau Séjour Bécot	16.6	41	85	
Château Bellevue	6.5	16	35	
Château Bergat	3	7.5	20	
Château Berliquet	9	22.5	60	
Château Cadet-Piola	6	15	20	
Château Canon-la-Gaffelière	22.5	45	125	
Château Cap de Mourlin	15.5	38.5	90	
Château-le-Chatelet	5	12.5	30	
Château Chauvin	9.5	24	70	
Château Corbin-Michotte	6	15	25	
Château Corbin (Giraud)	10	25	60	
Château Couvent-des-Jacobins	8	20	40	
Château Croque-Michotte	10	25	50	
Château Curé-Bon	5	12.5	20	
Château Dassault	18	45	70	
Château Faurie-de-Souchard	8.5	21	45	
Château Fonplégade	17	42.5	90	
Château Fonroque	18	45	60	
Château Franc-Mayne	6.5	16	35	
Château Grand-Barrail-Lamarzelle-Figeac	23.5	58	150	
Château Grand-Corbin	13.5	33	65	
Château Grand Corbin-Despagne	25.5	63	160	
Château Grand-Mayne	17.5	44	70	
Château Grand-Pontet	14	32.5	60	
Château Guadet-Saint-Julien	5.5	13	25	
Château Haut-Corbin	6	15	25	
Château Haut-Sarpe	7	15.5	60	
Clos des Jacobins	8	20	45	
Château La Clotte	4.5	11	25	
Château La Cluzière	3	7.5	12	
Château La Dominique	17	42.5	70	
Clos La Madeleine	2	5	10	
Château Lamarzelle	5.5	12	35	
Château La Tour-Figeac	16	40	100	
Château La Tour-du-Pin-Figeac (Beliner)	8.5	21	65	
Château La Tour-du-Pin-Figeac (Moueix)	7	17.5	45	
Château Laniotte	5	12.5	25	
Château Larcis-Ducasse	11	25	60	
Château Larmande	17	42.5	100	
Château Laroze	28	70	100	
Château La Serre	7	17.5	40	
Château Le Prieuré	4.5	11	25	
Château Matras	8.5	21	35	
Château Mauvezin	5	12.5	20	

	HECTARES	ACRES	TONNEAUX	CASES
Château Moulin du Cadet	5	12.5	30	
Château l'Oratoire	6	15	35	
Château Pavie-Decesse	8.5	21	40	
Château Pavie-Macquin	12	30	50	
Château Pavillon-Cadet	3.5	9	15	
Château Petit-Faurie-de-Souchard	9	22.5	50	
Château Ripeau	15	45	38	
Château Saint-Georges-Côte-Pavie	6	15	21	
Clos Saint-Martin	2.5	6	10	
Château Sansonnet	6.5	16	30	
Château Soutard	18	37.5	70	
Château Tertre-Daugay	8	20	34	
Château Trimoulet	16	40	70	
Château Troplong-Mondot	25	62.5	150	
Château Villemaurine	6.5	16	35	
Château Yon-Figeac	21	52.5	120	

V

GRAVES:
1959 OFFICIAL CLASSIFICATION

The vineyards of the Graves district were officially classified in 1953 and in 1959. Château Haut-Brion, the greatest of all Graves, is also officially classified with the great Médocs.

The following figures of production are approximate, and indicate average annual output, as given by the communes and taken from their Déclarations de Récoltes records.

CLASSIFIED RED WINES OF GRAVES

	COMMUNE	TONNEAUX	CASES
Château Haut-Brion	*Pessac*	140	13,000
Château Bouscaut	*Cadaujac*	120	10,000
Château Carbonnieux	*Léognan*	130	11,000
Domaine de Chevalier	*Léognan*	50	4,800
Château de Fieuzal	*Léognan*	60	5,500
Château Haut-Bailly	*Léognan*	100	9,000
Château La Mission-Haut-Brion	*Talence*	100	8,000
Château La Tour-Haut-Brion	*Talence*	18	1,500
Château La Tour-Martillac			
(Kressmann La Tour)	*Martillac*	80	7,000
Château Malartic-Lagravière	*Léognan*	60	5,000
Château Olivier	*Léognan*	90	8,000
Château Pape-Clément	*Pessac*	100	9,000
Château Smith-Haut-Lafitte	*Martillac*	200	18,000

CLASSIFIED WHITE WINES OF GRAVES

Château Bouscaut	*Cadaujac*	18	1,500
Château Carbonnieux	*Léognan*	130	12,000
Domaine de Chevalier	*Léognan*	10	950
Château Couhins	*Villenave-d'Ornon*	40	3,800
Château La Tour-Martillac			
(Kressmann La Tour)	*Martillac*	16	1,500
Château Laville-Haut-Brion	*Talence*	20	1,800
Château Malartic-Lagravière	*Léognan*	10	900
Château Olivier	*Léognan*	90	8,000
Château Haut-Brion*	*Pessac*	16	1,500

* Added to the list in 1960.

VI

POMEROL:
A PERSONAL CLASSIFICATION

The vineyards of Pomerol have not been classified by any officially recognized body. There is, however, an understood hierarchy of the vineyards, accepted by the experts of the regions in its broad outlines. The following list was compiled in consultation with the growers, shippers, and brokers most familiar with the wines in question.

	HECTARES	ACRES	TONNEAUX
CRUS HORS CLASSE (*Outstanding Growths*)			
Château Pétrus	12	30	40
CRUS EXCEPTIONNELS (*Exceptional Growths*)			
Château La Conseillante	11	28	40
Château L'Évangile	13	32.5	36
Château La Fleur-Pétrus	9	22	35
Château Lafleur	4	10	14
Château Trotanoy	9	22.5	30
GRANDS CRUS (*Great Growths*)			
Château Gazin	25	62	80
Château Latour Pomerol	9	22	40
Château Petit-Village	9	22.5	42
Vieux Château Certan	14	35	60
CRUS SUPÉRIEURS (*Superior Growths*)			
Château Beauregard	13	32	50
Château Certan-Giraud	2	5	12
Château Certan-de-May	4	10	18
Clos L'Église	5	12.5	24
Château L'Église-Clinet	4	10	21
Château Le Gay	8	20	25
Château Lagrange	8	20	30
Château La Grave Trigant de Boisset	8	20	30

	HECTARES	ACRES	TONNEAUX
Château Nénin	20	50	100
Château La Pointe	20	50	80

BONS CRUS (*Good Growths*)

	HECTARES	ACRES	TONNEAUX
Château Bourgneuf-Vayron	9	22.5	50
Château La Cabanne	9	22.5	35
Château Le Caillou	5	12.5	30
Château Clinet	6	15	39
Clos du Clocher	5	12.5	28
Château La Croix	8	20	23
Château La Croix-de-Gay	12	30	60
Clos de L'Église	5	12.5	25
Château L'Enclos	7	17.5	34
Château Gombaude-Guillot	6	15	30
Château Guillot	5	12.5	30
Château Moulinet	13	32.5	90
Clos René	10	25	55
Château Rouget	11	27	35
Château de Sales	46	115	220
Château du Tailhas	9	22.5	54
Château Taillefer	21	52.5	102
Château Vraye-Croix-de-Gay	4	10	13

VII

SAUTERNES-BARSAC:
CLASSIFICATION OF 1855

As in the Médoc, the Sauternes vineyards were officially classified in 1855. This classification is known as the Official Classification of the Great Growths of the Gironde.

The total production from these vineyards represents approximately 25 percent of the total Sauternes production, amounting roughly to 350,000 cases per year.

The following figures of production are approximate, and indicate average annual output, as given by the communes and taken from their Déclarations de Récoltes records.

FIRST GREAT GROWTH

	TONNEAUX	CASES	HECTARES	ACRES
Château d'Yquem (Sauternes)	80	5,600	91	226

FIRST GROWTHS

Château Guiraud (Sauternes)	90	8,000	43	107
Château La Tour-Blanche (Bommes)	50	4,800	24	60
Château Lafaurie-Peyraguey (Bommes)	50	4,800	19	47
Château de Rayne-Vigneau (Bommes)	180	16,000	67	166
Château Sigalas-Rabaud (Bommes)	35	3,000	14	35
Château Rabaud-Promis (Bommes)	75	7,000	30	75
Clos Haut-Peyraguey (Bommes)	25	2,200	20	50
Château Coutet (Barsac)	75	6,500	38	95
Château Climens (Barsac)	65	6,000	30	75
Château Suduiraut (Preignac)	74	9,000	66	164
Château Rieussec (Fargues)	90	8,000	61	151

SECOND GROWTHS

Château d'Arche Lafaurie (Sauternes)	50	4,000	27	67
Château Filhot (Sauternes)	50	4,000	54	134
Château Lamothe (Sauternes)	25	2,000	7	17
Château de Myrat*	0	0	0	0

	TONNEAUX	CASES	HECTARES	ACRES
Château Doisy-Védrines (Barsac)	35	5,700	20	50
Château Doisy-Daëne (Barsac)	30	1,900	10	25
Château Doisy-Dubroca (Barsac)	15	1,300	5	12
Château Suau (Barsac)	15	1,300	7	17
Château Broustet (Barsac)	30	2,700	15	37
Château Caillou (Barsac)	40	3,700	15	37
Château Nairac (Barsac)	40	3,000	17	42
Château de Malle (Preignac)	40	3,700	24	60
Château Romer (Fargues)	6	1,300	5	12
Château Romer-du-Hayot (Fargues)	60	2,600	19	47

* No longer in existence.

VIII

ALPHABETICAL LIST
OF V.D.Q.S. WINES

WINE	DEPARTMENT
Cabardès (see Côtes de Cabardès et de l'Orbiel)	*Aude*
Cabrières	*Hérault*
Coteaux de Châteaumeillant	*Cher · Indre*
Cheverny	*Loir-et-Cher*
Corbières	*Aude*
Corbières-Supérieures	*Aude*
Costières du Gard	*Gard · Hérault*
Coteaux d'Aix-en-Provence	*Bouches-du-Rhône, Var*
Coteaux des Baux-en-Provence	*Bouches-du-Rhône*
Coteaux d'Ancenis (followed by name of grape)	*Loire-Atlantique*
Coteaux du Giennois (see also Côtes de Gien)	*Loiret · Nièvre*
Coteaux de Gien	*Loiret*
Coteaux du Languedoc	*Gard · Hérault · Aude*
Coteaux du Lyonnais (see also Vin du Lyonnais)	*Rhône*
Coteaux de la Méjanelle	*Hérault*
Coteaux de Pierrevert	*Alpes-de-Haute · Provence*
Coteaux de Valençay	*Indre-Loir-et-Cher*
Coteaux du Vendômois	*Loir-et-Cher*
Coteaux de Vérargues	*Hérault*
Côtes d'Auvergne (see also Vin d'Auvergne)	*Puy-de-Dôme*
Côtes du Brulhois	*Lot et Garonne*
Côtes de Cabardès et de l'Orbiel (see also Cabardès)	*Aude*
Côtes du Forez	*Loire*
Côtes de Gien (see also Coteaux du Giennois)	*Loiret · Nièvre*
Côtes du Luberon	*Vaucluse*
Côtes de Malepère	*Aude*
Côtes du Marmandais	*Lot-et-Garonne*
Côtes du Porez	*Loire*
Côtes Roannaises	*Loire*
Côtes de Saint-Mont	*Gers*
Côtes de Toul	*Meurthe-et-Moselle*
Coteaux Varois	*Var*
Côtes du Vivarais	*Ardèche · Gard*

WINE	DEPARTMENT
Côtes du Vivarais (name followed by the cru: Orgnac, Saint-Montant, Saint-Remeze)	Ardèche · Gard
Gros Plant ou Gros Plant du Pays Nantais	Loire-Atlantique
La Clape	Aude
Lavilledieu (see Vin de Lavilledieu)	Tarn-et-Garonne
Les Fiefs Vendéens	Vendée
Minervois	Aude · Hérault
Minervois-Noble (see also Vin Noble du Minervois)	Aude · Hérault
Montpeyroux	Hérault
Mousseux ou Pétillant du Bugey (see Vin du Bugey)	Ain
Pic Saint-Loup	Hérault · Gard
Picpoul de Pinet	Hérault
Quatourze	Aude
Roussette du Bugey (see Vin du Bugey)	Ain
Roussette du Bugey (followed by name: Anglefort, Arbignieu, Chanay, Lagnieu, Montagnieu, Virieu le Grand)	Ain
Saint-Christol	Hérault
Saint-Drézery	Hérault
Saint-Georges-d'Orques	Hérault
Saint-Pourcain sur Sioule (see also Vin de Saint Pourcain sur Sioule)	Allier
Saint-Saturnin	Hérault
Sauvignon de Saint-Bris	Yonne
Vin d'Auvergne (see also Côtes d'Auvergne)	Puy-de-Dôme
Vin du Bugey (see also Mousseux ou Pétillant du Bugey)	Ain
Vin du Bugey (followed by the name: cru, Virieu le Grand, Montagnieu, Manicle, Machuraz, Cerdon)	Ain
Vin d'Entraygues et du Fel	Aveyron · Cantal
Vin d'Estaing	Aveyron
Vin du Haut Poitou	Vienne · Deux-Sèvres
Vin de Lavilledieu (see also Lavilledieu)	Tarn-et-Garonne
Vin du Lyonnais	Rhône
Vin de Marcillac	Aveyron
Vin de la Moselle	Moselle
Vin Noble du Minervois (see also Minervois-Noble)	Aude · Hérault
Vin de l'Orléanais	Loiret
Vin de Saint-Pourçain sur Sioule (see also Saint-Pourçain sur Sioule)	Allier
Vin du Thouarsais	Deux-Sèvres
Vins de Tursan	Landes

SUGGESTIONS FOR FURTHER READING

M. A. AMERINE and E. B. ROESSLER. *Wines: Their Sensory Evaluation*. W. H. Freeman and Company, San Francisco, 1976.

ALEXIS BESPALOFF, *The New Signet Book of Wine:* New American Library, New York, 1985.

P. BRÉJOUX. *Les Vins de Loire* and *Les Vins de Bourgogne*. Atlas de la France Vinicole, L. Larmat; Société Française d'Éditions Vinicoles, Paris, 1974.

J. M. BROADBENT. *Wine Tasting*. Wine & Spirit Publications Ltd., London, 1968.

MICHAEL BROADBENT. *The Great Vintage Wine Book*. Mitchell Beazley Publishers Ltd., London, and Alfred A. Knopf, New York, 1980.

PIERRE-MARIE DOUTRELANT. *Les bons vins et les autres*. Éditions du Seuil, Paris, 1976.

HUBRECHT DUIJIKER. *The Great Wine Châteaux of Bordeaux*. Amsterdam, 1975.

HENRI ENJALBERT. *Les Grands Vins de Saint-Emilion, Pomerol, Fronsac*. Paris, 1983.

CLIFTON FADIMAN and SAM AARON. *The Joys of Wine*. Harry N. Abrams, New York, 1975.

NICHOLAS FAITH. *Château Margaux*. Christie's Wine Publications, London, 1980.

CLAUDE FERET. *Bordeaux et ses Vins*. 13th ed. Bordeaux, 1982.

PATRICK FORBES. *Champagne: The Wine, the Land, and the People*. Reynal and Company, New York, 1967.

ROSEMARY GEORGE. *Chablis*. London, 1984.

PHILIPPE HUGUIER. *Vins de Provence*. A. Robert, 1977.

HUGH JOHNSON. *World Atlas of Wine*. Simon and Schuster, New York, 1985. *Pocket Encyclopedia of Wine*. Rev. ed. London and New York, 1985. *Modern Encyclopedia of Wine*. Simon & Schuster, New York, 1983.

HENRY CLOS JOUVE. *Itinéraires à travers les vins de France*. Denoël, Paris, 1980.

HENRI AND REMI KRUG. *L'Art de Champagne*. Paris, 1979.

ALEXIS LICHINE. *New Encyclopedia of Wines & Spirits*. Fourth Edition. Alfred A. Knopf, New York, and Cassells, London, 1985.

SALVATORE P. LUCIA, M.D. *Wine and Your Well-Being*. Popular Library, New York, 1971.

ROBERT PARKER. *Bordeaux*. Simon and Schuster. New York, 1985.

E. PENNING-ROWSELL. *The Wines of Bordeaux*. Allen Lane Books, London, 1979.

DAVID PEPPERCORN. *Bordeaux*. London, 1982.

ÉMILE PEYNAUD. *Connaissance et Travail du Vin*. Bordas, Paris, 1975.

CYRIL RAY. *Mouton-Rothschild: The Wine, the Family, the Museum*. Christie Wine Publications, London, 1975.

CYRIL RAY. *Lafite*. Peter Davies, London, 1968.

JEAN and GEORGES SAMALENS. *Le livre de l'amateur d'Armagnac*. Solar, Paris, 1975.

STEPHEN SPURRIER. *French Fine Wines*. London, 1984.

SERENA SUTCLIFFE. *André Simon's Wines of the World.* 2nd ed. Macdonald Futura Publishers, London, 1981.

FREDERICK S. WILDMAN, JR. *A Wine Tour of France.* Updated ed. Vintage Books, New York, 1976.

JULIUS WILE. *Frank Schoonmaker's Encyclopedia of Wine.* Hastings House, New York, 1978.

JON WINROTH. *Wine As You Like It.* The International Herald Tribune, Neuilly-Sur-Seine, 1981.

H. GAULT and C. MILLAU. *Guide France.* Le Nouveau Guide Gault-Millau, Paris.

Decanter Magazine, London.

Guide Michelin. Michelin et Cie., Clermont-Ferrand.

Le Bottin Gourmand, Paris.

La Revue du Vin de France, Paris.

Les Amis du Vin, Baltimore.

Les Grands Vins de Bordeaux. La Société d'Action et de Gestion Publicitaire, Bordeaux, 1979.

Vintage, New York.

Wine World, Los Angeles.

The author would like to acknowledge the help of the following individuals:

SAM AARON, New York

ANDRÉ-REGIS AFRE, Office of the Beaune Shippers' Association

PIERRE ARMENIER, Châteauneuf-du-Pape

CHARLES BAGNIS, Château de Cremant, Bellet

MARCEL BALY, Château Coutet, Barsac

ROSEMARY BARRY, New York

YVES BARSALOU, Narbonne

MICHEL BÉCOT, Château Beau-Séjour Bécot, Saint-Émilion

JEAN BELIARD, Paris

ROBERT BENAYOUNE, Chamber of Commerce, Bordeaux

JEAN BÉNÉTEAU, Hine et Cie., Jarnac

HENRI BERTRAND, I.N.A.O., Bordeaux

ALEXIS BESPALOFF, New York

MARCEL BLANCK, ex-I.N.A.O., Kaysersberg

PIERRE BRÉJOUX, ex-Inspector General of the I.N.A.O., Paris

MICHEL BRUN, Romanèche-Thorins

GEORGES BRUNET, Château Vignelaure, Rians

CATHERINE BUCZYNSKI, New York

COLIN CAMPBELL, Jas. Hennessy & Co., Cognac

PHILIPPE CAPBERN-GASQUETON, Saint-Estèphe

CLAIRE DE CAUMONT LA FORCE, Paris

ANDRÉ CAZES, Château Lynch-Bages, Mayor of Pauillac

JEAN-MICHEL CAZES, Château Lynch-Bages, Pauillac

CHRISTINE CLERC, Paris

JOSEPH CORSIN, Davayé and Fuissé

PHILIPPE COTTIN, Château Mouton-Rothschild, La Bergerie, Pauillac

ANNE COULON, London and Bordeaux

JEAN DELMAS, Château Haut-Brion, Pessac

PAUL DELON, Château Léoville-Las-Cases, Saint-Julien

The late MICHAEL DEMAREST, New York

JEAN DESCOMBES, Villié-Morgon

WILLIAM DEUTSCH, New York

A. DEVLATIAN, I.N.A.O., Paris

MARC DUBERNET, Narbonne

GEORGES DUBOEUF, Romanèche-Thorins

PHILIPPE DUFAYS, Châteauneuf-du-Pape

CHARLES ELLIOTT, New York

RENÉ ENGEL, Vosne-Romanée

HENRI ESTÉVENIN, Châteauneuf-du-Pape

The late M. FALLER, Domaine Faller, Kientzheim

PAUL FIGEAT, Les Loges, Pouilly-sur-Loire

FRANÇOIS DE GANAY, Armagnac de Montal

JEAN-PAUL GARDÈRE, Château Latour, Pauillac

BERNARD GINESTET, Margaux and Bordeaux

PIERRE GOFFRE-VIAUD, Libourne

BERNARD HARAMBOURE, Pauillac

THOMAS HEETER, Château Nairac, Barsac

NICOLE HEETER-TARI, Château Nairac, Barsac and Château Giscours, Labarde

BERNARD HINE, Jarnac

JACQUES HINE, Jarnac

OSCAR DE HORSCHITZ, Épernay

GASTON HUET, Mayor of Vouvray, I.N.A.O. des Vins de Touraine

GEORGES HUGEL, Riquewihr

JEAN HUGEL, Riquewihr

GÉRARD JABOULET, Tain l'Hermitage

MICHAEL JABOULET-VERCHERRE, Beaune and Pommard

JANE KETTLEWELL, London and New York

The late RENÉ KUEHN, Ammerschwihr

JOHN W. LAIRD, New York

509

JACQUES DE LAMY, Directeur du Conseil Interprofessionnel des Vins de Fitou, Corbières et Minervois, Lezignan

RENÉ LAPORTE, Saint-Satur-Sancerre

DANIEL LAWTON, Bordeaux

HUGUES LAWTON, Bordeaux

GUSTAVE LEDUN, Bureau National Interprofessionnel d'Armagnac, Eauze

PATRICK LÉON, Bordeaux

RAYMOND LESAUVAGE, former President of the Bordeaux Brokers' Association

PIERRE LIGIER, Directeur du Comité Interprofessionnel des Vins des Côtes du Rhône, Avignon

COMTE ALEXANDRE DE LUR-SALUCES, Château d'Yquem, Sauternes

ARMAND MABY, Tavel

JOSEPH MAGNET, I.C.V., Montpellier

GERARD MAGRIN, Directeur du Comité Interprofessionnel des Vins des Côtes de Provence, Les Arcs-sur-Argens

THIERRY MANONCOURT, Château Figeac, Saint-Émilion

HENRI MARTIN, Château Gloria, Saint-Julien

JEAN PAUL MARTIN, Sommelier des Templiers

JEAN-MARIE MAS, I.N.A.O., Angers and Bordeaux.

A. B. MESLIER, Château d'Yquem, Sauternes

HENRI MEURGEY, Beaune and Gevrey-Chambertin

CHRISTIAN MOUEIX, Libourne

MITCHELL NATHANSON, Syosset, N.Y.

JEAN-PIERRE MOUEIX, Libourne

MAURICE NINOT, Beaune

PIERRE PERROMAT, ex-Président de l'Institut National des Appellations d'Origine, Paris

PROFESSEUR ÉMILE PEYNAUD, Directeur Honoraire du Service des Recherches de la Station Agronomique et Oenologique de Bordeaux, Bordeaux

LUCIEN PEYRAUD (Bandol), Le Beausset

JEAN PIÉRARD, Comité Interprofessionnel des Vins de Champagne, Épernay

PRINCE EDMOND DE POLIGNAC, Reims

PRINCE GUY DE POLIGNAC, Bordeaux and Paris

PRINCE HENRI DE POLIGNAC, Paris, Reims

BRUNO PRATS, Cos d'Estournel, Saint-Estèphe, Président du Comité des Grands Crus Classés de Bordeaux

FRANK PRIAL, New York

CHARLES QUITTANSON, ex-Directeur de la Répression des Fraudes, Dijon

JEAN RENAUD, Pouilly-sur-Loire

BERTRAND DE RIVOYRE, Ambarès

M. ROSEAU, Cave Coopérative de Tavel

GEORGES ROUCOU, Comité de Promotion des Produits Agricoles du Languedoc-Roussillon, Montpellier

MAURICE RUELLE, Château Beychevelle, Saint-Julien

GEORGES SAMALENS, Laujuzan

JEAN SAMALENS, Laujuzan

CATRINE SANDISON, London and Bordeaux

ELIZABETH SCHUMANN, Bordeaux and London

GUY SCHŸLER, Bordeaux

MAURICE SEIGNOUR, Vacqueyras

MARY JO SMITH, London

DANIEL SENARD, ex-President of the Chamber of Commerce of Beaune and Propriétaire at Aloxe-Corton

JACQUES SEYSSES, Domaine Dujac, Morey-Saint-Denis

MARTIN SINKOFF, New York

PIERRE SYLVESTRE, Syndicat Général des Vignerons des Côtes du Rhône, Avignon

CLAUDE TAITTINGER, Reims

PIERRE TARI, Château Giscours, Labarde, Président de l'Union des Grands Crus de Bordeaux

JACQUES THÉO, former Président du Comité Interprofessionnel des Vins de Bordeaux and former President of Alexis Lichine & Co., Bordeaux

B. THEVENET, Comité Interprofessionnel des Vins de Touraine

ACKNOWLEDGMENTS

JOSEPH TOUCHAIS, Vice Président du
Conseil Général de Maine et Loire
and Président du Conseil Interprofessionnel des Vins d'Anjou
et de Saumur, Doué-la-Fontaine

MAURICE TOUTON, Bordeaux

JEAN TRAPET, Gevrey-Chambertin

GERARD DE VAINS, I.N.A.O., Montpellier

ALBERT VUILLIERS, Château Rieussec,
Preignac

ODILE WELTERT, New York

INDEX

A Note About the Author

ALEXIS LICHINE is a wine grower and wine merchant. He owns Château Prieuré-Lichine in the village of Margaux in the Médoc area near Bordeaux, and was for many years part-owner of Château Lascombes and three vineyards in Burgundy. His experience in selecting and purchasing wines for shippers began before World War II, and in 1955 he established his own firm, Alexis Lichine and Company, first in Margaux and then in Bordeaux. By the time he sold it in 1965, it had become one of the leaders in its field. Mr. Lichine subsequently continued in business with interests in the United States, Europe, and Africa, and in 1975 became an active wine merchant again as a director of and consultant to a major wine-importing firm in New York. He has produced a dramatized record album, *The Joys of Wine*. His magisterial *Encyclopedia of Wines and Spirits*, originally published in 1967 and recently re-issued in a third edition, is widely considered to be the most authoritative work on the subject. His first book, the celebrated *Wines of France*—an earlier version of *Alexis Lichine's Guide to the Wines and Vineyards of France*—was published in 1951.

Born in Moscow, Alexis Lichine went with his family to France after the Revolution and came to the United States in 1934. During the war he served with U.S. Army Intelligence in North Africa and Europe, reaching the rank of major. He is an Officer of the Legion of Honor and a member of the prestigious Académie des Vins de Bordeaux. Mr. Lichine now divides his time between New York City and his château in the Médoc, with frequent journeys through the vineyards of France, where he has probably spent more time than any other non-Frenchman.

A Note on the Type

The text of this book was set, via computer-driven cathode-ray tube, in Garamond, a modern rendering of the type first cut in the sixteenth century by Claude Garamond (1510–1561). Garamond was a pupil of Geoffroy Troy and is believed to have based his letters on the Venetian models, although he introduced a number of important differences, and it is to him we owe the letter which we know as old-style. He gave to his letters a certain elegance and a feeling of movement that won for their creator an immediate reputation and the patronage of Francis I of France.

The book was composed by American–Stratford Graphic Services, Inc., Brattleboro, Vermont; printed and bound by The Murray Printing Company, Westford, Massachusetts.

Typography and binding design by Earl Tidwell
Maps by Bernhard Wagner